AMNESTY INTERNATIONAL

Amnesty International is a global movement of more than 3 million supporters, members and activists who campaign for internationally recognized human rights to be respected and protected. Its vision is for every person to enjoy all of the human rights enshrined in the Universal Declaration of Human Rights and other international human rights standards.

Amnesty International's mission is to conduct research and take action to prevent and end grave abuses of all human rights – civil, political, social, cultural and economic. From freedom of expression and association to physical and mental integrity, from protection from discrimination to the right to housing – these rights are indivisible.

Amnesty International is funded mainly by its membership and public donations. No funds are sought or accepted from governments for investigating and campaigning against human rights abuses. Amnesty International is independent of any government, political ideology, economic interest or religion.

Amnesty International is a democratic movement whose major policy decisions are taken by representatives from all national sections at International Council meetings held every two years. The members of the International Executive Committee, elected by the Council to carry out its decisions, are Pietro Antonioli (Italy), Euntae Go (South Korea), Louis Mendy (Senegal), Christine Pamp (Sweden – Vice-Chair), Peter Pack (UK – Chair), Vanushi Rajanayagam Walters (New Zealand), Guadalupe Rivas (Mexico), Bernard Sintobin (Belgium Flemish – International Treasurer), Tjalling J.S. Tiemstra (Netherlands – co-opted member) and Julio Torales (Paraguay).

United against injustice, we work together for human rights.

First published in 2011 by
Amnesty International Ltd
Peter Benenson House
1 Easton Street
London WC1X 0DW
United Kingdom

© Amnesty International 2011
Index: POL 10/001/2011

ISBN: 978-0-86210-462-7
ISSN: 0309-068X

A catalogue record for this book
is available from the British
Library.

Original language: English

Printed on 100 per cent recycled
post-consumer waste paper by
Pureprint Group
East Sussex
United Kingdom

Pureprint is a CarbonNeutral®
company, and uses only
vegetable-oil-based inks.

amnesty.org

AMNESTY INTERNATIONAL

AMNESTY INTERNATIONAL REPORT 2011
THE STATE OF THE WORLD'S HUMAN RIGHTS

This report covers the period January to December 2010.

COUNTRY DATA

The facts at the top of each individual country entry in this report have been drawn from the following sources:

All **Life expectancy** and **Adult literacy** figures are from the UN Development Programme's Human Development Index, found at http://hdr.undp.org/en/media/HDR_2010_EN_Complete_reprint.pdf

The latest figures available were Life expectancy at birth (2010) and Adult literacy rate (percentage aged 15 and above, 2005-2008). For more information, see the UNDP website or www.uis.unesco.org

Some countries that fall into the UNDP's "high human development" bracket have been assumed by the UNDP to have a literacy rate of 99 per cent for purposes of calculating the Human Development Index. Where this is the case, we have omitted the figure.

All **Population** figures are for 2010 and **Under-5 mortality** figures are estimates for the period 2005-2010, both drawn from the UN Fund for Population Activities' Demographic, Social and Economic Indicators, found at www.unfpa.org/webdav/site/global/shared/swp/2010/swop_2010_eng.pdf

Population figures are there solely to indicate the number of people affected by the issues we describe. Amnesty International acknowledges the limitations of such figures, and takes no position on questions such as disputed territory or the inclusion or exclusion of certain population groups.

Some country entries in this report have no reference to some or all of the above categories. Such omissions are for a number of reasons, including the absence of the information in the UN lists cited above.

These are the latest available figures at the time of going to print, and are for context purposes only. Due to differences in methodology and timeliness of underlying data, comparisons across countries should be made with caution.

ABBREVIATIONS

ASEAN	Association of Southeast Asian Nations
AU	African Union
CEDAW	UN Convention on the Elimination of All Forms of Discrimination against Women
CEDAW Committee	UN Committee on the Elimination of Discrimination against Women
CERD	International Convention on the Elimination of All Forms of Racial Discrimination
CERD Committee	UN Committee on the Elimination of Racial Discrimination
CIA	US Central Intelligence Agency
ECOWAS	Economic Community of West African States
EU	European Union
European Committee for the Prevention of Torture	European Committee for the Prevention of Torture and Inhuman or Degrading Treatment or Punishment
European Convention on Human Rights	(European) Convention for the Protection of Human Rights and Fundamental Freedoms
ICRC	International Committee of the Red Cross
ILO	International Labour Organization
ILO Convention No. 169	ILO Convention No. 169 on Indigenous and Tribal Peoples
International Convention against enforced disappearance	International Convention for the Protection of All Persons from Enforced Disappearance
LGBT	lesbian, gay, bisexual and transgender
MDGs	UN Millennium Development Goals
NGO	non-governmental organization
OAS	Organization of American States
OSCE	Organization for Security and Co-operation in Europe
UN	United Nations
UN Convention against Torture	Convention against Torture and Other Cruel, Inhuman or Degrading Treatment or Punishment
UNDP	UN Development Programme
UNESCO	UN Educational, Scientific and Cultural Organization
UNHCR, the UN refugee agency	UN High Commissioner for Refugees
UNICEF	UN Children's Fund
UN Migrant Workers Convention	International Convention on the Protection of the Rights of All Migrant Workers and Members of Their Families
UN Refugee Convention	Convention relating to the Status of Refugees
UN Special Rapporteur on human rights defenders	Special Rapporteur on the situation of human rights defenders
UN Special Rapporteur on indigenous people	Special Rapporteur on the situation of human rights and fundamental freedoms of indigenous people
UN Special Rapporteur on racism	Special Rapporteur on contemporary forms of racism, racial discrimination, xenophobia and related intolerance
UN Special Rapporteur on torture	Special Rapporteur on torture and other cruel, inhuman or degrading treatment or punishment
UK	United Kingdom
USA	United States of America

A girl living in a Roma camp in Orly, near Paris, France, September 2010, where homes were spray-painted by local authorities. Roma faced forced evictions and continued to struggle to access housing, health services and education throughout Europe.

Salil Shetty, Secretary General of Amnesty International, speaking about human rights in China at a seminar hosted by Amnesty International Norway, Oslo, December 2010.

ACTIVISTS USE NEW TOOLS TO CHALLENGE REPRESSION

Salil Shetty, Secretary General

The year 2010 may well be remembered as a watershed year when activists and journalists used new technology to speak truth to power and, in so doing, pushed for greater respect for human rights. It is also the year when repressive governments faced the real possibility that their days were numbered.

Information is a source of power, and for those challenging the abuse of power by states and other institutions, it is an exciting time. Since Amnesty International's inception half a century ago, we have seen and shaped similar major shifts in the power struggle between those perpetrating abuses and the courageous and inventive individuals who expose their wrongdoing. As a movement dedicated to focusing global outrage in defence of beleaguered individuals, we are committed to supporting activists who imagine a world in which information is truly free and in which they can exercise their right to express dissent peacefully, beyond the control of the authorities.

For 50 years, Amnesty International has explored frontier technologies that can give voice to the powerless and abused. From teleprinters, photocopiers and fax machines through to radio, television, satellite communications, phones, emails and the internet, we have harnessed them all in support of mass mobilization. They have been tools that have aided the struggle for human rights, despite sophisticated government efforts to restrict the flow of information and censor communication.

This year Wikileaks, a website dedicated to posting documents received from a wide variety of sources, began publishing the first of hundreds of thousands of documents which were allegedly downloaded by a 22-year-old US Army intelligence analyst, Bradley Manning, who is currently in pre-trial detention and faces the possibility of more than 50 years in prison if convicted of espionage and other charges.

Wikileaks created an easily accessible dumping ground for whistleblowers around the world and showed the power of this platform by disseminating and publishing classified and confidential government documents. Early on, Amnesty International recognized Wikileaks' contribution to human rights activism when Wikileaks posted information related to violations in Kenya in 2009.

But it took old-fashioned newspaper reporters and political analysts to trawl through the raw data, analyze it, and identify evidence of crimes and violations contained in those documents. Leveraging this information, political activists used other new communications tools now easily available on mobile phones and on social networking sites to bring people to the streets to demand accountability.

A compelling and tragic example of the power of individual action when amplified through the new tools of the virtual world is the story of Mohamed Bouazizi. In December 2010, Mohamed Bouazizi, a street vendor living in Sidi Bouzid, Tunisia, set himself on fire outside the City Hall to protest police harassment, humiliation, economic hardship and the sense of powerlessness felt by young people like himself in Tunisia.

As word of his act of despair and defiance spread around Tunisia via mobile phones and the internet, it galvanized the long-simmering dissent against the country's oppressive government with unforeseen ramifications. Mohamed Bouazizi died from his burns, but his anger lived on in the form of street protests throughout the country. Activists in Tunisia – a group comprised of trade unionists, members of the political opposition, and youth – some of whom did their organizing via social networking sites – took to the streets to demonstrate their support for Mohamed Bouazizi's grievances. Experienced hands joined with young protesters in using new tools to challenge a repressive government.

The Tunisian government sought to enforce a tight media blackout and shut down individual access to the internet but news quickly spread thanks to new technologies. The protesters made it clear that their anger was about both the government's brutal repression of those who dared to challenge its authoritarianism as well as the lack of economic opportunity caused in part by government corruption.

In January, less than a month after Mohamed Bouazizi's desperate act, the government of President Zine El 'Abidine Ben 'Ali collapsed and he fled the country, seeking refuge in Jeddah, Saudi Arabia. The people of Tunisia celebrated the end of 20 plus years of unaccountable rule, setting the stage for the restoration of a participatory and rights-respecting government to be elected.

The fall of Ben 'Ali's government reverberated throughout the region and the world. Governments which rely on torture and repression to suppress dissent and which grow rich through corruption and economic exploitation were looking over their shoulders. The local elite and foreign governments which propped up these illegitimate regimes while pontificating on democracy and human rights, were also nervous.

In no time the upheaval in Tunisia triggered tremors in other countries. People took to the streets in Algeria, Bahrain, Egypt, Jordan, Libya and Yemen.

The tools in 2010 were new but the grievances were the same: the quest for a life lived with dignity, with the full range of civil, cultural, economic, political and social rights. Activists around the world who have too long endured the threat and reality of imprisonment, torture and other brutality because of their political opinion and beliefs or identity, imagined a world of possibilities including freedom from fear and meaningful political participation. What was clearly shown by the postings is that the lack of economic opportunity experienced by many in the region resonated deeply with those who were supporting the activists in Tunisia.

The frustration of people living under repressive governments is never far beneath the surface. For example, in Egypt, Khaled Said died following an assault by two police officers in an internet cafe in Alexandria in June 2010. His death provoked a public outcry – what in hindsight appears to be an early harbinger of the massive demonstrations in 2011. The police officers were charged with unlawfully arresting and torturing him, but not charged with direct responsibility for his death. In Iran, government officials restricted access to outside sources of information such as the internet as the discontent following the disputed election in 2009 continued and the wounds created by a brutal crackdown on protesters festered.

In China, the government attempted to bury the story of a young man who, when stopped by police after killing one woman and injuring another while driving drunk, dismissed them by proclaiming his relationship to a senior police official. The cry, "My father is Li Gang" became shorthand for lack of accountability and the story behind the line was posted and reposted on the internet throughout China even as the authorities struggled for control.

For those politicians who argue the primacy of civil and political rights over economic, social and cultural rights – or vice versa – the clarity with which activists have defined their frustration as related to the lack of political and economic opportunities demonstrates that this is a false dichotomy that ignores the experiences of millions, if not billions, of people throughout the world living without both.

Amnesty International, which began as an organization dedicated to the rights of prisoners of conscience, has long understood that it is just as important to point out the underlying violations that spur activists to write and to take to the streets as it is to ensure an end to detention and abuse of the activists. Social networking sites may be new, but they are important because they are a powerful tool that can facilitate camaraderie and support between disaffected critics living under similarly abusive governments around the world.

LEAKS AND REVELATIONS

In July, Wikileaks and several major newspapers began publishing nearly 100,000 documents related to the war in Afghanistan. Controversy regarding the content, the legality and the consequences of the leak erupted. The documents provided valuable corroboration of human rights violations documented by human rights activists and journalists – violations that the Afghan and NATO governments had denied. But human rights organizations were also alarmed when the Taleban announced that they were going through the documents on Wikileaks and would punish Afghans who had co-operated with the Afghan government or its international supporters. New technology, like all tools, presents risks as well as benefits; Wikileaks took steps to ensure that future document releases would incorporate the long-standing principle of "do no harm", a bedrock of Amnesty International's work over the past 50 years.

In response, the governments implicated in the abuses invoked the age-old excuse of claiming that the leaked documents highlighting government violations and failures were a threat to national security and therefore illegal. By and large they simply ignored the revelation of evidence of crimes under international law and their failure to investigate these crimes and prosecute those responsible.

In October, Wikileaks released nearly 400,000 documents related to the war in Iraq. Again, Amnesty International and other human rights organizations pointed out that even as the implicated governments cried national security, they were failing to meet their responsibility to investigate and prosecute those responsible for war crimes and other crimes under international law. The documents also confirmed that even as these governments were dismissing the reports of these violations by Amnesty International and other human rights organizations, they were in possession of documents that clearly verified the accuracy of these reports.

But these leaks were dwarfed by the final chapter in 2010 when Wikileaks and five major newspapers started to simultaneously publish the first 220 of 251,287 leaked confidential – but not top secret – diplomatic cables from 274 US embassies, consulates and diplomatic missions around the world, dated from 28 December 1966 to 28 February 2010. The newly available information, analysed by veteran newspaper reporters as well as new but passionate bloggers, fed into existing movements and inspired new actors.

TREMORS AROUND THE WORLD

There are differing perspectives on the Wikileaks drama, with some commentators describing it as operating in "a moral void" while others see it as the modern equivalent of the release of the Pentagon Papers. What is clear, however, is the impact that the leaks have had.

While the "Jasmine Revolution" in Tunisia would not have happened without the long struggle of brave human rights defenders over the last two decades, support for activists from outside the country may have been strengthened as people scrutinized the

Wikileaks documents on Tunisia and understood the roots of the anger. In particular, some of the documents made clear that countries around the world were aware of both the political repression and the lack of economic opportunity, but for the most part were not taking action to urge change. One leaked cable showed that the then Canadian envoy, the US ambassador and the UK ambassador all acknowledged that the Tunisian security forces torture detainees; that diplomatic assurances that the government will not torture detainees sent back to Tunisia are "of value" but unreliable; and that the ICRC does not have access to detention facilities run by the Ministry of Interior.

In another leaked cable, the US ambassador detailed how the Tunisian economy was in shreds due to the pervasiveness of corruption, ranging from shakedowns by the police to the long arm of "the Family" – that is members of President Ben 'Ali's immediate and extended family who used their power to amass wealth.

Which brings us back to Mohamed Bouazizi and so many other Tunisians who appear to have felt that all hope was lost in the face of torture, economic deprivation, government corruption, police brutality and the unrelenting repression of political opposition and any others who voiced dissent. He had no political avenue for demanding economic opportunities and when he tried to create his own by selling fruits and vegetables from a cart on the street, the police confiscated his goods. When he went to the political authorities to complain of police abuse, they declined to accept or investigate his complaint.

Mohamed Bouazizi's complaints were hardly unique. But his act of self-immolation happened around the same time as Wikileaks published documents showing that Western governments which had allied themselves with Ben 'Ali's government were aware of all these issues but apparently unwilling to exert external pressure on the government to respect human rights. The combination of these two events seems to have triggered widespread support for protesters in Tunisia. People from neighbouring countries were particularly supportive – some of whom face the same obstacles to enjoying their civil, cultural, economic, political and social rights.

A TELLING RESPONSE

Confronted with the situation in Tunisia and Egypt, the response of Western governments is instructive. The USA severed their long relationship with President Ben 'Ali of Tunisia. The French Minister of Foreign Affairs initially proposed helping the Ben 'Ali government to handle the protest, but outrage at such a position erupted in France and after Ben 'Ali fled Tunisia the French finally came out in support of the protesters. Faced with similar protests in Egypt, the USA and many European governments appeared caught off guard and unwilling to support the protesters' initial call for President Mohammad Hosni Mubarak to leave power.

The USA in particular has invested heavily in the stability of the Mubarak government despite ample evidence of its brutality over the last 30 years. In fact throughout the world, many governments that proclaim to value human rights and democracy explicitly supported political leaders, such as Hosni Mubarak in Egypt and Ben 'Ali in Tunisia, whom they knew were corrupt, repressive and indifferent to the rights of their own citizens. In fact, the first extraordinary renditions (outsourcing of torture) happened under the Bill Clinton administration which sent detainees to Egypt – a place well known for its systematic use of torture. The evidence of this hypocrisy – reinforced by the many diplomatic cables available through Wikileaks – exposes these governments and casts doubt on their commitments to human rights. In the end, the courage of peaceful protestors riskng their lives on the streets of Cairo and other cities proved too much for President Mubarak and his allies.

In the wake of the leaked diplomatic cables, governments have been scrambling to figure out what crimes may have been committed by Wikileaks (and Bradley Manning). There are troubling aspects to this response. The US government, which has been most vehement in attacking Wikileaks, had a different view when it was supporting new advances in disseminating information about other countries. In January 2010, US Secretary of State Hilary Clinton gave a speech aimed at encouraging governments around the world to ensure that their residents had access to the internet, comparing internet censorship to the Berlin Wall. "Information has never been so free", declared Hillary Clinton. "Even in authoritarian countries, information networks are helping people discover new facts and making governments more accountable."

She went on to relate how, during his visit to China in November 2009, President Barack Obama had "defended the right of people to freely access information, and said that the more freely information flows the stronger societies become. He spoke about how access to information helps citizens to hold their governments accountable, generates new ideas, and encourages creativity."

But the USA is not alone in wanting a well-behaved internet or in its willingness to use cyber technology to violate the right to privacy. The internet further exposes governments' desire to control access to information, as they seek to censor those using the internet when the content is perceived by those in power to be a threat even as they add hacking and surveillance to their own arsenals.

It is, however, clear that governments are not necessarily in the driver's seat, however much they might wish to be. In China, the so-called "Great Firewall" has played an important and damaging role in seeking to smother free discussion on the internet. Those who have overstepped the rules have been harassed or jailed. For example, in July 2010, Hairat Niyaz, a Uighur journalist and web editor, was sentenced to 15 years' imprisonment for "endangering state security". As evidence, the court cited interviews he had given to overseas media as well as his online translation of an overseas Uighur organization calling for protests against the government's handling of an incident in which at least two Uighur were killed when Han Chinese workers attacked Uighur workers in Shaoguan, Guangdong province, southern China. Again and again, however, despite the most sophisticated technology, the Chinese authorities have found themselves unsettled or outwitted by internet users – a wild colt that cannot be tamed, in the words of Cuban blogger Yoani Sánchez.

Take Liu Xiaobo, the scholar and co-author of the dissident document Charter '08. He was inspired by the activity of Eastern European intellectuals fighting against Communist authoritarianism in the 1970s and 1980s. They too benefited from new technologies – copying machines and faxes – to disseminate their ideas and challenge, and ultimately topple, abusive governments.

Liu Xiaobo was little known to most ordinary Chinese even after he was sentenced to 11 years imprisonment on Christmas Day 2009. And yet, when he was awarded the Nobel peace prize in October 2010 online activists around the world went into overdrive in seeking to acknowledge his role.

Chinese authorities were eager to shut the discussion down. Caught off balance by widespread support for the man they had officially described as a "traitor", they blocked searches for the phrase "empty chair" – a term many Chinese had begun to use in reference to the way that Liu Xiaobo was honoured at the prize-giving ceremony in Oslo, Norway.

Until Wikileaks, it appeared that governments believed they retained the upper hand. But when the companies that were necessary for Wikileaks to function withdrew their support – and it remains unclear whether this was as a result of direct government pressure – the companies and the governments that were condemning Wikileaks came under attack from hackers around the world.

This increased action by hackers and the continued dissemination of documents despite threats and outrage by various governments show how Wikileaks has changed the nature of the game with regard to who controls information. It also demonstrated a "take no prisoners" attitude among some hackers that threatened the privacy and security of individuals.

GETTING THE RIGHT BALANCE – A WORD OF CAUTION

As we have seen before, the desire to publicize information, if not balanced against individual rights, can lead to problems of its own. In August, two women filed criminal complaints against Julian Assange, the founder of Wikileaks, under the Swedish sexual offences act. Hackers published the names and identities of the women who had been vilified in the media as stooges of the US and Swedish governments. This demonstrates that in the new virtual universe women continue to be treated as pawns – or even worse – as acceptable collateral damage. To be clear, the women deserve to have their complaints fully investigated and if there is sufficient evidence, to see the alleged perpetrator prosecuted. Julian Assange must be accorded the presumption of innocence and given due process protections and a fair trial.

Human rights law is clear on this issue. Governments must be transparent and may only curtail freedom of expression (and the right to receive and impart information) to promote respect for the rights or reputations of others and to protect national security, public order and public health or morals. The claims by governments that national security is a carte blanche to restrict information is never justified – especially when the restriction appears to be covering up human rights and humanitarian law violations. But government hypocrisy and deception equally does not justify hacking into the prosecutor's office and violating the privacy of the women plaintiffs.

A DIGITAL FUTURE FOR HUMAN RIGHTS

There is nothing magical or deterministic about the internet and other communications technologies. Technology neither respects nor undermines human rights. It is and will continue to be a tool used by both those who want to challenge injustices around the world and those who want to control access to information and suppress dissenting voices. Arguably, FM Radio and mobile phones have done more to promote and protect human rights in Africa than most other conventional methods. Innovative use of crowdsourcing by the Ushahidi.com website in Kenya has opened up a whole new set of possibilities for conflict prevention.

Technology will serve the purposes of those who control it – whether their goal is the promotion of rights or the undermining of rights. We must be mindful that in a world of asymmetric power, the ability of governments and other institutional actors to abuse and exploit technology will always be superior to the grass-roots activists, the beleaguered human rights advocate, the intrepid whistleblower and the individual whose sense of justice demands that they be able to seek information or describe and document an injustice through these technologies.

In the debate surrounding Wikileaks, the dissemination of documents with apparent insufficient concern regarding the security of those exposed and the controversy surrounding the sexual offences case against Julian Assange made moral clarity difficult. It is not a case that allows for the moral clarity that – at least in retrospect – we associate with the publication of the Pentagon Papers. For those who find Wikileaks amoral, it is important to note that when those who should be speaking truth to power fail, those who live with the daily abuses of power may understandably celebrate Wikileaks. Their last hope for accountability is disclosure – however messy, embarrassing and apparently counter-productive it may be.

Nonetheless, these are amazing times for Amnesty International and other human rights activists who see the possibilities offered by technology for revealing the truth and holding debates that may evade state censorship and connect us across borders. We imagine the promise of living in a truly flat world in which all people have access to information in a meaningful way, in which all people can participate fully in decisions affecting their lives and in which no injustice goes unchallenged.

In 2011, Amnesty International celebrates its 50th anniversary. Described by a contemporary critic as "one of the larger lunacies of our time", the movement was ignited by a simple call to action from British lawyer Peter Benenson, asking society to remember "The Forgotten Prisoner". His passion was inspired when he learned of two Portuguese youths who had been imprisoned for raising their glasses in a toast to freedom.

Fortunately, for thousands of forgotten prisoners since, such "lunacy" not only prevailed, but continues, and we and our allies remain determined to promote the right to information and freedom of expression. Together we have successfully campaigned for the release of thousands of prisoners of conscience – some of whom, such as Ellen Johnson-Sirleaf – are today heads of states. Together we helped bring about the November 2010 release of Daw Aung San Suu Kyi, demonstrating yet again how unrelenting persistence can bring positive change. Together we have saved countless lives – most recently two activists challenging security forces of a mining operation who were about to stage a confrontation in order to rid themselves of activists who were willing to risk their lives by speaking truth to power.

Fifty years on the world has changed dramatically, but the imperative for individuals to stand together to fight injustice and protect the rights of human beings, wherever they may be, has not.

This anniversary is a moment to imagine how much individuals working together can achieve. If each of Amnesty International's members, more than 3 million people, reached out to just one more person to join our work for justice, we would double our impact. As we have seen in the Middle East and North Africa, the collective actions of individuals united in their quest for fundamental fairness can have the power to bring down repressive governments.

The need for individuals who value rights and freedoms to work in concert within and across borders remains great as governments persist in persecuting those who challenge abuse of power. While brave and determined individuals claim their rights and freedoms, governments, armed groups, corporations, and international institutions seek to evade scrutiny and accountability.

We draw inspiration from the release of Aung San Suu Kyi, the courage of Liu Xiaobo, the resilience of thousands of prisoners of conscience, the courage of countless human rights defenders and the tenacity, against all the odds, of hundreds of thousands of ordinary Tunisians who, confronted with the tragic story of Mohamed Bouazizi, determined to ensure his legacy through organizing against the abuse of power that led to his death. At Amnesty International, we commit ourselves to redouble our efforts to strengthen the global human rights movement and struggle to make sure no one else ever feels so alone in his or her despair as to see no way out.

A torchlight parade in Oslo, Norway, for Chinese political activist and Nobel peace prize winner, Liu Xiaobo, who is serving an 11-year prison sentence for "inciting subversion", December 2010. The Chinese government continued to persecute people for peacefully expressing their political and religious views.

AMNESTY INTERNATIONAL REPORT 2011
PART ONE: REGIONAL OVERVIEWS

11

A man stands in an oil slick covering a creek near Bodo City in Nigeria's Niger Delta, June 2010. Pollution and environmental damage caused by the oil industry continued to have a serious impact on people living in the region.

AFRICA

"Everybody knows the circumstances of my son's death but nobody will throw any light on his disappearance. We think they buried the problem along with the body. The state does not want to talk about it."

Mother of Dominique Lopy, who died after torture in custody in Senegal in 2007, talking to Amnesty International in 2010

A number of countries in Africa celebrated the 50th anniversary of their independence during the year while others prepared to do so soon. Despite the celebrations, the hopes and aspirations of many people in Africa remained unfulfilled, because their human rights were not respected and protected. The devastation caused can be seen in the hardship, repression and violence endured by people across the continent, such as those living in informal settlements in Port Harcourt, Nigeria, those languishing unfairly in prison in Angola despite the repeal of the law under which they were charged, the women and girls denied access to sexual and reproductive rights in Burkina Faso, and the millions of people who are still fleeing from armed conflict and poverty.

Conflict

During the past decade a number of long-standing civil wars have ended but other conflicts still continue to wreak havoc.

The armed conflict in Darfur, Sudan, intensified throughout the year, resulting in tens of thousands of newly displaced people, some of whom crossed into neighbouring Chad. Civilians were directly targeted in some attacks by armed groups and by government forces. Parts of Darfur remained inaccessible to humanitarian organizations and the joint UN-African Union (AU) mission in Darfur (UNAMID). Humanitarian workers and UNAMID staff were frequently abducted in Darfur, following a pattern similar to that seen in eastern Chad in recent years. Various mediation efforts during the year produced no tangible results. Repression by the Sudanese authorities continued in Darfur, with people being arbitrarily arrested, ill-treated and kept in detention without charge, primarily by the National Intelligence and Security Service (NISS). On a more positive note, preparations for the referendum on the secession of south Sudan did not lead to an increase in violence.

The relationship between Chad and Sudan improved, easing tensions between the two countries. A joint border patrol was set up, both countries promised not to support armed opposition groups in each other's country and there were reciprocal visits by the Heads of State. Even though Chad is a party to the Rome Statute of the International Criminal Court (ICC), it failed to arrest President Omar Al Bashir during his visit to Chad in July, despite the ICC arrest warrant against him on charges of war crimes, crimes against humanity and genocide. Kenya also failed to arrest President Al Bashir during his visit in August. Sudan continued to refuse to collaborate with the ICC over other outstanding arrest warrants. In July the AU Assembly reiterated its decision not to co-operate with the ICC over the arrest and surrender of President Al Bashir.

Chad called for the withdrawal of the UN Mission in the Central African Republic and Chad (MINURCAT) and the UN Security Council meekly complied, despite the potential negative impact on the protection of hundreds of thousands of refugees and displaced in eastern Chad. The displaced and refugees in eastern Chad remained at risk of human rights abuses, including violence against women and the recruitment and use of children by the Chadian armed forces and armed groups.

Large parts of the Central African Republic remained under the control of armed groups and were affected by violence, including attacks against civilians by the Uganda-based Lord's Resistance Army. Tens of thousands of people remained displaced and sexual violence remained prevalent.

In Somalia, the armed conflict between the Transitional Federal Government (TFG), supported by the African Union Mission in Somalia (AMISOM), and armed Islamist groups continued unabated, especially in Mogadishu. Hundreds of thousands of people were newly displaced and access for emergency humanitarian assistance was severely restricted because of insecurity, restrictions on humanitarian aid and because humanitarian workers were targeted by armed Islamist groups. The parties to the conflict did not take the necessary precautions to avoid civilian casualties during military confrontations and in some instances civilians were directly targeted. Children were forcibly recruited and used by the parties to the conflict. The international community remained more preoccupied with the problem of piracy off the Somali coast than with the plight of the civilian population. Military assistance to the TFG by various states, including the USA, without adequate safeguards may even have exacerbated the human rights and humanitarian situation. There was no strong impetus from the international community to hold those responsible for war crimes to account.

Limited progress was made to ensure accountability for crimes under international law, primarily due to lack of political will.

The conflict in the eastern Democratic Republic of the Congo (DRC) resulted in numerous violations of international human rights and humanitarian law. In Walikale, North Kivu, more than 300 people were raped in just four days by members of armed groups during a series of attacks against villages. Neither the Congolese armed forces (FARDC) nor the UN peace-keeping mission in the DRC (MONUC) intervened, even though they were stationed close by. The Congolese armed forces were also responsible for numerous human rights violations in the area. Hardly anyone was held to account for serious human rights violations, including rape and other forms of sexual violence. The Congolese authorities continued to refuse to hand over Bosco Ntaganda, a senior officer in the FARDC, to the ICC in spite of an arrest warrant against him for recruiting and using child soldiers.

In October, the UN released a report mapping gross violations of international human rights and humanitarian law in the DRC between 1993 and 2003. The report contains a wide range of recommendations to strengthen the Congolese justice system and address impunity which will require follow-up and political support. Criticism of the report by countries including Rwanda and Uganda, named in the report as perpetrators of human rights violations, was disappointing and reflects unwillingness to hold those responsible to account.

Limited progress was made in other countries to ensure accountability for crimes under international law, primarily due to lack of political will. In Burundi, the agreed Truth and Reconciliation Commission and the Special Tribunal had not yet been put in place by the end of the year. In Liberia, most recommendations of the Truth and Reconciliation Commission were not implemented, including the call for an extraordinary criminal tribunal to investigate and prosecute crimes under international law committed during the civil war. In Senegal, President Abdoulaye Wade said in December that he was no longer interested in pursuing the investigation and prosecution of former President Hissène Habré from Chad, even though funding for the judicial process seemed to have been secured. This in blatant disregard of Senegal's obligations under international law and the request of the AU. In another setback, the Kenyan parliament passed in December a motion to request the government to withdraw from the Rome Statute after the Prosecutor of the ICC presented an application for six Kenyan citizens to appear before the Court.

Public security concerns

Human rights violations by security and law enforcement forces continued to plague the region. Extrajudicial executions, torture and other ill-treatment, and excessive use of force, sometimes resulting in unlawful killings, were among the human rights violations documented.

The situation in the Niger Delta deteriorated during the year with armed groups and gangs kidnapping oil workers and their relatives and attacking oil installations. The reaction from the Nigerian security forces often led to human rights violations, including extrajudicial executions and torture. Human rights violations also remained the norm while enforcing the law in other parts of Nigeria with numerous cases of unlawful killings, including extrajudicial executions, enforced disappearances, arbitrary arrests, torture and other ill-treatment. Communal violence continued in Plateau State in Nigeria and led to hundreds of people being killed and thousands displaced.

Towards the end of the year a number of extrajudicial executions were reported in Burundi. The victims included people linked to the National Liberation Forces (FNL) opposition party. Although a judicial commission was established to investigate, no progress was made by the end of 2010.

In South Africa, numerous cases of torture and ill-treatment by police were reported, many of which were investigated by the Independent Complaints Directorate. Among the methods reported were beatings, electric shocks, suffocation and death threats. Human rights violations also occurred in Uganda after bomb attacks in July when at least 76 people were killed. Some people were arrested and kept in incommunicado detention; others were unlawfully transferred from Kenya to Uganda where they were detained.

In Mozambique, the police used live ammunition against people protesting against the high cost of living and killed at least 14 people. In Guinea, security forces shot with live ammunition at peaceful demonstrators. In Kenya, police killed seven men during a police operation in an informal settlement in Nairobi.

Deaths in custody, often after torture or other ill-treatment, occurred in a number of countries, such as in Burkina Faso, Cameroon, Republic of Congo, DRC, Eritrea, Ghana, Mauritania, South Africa and Swaziland. Prison conditions remained grim in many countries, including in Angola, Benin, Burundi, Liberia, Malawi, Sierra Leone and Tanzania.

In spite of a trend towards the abolition of the death penalty in Africa, Equatorial Guinea, Sudan and Somalia executed people sentenced to death, often after unfair trials. There was also one reported execution in Botswana. Gabon abolished the death penalty in law in 2010.

Elections in various countries were marred by violence and an increase in human rights violations. In nearly all cases, the human rights violations were committed with total impunity.

4

Repression of dissent

Elections in various countries were marred by violence and an increase in human rights violations. In nearly all cases, the human rights violations were committed with total impunity.

Presidential and parliamentary elections in Sudan in April led to a clampdown on freedom of expression. Media outlets were closed down, pre-print censorship was temporarily re-instated and journalists were arrested, some of whom were tortured. Many of the human rights violations were committed by the NISS but the National Security Act, which came into force in February, ensured that agents of the NISS enjoyed immunity from prosecution for human rights violations.

Elections in May in Ethiopia also led to restrictions on freedom of expression and assembly. Opposition parties stated that numerous members and activists were harassed, beaten and arrested prior to the elections, including in the Oromia region.

In Burundi, several people arrested during investigations into a series of grenade attacks before the elections were tortured by the National Intelligence Service. Although the Burundian government publicly stated it would initiate an investigation, no progress was made by the end of the year in holding those responsible to account. The government temporarily banned meetings of political opposition parties.

Rwanda also clamped down on freedom of expression and association before elections in August. Opposition political parties were not allowed to register, political opponents were arrested and a number of media outlets were closed. Journalists fled the country. Broad and ill-defined laws on "genocide ideology" and "sectarianism" were used to unduly restrict freedom of expression. The killings of a prominent politician and a journalist, as well as grenade attacks in which a number of people were killed, contributed to tension and insecurity in the run-up to the elections.

Presidential elections in Guinea led to increased violence and human rights violations. The security forces used excessive force, including by firing indiscriminately at protesters with live ammunition. Dozens of people were arbitrarily arrested during the electoral period and often denied access to their relatives, medical care or legal representation.

In Côte d'Ivoire, the results of the presidential elections in December were not accepted by incumbent President Laurent Gbagbo. Security forces loyal to him were responsible for a number of extrajudicial executions, enforced disappearances and arbitrary arrests. In spite of political pressure from the UN, the AU and the Economic Community of West African States (ECOWAS), Laurent Gbagbo refused to leave office, leading to a political stalemate and fears of rising violence.

In numerous other countries the rights to freedom of expression, association and peaceful assembly were not respected. Human rights defenders, journalists and members of the political opposition were at risk of harassment and intimidation, arbitrary arrest, torture or other ill-treatment, or unlawful killing.

Human rights defenders and activists were arbitrarily arrested and detained in Angola, the Central African Republic, Gambia, Niger and Zimbabwe, where in November the Supreme Court ruled that the 2008 arrest and detention of two members of Women of Zimbabwe Arise (WOZA) was wrongful and that their rights had been violated. The Court also ruled that the state had failed to protect the two human rights defenders from abuse. Human rights defenders received threats in Burundi and prominent human rights defender Floribert Chebeya was killed in the DRC. No progress was made in the investigation in Kenya into the killings of two human rights defenders in 2009, Oscar Kingara and Paul Oulu. In Ethiopia, the Charities and Societies Proclamation came into effect, imposing strict controls on civil society and severely hampering human rights work.

Peaceful demonstrations were banned – or participants arrested – in Angola, Benin, Cameroon, Swaziland and Togo.

Journalists were intimidated, threatened or arbitrarily arrested in Burundi, Chad, Côte d'Ivoire, the DRC, Equatorial Guinea, Ethiopia, Gambia, Ghana, Madagascar, Namibia, Nigeria, Rwanda, South Africa, Swaziland, Tanzania, Togo, Uganda and Zimbabwe.

Political opponents were unlawfully or arbitrarily arrested in Burundi, Equatorial Guinea, Madagascar, Niger and Togo. In Uganda, police officers and armed men disrupted an opposition rally and beat a number of participants.

In Eritrea, numerous activists, journalists, religious leaders, and others remained in detention, often incommunicado and at risk of ill-treatment.

In some countries, for example Somalia, armed groups such as al-Shabab were responsible for abuses against journalists and human rights defenders, including killings. Armed Islamist groups in Somalia were also responsible for stoning people to death and amputations. In various Sahel countries Al-Qa'ida in the Islamic Maghreb (AQIM) abducted individuals and held them hostage, killing some of them.

People on the move

Migrants continued to be exposed to discrimination and other human rights violations. Angolan security forces expelled more than 12,000 Congolese nationals between September and the end of December. Dozens of women and some men were reportedly raped during the

Millions of people in Africa living in slums and informal settlements were deprived of basic services, such as clean water, health care, education and effective policing.

expulsion and many were subjected to other abuses, arriving naked and without their belongings. Migrants, most of whom came from other West African countries, were arbitrarily detained in Mauritania to prevent them from trying to travel to Europe. Refugees and migrants were physically attacked in various parts of South Africa in spite of increased efforts by the authorities to respond to incidents of violence. Zimbabweans were given a chance to regularize their situation in South Africa.

In July, about 1,700 Rwandan rejected asylum-seekers, together with some recognized refugees, were forcibly returned to Rwanda from Uganda in violation of international law. Tens of thousands of other Rwandan refugees faced losing their refugee status by the end of 2011, putting them at risk of forcible return, partly because of pressure by Rwanda on neighbouring states. Thousands of Burundian refugees remained at risk of forcible return from Tanzania. Two people who were forcibly returned from Germany to Eritrea in 2008 fled once again and were granted refugee status in Germany. They had been detained in inhumane conditions after their forced return to Eritrea. Eritrea continued to implement a "shoot to kill" policy for anyone caught attempting to flee across the border.

Across the continent, millions of people remained displaced as a result of conflict and insecurity either within their own countries or as refugees. Kenya maintained its border closure with Somalia, hindering the assistance and protection of people fleeing from Somalia.

Housing – forced evictions

Millions of people in Africa living in slums and informal settlements were deprived of basic services, such as clean water, health care, education and effective policing. In many countries the authorities ignored their plight and excluded them from national plans and budgets. Lack of access to water and sanitation often led to further abuses, including sexual violence, as seen in informal settlements in Nairobi, Kenya.

There were mass forced evictions in several countries, including Angola, Ghana, Kenya and Nigeria, often driving people deeper into poverty. In Chad, Equatorial Guinea, Kenya and Zimbabwe thousands remained at risk of forced evictions. People who had been forcibly evicted in the past were often not given compensation or alternative accommodation and continued to live in destitution and with no security of tenure.

Maternal health

Progress was made in improving maternal health in Africa. Burkina Faso made commitments to lift all financial barriers to emergency obstetric care and access to family planning, but has now to live up to its promises. In Sierra Leone, a free health care service, abolishing user fees for pregnant women and children under five, was launched in April, but shortages of drugs and medical supplies led to problems as more women sought to use health facilities.

Other factors contributing to maternal mortality need to be urgently addressed in many countries, such as harmful traditional practices, discrimination against women, the lack of sexual and reproductive education and the absence of accountability mechanisms.

In July, the AU Assembly committed to a range of actions to reduce maternal mortality. These included spending 15 per cent of the public budget on health, launching a campaign to reduce maternal mortality, and a call for greater accountability in policy and financing decisions. The AU Commission was asked to set up a task force on maternal, newborn and child health to prepare and review reports on progress in the area of maternal and child health.

Discrimination

Violence and discrimination against women and girls continued to devastate their lives, restrict their opportunities and deprive them of their rights. In Sudan, the public order regime was used in the north to harass, arrest and ill-treat women and girls on the grounds of "indecent" or "immoral" dress or behaviour. Tens of thousands of cases of sexual violence were reported to the police in South Africa during the year. In Kenya, a survey indicated high levels of domestic violence, including marital rape, which is not a criminal offence under Kenyan law. In Liberia, the majority of reported rape cases involved girls under the age of 16. In many countries, women and girls subjected to sexual violence had no access to the police or justice system, were encouraged to reach out-of-court settlements, faced high medical costs and were ostracized by their communities. Women continued to be disproportionally affected by the HIV/AIDS pandemic, especially in southern Africa. Female genital mutilation continued to be practised in many countries even when prohibited in law, for example in Tanzania.

Discrimination against people based on their perceived or real sexual orientation remained widespread. In Cameroon, people were prosecuted on suspicion of same-sex activities and subjected to ill-treatment. In Malawi, two people were convicted of "gross indecency" and "unnatural acts" and sentenced to 14 years with hard labour. They were pardoned a few weeks later. A newspaper in Uganda published the photos and names of individuals it stated were homosexuals and messages inciting violence. The authorities failed to publicly denounce the newspaper, and a draconian anti-homosexuality bill remained pending in Parliament.

Violence and discrimination against women and girls continued to devastate their lives, restrict their opportunities and deprive them of their rights.

In Mauritania, the practice of slavery continued even though it is a criminal offence. Police did little to enforce the law and eight anti-slavery activists were arrested, reportedly ill-treated, and charged for bringing cases to the attention of the police.

Attacks against albino people continued in some countries. In Tanzania, the authorities' response remained inadequate, as they failed to investigate the attacks and past killings thoroughly, or to provide sufficient protection for activists campaigning for the rights of albino people.

During a visit to the Republic of Congo, the UN Special Rapporteur on indigenous people expressed concern about ongoing discrimination. In Eritrea, people continued to be persecuted and imprisoned on religious grounds; only members of permitted faiths were allowed to practise their religion.

The tide is turning

Amnesty International will shortly also celebrate its 50th anniversary. Since the first Amnesty International reports were published in the mid-1960s, their geographic scope and the range of human rights issues covered have expanded greatly. Numerous other human rights organizations have been created in the past half century, some of them inspired by Amnesty International's campaigning. In many countries in Africa there is now a vibrant civil society, which, although often still repressed, can no longer be ignored by those in power. A lot still needs to be achieved, but the tide is turning.

REGIONAL OVERVIEWS
AFRICA

AMERICAS

*"We have suffered too much with so much violence… we are not asking,
we are demanding rights: demarcation of our lands with urgency so that
we can return to live in peace, with happiness and dignity."*

Open letter from the Guarani-Kaiowá Indigenous People to Brazilian President Luiz Inácio Lula
da Silva, August 2010

In the Americas many human rights have been recognized in law, if not
always in practice, over the past 50 years. While abuses clearly persist –
particularly against vulnerable groups – the region has undeniably seen
progress, albeit slow and partial. Governments can rightly claim some
credit for these changes. However, it is the communities most affected by
human rights abuses who have been the real driving force behind these
advances. It is they who have spoken out and campaigned for change,
often at great personal risk. It is their determination and persistence that
have inspired millions and made it increasingly difficult for states to
ignore the growing clamour for fundamental and irreversible change.

The year began, however, with a sharp reminder of how fragile
these hard won rights can be. In January, a devastating earthquake hit
Haiti, leaving more than 230,000 people dead and millions homeless.
By the end of the year, more than 1,050,000 people displaced by the
disaster were still living in tents in makeshift camps, denied their rights
to adequate shelter and vulnerable to attack. The dramatic increase in
rapes was a clear indictment of the failure of the authorities to ensure
the security of women and girls living in the camps.

Haiti was a potent symbol of what the lack of political will to prioritize
the protection of rights can mean for ordinary people. However, it also
provided powerful evidence of the way grassroots organizations at the
forefront of human rights protection overcome seemingly insuperable
odds to keep hope and dignity alive. The Commission of Women Victims
for Victims (Komisyon Fanm Viktim pou Viktim, KOFAVIV) is one such
organization, offering support to the growing number of survivors of
sexual violence in Haiti's camps. Most KOFAVIV members are
themselves rape survivors and many lost everything in the earthquake.
Yet despite their own personal tragedies, they have stepped in to
provide survivors with the kind of medical, psychological and financial
support that the Haitian state should be providing, but does not.

Even in times of relative peace and stability, governments frequently fail to ensure that rights are upheld in practice, especially for those at greatest risk of abuse, such as people living in poverty, Indigenous Peoples, and women and girls. This is particularly true in cases where powerful economic interests view upholding the rights of poor and marginalized communities as contrary to their economic goals.

Human rights defenders

Defending human rights continued to be dangerous work in many countries in the region. Activists were killed, threatened, harassed or subjected to arbitrary legal proceedings in a number of countries including Brazil, Colombia, Cuba, Ecuador, Guatemala, Honduras, Mexico and Venezuela. Often they were targeted because their work threatened the economic and political interests of those in power.

In countries such as Colombia and Brazil, some protection measures were implemented to address the risks faced by human rights defenders. However, in others, the year ended without the creation of integrated measures to tackle the problem. For example, in Mexico, where there was growing concern about the security of activists, the authorities made little progress in implementing a protection programme, despite a commitment to do so first made in 2008.

Indigenous Peoples

Indigenous Peoples in the Americas have become increasingly vocal and organized in defence of their rights in recent years. Nevertheless, the legacy of widespread human rights abuses against them, and the failure to hold those responsible to account, helped perpetuate long-standing discrimination and poverty in Indigenous communities throughout the region.

The expansion of the agricultural and extractive industries and the introduction of huge development projects such as dams and roads into traditional Indigenous lands represented a significant and growing threat to Indigenous Peoples. In Argentina, Brazil, Chile, Colombia, Guatemala, Panama, Paraguay and Peru, Indigenous Peoples seen as standing in the way of commercial interests were threatened, harassed, forcibly evicted, displaced and killed as the drive to exploit resources intensified in the areas where they lived.

Although states in the Americas voted in favour of the 2007 UN Declaration on the Rights of Indigenous Peoples, by the end of 2010 none had enacted legislation ensuring that development projects affecting Indigenous Peoples could only be undertaken with the communities' free, prior and informed consent.

Haiti provided powerful evidence of the way grassroots organizations at the forefront of human rights protection overcome seemingly insuperable odds to keep hope and dignity alive.

Peru came close to approving landmark legislation in May when the Law on the Right of Indigenous People to Prior Consultation, drawn up with the participation of Indigenous Peoples, was passed by Congress. However, President García refused to promulgate it. Paraguay continued to fail to abide by two decisions handed down by the Inter-American Court of Human Rights in 2005 and 2006 ordering the state to return traditional lands to the Yakye Axa and Sawhoyamaxa. In August, the Court ruled on a third case involving Indigenous Peoples' rights and condemned Paraguay for its violation of the rights of the Xákmok Kásek. In Brazil, where the right of Indigenous Peoples to their "traditionally occupied lands" was enshrined in the Constitution as long ago as 1988, the Guarani-Kaiowá in Mato Grosso do Sul state faced numerous obstacles and protracted delays in getting their land claims settled. While their claims stalled in the courts, the Guarani-Kaiowá were harassed and attacked by gunmen hired by local farmers to remove them from the land.

Conflict

In Colombia, the 45-year internal armed conflict continued to take a heavy toll on the civilian population, which bore the brunt of the hostilities. Thousands of people were the victims of forced displacement, unlawful killing, kidnapping or enforced disappearance by guerrilla groups, the security forces and paramilitaries. The most marginalized groups – Indigenous, Afro-descendant and peasant farmer communities, as well as the urban poor – were targeted by the warring parties. Promises by the newly elected President, Juan Manuel Santos, that he would prioritize human rights and the fight against impunity raised hopes that his administration would show the political will to tackle the long-running human rights crisis in the country. However, continued attacks on human rights defenders, activists and community leaders, especially those working on land rights issues, showed the scale of the difficulties that lay ahead.

A number of countries, particularly in the Andean region, saw mass demonstrations against government policies and legislation on issues such as access to natural resources, land, education and public services. In September, Ecuador appeared to be on the brink of civil conflict after hundreds of police officers took to the streets in protest at government proposals to change their pay and benefits. President Correa, who became caught up in the protests, was briefly hospitalized for the effects of tear gas.

Public security

Poverty, criminal violence and the proliferation of small arms created and perpetuated the conditions in which human rights abuses

The expansion of the agricultural and extractive industries and the introduction of huge development projects represented a significant and growing threat to Indigenous Peoples.

flourished. Residents of poor urban neighbourhoods – particularly in parts of Mexico, Central America, Brazil and the Caribbean – continued to be caught between the violence of organized criminal gangs and human rights abuses by the security forces.

In many cases, endemic corruption in state institutions undermined their ability to respond adequately to organized crime. However, governments showed little appetite for addressing this long-standing and systemic problem. Rather, they increasingly resorted to the deployment of the military in response to organized crime and other perceived threats to security.

In Mexico, for example, the deployment of the military to combat organized crime resulted in numerous reports of serious human rights violations, including unlawful killings, enforced disappearances, torture and arbitrary detention. In Jamaica, a state of emergency was declared in May in parts of the country following an outbreak of gang violence. During the state of emergency, at least 4,000 people were detained and 76 killed, including three members of the security forces. More than half the killings were alleged to have been extrajudicial executions.

Counter-terror and human rights

US President Obama's promise that the Guantánamo detention centre would be closed by January 2010 was not fulfilled. By the end of the year, 174 people remained held in the prison. The only Guantánamo detainee so far transferred to the US mainland for prosecution in a federal court was tried and convicted. Two Guantánamo detainees were convicted by military commission during the year after pleading guilty. Revised rules, issued in April, governing military commission proceedings for so-called "war on terror" suspects showed that there was little hope that the US administration would make substantial reforms and uphold human rights.

Justice and impunity

In several Latin American countries, most notably the Southern Cone, there were continued and significant advances in efforts to bring to justice some of those responsible for serious and widespread human rights violations under past military regimes.

In Argentina, Reynaldo Bignone, former military general and former President, was found guilty in April of torture, murder and several kidnappings that occurred while he was commander of the notorious Campo de Mayo detention centre between 1976 and 1978. In July, General Luciano Benjamín Menéndez and Roberto Albornoz, former head of the intelligence police, were sentenced to life imprisonment for human rights violations committed at a secret detention centre in Tucumán province during the military regime (1976-1983).

There were continued and significant advances in efforts to bring to justice some of those responsible for serious and widespread human rights violations under past military regimes.

In July, Manuel Contreras, former head of the infamous Chilean National Intelligence Directorate (Dirección de Inteligencia Nacional, DINA), was sentenced to 17 years' imprisonment for his part in the killing in Argentina in 1974 of General Carlos Prats, a member of cabinet in the government of President Salvador Allende (1970-73), and his wife.

In a landmark ruling in October, the Uruguayan Supreme Court declared a 1986 amnesty law unconstitutional. However, the ruling was specific to the case against former President Juan María Bordaberry (1971-1976) and will not, therefore, lead to the reopening of previously archived cases.

Also in October, members of Peru's "Colina group" death squad and former high-ranking officials in the government of Alberto Fujimori (1990-2000) were convicted of the killing of 15 people and the enforced disappearance of 10 others in 1991 and 1992.

In Colombia, retired Colonel Luis Alfonso Plazas Vega was sentenced to 30 years' imprisonment in June for the enforced disappearance of 11 people in 1985 when the military stormed the Palace of Justice, where people were being held hostage by the M-19 guerrilla group.

However, in many cases progress was severely hampered by the fact that military institutions failed to co-operate with, and in some instances showed outright resistance to, investigations into human rights violations. In Bolivia, for example, officials investigating enforced disappearances dating from 1980-1981 continued to face obstacles in getting access to military archives, despite two Supreme Court orders for the declassification of the archives.

In Mexico and Colombia, the military justice systems continued to claim jurisdiction in cases of alleged human rights violations committed by members of the armed forces. New legislation in Colombia and proposed legal reforms in Mexico did not guarantee that all human rights violations would be excluded from military jurisdiction, despite clear evidence of the lack of independence and impartiality of military courts and prosecutors.

Efforts to introduce legislation to combat impunity stalled in some countries, while in others progress made in previous years was rolled back. For example, in April the Chilean Supreme Court upheld a decision that the 1978 Amnesty Law should apply in the case of Carmelo Soria Espinosa, a Spanish diplomat killed in 1976 by the security forces. Also, in April, the Brazilian Supreme Federal Tribunal upheld the interpretation that crimes committed by members of the military – extrajudicial executions, torture and rape – were political or related to political acts and, therefore, covered by an amnesty law passed by the military regime in 1979. However, in November the

Inter-American Court of Human Rights ruled that the 1979 Amnesty Law was null and void, and reminded the Brazilian authorities of their obligation to bring perpetrators to justice. Meanwhile in Peru, Congress voted to revoke Decree Law 1097, which effectively granted amnesties to human rights violators, but two decrees allowing members of the armed forces accused of human rights violations to be tried in military courts remained in place.

In El Salvador, President Funes signed into law an Executive Decree in January creating a new National Search Commission for Disappeared Children to search for children who disappeared during the armed conflict (1980-1992). By the end of the year, however, the new Commission was still not operational and the whereabouts of hundreds of disappeared children remained unknown.

Meanwhile, in the USA, those responsible for crimes under international law committed as part of the "war on terror", such as torture and enforced disappearance, were not held to account. In November, former President George W. Bush admitted that he had authorized the use of "water-boarding" (a form of torture in which the process of drowning a detainee is begun) during his administration. Nevertheless, accountability and remedy for human rights violations committed as part of the USA's programme of secret detention and rendition remained non-existent. In November, the US Department of Justice announced, without further explanation, that no one would face criminal charges in relation to the destruction in 2005 of 92 tapes depicting evidence of "water-boarding" and other torture techniques used against two detainees held in 2002.

International justice

In December, 14 people – 12 Chilean former military officials, including General Manuel Contreras; a Chilean civilian; and an Argentine former military official – were sentenced in absentia to between 15 years and life imprisonment by a court in France. The 14 were convicted in connection with the disappearance of four French-Chilean nationals during the early years of the Chilean military government of Augusto Pinochet (1973-1990).

Judges in the Americas made use of international human rights law to re-open cases of human rights violations that had been closed because statutes of limitations had expired. In Colombia, for example, the Supreme Court of Justice ruled in May that former Congressman César Pérez García should be prosecuted in connection with a 1988 massacre in Segovia by paramilitaries in which more than 40 peasant farmers were killed. The Court argued that the massacre amounted to crimes against humanity and was, therefore, not subject to the statute of limitations.

Accountability and remedy for human rights violations committed as part of the USA's programme of secret detention and rendition remained non-existent.

During 2010, St. Lucia became the 113th state to ratify the Rome Statute of the International Criminal Court. Paraguay and Brazil ratified the International Convention on enforced disappearance, but neither recognized the competence of the Committee against Enforced Disappearance to receive and consider communications from or on behalf of victims.

Death penalty

Forty-six prisoners – 45 men and one woman – were put to death in the USA during the year. This brought to 1,234 the total number of executions carried out since the US Supreme Court lifted a moratorium on the death penalty in 1976.

In Guatemala, Congress passed legislation in October that could lead to the resumption of the use of the death penalty. However, the President vetoed the bill, and in December Guatemala voted in favour of the UN General Assembly resolution calling for a moratorium on the use of the death penalty.

In December, Cuba commuted the sentences of the last three prisoners facing the death penalty.

Although death sentences were handed down in the Bahamas, Guyana, Jamaica and Trinidad and Tobago, no executions were carried out.

Freedom of expression

The Americas remained a dangerous region for those working in the media. Only Asia recorded more killings of journalists during 2010. Almost 400 media workers were threatened or attacked and at least 13 journalists were killed by unidentified assailants. Mexico accounted for more than half of these deaths, followed by Honduras, Colombia and Brazil. In many cases, those killed were believed to have been targeted because of their efforts to uncover corruption or to expose the links between officials and criminal networks.

A significant number of TV stations, particularly in Venezuela and the Dominican Republic, were forced to close temporarily; radio stations were also affected. In the Dominican Republic at least seven TV and radio stations had their transmission signal blocked or were forced to close temporarily in the run-up to the May elections. Some channels had still not been able to resume broadcasting by the end of the year.

In Cuba, journalists continued to be arbitrarily detained and all media remained under state control.

Inequality and development

Progress in poverty reduction was recorded in Argentina, Brazil, Mexico and Venezuela. However, although there was evidence that poverty was slowly decreasing in Latin America and the Caribbean, almost a fifth of the region's population continued to live in extreme poverty, including the vast majority of Indigenous Peoples. Despite a reduction in inequality in many countries, notably Venezuela, many of the least developed nations failed to show any tangible improvements and at the end of 2010 Latin America remained the most unequal region in the world.

Indigenous Peoples and Afro-descendant communities were disproportionately represented among those living in poverty, more so than any other group. The repeated, but false, claim that respect for the rights of Indigenous Peoples is incompatible with economic growth and development provided the backdrop to a persistent pattern of rights violations. In Guatemala, despite a request by the Inter-American Commission on Human Rights that operations at the Marlin 1 gold mine in San Marcos department be suspended, the mine was still operational at the end of the year. In Canada, the Toronto Stock Exchange took the decision in January to de-list the Copper Mesa Mining Corporation from the exchange. The company was the subject of a lawsuit presented by the Ecuadorian Intang Indigenous People who accused the company of responsibility for human rights violations. In May, an Ontario court struck out the lawsuit; an appeal was before the Ontario Court of Appeal at the end of the year.

Eighteen UN agencies working in Latin America issued a report in July on the progress made by states in achieving the Millennium Development Goals (MDGs). The report revealed that the MDG to reduce maternal mortality was the furthest off track. Tens of thousands of women continued to die from preventable pregnancy-related complications and wide disparities persisted in access to quality health care. The report attributed this to discrimination against women and their low status in society.

Laws banning abortion in all circumstances continued to deny women and girls in El Salvador, Chile and Nicaragua their right to sexual and reproductive health.

Violence against women and girls and the denial of reproductive rights

Violence against women and girls, including sexual violence, remained widespread and most survivors were denied access to justice and redress. Although states in the region introduced legislation to combat gender-based violence, in practice laws were seldom applied and investigations and prosecutions were rare. A new law in the USA offered hope to Indigenous women survivors of rape by establishing more robust systems to access justice. However, in countries such as Bolivia, Guatemala, Haiti and Nicaragua, failing justice systems helped perpetuate impunity for gender-based violence and so contributed to a climate where such violence proliferated.

Thousands of women in the region were raped, forcibly disappeared or killed during the year. Women in certain parts of Guatemala and Mexico and Indigenous women in Canada were at particular risk. The lack of resources available to investigate and prosecute these crimes raised questions about official willingness to address violence against women.

Many of those subjected to gender-based violence were girls under the age of 18. For example, in October, the UN Committee on the Rights of the Child requested that Nicaragua take urgent action to eradicate sexual violence against children, following increasing evidence of widespread sexual abuse of girls and teenagers in the country.

Laws banning abortion in all circumstances continued to deny women and girls in El Salvador, Chile and Nicaragua their right to sexual and reproductive health. Laws criminalizing abortion put anyone providing or seeking an abortion at potential risk of imprisonment, including girls and women who were pregnant as a result of rape or who experienced life-threatening complications in their pregnancies.

In some other countries, access to abortion granted in law was denied in practice because of protracted judicial procedures that made access to safe abortion almost impossible especially for those who could not afford to pay for private abortion services.

"I demand that the government respects our rights as women. We are girls and we have rights, and so long as they do not respect these rights, we will continue to fight to demand them," Clara, youth rights promoter, aged 18, Managua, Nicaragua.

REGIONAL OVERVIEWS
AMERICAS

Myanmar's pro-democracy leader Daw Aung San Suu Kyi addresses supporters following her release from house arrest, Yangon, Myanmar, 13 November 2010. The number of political prisoners in Myanmar reached an estimated 2,200 during 2010. Most were prisoners of conscience.

ASIA-PACIFIC

"I am innocent and I will prove my innocence. I will come out and resume my work towards the human rights and health rights of Adivasi communities in Chhattisgarh, regardless of the threats facing me and other human rights defenders."

Dr Binayak Sen, speaking to Amnesty International on 24 February 2010

In a region with almost two thirds of the world's population, stretching a third of the way around the planet, a few individual human rights defenders, like Binayak Sen, continued to dominate headlines and affect national and geopolitical events because of their courage in speaking truth to power. The events of 2010 highlighted the crucial role of brave individuals in demanding greater dignity and respect, but they also underscored the high price these human rights defenders pay – and the continuing need for global solidarity with them.

Fifty years after Amnesty International came into being dedicated to protecting the rights of those detained simply for their opinions, Asia-Pacific governments still made a habit of responding to critics with intimidation, imprisonment, ill-treatment and even death. Government repression did not distinguish between those who were clamouring for civil and political rights and those whose complaints were rooted in violations of economic, social and cultural rights.

There was good news in 2010. In mid-November, people around the world joined in celebrating with the people of Myanmar when Daw Aung San Suu Kyi was released upon the termination of her sentence, after spending 15 of the last 21 years in some form of detention.

For many years, Aung San Suu Kyi had the unfortunate distinction of being the only living recipient of the Nobel Peace Prize to be in detention. In December, she briefly shared that unwanted distinction with Liu Xiaobo, a writer and dissident serving a prison sentence in China for his role in drafting Charter 08, a manifesto for a more responsive and inclusive government in China.

The Chinese government responded by frying – and failing – to push the Norwegian government into rescinding the honour, and then by bullying and cajoling various governments to skip the award ceremony. In the end, the ceremony was well attended, but Liu Xiaobo languished in prison, while his wife Liu Xia was held under house arrest and other members of his family and fellow activists were barred from travelling to Oslo to receive the prize or participate in the festivities. This made Liu Xiaobo's the first Nobel Peace Prize to go physically uncollected since 1936, when the Nazi government in Germany prevented Carl von Ossietzky from attending the ceremony. The Nobel Committee's selection of Liu Xiaobo, and the Chinese government's petulant response, highlighted the ongoing – and even increasing – effort to silence government critics over the past three years.

The year ended with a life sentence imposed on Binayak Sen by a state court in India. Binayak Sen, a prisoner of conscience, is a physician and activist who has criticized both the Indian government and Maoist armed groups for the spiralling violence in central India. His trial was politically motivated, suffered from serious procedural and evidentiary flaws, and was roundly denounced by observers inside and outside India. Nevertheless, a sessions court in Chhattisgarh state sentenced Binayak Sen to life imprisonment for sedition – under the same problematic law used against Mahatma Gandhi by the British colonial government.

Aung San Suu Kyi, Liu Xiaobo, and Binayak Sen each served as symbols of resistance to injustice and indignity, but they are also individuals who keenly suffer the deprivations of detention. They may be at the centre of international attention, and even benefit from that attention, but in each case, government authorities have abused them and subjected their family members and associates to threats and harassment. In this sense, their plight is no different from that of thousands of activists and human rights defenders who suffer government persecution in the Asia-Pacific region but do not receive the attention of headline writers and policy-makers.

Aung San Suu Kyi, Liu Xiaobo and Binayak Sen each served as symbols of resistance to injustice and indignity. Their plight mirrors that of thousands of human rights defenders suffering government persecution in the region.

Freedom of expression

As even a cursory review of the events of 2010 shows, many journalists and activists across the Asia-Pacific region placed their lives and well-being on the line in order to challenge governments and other powerful actors to fulfil their obligations to respect the rights and dignity of all. As a result, many of those who dared exercise their right to express their opinions freely suffered violations of their civil and political rights. Paradoxically, it was often these civil and political violations that grabbed the headlines, and not the more complicated causes – often violations of economic, social and cultural rights – that prompted complaints and criticism in the first place.

Regardless of the reasons for dissent, most of the region's governments shared the desire to inhibit critics, notwithstanding political, religious, ethnic and cultural differences. Governments across the region also shared the routine invocation of "national security" or the maintenance of harmony and stability as the rationale for their attempts to silence dissent.

North Korea's government, beset by severe economic problems and increased political tensions with its neighbours, maintained its chokehold on all communications within the country. Vitit Muntarbhorn, the UN's Special Rapporteur on North Korea, ended his term by roundly condemning the country's singular lack of respect for nearly the entire gamut of internationally recognized human rights. There was no pretence of free expression or organized civil society, and the government severely punished efforts to even receive information from unauthorized sources, for instance via short-wave radio.

Few governments attempted to maintain this level of control over the opinions received and expressed by their citizens. Even in Myanmar, the government made an effort to reform its battered image (inside and outside the country) by holding parliamentary elections in November and replacing uniformed military rulers with civilian rulers (although often the very same people). The elections were widely viewed as problematic, since the electorate was denied the opportunity to debate the country's future and many, if not most, potentially critical candidates were barred from participation.

The Myanmar government may have tried to assuage some of the intense international and regional criticism by releasing Aung San Suu Kyi only a week after holding parliamentary elections. But the ongoing detention of thousands of prisoners, many of them held in horrific conditions, countered any pretence of real concessions. It has long been known that the authorities have detained some 2,200 political activists, many of them for supporting the cause espoused by Aung San Suu Kyi and her party, the National League for Democracy. But Amnesty International's research in 2010 uncovered how extensively the Myanmar military authorities have monitored and punished dissent among the country's many ethnic minority groups who have long been marginalized from power and seen their land and labour forcefully expropriated.

In most other countries in the region, authorities tried to control criticism even as old and new forms of expression spread. In Viet Nam, for instance, more than a dozen activists were convicted in faulty trials simply because they had peacefully voiced criticism of government policies. Most of those convicted faced charges under vague and poorly defined laws related to "national security".

China's government maintained intense pressure on some ethnic minority communities, in particular ethnic Tibetans, as well as Uighurs, a largely Muslim group from the resource-rich Xinjiang region. More

REGIONAL OVERVIEWS
ASIA-PACIFIC

than a year after violent riots erupted in Xinjiang, the Chinese government continued to persecute Uighur activists and muzzle those who criticized the government's conduct, justifying its repressive tactics by invoking the threat of "splittism" and vague and unsubstantiated threats to national security.

Critics of any ethnicity who directly challenged the Chinese government felt the heavy hand of repression. The Chinese government fell short even of the benchmarks it had established in its two-year human rights action plan, which ended in 2010. Contrary to the steady increase of public discussion on old-fashioned media platforms, such as newspapers, as well as social networking through the internet, voices that asked for a more representative government remained heavily restricted. The Chinese government showed that it is at once extremely sensitive to public criticism by the media and civil society and intensely afraid of trusting the country's citizens to play a greater role in their own governance.

> **The Chinese government showed that it is at once extremely sensitive to public criticism and intensely afraid of trusting the country's citizens to play a greater role in their own governance.**

Thailand, a country which boasts a more open media environment than most of its neighbours in Southeast Asia, witnessed greater government restrictions on free speech in the face of serious political unrest and street violence. As large, sometimes violent, protests broke out in Bangkok, the government imposed a state of emergency and cracked down on thousands of websites, shutting down tens of thousands of sites on grounds that they threatened national security or had somehow insulted the monarchy in violation of the country's harsh lese-majesty laws.

India has long prided itself on its vibrant media and powerful legal system – the bases of the country's boast of being the largest democracy in the world. Nevertheless, untenable and unsupported allegations of threats to national security undergirded the Indian government's case against Binayak Sen as well as hundreds of people detained in troubled Jammu and Kashmir state. Facing a significant escalation of protests against the Indian government's heavy-handed rule in the state, Indian authorities detained dozens of suspects and held many of them in administrative detention, without proper legal process.

The citizens of several other South Asian countries also suffered from significant restrictions on their free speech. In Sri Lanka, the curtailing of journalists and civil society continued apace as President Mahinda Rajapaksa won re-election in January. Journalists and activists who opposed his government reported intimidation and threats, bolstered by several incidents in which forces believed to be linked to the government harassed, detained or abducted journalists. Similarly, Afghan journalists faced increasing harassment and attacks by state and non-state actors, especially during the country's widely discredited parliamentary elections. But at least in government-controlled areas of Afghanistan, journalists bravely continued their work despite harassment and arbitrary detention by the authorities; unfortunately, in a growing swath of the country, the Taleban and other anti-government groups effectively shut down any critical debate.

In several instances, where governments did not directly interfere with freedom of expression, they did little to protect journalists or the space for public discourse. More than a year after the massacre of 33 journalists in the Philippines, the case against the alleged perpetrators dragged on, even as witnesses reported threats and intimidation. Pakistan was the scene of 19 lethal attacks on media workers in 2010, most of them without clear perpetrators – in different incidents, accusations ranged from the Pakistani Taleban to radical religious groups to the government's shadowy intelligence services. The government did little to protect journalists or bring their attackers to justice. Notwithstanding these attacks, many Pakistani journalists went to great lengths to report on the country's many ills.

Pakistan again suffered through a cataclysmic year, as unprecedented flooding in July and August submerged nearly a fifth of the country and affected some 20 million people. This catastrophe aggravated the misery facing millions of Pakistanis already afflicted by conflicted-related violence, displacement and extreme poverty. In north-west Pakistan, army personnel often violated the laws of war and human rights, arbitrarily arresting civilians and subjecting suspected insurgents to extrajudicial executions. The Pakistani Taleban and other insurgent groups in turn inflicted cruel punishments on the civilian population, targeted civilians and civilian property, including schools, and launched deadly suicide attacks in the major cities, causing hundreds of civilian deaths and injuries. In Balochistan, the bullet-riddled bodies of scores of missing Baloch activists were recovered across the province. The victims' relatives and activists accuse the Pakistani security forces of these "kill and dump" operations. The atrocities have only added to the climate of fear and the Baloch people's grievances of misgovernance and marginalization. But because reporting from these conflict-affected areas remained patchy and scarce, it provided only an inkling of the enormous human suffering in the province.

Similarly, in India, government restrictions and general insecurity dampened coverage (and hence understanding) of the escalating crisis posed by Maoist armed insurgencies in central and north-eastern India – referred to as India's gravest internal security challenge by Prime Minister Manmohan Singh. A potent combination of poverty, caste and ethnic discrimination, religious dogma, and corporate greed,

REGIONAL OVERVIEWS
ASIA-PACIFIC

laid the groundwork for a crisis pitting security forces and associated paramilitary groups against often indiscriminate militant groups, with civilians paying a heavy toll.

Corporate violations

It took the work of activists like Binayak Sen to focus attention on the difficulties gripping central India and in particular Chhattisgarh state. Activists have long pointed out that the conflict across central India was fuelled by government policies that aggravated the region's poverty, government inaction in the face of corporate wrongdoing after the 1984 Union Carbide gas disaster in Bhopal, and more recent attempts to pursue economic development without adequately consulting the region's residents.

In a positive move, the Indian government put the brakes on the development of a large-scale aluminium mining project by UK-based Vedanta Resources and the state-owned Orissa Mining Corporation after an administrative panel found that the companies had proceeded without securing the free, prior, informed consent of the region's Indigenous Adivasi population, for whom the area of the mine was of supreme religious importance. The decision was the first of its kind in India and raised hopes that the Indian government would provide greater attention to the Adivasi population, as well as other groups facing institutionalized poverty and marginalization.

The reversal of the Vedanta decision was the result of intense campaigning by Adivasis in close association with international groups – including Amnesty International – which marshalled global economic and public relations pressure. In London, where Vedanta shareholders were meeting in July 2010, activists used international law, economics, celebrity advocates, and even painted themselves blue to invoke the recent science fiction blockbuster film *Avatar*, whose plot of a native population battling corporate interlopers superficially resembled the situation in Orissa.

Access to health care and maternal mortality

In other areas, the campaign for maintaining the dignity and defending the rights of the poor and the marginalized remained fraught. In Indonesia, local groups combating the country's disproportionately high rate of maternal mortality have recently stepped up their efforts to reverse the trends by reforming the discriminatory laws and problematic societal attitudes at the heart of the statistics. Even as thousands of Indonesian women die needlessly through pregnancy and childbirth, it has proved difficult to garner sufficient public support – and therefore government attention and resolve – to address the problem.

> **Afghanistan still suffered from one of the worst maternal mortality rates in the world: one in eight Afghan women died of pregnancy-related complications.**

The Indonesian government has nevertheless committed itself to improving the conditions of the country's populace, and in particular of Indonesian women and girls. It has proved far more difficult to fight for the rights of citizens of countries whose governments, to a greater or lesser extent, simply ignore their obligations.

In North Korea, millions of people suffer from insufficient food and lack of access to medicine and health care. Egregious government mismanagement, coupled with naturally occurring draught, have led to extreme shortages so that people in many circumstances have had to supplement their food with inedible plants and make do without even basic health care. Despite these difficulties, the North Korean government has restricted the distribution of international aid.

Afghanistan still suffered from one of the worst maternal mortality rates in the world: one in eight Afghan women died of pregnancy-related complications. Early marriage – often under the age of 15 – and lack of access to medical intervention until complications become severe, are two factors that have hampered improvement in the situation.

Few situations are as extreme as in North Korea and Afghanistan. But the wilful violation of international human rights can occur even in a much wealthier country like Malaysia, where the government has defied the international prohibition of torture by continuing to allow the caning of thousands of people detained on allegations of immigration violations and petty criminal activity. According to the government's own records, over the past decade, tens of thousands of people have been caned, a practice that causes victims extreme pain and permanent scarring. In February, three women were caned for allegedly violating religious law, or Shari'a, the first time women had received such a punishment. The Malaysian government has even enlisted physicians to aid the process by ensuring that victims of caning are prepared for the punishment, a clear violation of medical ethics and the physicians' obligation to prevent harm to those in their care.

Unfortunately, instead of acting immediately to end this shameful practice, the Malaysian government attempted to stifle internal debate and even resorted to physically blacking out copies of the international weekly *Time* magazine that carried a reference to the "epidemic" of caning in Malaysia.

International justice

Media attention and public pressure are only one of the components necessary to ensure that our leaders are responsive and accountable for respecting international human rights. The restrictions governments placed on monitoring suggested how important it has

REGIONAL OVERVIEWS ASIA-PACIFIC

been to bear witness and speak the truth. But without some mechanism to translate this testimony into justice, powerful people all too often get away with wrongdoing. In 2010, the scales of justice in the Asia-Pacific region remained decidedly out of balance in favour of the perpetrators.

The government of Sri Lanka spent the year trying to avoid accountability for the war crimes and human rights violations that characterized the long conflict which ended in the military annihilation of the armed group, the Liberation Tigers of Tamil Eelam (themselves responsible for numerous human rights abuses) – at the cost of thousands of civilians killed, injured and detained. Despite a promise to the UN to provide justice, the government established a Lessons Learnt and Reconciliation Commission whose mandate made no mention of accountability. The Commission seemed destined to join the other ultimately futile special bodies established over the last two decades to address impunity in Sri Lanka, without actually leading to justice. Hope for accountability centred on an advisory panel of experts assigned to assist UN Secretary-General Ban Ki-moon in assessing the need for an international accountability mechanism.

Existing international accountability mechanisms had a mixed record in 2010. In Cambodia, the notorious Khmer Rouge prison official Kaing Guek Eav, also known as "Duch", was sentenced in July to 35 years in jail for crimes against humanity and war crimes, the first such conviction by the Extraordinary Chambers in the Courts of Cambodia (ECCC), the UN-backed Khmer Rouge tribunal. Four more Khmer Rouge leaders remain in custody pending hearings, a small but decidedly significant step forward in the search for accountability for the country's killing fields. Cambodia's leader, Hun Sen, publicly called for the ECCC to limit its activity to these five people.

In 2010, the notion that heads of state can be subject to justice was no longer alien, as demonstrated by the lengths to which they went to pay lip service to justice while carefully evading legal liability.

Similarly, in March, President José Ramos-Horta of Timor-Leste told the UN Human Rights Council that "in the efforts to bring about peace between long-standing rival communities, often we have to compromise on justice." This statement flew in the face of recommendations from Timor-Leste's own Commission for Reception, Truth and Reconciliation in 2005, as well as by Timorese victims, national human rights groups and UN justice experts.

So far, the principle of international justice in the Asia-Pacific region has been honoured more in the breach than in actual practice. But in 2010 the notion that powerful people – even heads of state – can and should be subject to justice was no longer alien, as demonstrated by the lengths to which governments, corporations and armed groups went to pay lip service to the notion of justice while carefully evading legal liability.

The heart of the struggle

Some activists in the Asia-Pacific region, like Aung San Suu Kyi, Liu Xiaobo and Binayak Sen, have achieved global prominence, and they each have used their fame, and faced unfair punishments, to push for improvements in the rights of the people of the Asia-Pacific region. The most important contribution made by these human rights defenders is not through their iconic status, but rather, through describing that what happened to them has happened to hundreds of less famous other brave critics and activists. Ultimately, it is crucial to maintain a focus on the violations they have suffered, because, as shown by the case of Duch, as well as other successful international prosecutions, it takes only one case, one set of individual facts, to secure a conviction for violations of international human rights law. That is why in 2010, as in years past, the work of individual human rights defenders remained at the heart of the struggle for human rights worldwide, even when they were addressing massive and systematic violations in a region that houses nearly two thirds of the world's population and stretches a third of the way around the globe.

REGIONAL OVERVIEWS
ASIA-PACIFIC

A man and young boy stare at a burned-out house in an Uzbek district of Osh city, southern Kyrgyzstan, June 2010. Violent clashes between ethnic Kyrgyz and ethnic Uzbek gangs left hundreds dead and forced hundreds of thousands to flee their homes.

EUROPE AND CENTRAL ASIA

"The great lie has been laid bare. The truth has been brought home at last."

Tony Doherty, whose father Paddy died on Sunday 30 January 1972 in Derry, Northern Ireland, when soldiers opened fire on a civil rights march.

The right to truth and justice, and the determination of victims and their relatives to achieve this however long and however hard the struggle, remained a key part of the human rights landscape across the Europe and Central Asia region throughout the year.

On 15 June, families gathered in a council building in Northern Ireland in the UK to have first sight of the findings of a long-running – and long-awaited – inquiry into the killing of 13 people by the British army on a day that became known as Bloody Sunday.

They had waited nearly four decades for justice, and their jubilation when it came was unrestrained. The inquiry rejected all claims from earlier government reports that any of those killed and injured by soldiers were posing a threat, were armed with a firearm, or threw a nail or petrol bomb. It vindicated all their loved ones of any responsibility for the shootings. The report confirmed that several of the victims had been shot in the back while running away, and found that accounts by many of the soldiers were manifestly untrue. In response, the UK Prime Minister gave a public state apology.

Freedom of expression

For a region that prides itself as a beacon for free expression, the real picture was very different for many seeking to publicize abuses, articulate alternative views, or hold governments and others to account. Freedoms of expression and association remained under attack – as did human rights defenders themselves.

In Turkey, despite increasingly open debate regarding previously taboo issues, numerous criminal prosecutions followed the expression of dissenting opinions: especially those relating to criticism of the armed forces, the position of Armenians and Kurds in Turkey and ongoing criminal prosecutions. Alongside various articles of the Penal Code, anti-terrorism laws carrying higher prison sentences and resulting in pre-trial detention orders were frequently used to stifle legitimate free expression. Kurdish political activists, journalists and human rights defenders were among those most frequently prosecuted. Arbitrary restrictions continued to be imposed, blocking access to websites, and newspapers were issued with temporary closure orders. Threats of violence against outspoken individuals continued.

Elsewhere, the clampdown remained depressingly familiar. Virtually any form of dissent was suppressed in Turkmenistan. Journalists working with foreign media faced harassment and intimidation, and independent civil society activists were unable to operate openly. Fears for their safety were heightened after the President called on the Security Ministry to fight those who "defame our law-based democratic state". In Uzbekistan, human rights defenders and independent journalists were harassed, beaten, detained and imprisoned after unfair trials. A similar pattern was seen in Azerbaijan, with criminal and civil defamation laws used to silence criticism, and Serbia, where human rights defenders and journalists continued to be subject to threats, attacks and hate speech.

By making unsubstantiated links between immigration status and crime, some politicians and government representatives themselves contributed to fostering a climate of intolerance and xenophobia.

In Russia, the authorities continued to send out mixed messages on freedom of expression. They promised respect and protection for journalists and civil society activists, while at the same time launching, or failing to curb, smear campaigns against prominent government critics. The environment for human rights defenders and independent NGOs remained difficult. Threats, assaults, administrative harassment and public attacks on their character and integrity continued, with the intention of impeding their work and undermining their credibility. Investigations into attacks on, and the murders of, other prominent human rights defenders and journalists produced few results. The clampdown on social activism also continued, including through the banning of demonstrations, their violent dispersal and the prosecution of individuals under anti-extremism legislation.

In a worrying new trend, the picture darkened in Ukraine for human rights defenders. They were physically attacked, and faced harassment from law enforcement officers, in connection with their legitimate human rights work. There was a fresh assault on civil society in Belarus, obliterating the fragile signs of openness in the run-up to the presidential election in December. In the aftermath of the election, which was marred by irregularities, riot police violently dispersed mainly peaceful demonstrators. By the end of the year, 29 people, including six opposition presidential candidates, members of their campaign teams and journalists, faced trumped-up charges of organizing mass disorder – and up to 15 years' imprisonment – in connection with the demonstrations. In Kyrgyzstan, in a climate of mutual blame and growing nationalist discourse following the June violence which left hundreds dead, human rights defenders faced the difficulty of having to justify their work protecting different ethnic communities, and obstruction from the authorities, when trying to document the events.

The situation also worsened for women who chose to wear a full face veil as an expression of their religious, cultural, political or personal identity or beliefs. Legislation banning the wearing in public of clothing intended to conceal the face was discussed in the parliaments of Bosnia and Herzegovina and Italy, proposed by the new government of the Netherlands, was voted for in the Belgium parliament and was adopted in France. Several municipalities in Spain also passed regulations banning the wearing of full-face veils in municipal buildings. In Turkey, no progress was made in removing legal barriers preventing women wearing the headscarf in universities, although implementation of the ban relaxed during the year.

People on the move

Despite the economic downturn, Europe remained a destination for those seeking to escape poverty, violence or persecution. Large numbers of migrants and asylum-seekers continued to travel along routes which evolved in response to states' efforts to thwart arrivals, including policies of interception at sea, readmission agreements with countries of origin and transit, and strengthened border controls. The main routes of previous years from western Africa and Libya to the maritime borders of Spain, Italy and Malta saw much-reduced flows, with the migration focus into the EU shifting to the land borders of Greece with Turkey.

The global economic crisis also exacerbated the vulnerability of asylum-seekers and migrants, in particular to trafficking and smuggling networks, and pushed others into the informal economy, with restrictions in access to economic and social rights. In many countries across the region authorities failed to adequately protect foreign nationals in their territory, including refugees, asylum-seekers and migrants, from rising hostility and racially motivated violence. By making unsubstantiated links between immigration status and crime, some politicians and government representatives themselves contributed to fostering a climate of intolerance and xenophobia.

The signature response of European states to the challenges of significant and complex flows of mixed migration remained repressive, resulting in a consistent pattern of human rights violations linked to the interception, detention and expulsion by states of foreign nationals, including those eligible for international protection. Detaining asylum-seekers and irregular migrants as a tool of deterrence and control was widespread, rather than a last, legitimate resort.

REGIONAL OVERVIEWS
EUROPE AND CENTRAL ASIA

Asylum systems in the region also frequently failed those seeking protection, with asylum-seekers facing a range of violations including being blocked from access to territory and asylum procedures; detained unlawfully; denied necessary guidance and support to pursue their claims; forced into destitution; unlawfully expelled before their claims could be heard; and sent to countries where they were at risk of grave human rights violations.

One depressing trend was the willingness of states to send people back to places where they faced a real risk of persecution or serious harm. Belgium, Denmark, the Netherlands, Norway, Sweden and the UK sent rejected asylum-seekers back to Iraq, despite recommendations by the UNHCR, the UN refugee agency. EU countries and Switzerland also continued to forcibly return Roma to Kosovo, contrary to the advice of the Council of Europe Commissioner for Human Rights: many of those returned were denied basic rights and were at risk of cumulative discrimination amounting to persecution. A number of EU countries sent asylum-seekers back to Greece under the Dublin II Regulation, despite that country's lack of a functioning asylum system. People were returned from Italy and Turkey without even being able to access the asylum systems there. Kazakhstan stepped up efforts to forcibly return asylum-seekers and refugees to China and Uzbekistan under national security and counter-terrorism measures.

In a positive move, however, a number of European states including Albania, Bulgaria, Georgia, Germany, Latvia, Slovakia, Spain and Switzerland accepted former Guantánamo Bay detainees who could not be repatriated to their home countries as they might be at risk of torture and other ill-treatment.

Across the region, hundreds of thousands of people also remained displaced by the conflicts that accompanied the collapse of the former Yugoslavia and the Soviet Union, often unable to return owing to their legal status – or lack of it – and discrimination in access to rights including property tenure.

A continuing rise in racism and hate speech in public discourse in many countries served to further marginalize those already sidelined by poverty or discrimination.

Discrimination

A continuing rise in racism and hate speech in public discourse in many countries served to further marginalize those already sidelined by poverty or discrimination.

One of the most profound illustrations of systemic discrimination was against the Roma, who remained largely excluded from public life and often the focus of overt public hostility and xenophobic political discourse. Roma remained one of the few groups in respect of which openly racist comments and attitudes were not just tolerated, but widely shared. Roma families were frequently unable to enjoy full access to housing, education, employment and health services.

Many Roma continued to live in informal settlements or slums lacking even a minimum degree of security of tenure, because of the irregular status of the settlements or their lack of official documents to confirm tenure arrangements. They remained vulnerable to forced evictions, in places such as Italy, Greece, France, Romania and Serbia, driving them further into poverty and marginalization with little hope of redress. In Italy, for example, some families were subjected to repeated forced evictions, which disrupted their communities, their access to work and made it impossible for some children to attend school. In France, a speech by the President describing the camps inhabited by Roma as sources of criminality was followed by a ministerial instruction (later reworded but the effect remained the same) to dismantle them. The incident revealed the tensions resulting from lack of attention over decades to the situation of the Roma in Europe, provoking calls for the EU to do more to engage states on respect for the rights of Roma.

Millions of Roma across Europe also remained severely disadvantaged by low levels of literacy and poor or incomplete education. One of the routes out of the vicious cycle of poverty and marginalization, education, was denied to many Romani children who continued to be placed in substandard, segregated classes or schools, including in Croatia, the Czech Republic, Greece, Hungary, Romania and Slovakia. Negative stereotyping, as well as physical and cultural isolation, also blighted future prospects.

Authorities in a number of countries also fostered a climate of intolerance for lesbian, gay, bisexual and transgendered (LGBT) communities. In Italy, against a backdrop of derogatory remarks by some politicians and officials, accompanied by a significant rise in intolerance and hate speech against the communities, violent homophobic attacks continued. In Turkey, the Minister for Women and the Family stated that homosexuality was a disease and required treatment.

In Lithuania, legal provisions entered into force which attempted to stifle any public discussion of homosexuality or public expression of the identity of LGBT people. The country's first Pride march took place, however, despite efforts by certain authorities to ban it. Such efforts elsewhere were unfortunately successful, with marches banned or impeded in Belarus, Moldova and Russia.

Regrettably, member states continued to block a new EU-wide directive on non-discrimination, which would simply close a legal protection gap for those experiencing discrimination outside of employment on the grounds of disability, belief, religion, sexual orientation and age. EU laws in this field would make a crucial difference to how all forms of discrimination are tackled across Europe.

REGIONAL OVERVIEWS
EUROPE AND CENTRAL ASIA

Counter-terror and security

In spite of the lack of political will and outright obstruction by some governments, there were some small but significant steps towards insight into, and accountability for, European governments' roles in the CIA-operated rendition and secret detention programmes.

A criminal investigation into Poland's complicity in such programmes continued, and in July it was confirmed that CIA-operated flights had landed at an airport near an alleged secret detention centre at Stare Kiejkuty. In September, the Prosecutor's Office confirmed that it was investigating claims by a Saudi Arabian national that he had been held in a secret detention centre in Poland. He was granted "victim" status in October, the first time a rendition victim's claims had been acknowledged by the authorities anywhere in Europe. New evidence of Romania's participation in the rendition and secret detention programmes came to light when the Polish Border Guard office released information that a flight from Poland carrying passengers had continued on to Romania – although the government there maintained its increasingly implausible denials of involvement.

In the face of mounting pressure the UK announced an inquiry into allegations that state actors had been involved in the rendition, secret detention and/or torture and other ill-treatment of a number of detainees held abroad. A delegation from the European Committee for the Prevention of Torture visited two secret prison sites in Lithuania, where a criminal investigation was ongoing into the establishment and operation of the sites, although there were concerns that this investigation would be closed prematurely. In Italy, an appeal court upheld the first and only convictions to date in relation to human rights violations in connection with the rendition and secret detention programmes. Twenty-five individuals, - 22 CIA agents, a US military official, and two Italian intelligence operatives - had been convicted for their involvement in the abduction of an Egyptian national from a street in Milan. He was subsequently unlawfully transferred by the CIA from Italy to Egypt where he was held in secret and allegedly tortured. The Italian government's claims of "state secrecy", however, resulted in the dismissal of charges on appeal against five Italian high-ranking intelligence officials.

As in previous years, however, the watchwords of security and state secrecy were too often used to drive policies and practices that undermined rather than strengthened human rights. For example, governments continued to use unenforceable diplomatic assurances to rid themselves of foreigners alleged to be involved in acts of terrorism, instead of prosecuting those people for any crimes of which they were accused. The UK, for example, continued to deport

> As in previous years the watchwords of security and state secrecy were too often used to drive policies and practices that undermined rather than strengthened human rights.

individuals alleged to pose a threat to "national security" to countries where they would be at risk of torture and other ill-treatment.

While constitutional amendments in Turkey and revisions to the Anti-Terrorism Law represented positive steps, unfair trials under anti-terrorism legislation continued, and anti-terrorism laws carrying higher prison sentences and resulting in pre-trial detention orders were frequently used to stifle freedom of expression.

The security situation in Russia's North Caucasus remained volatile, with violence affecting Chechnya, Ingushetia, Dagestan and neighbouring regions. Government authorities publicly acknowledged that measures to combat armed violence were not effective. High numbers of law enforcement officials, as well as civilians, were killed in attacks by armed groups.

Armed groups also caused death and destruction elsewhere in the region, including those based in Greece, Spain and Turkey. In September, the armed Basque separatist group Euskadi Ta Askatasuna (ETA) announced that it would not carry out any "offensive armed actions".

Death penalty

Mixed signals continued from Belarus, the last executioner in the region. In a continuing positive trend state representatives expressed their willingness to engage with the international community regarding the death penalty, and their intention to mould public opinion in favour of abolition. Despite this, three death sentences were handed down and two people executed within a flawed criminal justice system which continued to shroud the process in secrecy. Prisoners and their relatives had no advance warning about the date of execution, and relatives were denied permission to claim the body or even to know where the burial place was. The executions were carried out despite a request for a stay by the UN Human Rights Committee so it could consider the men's cases.

Impunity in post-conflict situations

Some progress was made in tackling impunity for crimes committed on the territory of the former Yugoslavia during the wars of the 1990s, both through the domestic courts and through international discourse. In notable moves the Croatian President apologized to families and victims, and the Serbian parliament condemned crimes committed against the Bosniak (Bosnian Muslim) population of Srebrenica in July 1995 – while falling short of referring to them as genocide.

Fundamental problems remained, however. In spite of the President's stance in Croatia, the political will to implement justice system reforms and tackle impunity, including for ethnic bias in prosecutions, was still largely missing. Allegations pointing to command responsibility for war crimes against several high-profile political and military leaders remained uninvestigated. In Bosnia and Herzegovina, verbal attacks on the justice system and denial of war crimes by high-ranking politicians, including of the genocide in Srebrenica in July 1995, further undermined the country's efforts to prosecute war crimes cases. In both countries witness support and protection measures remained inadequate, and continued to be one of the main obstacles for victims of war crimes and their families in seeking justice. Little progress was made in Kosovo and Serbia in establishing the fate of those missing since the 1999 war. The International Tribunal for the Former Yugoslavia urged Serbia to take more proactive measures to arrest former Bosnian-Serb General Ratko Mladić and former Croatian Serb leader Goran Hadžić.

None of the sides to the 2008 conflict between Russia and Georgia conducted comprehensive investigations, in spite of a report by an international fact-finding mission commissioned by the EU the following year which confirmed that violations of international human rights and humanitarian law had been committed by Georgian, Russian and South Ossetian forces.

Torture and other ill-treatment

Victims of torture and other ill-treatment were likewise too often failed by justice systems which did not hold those responsible to account. Obstacles to accountability included lack of prompt access to a lawyer, failure by prosecutors to vigorously pursue investigations, victims' fear of reprisals, low penalties imposed on convicted police officers, and the absence of properly resourced and independent systems for monitoring complaints and investigating serious police misconduct.

Too often, the rhetoric of compliance masked continuation in practice. In Kazakhstan and Uzbekistan, for example, reports of torture and other ill-treatment continued unabated despite government promises to adopt a zero-tolerance policy, or assertions that the practice had decreased. In Russia, in spite of a stated desire for police reform, corruption and collusion between the police, investigators and prosecutors were widely perceived as undermining the effectiveness of investigations and obstructing prosecutions. Detainees frequently reported unlawful disciplinary punishments and the denial of necessary medical care.

A landmark judgment in Turkey, however, saw 19 officials including police officers and prison guards convicted for their part in the torture that resulted in the death of political activist Engin Çeber in Istanbul in October 2008. Four of those convicted were sentenced to life imprisonment, the first time in Turkish legal history that state officials

Allegations pointing to command responsibility for war crimes against several high-profile political and military leaders remained uninvestigated.

had received such a sentence for causing death through torture. Regrettably, this contrasted starkly with other cases involving alleged torture committed by state officials where criminal investigations and prosecutions of law enforcement officials remained ineffective.

Violence against women

Violence against women and girls in the home remained pervasive across the region for all ages and social groups. Only a small proportion of women officially reported this abuse. They were deterred by fear of reprisals from abusive partners, the idea of bringing "shame" on their family, or for reasons of financial insecurity. Migrant women in an irregular situation in particular feared registering a complaint with the police due to the risk of expulsion should their lack of status be discovered. Mostly, the widespread impunity enjoyed by perpetrators meant they knew there was little point.

Those who did come forward were too often failed by justice and support systems which were inadequate and unresponsive. In some countries such as Albania domestic violence was not a specific criminal offence. Many countries lacked functioning nationwide cross-referral systems and the services to protect survivors of domestic violence, such as shelters and adequate and safe alternative housing, were woefully inadequate. Armenia, for example, had only one shelter, funded by foreign donations.

Justice and impunity

Across the region the desire for truth, justice and redress remained unquenchable. For some, these came through a shift in the political will to address the past, or the indefatigable refusal of friends, family and advocates to give up. For many, the wait was long, but always worth it: people like the family of Himzo Demir, who was abducted and subjected to enforced diasappearance in 1992 during the Yugoslav wars. In October, they finally received confirmation that his remains had been among those buried as unidentified in a mass grave in Višegrad. The search was over and they could finally hold the funeral.

What is striking among so many inspiring stories, however, is how many people are still waiting because states have sought to block access to the truth, obstruct justice, and default on redress. Particularly in a region which has a human rights architecture unrivalled elsewhere in the world.

It is time Europe's governments realize that efforts at denial and obfuscation – by themselves or their allies – will not in the end prevail against those courageous people who dare to stand up, whatever the personal cost, and hold them accountable.

In Lebanon in 2010, Amineh 'Abd al-Husri holds a picture of her son, Ahmed Zuhdi al-Sharqawi, who disappeared in 1986. Successive Lebanese governments have made little effort to investigate the fate of thousands of individuals missing since the 1975-90 civil war.

MIDDLE EAST AND NORTH AFRICA

"We want both: the freedom to work and the freedom to speak. Instead, I got beaten."

Walid Malahi, who was beaten by Tunisian riot police during an anti-government protest, speaking to Amnesty International researchers in Tunisia.

2010 dawned with Yemen an unusual focus of international attention following an alleged terrorist incident. It closed with many eyes transfixed by the emergent people's power in Tunisia and the chain reaction it was setting off elsewhere in the region. Both involved suicide – the first, an alleged suicide bomber aiming to kill passengers on a commercial jet; the second, the self-immolation by a young man in despair at his lack of work or opportunity and worn down by political repression.

These events were not simply the bookends of a year. Both also illuminated key currents affecting the states of the Middle East and North Africa – governments' preoccupation with their political security but neglect of their people's human security and failure to uphold the human rights on which that depends.

In January, Yemen was in the grip of a bloody conflict in its impoverished northern Sa'dah region and the government faced a swelling secessionist movement in the south. Yet it was neither of these, despite the human rights abuses that they spawned, that moved Yemen up the international political agenda. The cause, rather, was an incident that happened on 25 December 2009, thousands of miles away, when a Nigerian man said to have received training from al-Qa'ida in Yemen allegedly tried to blow up an airliner over the US city of Detroit. That act cast an immediate spotlight on Yemen as a potential base for al-Qa'ida at Saudi Arabia's southern border and just a short Red Sea crossing from the conflict-ridden state of Somalia, particularly after reports of the formation of al-Qa'ida in the Arabian Peninsula as a merger of al-Qa'ida forces in Yemen and Saudi Arabia.

Yemen, the poorest country in the region, was already suffering acute social, economic and political ills – a predominantly young population facing increasing poverty and unemployment; a country whose oil reserves and water supplies are nearing exhaustion; a government headed by a President in power since 1978 exhibiting increasing intolerance of dissent. This, together with the Sa'dah conflict and the growing calls for secession in the south, implied that Yemen could soon become again the focus of international attention, as concerns mounted that any further deterioration in such an extensively armed tribal country could lead to a total breakdown of law and order.

That it had already become such, to some extent, became clear during a visit to the country by Amnesty International researchers in March. They saw evidence of the weaponry used to attack an alleged al-Qa'ida camp in December 2009. That attack, carried out just over a week before the Detroit airline bomb incident, killed 41 Yemeni civilians, mostly women and children. Markings on the weapon remnants indicated that they came from a Tomahawk cruise missile carrying cluster bombs and that the attack must have been carried out by US forces, probably from a US warship off Yemen's coast, rather than by Yemeni security forces. US government files subsequently confirmed this; a record of a meeting between Yemen's President and a senior US official revealed the President ruefully acknowledging that he had lied to his own people by telling them that Yemeni forces had been responsible for the attack to cover up what he saw as a politically damaging truth – that the deaths of Yemeni civilians had resulted directly from a US attack.

In Tunisia, 24-year-old Mohamed Bouazizi's act of despair on 17 December – he set himself alight after a local official in the town of Sidi Bouzid prevented him from selling vegetables from his handcart and reportedly assaulted him – was a lone and ultimately fatal expression of protest that struck a chord with thousands of his fellow Tunisians and hundreds of thousands more in Egypt, Algeria and other states across the region. It unleashed a surge of protests that spread like wildfire across the country. Mohamed Bouazizi's act screamed out the frustration felt by so many of his generation at the abusive nature of governments across the Middle East and North Africa in which a few monopolize virtually all political and economic power – unaccountable, repressive, intolerant of dissent and content to rely on brutal, omnipotent and ubiquitous security and intelligence forces to maintain their grasp on the state and its resources, as they have in many cases for decades. True to form, faced with popular protests, the Ben 'Ali government resorted to force, shooting down demonstrators as they had done in Gafsa in 2009. This time, however, the demonstrators would not be cowed and became even more determined to achieve their aim of ridding their country of President Ben 'Ali.

Many eyes were transfixed by the emergent people's power in Tunisia and the chain reaction it was setting off elsewhere in the region.

Conflict and insecurity

Yemen's largely unreported Sa'dah conflict, which had seen Saudi Arabian jets pound towns and villages and contributed to some 350,000 people fleeing their homes, ended with a ceasefire in February. The conflict in Iraq, however, raged on as US troop numbers were scaled down and the USA completed its handover of prisons and thousands of untried detainees to Iraqi government control. They did this despite continuing revelations about the Iraqi government's use of secret prisons and Iraqi security forces' use of torture on an epidemic scale. The US government simply preferred to look away rather than meet its obligation to protect detainees at risk of torture. It also consigned around 3,400 Iranian exiles living at Camp Ashraf, north of Baghdad, to an uncertain and insecure future after US forces handed control of the camp to Iraqi authorities.

Armed groups in Iraq continued relentlessly to detonate bombs that killed and maimed civilians. Shi'a pilgrims and Christians were among those targeted by Sunni armed groups determined to show their muscle and to sow further sectarian division, intensifying their attacks during the months of political limbo that followed the inconclusive outcome of Iraq's national elections in March.

The Iraqi government's riposte was to sweep up suspects, torture them to extract "confessions", cart them before the courts and sentence scores to death after grossly unfair trials. Continuing attacks by suicide bombers defied assertions of the death penalty's deterrent effect.

The other regional pivot of conflict remained the continuing struggle between Israelis and Palestinians. Unusually, one round of this was played out on the high seas when Israeli soldiers intercepted in May a six-ship flotilla seeking to break Israel's military blockade of Gaza to bring humanitarian relief to the 1.5 million Palestinians confined there. Nine people were killed aboard the Turkish *Mavi Marmara* after it was boarded by Israeli troops, provoking an international outcry so strong that Israel felt obliged to slightly relax the Gaza blockade. A UN investigation concluded that at least six of the nine deaths appeared to be "extra-legal, summary and arbitrary executions" by Israeli forces. The outcome of Israel's own domestic investigation was still awaited at the end of the year; it lacked independence.

December saw the second anniversary of the launch of Operation "Cast Lead", Israel's 22-day military assault on Gaza that killed nearly 1,400 Palestinians, over 300 of them children. In 2009, a UN fact-finding inquiry headed by Justice Richard Goldstone had accused both Israel and the Palestinian side of war crimes and possible crimes against humanity, and called for investigations and accountability.

REGIONAL OVERVIEWS
MIDDLE EAST AND NORTH AFRICA

Yet, by the end of 2010 the victims were still waiting for justice and reparation. Israel's domestic investigations were flawed, lacking independence and even acknowledgement of the extent of civilian casualties that Israeli forces had caused, while Hamas failed to conduct even the semblance of an investigation maintaining, against all evidence, that it had targeted only military installations when firing indiscriminate rockets and other weapons into Israeli civilian areas. The matter was due to come before the UN Human Rights Council in March 2011 for decision on whether to allow the abusive parties yet more time to ignore the claims of their victims or to turn the matter over to international justice mechanisms.

Repression of dissent

Freedom of expression, a cornerstone right vital for its own sake and for accessing other human rights, was everywhere curtailed by governments across the region. So too were the closely related rights to freedom of association and assembly, with state authorities impeding the development of human rights NGOs and a vibrant civil society and seeking often to prevent public expressions of dissent.

The conflict in Iraq raged on. The US government preferred to look away rather than protect detainees at risk of torture. Armed groups continued relentlessly to detonate bombs that killed and maimed civilians.

In countries including Iran, Libya, Saudi Arabia and Syria, those who dared speak out in favour of greater freedoms, against their government or in defence of human rights, did so at their peril. In these and other states, the forces of repression – the shadowy, all-powerful and unaccountable secret police – were never far away. Government critics were harassed and intimidated, arrested and detained, and sometimes tortured or tried and jailed on trumped-up charges to silence them and to send a message to others who might have the temerity to speak out. In Iran, several ethnic minority activists were summarily hanged in reprisal for an armed attack carried out when they were already in prison. In Syria, the national bar association appeared to have been co-opted to target and strike off a leading human rights lawyer who had reported on trials before Syria's unfair special security court. In the West Bank, the Fatah-dominated Palestinian Authority targeted suspected supporters of Hamas, while in Gaza, the Hamas de facto administration similarly turned the screw on supporters of Fatah. In the Western Sahara, under Moroccan administration since 1975, Moroccan authorities targeted Sahrawi human rights defenders and advocates of self-determination for the territory's people. In Bahrain, a leading human rights NGO was effectively taken under government control after it spoke out about the alleged torture of leading members of the Shi'a community detained in August and September.

Freedom of expression and the media

State authorities strove to maintain their control over the free flow of information using methods both familiar and time-worn, but faced an increasing challenge from the rise and accessibility of social media and a populace increasingly determined to have their say. In Egypt, Syria and elsewhere, bloggers were arrested and detained. In Iran, Tunisia and elsewhere governments blocked access to the internet and cut mobile phone lines in their efforts to staunch protests. In Yemen, a leading journalist was abducted from the street and detained, and a press court targeted editors and journalists who failed to toe the government's line. There, as elsewhere in the region, the authorities resorted to criminal defamation prosecutions to chill debate and deter journalists from exposing human rights abuses or corruption in high circles.

But, as the protests in Tunisia showed, governments who obstructed access to the internet or cut mobile phone networks were doing no more than sticking a finger in the dyke. Activists turned in increasing numbers to social networking sites to keep one jump ahead of the authorities and to publish damning evidence of state abuse. One very positive sign emerging in 2010 was that the battle for control of access to information was finally turning in favour of the citizen activist.

Public 'security'

Torture and other ill-treatment of detainees remained an abiding feature across the region. The victims frequently were political suspects who were detained, often at undisclosed locations where they were subject to interrogation and held incommunicado for weeks at a time, or even longer. Police violence against ordinary criminal suspects was also endemic in Egypt and other countries. Where there were trials, international fair trial standards were routinely ignored, especially in cases involving dissent or outright opposition to those in power.

In Iran, "show trials" continued of people who had protested against the official result of the 2009 presidential election leading to at least two executions. In Saudi Arabia, trials of security suspects continued to be held behind closed doors amid the tightest security. In Egypt, civilian political activists and other suspects continued to face trial before military or emergency courts at the direction of the country's President.

Egypt's 30-year national state of emergency was again renewed by a compliant parliament in May; similarly, the Algerian and Syrian governments maintained long-running states of emergency under which their security forces, like those in Egypt, were equipped with extraordinary powers of arrest and detention, which were used to suppress legitimate political activities and expression of human rights.

REGIONAL OVERVIEWS
MIDDLE EAST AND NORTH AFRICA

Several governments maintained and made extensive use of the death penalty and other cruel punishments, such as amputation and flogging. Indeed, it was ironic given the mutual antipathy of their leaders and governments that the twin Gulf superpowers of Iran and Saudi Arabia were at one in their continuing devotion to the death penalty and other cruel punishments, which they justified in the name of Shari'a (Islamic law) but utilized in a manner that often suggested a more cynical, political motivation. This was particularly so in Iran, where the authorities carried out more executions than in any country other than China and did so with evident intent to terrorize. Some 252 executions were recorded in Iran, though the true total may have been far higher. So great was the wave of international revulsion against the planned stoning to death of Sakineh Mohammadi Ashtiani, however, that she was still alive at the end of the year though facing an uncertain future as various Iranian authorities went through contortions to try and justify her execution. The anger that her case prompted both at home and abroad provided a telling sign of the impact that international public opinion can have in averting a serious human rights violation.

In Saudi Arabia, at least 27 prisoners were executed, although this marked a significant reduction on the previous two years and hopefully augured a long-term positive trend, though this was by no means assured. Hard-line governments also continued to carry out executions in Egypt, Iraq, Libya, Syria and Yemen, and Hamas carried out five executions in Gaza, but increasingly these appeared out of step with the worldwide trend towards abandonment of this most cruel expression of state violence, a trend reflected by the maintenance of moratoriums on executions in the states of the Maghreb, Jordan and Lebanon.

Economic concerns – housing and livelihoods

The 1.5 million Palestinians who live crowded into the Gaza Strip endured another year of extreme hardship under an Israeli military blockade that constituted collective punishment, a breach of international law, and effectively confined them to the tiny, war-ravaged enclave. Twice Israel announced some easing of the blockade, but with little effect. Some 80 per cent of Gaza's people continued to rely on international humanitarian assistance and food aid for their survival.

Elsewhere in the region, there was severe impoverishment in many communities as the global recession bit deep, exacerbated by a lack of infrastructure and other development, official corruption and plain misgovernment. It was reflected in high rates of unemployment, especially among the young, fuelling a sense of marginalization and demands for change, the driving forces of the Tunisian uprising in

State authorities faced an increasing challenge from the rise and accessibility of social media and a populace increasingly determined to have their say.

December. So often, it was those forced to the margins of society who felt the full force of police brutality or official unconcern.

In Egypt, workers and others continued to stage protests against rising living costs and to demand better wages and working conditions. Among the millions of people living in the country's sprawling informal settlements (slums), thousands in Cairo faced forced eviction from areas declared "unsafe" or because their "shack areas" had been earmarked for development and gentrification. All too frequently, those to be removed were not consulted in advance or allowed a voice in official decisions about their relocation, and some were left homeless. They were made to feel that they had no rights by the very authorities whose responsibility it is to uphold and respect their human rights.

Discrimination

2010 saw little improvement in the status of women and girls who, across the region, continued to face discrimination and violence, including within the family. Men remained superior under family and personal status laws in matters such as marriage, divorce, child custody and inheritance, and women continued to be accorded inferior status under the criminal law. Particularly in more traditional areas, girls were subject to early and forced marriage and women who challenged strict dress codes or were seen by male relatives as not conforming to their particular notions of family "honour" risked violent reprisals and even murder at the hands of their fathers, brothers, husbands or other male relatives. In all too many cases, men who cited "honour" as a mitigating factor escaped any or appropriate punishment for crimes of violence committed against female members of their families.

While virtually all women were at risk of gender-based violence, women migrant domestic workers were particularly exposed. Mostly, these were women from poor and developing countries in Asia and Africa who worked in countries in the Gulf as well as in Jordan and Lebanon. They were generally excluded altogether from local labour laws, where these exist, and were triply vulnerable – as foreigners, as migrants and as women – to exploitation and abuse, including sexual and other violence, at the hands of their employers. Two of the most disturbing cases that came to light in 2010 involved women employed as domestic servants in oil-rich Saudi Arabia: one, a Sri Lankan national, alleged that her employer had driven more than 20 nails into her hands, leg and head after she complained that she had too much work to do; another, an Indonesian national, was cut on the face with scissors, burned with a hot iron and beaten to the point were she required admission to hospital.

Severe impoverishment blighted many communities as the global recession bit deep, exacerbated by a lack of infrastructure, official corruption and plain misgovernment.

Migrants from sub-Saharan Africa who sought to find work in North Africa or to transit them and gain entry to European states were liable to summary arrest and detention or deportation. Those at risk included refugees and asylum-seekers. In Egypt, border guards continued their policy of shooting migrants attempting to cross the country's border into Israel, killing at least 30. In Libya, thousands of suspected irregular migrants, including refugees and asylum-seekers, were held in severely overcrowded and unhygienic detention centres and faced habitual abuse, sometimes amounting to torture.

Members of ethnic and religious minorities also faced discrimination, as in Iran, or were targeted for attack by armed groups, as in Iraq. In Egypt, Coptic Christians were attacked. In Lebanon, Palestinian refugees continued to be barred from various professions and prevented from accessing other basic rights. In Syria, Kurds faced continuing discrimination and restrictions on use of their language and cultural expression. Life in the region was hard, especially hard, for migrants, refugees and members of minority groups.

Accounting for the past

The long-running truth and reconciliation process launched with some fanfare in Morocco and Western Sahara in 2004 continued its snail-like progress and continued to disappoint. From the outset, the process explicitly omitted any consideration of justice as a means to remedy the gross violations committed by government forces between 1956 and 1999 and, in practice, it largely failed even to provide the truth about what happened to those who disappeared or suffered other grave abuses. On top of this, the Moroccan authorities showed little sign of implementing the far-reaching legal and institutional reforms that had been due to flow from the process, to hold the security forces accountable under the law and eradicate the use of secret detention and torture. Underscoring this failure, in 2010 new reports emerged of torture of suspects by Morocco's secret police.

Meanwhile, the work of the Special Tribunal for Lebanon (STL), set up under UN auspices in the wake of the assassination of former Lebanese Prime Minister Rafic Hariri in 2005, provoked a political storm that threatened the coalition government headed by the late Prime Minister's son. Tension mounted after reports that the STL intended to indict several members of Hizbullah, Lebanon's most powerful political force and a partner in the coalition government, leading Hizbullah to accuse the STL of being politically driven. At the end of 2010, the facts were still to emerge, but it was hard to escape the conclusion that the STL had been from the outset an exercise in selective justice. Its mandate and jurisdiction were limited, covering

Twenty years after the Lebanese civil war ended, people still gather in a Beirut park clutching precious but yellowing photographs of their missing relatives, demanding to know what became of them.

only the Hariri assassination and some associated attacks. Few or no steps have been taken by any Lebanese government to investigate the thousands of disappearances, abductions, killings and other abuses that were committed during the bitter 15-year civil war that ended in 1990, nor even to adequately protect mass graves, despite the pleas of the now ageing relatives of the thousands of missing people. The legacy of that darkest of periods in Lebanon's recent history has yet to be addressed. As a reminder of this, each day a solemn group of people gather quietly in a Beirut park clutching precious but yellowing photographs of their long-lost but not yet forgotten loved ones, to ask what became of them and where their remains lie. It is a poignant sight. Sadly, 20 years on, there has still been no UN Security Council demand, nor barely any international pressure, to provide them with the answers that are their due.

REGIONAL OVERVIEWS
MIDDLE EAST AND NORTH AFRICA

A confrontation between protesters calling for change and security forces in the Tunisian capital, Tunis, December 2010. During the wave of protests security forces used excessive force, including live ammunition, rubber bullets and tear gas, against mostly peaceful demonstrators, leaving more than 100 people dead.

AMNESTY INTERNATIONAL REPORT 2011
PART TWO: COUNTRY ENTRIES

11

A camp for displaced people near Port au Prince airport following a massive earthquake, Haiti, January 2010. By year's end more than a million people remained displaced because of the disaster, living in makeshift camps where violence against women and girls was increasing.

AFGHANISTAN

ISLAMIC REPUBLIC OF AFGHANISTAN

Head of state and government:	Hamid Karzai
Death penalty:	retentionist
Population:	29.1 million
Life expectancy:	44.6 years
Under-5 mortality (m/f):	233/238 per 1,000

Conflict-related violence, and attendant human rights violations, increased throughout the country, including in northern and western Afghanistan, areas previously considered relatively safe. The Afghanistan NGO Security Office (ANSO), which advises organizations on safety conditions in Afghanistan, recorded 2,428 civilians killed in 2010 as a result of the conflict, with the majority attributed to the Taleban and other anti-government forces. There was a significant rise in the numbers of assassinations and executions of civilians by the Taleban for "supporting" the government or "spying" for the international forces. Violence caused by insurgents intensified, triggering widespread human rights abuses. In light of the spiralling conflict and the absence of an adequate domestic judicial system, Amnesty International called on the International Criminal Court to investigate war crimes and crimes against humanity. The international community increasingly discussed ending its military presence in the country. The Afghan people continued to lose confidence in the ability of the government and the international security forces to uphold the rule of law and deliver essential social services. Health care, education and humanitarian aid remained out of reach for people in most rural areas, particularly in the south and south-east where the conflict was most intense.

Background

Parliamentary elections held on 18 September were marred by nearly 6,000 allegations of electoral irregularities and fraud, attacks on candidates, and intimidation and attacks by the Taleban on voters, electoral workers and candidates.

Following the International Conference on Afghanistan held on 28 January in London, UK, and the National Consultative Peace Jirga held 2-4 June in Kabul, President Karzai established a 68-member High Peace Council in September to pursue peace negotiations with insurgent groups. The High Peace Council included figures widely accused of committing human rights abuses and war crimes. Only 10 women were appointed to the High Peace Council despite strong national and international pressure for adequate representation of women in negotiating teams and forums.

Afghan civil society groups, in particular women's groups, war victims, and those who suffered at the hands of the Taleban, called on the government to ensure that the protection and promotion of human rights would not be sacrificed to facilitate negotiations with the Taleban and other insurgent groups.

The National Stability and Reconciliation bill was officially promulgated, granting immunity from criminal prosecution to people who committed serious human rights violations and war crimes over the past 30 years. The law was passed in March 2007 but not publicized and promulgated until early 2010.

Nine million Afghans, more than 30 per cent of the population, lived on less than US$25 a month and could not meet their basic needs. According to UNICEF, Afghanistan's maternal death rate of 1,800 per 100,000 live births continued to be the second worst in the world. It was estimated that more than half a million Afghan women died every year during childbirth or after giving birth.

Abuses by armed groups

The Taleban and other armed groups (some anti-government and others ostensibly supporting the government) targeted, abducted, indiscriminately attacked and unlawfully killed civilians, committing human rights abuses and gross violations of international humanitarian law. According to ANSO, the Taleban and other anti-government armed groups were responsible for 2,027 casualties, up more than a quarter from 2009. The number of civilians assassinated or executed by armed groups surged by more than 95 per cent, including public executions of children. The victims were accused of "supporting" the government or "spying" for the international forces.

Suicide attacks
■ On 18 January, Taleban suicide bombers and gunmen attacked major government buildings, the Kabul Serena Hotel, a shopping mall and cinema in central Kabul. Seven people, including a child, were killed and at least 35 civilians were injured.

■ On 26 February, four suicide bombers attacked a guesthouse in Kabul city. At least 16 people, most of them foreign medical staff, were killed and more than 50 were injured. The Taleban claimed responsibility for the attack but the Afghan government blamed the Pakistan-based armed group Lashkar-e Taiba for the attack.

■ On 3 May, Taleban suicide bombers and gunmen attacked government buildings in Nimroz province and killed 13 people, including Gul Makai Osmani, a legislator.

■ On 9 June, at least 40 people were killed and more than 70 wounded when a suicide bomber struck a wedding celebration in the southern province of Kandahar. Fourteen children were among the dead.

Abductions

■ On 26 September, Linda Norgrove, a Scottish aid worker, and three Afghan colleagues, were kidnapped by members of the Taleban in Kunar province, eastern Afghanistan. The three kidnapped Afghan aid workers were released on 3 October but Linda Norgrove was apparently killed by US special forces during a rescue attempt.

Unlawful killings

■ On 8 June, the Taleban hanged a seven-year-old boy, accusing him of spying for British forces in southern Helmand province.

■ On 5 August, 10 members of the International Assistance Mission, an aid organization, were killed in southern Badakhshan province on their return from a medical mission. Both the Taleban and Hezb-e Islami claimed responsibility for the attack and accused the victims of being missionaries.

Violations by Afghan and international forces

ANSO reported that 401 civilians were killed by international and Afghan security forces, a decrease of 14 per cent from 2009. Air attacks remained the most harmful operations tactic, accounting for 53 per cent of civilian deaths attributed to international and Afghan security forces. Thirty-seven per cent of the deaths occurred during ground operations, including night raids.

The International Security Assistance Force (ISAF) issued tactical directives in March and August to lessen the impact of fighting on civilians. The former sought to regulate night raids and the latter was aimed at regulating aerial strikes and indiscriminate fire on residential compounds. However, there was an increase in the number of night raids, particularly in the eastern and southern region of Afghanistan, which often resulted in civilian casualties.

■ On 21 February, 27 civilians were killed and 12 others wounded near the border of Dai Kundi and Uruzgan provinces, when two US military helicopters fired on several civilian vehicles mistakenly believed to be carrying insurgents.

■ On 23 July, as many as 45 civilians, including children, were killed in a NATO air strike in Helmand province.

■ On 4 August, more than 12 Afghan civilians died during a night raid by US troops hunting for Taleban in Nangarhar province.

■ On 11 August, three brothers were killed during a night raid by NATO and US forces in Wardak province. The deaths sparked an anti-American protest in the area, where villagers said the brothers were civilians and not insurgents.

Neither the Afghan judiciary, nor the governments contributing to ISAF, demonstrated the ability or willingness to provide proper accountability or compensation for victims of violations by pro-government forces.

Freedom of expression

Afghan journalists continued to report critically on events, risking harassment, violence, and censorship. The Afghan authorities, especially the intelligence service, the National Directorate of Security (NDS), arbitrarily detained journalists. The Attorney General's Office illegally closed down radio stations and censored other media outlets. One of the most common grounds for applying such restrictions was the vague and undefined charge of being anti-Islamic.

The Taleban and other anti-government groups continued to target journalists and blocked almost all reporting from areas under their control.

■ On 5 September, Sayed Hamed Noori, a presenter, journalist and Deputy Chairman of Afghanistan National Journalists Union, was murdered in Kabul.

■ On 18 September (election day), Radio Kapisa FM director Hojatullah Mujadadi was arrested by the NDS at a voting station in Kapisa province. He claimed he was threatened by both the governor and NDS officials because of his independent coverage of the situation in the province.

■ Japanese freelance journalist Kosuke Tsuneoka was kidnapped in late March during a reporting assignment in a Taleban-controlled region of northern Afghanistan. His captors released him to the Japanese Embassy on

7 September. After his release, he said that his captors were not Taleban insurgents, but "a group of corrupt armed factions" with links to the Afghan government.

Freedom of religion

People converting to other religions were prosecuted by the Afghan judiciary. Three Afghans who converted to Christianity were arrested and detained by the NSD. Faith-based NGOs accused of proselytizing were forced to temporarily suspend their activities.

■ In October, Shoib Asadullah was arrested for converting from Islam to Christianity. A primary court in the northern city of Mazar-e-Sharif threatened to execute him for apostasy if he refused to recant.

Violence against women and girls

Afghan women and girls continued to face endemic violence and discrimination at home and in the public sphere. The Afghanistan Independent Human Rights Commission documented 1,891 cases of violence against women, but the true number may be higher.

■ In March, 18-year-old Bibi Aysha had her nose and ears cut off by her husband in Uruzgan province, southern Afghanistan, apparently on the order of a Taleban commander acting as "judge" for the crime of running away from her abusive in-laws.

■ On 9 August, the Taleban shot dead a woman, after forcing her to abort her foetus, in Badghis province on accusations of adultery.

■ On 16 August, the Taleban stoned to death a couple for alleged adultery and elopement in Imam Sahib district, Kunduz province.

Afghan women and female politicians, including parliamentary election candidates, were increasingly attacked by the Taleban and other armed groups.

■ In March, Member of Parliament Fawzia Kofi was injured by gunfire by unknown gunmen while travelling from Jalalabad to Kabul.

■ In April, Nadia Kayyani, a Provincial Council member, was left in a critical condition after being attacked in a drive-by shooting in Pul-e-Khumri, the provincial capital of Baghlan, northern Afghanistan.

■ Two Afghan aid workers were killed in Helmand after returning from Garmseer district where they were running a project for women's economic empowerment. Both women were forced out of their car by a group of armed men. Their bodies were found the next day near Garmseer district centre.

Refugees and internally displaced people

UNHCR reported that 102,658 Afghans were forced to flee their homes in 2010 as a result of the armed conflict, bringing the total number of internally displaced people to 351,907.

■ Around 26,000 people were displaced in Helmand province between February and May after NATO launched a major military operation against insurgent groups in Marjah district, Helmand province.

■ More than 7,000 people were displaced from the Zhari and Arghandab districts of Kandahar province after a major NATO military operation in the area in September. The warring parties failed to ensure adequate humanitarian assistance for the displaced.

According to UNHCR, 2.3 million Afghans continued to live abroad as refugees, the majority in neighbouring Iran and Pakistan. Fewer refugees chose to return to Afghanistan as a result of increased insecurity, poor infrastructure, scarce employment opportunities and lack of basic services, including education and health. Most of the displaced living in informal settlements in urban areas lacked similar basic services, and were at risk of forced evictions.

Justice and security forces

The formal justice system remained inaccessible to most Afghans. Concerns about corruption, inefficiency and high costs led many citizens to resort to traditional methods of dispute resolution, as well as seeking "justice" in Taleban courts, which operated without basic safeguards of due process and rule of law, meted out brutal punishments and routinely discriminated against women.

The government initiated efforts to increase the number of police from 96,800 to 109,000 in 2010, and to improve police performance at the district level. However, Afghan police faced widespread allegations of involvement in illegal activities including smuggling, kidnapping, and extortion at checkpoints.

In the absence of a practical justice system to address the lack of accountability by the warring parties, Amnesty International urged the Afghan government to ask the International Criminal Court to investigate allegations of war crimes and crimes against humanity committed by all parties to the conflict.

Death penalty

At least 100 people were sentenced to death, had their sentences confirmed by the Supreme Court, and were awaiting consideration of their clemency appeals by the President. On 24 October, Hamid Karzai ordered the judiciary to review all death row cases.

Amnesty International visits/reports
🚗 Amnesty International delegates visited Afghanistan in February and July.

📄 Afghanistan: Human rights must be guaranteed during reconciliation talks with the Taleban (ASA 11/003/2010)

📄 Open letter to delegates of the International Conference on Afghanistan, Kabul, 20 July 2010 (ASA 11/009/2010)

📄 Afghan civilians at risk during NATO offensive against Taleban, 17 February 2010

📄 Afghan women human rights defenders tell of intimidation and attacks, 8 March 2010

📄 Afghanistan leak exposes NATO's incoherent civilian casualty policy, 25 July 2010

ALBANIA

REPUBLIC OF ALBANIA

Head of state:	Bamir Topi
Head of government:	Sali Berisha
Death penalty:	abolitionist for all crimes
Population:	3.2 million
Life expectancy:	76.9 years
Under-5 mortality (m/f):	18/17 per 1,000
Adult literacy:	99 per cent

Domestic violence remained widespread and the trafficking of women and young girls for forced prostitution continued. There were some allegations of ill-treatment by police. Detention conditions in police stations were often very poor, but the conditions and treatment of remand and convicted prisoners improved. Homeless people with "orphan status" were denied their right under domestic law to priority with housing.

Background
The political stalemate following the contested June 2009 national elections continued. Although the main opposition party, the Socialist Party, ended its boycott of parliament in May, it frequently withdrew from parliament in protest. Legislative work was delayed, including electoral reform. Adopted legislation included an anti-discrimination law and a law protecting children's rights. Politicians accused each

other of corruption; investigations were opened into some of these allegations. Public confidence in the judiciary remained low. In November, the European Commission concluded that Albania had not fulfilled the criteria for candidate status for EU membership, and urged further reforms.

Violence against women and children
Domestic violence was widespread, but there was progress in countering it, both through legislation and in practice. Although domestic violence was still under-reported, reported incidents increased to 1,423 in the first nine months of the year, 433 more than for the same period in 2009. Domestic violence was not a specific criminal offence and, except in cases of serious injury or death, was only prosecuted on the victim's request. Victims increasingly sought protection through civil proceedings, although most later withdrew because of economic and social pressures and the lack of free legal aid available to them. As a result, courts issued comparatively few protection orders. For example, during the year Tirana District Court received 538 petitions from victims, the majority women, but issued only 129 protection orders.

The government initiated monitoring of incidents of domestic violence to assist policy-making. Health workers were trained in the identification and treatment of victims of domestic violence. In September, parliament adopted amendments to the 2006 law "On measures against violence in family relations". These provided for the establishment of a shelter for victims of domestic violence, mechanisms for co-ordinating responses to domestic violence referrals, and free legal aid for petitioners for protection orders, with court expenses to be paid by the perpetrators.

Trafficking in human beings
Trafficking of human beings, primarily young women and girls for forced prostitution, continued.
■ In May, Kristaq Prifti and Roland Kuro were arrested on a charge of trafficking a 14-year-old girl to Greece, where they allegedly forced her to work as a prostitute for five years.

In June, the US State Department Trafficking in Persons Report acknowledged the Albanian authorities' efforts to counter trafficking, but urged that assets seized from convicted traffickers be used to fund victim protection and integration; it also called for improved identification and protection for trafficked child victims and for rigorous prosecution of law enforcement officials complicit in human trafficking.

Enforced disappearances

■ The fate of Remzi Hoxha, an ethnic Albanian from Macedonia who disappeared in 1995, remained unknown, although the trial continued in Tirana of former officers of the National Intelligence Service. Ilir Kumbaro, Arben Sefgjini and Avni Koldashi were charged with the abduction and "torture with serious consequences" of three men, including Remzi Hoxha. Ilir Kumbaro was tried in his absence. He had been arrested in the UK in 2008, but in December 2009 was released after his appeal against extradition was upheld by a UK court on the grounds that his arrest warrant was no longer valid. In August 2010 he was rearrested in London on the basis of a new warrant, but was released on bail a week later.

Counter-terror and security

In February, three detainees from Egypt, Tunisia and Libya were transferred from US detention in Guantánamo Bay to Albania. Since 2006, Albania has accepted 11 former Guantánamo Bay prisoners who could not be repatriated to their home countries for fear of persecution.

Justice system

In November, the Council of Europe's Parliamentary Assembly criticized the Albanian authorities' decision to extradite Almir Rrapo, a dual US/Albanian national, to the USA on charges including murder. The decision ignored a binding interim measure by the European Court of Human Rights suspending his extradition. Tirana Appeal Court had ruled in favour of his extradition without a durable guarantee by the competent US authority that he would not face the death penalty. Following his extradition, the Albanian High Court overturned the Appeal Court's decision.

Torture and other ill-treatment

Charges of torture continued to be brought very rarely, except where incidents of ill-treatment by police resulted in serious injury or death; police officers were generally prosecuted for the lesser offence of "arbitrary acts", usually punished by a fine.
■ In April, on the recommendation of the Ombudsperson, an investigation was begun against two police officers in Tirana suspected of torture. They

were accused of having severely beaten three young men during and after their arrest in 2009. On completion of the investigation in December, the two police officers were charged with "arbitrary acts".
■ In October, Tirana District Court found police officer Vlash Ashiku guilty of having, while on duty, punched Tomor Shehu around the face and head in 2008. He was convicted of "arbitrary acts" and sentenced to a small fine (US$15).

The European Committee for the Prevention of Torture visited Albania in May to review measures taken to implement its previous recommendations.

Detention conditions

Despite renovation work in some police stations, detention conditions remained very poor in many others, and separate rooms for the detention of women and children were often lacking. There were some improvements in conditions of detention in prisons and remand centres: work began on the construction of two new remand centres, educational programmes were started in at least five prisons, and special sections for prisoners with mental illnesses or drug dependency were opened in six prisons.

Overcrowding was reduced by the release of about 1,000 prisoners on probation. However, considerable problems remained, often related to the dilapidated state of some prison buildings. In April, the Ombudsperson noted poor conditions in the women's section of remand prison 313 due to damp, poor heating and sanitation and infestations of vermin.

Right to adequate housing – orphans

Under Albanian law, registered orphans up to the age of 30 who are homeless are among the vulnerable groups to be prioritized when social housing is allocated. However, the law was not implemented and many, including young people raised in state care who were not eligible for orphan status, continued to live in dilapidated disused school dormitories or struggled to pay for low-grade private rented accommodation. The income criteria for eligibility for the main social housing programme, offering state-subsidized mortgages, were set too high for this group. A social housing project, assisted by a Council of Europe Development Bank loan, aiming to construct 1,100 apartments for rent by low-income families had not been completed by the end of the year.

Amnesty International visits/reports

🚌 An Amnesty International delegate visited Albania in November.

📘 Ending domestic violence in Albania: The next steps (EUR 11/001/2010)

📘 In search of shelter: Leaving social care in Albania (EUR 11/004/2010)

ALGERIA

PEOPLE'S DEMOCRATIC REPUBLIC OF ALGERIA

Head of state:	Abdelaziz Bouteflika
Head of government:	Ahmed Ouyahia
Death penalty:	abolitionist in practice
Population:	35.4 million
Life expectancy:	72.9 years
Under-5 mortality (m/f):	35/31 per 1,000
Adult literacy:	72.6 per cent

Human rights defenders and others were banned from holding some meetings and demonstrations. People suspected of security-related offences were arrested and detained incommunicado. Women victims of gender-based violence were not provided with redress. Foreign nationals were arrested and expelled without recourse to appeal. Christians were prosecuted for practising their faith without permission, and others faced trial for offending Islamic tenets. No executions were carried out, but over 130 people were sentenced to death. The authorities failed to take any steps to combat impunity for enforced disappearances and other serious past human rights abuses.

Background

The government maintained the state of emergency in force since 1992.

At least 45 civilians and some 100 members of the military and security forces were killed in continuing political violence, mainly in bomb attacks by armed groups, particularly Al-Qa'ida Organization in the Islamic Maghreb. Over 200 alleged members of Islamist armed groups were reported to have been killed by security forces in skirmishes or search operations, often in unclear circumstances, prompting fears that some may have been extrajudicially executed.

Strikes, riots and demonstrations by people demanding jobs, housing and better salaries punctuated the year. Some protesters were arrested and prosecuted.

The government said it had invited seven UN Special Rapporteurs to visit Algeria but it did not extend invitations to the Special Rapporteur on torture or the UN Working Group on Enforced or Involuntary Disappearances, despite their long-pending requests to carry out investigative visits.

Freedom of expression, association and assembly

The authorities banned some meetings and demonstrations by human rights defenders, journalists and families of victims of enforced disappearance.

■ In March, the authorities stopped the Algerian League for the Defense of Human Rights from using its intended venue to hold its annual conference, forcing the organization to change venue at short notice.

■ The authorities banned a protest by journalists and others calling for more press freedom, scheduled for 3 May in Algiers, and briefly detained four of the organizers.

■ From August, the authorities prevented relatives of victims of enforced disappearance from holding public protests in front of the National Advisory Commission for the Promotion and Protection of Human Rights (CNCPPDH) without giving an official reason, and police used violence to disperse protesters who sought to defy the ban.

Journalists and human rights defenders faced defamation or other criminal charges apparently for criticizing state officials or institutions, or alleging corruption.

■ Belhamideche Belkacem, director of the daily *Réflexion,* and two other men were sentenced to six months' imprisonment on 13 May after being convicted of defaming the Mayor of Ain-Boudinar in an article about alleged corruption published in the newspaper in June 2009. All three remained at liberty awaiting the outcome of an appeal.

■ Anti-corruption activist and journalist Djilali Hadjadj was arrested on 5 September at Constantine airport on the basis that he had previously been convicted in his absence of forgery. He was retried on 13 September in Algiers. He was convicted and sentenced to a suspended six-month prison term and fined, then released.

Counter-terror and security

Officers of the Department of Information and Security (DRS), military intelligence, continued to arrest security suspects and detain them incommunicado, in some cases for more than the 12 days permitted by law, at unrecognized detention centres where they were at risk of torture or other ill-treatment. Impunity for torturing or otherwise abusing security suspects remained entrenched.

■ Salah Koulal was arrested on 5 September in Baghtiya, Boumerdès province, by plain-clothed security officers and detained for 13 days in an unrecognized detention centre in Blida. He remained in El Harrach prison at the end of the year, awaiting trial on a charge of being an "apologist" for terrorism-related activities.

■ Mustapha Labsi was detained for 12 days by the DRS after he was forcibly returned to Algeria from Slovakia on 19 April. He was then transferred to El Harrach prison. At the end of 2010, he was awaiting trial on charges of belonging to a "terrorist group abroad".

■ In April, security suspects held in El Harrach prison went on hunger strike to protest against alleged ill-treatment by guards who, they said, had insulted, slapped and humiliated them. No official investigation into their allegations was held.

Suspects in terrorism-related cases faced unfair trials. Some were convicted on the basis of "confessions" that they alleged were extracted under torture or other duress, including some who were sentenced to death by military courts. Some were denied access to lawyers of their choice. Other security suspects were detained without trial.

■ The trial of Malik Medjnoun and Abdelhakim Chenoui had not resumed by the end of 2010. Accused of murdering famous Kabyle singer Lounès Matoub, and of terrorism-related offences, they have spent over 10 years in detention without trial. Both were tortured during prolonged incommunicado detention following their arrest in 1999.

■ Hasan Zumiri and Adil Hadi Bin Hamlili were transferred to Algeria from US custody in Guantánamo Bay in January; Abdelaziz Naji was transferred in July. All three remained at liberty while investigations continued to determine whether they would face charges of belonging to a "terrorist group abroad". Two former Guantánamo detainees, Mustafa Ahmed Hamlily and Abdul Rahman Houari, were acquitted of similar charges in February and November, respectively. Another former Guantánamo detainee, Bachir Ghalaab, was sentenced to a suspended prison term.

Discrimination and violence against women

In November, the UN Special Rapporteur on violence against women visited Algeria. Despite efforts to implement a national strategy to combat violence against women, the authorities had yet to criminalize domestic violence, including marital rape, and individuals responsible for gender-based violence were not brought to justice.

■ In March and April, a series of attacks targeting women living alone took place in the "36 dwellings" and "40 dwellings" areas in the town of Hassi Messaoud. Groups of men forcibly entered the women's homes, and robbed and physically assaulted them. Some women were also sexually abused. Complaints led to tighter security around the targeted areas, but did not result in prosecutions of alleged perpetrators.

Impunity – enforced disappearances

No steps were taken to investigate the thousands of enforced disappearances and other serious abuses that took place during the internal conflict in the 1990s. The authorities continued to implement the Charter for Peace and National Reconciliation (Law 06-01), which gave impunity to the security forces, criminalized public criticism of their conduct and amnestied members of armed groups responsible for gross human rights abuses. In October, a senior official claimed that 7,500 "repented terrorists" had been granted amnesties since 2005. He also said that 6,240 families of people who had disappeared had accepted financial compensation, and that only 12 families "manipulated by NGOs and foreign bodies" were refusing compensation. Under Law 06-01, relatives can seek compensation if they obtain a death certificate from the authorities for the person who disappeared.

Families of the disappeared continued to hold protests in several cities, including Algiers, Constantine and Jijel. The head of the CNCPPDH declared in August that demands by families for truth and justice were unrealistic due to the absence of testimonies and the impossibility of identifying perpetrators.

In July, the UN Human Rights Committee said that the authorities should investigate the disappearance of Douia Benaziza, who was arrested by security forces in June 1996, and provide her family with an adequate remedy. The Committee found that the authorities had breached her right to liberty and security of person, and her right not to be tortured or ill-treated.

A

Freedom of religion

Amid a continuing crackdown on Protestant churches, Christians, including converts, faced judicial proceedings for "practising religious rites without authorization" under Ordinance 06-03 regulating religious faiths other than Islam. The Constitution guarantees freedom of religion but makes Islam the state religion.

■ A Protestant church in Tizi Ouzou was pillaged in January; the authorities failed to investigate.

■ In August, the trial began in the town of Al-Arba'a Nath Irathen of Mahmoud Yahou, who had established a Protestant church earlier in the year in Tizi Ouzou province, and three other converts to Christianity. They were accused of breaching Ordinance 06-03. The church was not registered apparently as a result of the authorities' refusal to establish any new Protestant churches. In December, the four men were sentenced to suspended prison terms and fined.

Individuals were prosecuted for breaking fast during the holy month of Ramadan under Article 144 bis 2 of the Penal Code. Courts were not consistent in their sentencing, in some cases dropping the charge and in others imposing prison terms and fines.

■ On 5 October, a court in Ain El-Hammam cleared two Christian converts, Hocine Hocini and Salem Fellak, of all charges. They were prosecuted for eating during daylight hours in Ramadan.

Death penalty

Algeria co-sponsored the UN General Assembly resolution calling for a moratorium on the death penalty, and maintained a de facto moratorium on executions that has been in force since 1993. Nonetheless, more than 130 people were sentenced to death, many·in their absence, mostly for terrorism-related offences.

Migrants' rights

Thousands of Algerians and sub-Saharan Africans continued to attempt to migrate to Europe from Algeria, undeterred by amendments to the Penal Code introduced in 2009 that criminalized "irregular exit" from Algeria. Some perished in the desert or at sea; some were intercepted by border control authorities.

According to police statistics, 34 foreign nationals were expelled while 5,232 were deported from Algeria between January and June. Law 08-11, which regulates the entry, stay and movement of foreigners

in Algeria, allows provincial governors to order deportations of individuals who have entered or remain in Algerian territory "illegally", without guaranteeing their right to appeal.

In May, the UN Committee on Migrant Workers expressed concern that Algerian legislation allows for the indefinite detention of irregular migrants and that the authorities had failed to investigate reports of collective expulsions.

Amnesty International visits/reports

🚍 Amnesty International's request to conduct a fact-finding visit to the country was not granted. The authorities said that the organization could only visit the Sahrawi refugee camps in Tindouf, run by the Polisario Front, but not the remainder of the country.

▨ Algeria: Investigate and prosecute attacks against women (MDE 28/002/2010)

▨ Algeria: Release Malik Medjnoun (MDE 28/008/2010)

ANGOLA

REPUBLIC OF ANGOLA

Head of state:	José Eduardo dos Santos
Head of government:	António Paulo Kassoma
Death penalty:	abolitionist for all crimes
Population:	19 million
Life expectancy:	48.1 years
Under-5 mortality (m/f):	220/189 per 1,000
Adult literacy:	69.6 per cent

Several people were arrested and accused of crimes against the state. Some remained in detention without trial. Two prisoners of conscience and several possible prisoners of conscience were convicted of crimes against the security of the state. Forced evictions continued to be carried out. Several planned demonstrations were arbitrarily prohibited. Police officers were brought to justice in at least one case of extrajudicial execution, but police continued to violate human rights. Despite an agreement between Angola and the Democratic Republic of the Congo (DRC) to stop mass expulsions of the other country's nationals, Angola continued these expulsions, during which human rights violations were committed.

Background

On 8 January, the Togo football team was attacked in Cabinda as it travelled to play in the African Cup of Nations football tournament being hosted by Angola. Two people were killed and several injured during the attack. A faction of the Front for the Liberation of the Cabinda State, FLEC/PM, claimed responsibility for the attack, stating that it did not intend to attack the team, only the Angolan Armed Forces members (FAA) escorting the team. A few days later another faction, FLEC-Fac, reportedly also claimed responsibility. Two men, João António Puati and Daniel Simbai, were arrested on suspicion of carrying out the attack. João António Puati was convicted and sentenced to 24 years' imprisonment for the attack, while Daniel Simbai was acquitted. At least 14 others were arrested following the attack, although not accused directly of carrying it out. There were further attacks by FLEC in Cabinda during 2010.

In January, parliament approved a new Constitution which provides for the President to be elected by parliament. The Constitution also allows President dos Santos, who has been in office for over 30 years, to serve two more five-year terms. In addition, it replaces the Prime Minister with a Vice-President selected by the President.

In September, the Angolan Bar Association asked the Constitutional Court to rule on the legality of Article 26 of the Law on crimes against the security of the state. The article stated that "all and every act, not foreseen in the law that puts at risk or could put at risk the security of the state will be punishable". In December the Court decided it did not have to make a ruling on this due to a new Law on crimes against the security of the state approved by parliament in November. The new law repeals Article 26 of the old law, but makes it a criminal offence to insult the Republic, the President or any organ of power of the state.

In February, Angola's human rights record was assessed under the UN Universal Periodic Review. In September Angola presented its report to the Committee on the Rights of the Child.

Right to adequate housing – forced evictions

In October, President dos Santos reiterated the government's commitment to enabling Angolan families to obtain their own houses and in November he launched a slum restoration project. Despite this, forced evictions continued in the capital, Luanda and there were large-scale forced evictions in Huíla province. There were also threats of forced evictions in other parts of the country.

■ In March over 3,000 homes near the railway line in Lubango, Huíla province, were demolished to make way for railway upgrades. At least two children died during these forced evictions; one when debris fell on him and another apparently due to poor living conditions following the demolitions. Those forcibly evicted were moved to Tchavola neighbourhood, on the outskirts of Lubango, and left without access to clean water or basic services and exposed to extremes of weather. Only 600 tents were provided for all the families. In April, the Huíla provincial government apologized for the demolitions. However, there were reports of further forced evictions in Lubango in August and in September.

Unlawful killings

In March, seven police officers were convicted and sentenced to 24 years' imprisonment by the Luanda Provincial Court for killing eight youths in the Largo da Frescura area of Luanda in July 2008. However, many police officers continued to violate human rights with impunity.

■ In May, the bodies of William Marques Luís "Líro Boy" and Hamilton Pedro Luís "Kadú" were found by their family in the Central Morgue of Luanda. They had been arrested without a warrant at their home in Luanda's Benfica neighbourhood by several police officers and were subsequently extrajudicially executed. "Kadú" was reportedly beaten by the police outside his home before he and "Líro Boy" were taken away. "Kadú" had been shot in the head and abdomen and his body showed signs of having been beaten. "Líro Boy" had been shot several times in the head and his body showed signs of torture, including broken limbs. In November police authorities announced that those responsible for the deaths had been detained. No further details were provided.

■ In July, 19-year-old Valentino Abel was killed when a police officer opened fire in the Belo Horizonte area of Kunhinga Municipality in Huambo. The police officer had apparently intervened to stop an altercation and had been slapped. He then reportedly became enraged and started shooting indiscriminately. Three shots hit Valentino Abel in the thorax, killing him. The Municipal Police Commander stated that the police officer had been drunk and had run away following the incident, but was captured two days later. However, no information was available concerning any proceedings against him.

Freedom of assembly

Despite provisions of the new Constitution guaranteeing the right to demonstrate peacefully without the need for authorization, this right was denied on a number of occasions.

■ On 1 April, OMUNGA, an NGO based in Benguela, informed the Benguela provincial government of its intention to hold a peaceful march on 10 April in protest against forced evictions in Huíla province and in solidarity with the victims. A similar march planned in March had not been allowed, allegedly because not all the requirements of the law had been complied with. Although the organizers had complied with national law, the Benguela provincial government once again refused to authorize the march planned for April, on the grounds that there had been no forced evictions in the province. Nevertheless, the demonstration went ahead peacefully on the day.

■ In May, the Cabinda provincial government refused to allow a planned march in protest against the arbitrary arrest and detention of people in connection with the attack on the Togo football team, even though the organizers of the march had complied with all the requirements of the law.

In June, the President of the Constitutional Court stated that Angolan national law does not require prior authorization from administrative authorities for demonstrations to occur. However, authorities continued to prevent peaceful demonstrations.

Prisoners of conscience and possible prisoners of conscience

Between January and April, at least 14 people were arrested in Cabinda on charges related to the January attack on the Togo football team. Two were prisoners of conscience and a number of others were possible prisoners of conscience. Seven were released without charge, while the others were charged with crimes against the security of the state. Of these one had the charges dropped after seven months' detention, another was acquitted, while five were convicted but later released due to the repeal of article 26 of the Law on crimes against the security of the state under which they were convicted. There were also other arrests in other provinces of possible prisoners of conscience.

■ In August, prisoners of conscience Francisco Luemba, a lawyer, and Raul Tati, a Catholic priest, were convicted of being the "moral authors of the crime of other crimes against the security of the state" and sentenced to five years' imprisonment by the Cabinda Provincial court. They were tried along with two other men who might also have been prisoners of conscience, José Benjamin Fuca and Belchior Lanso Tati, who were sentenced to three and six years respectively. Police arrested all four men shortly after the attack in January. They had documents on Cabinda and had recently attended a conference aimed at finding a peaceful resolution to the situation. José Benjamin Fuca and Belchior Lanso Tati allegedly also confessed to being members of FLEC. They appealed to the Supreme and Constitutional Courts. On 22 December, all four men were unconditionally released by the Cabinda Provincial Court due to the repeal of the law under which they were convicted.

■ Police arrested more members of the Commission of the Legal Sociological Manifesto of the Lunda Tchokwe Protectorate. Between January and October, at least 24 members were reportedly arrested in Luanda and Lunda Norte province. Thirteen were reportedly released without charge after varying periods in pre-trial detention. Three, Sebastião Lumani, José Muteba and José António da Silva Malembela, were convicted of crimes against the security of the state by the Lunda-Norte Provincial Court. They were sentenced to six years', five years' and four years' imprisonment respectively and remained in prison at the end of the year despite the repeal of the law under which they were convicted. Domingos Manuel Muatoyo and Alberto Cabaza, who were arrested in Luanda in July, were accused of demonstrating against the government and remained in pre-trial detention at the end of the year. A further six people remained in detention without charge. Other members of the Commission arrested in 2009 remained in prison without trial at the end of the year despite the repeal of the law under which they were charged.

Migrants' rights

Despite an agreement in 2009 to stop expulsions between Angola and the DRC, the Angolan authorities continued to expel Congolese nationals and the expulsions were accompanied by human rights violations, including sexual violence. The UN Office for the Coordination of Humanitarian Affairs (OCHA) reported that over 12,000 migrants had been expelled to Bandundu, Bas-Congo and Kasai provinces between

September and the end of the year. According to OCHA, 99 women and 15 men were raped during the expulsion. One woman reportedly died in hospital after being raped. Other human rights violations included torture and other ill-treatment, and many of the migrants arrived naked and without their belongings. There were other expulsions in the course of the year.

No one is known to have been held responsible for human rights violations associated with these expulsions or similar expulsions in previous years.

Amnesty International visits/reports

🚂 Amnesty International delegates were not granted access to Angola for more than two years. Visa applications submitted in October 2008 and October 2009 had still not been granted by the end of 2010. In November, Amnesty International once again applied for visas to attend a conference organized by the Angolan Council of Churches for the end of November. These visas were not granted by the end of the year.

📄 Angola: Death of Muatxihina Chamumbala in Conduege Prison and concern for the remaining 32 prisoners (AFR 12/012/2010)

📄 Angola: Benguela Provincial Authorities must not unreasonably prevent peaceful demonstration (AFR 12/006/2010)

📄 Angolan activists jailed over attack on Togo football team, 3 August 2010

ARGENTINA

ARGENTINE REPUBLIC
Head of state and government:	**Cristina Fernández**
Death penalty:	**abolitionist for all crimes**
Population:	**40.7 million**
Life expectancy:	**75.7 years**
Under-5 mortality (m/f):	**17/14 per 1,000**
Adult literacy:	**97.7 per cent**

Women and girls who were pregnant as a result of rape continued to face major obstacles in getting access to legal abortions. Excessive use of force by the police and inhumane prison conditions remained serious concerns. Legal proceedings against those responsible for past human rights violations during the military regimes continued.

Background

In June, Argentina became the first country in Latin America to legalize same-sex marriage. In July,

President Cristina Fernández passed a decree to implement legislation passed in 2009 to prevent and punish violence against women. In December, following a process of national consultation, a National Human Rights Plan was made public.

Sexual and reproductive rights

The CEDAW Committee and the UN Human Rights Committee called on Argentina to amend legislation criminalizing abortion in some cases. Misinterpretation of the Criminal Code resulted in pregnant rape survivors facing serious obstacles in getting legal abortions. The status of the long-awaited Guide for the Integral Attention of Non-Punishable Abortion Cases was put in doubt and there were concerns that the lack of clear institutional guidelines on abortion would continue.

■ In March, two 15-year-old girls from the southern province of Chubut, both of whom had allegedly been raped by their stepfathers, were denied legal abortions by two different judges, causing delays and endangering their lives. Both judicial decisions were subsequently overturned.

Torture and other ill-treatment

The UN Human Rights Committee, the UN Committee on the Rights of the Child and the Inter-American Commission on Human Rights expressed serious concerns at reports of torture and other ill-treatment in prisons and police stations, particularly in Buenos Aires and Mendoza provinces. In January, a Provincial Mechanism for the Prevention of Torture was approved by legislators in Chaco province. However, a similar national mechanism, which is required under the Optional Protocol to the UN Convention against Torture, had still not been put in place by the end of the year.

Police and security forces

Excessive use of force by security forces leading to injury and deaths was reported. In separate incidents in June and October, two teenage boys were shot dead by police officers in Río Negro province.

■ On 15 February, police violently broke up a protest by residents in the town of Andalgalá, Catamarca province, against open-pit mining in the area. A few hours later, thousands of people gathered in the local square in solidarity with the protesters. The security forces allegedly responded by beating demonstrators with truncheons and firing tear gas and rubber bullets indiscriminately.

A

During the incidents, some protesters also damaged the local municipal building. Several people were arrested and around 70 people were injured.

Impunity

According to official data, by the end of the year, 110 people had been convicted for their role in human rights violations committed under the military regimes of the past; 820 more were facing criminal charges; and 13 trials were continuing. Despite progress in bringing to justice perpetrators of past human rights violations, a report by the Supreme Court admitted that there had been some delays, in particular in provincial courts.

■ On 20 April, Reynaldo Bignone, a former military general and former de facto President, was found guilty of torture, murder and several kidnappings that occurred while he was commander of the notorious Campo de Mayo detention centre between 1976 and 1978.

■ In July, former General Luciano Benjamín Menéndez and Roberto Albornoz, former head of the intelligence police, were sentenced to life imprisonment for human rights violations committed at a secret detention centre in Tucumán province during the military regime (1976-1983).

■ In December, Jorge Videla, de facto President of Argentina between 1976 and 1981, was found criminally responsible for the torture and deaths of over 30 prisoners in Córdoba in 1976. The court found a further 22 military and police officers guilty of these crimes.

Indigenous Peoples' rights

Concerns remained at the failure to implement the 2006 national emergency law which temporarily suspends the execution of eviction orders or the removal of Indigenous communities from traditional lands until an appropriate nationwide survey has been carried out.

■ In November, 400 police officers violently dispersed members of the Toba Qom Indigenous community who had mounted a roadblock in protest at plans to build a university on traditional lands. The police also burned down the community's temporary homes. At least one police officer and one member of the Indigenous community were killed.

Right to health – land and environment

An NGO report published in early 2010 identified 120 land-ownership and environment-related conflicts in the Chaco area of northern Argentina, affecting over half a million people, mainly from peasant and Indigenous communities.

Despite growing evidence of the negative impact on health of chemicals used on soya and rice plantations in several northern provinces, by the end of the year no systematic epidemiological study or investigation had been initiated to evaluate the extent and gravity of the problem.

International justice

In September, the Supreme Court unanimously ruled in favour of the extradition of Sergio Galvarino Apablaza Guerra to Chile where he faced charges in connection with the murder of Senator Jaime Guzmán and the kidnapping of Cristián Edwards in 1991. However, in October, a federal judge closed the case for his extradition after the National Commission for Refugees granted him refugee status.

Amnesty International visits/reports

Argentina: "Exigimos respeto" – los derechos de los pilagá del Bañado la Estrella (AMR 13/001/2010)

ARMENIA

REPUBLIC OF ARMENIA

Head of state:	Serzh Sargsyan
Head of government:	Tigran Sargsyan
Death penalty:	abolitionist for all crimes
Population:	3.1 million
Life expectancy:	74.2 years
Under-5 mortality (m/f):	29/25 per 1,000
Adult literacy:	99.5 per cent

Perpetrators of human rights violations continued to enjoy impunity. Protection for women and girls still failed to meet international standards. No genuine civilian alternative to military service was introduced.

Deaths in custody

Following its visit to Armenia in September, the UN Working Group on Arbitrary Detention expressed concern about ill-treatment and beatings of detainees and prisoners. It also expressed concern over detainees being pressured in order to extract confessions.

■ In April, Vahan Khalafian died in hospital hours after being detained at the police precinct in Charentsavan on charges of theft. The authorities claimed that he had stabbed himself after being ill-treated by police officers but his family disputed the suicide account. In November, two police officers were sentenced for abuse of official authority, which allegedly caused the suicide; one to eight years' imprisonment and his subordinate to two years' suspended sentence.

Impunity

At the end of the year there had still been no independent inquiry into allegations of excessive use of force against members of the public during post-election protests in 2008; no one had been brought to justice in connection with 10 deaths, including of two police officers, that occurred during the violent demonstrations. The families of nine victims initiated proceedings against the General Prosecutor's Office for failing to investigate the deaths. The General Jurisdiction Court dismissed their complaints and its decisions were upheld by the Appeal Court and the Supreme Court.

Freedom of expression

In November, Nikol Pashinian, an opposition activist and editor-in-chief of *Haikakan Zhamanak*, was reportedly assaulted by unidentified men while serving a revised prison sentence of three years and 11 months. He was originally sentenced in January to seven years' imprisonment on charges of organizing mass disorder in 2008. He continued to write articles for his newspaper while in detention. His lawyer reported that Nikol Pashinian had earlier been threatened with harm unless he stopped exposing in his newspaper allegedly corrupt practices in the penitentiary system. Following the assault, the journalist was moved to another prison.

Violence against women and girls

In March, the government set up the State Interagency Committee to Combat Gender-Based Violence following a decree by the Prime Minister. However, no progress had been made by the government on enacting legislation specifically addressing violence against women and the setting up of shelters, contrary to a 2009 CEDAW recommendation. There was currently only one shelter in the country, run by the NGO, Women's Rights Centre, with foreign donor funding.

In October, 20-year-old Zaruhi Petrosian, a victim of ongoing domestic violence, died, reportedly after being severely beaten by her husband and mother-in-

law. According to her sister, Zaruhi Petrosian had approached police on two occasions to report the abuse and seek help but they reportedly dismissed her case as "unimportant" and "irrelevant". Following extensive publicity about the case, the authorities arrested her husband and charged him with "causing wilfully heavy damage to health".

Prisoners of conscience

At the end of the year, 73 men were serving prison sentences for refusing to do military service on grounds of conscience. The alternative service remained under military control. In November the Grand Chamber of the European Court of Human Rights considered an appeal by the conscientious objector Vahan Bayatyan against the Court's 2009 ruling that his right to freedom of conscience and religion had not been violated when he was convicted of evading the draft in 2002. In 2009, the Court held that the Convention did not guarantee the right of conscientious objection; a dissenting judge issued an opinion stating that the majority's finding failed to reflect that the right to conscientious objection is almost universally accepted to be fundamental to the rights to freedom of thought, conscience and religion.

A

AUSTRALIA

AUSTRALIA	
Head of state:	Queen Elizabeth II, represented by Quentin Bryce
Head of government:	Julia Gillard (replaced Kevin Rudd in June)
Death penalty:	abolitionist for all crimes
Population:	21.5 million
Life expectancy:	81.9 years
Under-5 mortality (m/f):	6/5 per 1,000

The government reinstated the Racial Discrimination Act but only partially restored protection of human rights. The UN Committee on the Elimination of Racial Discrimination (CERD Committee) criticized the government for the continued discrimination against Indigenous Peoples and the high level of disadvantage they faced. The government temporarily suspended processing asylum claims for Sri Lankans and Afghans, but committed to releasing a number of children and families from immigration detention.

Indigenous Peoples' rights

In June, the Federal Government reinstated the Racial Discrimination Act. The Act had been suspended in Northern Territory Aboriginal communities since 2007 when the government launched the Northern Territory intervention in response to a report citing high levels of sexual abuse. Aboriginal people were subjected to racially discriminatory measures, including compulsory income management. However, the reinstatement only partially restored human rights protection and did not provide remedies for ongoing discrimination or avenues of redress for damage suffered.

In August, Australia appeared before the CERD Committee. Key concerns of the Committee were the lack of protection against racial discrimination in the Australian Constitution, the partial reinstatement of human rights protection, disproportionate imprisonment rates for Indigenous people and continued Indigenous deaths in custody.

Refugees and asylum-seekers

In April, the government suspended asylum applications for Sri Lankan and Afghan nationals for three and six months respectively.

In June, the government reopened the controversial Curtin detention centre and detained some families in the remote mining town of Leonora in Western Australia.

In September, the Minister for Immigration announced plans to detain 300 asylum-seekers on an air force base at Weipa in the far north of Queensland.
■ Three Sri Lankan asylum-seekers who had been forcibly returned to Sri Lanka from Australia were subsequently arrested and tortured.

Mandatory, indefinite detention, coupled with poor conditions in some detention facilities, put a large number of detained asylum-seekers at risk of self-harm and mental illness.

In October, the government committed to releasing several hundred children and families held under Australia's mandatory detention regime. However, the government announced it would establish two new centres to increase Australia's detention capacity by 1,200 places, many of which were intended for children and families.

Violence against women and girls

In September, the government released a draft of its National Plan to Reduce Violence against Women and their Children.

Legal, constitutional or institutional developments

In April, laws were introduced that created a specific torture offence and ensured that the death penalty could not be reintroduced anywhere in Australia.
■ In October, a young couple facing criminal charges in the state of Queensland for self-procuring an abortion were acquitted. This highlighted inconsistencies in abortion laws across state jurisdictions and the need to regulate abortion under health legislation.

A Federal Human Rights Act was recommended by a government-appointed committee after widespread public consultation. However, the government did not adopt the recommendation.

AUSTRIA

REPUBLIC OF AUSTRIA

Head of state:	Heinz Fischer
Head of government:	Werner Faymann
Death penalty:	abolitionist for all crimes
Population:	8.4 million
Life expectancy:	80.4 years
Under-5 mortality (m/f):	6/5 per 1,000

Allegations of police ill-treatment, including racially motivated abuses, continued. Asylum seekers were forcibly returned to Greece under the Dublin II Regulation.

Racism

Reports of racially motivated police misconduct towards foreign nationals and ethnic minorities continued. Structural shortcomings within the criminal justice system when responding to discrimination, such as the failure to promptly and thoroughly investigate allegations of racially motivated ill-treatment and excessive use of force, and the absence of a comprehensive and coherent system to record incidents of racist misconduct, were not adequately addressed.

Torture and other ill-treatment

In May 2010, the UN Committee against Torture reiterated its concerns regarding the absence of the crime of torture in Austria's Criminal Code, the high level of impunity for abuses by police and the lenient sentences imposed by courts in cases of torture or other ill-treatment.

■ The European Court of Human Rights began to examine the complaint of Gambian national Bakary J., alleging that his expulsion from Austria would result in a violation of his right to family life and his right not to be ill-treated. Bakary J., who was tortured by four police officers in 2006 following an unsuccessful deportation, has yet to receive reparation. The officers received suspended sentences of less than one year in August 2006.

■ In November, proceedings against a police officer charged with grievous bodily harm continued before the Regional Criminal Court in Vienna. US citizen Mike B., an African-American teacher, was injured by an undercover policeman on 11 February 2009 in an underground station in Vienna.

Police and security forces

At the Vienna Regional Criminal Court in November, the trial began of the individuals accused of killing Chechen refugee Umar Israilov on 13 January 2009. The proceedings to determine if the police failed to provide protection to Umar Israilov upon the request of his lawyer were pending before the Independent Administrative Tribunal.

Migrants' and asylum-seekers' rights

Austria continued to transfer asylum-seekers to Greece under the Dublin II Regulation, despite the lack of a functioning asylum system there. In some cases, such transfers were stopped by interim measures of the European Court of Human Rights. In November, the Court sent a letter to the government asking it to stop transfers to Greece but the authorities decided to maintain the practice of individual assessment of each case.

■ On 19 July, Reza H., an Afghan asylum-seeker who had alleged that he was 16 years old, died following a suicide attempt carried out during his detention at the Police Detention Centre in Hernals, Vienna, pending his transfer back to Sweden. During the interview by the Federal Asylum Office held in May, Reza H. stated repeatedly that he had been raped while in a hostel for asylum-seekers in Sweden, where he had previously sought asylum. Despite this, he was detained without

the provision of psychological counselling. Inquiries were initiated by the Austrian Ombudsperson's Office and the Ministry of Interior.

Amnesty International visits/reports

🗐 Austria: Submission to the UN Universal Periodic Review, January 2011 (EUR 13/002/2010)

AZERBAIJAN

REPUBLIC OF AZERBAIJAN

Head of state:	Ilham Aliyev
Head of government:	Artur Rasizade
Death penalty:	abolitionist for all crimes
Population:	8.9 million
Life expectancy:	70.8 years
Under-5 mortality (m/f):	54/52 per 1,000
Adult literacy:	99.5 per cent

Journalists and civil society activists continued to face intimidation. The authorities continued to ban demonstrations in the centre of Baku. NGOs and religious organizations faced restrictions in obtaining registration.

Background

The parliamentary elections on 7 November were described by the OSCE as "peaceful" but "not sufficient to constitute meaningful progress in the democratic development of the country."

Against a backdrop of skirmishes along Azerbaijan and Armenia's ceasefire line and an increase in their defence budgets, little progress was made in the negotiations to resolve the Nagorno-Karabakh conflict under the aegis of the OSCE Minsk Group. Some 600,000 people internally displaced by the conflict continued to suffer discriminatory registration requirements and inadequate housing.

Freedom of expression

Threats, harassment, and acts of violence against journalists and civil society activists continued with impunity, leading to an increase in self-censorship. Criminal and civil defamation laws were used to silence criticism, resulting in prison sentences and heavy fines against journalists.

On 12 February, the parliament (Milli Mejlis), approved a ban on the use of video, photo, or voice recordings without the subject's prior knowledge or consent. Only law enforcement officials were exempt.

Journalists and civil society activists were frequently subjected to violence and prevented from carrying out their work, sometimes through excessive use of force by police officers.

■ Seven journalists, attempting to cover the 27 April protests against the government's clampdown on the freedoms of expression and assembly, were detained by police officers. Two journalists, Mehman Huseynov from the Institute for Reporter Freedom and Safety, and Afgan Mukhtarli from the *Yeni Musavat* newspaper, reportedly had their cameras broken. Mehman Huseynov's leg was allegedly injured during the dispersal.

During the election period, a number of journalists were forcibly expelled from polling stations and detained by the police when trying to record electoral violations such as ballot stuffing.

■ On 18 November, Bakhtiyar Hajiyev, a youth activist and parliamentary candidate who exposed electoral violations, was detained on the Azerbaijan/Georgia border and held overnight at a military drafting centre before being released. He was threatened with forcible conscription into the army, despite being excused from military service as a registered student and a parliamentary candidate.

On 22 April, the European Court of Human Rights ruled that Eynulla Fatullayev, a newspaper editor and journalist, was unlawfully imprisoned, and ordered his immediate release. He had been sentenced to eight and a half years in prison on charges of defamation, incitement to ethnic hatred, terrorism and tax evasion. He remained in prison and, on 6 July, a Baku court convicted and sentenced him to two and a half years in prison for possession of illegal drugs. On 11 November the Supreme Court annulled the charges of defamation, incitement to ethnic hatred and terrorism. However, Eynulla Fatullayev remained in prison on the drug-related charges, which were widely believed to have been fabricated.

Two youth activists and bloggers, Adnan Hajizade and Emin Abdullayev (blogger name Emin Milli), held on fabricated charges of "hooliganism" since 8 July 2009, were conditionally released on 18 and 19 November, having served 16 months of their respective 24 and 30 month prison sentences. By the end of the year, their convictions had not been overturned.

Freedom of assembly

Demonstrations continued to be banned in Baku's city centre. Throughout the year, especially during the election period, opposition parties were prevented from holding rallies or demonstrations, or were allocated unsuitable locations such as building sites.

■ On 27 April, around 80 people, travelling to a rally in Baku in defence of the rights to freedom of expression and assembly, were seized by police officers, who pushed them into minibuses and police cars. Forty were driven to the outskirts of the city and released immediately and another 30 were taken to a police station and released after five hours. Ten were charged with resisting arrest and violating public order, and released in the late evening. On 13 April, police had broken up a similar protest at the same location organized by the opposition Musavat party, arrested 47 people and released them after several hours.

Freedom of association

Loopholes in the law relating to the registration of NGOs continued to be used to prevent organizations from registering legally. Some religious communities were also denied registration or faced difficulties re-registering, following the 2009 amendments to the Law on Freedom of Religion which made unregistered activity illegal. According to a report published in June by the Council of Europe Commissioner for Human Rights, fewer than half the 534 previously registered religious communities were able to re-register.

Violence against women

On 25 May, parliament adopted the Draft Law on Domestic Violence, criminalizing domestic violence and providing for the creation of aid centres for victims of violence.

Amnesty International visits/reports

- Azerbaijan: Continuation of crackdown on dissent (EUR 55/001/2010)
- Azerbaijani bloggers lose appeal against fabricated charges, 10 March 2010
- Imprisoned Azerbaijani journalist faces new jail term, 5 July 2010
- Azerbaijan urged to release journalist after court revokes charges, 12 November 2010
- Azerbaijan urged to end harassment of activists, 19 November 2010

BAHAMAS

COMMONWEALTH OF THE BAHAMAS
Head of state: Queen Elizabeth II, represented by Sir Arthur
              Alexander Foulkes (replaced Arthur Hanna in April)
Head of government: Hubert Ingraham
Death penalty: retentionist
Population: 0.3 million
Life expectancy: 74.4 years
Under-5 mortality (m/f):   14/12 per 1,000

There were concerns about the treatment of Haitian migrants. At least five people were sentenced to death; no executions were carried out.

Police and security forces

Members were appointed to a new Police Complaints Inspectorate, which is mandated to review complaints of abuses by police officers and ensure investigations are conducted impartially. The Inspectorate was established to address long-standing impunity for past cases of police abuses.

Refugees and migrants

Following the earthquake in Haiti in January, the authorities announced that they would suspend the repatriation of Haitian migrants. However, soon afterwards, there were reports that Haitian migrants who landed in the Bahamas were being charged with illegal landing and repatriated. By the end of the year hundreds of Haitians had been repatriated.

The government failed to publish a report by the Department of Immigration into reports of ill-treatment of scores of migrants held in the Carmichael Detention Center in 2009.

Violence against women and girls

The bill introduced in July 2009 to amend provisions of the 1991 Sexual Offences and Domestic Violence Act, which excludes rape within marriage from the definition of the criminal offence of rape, had still not been discussed in Parliament by the end of 2010.

Death penalty

At least five people were sentenced to death. Thirteen of those under sentence of death were awaiting retrials following a ruling in 2006 by the UK-based Judicial Committee of the Privy Council abolishing mandatory death sentences for murder. In December,

the Bahamas voted against a UN General Assembly resolution calling for a moratorium on the use of the death penalty.

BAHRAIN

KINGDOM OF BAHRAIN
Head of state: King Hamad bin 'Issa Al Khalifa
Head of government: Shaikh Khalifa bin Salman Al Khalifa
Death penalty: retentionist
Population: 0.8 million
Life expectancy: 76 years
Under-5 mortality (m/f):   13/13 per 1,000
Adult literacy: 90.8 per cent

Scores of anti-government activists were arrested. Twenty-five leading opposition activists were on trial, two in their absence, accused of plotting to overthrow the government; the 23 were initially denied access to lawyers after their arrest and some said they were tortured. Other unfair trials took place. The authorities restricted freedom of expression, including by shutting down several websites and political newsletters. The government suspended board members of an independent human rights organization. One person was executed.

Background

In April, the King appointed the 23 members of the board of the National Human Rights Institution, established in November 2009. In September, however, the board's President resigned amid disagreement between its members about how the institution should respond to political arrests.

During 2010, sporadic protests took place in predominantly Shi'a villages against alleged government discrimination in relation to housing and employment opportunities. In some cases, protesters blocked highways with burning tyres and threw home-made petrol bombs at the police and security forces. Hundreds of people were arrested, particularly in August and September, in connection with protests and riots, including many leading opposition figures, most from the Shi'a majority community. Many were allegedly arrested without warrants and held incommunicado for up to two weeks after arrest.

B

Independent and Shi'a Islamists won the majority of seats in parliamentary elections in October.´

Unfair trials, torture and other ill-treatment

Trials of people arrested in connection with the protests started; some were marred by allegations of torture, denial of access to lawyers and other abuses.

■ The trial began on 28 October before the High Criminal Court in Manama of 25 prominent activists, most associated with al-Haq, an unauthorized opposition group. They were charged under the 2006 anti-terrorism law with "forming and funding an illegal organization with the aim of overthrowing the government and dissolving the constitution" and other offences. Two of them, who live abroad, were tried in their absence. All were accused of fomenting protests and inciting public unrest. The 23 arrested were held incommunicado for two weeks before they were charged. Some told the Public Prosecutor that they had been tortured and otherwise ill-treated by National Security Agency officials and had signed "confessions" under duress; several were referred for medical examination, but a government forensic doctor was reported to have found no physical evidence of torture. During the initial stages of the trial, defence lawyers complained about continuing restrictions on their access to their clients, and most of the accused repudiated their "confessions" and repeated to the court that they had been tortured or ill-treated. No independent investigation was initiated into the torture allegations, and only two defendants were referred to an independent medical doctor for examination. In December, the defence lawyers of the 23 withdrew from the case because the court ignored their requests, and the defendants refused to recognize or co-operate with lawyers subsequently appointed. The trial was continuing at the end of the year.

Other trials were held of people accused of murder and burning cars, tyres and other property while participating in anti-government demonstrations and riots in previous years. In some, the defendants alleged they had been tortured or ill-treated to make them "confess".

■ In March, the Supreme Appeal Court convicted 19 men accused of killing a police officer during an anti-government demonstration in 2008 in Karzakan and sentenced them to three years in prison. In October 2009 a lower court had acquitted them, finding that there was extensive evidence that the accused had been tortured in pre-trial detention to force them to "confess". This finding was ignored by the Supreme Appeal Court. No steps were taken to investigate the men's torture allegations.

Other cases of torture were also reported.

■ Two men, who were detained for the alleged attempted murder in August of a newspaper editor, were said to have been tortured to obtain detailed confessions used in court. They were released in December after the victim told the court that they were not the people who had attacked him.

Excessive use of force

Several times during the year security forces were reported to have fired shotguns at protesters and others. In October, the Interior Minister told Amnesty International that the security forces had tried to contain protests and violence without using excessive force and that no one had been wounded by their actions.

■ In March, Ibrahim al-Dumistani and 'Abdel-'Aziz Nasheeb, both nurses, were arrested after they assisted Hussain 'Ali Hassan al-Sahlawi who had been shot, apparently by police trying to disperse a protest in Karzakan in which demonstrators had burned tyres. The injured man said he had not been protesting and was shot by police outside his home. The nurses were charged with assisting a "cover up" and "abusing their medical profession", and quickly released on bail.

Freedom of expression

Critics of the monarchy and government were warned that they would be prosecuted under the 2002 Press and Publications Law, which prescribes prison terms for those criticizing the King or "inciting hatred of the regime", although no such prosecutions were reported.

The government clamped down further on dissent after the arrest of the 23 opposition activists. On 28 August, the Public Prosecutor invoked Article 246 of the Penal Code to prohibit the media and others from publishing or broadcasting information about the arrests; breaches would be punishable by up to one year in prison. Although no prosecutions were reported, the government banned and shut down various publications and blogs. Among them was the Bahrain Online forum, which the Director of the National Information Agency said in October had been closed because it was deemed to have incited hatred and violence. He also said that other websites had been blocked because they had published material that breached Bahraini law, and that newsletters of political associations had been banned as the law only allows their circulation to members whereas these had been distributed to the public.

Freedom of association

In September, the government suspended the board of the independent NGO Bahrain Human Rights Society, accusing it of "legal and administrative irregularities" and "co-operating with illegal organizations". Shortly before, the NGO had published on their website allegations of torture relating to the 23 detained Shi'a activists. The government appointed a temporary administrator, severely compromising the society's independence.

Several human rights activists were prevented from travelling abroad, although the government denied that travel bans had been issued against them.

■ Nabeel Rajab, Director of the Bahrain Centre for Human Rights that was banned in 2004, was prevented at the border from travelling to Saudi Arabia on 27 September, prompting international protests. In October, he was allowed to travel.

Migrants' rights

Foreign migrants, especially domestic workers, continued to be exploited and abused despite revisions to the *kafala* (sponsorship system) made in 2009 to enable foreign workers to change jobs without obtaining their employer's consent. In several reported cases, employers confiscated foreign domestic workers' passports to prevent them seeking alternative employment. A number of migrant workers were reported to have committed suicide on account of their poor living and working conditions. Bahraini law affords little protection to foreign domestic workers; for example, it contains no provisions establishing a minimum wage or rest time.

Death penalty

At least one person was sentenced to death and one man was executed. As in the previous 10 years, the death penalty was only used against foreign nationals.

■ In March, Russell Mezan, a Bangladeshi national, was sentenced to death for murdering a Kuwaiti man. The death sentence was upheld on appeal in October and by the Cassation Court later in the year.

■ In July, Jassim Abdulmanan, a Bangladeshi national, was executed. He had been sentenced in 2007 for murdering another Bangladeshi national in 2005.

In December, Bahrain abstained on a UN General Assembly resolution calling for a worldwide moratorium on executions.

Amnesty International visits/reports

🚍 An Amnesty International delegation visited Bahrain in October for research purposes and meetings with the government. The delegation observed the first session of the trial of 23 Shi'a activists arrested in August and September.

▤ Bahrain: Detained Shi'a Muslims at risk (MDE 11/005/2010)

▤ Bahrain: Fair trial and freedom of expression must be guaranteed (MDE 11/009/2010)

B

BANGLADESH

PEOPLE'S REPUBLIC OF BANGLADESH

Head of state:	Zillur Rahman
Head of government:	Sheikh Hasina
Death penalty:	retentionist
Population:	164.4 million
Life expectancy:	66.9 years
Under-5 mortality (m/f):	58/56 per 1,000
Adult literacy:	55 per cent

Rapid Action Battalion (RAB) personnel and other police officers detained more than 1,500 people, many of them arbitrarily, during demonstrations. They used excessive force against demonstrators, injuring hundreds. RAB and the police continued to be implicated in extrajudicial executions. At least six detainees died in police custody, allegedly from torture. Nine men were executed and at least 32 men were sentenced to death. Six people were detained for war crimes. The government failed to adequately protect the Jumma Indigenous people of the Chittagong Hill Tracts against attacks from Bengali settlers.

Background

In February, the Supreme Court upheld a 2005 High Court judgement that declared the Fifth Amendment to the Constitution unlawful. The ruling did not provide new scope for investigation of human rights violations committed between August 1975 and April 1979, which the Amendment had shielded.

In March, Bangladesh ratified the Rome Statute of the International Criminal Court.

Violence against women and girls

According to government figures, violence against women topped all crimes reported to the police in the first six months of the year. Of 7,285 complaints made, 1,586 were rape cases. Parliament passed the Domestic Violence (Prevention and Protection) Bill in October.

Arbitrary arrests and detentions

RAB and other police officers detained more than 1,500 opposition supporters, many of them arbitrarily, for between one week and two months during student protests or street rallies, which were at times violent. Dozens of the detainees were charged with violent criminal activity. The rest were released without charge.

■ In February, police arrested some 300 supporters of Islami Chhatra Shibir, the student wing of the opposition party Jamaat-e-Islami, and detained them for up to two months in Dhaka, Rajshahi, Chittagong and other cities. The arrests followed a wave of student violence at major university campuses. Four students died during clashes between rival groups. Scores of Awami League party student activists were also reported to be involved in the violence. Police detained around a dozen of them.

■ In June, more than 200 people, including 20 leading members of the opposition Bangladesh Nationalist Party (BNP), were arrested and detained for between one and five weeks, during and immediately after a general strike called by the party.

Excessive use of force

■ On 27 June, RAB personnel used excessive force during a raid on the house of Mirza Abbas, a leading BNP politician and former mayor of Dhaka. They attacked those gathered peacefully inside the house during the general strike called by the opposition. They beat and injured at least 20 people, mostly women.

■ Dozens of people were injured in June and August as police clashed with hundreds of striking textile workers calling for higher wages. No RAB or other police personnel were charged for the attacks.

Extrajudicial executions

The government failed to fulfil its pledge to end extrajudicial executions. Bangladeshi human rights groups estimated the number of suspected extrajudicial executions by RAB and other police officers at more than 60 for the first 10 months of the year.

■ On 3 May, witnesses saw police officers arresting Abdul Alim, aged 32, in Kolabaria village, Kushtia District. The next morning, the family discovered he had been killed. A police officer claimed that Abdul Alim was killed while resisting arrest. In July, the family filed a complaint before a Kushtia court accusing several police officers of unlawfully killing Abdul Alim. Kushtia police investigated the incident and submitted a report in August – on a court order. The report reiterated the police's initial account of Abdul Alim's death. The family challenged the validity of the report before the court. A decision on this challenge remained pending.

Torture and other ill-treatment

Torture of detainees held by the police or other security forces reportedly led to the death of at least six individuals. Six police officers were reportedly investigated for torturing detainees but no one was brought to trial. A private member's bill criminalizing torture remained pending before parliament.

■ Mahmoodur Rahman, editor of *Amar Desh* newspaper, was detained on 2 June for allegedly running the paper without a valid licence. He testified before a magistrate that police officers had beaten him severely while he was in custody.

■ At least six garment workers detained in early August, one of whom was pregnant, were beaten by police officers during interrogation. Their arrest followed a wave of garment workers' street rallies calling for higher wages.

Death penalty

Five men found guilty of killing the country's founding leader, Sheikh Mujibur Rahman, in 1975 were executed in January. Their hasty execution – less than 24 hours after their final conviction – was unprecedented. Contrary to usual practice, the President dismissed clemency petitions by three of them before the court's final verdict. Four other men were executed in three different jails on 15 September.

Impunity

In March, the government set up the International Crimes Tribunal to try "those who committed crimes, assisted criminals and took part in the genocide during the Liberation War". Between August and November, the Tribunal ordered the arrest of five leaders of the Jamaat-e-Islami for war crimes. They were Motiur Rahman Nizami, Ali Ahsan Muhammad Mojahid,

Muhammad Kamaruzzaman, Abdul Quader Molla and Delwar Hossain Sayeedi. Salauddin Quader Chowdhury, a BNP leader detained since mid-December, was later declared a war crimes suspect. They all had been arrested initially on unrelated charges. The International Crimes (Tribunal) Act 1973 and its 2009 amendment, under which the trials were being held, lacked adequate fair trial safeguards. It denied, among other things, the right to challenge the jurisdiction of the Tribunal, the right to the possibility of bail and the right to challenge the impartiality of the judges.

Indigenous Peoples' rights

The government's failure to ensure the security of Jumma inhabitants of the Chittagong Hill Tracts often exposed the Jumma to attacks from Bengali settlers encroaching on their land. At least two Jumma Indigenous people died on 20 February after the army, which maintained a heavy presence in the area, opened fire on hundreds of Jumma Indigenous demonstrators. They were peacefully demanding protection after Bengali settlers had set fire to at least 40 of their houses in the Baghaichhari area of the Rangamati district on the night of 19 February. There were no reports of an investigation or of anyone being prosecuted for the attacks or the killings.

Amnesty International visits/reports

🚗 Amnesty International delegates visited Bangladesh in June and September.

📄 Bangladesh: Transparency needed over hasty executions and safety of family members must be ensured (ASA 13/003/2010)

📄 Bangladeshi security forces used excessive force during raid, 30 June 2010

BELARUS

REPUBLIC OF BELARUS

Head of state:	Alyaksandr Lukashenka
Head of government:	Syarhey Sidorski
Death penalty:	retentionist
Population:	9.6 million
Life expectancy:	69.6 years
Under-5 mortality (m/f):	14/9 per 1,000
Adult literacy:	99.7

Three death sentences were handed down and two people were executed. The rights to freedom of expression and assembly were severely restricted and peaceful demonstrators were detained and fined. Allegations of torture and other ill-treatment were not investigated promptly and impartially. Prisoners of conscience were denied access to medical and legal assistance.

Background

In December, President Alyaksandr Lukashenka was re-elected for the fourth time by 79.7 per cent of the votes in elections that international observers judged fell short of OSCE standards. Riot police violently dispersed a mainly peaceful demonstration held by opposition supporters at close of voting on 19 December. The events were followed by a clampdown on opposition activists, human rights defenders and journalists who were subjected to arbitrary detention, searches, threats and other forms of harassment by the authorities.

Death penalty

State representatives expressed their willingness to engage with the international community regarding the death penalty. In February, a Parliamentary Working Group on the Death Penalty was established. In September, the government acknowledged the need to abolish the death penalty to the UN Human Rights Council; it stated its intention to mould public opinion in favour of abolition and to continue its co-operation with the international community. Despite this, Belarus continued to hand down death sentences and to carry out executions.

■ Vasily Yuzepchuk and Andrei Zhuk, who had been sentenced to death in June and July 2009 respectively, were executed in March. As in all death penalty cases in Belarus, neither the prisoners nor their relatives were informed of the date in advance. Andrei Zhuk's mother

B

only learnt of her son's execution afterwards when she tried to deliver a food parcel on 19 March. The execution was carried out despite the fact that both men had applied to the UN Human Rights Committee, and on 12 October 2009 the Committee had made a request to the government not to execute the two men until it had considered their cases.

■ Oleg Grishkovtsov and Andrei Burdyko were sentenced to death on 14 May by Hrodna Regional Court for premeditated murder, armed assault, arson, kidnapping of a minor, theft and robbery. Their appeals were turned down by the Supreme Court on 17 September 2010.

■ On 14 September, Ihar Myalik was sentenced to death by Mahilyou Regional Court for a series of armed assaults and murders committed in 2009 on the Mahilyou-Homel highway. A second man was sentenced to life imprisonment for the same crime, and a third died in custody before the end of the trial.

Freedom of expression

In May, the OSCE Representative on Freedom of the Media expressed concern in a letter to the Belarusian authorities about pressure placed on independent media in the country and stated that "Intimidation of journalists exerts a 'chilling' effect on already weakened investigative journalism in Belarus."

■ On 3 September Aleh Byabenin, the editor and founder of the unofficial news website Charter '97, was found dead, suspended from the banisters of his dacha with a rope around his neck. On 4 September, the initial conclusions of a forensic medical examination were announced, which found that the most likely cause of death was suicide. However, colleagues and family members questioned the official verdict, pointing out a number of inconsistencies about the way his body was found, the fact that he had been targeted by the authorities in the past, and that shortly before his death he had joined the campaign team of Andrei Sannikau, an opposition presidential candidate.

On 1 July, Presidential Decree No. 60 "On measures to improve the use of the national segment of the internet" came into effect. The decree requires among other things that internet service providers check the identity of subscribers in person, and make information about subscribers available to the authorities; and measures have been introduced to limit access to information that could be classed as extremist, pornographic, or that promotes violence and other illegal acts. According to a study

commissioned by the OSCE, these measures "lead to unsubstantiated restrictions of a citizen's right to receive and disseminate information", and give the authorities extremely broad powers to limit access to certain sources of information.

Freedom of assembly

The restrictive "Law on Mass Actions" continued to limit freedom of assembly and expression. The law requires demonstrators to apply for permission to the local authorities and stipulates that public events cannot take place within 200m of underground stations and pedestrian crossings. It also requires organizers to take responsibility for public safety measures, as well as measures connected with medical services and cleaning up after the action, all of which they need to finance. As a result of these provisions, many applications were turned down.

■ On 8 May, the Minsk City Executive Committee refused permission for a march to celebrate Slavic Pride on 15 May because the proposed route was within 200m of underground stations and pedestrian crossings. A group of demonstrators organized a march on 15 May regardless of the ban. Eight of the demonstrators were detained over the weekend and five of them were charged with taking part in an unauthorized demonstration and fined.

■ A mainly peaceful demonstration after the presidential elections on 19 December was violently dispersed by riot police and over 700 people were charged with administrative offences and detained for 10 to 15 days. They were arbitrarily detained for the peaceful exercise of their right to freedom of expression and many demonstrators were subjected to disproportionate force by law enforcement officers.

Torture and other ill-treatment

In August, Belarus submitted its fourth periodic report to the UN Committee against Torture. The report rejected the recommendation made by the Committee in 2000 to introduce a definition of torture into the Criminal Code in accordance with the definition in the UN Convention against Torture, and claimed that all allegations of torture and other ill-treatment were examined by prosecutors. However, according to a shadow report submitted by NGOs in December, complaints to the Prosecutor's Office rarely led to criminal investigations for torture and were usually subject to a superficial investigation which did not extend beyond interviewing the police officers alleged to be the perpetrators.

On 18 January the Prosecutor of Soviet district in Minsk turned down a request for a criminal investigation into allegations of torture made by Pavel Levshin. He had been detained by police officers from Soviet district police station on 9 December 2009 on suspicion of theft. Pavel Levshin claims that on 10 December from 5pm to 8pm police officers subjected him to torture and other ill-treatment. In his complaint to the prosecutor he claimed that police handcuffed him, laid him on his stomach and inserted his feet behind his hands in a position known as "the swallow". They beat him with a rubber truncheon and with plastic bottles filled with water. They also put a plastic bag over his head and held it there five times until he came close to suffocating. A forensic medical report confirmed that he had injuries consistent with his allegations, but the Prosecutor quoted the police report and stated that no evidence of torture had been found.

Prisoners of conscience

By the end of the year, 29 people including six opposition presidential candidates, members of their campaign teams and journalists were charged with "organizing mass disorder" in connection with the demonstrations on 19 December. They faced a possible maximum prison sentence of 15 years. Many of them had been charged solely for the peaceful expression of their views; at least 16 of them were prisoners of conscience.

■ Andrei Sannikau, an opposition presidential candidate, was detained during the demonstration on 19 December. He was beaten by riot police and suffered injuries to his legs. He was being driven to hospital with his wife, the journalist Iryna Khalip, when the car was stopped by law enforcement officers and he was taken into custody. On 27 December, employees of child welfare services visited their three-year-old son, Danil, and informed his grandmother that she would need to complete procedures to establish her custody over the child or he would be taken into care. On 29 December Andrei Sannikau was charged with the criminal offence of organizing mass disorder. Iryna Khalip was subsequently also detained and charged. Andrei Sannikau's lawyer was granted only intermittent access to him and expressed fears that he was not receiving adequate medical attention for his injuries. The lawyer was subsequently threatened with disbarment for raising concerns about his client's health.

Military service remained compulsory, but discussions were ongoing with regard to a draft law on alternative service and two conscientious objectors were acquitted during the year.

Amnesty International visits/reports

🚌 Amnesty International delegates visited the country in September.

BELGIUM

KINGDOM OF BELGIUM

Head of state:	King Albert II
Head of government:	Yves Leterme (interim government from 26 April 2010)
Death penalty:	abolitionist for all crimes
Population:	10.7 million
Life expectancy:	80.3 years
Under-5 mortality (m/f):	6/5 per 1,000

Reception conditions for asylum-seekers continued to be inadequate. The policy of forcibly returning rejected asylum-seekers to Iraq was maintained. Allegations of excessive use of force by the police persisted. There were concerns that a draft law banning the full-face veil in public would violate freedoms of expression and religion.

Refugees and asylum-seekers

Reception conditions for asylum-seekers were inadequate. According to local NGOs, between October 2009 and December 2010 the federal government agency responsible for the reception of asylum-seekers (Fedasil) failed to provide a total of 7,723 asylum-seekers with accommodation. At the end of the year, 1,203 asylum-seekers were still temporarily housed in hotels, without any medical, social or legal assistance. The government took some measures in the course of the year, including the creation of a number of emergency shelters, but they were insufficient and did not adequately address the deficiencies.

On 19 January, the European Court for Human Rights ruled in *Muskhadzhiyeva and others v. Belgium* that, by detaining four young children and their mother in a secure detention centre for over a month before sending them back to Poland in January 2007, Belgium had violated the prohibition of torture and other ill-treatment and the right to liberty in respect of the four children. Since October 2009, families with children had been accommodated in so-called "living units" and were no longer held in detention centres.

Belgium maintained its policy on forcible returns to Iraq, despite guidelines from UNHCR, the UN refugee agency, which called on states not to forcibly remove anyone to the provinces of Ninewa (Mosul), Kirkuk, Diyala, Salah al-Din and Baghdad, as well as to other particularly dangerous areas such as parts of Al Anbar province.

■ In October, the authorities finally managed to coerce Saber Mohammed, an Iraqi asylum-seeker, into giving up his fight against removal and returned him to Iraq. This happened in spite of the Belgian Commissioner for Refugees and Stateless Persons confirming in September that, if returned to Iraq, Saber Mohammed would be exposed to a real risk of torture or other ill-treatment. In 2005, he had been convicted of terrorism-related offences in Belgium and imprisoned. Immediately after completing this sentence, he was detained again pending removal to Iraq. Except for a period under a compulsory residence order, he remained in administrative detention until his removal to Iraq. The Belgian authorities' coercive methods included hinting that they would continue to subject him to successive periods of detention. He was detained upon arrival in Iraq on 27 October without access to his family or lawyers until his release on 23 November.

Excessive use of force

Police were alleged to have used excessive force during several demonstrations.

There were allegations from protesters of excessive use of force by the police following two demonstrations in Brussels, in September and October. In October, the Permanent Oversight Committee on the Police Services opened investigations into the allegations.

■ At the end of the year there had still been no investigation into allegations of excessive use of force by law enforcement officials against Ebenizer Sontsa, a rejected asylum-seeker from Cameroon, during their attempt to forcibly return him to Cameroon in April 2008. In May 2008 Ebenizer Sontsa killed himself.

International justice

On 8 December the Brussels Civil Court delivered its first findings in a case brought by nine survivors of the Rwandan genocide against the Belgian state and three Belgian soldiers. The Court found that the Belgian state was responsible for ordering the prompt return of Belgian peacekeepers from Kigali in 1994, leaving behind an estimated 2,000 people in a school building that was under Belgian control when the peacekeepers withdrew. Many of them were killed shortly after the departure of the peacekeepers. The Court also ruled that by obeying those orders the three soldiers had engaged their own responsibility.

Discrimination

On 29 April, the lower house of the Belgian parliament voted in favour of legislation banning the partial or complete covering of the face in public with clothing in a way that makes the wearer no longer identifiable. There were concerns that a general prohibition on wearing full-face veils would violate the rights of those women who choose to wear a full-face veil as an expression of their religious, cultural, political or personal identity or beliefs. At the end of the year the draft law was pending consideration by the Senate.

BENIN

REPUBLIC OF BENIN

Head of state and government:	Thomas Boni Yayi
Death penalty:	abolitionist in practice
Population:	9.2 million
Life expectancy:	62.3 years
Under-5 mortality (m/f):	123/118 per 1,000
Adult literacy:	40.8 per cent

Freedom of expression and assembly was restricted. At least one person was sentenced to death. Prison conditions remained poor due to overcrowding.

Freedom of expression and assembly

In October, the Ministry of Interior banned all demonstrations calling for information on the whereabouts of Pierre Urbain Dangnivo, a Ministry of Finance official who disappeared in August. Suspicions about the possible involvement of government officials in his disappearance provoked protests from the press, civil society and opposition political parties. An official inquiry failed to clarify his fate by the end of the year. Many civil society groups, including trade unions, denounced restrictions on freedom of expression and assembly.

Death penalty

In May, Susanne Lanmanchion was sentenced to death in her absence by the Assize Court of Abomey (in the centre of the country) for killing her mother.

Prison conditions

Prisons remained overcrowded. The prison of Cotonou (the main city) held six times its capacity, resulting in harsh conditions. Of the 2,500 inmates held, 80 per cent were in pre-trial detention.

BOLIVIA

PLURINATIONAL STATE OF BOLIVIA

Head of state and government:	**Evo Morales Ayma**
Death penalty:	**abolitionist for ordinary crimes**
Population:	**10 million**
Life expectancy:	**66.3 years**
Under-5 mortality (m/f):	**65/56 per 1,000**
Adult literacy:	**90.7 per cent**

Institutional developments in the justice system gave rise to serious concerns. Key trials for past human rights violations and investigations into allegations of violence by the security forces and by private individuals progressed slowly.

Background

Lack of consultation and agreement on political reforms increased political tensions. Some Indigenous groups and trades unions initiated protests. In May, the Bolivian Trades Union Confederation (Central Obrera Boliviana) called a strike over pay and pension reforms. In June, the Confederation of Indigenous Peoples of Bolivia (Confederación de Pueblos Indígenas de Bolivia) began a protest march in the town of Trinidad, Beni department, against elements of the proposed autonomy law and the lack of progress in land allocation. A negotiated resolution was reached in July. Tensions between the local and national authorities arose in Potosí department in July and

August following a 19-day strike by *campesino* (peasant farmer) organizations, the local civic committee and some local government authorities over land and environmental and infrastructure issues. In December, President Evo Morales rescinded plans to end government subsidies on petrol and diesel after a sharp increase in prices provoked mass protests.

High-ranking government officials publicly questioned the legitimacy of NGOs and social movements expressing dissent to government policies and actions.

In February Bolivia's human rights record was assessed under the UN's Universal Periodic Review. A number of states raised concerns around the independence of the judiciary, impunity and access to justice, the rights of women, and discrimination on grounds of sexual orientation.

Legal, constitutional or institutional developments

Ambitious deadlines for passing new legislation and a lack of procedural transparency hampered meaningful consultation over the far-reaching reforms.

A new Human Rights Ombudsman took office in May, amid concerns that objective criteria had not been taken into consideration in the first round of selection.

A law passed in February empowered the President to designate by decree interim judges to vacant posts in the Supreme and Constitutional Courts. These temporary mandates were extended following delays in the selection and election of new judges. The tenure of judges already sitting in these Courts, appointed by previous administrations, was due to end once this process was completed.

Interim judges in the Constitutional Court were mandated to deal exclusively with the backlog of cases lodged prior to February 2009. As a result, the Court could not exercise constitutional oversight of new legislation. There were a number of concerns about the compatibility of new legislation with international human rights standards. These included the retroactive effect of the anti-corruption law, heavy criminal penalties established in the anti-racism law and, in the judiciary law, the "litigant's defence" role which exercises a supervisory function while depending on the executive.

Police and security forces

There were continuing concerns over human rights violations during security operations and in police and military establishments.

■ Two people died from gunshot wounds and at least 30 people were injured when police attempted to disperse protesters who had mounted a roadblock in Caranavi province. The protesters were concerned about indications that the government might renege on an electoral promise to build a citrus-processing plant there. A report by the Human Rights Ombudsman, later challenged by the government, criticized the use of disproportionate and excessive force, arbitrary arrests, as well as inhumane and degrading treatment during detention. Investigations into the case were continuing at the end of the year.

■ In September, a video came to light showing an army conscript in Challapata, Oruro department, being submerged repeatedly in water in 2009 by people in military uniform. The video re-awakened concerns about the prevalence of violence within the military. Four military officers were under *ex officio* investigation at the end of the year.

Unlawful killings

A number of cases of "lynching" came to light during the year.

■ Four police officers were killed between 23 May and 1 June after being held captive by private individuals in Saca Saca, near Uncía, Oruro department. One officer was believed to have been tortured for several days before being killed. Indigenous authorities in the community accused the police of killing a taxi driver and extortion, and rejected the presence of prosecutors investigating the case. Six suspects were under investigation at the end of the year.

Impunity

There were continued delays in bringing to justice those responsible for human rights violations committed under past military regimes and since the return to democratic rule, and in providing reparation to victims.

■ In August, the Supreme Court sentenced Oscar Menacho Vaca and Justo Sarmiento Alanez, two former political officials in the military government of Hugo Banzer (1971-1978), to 20 years' imprisonment, and a third agent to 15 years, for their role in the enforced disappearances of José Carlos Trujillo Oroza and José Luis Ibsen Peña in 1972 and 1973.

■ In September, the Inter-American Court ruled that Bolivia had failed in its responsibility to investigate and bring to justice those responsible for the enforced disappearances of activist José Luis Ibsen Peña and his son Rainer Ibsen Cárdenas between 1971 and 1973.

■ Prosecutors attempting to access military archives as part of their investigations into enforced disappearances in 1980-1981 faced continuing obstacles, despite two Supreme Court orders to declassify the archives in April.

■ Trial proceedings relating to the "Black October" events of 2003, in which at least 67 people were killed and more than 400 injured in clashes between the security forces and demonstrators, were subject to delays. Limited resources hindered the ability of witnesses and victims to attend court.

■ There were continued delays in the trial connected to the Pando massacre in 2008. The former departmental prefect accused of intellectual authorship of the human rights violations committed remained under preventive detention at the end of the year.

According to NGOs, only 218 of the 6,000 victims of human rights violations who had applied for reparations under a 2004 law had been granted benefits.

NGOs reported that 82 per cent of cases of sexual violence that reached the courts in the rural municipality of Quillacollo, Cochabamba department, between 2008 and mid-2010 had either been abandoned or remained without final sentence.

Maternal mortality

Figures available as part of the 2008 national Demographic and Health Survey demonstrated an increase in the country's maternal mortality ratio, from 230 deaths per 100,000 live births in 2003 to 310 in 2008. The methodological basis for the figures was questioned, but authoritative sources suggested that the same methodology had been used in arriving at both sets of statistics.

Amnesty International visits/reports

🚍 Amnesty International delegates visited Bolivia in June.

BOSNIA AND HERZEGOVINA

BOSNIA AND HERZEGOVINA

Head of state:	rotating presidency – Željko Komšić, Nebojša Radmanović, Bakir Izetbegović (replaced Haris Silajdžić in November)
Head of government:	Nikola Špirić
Death penalty:	abolitionist for all crimes
Population:	3.8 million
Life expectancy:	75.5 years
Under-5 mortality (m/f):	17/12 per 1,000
Adult literacy:	97.6 per cent

Nationalistic rhetoric was widespread. Prosecution of war crimes cases continued, but progress remained slow. Civilian victims of war continued to be denied access to justice and reparations.

Background

In the run-up to the October general elections, relations between the main ethnic groups – Bosnian Muslims (Bosniaks), Croats and Serbs – continued to be marked by nationalistic rhetoric. Continuous calls for separation by several high-level politicians in the Serb entity of Republika Srpska in Bosnia and Herzegovina (BiH) threatened the stability of the country. On some occasions Croat politicians also proposed the creation of a Croat-dominated entity within BiH.

In July, just before the 15th anniversary of the genocide at Srebrenica in 1995, several high-level politicians of Republika Srpska made statements glorifying the perpetrators of this crime and other people accused of being responsible for it, including Radovan Karadžić. Some of them denied the fact that genocide had taken place in Srebrenica.

The main ethnic parties representing Serbs and Bosniaks – the Alliance of Independent Social Democrats (SNSD) and the Party of Democratic Action respectively – secured most seats in the decision-making institutions of the country. However, the elections also introduced a non-ethnic political party – the Social Democratic Party (SDP) which gained the majority of seats in the Federation of BiH (the predominantly Bosnian Muslim and Croat entity).

The international community continued to maintain its presence in BiH, and Valentin Inzko continued to serve as the High Representative – head of the civilian peace implementation agency created by the 1995 Dayton Peace Agreement. The High Representative also acted as the EU Special Representative.

The EU maintained its peacekeeping force with approximately 1,600 troops as well as a police mission with just under 300 staff.

The accession negotiations with the EU continued. As part of the process, in December the country entered into a visa liberalization agreement which allowed citizens of BiH to travel freely in the 25 countries within the Schengen area of Europe.

In January, BiH started to serve its two-year term as a non-permanent member of the UN Security Council.

Justice system – crimes under international law

Prosecution of crimes under international law continued before the domestic judiciary in BiH, at a slow pace.

The War Crimes Chamber (WCC) of the State Court continued to play the central role in war crimes prosecutions in BiH. At the end of September, 50 war crimes trials were pending before the WCC. A further 20 cases were on trial in the Federation of BiH and 13 in the Republika Srpska. The Brcko District had four pending cases. Prosecution of rape and other war crimes of sexual violence continued to receive little attention. Fewer than 20 such cases had been prosecuted in total by the WCC since its creation in 2005.

However, it was estimated that there was a backlog of up to 10,000 untried war crimes cases. The implementation of the State Strategy for the Work on War Crimes, which was adopted in 2008 in order to address the issue, was delayed.

Witness support and protection measures in BiH remained inadequate, and continued to be one of the main obstacles for victims of war crimes and their families in seeking justice.

Despite some efforts, the authorities failed to grant access to reparation for many victims of war crimes, including survivors of sexual violence, families of those forcibly disappeared and victims of torture.

Verbal attacks on the justice system and denial of war crimes – including of the genocide in Srebrenica in July 1995 – by high-ranking politicians further undermined the country's efforts to prosecute war crimes cases.

International justice

At the end of 2010, six war crimes cases concerning BiH were pending before the Trial Chamber of the International Criminal Tribunal for the former Yugoslavia (Tribunal). In addition, two cases were on appeal.

■ In June, the Trial Chamber of the Tribunal convicted seven former Bosnian Serb high-ranking military and police officials on charges related to crimes under international law committed in 1995 in Srebrenica and Žepa. Vujadin Popović and Ljubiša Beara were found guilty of genocide along with other charges and sentenced to life imprisonment. Drago Nikolić was convicted of aiding and abetting genocide, extermination and murder, among other charges, and sentenced to 35 years in prison. Ljubomir Borovčanin, who was found guilty of aiding and abetting extermination, murder, persecution and forcible transfer, was sentenced to 17 years in prison. Radivoje Miletić, convicted of murder, persecution and forcible transfer, was sentenced to 19 years' imprisonment. Milan Gvero was found guilty of persecution and inhumane acts and sentenced to five years. Vinko Pandurević was found guilty of aiding and abetting murder, persecution and inhumane acts and was sentenced to 13 years' imprisonment.

The Trial Chamber found that at least 5,336 individuals were killed in several executions following the fall of Srebrenica but noted that the final number of victims could be as high as 7,826.

■ The proceedings against Radovan Karadžić continued before the Trial Chamber on various charges, including two counts related to genocide. The first related to the crimes committed between 31 March and 31 December 1992 in a number of municipalities in BiH, including killings, torture and forcible transfer or deportation, and whose aim was the destruction of Bosnian Croats and Bosnian Muslims as ethnic or religious groups. The second referred to the killing of more than 7,000 men and boys in July 1995 in Srebrenica. There were also five counts of crimes against humanity, including persecution, extermination, murder and deportation of non-Serbs. The indictment also contained four charges of violations of the laws or customs of war such as hostage-taking and spreading terror among the civilian population.

During the proceedings Radovan Karadžić rejected all charges, claiming that both Sarajevo and Srebrenica were legitimate military targets.

■ The appeals proceedings in the case against Rasim Delić started in January. He had been found guilty of failing to take necessary and reasonable measures to prevent and punish the crimes of cruel treatment committed by members of the El Mujahedin Unit of the Army of BiH. He had been sentenced to three years' imprisonment by the Trial Chamber in September 2008. On 16 April, while on provisional release, Rasim Delić died. In June, the Appeals Chamber terminated the appeals proceedings and announced that the Trial Chamber judgement should be considered as final.

Some victims and their families sought justice before other international courts.

■ On 28 January 2010, the Court of Appeals in The Hague heard a civil case filed by 6,000 relatives of the victims of genocide in Srebrenica (the "Mothers of Srebrenica") against the Netherlands and the UN.

The applicants claimed compensation from the Dutch authorities and the UN for having failed to protect them and their families from genocide committed in Srebrenica in July 1995 by members of the Bosnian Serb Army led by General Ratko Mladić. In the first instance judgement in July 2008, the District Court in The Hague had stated that it had no jurisdiction over actions by the UN personnel. It also discharged any responsibility of the Dutch government.

On 30 March, the Court of Appeals in The Hague rejected the appeal in the case. The court stated that the immunity of the UN from prosecution was absolute and that it was not competent to deal with the compensation claim.

Women's rights

Survivors of war crimes of sexual violence
Despite some efforts by the Ministry for Human Rights and Refugees to introduce relevant state laws and policies, survivors of war crimes of sexual violence continued to be denied access to economic and social rights.

Many women who were raped during the war continued to live in poverty. They were unable to find work as they still suffered from the physical and psychological consequences of their war-time experience.

In July, the Ministry, together with the UN Population Fund and NGOs, started work on a state strategy for reparation for these survivors. However, crucial political support for the initiative was missing.

A lack of government support for psychological support for the survivors meant that services were almost exclusively provided by NGOs, and often had limited reach. Many survivors of war crimes of sexual violence could not access the health care system. They were also discriminated against in access to social benefits compared to other groups of victims of war, such as war veterans.

At the November session of the UN Committee against Torture, the government acknowledged that only 2,000 women survivors of war crimes of sexual violence were receiving social benefits in the country based on their status of civilian victims of war.

Freedom of expression

In August the Serb SNSD party proposed in the State Parliament of BiH a draft law which would prohibit wearing clothes in public which prevent identification. Concerns were expressed that the draft law, if adopted, would violate the rights of women who choose to wear a full-face veil as an expression of their religious, cultural, political or personal identity or beliefs, and would violate their right to freedom of expression and religion.

Enforced disappearances

Progress in identifying the whereabouts of victims of enforced disappearance during the 1992-1995 war was slow. Due to the inadequate response of the justice system, those responsible often enjoyed impunity.

Although exhumations conducted by the Missing Persons Institute continued at various locations, the whereabouts of between 10,000 and 11,500 people remained unknown.

The state authorities failed to create a database of the missing people and to open the Fund for Support to the Families of Missing Persons – both of which were envisaged by the Law on Missing Persons adopted in 2004.

In June, the UN Working Group on Enforced or Involuntary Disappearances visited BiH and urged the authorities to implement in full the 2004 law. It also noted with concern that many judgements of the Constitutional Court of BiH in cases involving enforced disappearances remained unimplemented. It recommended that the authorities establish a national programme on reparations for relatives of victims of enforced disappearance, which should include measures such as compensation, restitution, rehabilitation, satisfaction and guarantees of non-repetition.

Discrimination
Minority rights

The authorities failed to implement the December 2009 judgement of the European Court of Human Rights in the case brought by Dervo Sejdić (a Romani man) and Jakob Finci (a Jewish man). The applicants complained that, as they did not belong to any of the main ethnic groups, they were denied the right to be elected to the state institutions (as under the current legal framework this right was restricted to Bosniaks, Croats and Serbs). The Court had ruled that the constitutional framework and the electoral system discriminated against the applicants and the authorities were obliged to amend it. However, political attempts to change the constitutional framework, the electoral system and to reform the state institutions failed.

Roma

In August, the CERD Committee expressed concerns about discrimination of Roma in access to adequate housing, health care, employment, social security and education. The Committee also recommended that the authorities take measures to ensure that all Roma had access to identity documents.

Counter-terror and security

The authorities of BiH continued to violate the rights of some people who had settled in BiH during or after the war and who had subsequently been granted BiH citizenship. As a result of decisions by the State Commission for the Revision of Decisions on Naturalization of Foreign Citizens, some of them lost their citizenship and deportation procedures were initiated against them.

Several individuals were placed in prolonged detention in the immigration deportation centre in Lukavica awaiting deportation to their countries of origin. They included Imad Al-Husein (detained since October 2008), Ammar Al-Hanchi (detained since April 2009), Fadil El-Hamdani (detained since June 2009) and Zijad al-Gertani (detained since May 2009). The authorities continued to imprison these people, whose citizenship had been revoked, on the grounds of unspecified national security concerns. If deported, they would be at risk of torture or the death penalty in their countries of origin.

There was no legal provision for the four men to examine the evidence brought against them, and consequently they could not effectively challenge the decisions on their detention before the courts in BiH.

B

Two of the detainees appealed to the European Court of Human Rights against the revocation of their citizenship and their subsequent removal from the country. In both cases, the Court granted temporary measures against their deportation.

In November, the UN Committee against Torture recommended among other things that the authorities ensure that national security considerations did not undermine the principle of *non-refoulement*. The Committee urged BiH to fulfil its obligations to respect the principle of absolute prohibition of torture in all circumstances.

Amnesty International visits/reports

🚘 Amnesty International delegates visited Bosnia and Herzegovina in March and December.

📋 Bosnia and Herzegovina: Amnesty International calls for justice and reparation for survivors of war crimes of sexual violence (EUR 63/002/2010)

📋 Bosnia and Herzegovina: Briefing to the UN Committee against Torture (EUR 63/005/2010)

📋 Bosnia and Herzegovina must reject Burqa ban, 31 August 2010

BRAZIL

FEDERATIVE REPUBLIC OF BRAZIL

Head of state and government:	**Luiz Inácio Lula da Silva**
Death penalty:	**abolitionist for ordinary crimes**
Population:	**195.4 million**
Life expectancy:	**72.9 years**
Under-5 mortality (m/f):	**33/25 per 1,000**
Adult literacy:	**90 per cent**

Communities living in poverty continued to face a range of human rights abuses, including forced eviction and lack of access to basic services. Although some cities saw a reduction in homicide rates, high levels of police and gang violence in shanty towns further entrenched inequalities. Torture, overcrowding and degrading conditions continued to characterize the prison and juvenile detention systems where lack of effective control led to riots resulting in a number of deaths. Indigenous Peoples, *Quilombolas* (members of Afro-descendant communities) and landless workers faced threats, intimidation and violence in the context of land disputes. Human rights defenders remained at risk and often had difficulty accessing state protection.

Background

As Luiz Inácio Lula da Silva ended his second and final term as President, Brazil was enjoying a surging economy, political stability and a high profile on the international stage. Considerable progress had been made in reducing poverty, but stark inequalities remained. Dilma Rousseff won the presidential elections in the second round in October, promising continuity and was due to take office in January 2011. She said that public security, health and the eradication of poverty would be priorities for her administration.

President Lula approved a modified version of the Third National Human Rights Plan in May, amid criticisms that references to the decriminalization of abortion, mediation in agrarian conflicts and sections relating to crimes committed during the military regime (1964-85) had been removed.

In October, in a landmark ruling, the Brazilian High Court of Justice voted to bring the investigation and judicial proceedings relating to the killing of Manoel Mattos, a former councillor and human rights activist, under federal jurisdiction. This was the first time a case had been moved to federal jurisdiction since a 2004 constitutional amendment allowed for cases of grave human rights abuses to be heard at the federal level. Manoel Mattos had exposed the activities of death squads in the border region of Paraíba and Pernambuco states and investigations into his death were hampered by threats against witnesses.

The controversial Belo Monte hydroelectric dam project on the Xingu River in Pará state was granted an environmental licence in February by the Brazilian environmental agency amid opposition from Indigenous and other rural communities, human rights and environmental groups and federal prosecutors. Local NGOs argued that the dam project could displace thousands of families, and flood vast tracts of traditional Indigenous lands. In October, in a positive step, the federal government issued a decree providing for the creation of a socio-economic register including a public record of all those affected by dams.

In February, Brazil approved a constitutional amendment which added the right to food to existing economic, social and cultural rights. In November, Brazil ratified the International Convention against enforced disappearance. However, Brazil did not recognize the competence of the Committee on Enforced Disappearances to receive complaints from or on behalf of victims or states when the national authorities fail to fulfil their obligations.

Public security

Criminal and police violence continued to be a serious problem in Brazil's largest cities. In a progress report, the Special Rapporteur on extrajudicial, summary or arbitrary executions wrote that "the norm remains that citizens, especially residents of favelas (shanty towns), remain hostage to violence from gangs, militias and the police" and that "extrajudicial killings remain widespread".

In Rio de Janeiro, further Police Pacification Units were installed in favelas, achieving reductions in violence. However, outside of these projects, police violence, including killings, remained widespread. According to official statistics, police killed 855 people in situations described as "acts of resistance" in 2010.

In November, in response to gang violence, including the burning of more than 150 vehicles and attacks on police posts, police mounted operations across the city. More than 50 people were killed in confrontations between police and drug gangs in the space of a week. Civil Police killed seven people in a single operation in the community of Jacarezinho. In the community of Vila Cruzeiro, a 14-year-old girl was killed inside her house when she was hit by a stray bullet. At the end of the week, over 2,600 men, supported by the army and the navy, staged a major operation in the Complexo do Alemão, a group of shanty towns in the city's northern zone where Rio's largest drug faction had set up headquarters. The complex was swiftly taken and at the end of the year was under the control of the army, awaiting the possible future deployment of a Police Pacification Unit.

Militias and death squads

Militias (armed paramilitary-style groups) continued to dominate many areas of Rio de Janeiro and a large number of the recommendations of the 2008 parliamentary inquiry into the militias had not been implemented by the end of 2010.
■ In September, Leandro Baring Rodrigues was shot dead as he drove his car. A year earlier, he had witnessed the killing of his brother, Leonardo Baring Rodrigues, who had testified against the militias in the case of a massacre of seven people in the Barbante favela in 2008.

Death squads, many made up of off-duty law enforcement officers, continued to operate in many states. In August, a report presented by the Council for the Defence of Human Rights – a federal body which investigates human rights violations – concluded that death squads, often contracted by local businesses to threaten, torture and kill petty thieves, were operating with impunity in Ceará state.
■ More than 30 people living on the streets were killed in Maceió, the capital of Alagoas state, in what state prosecutors suggested could be attempts by vigilantes to "clean up" the city. Investigations into the killings were slow; by November, investigations into only four cases had been completed and passed on to the prosecution services.

There was a spate of multiple homicides in São Paulo in which the perpetrators were suspected of having links to police death squads and criminal gangs. According to official figures, between January and the end of September, 240 people had been killed in 68 separate incidents across the capital and greater São Paulo.

Torture, other ill-treatment and prison conditions

Torture was widespread at the point of detention and in police cells, prisons and juvenile detention systems.
■ In April, a motorcycle courier was tortured to death inside a military police base in São Paulo. He died after being repeatedly kicked in the face and beaten with sticks and a chain by a group of police officers. Twelve police officers were later charged in connection with the death.

Prisons remained severely overcrowded and inmates were held in conditions amounting to cruel, degrading or inhuman treatment. The authorities had effectively lost control of many facilities, leading to a series of riots and homicides.
■ In October, rival factions killed 18 prisoners, four of whom were decapitated, in two facilities in Maranhão state. The riots began after prisoners complained about overcrowding, the poor quality of the food and lack of access to water.

In November, following criticism by the state Human Rights Commission and local NGOs, the Espírito Santo state authorities closed the Judicial Police Department in Vila Velha, which had been holding up to eight times as many prisoners as it was designed to house and which had been the subject of repeated torture allegations. The controversial use of shipping containers to house prisoners in several units was also stopped. Nevertheless, inspections by the National Council of Justice reported continuing problems, including overcrowding and insanitary conditions, especially in the Tucum Women's Prison.

At the end of the year, proposals for a federal law to introduce preventative mechanisms in line with the

Optional Protocol to the Convention against Torture – ratified by Brazil in 2007 – remained stalled in the Office of the President's Chief of Staff. Meanwhile, two states, Alagoas and Rio de Janeiro, approved laws to implement the Optional Protocol in May and June respectively.

Right to adequate housing

Hundreds died and tens of thousands were made homeless in floods that swept across São Paulo, Rio de Janeiro, Alagoas and Pernambuco states in the first half of the year. The floods exposed the inadequacy of much of the housing and the negligence of authorities in addressing clear potential risks.

Other communities faced threats of forced eviction due to infrastructure works planned for the World Cup and the Rio Olympics.

■ In Niteroi municipality, Rio de Janeiro state, more than 100 people died after part of the Morro do Bumba favela collapsed in mudslides. The favela had been built on a garbage dump and, despite many warnings of high toxicity and instability, including a study carried out by the Fluminense Federal University in 2004, no attempts had been made to mitigate risks or resettle residents. At the end of the year, survivors of the floods, including residents of the Morro do Bumba, were being housed in abandoned military barracks in extremely precarious conditions. They told Amnesty International that more than six months after being made homeless, the municipal authorities had not offered them any alternative housing and that the rent assistance they were receiving was unreliable and insufficient.

■ After months of threats, on 22 October at 9am, council workers accompanied by heavily armed civil and military police began bulldozing a commercial district that had existed for more than 20 years, destroying five shops in the community of Restinga, in Recreio dos Bandeirantes, Rio de Janeiro. The works were undertaken as part of the construction of the Transoeste bus corridor. The community was not given any prior warning of the operation.

■ Residents of the favela do Metrô, near Rio's Maracanã stadium, were repeatedly threatened with eviction. Without any information, consultation or negotiation, municipal workers spray-painted houses to be demolished in June. They told residents that they would either be moved to housing estates in Cosmos, some 60km away on the outskirts of Rio de Janeiro, or into temporary shelters and that no compensation would be offered.

■ In October, 3,000 people from the homeless movement occupied four abandoned buildings in the centre of São Paulo. Police initially stopped food and water from entering the buildings. After families were evicted from one of the buildings in November, they set up a protest camp in front of the council offices. On 22 November, in the middle of a storm, members of the Municipal Guard violently removed the families, using tear gas, pepper spray and truncheons. Ten women and seven men were injured.

Indigenous Peoples' rights

Indigenous Peoples fighting for their constitutional rights to traditional lands continued to face discrimination, threats and violence. The situation was particularly grave in the state of Mato Grosso do Sul, where Guarani-Kaiowá communities faced persistent persecution from gunmen hired by local farmers. In spite of efforts on the part of federal prosecutors to speed up the process to recognize the rights of Indigenous Peoples to traditional lands, the process remained stalled.

The Guarani-Kaiowá communities of Y'poí, Ita'y Ka'aguyrusu and Kurusú Ambá in the south of Mato Grosso do Sul state were harassed and attacked by hired gunmen. In the community of Kurusú Ambá, a three-year-old Indigenous boy died after suffering bouts of diarrhoea in September. At the time the security situation had been deemed so dangerous that the Federal Health Agency had suspended visits.

■ In October in the south of Bahia state, Pataxó Hã-Hã-Hãe leader José de Jesus Silva (known as Zé da Gata) was shot dead by a gunman riding on a motorcycle. José de Jesus Silva was trying to deliver supplies to an Indigenous occupation of traditional lands. A decision relating to the demarcation of Pataxó Hã-Hã-Hãe lands had been pending in the Supreme Court since 1983.

Land disputes

Threats and violence against landless workers continued, often carried out by gunmen hired by farmers. Few cases were adequately investigated.

■ In the municipality of São Vicente de Férrer, Maranhão state, local farmers repeatedly threatened the Charco community, which was campaigning to have its land recognized as a *Quilombola* settlement. On 30 October, community leader Flaviano Pinto Neto was shot seven times in the head. Another community leader, Manoel Santana Costa, received repeated death threats, as did 20 fellow members of the community.

B

Workers' rights

Degrading labour conditions persisted across Brazil. In May, the UN Special Rapporteur on contemporary forms of slavery visited Brazil. She concluded that forced labour and "slave-like" practices were most prevalent in the cattle sector, followed by sugar cane plantations. She urged the federal authorities to pass a constitutional amendment that would allow for the expropriation of land where forced labour is used. The amendment, which was proposed in 1999, remained stalled in Congress at the end of the year.

Human rights defenders

By the end of the year the National Programme for the Protection of Human Rights Defenders had expanded its operations to six states. However, inconsistent funding and a lack of co-ordination between state and federal authorities meant that many human rights defenders included in the programme remained without protection.

■ In May, Josilmar Macário dos Santos was shot at as he drove his taxi along a viaduct in the neighbourhood of Catumbi, in Rio de Janeiro city. At the time of the attack, hearings were taking place in the case against four police officers accused of killing six young men, including Josilmar Macário dos Santos' brother, Josenildo dos Santos. Although included in the National Programme, Josilmar Macário dos Santos did not receive adequate protection.

■ Alexandre Anderson de Souza, President of a fishermen's association in Magé, Rio de Janeiro state, received a series of death threats related to his work as a community leader. He was involved in protests against the environmental impact of the construction of a pipeline in the bay where the community fishes.

Impunity

Brazil continued to lag behind the rest of the region in its response to grave human rights violations committed during the military era. In April, the Supreme Court ruled against a challenge to interpretations of the 1979 Amnesty Law. Current interpretations have resulted in impunity for officers accused of grave human rights violations including torture, rape and enforced disappearance during Brazil's military dictatorship (1964-85).

■ In November, the Inter-American Court of Human Rights ruled that Brazil was responsible for the enforced disappearance of 62 guerrillas in Pará state between 1970 and 1972. The court found that Brazil had violated the right to justice by not adequately investigating the cases and withholding information, and that the 1979 Amnesty Law runs counter to Brazil's obligations under international law and cannot be used to block prosecutions in cases of grave human rights violations.

By the end of the year, President Lula had not fully complied with a 2009 ruling of the Inter-American Court of Human Rights ordering that compensation be paid to the family of landless worker Sétimo Garibaldi. According to witnesses, Sétimo Garibaldi was shot dead by hooded gunmen on the Fazenda São Francisco, in Querência do Norte in the north-east of Paraná state, in November 1998.

Amnesty International visits/reports

B

🚌 Amnesty International delegates visited Brazil in October.

📄 "We know our rights and we will fight for them": Indigenous rights in Brazil – the Guarani-Kaiowá (AMR 19/014/2010)

BULGARIA

REPUBLIC OF BULGARIA

Head of state:	Georgi Parvanov
Head of government:	Boyko Borissov
Death penalty:	abolitionist for all crimes
Population:	7.5 million
Life expectancy:	73.7 years
Under-5 mortality (m/f):	17/13 per 1,000
Adult literacy:	98.3 per cent

Roma faced widespread discrimination. Demolitions of Romani homes and evictions of families continued. An NGO investigation found that children had died in care homes due to preventable causes, including starvation, neglect or cold, between 2000 and 2010.

Discrimination – Roma

Discrimination faced by Roma remained widespread and the legal framework for the protection against discrimination of ethnic minorities was deficient. In April, the Council of Ministers submitted a proposal for an amendment of the Protection Against Discrimination Act to parliament. It suggested that the equality body entrusted with monitoring the anti-discrimination law and the examination of individual complaints should be reduced from nine to five members. NGOs raised concern that this would seriously jeopardize protection against discrimination.

■ In March, the European Court of Human Rights found Bulgaria in violation of the prohibition of discrimination and the right to a fair trial. A district court had imposed a custodial sentence on a Romani woman convicted of fraud in 2005 despite the prosecution's recommendation for a suspended sentence.
The district court had reasoned that, especially among members of minority groups, a suspended sentence would not be considered as a punishment. The European Court concluded that such reasoning amounted to differential treatment on the ground of ethnicity.

■ Following the forced eviction of 200 Roma and the dismantling of their houses in 2009, in January, the municipality of the town of Bourgas reportedly ordered the demolition of 20 homes by bulldozers. The mayor was quoted in local media reasoning that the municipality would not allow "roaming Roma" and was "trying to get the message across" that every time illegal construction took place, it would be cleared.

■ In April, a Romani settlement in the Sofia borough of Vrubnitsa was demolished in what the municipality called a "spring clean-up operation", reportedly following a petition of residents of the borough in January demanding the eviction of Roma living in the settlement.

Torture and other ill-treatment
Serious concerns were raised over the treatment of children in social care homes, and the adequacy of previous investigations into excessive use of force.

Children in social care homes
■ In September, the Bulgarian Helsinki Committee published the results of its investigation into cases of deaths of children with mental disabilities in social care homes carried out in collaboration with the Prosecution Service. The investigation found evidence of 238 deaths which occurred between 2000 and 2010. The causes of death established during the research included starvation, neglect, general physical deterioration, infections, freezing to death, pneumonia and also violence. The NGO suggested that at least three quarters of these deaths could have been avoidable and that a large number of these deaths had never been investigated. Following publication, criminal investigations were reportedly initiated into 166 cases.

Excessive use of force
The Bulgarian Helsinki Committee reported in July that excessive use of force and firearms by law enforcement officers continued to be practised by and large with impunity.

■ In January, the Supreme Court of Cassation revoked the prison sentences of five police officers, who had been initially sentenced to a total of 82 years for beating Angel Dimitrov to death in 2005. The Court referred the case back to the Military Court of Appeal, reportedly due to procedural violations and mainly a failure to adequately assess the cause of death. In November, the Military Court of Appeal halved the initial prison sentences of the police officers.

■ In July, the European Court of Human Rights established a violation of the right to life of Gancho Vachkov, fatally shot in the head by the police during a pursuit in Sofia on 6 June 1999. The Court concluded that the shooting "was not absolutely necessary", and that the subsequent investigation failed to be thorough, impartial and effective.

■ In October, the European Court found in the case of *Karandja v. Bulgaria* that the state had violated the right to life of Peter Karandja in June 1997. Domestic legislation allows the use of firearms to arrest a suspect, regardless of the seriousness of the alleged offence or the threat to other people. However, the shooting of Peter Karandja, resulting in his death, was found unlawful. It was established that there were shortcomings in the collection of evidence, witness statements and the evaluation of facts, and the state failed to inform the victim's relatives about the results of the investigation.

Racism
In June, NGOs reported an increase in attacks by far-right groups and inadequate reactions from the police and the government. There were reports of attacks against Roma, foreign nationals, Muslims and LGBT people.

■ On 6 June, four young people were reported to have been severely beaten on a tram by a group of about 20 masked men – allegedly self-identified neo-Nazis – in the capital, Sofia. The assailants, armed with knuckle dusters and knives, attacked the four men on their way to a demonstration at the temporary accommodation centre in Busmantsi against the detention of foreign nationals. Six of the alleged perpetrators were arrested.

Refugees, asylum-seekers and migrants

Local NGOs reported a tendency towards abuses of power by the authorities in the expulsion of foreign nationals.

■ In February, the European Court of Human Rights held that Bulgaria would violate the right to family life and the right to an effective remedy of Pakistani national Ali Raza, if he were deported to Pakistan. Ali Raza, who married a Bulgarian national in 2000, had been placed in a detention centre between 2005 and 2008 pending his deportation. An expulsion order in 2005 alleged he would constitute a serious threat to national security, but did not provide factual grounds. While the Court recognized that the use of confidential material may "prove unavoidable where national security is at stake", it held that the complete concealment of the judicial decision from the public cannot be regarded as warranted. Since the only known allegation against Ali Raza was "information that [he] had been involved in human trafficking", the Court concluded that the notion of national security was stretched "beyond its natural meaning" and the authorities failed to specify further particulars about the alleged threat.

Amnesty International visits/reports

📰 Europe: Stop forced evictions of Roma in Europe (EUR 01/005/2010)

BURKINA FASO

BURKINA FASO

Head of state:	Blaise Compaoré
Head of government:	Tertius Zongo
Death penalty:	abolitionist in practice
Population:	16.3 million
Life expectancy:	53.7 years
Under-5 mortality (m/f):	160/154 per 1,000
Adult literacy:	28.7 per cent

A man died as a result of ill-treatment by police; two others were shot dead by members of the security forces during the resulting protests. At least one person was sentenced to death. Despite an official commitment to improve access to maternal health care, maternal mortality remained high.

Death in custody and extrajudicial executions

In June, Arnaud Somé, an alleged drug trafficker, was arrested by police in Gaoua, 400km north of Ouagadougou, the capital. He was beaten and severely ill-treated, and died in hospital as a result of his injuries. In the following days, protests against torture in custody in Gaoua became violent and were repressed by the police. Using live ammunition, police killed two people – Sié Bouréïma Kambou and Etienne Da. An inquiry was opened, but by the end of 2010 the findings had not been made public.

Death penalty

In June, Alaye Diakité was sentenced to death by the Criminal Chamber of the Appeal Court of Bobo Dioulasso for the murder of his half-brother.

Right to health – maternal mortality

In February, during a meeting with Amnesty International's interim Secretary General, President Blaise Compaoré committed to lifting all financial barriers to emergency obstetric care and access to family planning, as part of a strategy to combat maternal mortality.

In April, Burkina Faso co-sponsored a resolution on maternal mortality at the UN Human Rights Council. It called for a human rights perspective to address preventable maternal mortality and morbidity and greater commitment and political will.

Despite these commitments, by the end of 2010 no real measures had been taken to improve maternal health services. In particular, women were required to pay fees if they gave birth in government facilities. Access to family planning and to contraceptive services remained very low.

Amnesty International visits/reports

🚌 A high-level Amnesty International mission visited Burkina Faso in February.

📰 Burkina Faso: Giving life, risking death (AFR 60/001/2010)

📰 Burkina Faso: President commits to lifting financial barriers to maternal health in a meeting with Amnesty International, 12 February 2010

📰 Burkina Faso: Briefing to the UN Committee on the Elimination of Discrimination against Women (AFR 60/012/2010)

B

BURUNDI

REPUBLIC OF BURUNDI

Head of state and government:	**Pierre Nkurunziza**
Death penalty:	**abolitionist for all crimes**
Population:	**8.5 million**
Life expectancy:	**51.4 years**
Under-5 mortality (m/f):	**177/155 per 1,000**
Adult literacy:	**65.9 per cent**

The government intensified restrictions on freedom of expression and freedom of association during and after the elections. Human rights defenders and journalists were increasingly at risk. Magistrates were subject to pressure from the executive. Government promises to investigate torture committed by the intelligence service and reported extrajudicial executions by the police and army did not yield results. Women and girls continued to be victims of rape and other sexual violence, often committed with impunity.

Background

The government imposed growing restrictions on freedom of association and freedom of expression before, during and after municipal, presidential, legislative and communal elections held between May and September.

The ruling party, the National Council for Defence of Democracy-Forces for Defence of Democracy (CNDD-FDD) won 64 per cent of the vote in May's municipal elections. International and national election observers noted "irregularities", but found the elections to be broadly free and fair. Some election observers noted pre-electoral intimidation. Opposition parties rejected the results, claiming that there had been massive fraud. In early June, they withdrew from June's presidential elections leaving President Nkurunziza as the only candidate. Most opposition parties also boycotted the legislative elections in July, leading to a CNDD-FDD landslide.

After the opposition's boycott of the presidential elections, the government imposed a temporary ban on opposition party meetings. Campaigning for the presidential elections was marked by political violence, including numerous grenade and arson attacks, mainly targeting the CNDD-FDD party.

There was a rise in insecurity and criminality from September onwards in areas that were former National Liberation Forces (FNL) strongholds. The government called these groups "bandits", but others saw this as a possible precursor to renewed armed opposition.

Several acts of politically motivated violence in the weeks leading up to the communal elections were not fully investigated by the police. Statements by senior government officials that individuals should be prosecuted often failed to result in appropriate judicial action.

Between January and November, 4,752 Burundian refugees returned.

Freedom of association and assembly

A government ban issued on 8 June on meetings by political opposition parties, after their boycott of the presidential elections, unlawfully restricted the right to freedom of assembly. Opposition parties still encountered problems holding meetings even after the ban was lifted following the presidential elections.

Searches of houses and offices of opposition members were often conducted without the necessary authorizations or at night, violating the Burundian code of criminal procedure.

UN human rights observers documented at least 242 election-related arrests, most from the opposition, between 1 May and 20 July. Some individuals were accused, and others charged, with offences of threatening state security, grenade attacks, burning CNDD-FDD offices and illegal arms possession. The UN found that 62 of the 242 arrests could be politically motivated. These included charges of holding illegal meetings, encouraging the population not to vote, and one charge of being "FNL". Some opposition detainees were held by the National Intelligence Service (SNR) for longer than the two weeks allowed by law before being charged. Most have since been released.

Extrajudicial executions

UN human rights monitors confirmed nine reports of extrajudicial executions by the police and army between August and mid-October. These included three FNL members found dead in the Ruzizi River in October shortly after their release from police custody in Cibitoke. The government established a judicial commission in late October to investigate these reports.

Torture and other ill-treatment

Between the end of June and early July, the SNR reverted to old practices of torture not seen in recent years. Twelve individuals arrested as part of the

B

government's investigations into grenade attacks were allegedly subjected to physical and psychological torture and other ill-treatment by the SNR. They were slapped, kicked and hit with batons and reported receiving death threats as security agents tried to extract confessions.

Only one further torture case was reported after the UN, the diplomatic community and human rights organizations raised these cases with the government. The government committed to opening investigations, but had not done so by the end of year. None of the suspected perpetrators were suspended pending investigations.

Three police officers were convicted on 7 June by the High Court in Muramvya of ill-treating detainees thought to be FNL members in Rutegama in October 2007. However, authorities failed to execute the judgement; two officers were still serving in the police force by the end of the year and a third had been jailed on other charges in 2009.

Illegal extradition

Déogratias Mushayidi, a Rwandan opposition politician, was detained in Burundi on 3 March by Burundian security forces and handed over to Rwanda two days later. His arrest appeared to contravene formal extradition proceedings.

Freedom of expression

Human rights defenders

The government discussed the status of the Forum for the Strengthening of Civil Society (FORSC), whose legal position remained unclear after its suspension in 2009. This positive development was overshadowed by judicial harassment of human rights defenders, threats by government officials to arrest defenders or suspend their organizations, and enhanced surveillance and intimidation by individuals thought to be intelligence agents. Prominent individuals campaigning for justice for Ernest Manirumva, an anti-corruption activist killed in 2009, were at risk. The government also expelled a staff member of Human Rights Watch from Burundi.

■ The trial of the killers of Ernest Manirumva opened on 14 July. Civil society criticized the prosecution for failing to investigate leads which might implicate senior intelligence officials and police. The case, twice adjourned, was slow to progress.

■ In March, Pierre Claver Mbonimpa, President of the Association for the Protection of Human Rights and Detained Persons (APRODH) and Gabriel Rufyiri, President of the Anti-Corruption and Economic Malpractice Observatory (OLUCOME), stated that they were under surveillance and warned of potential assassination plots against them. In May, Pierre Claver Mbonimpa was summoned by the prosecution to respond to questions about his work on the Justice for Ernest Manirumva campaign. In October, the Interior Minister told him in a private meeting that he could be removed as President of APRODH if he continued to denounce abuses involving the police. In a press conference at the same time as the meeting, a police spokesperson threatened to arrest him on account of statements he made alleging extrajudicial executions by police.

■ Staff members of OLUCOME and their families received death threats in October and November.

Journalists

Burundi's independent media remained vibrant and journalists continued to criticize the government despite attempts to silence them. The government unduly restricted freedom of speech through harassment by judicial authorities and prolonged pre-trial detention. Some death threats received by journalists appeared to come from state agents.

■ In July, Jean Claude Kavumbagu, editor of Net Press, was arrested for an article questioning the capacity of Burundi's security forces to defend Burundi from an attack by the Somali armed group Al-Shabaab. He was charged with treason, an offence only applicable under Burundian law in time of war. He remained in detention at the year's end.

■ Journalists from African Public Radio (RPA) received death threats and anonymous phone calls, and were harassed, including by individuals who appeared to be state agents.

Political parties

In September, François Nyamoya, a lawyer and Movement for Solidarity and Democracy (MSD) spokesperson, was arrested on defamation charges after the SNR's General Administrator, Adolphe Nshimirimana, lodged a complaint against him. François Nyamoya had publicly criticized human rights violations by the SNR and the police and called for the dismissal of Adolphe Nshimirimana and the Deputy Director of the Police. Adolphe Nshimirimana accused François Nyamoya of calling him a "bandit". He was detained in Mpimba Prison until being conditionally released in October.

Justice system

Magistrates came under pressure and were moved to different provinces if they took decisions that were seen as unfavourable to the executive. President Nkurunziza continued to preside over the Superior Council of the Magistracy, the institution responsible for selecting, promoting and demoting magistrates.

■ In July, a magistrate decided that there was insufficient evidence to charge Gabriel Rufyiri of OLUCOME after a complaint from the director of a parastatal organization that OLUCOME had falsely accused him of using a state vehicle to campaign for CNDD-FDD. The following day the magistrate was transferred to a rural area.

Prison conditions

Prisons were overcrowded and under-resourced. Despite steps to expedite bail hearings, the judiciary's continued lack of capacity contributed to continued overcrowding.

Transitional justice

President Nkurunziza committed to moving forward with the creation of a Truth and Reconciliation Commission (TRC) in his inauguration speech in September. The President received the report on the 2009 national consultations on transitional justice in November. Publishing the report was a prerequisite to establishing the TRC and a Special Tribunal within the Burundian justice system. Impunity persisted for serious past abuses by the FNL, CNDD-FDD and the former Burundian army.

Independent National Human Rights Commission

At the year's end, the Independent National Human Rights Commission (CNIDH) had not been established. Parliament adopted a bill in December setting up the CNIDH, which awaited presidential assent at the year's end.

The UN renewed the mandate of the Independent Expert on the human rights situation in Burundi pending the creation of the CNIDH, but with restricted reporting capacities. The Independent Expert was allowed to visit Burundi in November after his previous visit was blocked by the government.

Amnesty International visits/reports

🚗 Amnesty International delegates visited Burundi in July and October 2010.
📄 Burundi: Protect independent human rights reporting (AFR 16/001/2010)
📄 Burundi: "A step backwards" – torture and other ill-treatment by

Burundi's National Intelligence Service (AFR/16/002/2010)
📄 Burundi: Demand release of online editor: Jean Claude Kavumbagu (AFR 16/004/2010)
📄 Burundi: Still no justice for Burundi massacre victims (AFR 16/005/2010)
📄 Burundi: Ensure justice over activist's killing, 8 April 2010
📄 Burundi: Investigate those accused of torturing opposition politicians, 23 August 2010

CAMBODIA

KINGDOM OF CAMBODIA

Head of state:	King Norodom Sihamoni
Head of government:	Hun Sen
Death penalty:	abolitionist for all crimes
Population:	15.1 million
Life expectancy:	62.2 years
Under-5 mortality (m/f):	92/85 per 1,000
Adult literacy:	77 per cent

Forced evictions, land grabs and land disputes remained among the most serious human rights issues. Protests by affected families and communities increased. Activists and human rights defenders protecting the right to adequate housing faced legal action and imprisonment on spurious charges. The judiciary and the courts continued to lack independence and were used to stifle freedom of expression, association and peaceful assembly; journalists, trade unionists and opposition politicians were targeted. Impunity for human rights violations remained an overriding concern. Kaing Guek Eav, aka Duch, was the first defendant to be convicted by the Extraordinary Chambers in the Courts of Cambodia (ECCC) for crimes against humanity committed during the Khmer Rouge period.

Background

The authorities accepted all 91 recommendations made by UN member states under the Universal Periodic Review in March to improve human rights, including on measures to combat impunity, forced evictions and involuntary relocation and to reform the judiciary.

In June, a visit by the UN Special Rapporteur on the situation of human rights in Cambodia focused on the judiciary, which he described as lacking independence and the capacity to deliver justice to all.

A new Penal Code came into force in December which included controversial provisions that limited freedom of expression.

Forced evictions

Thousands of people around the country, including Indigenous populations, were adversely affected by forced evictions, land grabs and land disputes, some in connection with economic land concessions granted to powerful companies and individuals. Increasing numbers of individuals and communities protested and petitioned the authorities in defence of their rights to adequate housing.

In May the authorities approved a Circular on "temporary settlements on illegally occupied land", aimed at relocating long-standing communities, some with legal tenure, from the capital, Phnom Penh and other urban areas.

■ The forced eviction of 20,000 people living around Boeung Kak Lake in Phnom Penh gathered pace as the private company developing the site filled the lake with sand. Homes were flooded and belongings destroyed by water displaced by the sand. Company representatives intimidated and harassed villagers in attempts to force them to accept inadequate compensation or resettlement, despite many of them having legal tenure under the 2001 Land Law. Police harassed activists protesting the forced eviction.

■ Police used unnecessary force, including electric batons, to break up a peaceful protest by Boeung Kak Lake villagers during the visit of the UN Secretary-General in October. Suong Sophorn was beaten unconscious and detained by police until the departure of the Secretary-General. He had previously been arrested and fined in 2009 for painting "Stop Eviction" on his house.

International justice

In a landmark decision in July, the Extraordinary Chambers in the Courts of Cambodia (ECCC) convicted Kaing Guek Eav (known as Duch) for crimes against humanity and grave breaches of the Geneva Conventions for his role in mass executions, torture and other crimes during the Khmer Rouge period. Duch was the commander of security prison S-21, where at least 14,000 people were tortured and killed. He was sentenced to 35 years' imprisonment, reduced by 16 years for time served and illegal detention. Both the prosecution and defence appealed against the sentence.

■ In September, Ieng Sary, Ieng Thirith, Khieu Samphan and Nuon Chea were charged with genocide of the Cham and Vietnamese, crimes against humanity, war crimes, and other crimes.

■ Prime Minister Hun Sen undermined progress on an additional two cases covering five individuals by warning that he would not allow further prosecutions.

Human rights defenders

Scores of people were arrested for defending the right to housing and protesting against land grabs and forced evictions, with dozens serving sentences imposed in previous years. Most were charged with fabricated, groundless or spurious offences, such as damage to private property, incitement, robbery, and assault.

■ Trials continued of villagers involved in protests over loss of farmland in a dispute in Chikreng district of Siem Reap province. Hundreds of villagers attended the trials to support the defendants, including Buddhist monk Luon Savath, who was harassed by security forces and threatened with defrocking for his peaceful activities. He had documented the aftermath of the shooting of Chikreng protesters by security forces in March 2009.

■ In May, community leaders Long Sarith and Long Chan Kiri were sentenced to two years' imprisonment for "clearing state forest" in connection with a land dispute involving a sugar company and residents of Bos village in Samrong district of Oddar Meanchey province. The homes of 100 families in the village were destroyed by security forces four days after their arrest in October 2009.

Freedom of expression and association

The courts were used to curtail freedom of expression and association of journalists, trade union members and opposition parliamentarians.

■ After two trials in January and September, Sam Rainsy, leader of the largest opposition party, was sentenced in absentia to 12 years' imprisonment concerning protests over disputed territory on the Cambodia-Viet Nam border. He lived in exile.

■ In September, around 200,000 workers took part in a four-day nationwide strike to protest over an inadequate increase in the minimum wage. Union leaders and activists were threatened with legal action, including charges of "incitement". Factory owners suspended union leaders and protesting workers were fired from their jobs. Even after intervention by the

C

authorities, by December around 370 workers and union leaders had not been reinstated. Several court cases were ongoing at the end of the year.

Violence against women and girls

No comprehensive, reliable official data was available on incidents of violence against women and girls, including sexual violence, or on the number of prosecutions of suspected perpetrators. Victims faced obstacles in obtaining justice due to criminal justice system failures and out of court settlements. A shortage of services to aid and support victims added to their trauma.

■ Meas Veasna was reportedly raped by a monk at a pagoda in Prey Veng province in June 2009 just weeks after giving birth. Although she reported the crime to the police and attended a meeting with pagoda leaders, police, local authorities and the alleged perpetrator, no prosecution was made. Instead, a pagoda representative gave her USD250 for medication. She now lives in a different town from her husband and young children because of the stigma attached to rape.

Amnesty International visits/reports

🚗 Amnesty International delegates visited Cambodia in February/March.

📄 Breaking the silence: Sexual violence in Cambodia (ASA 23/001/2010)

CAMEROON

REPUBLIC OF CAMEROON

Head of state:	Paul Biya
Head of government:	Philémon Yang
Death penalty:	abolitionist in practice
Population:	20 million
Life expectancy:	51.7 years
Under-5 mortality (m/f):	151/136 per 1,000
Adult literacy:	75.9 per cent

The government continued to restrict the activities of political opponents and journalists and to stifle freedom of expression. One journalist died in custody. Detention conditions remained harsh and often life-threatening. People engaging in same-sex sexual relations faced arrest and imprisonment. Members of the security forces implicated in human rights violations in February 2008 continued to enjoy impunity. At least 77 prisoners were on death row.

Background

Ahead of elections scheduled for late 2011, fears grew of potential instability after 28 years of rule by President Paul Biya. Opposition leaders accused the President of undermining the powers of the electoral commission, known as Election Cameroon (ELECAM). Parliament, dominated by the ruling Democratic Assembly of the Cameroonian People (RDPC), passed a bill in March giving the government oversight of poll preparations through the Ministry of Territorial Administration – a task previously carried out by ELECAM.

In September, President Biya reshuffled his government and replaced senior security service officials.

Armed clashes in the Bakassi region continued during the year. On 18 March the government announced that 19 soldiers of the elite Delta Rapid Intervention Battalion had been convicted for "acts of brutality against civilians" following clashes in February in the Bakassi Peninsula in which 24 civilians had been injured. Insecurity increased off the Bakassi coast, with boats being captured by a group calling itself African Marine Commando, and sailors being held hostage or killed.

In May, a Cameroon-Nigeria mixed commission started further demarcation of a disputed boundary that was settled by a decision of the International Court of Justice in 2002.

The government was reportedly planning to abolish female genital mutilation in its revision of the Penal Code.

Corruption charges

Dozens of former government officials and heads of state companies, some of them arrested during 2010, remained in custody awaiting trial on charges of corruption. Many of them claimed that the charges against them were motivated by political differences or jealousy.

■ At the end of the year, prisoners Titus Edzoa and Thierry Atangana were on trial on new charges of corruption brought against them, barely two years before they were due to complete the 15-year prison sentence they received in 1997. Their trial in 1997 had been unfair – it ended in the early hours of the morning, without the assistance of legal counsel – and was apparently politically motivated. Titus Edzoa had resigned as a senior government official to stand for president and Thierry Atangana was accused of being his campaign manager.

Freedom of expression

The government sought to silence critics of its policies, including journalists and human rights defenders.

■ Germain Cyrille Ngota, managing editor of the *Cameroon Express*, one of three journalists detained in March, died in custody in April. He was allegedly not given any medical treatment during his detention and members of his family claimed he had been tortured. A government inquiry, whose proceedings were not public, concluded that he had died from natural causes but its findings were disputed by journalists and human rights defenders. Robert Mintya, director of the magazine *Le Devoir*, and Serge Sabouang, director of the bi-monthly *La Nation*, who had been arrested with Germain Cyrille Ngota and claimed to have been tortured, continued to face charges of fraud and using false documents. Robert Mintya was assaulted by a fellow inmate in August and was hospitalized for several weeks as a result. Robert Mintya and Serge Sabouang were released in November, reportedly on the orders of President Paul Biya, but the charges against them were not dropped.

■ The trial of three journalists and a teacher arrested after a televised debate in 2008 opened in January but was postponed at least six times during 2010. Alex Gustave Azebaze and Thierry Ngogang of the independent television channel STV2, Anani Rabier Bindji of Canal2 and university teacher Aboya Manassé faced charges of revealing confidential information for discussing Operation Epervier, a government anti-corruption initiative.

■ Lewis Medjo, director of *La Détente Libre* newspaper, who was sentenced to three years' imprisonment in January 2009, was released in June.

■ Former mayor Paul Eric Kingué and musician Pierre Roger Lambo Sandjo were serving prison sentences after they were convicted of involvement in the February 2008 riots. Human rights defenders in Cameroon maintained that Paul Eric Kingué was detained because he protested against unlawful killings of alleged rioters and Pierre Roger Lambo Sandjo because he composed a song criticizing the amendment of the Constitution that allowed President Biya to stand for president again.

Freedom of association and assembly

The government continued to curtail the activities of the Southern Cameroons National Council (SCNC), a non-violent secessionist group, whose members faced arrest and imprisonment. Non-violent activities of political organizations and civil society groups were similarly subject to official sanction.

■ In November, seven trade union members were arrested following a public demonstration organized by the Central Public Sector Union (CSP) in front of the office of the Prime Minister in Yaoundé. They included Jean-Marc Bikoko, President of the CSP, and leading members of several education trade unions. They were charged with offences relating to an unauthorized demonstration, and their trial was continuing at the end of the year.

■ Journalists protesting against the death in custody of newspaper editor Germain Cyrille Ngota were prevented by police from staging a sit-down protest on World Press Freedom Day in May. Some claimed to have been beaten by police.

Rights of lesbian, gay, bisexual and transgender people

The Penal Code criminalizes same-sex sexual relations and even the National Human Rights Commission refuses to recognize and defend the rights of lesbian, gay, bisexual and transgender (LGBT) people. Arrests, prosecutions and trials of gay men continued during 2010 on a regular basis. Those imprisoned were prisoners of conscience.

■ Fabien Mballa and Aboma Nkoa Emile were arrested on 24 March by gendarmes in Camp Yeyap, Yaoundé. They were sentenced by the criminal court of Yaoundé to five months' imprisonment and fines, and were held in Kondengui prison.

■ Roger Bruno Efaaba Efaaba and Marc Henri Bata, who were arrested in September on suspicion of theft, but then accused of same-sex activities, were subjected to forced anal medical examinations in October, a form of cruel, inhuman and degrading treatment. They remained in custody at the end of the year.

Prison conditions

Prisons and other detention centres were overcrowded and conditions were often life-threatening. Medical care and food were often not provided or were inadequate. Disturbances and escape attempts were frequent, and several prisoners were killed during escape attempts. Prison guards were poorly trained, ill-equipped and their numbers inadequate for a large prison population.

Kondengui prison, which was built for 700 inmates, was holding 3,852 in August. Food, water and medical supplies were all in short supply. In one wing, known as Kosovo, there was not enough room for prisoners to sleep lying down. Another wing held mentally ill detainees who did not receive any psychiatric care.

Douala (New Bell) prison, with an official capacity of 700, held more than 2,453 inmates in August. Many of its inmates were in pre-trial detention and were held together with convicted prisoners. Some prisoners were held in leg irons.

Prisoners were reported to have died in Maroua prison because of the scorching heat, and in Ngaoundere prison as a result of cholera.

Impunity

Government officials confirmed that no action had been taken against members of the security forces accused of human rights violations in 2008, when as many as 100 people were killed during protests against price rises and against a constitutional amendment that removed limits on presidential terms of office.

Death penalty

At least 77 prisoners were on death row, although no executions have been reported since 1997. There were concerns that a presidential decree issued in May to commute some death sentences to life imprisonment had not yet been fully implemented. Prisoners on death row were not informed why their sentences were not commuted.

Amnesty International visits/reports

Amnesty International delegates visited Cameroon in August, meeting government officials for the very first time, and carrying out research.

CANADA

CANADA
Head of state: Queen Elizabeth II, represented by Governor General David Johnston (replaced Michaëlle Jean in October)
Head of government: Stephen Harper
Death penalty: abolitionist for all crimes
Population: 33.9 million
Life expectancy: 81 years
Under-5 mortality (m/f): 6/6 per 1,000

Indigenous Peoples faced ongoing, systematic violations of their rights. There were fears that proposed new legislation could result in the prolonged detention of asylum-seekers. Concerns about human rights violations associated with counter-terror and security operations persisted.

Background

A proposed bill to create a national housing strategy consistent with international human rights standards was pending at the end of the year.

In June, Parliament passed legislation to implement a free trade agreement with Colombia but this did not include a credible, independent human rights impact assessment. In October, a bill to develop national human rights standards and an associated enforcement scheme for businesses was narrowly defeated by the House of Commons.

In June a national coalition was launched, Voices/Voix, responding to government funding cuts and other measures that impeded civil society advocacy in such areas as women's equality and the rights of Palestinians.

Indigenous Peoples' rights

The traditional lands of the Lubicon Cree continued to be exploited for oil and gas development authorized by the Alberta provincial government without the free, prior and informed consent of the Lubicon. In September, the UN Special Rapporteur on indigenous people called for "renewed and resolute" action to protect the rights of the Lubicon.

There were continuing concerns about failure to investigate excessive use of force by police during protests over land rights in Tyendinaga Mohawk Territory in Ontario. Progress in implementing related reforms proposed by the 2007 Ipperwash Inquiry remained slow.

A Canadian Human Rights Tribunal hearing continued into a complaint that the federal government spends substantially less on child and family services in First Nations communities than is provided in predominantly non-Indigenous communities.

The Inter-American Commission on Human Rights proceeded with a review of a complaint from the Hul'qumi'num Treaty Group, alleging violations of Indigenous land rights on Vancouver Island in British Columbia.

In November, Canada endorsed the UN Declaration on the Rights of Indigenous Peoples. Indigenous Peoples' organizations urged the government to implement the Declaration in a principled manner.

Women's rights

In June, as host of the G8 Summit, the government announced a global child and maternal health initiative. There was controversy about the lack of a comprehensive approach on sexual and reproductive rights.

In September, the British Columbia government announced an inquiry into the police response to cases of missing and murdered women in Vancouver, many of whom were Indigenous. There were concerns that the inquiry might not analyse the underlying factors that put these women at risk.

The federal government failed to work with Indigenous women to establish a national action plan to address the high levels of violence they face. A government funding announcement in October left substantial gaps in the protection afforded Indigenous women.

In October the federal government released an Action Plan for the Implementation of UN Security Council Resolutions on Women, Peace and Security.

Counter-terror and security

In January, the Supreme Court of Canada ruled that Canadian officials violated the rights of Canadian citizen Omar Khadr during interrogations at Guantánamo Bay in 2003 and 2004. He had been apprehended by US forces when he was 15 years old. (See USA entry.)

Hearings by the Military Police Complaints Commission into concerns that Canadian soldiers transferred prisoners in Afghanistan to the custody of Afghan officials, despite a serious risk they would be tortured, continued throughout the year.

Refugees

In June, Parliament passed the Balanced Refugee Reform Act, instituting an appeal for refused refugee claimants and introducing a safe country of origin list to be used for expediting some refugee claims.

In October, the government proposed legislation to crack down on human smuggling, which penalizes refugee claimants arriving in Canada in an "irregular" manner. The proposals included mandatory detention for one year without access to a detention review.

Policing and justice

In April, the Royal Canadian Mounted Police revised its policy, limiting the use of conducted energy devices to situations where individuals are "causing bodily harm" or "will imminently cause bodily harm."

Aron Firman died in June, after being stunned with a Taser by members of the Ontario Provincial Police in Collingwood, Ontario. Federal Guidelines for the Use of Conducted Energy Weapons, released in October, did not set a threshold of risk for Taser use.

In June, more than 1,000 people were arrested in Toronto during protests related to the G8 and G20 Summits. The federal and Ontario governments rejected calls for a comprehensive public inquiry.

C

CENTRAL AFRICAN REPUBLIC

CENTRAL AFRICAN REPUBLIC

Head of state:	François Bozizé
Head of government:	Faustin Archange Touadéra
Death penalty:	abolitionist in practice
Population:	4.5 million
Life expectancy:	47.7 years
Under-5 mortality (m/f):	196/163 per 1,000
Adult literacy:	54.6 per cent

Much of the country was not under the control of central government, and attacks on civilians by armed groups increased. Gross human rights abuses by armed groups and members of the security forces were committed with virtually total impunity. The trial of Jean-Pierre Bemba started before the International Criminal Court (ICC). People accused of witchcraft were tortured and killed.

Background

Elections planned for April and October were postponed until January 2011. In October 2010 the independent electoral commission announced that the voter census had been completed successfully. However, election officials were abducted and held hostage by armed groups in parts of the country. Leaders of opposition parties, including the President of the Liberation Movement for the People of Central Africa (MLPC), were subjected to harassment and prevented from travelling abroad, without explanation.

As much as two thirds of the country was beyond the control of the government. Thousands of people were forced to flee their homes because of armed attacks, and as many as 200,000 remained internally displaced. There were also about 200,000 refugees in neighbouring countries.

The north-west of the country was under the effective control of the Popular Army for the Restoration of Democracy (APRD), an armed group which had signed a peace agreement with the government but not disarmed. In the south-east and east the Lord's Resistance Army (LRA) increased the number and severity of its attacks.

The AU announced in October the formation of a joint military force, with troops provided by the Central African Republic (CAR), the Democratic Republic of the Congo (DRC), Sudan and Uganda, to fight the LRA, which had moved to the CAR, DRC and Southern Sudan after being ousted from northern Uganda.

In May, US President Barack Obama signed a law committing his government to help the CAR and other countries in the region to eliminate the threat posed to them by the LRA. In June, members of US Special Forces visited south-eastern CAR to assess potential assistance to the CAR government against the LRA. In November, President Obama submitted to the US Congress a "Strategy to Support the Disarmament of the Lord's Resistance Army".

In May, the UN Security Council decided to end the mandate of the UN Mission in the Central African Republic and Chad (MINURCAT) after the Chadian government asked for the peacekeepers to be withdrawn. The 4,375-strong force was to pull out from the two countries in stages by the end of 2010.

A 500-strong peacekeeping force known as the Mission for the Consolidation of Peace in Central African Republic (MICOPAX) continued to be deployed under the aegis of the Economic Community of Central African States.

The Ugandan army continued to deploy thousands of troops in the east of the country.

International justice

The trial of Jean-Pierre Bemba, former Vice-President of the DRC, started in November. In October, an appeals panel at the court in The Hague had rejected an appeal from his lawyers to dismiss the case, the final obstacle to starting the trial. The ICC said that Jean-Pierre Bemba would face two counts of crimes against humanity and three counts of war crimes. He is accused of leading militias in the CAR in 2002 and 2003 that killed and raped civilians.

Abuses by armed groups

Armed groups killed and injured civilians with impunity in parts of the country affected by the armed conflict. Other abuses frequently reported included rape of women and girls, looting and burning down of homes, granaries and shops. Widespread insecurity in the region made it very difficult for human rights and humanitarian organizations to establish the number of victims and the identity of the perpetrators.

The APRD mounted roadblocks and extorted "taxes" in the north of the country.
■ According to Jean-Jacques Demafouth, political leader of the APRD, Souleymane Garga, President of the National Federation of Central African Cattlekeepers, had been killed in April 2009 by or on the orders of an APRD commander in Paoua. The APRD reportedly paid compensation to Souleymane Garga's family, and the family accepted the APRD's apologies.

The LRA carried out hundreds of attacks in the CAR, abducting people, including girls, looting and pillaging, and killing hundreds of civilians.
■ On 4 July, the LRA attacked Mada-Bazouma near the town of Bangassou. According to reports, four people, two of them women, were mutilated; seven, including a 14-year-old girl, were abducted, while a military detachment stationed some 15km away did not arrive until the following day.
■ A spokesman for UNHCR, the UN refugee agency, said that LRA rebels attacked the northern town of Birao on 10 October, abducting young girls, looting property and setting shops on fire. He added that the LRA had already carried out more than 240 deadly attacks in 2010, killing at least 344 people.

The Convention of Patriots for Justice and Peace (CPJP), one of the armed groups that refused to sign a peace agreement with the government, was accused of rapes, killings, looting and extortion in north-eastern CAR.

■ On 30 October, members of the CPJP abducted 21 census agents who were updating voters' rolls for elections planned for late October. The agents were reportedly seized as they approached the town of Birao and their records were destroyed.

The Ugandan army maintained its presence in the east of the country. In January, it reportedly killed Bok Abudema, second-in-command of the LRA, north of the town of Djema. A Ugandan soldier shot dead a young CAR national and injured his father in October.

Police and security forces

Government forces were responsible for unlawful killings and other human rights violations in areas of the country where they were engaged in conflict with armed groups. The government was also responsible for arbitrary arrests, enforced disappearances and torture and other ill-treatment.

■ Two sisters of Hassan Ousman, leader of the former rebel movement, National Movement for the Salvation of the Homeland (MNSP), were arrested in March. They had been searching for information about their brother, who disappeared in December 2009. Hassan Ousman was the Chair of the Subcommittee on Security and Armed Forces of the Dialogue Follow-up Committee. His two sisters were charged with espionage and collaboration with a foreign power.

■ Charles Massi, a former government minister and leader of the CPJP, disappeared in January. He was believed to have been tortured to death by government forces. He had been handed over to the CAR authorities by members of the Chadian security forces.

Prisoners of conscience

Suspected critics of the government, and their associates and relatives, were imprisoned on false charges.

■ Eleven people were detained in June because they had links to a lawyer and a businessman sought for arrest by the authorities. Symphorien Balemby, President of the CAR Bar Association, and businessman Jean-Daniel Ndengou fled the country when they were publicly accused of responsibility for the burning of a privately owned supermarket in the capital, Bangui, on 9 June. The 11 detainees included Albertine Kalayen Balemby, wife and secretary to Symphorien Balemby, and Gabin Ndengou, brother of

Jean-Daniel Ndengou and a driver for the World Health Organization. The detainees were reported to have been charged with arson, incitement to hatred and criminal association, but Amnesty International considered them prisoners of conscience, falsely charged because of their association with the two men.

■ Human rights defender Lewis-Alexis Mbolinani, Co-ordinator of the NGO Youth United for Environmental Protection and Community Development (JUPEDEC), remained in detention without trial until late March. He had been arrested in December 2009 by members of the Research and Investigation Division (SRI) of the police, and falsely accused of collaborating with the LRA. He was released provisionally in April, and after his release, he said that he had been tortured in detention. In October, the Bangui High Court Prosecutor declared that Lewis-Alexis Mbolinani had no case to answer.

Torture and killings of people accused of witchcraft

Women and men accused of witchcraft were frequently subjected to torture and other ill-treatment, or even killed. Government and security officials condoned the accusations and the ill-treatment, and took no action to protect the victims or bring those responsible for abuses to justice.

■ Betty Kimbembe, the 35-year-old mother of a four-month-old baby, and two men were severely beaten in April by government soldiers and a son of President Bozizé, reportedly after the president's son accused them of witchcraft.

Death penalty

Fourteen people were sentenced to death in their absence for murder by the Bangui Criminal Court. No other death sentences or executions were reported.

Amnesty International visits/reports

🚍 Amnesty International delegates visited the CAR in July.

CHAD

REPUBLIC OF CHAD

Head of state:	Idriss Déby Itno
Head of government:	Emmanuel Djelassem Nadingar
	(replaced Youssouf Saleh Abbas in March)
Death penalty:	retentionist
Population:	11.5 million
Life expectancy:	49.2 years
Under-5 mortality (m/f):	220/201 per 1,000
Adult literacy:	32.7 per cent

The political situation remained tense, especially in eastern Chad, despite normalization of relations with Sudan and peace agreements with leaders of some armed groups. Inter-ethnic clashes erupted and human rights violations were committed with almost total impunity. Civilians and humanitarian workers were killed and abducted; women and girls were victims of rape and other violence; and children were recruited as soldiers or abducted for ransom. Journalists and human rights defenders faced harassment and intimidation. Forcible evictions continued. The UN Mission in the Central African Republic and Chad (MINURCAT) was withdrawn on 31 December.

Background

In January, the government asked the UN Security Council to withdraw MINURCAT. At the time, agreed benchmarks to measure MINURCAT's success had not yet been achieved. On 25 May, under pressure from Chad, the UN Security Council resolved to end MINURCAT by 31 December 2010. The Chadian government indicated it would assume full responsibility for protecting civilians on its territory. In October, Chad presented a protection plan – centred around the Détachement Intégré de Sécurité (DIS) security force – and requested financial assistance.

On 15 January Chad and Sudan signed an agreement to deny armed groups the use of their respective territories and to normalize relations. The Chad-Sudan border that had been closed since 2003 reopened in April. In March, Chad and Sudan deployed a joint border monitoring force to counter criminal activity and armed groups. In May, Khalil Ibrahim, leader of the Sudanese armed group, the Justice and Equality Movement, was denied access to Chad, although his forces had been based in Chad for years. In July, Sudanese President Omar Al-Bashir

visited Chad for a meeting, despite facing an International Criminal Court arrest warrant. President Al-Bashir also asked Chadian armed group leaders Timane Erdimi, Mahamat Nouri and Adouma Hassaballah to leave Sudan.

The electoral census started in May. In October, President Déby announced that legislative and local elections planned for November were postponed and would take place in 2011 together with the presidential elections.

Most of the recommendations of a commission of inquiry into events in the capital, N'Djamena in February 2008 had not been implemented by the end of 2010. During the fighting, serious human rights violations had been committed including the disappearance of opposition leader Ibni Oumar Mahamat Saleh.

At least 150,000 people in many parts of the country were forced to leave their homes because of heavy rains and floods. Around 68,000 refugees from the Central African Republic continued to live in camps in southern Chad.

Chadian authorities organized a national human rights conference in March with support from MINURCAT, but most local human rights organizations refused to participate. In June, the government organized a regional conference on ending the use and the recruitment of child soldiers.

Eastern Chad

The security situation remained volatile in the east. More than 262,000 Sudanese refugees from Darfur were living in 12 refugee camps and around 180,000 internally displaced persons (IDPs) in 38 IDP sites. In May, at least 5,000 new refugees arrived following fighting in Darfur. According to the UN, 48,000 IDPs returned to their home villages, mainly in the Ouaddai and the Dar Sila region. Most were reluctant to return because of the insecurity in their villages, the proliferation of small arms and the lack of basic services such as water, health and education.

Human rights abuses continued, including rape of girls and women, recruitment of children, kidnapping of humanitarian personnel and killings of civilians. Fighting between the national army, the Armée Nationale Tchadienne (ANT), and armed groups also continued. In April, fighting erupted between the ANT and the opposition Front populaire pour la renaissance nationale (FPRN) around Tissi and For Djahaname on the Darfur border.

Tensions between Chadian ethnic groups were high.

■ In March, a man was killed following fighting between members of the Arab and Dadjo communities in Goz Beida. One person was arrested in connection with this incident.

■ Increasing ethnic violence between President Déby's ethnic group, the Zaghawa, and the Tama was a major concern. On 21 October, Colonel Dongui, a member of the Zaghawa ethnic group and head of military intelligence in the Dar Tama region, shot dead Colonel Ismael Mahamat Sossal, a Tama and Commandant of the military region. In response, Colonel Sossal's bodyguards killed Colonel Dongui. Other people were injured in this incident. Several people were subsequently arrested, including two Tama army officers.

There were fears that the full withdrawal of MINURCAT would lead to a further deterioration in the human rights and humanitarian situation. Chadian authorities delayed the implementation of plans presented to the UN Security Council in October.

Abuses by armed groups and bandits

Serious incidents of banditry and armed attacks against humanitarian workers occurred in eastern Chad, especially between May and July. Numerous abductions of humanitarian personnel, carjackings and robberies were reported.

■ An ICRC staff member, agronomist Laurent Maurice, was released in February after being abducted and held for 89 days by armed men.

■ On 6 June, three Oxfam personnel were abducted in Abéché. Two were released later that day, but the third was held until 15 June. According to the authorities, he was freed by the joint Chadian/Sudanese military force at Sarne, in eastern Chad. The authorities stated that those responsible had been arrested but no trial had started by the end of 2010.

■ On 10 July, a vehicle belonging to the French Red Cross was stolen by six armed men near the village of Boulala. The driver and his colleague were held and later released near Moussoro.

Violence against women and girls

Rape and other forms of violence against women and girls continued to be perpetrated by members of their communities, armed groups and the security forces. In most of the cases documented, the victims were children and the suspects enjoyed impunity.

■ Two refugee girls aged 13 were raped on 16 July by a group of men near Farchana refugee camp. The girls had gone to search for firewood. The Chadian gendarmerie and the DIS reportedly opened an investigation into the case.

■ On 6 September a 14-year-old refugee girl from Am Nabak camp was raped at the village of Shandi by a local cattle herder, who paid the village chief compensation in Sudanese money before leaving the area. Clashes erupted over the camels he left behind, in which one person was killed.

■ The UN reported that army soldiers allegedly committed at least 11 cases of violence against women between February and April. Although senior officers reportedly said that they would take appropriate action, it was unclear at the end of the year whether any action had been taken against the suspects.

Child soldiers

The recruitment and use of children by armed forces and groups continued and recruiters enjoyed total impunity. The UN stated in 2007 that between 7,000 and 10,000 children might have been used as fighters or associated with Chadian and Sudanese armed groups and the Chadian army. Less than 10 per cent had officially been released from these armed forces and groups by the end of 2010.

Children from villages in eastern Chad, refugee camps and IDP sites continued to be used by the Chadian security forces, and some senior ANT officers were involved in recruiting children during the year.

■ Following a peace agreement signed in April with the Chadian government, the Movement for Democracy and Justice in Chad (Mouvement pour la Démocratie et la Justice au Tchad, MDJT) released 58 children, including 10 girls, in August.

■ In September, after a Sudanese armed group organized meetings to recruit children in the Goz Amir refugee camp, members of the DIS arrested 11 individuals. It was later established that these individuals regularly organized such meetings.

Unlawful killings

Members of the Chadian security forces, Sudanese and Chadian armed groups were responsible for unlawful killings committed with impunity in the context of ongoing insecurity.

■ On 19 October Defa Adoum, a Tama farmer suspected of possessing firearms, was arrested by Colonel Dongui, head of military intelligence in the Dar Tama region, who was based in Guéréda and a member of the Zaghawa ethnic community. The farmer reportedly died as a result of torture.

C

Arbitrary arrests and detentions

The authorities continued to arrest and arbitrarily detain people without charge. People were detained in secret detention facilities where visits were not allowed, such as the Korotoro detention centre.

Freedom of expression – journalists

Journalists continued to face intimidation and harassment by government officials.

Decree No. 5, which restricted freedom of expression and had been issued during the state of emergency in February-March 2008, was lifted. The government passed a new media law in August. The new law introduces prison sentences of one to two years, fines and a ban on publication for up to three months for "inciting racial, ethnic or religious hatred and condoning violence".

■ On 18 October, Prime Minister Emmanuel Nadingar threatened to close *Ndjamena Bi-Hebdo* after the newspaper published an article comparing Chad with Sudan. Journalists from the newspaper feared for their safety following the Prime Minister's press conference on the matter.

Forced evictions

Hundreds of people were forcibly evicted and their houses destroyed in various areas of N'Djamena. Evictions were conducted without due process, adequate notice or consultation. Most of the families who had lost their homes since the beginning of this eviction campaign in February 2008 had not received alternative housing or any other form of compensation. Some won court cases against the government, but in most cases the court decisions were not respected.

■ In May, the authorities told people living in Ambatta, N'Djamena, to leave their homes by the end of the rainy season, around mid-October, to enable the construction of modern houses. Around 10,000 people were at risk of forced eviction; they were not consulted or offered any alternative housing. The evictions had not happened by the end of 2010.

■ At least three people were killed on 19 July during an operation conducted by the police to forcibly evict security officers from government houses in the centre of N'Djamena.

Children's rights – abductions

Dozens of children, some as young as 10, were abducted for ransom. Some were released when their families paid large sums. The fate of others remained unknown at the end of the year.

■ On 23 September, at least five young boys were abducted from their homes in the Léré Lake region by armed men who demanded money for their release.

■ At the end of October, three young boys were taken from their home at Bodoro, 3km from the Cameroonian border, by 11 armed men. The elder brother of one of the children was killed when he alerted other villagers during the attack. They were released after three days in captivity.

Death penalty

On 27 July, an N'Djamena criminal court sentenced Guidaoussou Tordinan to death for shooting dead his wife and injuring his mother-in-law in November 2009. No further information was available on the application of the death penalty or the number of people on death row.

Amnesty International visits/reports

🚍 Amnesty International delegates visited Chad in March, May, June and September.

📄 Chad: UN Security Council must work to ensure further extension of UN mission mandate (AFR 20/004/2010)

📄 Chad: "We too deserve protection" – human rights challenges as UN mission withdraws (AFR 20/009/2010)

📄 Chad: 10,000 at imminent risk of forced eviction (AFR 20/011/2010)

📄 Still in need of safety: The internally displaced in eastern Chad (AFR 20/012/2010)

CHILE

REPUBLIC OF CHILE
Head of state and government: Sebastián Piñera (replaced
                                Michelle Bachelet in March)
Death penalty: abolitionist for ordinary crimes
Population: 17.1 million
Life expectancy: 78.8 years
Under-5 mortality (m/f):   10/8 per 1,000
Adult literacy: 98.6 per cent

Indigenous Peoples continued to campaign for their rights to be respected. Some progress was made in bringing to justice those responsible for past human rights violations. Legal obstacles to the enjoyment of sexual and reproductive rights persisted.

Background

A devastating earthquake and tsunami in February in southern Chile left up to 500 dead and caused widespread damage.

In August, the collapse of a copper-gold mine in the Atacama desert trapped 33 miners 700m below ground. After 69 days, an operation to save the miners was successfully concluded. The accident drew attention to issues around safety in the extractive industries. Eighty-three people died in a fire in the overcrowded San Miguel prison in December, drawing attention once again to the terrible conditions in many prisons in the country.

In January, Chile's Memory Museum was opened to the public, providing a space to acknowledge human rights violations committed between 1973 and 1990. The process of setting up a National Human Rights Institute started in July, though concerns that its autonomy was not constitutionally recognized remained.

Police acknowledged "errors" in their response, using teargas and water cannon, to a peaceful student protest in Santiago in August.

The modification of existing legislation allowing civilians to be tried in military courts was discussed in Congress in October.

Indigenous Peoples' rights

In July, 23 Mapuche prisoners began a hunger strike in protest at the use of anti-terrorist legislation against them and at alleged violations of due process, among other things. At its peak, 34 prisoners were participating in the hunger strike. Following negotiations between representatives of the prisoners and the government, mediated by Archbishop Ricardo Ezzati, the strike ended in October. An accord signed by all parties stipulated that all the cases brought under anti-terror legislation would be transferred to criminal law; that the government would pursue reforms to the Code of Military Justice; and that other measures to address Mapuche demands would be taken in line with international human rights standards.

From August onwards, Indigenous groups on Rapa Nui (Easter Island) protested against the continuing failure to return traditional land. In response, the government set up working groups to discuss their concerns in September, but many clan members objected to the terms of the discussion. In December, more than 20 people were injured in violent clashes between security agents and clan members occupying buildings and land.

A draft bill before Congress proposing constitutional recognition of Indigenous Peoples was given urgent status in September, but this was withdrawn in October. The bill had not been discussed by the end of the year.

Impunity

A decree signed in January by the outgoing President established a commission to allow the cases of those who had been subjected to political imprisonment, torture or enforced disappearance between 1973 and 1990 – and who had not yet been identified by the Rettig or Valech Commissions – to be presented. Victims and their relatives were given six months to present their cases, after which the commission would review the cases and produce a list of names of those who qualified for the same benefits as those granted under the Rettig and Valech Commissions.

In July, two proposals for the granting of pardons to coincide with the country's bicentenary were presented by the Catholic Church and representatives of evangelical churches. President Piñera ruled out the granting of pardons for crimes against humanity and stated that any pardons granted on humanitarian grounds would be decided on a case-by-case basis.

Victims' groups continued to present cases for prosecution.

■ In August, 438 cases were presented by a group of ex-conscripts, accusing the Army of human rights violations against army recruits between 1973 and 1990.

- In October, a group representing the families of those executed on political grounds announced they had presented a total of 300 cases to the judiciary.
- In April, the Supreme Court upheld the decision to ratify the application of the amnesty law in the case of Carmelo Soria, a Spanish diplomat killed in 1976 by security forces.
- In July, Manuel Contreras, former head of the National Intelligence Directorate (Dirección de Inteligencia Nacional, DINA), was sentenced to 17 years' imprisonment for his involvement in the 1974 homicide of General Carlos Prats and his wife Sofía Cuthbert in Buenos Aires, Argentina.

Discrimination

In September, the Inter-American Commission on Human Rights filed an application with the Inter-American Court of Human Rights in the case of Karen Atala, a Chilean judge who was denied custody of her three daughters on the grounds of her sexual orientation. It also found that the Chilean legal system did not take into account the best interests of the children when granting custody to their father.

NGOs denounced a campaign to stop a film festival on sexual diversity in October. Leaflets distributed and letters sent to festival locations and supporters opposed the "promotion" of homosexual relationships in the festival.

Sexual and reproductive rights

Abortion remained criminalized in all circumstances. Two draft laws seeking to limit the scope of criminal provisions applicable in abortion cases were presented to Congress in December.

An NGO reported on the discrimination faced by HIV-positive women in accessing health services, and systematic violations of their right to medical confidentiality. It also identified a number of cases of coercive or forced sterilization.

Amnesty International visits/reports

Open Letter to President Piñera (AMR 22/003/2010)

CHINA

PEOPLE'S REPUBLIC OF CHINA

Head of state:	Hu Jintao
Head of government:	Wen Jiabao
Death penalty:	retentionist
Population:	1,354.1 million
Life expectancy:	73.5 years
Under-5 mortality (m/f):	25/35 per 1,000

The Chinese government responded to a burgeoning civil society by jailing and persecuting people for peacefully expressing their views, holding religious beliefs not sanctioned by the state, advocating for democratic reform and human rights, and defending the rights of others. Popular social media sites remained blocked by China's internet firewall. The authorities continued to repress Tibetan, Uighur, Mongolian and other ethnic minority populations. On the international stage, China grew more confident and more aggressive in punishing countries whose leaders spoke publicly about its human rights record.

Background

China maintained a relatively high level of economic growth compared to other major economies, despite the continuing global recession. However, it faced intensifying domestic discontent and protests stemming from growing economic and social inequalities, pervasive corruption within the judicial system, police abuses, suppression of religious freedoms and other human rights, and continuing unrest and repression in the Tibetan and Uighur regions of the country. Despite a rise in average incomes, millions had no access to health care, internal migrants continued to be treated as second-class citizens, and many children were unable to pay school fees.

The authorities renewed their commitment to strengthening the rule of law. However, access to justice remained elusive for those considered a political threat to the regime or to the interests of local officials. Political influence over and corruption within the judiciary remained endemic.

Reflecting its growing international economic and political influence, China increasingly threatened economic and political retaliation against countries that criticized its human rights record. Many countries appeared reluctant to publicly challenge China on its

C

lack of progress on human rights, and bilateral channels, such as human rights dialogues, proved largely ineffective. The authorities reacted angrily to the news that the Nobel Peace Prize had been awarded to long-time Chinese political activist Liu Xiaobo, indefinitely postponing bilateral trade talks with Norway. Foreign diplomats reported being pressured by China not to attend the award ceremony on 10 December in Oslo.

Freedom of expression

The authorities stopped people from speaking out about or reporting on politically sensitive issues by accusing them of divulging "state secrets", "splittism" (ethnic minority nationalism), slander, and the crime of "subversion". Vague regulations were used to tightly control publication of politically sensitive material, including references to the 1989 Tiananmen Square demonstrations, human rights and democracy, Falun Gong, and Tibetan and Uighur issues. Official censorship relied heavily on "prior restraint", a form of self-censorship, and the use of an internet "firewall" that blocked or filtered out sensitive content.

The amended state secrets law, effective 10 October, added a new provision, Article 28, which requires internet and other telecommunications companies to co-operate in investigations of "state secret" leaks, or face prosecution. The authorities maintained tight control over online news reports, restricting licences to large, government-backed websites. Many social media sites remained blocked, including Facebook, Twitter, YouTube and Flickr.

■ On 5 July, Liu Xianbin, a member of the banned Chinese Democracy Party, was detained in Suining city, Sichuan province, for "inciting subversion of state power". The charge was linked to his support for human rights activists and articles he posted on overseas websites.

■ In July, Gheyret Niyaz, an ethnic Uighur, was sentenced to 15 years in prison for "leaking state secrets". Evidence used against him included essays he had written on the economic and social conditions of Uighurs in China. It was reported that his sentence was also linked to comments he made to foreign media which criticized government policies in the Xinjiang Uighur Autonomous Region (XUAR).

Freedom of religion

The state required all religious groups to register with the authorities, and controlled the appointment of religious personnel. Followers of unregistered or banned religious groups risked harassment, persecution, detention and imprisonment, with some groups labelled "heretical cult organizations" by the authorities. Churches and temples constructed by religious groups deemed illegal by the state risked demolition. More than 40 Catholic bishops of unregistered "house churches" remained in detention, under house arrest, in hiding or unaccounted for.

■ In December, over 100 students from a Catholic seminary in Hebei province protested against the appointment of a non-Catholic government official as school head – the first protest of its kind since 2000.

■ Alimjan Yimit's 15-year sentence was upheld on appeal by the XUAR People's High Court in March. Alimjan Yimit was detained for "leaking state secrets" after he spoke twice with an American Christian in Urumqi city in April and May 2007.

Falun Gong

The authorities renewed the campaign to "transform" Falun Gong practitioners, which required prison and detention centres to force Falun Gong inmates to renounce their beliefs. Those considered "stubborn," that is, those who refuse to sign a statement to this effect, are typically tortured until they co-operate; many die in detention or shortly after release.

Falun Gong members continued to be targeted in security sweeps carried out prior to major national events. Falun Gong sources documented 124 practitioners detained in Shanghai prior to the World Expo, with dozens reported to have been sentenced to terms of Re-education through Labour or prison. Human rights lawyers were particularly susceptible to punishment by the authorities for taking on Falun Gong cases, including losing their licences, harassment and criminal prosecution.

■ Guo Xiaojun, a former lecturer at a Shanghai university and a Falun Gong practitioner, was detained in Shanghai in January and later charged with "using a heretical organization to subvert the law". He was sentenced to four years in prison for allegedly having distributed Falun Gong materials. He was tortured in detention, kept in solitary confinement and eventually signed a confession that was used to uphold his sentence at a closed appeal hearing. He had already previously served a five-year prison term for his beliefs.

■ Lawyers Tang Jitian and Liu Wei had their licences permanently revoked in April by the Beijing Municipal

C

Justice Bureau, on grounds of "disrupting the order of the court and interfering with the regular litigation process". The two had represented a Falun Gong practitioner in April 2009 in Sichuan Province.

Human rights defenders

Civil society continued to expand, with increased numbers of NGOs operating in the country. However, the authorities tightened restrictions on NGOs and human rights defenders. In May, under pressure from the authorities, Beijing University severed links with four civil society groups, including the Center for Women's Law and Legal Services.

■ Prominent human rights lawyer Gao Zhisheng, who had "disappeared" while in the custody of public security officials in February 2009, remained unaccounted for after briefly resurfacing in April.

■ Chen Guangcheng, who was released from prison on 9 September, and his wife, remained under house arrest. They could not leave their home, even to seek medical care.

■ Tian Xi, who contracted HIV and hepatitis B and C through a blood transfusion in 1996 when he was nine years old, was tried on 21 September on charges of "intentionally damaging property". For years, Tian Xi had lobbied the hospital for compensation for himself and others infected through blood transfusions there. On 2 August, he lost his temper in a meeting at the hospital and knocked some items off a desk. Through a legal loophole his trial was suspended, allowing the authorities to keep him in indefinite detention.

Detention without trial

The use of illegal forms of detention expanded, including prolonged house arrest without legal grounds, detention in "black jails", "brain-washing" centres, psychiatric institutions, and unidentified "hotels". The government did not make any progress on the reform or abolition of systems of administrative detention, including Re-education through Labour, used to detain people without charge or trial. Hundreds of thousands continued to be held in such facilities.

Torture and other ill-treatment

Torture and other ill-treatment remained endemic in places of detention. Amnesty International received reports of deaths in custody, some of them caused by torture, in a variety of state institutions, including prisons and police detention centres. In July, new regulations were introduced to strengthen prohibitions

against the use of illegal oral evidence in criminal cases, including coerced confessions. However, China's Criminal Procedure Law had not yet been amended to explicitly prohibit the use of confessions obtained through torture and ill-treatment as evidence before the courts.

Death penalty

Statistics on death sentences and executions remained classified. However, publicly available evidence suggested that China continued to use the death penalty extensively, with thousands being executed after unfair trials. A number of cases where innocent people were sentenced to death or executed became heated topics of public debate, putting pressure on the authorities to address the issue.

Xinjiang Uighur Autonomous Region

The authorities failed to independently investigate the clashes of July 2009 in Urumqi city, including possible abuse of state power. People involved in the clashes continued to be sentenced after unfair trials. In March, Nur Bekri, governor of the XUAR, announced that 97 cases involving 198 individuals had been tried; however, only 26 cases involving 76 individuals were made public. The authorities continued to warn human rights lawyers against taking up these cases and in January the XUAR High People's Court issued "guiding opinions" to the courts specifying how such trials should be conducted.

Security measures were tightened in the XUAR, including revision of the Comprehensive Management of Social Order, effective 1 February. This renewed the authorities' commitment to "strike hard" against crime in the region, in particular crimes of "endangering state security". The authorities announced that 376 such cases had been tried in 2010 in the XUAR, up from 268 in 2008.

Freedom of expression

Freedom of expression in the XUAR was severely curtailed by laws criminalizing the use of the internet and other forms of digital communication. Infractions included vaguely defined crimes of "ethnic separatism", such as "inciting separatism", and distributing materials and literary works with "separatist content". After partial restoration of text messaging in January, over 100 people were detained for "spreading harmful information" and "harming ethnic unity" by sending text messages, five of whom were taken into criminal custody. The complete block

C

on information and communications imposed across the XUAR in the aftermath of the July 2009 unrest was almost fully lifted in May; however, several popular Uighur websites remained banned.

A "central work forum" held in May set out ambitious economic and political plans for the region, but did not address long-standing grievances of Uighurs, including serious employment discrimination. The XUAR authorities pushed forcefully ahead with the "bilingual education" policy which in practice promotes the use of Mandarin Chinese as the language of instruction while marginalizing Uighur and other ethnic minority languages, even in ethnic minority schools.

■ In July, Uighur website managers Nureli, Dilixiati Perhati and Nijat Azat were sentenced to three, five and 10 years respectively in July for "endangering state security" through postings on their websites.

■ On 1 April, the Urumqi Intermediate People's Court sentenced Gulmira Imin, a Uighur website administrator, to life in prison for "splittism, leaking state secrets, and organizing an illegal demonstration". It was believed the charges were linked to regular postings she made to the website Salkin, which was one of the websites on which the call to join the protests on 5 July 2009 was published.

Tibet Autonomous Region

The authorities continued to crack down on local protests associated with the March 2008 protests. Leading Tibetan intellectuals were increasingly targeted, with a number of well-known people in arts, publishing and cultural circles being sentenced to harsh sentences on spurious charges. Providing information on politically sensitive topics to foreigners was severely punished. Thousands of Tibetan students demonstrated against an official language policy which imposed Mandarin Chinese as the main language of instruction in schools at the expense of Tibetan. The policy is widely seen by Tibetans as a threat to the preservation of their culture. Although the authorities did not suppress these protests, they reiterated their commitment to the policy. Demonstrations by hundreds of Tibetan students against this policy spread to the Beijing National Minorities University in October.

The authorities continued to restrict freedom of religion. The official Buddhist Association of China issued measures, effective 10 January, calling for the Democratic Management Committees of monasteries and nunneries to verify the "conformity" of religious personnel with political, professional and personnel criteria, giving the authorities another way to weed out politically "unreliable" religious leaders.

■ In May, Tagyal, a Tibetan intellectual who worked in a government publishing house, was charged with "inciting splittism" after he warned Tibetans to avoid corrupt official channels when donating money to victims of the April Yushu earthquake in Qinghai. Tagyal had also published a book on the 2008 Tibetan protests.

Hong Kong Special Administrative Region

The government proposed amendments allowing limited reform of the methods for electing the Legislative Council (LegCo) and selecting the Chief Executive in 2012. This prompted calls for speedy progress towards universal suffrage as stipulated in the Basic Law. LegCo passed the amendments in June, only after a controversial last minute compromise between the central government and the Democratic Party. This extended a second vote to all the electorate via a functional constituency composed of district councillors.

Freedom of expression, association and assembly

Foreign nationals denied entry to Hong Kong included Chen Weiming, sculptor of the Goddess of Democracy statue used in the 4 June 1989 Tiananmen vigil, and six Falun Gong dance troupe technicians.

■ In January, police used pepper spray to disperse thousands of demonstrators surrounding the LegCo building during voting on a HK$66.9 billion (US$8.6 billion) rail link with Guangdong province. Protesters highlighted inadequate consultation or compensation for those evicted.

■ On 29 and 30 May, police arrested 13 activists and twice confiscated Goddess of Democracy statues displayed in Times Square. Using new tactics, hygiene department officials pursued prosecution for failure to obtain a "public entertainment" licence. Following public criticism, the statues were returned before the Tiananmen vigil which attracted between 113,000 and 150,000 participants.

Several activists prosecuted for unlawful assembly or assaulting officers while demonstrating outside the Central Government Liaison Office were acquitted. In August, police issued internal guidelines on charging individuals for assaulting security officers after public criticism of cases perceived as frivolous prosecutions or biased sentencing.

C

Discrimination

In April, the government issued administrative guidelines on promoting racial equality.

■ In May, a coroner's jury returned a verdict of lawful killing over the March 2009 hillside shooting of Hong-Kong born Nepali street sleeper, Dil Bahadur Limbu, by a police constable investigating a nuisance complaint. Ethnic minority groups had called for an independent commission of inquiry. Application for judicial review by Dil Bahadur Limbu's widow was pending.

■ In October a post-operative transsexual woman lost her legal challenge for the right to marry her boyfriend in her reassigned sex.

Refugees and asylum-seekers

A 2009 pilot scheme, screening applicants opposing deportation on grounds that they would be at risk of torture, completed 122 applications in 10 months, leaving a backlog of 6,700.

■ In November three UNHCR mandated refugees and one successful torture claimant long resident in Hong Kong challenged the constitutionality of policies denying them legal status, visas and the right to work.

COLOMBIA

REPUBLIC OF COLOMBIA
Head of state and government: **Juan Manuel Santos Calderón**
(replaced Álvaro Uribe Vélez in August)
Death penalty: **abolitionist for all crimes**
Population: **46.3 million**
Life expectancy: **73.4 years**
Under-5 mortality (m/f):   **30/22 per 1,000**
Adult literacy: **93.4 per cent**

The civilian population, especially rural and poor urban communities, continued to bear the brunt of the long-running armed conflict. Guerrilla groups, paramilitaries and the security forces were responsible for serious and widespread human rights abuses and violations of international humanitarian law, including war crimes.

President Juan Manuel Santos, who assumed office in August, said he would prioritize human rights and the fight against impunity. In marked contrast to the previous government, he adopted a less hostile stand towards human rights defenders.

The new government presented legislation on reparation for victims and land restitution, which it claimed would benefit those affected by human rights abuses. However, victims' and human rights organizations expressed reservations about the legislation and human rights defenders and social leaders continued to be threatened and killed. Those campaigning for the return of lands misappropriated during the conflict, mainly by paramilitary groups, were at particular risk. Human rights defenders, judges, lawyers, prosecutors, witnesses, and victims and their families involved in human rights-related criminal cases were also threatened and killed.

Background

In February, the Constitutional Court blocked a proposed referendum which could have allowed President Álvaro Uribe to stand for a third consecutive term of office.

The administration of President Uribe waged a campaign to discredit the Supreme Court of Justice, partly because of the Court's investigations into links between members of Congress, including his cousin Mario Uribe, and paramilitary groups. However, relations with the Court appeared to improve under the government of President Santos.

The main guerrilla group, the Revolutionary Armed Forces of Colombia (FARC), suffered another serious setback in September, when the security forces killed one of their historic leaders, Víctor Julio Suárez Rojas, alias "Mono Jojoy", during a military operation.

On 19 October, Congress adopted the International Convention against enforced disappearance.

The internal armed conflict

The warring parties did not distinguish between civilians and combatants, resulting in forced displacement, unlawful killings, kidnappings and enforced disappearances. Indigenous Peoples, Afro-descendant and peasant farmer communities, and their leaders, continued to be directly targeted by the warring parties. According to the National Indigenous Organization of Colombia at least 122 Indigenous people were killed in 2010.

■ On 28 September, Indigenous leaders María Elena Galíndez and Ramiro Inampués were found shot dead in Guachucal Municipality, Nariño Department. Together with other Indigenous activists, they had been about to start talks with the government on land rights issues.

C

■ On 17 July, Jair Murillo was shot dead in the city of Buenaventura. He had been co-ordinating the participation of displaced Afro-descendants in a march scheduled to take place in Bogotá the following day. Jair Murillo's organization, the Integral Foundation of the Pacific Coast of Nariño, and other Afro-descendant organizations, had been named in a paramilitary death threat on 14 May.

More than 280,000 people were forcibly displaced in 2010, compared with 286,000 in 2009. Between 3 and 5 million people have been displaced in the last 25 years.

In November, the Human Rights Ombudsman expressed his concern at the increase in massacres in 2010. Paramilitaries and drug traffickers were thought to be mainly responsible.

Several bombings in urban areas, some of which the government attributed to the FARC, killed and injured civilians.

■ On 24 March, a car bomb exploded near the Office of the Attorney General in Buenaventura killing at least nine people and injuring dozens.

Impunity

There were several important judicial rulings in human rights-related criminal cases.

■ On 10 September, six army soldiers were each sentenced to 40 years' imprisonment for the killing in December 2008 of Edwin Legarda, the husband of Indigenous leader Aída Quilcué.

■ On 8 June, retired Colonel Luis Alfonso Plazas Vega was sentenced to 30 years' imprisonment for the enforced disappearance of 11 people in November 1985, after military forces stormed the Palace of Justice where people were being held hostage by members of the M-19 guerrilla group. Luis Alfonso Plazas Vega appealed against the sentence. The presiding judge left the country after the ruling following threats.

However, most perpetrators of human rights abuses continued to evade justice. The fight against impunity was undermined by threats against and killings of those involved in human rights trials.

Land rights

President Santos stated that returning some of the more than 6 million hectares of land misappropriated during the conflict to peasant farmers, Indigenous Peoples and Afro-descendant communities would be a priority for his presidency. In October, the government announced it would return 312,000 hectares of land to around 130,000 displaced families by April 2012, and a total of 2 million hectares by the end of its four-year term in office. However, increasing threats against and killings of leaders of displaced communities and of those seeking the return of stolen lands threatened to undermine these efforts.

■ On 19 September, Hernando Pérez, a leader of the Association of Victims for the Restitution of Land and Property, was killed in Necoclí Municipality, Antioquia Department. Hours earlier, he had participated in an official ceremony in Nueva Colonia, Antioquia Department, to return land to dozens of peasant farmer families forcibly displaced by paramilitaries.

The Justice and Peace process

The Justice and Peace process continued to fall short of international standards on victims' rights to truth, justice and reparation, although some truths about human rights violations did emerge. Through the process, which began in 2005, around 10 per cent of the more than 30,000 paramilitaries who supposedly demobilized qualified for reduced prison sentences in return for laying down their arms, confessing to human rights abuses and returning stolen lands. The rest received de facto amnesties. However, in November the Constitutional Court rejected a law, passed in 2009, which would have confirmed such amnesties for 19,000 of these paramilitaries, arguing that it ran counter to the right to truth, justice and reparation. In December, Congress passed a law again granting de facto amnesties to these paramilitaries in return for them signing an Agreement to Contribute to the Historic Truth and Reparation.

In June, a Justice and Peace judge sentenced two paramilitaries to eight years in prison each for human rights violations, while a third paramilitary received the same sentence in December. These were the only sentences that had been passed under the process by the end of 2010.

In February, the Supreme Court of Justice refused to authorize further extraditions of paramilitaries to the USA because of concerns that most of the paramilitary leaders extradited to the USA in 2008 on drugs charges were not co-operating with the Colombian justice system in its investigation into human rights violations.

Extrajudicial executions by the security forces

Extrajudicial executions were reported, although in fewer numbers than in previous years. However,

C

progress in criminal investigations by the Office of the Attorney General into more than 2,300 such killings carried out since 1985 continued to be slow.

There were concerns that the provisional release during 2010 of dozens of army soldiers held on remand for their alleged part in extrajudicial executions could undermine criminal investigations into such cases.

The military justice system continued to claim jurisdiction in some of the cases implicating members of the security forces in human rights violations. Many such cases were closed without any serious attempt to hold those responsible accountable. A new military criminal code approved in August was ambiguous on whether extrajudicial executions and rape were to be excluded from military jurisdiction.

In September, the Office in Colombia of the UN High Commissioner for Human Rights published a report confirming the presence of at least 446 unidentified bodies in a cemetery next to an army base in La Macarena, Meta Department. The UN called for a thorough investigation to ascertain how many were victims of extrajudicial executions. On 22 July, NGOs had reported in a public meeting that there were unidentified bodies in the La Macarena cemetery. Three days later, President Uribe said of these NGOs: "Terrorism … while it proposes peace through some of its spokesmen, through other spokesmen it comes here to La Macarena to find how to discredit the armed forces and how to accuse them of human rights violations".

Some of those involved in exposing extrajudicial executions were threatened or killed.

■ On 13 August, the body of Norma Irene Pérez, one of the organizers of the public meeting, was found with gunshot wounds in La Macarena.

The 'Parapolitical' scandal

The Supreme Court of Justice continued to make progress in its investigations into illegal links between politicians and paramilitary groups. Dozens of former members of Congress were investigated, many of whom were convicted and imprisoned.

On 4 March, the Supreme Court issued a statement warning that the killing of members of the judiciary threatened the rule of law. The statement followed claims that several magistrates investigating the scandal had received death threats.

In September, the Procurator General banned Senator Piedad Córdoba from public office for 18 years. He argued she had exceeded her role as a mediator in talks with the FARC designed to secure the release of hostages by giving political advice to the guerrilla group. Piedad Córdoba denied all the allegations.

The civilian intelligence service

In January, the Office of the Attorney General charged seven senior officials of the civilian intelligence service, the Departamento Administrativo de Seguridad (DAS), with illegal wiretapping and membership of paramilitary groups, and continued to investigate several former DAS directors and government officials. In 2009, the media revealed that the DAS, which operates under the direct authority of the President, had been involved in a massive, long-standing, illegal "dirty tricks" campaign against human rights defenders, politicians, judges and journalists.

In October, Congress opened an investigation into the role played in the scandal by former President Uribe. Earlier that month, the Office of the Procurator General announced disciplinary sanctions against several public officials for their role in the scandal, including three former DAS directors and President Uribe's chief of staff, Bernardo Moreno.

In October and December, two senior DAS officials, Jorge Alberto Lagos and Fernando Tabares, were each sentenced to eight years in prison for their role in these crimes.

In November, one of the former DAS directors under investigation, María del Pilar Hurtado, asked for and was granted asylum in Panama, increasing concerns that criminal investigations against senior DAS and government officials could stall.

Paramilitary groups

Paramilitaries continued to kill civilians; threaten and kill human rights defenders and social leaders; recruit children; and carry out acts of "social cleansing". These groups continued to expand and became organizationally more sophisticated. Collusion with the security forces continued in many parts of the country.

■ On 4 September, peasant farmers Luis Alberto Cortés Mesa, José Wilmer Mesa Mesa and Ilfo Boanerge Klinger Rivera were stopped by members of the Black Eagles paramilitary group as they walked home along the river Telembí in Barbacoas Municipality, Nariño Department. On 5 September, the bodies of the three men were found hacked to death and bearing signs of torture.

■ On 15 August, two young men, Diego Ferney Jaramillo Corredor and Silver Robinson Muñoz, were shot dead by gunmen outside the city of Puerto Asís, Putumayo Department. On 20 August, a third man, Norbey Álvarez Vargas, was killed by gunmen in the city. The three were the first three names on a death list of 65 young men from Puerto Asís circulated on the Internet, reportedly by paramilitary groups. On 20 August, a further list was circulated with the names of 31 local young women.

Guerrilla groups

The FARC and the smaller National Liberation Army (Ejército de Liberación Nacional, ELN) committed serious human rights abuses and violations of international humanitarian law, including unlawful killings, hostage-taking and the recruitment of children.

The FARC in particular carried out indiscriminate attacks in which civilians were put at risk through the use of low-precision explosive devices.

According to government figures, 35 members of the security forces and one civilian were killed in 2010 and 363 injured by anti-personnel mines employed predominantly by the FARC.

According to government figures, there were 282 kidnappings in 2010, compared with 213 in 2009. Most were attributed to criminal gangs, but guerrilla groups were responsible for most conflict-related kidnappings. However, the main NGO supporting victims of kidnapping, País Libre, criticized the government agency responsible for compiling kidnapping statistics, Fondelibertad, for claiming that only 79 people remained in captivity as of February.

■ Lizbeth Jaime, Mónica Duarte and Nohora Guerrero, members of the NGO Fundación Progresar, and María Angélica González, from the Office of the Vice-President, were kidnapped by the ELN on 9 July. They were released on 22 July.

Several soldiers and police officers held by the FARC were freed.

Human rights defenders and other activists

Human rights defenders, trade unionists and social leaders continued to be threatened and killed, mainly by paramilitary groups. In 2010, at least 14 human rights defenders were killed. The National Trade Union School reported that 51 members of trade unions were killed during the year.

■ On 10 October, the paramilitary Black Eagles Central Bloc sent an email death threat to 20 individuals and 69 human rights and social organizations, most of which were campaigning for reparation for victims of human rights violations, and for the return of stolen lands.

■ On 17 June, in Barrancabermeja, Santander Department, gunmen on a motorcycle shot and killed Nelson Camacho González, a member of the oil workers' union. The killing followed a death threat sent on 26 May by the paramilitary Joint Cleansing Command to 17 NGOs, trade unions, peasant farmer organizations, and groups representing forcibly displaced people working in Barrancabermeja and the surrounding area.

Human rights defenders and social activists accused of links with guerrilla groups continued to face criminal proceedings, often based solely on the statements of informants.

Violence against women and girls

All parties to the conflict subjected women to sexual abuse and other forms of gender-based violence.

■ In November, an army lieutenant was arrested in connection with the killing of two brothers aged nine and six, and the rape and killing of their sister, aged 14, in Tame, Arauca Department. The three children had disappeared on 14 October.

Women activists working with displaced women were threatened and killed.

■ On 5 November, Elizabeth Silva Aguilar, President of the Association of Homeless and Displaced People of Bucaramanga, was killed by gunmen who entered her home.

■ The NGO Sisma Women's Corporation received an email death threat on 27 January from the paramilitary Central Bloc of the Black Eagles Truth and Death.

US assistance

In 2010, the USA allocated US$667 million in military and non-military assistance for Colombia. This included US$508.2 million from the State and Foreign Operations funding bill. The security forces were allocated S$256 million of this, of which approximately US$100 was earmarked for the armed forces. Payment of 30 per cent of the US$100 million was conditional on the Colombian authorities meeting certain human rights requirements. In September, the US authorities determined that the Colombian government had made significant progress in improving the human rights situation in the country and released some US$30 million in security assistance funds.

C

In August, the Constitutional Court ruled that the agreement to allow the US military to use seven Colombian military bases, signed in 2009, could not be implemented until it was submitted to and approved by Congress and then by the Court itself.

International scrutiny

The report on Colombia of the Office of the UN High Commissioner for Human Rights, published in March, said the main challenge for 2010 would be the effective implementation of UN recommendations, including "all previous pending recommendations of the High Commissioner".

In October, the government renewed the mandate of the Office in Colombia of the UN High Commissioner for Human Rights for a further three years.

Several UN Special Rapporteurs – including those on extrajudicial and summary executions; on indigenous people; and on the independence of judges and lawyers – presented reports on Colombia to the UN Human Rights Council. Colombia was also reviewed by the UN Committee on Economic, Social and Cultural Rights, the Committee on the Rights of the Child, and the Human Rights Committee. The UN Independent Expert on minority issues visited Colombia in February.

Amnesty International visits/reports

🚗 Amnesty International delegates visited Colombia in April, July and September.

📰 The struggle for survival and dignity: Human rights abuses against Indigenous Peoples in Colombia (AMR 23/001/2010)

📰 Colombia: Seeking Justice – the mothers of Soacha (AMR 23/002/2010)

📰 Open letter to Presidential Candidates: What will you do to protect the human rights of all Colombians? (AMR 23/013/2010)

CONGO (REPUBLIC OF)

REPUBLIC OF CONGO

Head of state and government:	Denis Sassou-Nguesso
Death penalty:	abolitionist in practice
Population:	3.8 million
Life expectancy:	53.9 years
Under-5 mortality (m/f):	135/122 per 1,000

Torture and other ill-treatment by members of the security services were reported in detention centres, including the central prison in Brazzaville. Three asylum-seekers from the Democratic Republic of the Congo (DRC) spent a sixth year in military detention without charge or trial.

Background

Frédéric Bintsamou, a former leader of the National Resistance Council, an armed group which became a political party, the National Republican Council (CNR), stood as a candidate in a parliamentary by-election in the Pool region in July. The election was won by a candidate from the ruling coalition.

In October, the EU and the Republic of Congo agreed a project to remove mines and other explosives from around the international airport in the capital, Brazzaville. In December, France signed an agreement to support a regional military school and health services for Congolese armed forces.

The government announced in October that it was deploying soldiers, gendarmes and police to restore law and order in the Pool region which had been affected by armed conflict between 1998 and 2003. Leaders of the CNR expressed concern that they had not been consulted about the operation.

The UN Special Rapporteur on indigenous people visited the country in November. The Special Rapporteur expressed concern that Indigenous Peoples were discriminated against and deprived of social and health services, and worked in conditions similar to serfdom. The National Assembly adopted in late December a law to protect Indigenous people known locally as Pygmies. The law seeks to strengthen the protection and promotion of the rights of Pygmies and provide resources for their socio-economic development.

C

President Sassou-Nguesso granted an amnesty to former President Pascal Lissouba who had been sentenced in 2001 to 30 years' imprisonment with hard labour for treason and corruption. Pascal Lissouba has been living in exile since being overthrown by an armed group led by Denis Sassou-Nguesso in 1997.

In November, the French Cassation Court ruled that a complaint of corruption by the French branch of Transparency International against the Congolese President, the President of Equatorial Guinea and the former President of Gabon, could be heard in French courts. Transparency International asked the French judiciary to inquire into how the three had acquired property in France.

In late December, the Brazzaville Court of Appeal acquitted former army colonel Ferdinand Mbahou of endangering the security of the state. He had been arrested in July 2009 in connection with speeches he had made while living in France, and was granted provisional release in January 2010.

Enforced disappearances

In November, the Republic of Congo withdrew a case against France that it had lodged with the International Court of Justice (ICJ) in 2002. The Republic of Congo had asked the ICJ to nullify a case against President Sassou-Nguesso and other senior government officials in a French court in connection with the disappearance in 1999 of more than 350 Congolese nationals after their return from the DRC. In 2005, a Congolese court found the Congolese government responsible for many of the disappearances but acquitted all security and government officials on trial. By the end of 2010, there had been no inquiry to establish the identities of those who had ordered, carried out or condoned the disappearances.

Torture and other ill-treatment

Torture and ill-treatment by members of the security services were reported in detention centres, including the central prison in Brazzaville.

■ Ferdinand Mbourangon died in September after being beaten by gendarmes at the central prison in Brazzaville. He had been part of a protest against the prison authorities' refusal to allow a fellow inmate to attend his child's funeral. Ferdinand Mbourangon was taken to a military hospital for treatment but prison authorities rejected a doctor's recommendation that he should be hospitalized. An autopsy reportedly established that he had suffered internal bleeding. It was unclear whether the authorities took any action in connection with his death.

■ André Bakekolo, a retired police officer, was severely beaten when he went to Ouenze police station in Brazzaville to complain that police officers had taken his property. The police had been looking for his son, who had been involved in a traffic accident. The commander of the police station was reportedly suspended after André Bakekolo complained to the authorities.

Refugees and asylum-seekers

Three asylum-seekers from the DRC spent a sixth year in military detention without charge or trial. Germain Ndabamenya Etikilime, Médard Mabwaka Egbonde and Bosch Ndala Umba were arrested in 2004 in Brazzaville. The authorities continued to refuse to disclose the basis for their detention.

In June, the governments of the Republic of Congo and the DRC and UNHCR, the UN refugee agency, signed an agreement to repatriate about 150,000 people who had fled from the DRC in 2009. It was unclear whether the agreement provided for continued protection in the Republic of Congo for refugees who feared returning to the DRC. The DRC government demanded the extradition of suspected leaders of an armed group accused of causing violence in north-eastern DRC and who were being detained in the Republic of Congo. They had not been extradited by the end of the year.

During a visit by Rwandan President Paul Kagame in November, President Sassou-Nguesso announced that the stay of some 8,000 Rwandan refugees in his country would expire at the end of 2011.

C

CÔTE D'IVOIRE

REPUBLIC OF CÔTE D'IVOIRE

Death penalty:	abolitionist for all crimes
Population:	21.6 million
Life expectancy:	58.4 years
Under-5 mortality (m/f):	129/117 per 1,000
Adult literacy:	54.6 per cent

Tensions rose dramatically after presidential elections in November that led to a political stalemate and to serious human rights violations, mostly committed by security forces loyal to the outgoing President, Laurent Gbagbo. Dozens of people were killed, detained, abducted or disappeared. Several thousand people fled to neighbouring countries or became internally displaced. Throughout the year, the New Forces (Forces Nouvelles) a coalition of armed groups in control of the north of the country since 2002, continued to commit human rights abuses. Harassment and physical assault remained rampant, notably at roadblocks.

Background

The presidential election postponed since 2005 was finally held in November, and led to a political stalemate. Both the outgoing President, Laurent Gbagbo, and his opponent, Alassane Ouattara, declared themselves winners of the election and appointed rival governments.

The international community, including the AU and ECOWAS, unanimously recognized Alassane Ouattara as the winner of the election. Sanctions against Laurent Gbagbo and some of his close supporters were adopted by the EU and the USA.

In December, Laurent Gbagbo called for the United Nations Operation in Côte d'Ivoire (UNOCI) and the French peacekeeping force, Licorne, to leave the country. The Security Council turned down this request and extended the mandate of UNOCI for an additional six months. The French government also said that its force would remain.

Despite several mediation efforts led by the AU and ECOWAS, no political solution was found by the end of the year, against a background of deepening shortages and rising prices of basic commodities.

Despite the fact that several thousand members of the New Forces were integrated into the national army, full disarmament of the New Forces and of pro-government militias, as set out in the 2007 Ouagadougou peace agreement, was not achieved by the end of 2010. This fuelled the political crisis, as both sides used their armed members to quell and intimidate political opponents.

Police and security forces

Throughout the year the security forces used excessive force in dispersing protests, unlawfully killing a number of people. They were also responsible for widespread abuses committed to extort money at checkpoints and during inspections of identity documents.

■ In February, the security forces violently repressed several demonstrations, particularly in the town of Gagnoa, where at least five demonstrators were shot dead. They were protesting against President Gbagbo's decision to dissolve the government and the electoral commission.

After the disputed presidential election, security forces loyal to Laurent Gbagbo committed extrajudicial executions, arbitrary arrests and enforced disappearances.

■ On 1 December, security forces in Abidjan led a raid on the offices of the Rally of Republicans (RDR), the party of Alassane Ouattara which left at least four people dead and several wounded.

■ On 16 December, security forces and militiamen loyal to Laurent Gbagbo killed at least 10 unarmed protesters in Abidjan during mass protests over the political deadlock. Salami Ismaël, a car washer, who was nearby and not participating in the march, was shot dead by two hooded men wearing military uniforms.

■ On 18 December, Brahima Ouattara and Abdoulaye Coulibaly, members of an organization called Alliance pour le changement (APC), were arrested in a neighbourhood of Abidjan by Republican Guards. By the end of the year, their fate and whereabouts remained unknown.

Abuses by armed groups

Fighters and supporters of the New Forces were responsible for human rights abuses, including torture and other ill-treatment, arbitrary detention and widespread extortion. A climate of impunity prevailed due to the absence of a functioning judicial system in the north of the country.

■ In April, a student, Amani Wenceslas, was killed by a stray bullet during an exchange of fire between two factions of the New Forces in Bouaké. Two armed fighters were also killed during this clash.

After the November election, the New Forces in the border region with Liberia in the west of the country reportedly threatened and harassed people accused of being supporters of Laurent Gbagbo. As a result, thousands of people fled to Liberia.

Violence and impunity in the west of the country

Throughout the year, people living in the west of the country were physically and sexually abused by criminal gangs and militiamen close to President Gbagbo's party. Neither the state security forces nor the New Forces, which each controlled parts of the area, provided protection. Both forces extorted money and attacked people at checkpoints with complete impunity.

After the November election, there were several reports of clashes between supporters of the two presidential candidates.

■ In November, in Sinfra, a retired gendarme shot at a group of alleged supporters of Alassane Ouattara, who then went to the retired gendarme's home and killed his wife.

Freedom of expression – media

Several journalists, newspapers and media outlets were harassed and threatened by the authorities.

■ In May, Dembélé Al Seni, editor of the daily *L'Expression,* and one of his journalists were summoned to the headquarters of the Directorate for Surveillance of the Territory (DST). They were interrogated for several hours about their coverage of opposition demonstrations in February in Gagnoa. They had provided video footage of the violent reaction of the security forces to the French TV news station France 24, which was suspended for several days for reporting these events.

After the November election, several newspapers close to Alassane Ouattara were prevented from publishing for several days in December. Foreign media including Radio France Internationale and France 24 were also banned from broadcasting until the end of the year.

Corporate accountability

More than one year after reaching an out-of-court settlement with the oil-trading company Trafigura over waste dumping in Côte d'Ivoire, thousands of victims were still waiting to receive their compensation money.

In January, an Ivorian appeal court ruled that the compensation money should be transferred to a group called the National Coordination of Toxic Waste Victims of Côte d'Ivoire (CNVDT-CI), which falsely claimed to represent the 30,000 victims involved in the UK settlement.

Following the court's decision to transfer the compensation to CNVDT-CI, the claimants' legal representatives saw no option but to reach an agreement with CNVDT-CI to distribute the funds jointly. The joint distribution process which followed was plagued by repeated delays and concerns over CNVDT-CI's role. By July, an estimated 23,000 people had received compensation, but the joint distribution process came to a halt shortly thereafter. In September, CNVDT-CI began a new distribution process that was again halted. By the end of the year, thousands of legitimate claimants were still awaiting payment and there were serious concerns about the future of the remaining compensation funds given the lack of transparency of the process and allegations regarding misappropriation of funds.

Amnesty International visits/reports

📖 Côte d'Ivoire: Thousands still waiting to receive compensation over toxic waste dumping (AFR 31/002/2010)

📖 Côte d'Ivoire security forces urged to protect civilians as tensions rise, 6 December 2010

📖 Côte d'Ivoire: Security forces kill at least nine unarmed demonstrators, 16 December 2010

📖 Côte d'Ivoire: Injured protesters denied medical care, 17 December 2010

📖 Côte d'Ivoire: Defenceless people need urgent protection from escalating violence, 21 December 2010

📖 Côte d'Ivoire: Human Rights Council special session misses opportunity to protect Ivorian population, 24 December 2010

C

CROATIA

REPUBLIC OF CROATIA

Head of state:	Ivo Josipović (replaced Stjepan Mesić in February)
Head of government:	Jadranka Kosor
Death penalty:	abolitionist for all crimes
Population:	4.4 million
Life expectancy:	76.7 years
Under-5 mortality (m/f):	8/7 per 1,000
Adult literacy:	98.7 per cent

Despite pressure from the international community, progress prosecuting crimes committed during the 1991-1995 war continued to be slow. Many crimes allegedly committed by members of the Croatian Army and police forces remained unaddressed. Some political efforts were undertaken by the President to deal with the wartime past. However, both the government and the judicial authorities failed to take targeted action to resolve the issue of war crimes. Discrimination against Roma, Croatian Serbs and LGBT people continued.

Background

Accession negotiations with the EU progressed and several negotiation chapters were successfully closed. In June, negotiations on justice and fundamental rights were opened and specific benchmarks were set by the EU.

In the December report to the UN Security Council, the Chief Prosecutor for the International Criminal Tribunal for the former Yugoslavia (the Tribunal) stated that Croatia continued to fail to submit all outstanding military documents related to "Operation Storm", a large-scale military operation conducted by the Croatian Army in 1995.

Justice system – crimes under international law

Progress prosecuting crimes committed during the 1991-1995 war continued to be slow.

The capacity of the Croatian justice system to prosecute war crimes remained low. On average, fewer than 18 cases were completed each year. Hundreds of cases, especially those in which the victims were Croatian Serbs and those allegedly responsible were members of the Croatian Army and police forces, remained unaddressed.

The courts adjudicating in those cases continued to apply the 1993 Basic Criminal Code which was not in accordance with international standards. The Code lacked clear definitions of crucial criminal concepts such as the principle of command responsibility, war crimes of sexual violence and crimes against humanity. Its application resulted in impunity for many crimes.

Witness intimidation in the courtroom continued. Measures to provide victims and witnesses with support and protection remained inadequate. Only four courts in Croatia had the facilities and staff to provide witness support.

Legislation adopted in 2003, aimed at addressing the issues that prevent war crimes prosecutions, remained largely unimplemented. The political will to implement justice system reforms and tackle impunity was largely missing.

The authorities failed to provide victims of war crimes and their families with access to reparation.

■ In July, the Supreme Court upheld the conviction of Branimir Glavaš and five others, who in 2009 were found guilty by the Zagreb County Court of crimes committed against Croatian Serbs in Osijek during the war. However, the sentence was reduced by the Supreme Court, based on the extensive application of mitigating factors. Some mitigating factors such as the accused being in the service of the Croatian Army were in contravention of international standards.

Previously in May 2009, Branimir Glavaš, who held a Bosnian passport, had fled to Bosnia and Herzegovina (BiH). In September 2010, the July verdict of the Supreme Court of Croatia was confirmed by the State Court of BiH, which resulted in the arrest of Branimir Glavaš on 28 September. In October 2010, an investigation was launched by the Office for the Suppression of Corruption and Organized Crime against five people, including a member of the Croatian Parliament. In June and July, the group had allegedly tried to recruit people to bribe judges adjudicating in the Branimir Glavaš case in order to secure a more favourable sentence.

■ In March, the Supreme Court of Croatia upheld the conviction of Mirko Norac and the acquittal of Rahim Ademi which had been handed down by the Zagreb County Court in 2008. The accused were both indicted for war crimes, including murder, inhumane treatment, plunder and wanton destruction of property, against Croatian Serb civilians and prisoners of war during military operations in 1993. In its verdict, the Supreme

C

Court of Croatia reduced the sentence against Mirko Norac from seven to six years' imprisonment, based on the application of mitigating factors, many of which were in contravention of international law. Factors included the crimes being committed during a lawful military action by the Croatian Army and his participation in the war for independence.

In June, the Council of Europe Commissioner for Human Rights urged the Croatian authorities to take effective measures to ensure that war crimes cases were prosecuted in an unbiased manner, independent of the alleged perpetrator's ethnic or other background and in accordance with the general prohibition of discrimination. He concluded that service in the Croatian Army or police forces should not be drawn on as a mitigating circumstance for serious human rights violations.

In November the European Commission, in its progress report on Croatia, observed that impunity for war crimes remained a problem, especially when victims were ethnic Serbs and alleged perpetrators were members of the Croatian Army.

■ On 10 December, Tomislav Merčep was arrested in Zagreb. In a report published the day before, Amnesty International had identified him as one of several high-profile individuals suspected of war crimes. The investigation against Tomislav Merčep included his alleged command responsibility for the unlawful killing and enforced disappearance of 43 individuals in Zagreb and Pakračka Poljana during the 1991-1995 war.

International justice

Several cases related to crimes under international law committed on Croatian territory during the 1991-1995 war were pending before the Tribunal in The Hague.

■ Between July and September, the Tribunal's Prosecutor and the defence teams delivered their final briefs in the case against three retired Croatian generals, Ante Gotovina, Ivan Čermak and Mladen Markač. They were indicted on nine counts of crimes against humanity and violations of the laws or customs of war allegedly committed against the Serb population in 14 municipalities in the southern part of Croatia during "Operation Storm" in 1995. The judgement was expected to be announced in 2011.

Controversy remained around Croatia's willingness to co-operate with the Tribunal Chief Prosecutor's Office. In July, the Trial Chamber emphasized that the Croatian authorities were obliged to co-operate yet it

had rejected the Tribunal Prosecutor's application for an order to the authorities to produce evidence relating to the case. The Trial Chamber observed that due to the nature of the proceedings it was unable to establish whether the authorities were in a position to comply with the order if it had been issued. The Trial Chamber also refrained from deciding whether the documents sought existed.

■ The trial proceedings against Vojislav Šešelj, who was accused of crimes in BiH, Croatia and Serbia (Vojvodina), continued. He was indicted on several counts related to crimes against humanity such as persecutions on political, racial or religious grounds, deportation and inhumane acts. The indictment included violations of the laws or customs of war such as murder, torture, cruel treatment, wanton destruction of villages, or devastation not justified by military necessity, destruction or wilful damage done to institutions dedicated to religion or education, and plunder of public or private property.

■ The trial of Momčilo Perišić, which included charges related to the shelling of Zagreb in May 1995, continued before the Trial Chamber of the Tribunal. In November, the Trial Chamber allowed the Prosecutor's motion for new evidence to be presented in the case.

■ The trial of Jovica Stanišić and Franko Simatović continued. Charges included racial and religious persecution, murder, deportation and inhumane acts against the non-Serb population in the Serb-controlled areas of Croatia during the 1991-1995 war. In October, new evidence was added to the case. During the year the Trial Chamber made adjustments to the trial schedule to accommodate Jovica Stanišić's poor health. The death of the lead counsel for Franko Simatović in 2009 also caused delays.

■ In December, the conviction of Veselin Šljivančanin for aiding and abetting the murder of 194 prisoners of war after the fall of Vukovar in November 1991 was revised by the Tribunal Appeals Chamber. As a result the Chamber reduced Veselin Šljivančanin's sentence from 17 to 10 years' imprisonment.

Freedom of assembly

Concerns were raised about the right to freedom of assembly when at least 140 people were detained for a short time during a peaceful demonstration in Zagreb on 15 July.

The protests were organized by the civil society initiative Pravo na Grad (Right to a City) in order to protect Varšavska Street in the historic part of Zagreb

C

from being partially destroyed during the construction of a shopping centre entry-exit ramp. The construction works involved cutting down several trees and turning a public walkway into an entry to a private property.

Discrimination
Ethnic minorities
Roma continued to face discrimination in access to economic and social rights, including education, employment and housing. Measures undertaken by the authorities remained insufficient.

In March, the Grand Chamber of the European Court of Human Rights announced its judgement in the case of *Oršuš and Others v. Croatia*. The Grand Chamber concluded that the placement, in 2002, of 14 Romani schoolchildren in separate classes based on their command of the Croatian language amounted to discrimination on the basis of ethnicity.

In particular, the Grand Chamber concluded that rather than assessing their language skills as the government had claimed, the tests that were supposed to determine the placement of children in Roma-only classes assessed only their general psycho-physical conditions. Once placed in Roma-only classes the children were not provided with any measures to address their alleged lack of knowledge of the Croatian language. Subsequently, there was no system in place to monitor the children's progress in learning Croatian. The curriculum taught in Roma-only classes was significantly reduced and had 30 per cent less content than the curriculum followed in mainstream classes.

In June 2010, the Commissioner for Human Rights of the Council of Europe reported that "de facto segregation" of Roma pupils persisted in some schools in the country.

In July, the UN Special Rapporteur on adequate housing visited Croatia and concluded that the current housing situation was strongly shaped by the legacy of armed conflict and by the transition from a socially owned housing model to the private market. This affected the most vulnerable groups, including Roma and Croatian Serbs. The Rapporteur also expressed concern at the living conditions in Roma settlements. Furthermore, she observed that more than 70,000 Croatian Serbs were still refugees residing in neighbouring countries, at least 60,000 of whom were in Serbia.

Rights of lesbian, gay, bisexual and transgender people
On 19 June, the Zagreb Pride took place. Some 500 people who participated were protected by the police and no major incidents were recorded. However, when the main event had finished two participants were physically attacked by a group of young men. An investigation was opened to identify those responsible but, at the end of the year, it had failed to yield results.

Amnesty International visits/reports
🚍 Amnesty International delegates visited Croatia in January, March-April and December.

🗐 Croatia: Briefing to the United Nations Committee against Torture (EUR 64/001/2010)

🗐 Briefing to the European Commission and member states of the European Union (EU) on the progress made by the Republic of Croatia in prosecution of war crimes (EUR 64/002/2010)

🗐 Behind a wall of silence: Prosecution of war crimes in Croatia (EUR 64/003/2010)

🗐 Croatia: Authorities must guarantee freedom of assembly (EUR 64/004/2010)

🗐 Croatian war crimes suspect arrested, 10 December 2010

CUBA

REPUBLIC OF CUBA

Head of state and government:	**Raúl Castro Ruz**
Death penalty:	**retentionist**
Population:	**11.2 million**
Life expectancy:	**79 years**
Under-5 mortality (m/f):	**9/6 per 1,000**
Adult literacy:	**99.8 per cent**

Forty-three prisoners of conscience were released throughout the year. The rights to freedom of expression, association and assembly continued to be restricted and scores of critics of one-party government were harassed. The US embargo against Cuba remained in force.

Background
Prisoner of conscience Orlando Zapata Tamayo died on 23 February following a prolonged hunger strike. He was one of 75 people arrested during a crackdown by the authorities in March 2003, and was serving a 36-

year prison term at the time of his death. A few months later, between July and December, the Cuban government released 41 prisoners of conscience following an agreement with the Spanish government and dialogue with the Catholic Church. All of those released, except one, left Cuba with their relatives.

In October the Council of the EU decided to maintain its Common Position on Cuba for another year. This calls on the Cuban government to improve respect for human rights.

The visit of the UN Special Rapporteur on torture was postponed on at least two further occasions during 2010. The Cuban authorities had extended an invitation to the Special Rapporteur to visit the country in 2009.

Cuba had not ratified the International Covenants on Civil and Political Rights and on Economic, Social and Cultural Rights by the end of the year, despite having given an undertaking to do so at the UN Human Rights Council in February 2009.

In October, Raúl Castro announced the next Congress of Cuba's Communist Party for April 2011, the first to take place in 16 years.

Freedom of expression – dissidents and journalists

All media remained under state control, impeding Cubans' free access to independent sources of information. Content on and access to the internet continued to be monitored and, on occasion, blocked. Police and state security officials continued to intimidate and harass independent journalists, scores of whom were arrested and imprisoned only to be released days or weeks later without charge or trial. Many of the detainees reported that they were put under pressure to stop taking part in dissident activities, such as anti-government demonstrations, or sending reports to foreign media outlets.

■ Calixto Ramón Martínez, a journalist for the independent news agency Hablemos Press, was arrested on 23 April as he tried to cover a private function in Havana in honour of Orlando Zapata Tamayo. Calixto Ramón Martínez was released the following day, but rearrested moments later. He was detained at a police station for seven days and then transferred to Valle Grande, a maximum security prison on the outskirts of Havana. He was released on 14 May and threatened with charges of "contempt of authority" and "aggression". State security officials also asked him to stop his reporting activities.

Prisoners of conscience

Eleven prisoners of conscience from the group of the 75 arrested in March 2003, remained in prison at the end of 2010.

■ Darsi Ferrer, who had been arrested in July 2009, was finally brought to trial on 22 June 2010. He was sentenced to one year's imprisonment and three months' "correctional work" outside the prison after being found guilty of receiving "illegally obtained goods" and "violence or intimidation against a state official". He was immediately released as he had already been held in prison for almost a year. Amnesty International considered Darsi Ferrer to be a prisoner of conscience held on politically motivated charges brought by the state in reprisal for his human rights activism.

Arbitrary detention

Dissidents continued to be arbitrarily detained in order to prevent them from exercising their rights to freedom of expression, association and assembly.

■ On 15 February, Rolando Rodríguez Lobaina, José Cano Fuentes and other members of the Eastern Democratic Alliance were arrested by state security officials in Guantánamo and held in detention to prevent them from taking part in the Alliance's anniversary celebrations. They were released without charge four days later.

■ On 12 August, state security officials detained Néstor Rodríguez Lobaina, his brother Rolando, and three other members of the organization Youth for Democracy at Néstor Rodríguez' house in the town of Baracoa, Guantánamo Province. The five were protesting at the arrest of two other members of the organization at the time. The two initial detainees were released on 16 August without charges while Néstor Rodríguez Lobaina and the four others were released after nearly three weeks in detention and warned that they would be charged with "public disorder". However, no formal charges had been filed against the five men by the end of the year.

Death penalty

In December, the People's Supreme Court commuted the death sentences of Salvadoran nationals Raúl Ernesto Cruz León and Otto René Rodríguez Llerena to 30 years in prison. They were both convicted of terrorism charges in 1999. On 28 December, Humberto Eladio Real Suárez, a Cuban national sentenced to death in 1996 for the killing of a police officer in 1994, had his sentence commuted to 30 years in prison. By the end of 2010, no prisoners remained on death row.

Freedom of movement
■ Guillermo Fariñas, a psychologist, independent journalist and political dissident, was forbidden from travelling to Strasbourg in December to collect the 2010 Sakharov Prize for Freedom of Thought awarded by the European Parliament. He was the third Cuban dissident awarded the prize since 2002 who had been prevented by the authorities from travelling outside Cuba. Guillermo Fariñas went on hunger strike for more than four months. He ended the protest in July when the Cuban government announced the release of prisoners of conscience.

US embargo against Cuba
The US embargo continued to affect the economic, social and cultural development of the Cuban people and in particular the most vulnerable groups.

According to the UN Population Fund, treatments for children and young people with bone cancer and for patients suffering from cancer of the retina were not readily available because they were commercialized under US patents. The embargo also affected the procurement of antiretroviral drugs used to treat children with HIV/AIDS. Under the terms of the US embargo, medical equipment and medicines manufactured under US patents cannot be sold to the Cuban government.

In September, US President Barack Obama renewed the extension of economic and financial sanctions against Cuba as provided for in the Trading With the Enemy Act. In August, he relaxed travel restrictions on academic, religious and cultural groups under the "people-to-people" policy. For the 19th consecutive year, a resolution calling on the USA to end its embargo against Cuba was adopted by an overwhelming majority (187 votes to two) in the UN General Assembly.

Amnesty International visits/reports
🚗 The Cuban authorities have not granted Amnesty International access to the country since 1990.
📄 Restrictions on freedom of expression in Cuba (AMR 25/005/2010)

CYPRUS

REPUBLIC OF CYPRUS

Head of state and government:	Demetris Christofias
Death penalty:	abolitionist for all crimes
Population:	0.9 million
Life expectancy:	80 years
Under-5 mortality (m/f):	7/6 per 1,000
Adult literacy:	97.8 per cent

A number of rejected asylum-seekers were forcibly removed to Syria. In a landmark ruling in a human trafficking-related case, Cyprus was found in violation of the rights to life and to protection from forced labour.

Background
Negotiations between Greek Cypriot and Turkish Cypriot leaders continued during the year. Among the areas covered were governance and power-sharing, EU-related and economic matters and property issues. In November, both sides agreed to intensify their contacts. The UN Committee on Missing Persons in Cyprus continued its work. By the end of December it had exhumed in total the remains of 767 people. Several racially motivated attacks were reported during the year.

Refugees and asylum-seekers
In late May, around 250 Syrian Kurd protesters camped outside the "EU House" in Nicosia to protest against the authorities' rejection of their asylum claims and to protest about residence rights. On 11 June, 143 of the protesters, including children, were reportedly arrested during an early morning police operation. Several of them were released immediately but, according to reports, 23 were forcibly removed to Syria that day. On 14 June, the European Court of Human Rights issued interim measures requesting that Cyprus suspend the removal of the 44 who were still in detention. Seven of these were then released, either because they had pending asylum applications or were stateless. According to reports, of those remaining, 32 were forcibly removed to Syria after the European Court lifted the interim measures in their cases in September. The remaining five continued to be detained in Cyprus. Seventeen of those forcibly removed were reportedly arrested and detained upon or after their arrival in Syria.

Policing

■ In November, people taking part in the Rainbow Festival, an anti-racism event in Larnaka, were reportedly attacked by people from an anti-migrant demonstration held on the same day and at the same place. Concerns were expressed over the police's handling of the events. There were also allegations that the police used excessive force against the festival-goers to open the way for the anti-migrant demonstrators. The police reportedly arrested six festival-goers, but none of the demonstrators.

Trafficking in human beings

■ In a landmark ruling in January on the death of Oxana Rantseva, a victim of human trafficking, the European Court of Human Rights found Cyprus in violation of the right to life due to its failure to conduct an effective investigation. The Court also found Cyprus in violation of the right not to be subjected to slavery and forced labour, due to the authorities' failure to put in place an appropriate framework to counter trafficking and the failure of the police to take measures to protect Oxana Rantseva from trafficking. In March 2001 in Limassol, Oxana Rantseva fell to her death in suspicious circumstances while trying to escape from a fifth-floor flat owned by an employee of her former employer.

Rights of lesbian, gay, bisexual and transgender people

In March, the Authority against Racism and Discrimination recommended the legal recognition of cohabitation between same-sex couples.

CZECH REPUBLIC

CZECH REPUBLIC
Head of state: Václav Klaus
Head of government: Petr Nečas (replaced Jan Fischer in
                                                     July)
Death penalty: abolitionist for all crimes
Population: 10.4 million
Life expectancy: 76.9 years
Under-5 mortality (m/f):   5/4 per 1,000

Several trials were ongoing in cases of violent attacks against Roma and some defendants received heavy sentences. The government continued to fail to eliminate segregation of Romani children in the educational system. Concerns were raised over amendments to the law on treatment of migrants.

Background

Following parliamentary elections in May, the President appointed a new centre-right coalition government in July. In September, the government dismissed the state Human Rights Commissioner. No successor had been appointed to the post at the end of the year.

In October, two high-level officials at the Ministry of Education responsible for integration of Romani children into mainstream education resigned from their posts in protest against the new government's failure to prioritize equal education for Romani children.

The Supreme Administrative Court decided to dissolve the Workers Party (Dělnická strana) on the grounds that its programme involved incitement to national, racial, ethnic and social hatred and that it presented a threat to democracy.

Discrimination – Roma

Roma faced overt public hostility and several trials of attacks against Roma were pending. Roma continued to experience discrimination, including segregation in schools and housing.

Violent attacks

■ On 14 March, Molotov cocktails were thrown into the home of a Romani family in the Bedřiška settlement in the town of Ostrava. In November, the State Prosecutor charged one of the family's neighbours and her teenage son with attempted murder. The police investigation ruled out racial motivation for the crime and concluded the attack was a result of a neighbourly dispute. In December, the Regional Court in Ostrava gave the perpetrators suspended sentences.

■ On 20 October, the Regional Court in Ostrava found four men guilty of attempted homicide and property damage in an arson attack against a Romani family in the village of Vítkov in April 2009. It held that the crime was premeditated and racially motivated. Three of the perpetrators were each sentenced to 22 years' and the fourth to 20 years' imprisonment. All of them appealed the verdict. The attack had destroyed the house of a Romani family. A two-year-old girl had suffered burns over 80 per cent of her body and had been in an induced coma for three months.

■ The trial against eight suspects accused of attacks on Roma in Havířov was pending. During one of the attacks in November 2008, a group of alleged neo-Nazis attacked several people and severely injured one man.

Education

Segregation of Roma children in schools for pupils with "mild mental disabilities" and Roma-only schools and classes continued. Three years after the judgement of the European Court of Human Rights, which confirmed the prohibition of separate and inferior education of Roma, the government still failed to eliminate discrimination within the country's educational system.

The Czech School Inspectorate found in March that 35 per cent of all children diagnosed with "mild mental disability" were Roma, while in some regions the percentage amounted to more than 50 per cent.

In reaction to the report, the Public Defender of Rights (Ombudperson) stated in April that "the consequence of the assessment method applied to Romani children by psychologists of School Advisory Centres is their segregation outside the mainstream education, thus resulted in them being denied access to good quality education." The Ombudsperson also found that it was discriminatory that one third of the children diagnosed as mentally disabled were Roma.

The government had adopted a National Action Plan for Inclusive Education in March, although it did not address discrimination on the basis of ethnic origin nor did it include a concrete timeline for the desegregation of Czech schools. The implementation of the Action Plan was then postponed by the new Minister of Education, who also rejected amendments to two Ministry Regulations aimed at eliminating some of the discriminatory barriers faced by Romani children in accessing education in mainstream schools.

After his November visit, the Council of Europe Commissioner for Human Rights stated that "[t]here has been virtually no change on the ground in the Czech Republic since the European Court ... found three years ago that the country had discriminated against Roma children by educating them in schools for children with mental disabilities." On 2 December, in the review of the implementation of the judgement, the Committee of Ministers of the Council of Europe encouraged the government to implement the Action Plan without delay, and to address the situation of pupils placed in the wrong schools.

Housing

The Ombudsperson found in September that the municipality of Vítkovice district in Ostrava significantly violated legal regulations in cases of Roma applicants for permanent residence. He raised concerns that additional administrative requirements – such as an interview with officials – for Roma when applying for permanent domicile might constitute discrimination. The NGO Zšvůle práva representing the Roma applicants had notified the Ombudsperson's Office and also filed a civil complaint in 2009 against the practice of the municipality. The civil case was pending at the end of the year.

■ The case of the 2006 eviction of Roma from the town of Vsetín was referred back to the Regional Court of Ostrava in October by the Appeals Court, as the Regional Court had failed to assess a large part of the evidence presented by the complainants. The Ombudsperson had stated in 2007 that the eviction amounted to a substantial violation of the right of the inhabitants to human dignity and to the protection of private and family life. Some families alleged that they were threatened with homelessness if they did not agree to the eviction. Some of the evictions were carried out at night and the alternative housing provided was reportedly inadequate.

Enforced sterilization of Romani women

Despite expressing regret over past enforced sterilizations, the government failed to implement legislative changes to ensure free, prior and informed consent for sterilizations. In October, the CEDAW Committee recommended that the government review the three-year time limit in the statute of limitation for the enforcement of compensation claims in cases of enforced sterilizations.

■ In January, the High Court in Prague awarded 200,000 Czech koruna (approximately 8,100 euros) compensation to two Romani women who underwent enforced sterilization.

Refugees' and migrants' rights

The parliament adopted an amendment to the Act on the Stay of Foreigners in December. The new legislation, extending the maximum period of immigration detention from six to 18 months, gave rise to concern.

Amnesty International visits/reports

🚗 Amnesty International delegates visited the Czech Republic in January.

📄 Injustice renamed: Discrimination in education of Roma persists in the Czech Republic (EUR 71/003/2009)

📄 Czech Republic: Four convicted of racially-motivated attacks in Vítkov (EUR 71/007/2010)

📄 Romani children continue to be trapped in separate and unequal education, despite judgments by the European Court of Human Rights (EUR 01/029/2010)

DEMOCRATIC REPUBLIC OF THE CONGO

DEMOCRATIC REPUBLIC OF THE CONGO

Head of state:	Joseph Kabila
Head of government:	Adolphe Muzito
Death penalty:	retentionist
Population:	67.8 million
Life expectancy:	48 years
Under-5 mortality (m/f):	209/187 per 1,000
Adult literacy:	66.6 per cent

Civilians in eastern Democratic Republic of the Congo (DRC) were subjected to serious human rights violations throughout the year by government forces and armed groups. An armed group besieged Mbandaka in April; the town returned to government control after two days of fighting during which soldiers allegedly committed extrajudicial executions, rapes and arbitrary detentions. Foreign and Congolese armed groups committed abuses, including the mass rape of more than 300 people in July and August in North Kivu. The security services were also responsible for politically motivated human rights violations. Prominent human rights defender Floribert Chebeya was killed in June.

Background

The national army, Forces Armées de la République Democratique du Congo (FARDC), led several military operations against armed groups in eastern and northern DRC. Operation Amani Leo, which was launched in January against the Democratic Liberation Forces of Rwanda (FDLR), conducted operations throughout North and South Kivu. FARDC soldiers reportedly subjected civilians to forced labour and arbitrary detentions as well as seizing property and livestock. The UN provided some logistical and planning support to Amani Leo. The FARDC also led operations against the Lord's Resistance Army (LRA) in Province Orientale and against the Allied Democratic Forces/National Army for the Liberation of Uganda (AFD/NALU) in the Grand Nord region of North Kivu, which led to displacement of civilians.

On 4 April, an armed group, the Mouvement de libération indépendante des alliés (MLIA), attacked Mbandaka, capital of Equateur province, controlling parts of the city for two days. Congolese security forces deployed in response allegedly killed, raped and arbitrarily detained civilians.

Impunity for human rights violations remained rife. Known perpetrators of crimes under international law were not removed from their posts or brought to justice. In March the President announced that the UN peacekeeping mission in the DRC (MONUC) was to leave by June 2011. The mission was renamed the UN Stabilization Mission in the DRC (MONUSCO) from 1 July as part of a compromise with the DRC government. MONUSCO's mandate was extended until at least June 2011, and the government agreed that UN troops would be withdrawn only after demonstrable improvements in security.

In September, the DRC ratified the Optional Protocol to the UN Convention against Torture, which requires it to grant access to places of detention to national and UN observers. In March, during the UN Universal Periodic Review, the government opposed a recommendation to grant UN observers access to detention centres, including those of the National Intelligence Agency (Agence nationale de renseignements, ANR) and the National Guard.

A government reshuffle in March removed the position of Minister for Human Rights. Responsibility for human rights promotion was transferred to the Minister of Justice. In April the government launched a Human Rights Liaison Committee to improve communications between human rights organizations and the authorities.

D

In December, opposition leaders announced their candidacy for presidential elections in 2011. The announcement coincided with incidents of violations of the rights of journalists and opposition parties to freedom of expression and to freedom of assembly.

Abuses by armed groups

Attacks on civilians by the LRA were particularly intense in February and March. The LRA abducted civilians and forced them to fight. In the Bas Uélé district of Province Orientale, 80 people were reportedly killed by the LRA between 22 and 26 February. As of July, over 300,000 people were displaced in Haut and Bas Uélé as a result of LRA attacks.

The FDLR were a constant threat to the civilian population in the Kivus and Maniema province and were responsible for unlawful killings, abductions, looting and burning of homes. An FDLR battalion in Walikale territory, North Kivu, joined forces with the Sheka Mayi-Mayi group and perpetrated a number of abuses in the territory. Shabunda territory in South Kivu was regularly attacked by the FDLR; 40 villagers were abducted in March.

Other local armed groups, including the Mayi-Mayi, the Alliance Pour le Congo Libre et Souverain (APCLS) in Masisi, the Coalition of Congolese Patriotic Resistance (PARECO) in North Kivu, the Forces Républicaines Fédéralistes (FRF) in Fizi in South Kivu, the Front de Résistance Patriotique d'Ituri (FRPI) and the Front Populaire pour la Justice au Congo (FPJC), were also active. Armed groups attacked MONUSCO bases in North Kivu in August and October, and attacked and abducted humanitarian workers on a number of occasions.

Unlawful killings

Armed groups and government forces were responsible for hundreds of unlawful killings of civilians and attacks on humanitarian personnel. Civilian resistance to theft, forced labour and other abuses by armed forces was frequently met with unlawful killings and other acts of violence.
■ In February, the FDLR allegedly abducted 15 women and killed five of them in Mwenga territory, South Kivu.
■ At least 20 people detained in the military jails of Mbandaka, Equateur province, were allegedly executed by FARDC soldiers on the night of 4/5 April.
■ On 21 May, a woman was allegedly shot dead in Kalehe, South Kivu, by an FARDC soldier for refusing to carry military supplies.

■ On 1 July, two FARDC soldiers reportedly killed a man, raped his 12-year-old daughter and killed another man who tried to rescue them in a village in Walungu territory, South Kivu. Two other women in the household were ill-treated and several houses were looted.

Sexual violence

Rape and other forms of sexual violence were widespread, committed by government security forces, including the National Police, and armed groups. Insufficient access to health care and impunity for perpetrators aggravated the situation for rape survivors. Members of security forces responsible for sexual violence were often protected by superior officers or allowed to escape by prison staff.
■ Between 30 July and 2 August, more than 300 women, men and children were raped in a series of attacks on 13 villages in the Walikale territory, North Kivu, by a coalition of the FDLR, Mayi-Mayi and deserters from the FARDC. During the attacks, villagers were rounded up, roads and communication were blocked and the assailants systematically looted houses and raped those seeking to hide or escape.
■ Within one week in April, 16 cases of rape by government forces were reported, including a case of gang rape by National Police officers, during fighting in Mbandaka, Equateur province.
■ On 6 August, 10 women were reportedly raped in Katalukulu, Fizi territory, by FARDC soldiers, apparently in reprisal for a Mayi-Mayi attack.

Child soldiers

Children continued to be recruited and used by armed groups in eastern DRC. The LRA and the FDLR abducted children and used them as fighters or as domestic and sexual slaves.

Many children also served in the FARDC. Some were former members of armed groups who had not been identified during integration into the FARDC in March 2009. Others were new recruits. Although the FARDC formally ended recruitment of children in 2004, the Child Protection Code adopted in January 2009 was largely unimplemented and the government had no plan of action to separate children from armed forces as required by UN Security Council resolutions 1539 (2004) and 1612 (2005).

Internally displaced people and refugees

The number of internally displaced people rose to nearly two million in August. Most were in North and

South Kivu and Orientale provinces. Living conditions were very poor both within camps and within host communities and the displaced were vulnerable to attacks by armed groups.

After the attack on Mbandaka in April, the number of refugees in neighbouring Republic of Congo reached more than 114,000, with about 18,000 in the Central African Republic. About 33,000 people were internally displaced within Equateur province. In Province Orientale, the LRA attacks of December 2009 and February and March 2010 led to the displacement of over 300,000 people.

Between September and November, more than 6,000 Congolese citizens were expelled from Angola. According to humanitarian workers, more than 100 reported having been raped in Angola (see Angola entry).

Torture and other ill-treatment

Acts of torture and other ill-treatment were committed by armed groups and government security forces.
■ On 20 August, FARDC soldiers in Kasando, North Kivu, reportedly tortured five people, including two children, arrested after an attack on the MONUSCO base in Kirumba. They received between 40 and 120 lashes each, and some had their feet and hands burned and mutilated. They were transferred to the Military Prosecutor in Goma.

Death penalty

Military courts sentenced scores of people to death during the year, including civilians. No executions were reported. On 25 November, the National Assembly rejected the proposal to discuss a draft law on the abolition of death penalty.

Administration of justice

Lack of resources and political interference paralyzed courts throughout the country and led to strikes by magistrates in March in Kisangani and Kasai Oriental. Courts were overwhelmed with cases, resulting in excessive periods of pre-trial detention. Trials fell short of fair trial standards, judgements were seldom enforced and victims rarely received reparations. Military authorities and the government interfered in cases before the military and civilian justice system. Commanders in the field ignored arrest warrants issued by military prosecutors against members of their units, blocking the work of military justice authorities.

Scores of civilians were tried in front of military courts in breach of international fair trial standards. In October, the National Assembly started to discuss a draft law on implementation of the Rome Statute of the International Criminal Court which would require war crimes and crimes against humanity to be tried by civilian courts.

On 12 August, an FARDC company of former armed group members laid siege to the Military Prosecutor's Office in Goma. They succeeded in forcing the release of a commander who had been arrested for refusing in July to redeploy his troops to the area in Walikale where mass rapes by armed groups took place a few weeks later.

Prison conditions

Prisons lacked the resources to meet international minimum standards. Prisoners were not guaranteed even one meal a day and had inadequate access to health care. Dozens died in prison as a result of the poor conditions, and many more died in hospital after undue delays in being transferred. Prison facilities were in a state of decay that impeded the effective separation of women from men, and of detainees from convicted prisoners. Cases of rape within prison and police detention facilities were reported.

Human rights defenders

Human rights defenders were attacked, abducted, and subjected to death threats and other forms of intimidation by government security forces and armed groups. Many defenders in North Kivu who spoke out against abusive army commanders were forced into hiding or to flee the region. Others were targeted because of their advocacy in individual human rights cases. The ANR, which was subject to no independent oversight or judicial control, violated the right to freedom of expression of human rights defenders and journalists.
■ On 2 June, Floribert Chebeya, a prominent human rights defender, was found dead in his car in Kinshasa. He and his driver had gone missing the day before after going to meet the General Inspector of Police, at his request. The driver remained missing. Eight police officers were charged with the murder and their trial began in November. The General Inspector of Police was suspended but not charged.

Freedom of expression – journalists

Scores of journalists throughout the country were threatened, arbitrarily arrested, prosecuted, intimidated, warned by state authorities not to report on certain subjects, and sometimes killed for their work. Radio France International broadcasts were restored after a year's suspension by the government, which had banned international reporting on military operations.

■ On 5 April, cameraman Patient Chebeya was killed by armed men in front of his house in Beni, North Kivu.

International justice

On 1 October, the UN reported on a mapping exercise documenting the most serious violations of human rights and international humanitarian law committed within the DRC between March 1993 and June 2003. The report raised hopes of justice for crimes under international and national law for thousands of victims and human rights defenders. While not binding under Congolese law, the report amplified the obligation of the government to investigate the violations, bring those responsible to justice, and ensure victims received effective reparation.

■ Proceedings continued before the International Criminal Court (ICC) against Thomas Lubanga, charged with recruiting and using children under the age of 15 for the armed group Union des Patriotes Congolais (UPC) in Ituri. In July, the trial nearly collapsed when the Prosecutor refused to comply with a ruling by ICC judges to disclose the identity of an intermediary to defence lawyers. The appeal chamber ruled in October that the trial could continue.

■ On 11 October, French authorities arrested Callixte Mbarushimana, Secretary of the FDLR, following an arrest warrant issued by the ICC. He had been living as a refugee in France.

■ In October, the DRC Minister of Justice reiterated the government's refusal to surrender Bosco Ntaganda to the ICC, which had sought him since 2006 on charges of recruitment and use of children.

■ Proceedings in the ICC case of Jean-Pierre Bemba, former Vice President of the DRC charged with crimes against humanity committed in the Central African Republic, were dominated by challenges to the ICC's jurisdiction by defence lawyers. The trial eventually began on 22 November.

Amnesty International visits/reports

🚌 Amnesty International delegates visited the country in August and December.

📄 Human rights defenders under attack in the Democratic Republic of the Congo (AFR 62/001/2010)

📄 Democratic Republic of the Congo: Open Letter to His Excellency President Joseph Kabila – commission of inquiry on the death of Floribert Chebeya Bahizire (AFR 62/007/2010)

📄 Democratic Republic of the Congo:Mass rapes in Walikale - Still a need for protection and justice in Eastern Congo (AFR 62/011/2010)

📄 UN forces must remain in the Democratic Republic of the Congo, 5 March 2010

📄 Democratic Republic of the Congo must investigate activist's death, 2 June 2010

📄 Human rights activists targeted in the Democratic Republic of the Congo, 29 June 2010

📄 Justice urged for murder of human rights defender in the Democratic Republic of the Congo, 30 July 2010

📄 Action needed to investigate decade of crimes in the Democratic Republic of the Congo, 1 October 2010

D

DENMARK

KINGDOM OF DENMARK

Head of state:	Queen Margrethe II
Head of government:	Lars Løkke Rasmussen
Death penalty:	abolitionist for all crimes
Population:	5.5 million
Life expectancy:	78.7 years
Under-5 mortality (m/f):	6/6 per 1,000

Counter-terrorism legislation continued to give rise to concern. Forced returns contrary to international guidelines, including to Iraq, continued. Women were not adequately protected against violence in legislation or practice.

Counter-terror and security

Counter-terrorism legislation continued to impact on human rights. Judicial control of police access to private and confidential information was weak (for example, intercepting telephone and computer communications) and proceedings by which deportations and expulsions on national security grounds could be challenged remained unfair.

In September, the government published a review of counter-terrorism legislation adopted since 2001. The review was criticized for its lack of thoroughness and for failing to include the views of different stakeholders. Based on statements by the Director of Public Prosecutions, the National Police and the Police Security and Intelligence Service exclusively, the review concluded that the increased powers given to the latter had enhanced terrorism prevention.

In December, the Eastern High Court annulled an order to expel a Tunisian citizen, Slim Chafra, on the grounds that he was considered a threat to national security. The Court found that Slim Chafra had not been able to effectively challenge the decision to expel him, because it was based primarily on secret material, presented in closed hearings, which he and his lawyers did not have access to. Consequently, he had not had fair or reasonable means of defending himself.

Torture and other ill-treatment

In November, a local court ruled that the extradition of Niels Holck, a Danish national, to India could not proceed after determining that diplomatic assurances negotiated between the Danish and Indian government did not offer sufficient protection against the risk of torture and other ill-treatment. The government appealed the case, which at the end of the year remained pending at the High Court.

In December, the Copenhagen Municipal Court ruled that the mass pre-emptive arrests of 250 people during the 2009 Climate Change Conference in Copenhagen were unlawful, and furthermore that the circumstances under which the arrests took place in 178 of those cases constituted degrading treatment, in violation of article 3 of the European Convention on Human Rights.

The problem of minors on remand being detained in the same facilities as adult inmates persisted.

Refugees and asylum seekers

In May, the government amended its policy regarding transfers of asylum-seekers to Greece under the Dublin II Regulation. Despite the lack of protection under the current Greek asylum determination procedure, the government announced that it would no longer wait for Greece to explicitly accept responsibility for a case before transfer. The European Court of Human Rights granted interim measures halting transfer in at least 304 cases, and effectively prevented the majority of transfers taking place. However, the Danish Minister of Refugees, Immigration and Integration did not declare a halt of all Dublin transfers to Greece. By the end of the year 20 people had been transferred to Greece under the Regulation.

Despite recommendations from UNHCR, the UN refugee agency, at least 62 Iraqis were returned to Baghdad, Iraq, despite the real risk of persecution or serious harm.

Violence against women

Legislation did not adequately protect women against sexual violence. An expert committee, commissioned by the government in 2009 to examine existing legislation on rape had not yet submitted its findings by the end of the year. For example, legislation provides that if the perpetrator enters into or continues a marriage or registered partnership with the victim after the rape, it gives grounds for reducing or remitting the punishment.

On average only 20 per cent of reported rapes result in a conviction, the majority of cases are closed by the police or prosecution and are never brought to trial, leading to a high risk of impunity for perpetrators.

Discrimination

In August, the CERD Committee called on the government to provide adequate shelter for Roma and Travellers in the country, facilitate their access to public services and provide effective protection against discrimination and hate crimes.

The Committee also reported that the introduction in May of a new point-based system for individuals seeking permanent residence introduced "onerous and stringent requirements" that may unfairly exclude vulnerable individuals.

Amnesty International visits/reports

Case closed: Rape and human rights in the Nordic countries – summary report (ACT 77/001/2010)

Dangerous deals: Europe's reliance on 'diplomatic assurances' against torture (EUR 01/012/2010)

DOMINICAN REPUBLIC

DOMINICAN REPUBLIC

Head of state and government:	Leonel Fernández Reyna
Death penalty:	abolitionist for all crimes
Population:	10.2 million
Life expectancy:	72.8 years
Under-5 mortality (m/f):	37/29 per 1,000
Adult literacy:	88.2 per cent

Unlawful killings by police were reported. People of Haitian descent continued to face entrenched discrimination and social exclusion. Violence against women and girls remained widespread.

Background

A new constitution entered into force on 26 January. In April, the Dominican Republic's human rights record was assessed under the UN's Universal Periodic Review (UPR) and the Dominican authorities undertook to implement 74 of the 79 recommendations made by the UN Human Rights Council. The Dominican Republic provided significant support to humanitarian operations in Haiti following the earthquake there in January.

Police and security forces

According to police statistics, 167 people were killed by police officers between January and September. Evidence suggested that many of these killings may have been unlawful.

■ On 27 June, police shot and killed student Abraham Ramos Morel in Santo Domingo. A police motorbike patrol had ordered him to stop his car and then opened fire, even though Abraham Ramos Morel signalled that he would stop further on in a clearer area. Two police officers were on trial at the end of the year.

There were several reports of torture and other ill-treatment during police interrogation.

■ Juan Carlos Santiago was detained by police in August and questioned about the whereabouts of his brother, who was wanted on suspicion of murder. Juan Carlos Santiago reported that he was beaten while held handcuffed during interrogation at the police headquarters in Santo Domingo.

Police and judicial officials failed to establish the whereabouts of Juan Almonte Herrera who was abducted in Santo Domingo on 28 September 2009 by four men identified by eyewitnesses as police officers.

Discrimination – Haitian migrants and Dominico-Haitians

A UN report on human development found that the economic situation of most Haitians living in the Dominican Republic was worse than that of the poorest fifth of the Dominican population. The failure of the government to adequately regulate migration law contributed to the continuing exclusion and vulnerability of Haitian migrants.

Access to nationality

Thousands of Dominicans of Haitian descent were refused identity documents on the basis of a directive issued in March 2007 by the Dominican Electoral Board. Without identity documents, Dominico-Haitians were effectively denied other rights, including the rights to education, employment and citizenship.

■ Altagracia Polis' repeated requests for an identity card since 2007 were refused on the grounds that her parents are Haitians. Unable to present valid identity documents, she lost her job and was unable to continue her studies or register the birth of her daughter. Altagracia Polis was born in the Dominican Republic; her brothers, who applied for their documents before 2007, were issued with Dominican identity cards.

During the UPR, the Dominican Republic undertook to adopt comprehensive strategies to combat racism, including specific measures to protect people of Haitian origin, and to protect the rights of migrants. However, the government rejected the recommendation that it adopt measures to ensure that Dominicans of Haitian descent were not denied citizenship or arbitrarily subjected to retroactive cancellation of birth and identity documents.

Migrants' rights – expulsions

In the aftermath of the earthquake which struck Haiti, the Dominican authorities announced a halt to the deportations of irregular Haitian migrants. According to human rights organizations, the deportations were re-activated in July despite calls for them to be halted unless they could be conducted in safety and dignity. In many cases, expulsions appeared to be arbitrary and without the possibility of challenging the decision.

Trafficking in human beings

After the earthquake in Haiti, human rights organizations reported an increase in the number of Haitian children being trafficked into the Dominican Republic.

The authorities announced the creation of a specialized centre in Haina to provide immediate assistance to trafficked children. However, no information was available on the effectiveness of the measures taken by the authorities to dismantle trafficking networks.

Violence against women and girls

According to the General Prosecutor's Office, there was a 20 per cent increase in the number of women killed by their partners or former partners between January and July 2010, compared with the same period in 2009.

Sexual violence remained widespread, with girls being particularly vulnerable.

According to women's organizations, the national health system was largely unable to provide adequate medical and psychological care to victims of gender-based violence. However, protocols for the provision of comprehensive care for survivors of domestic and other gender-based violence against women were adopted by the Ministry of Public Health.

Freedom of expression – journalists

The Dominican National Union of Press Workers reported that at least seven TV channels were forced to temporarily close or their transmission signal was blocked during the electoral campaign as a consequence of political pressures.

The Union also announced in November that scores of journalists and other media workers had been harassed or physically attacked during the year. In most cases perpetrators were not brought to justice.

Amnesty International visits/reports

🚍 Amnesty International delegates visited the country in October 2010.

📄 Dominican Republic: Protection urged after killing and threats (AMR 27/002/2010)

📄 One year on, Juan Almonte's fate continues to be unknown: Possible enforced disappearance in the Dominican Republic (AMR 27/003/2010)

ECUADOR

E

REPUBLIC OF ECUADOR

Head of state and government:	**Rafael Vicente Correa Delgado**
Death penalty:	**abolitionist for all crimes**
Population:	**13.8 million**
Life expectancy:	**75.4 years**
Under-5 mortality (m/f):	**29/22 per 1,000**
Adult literacy:	**84.2 per cent**

Spurious criminal charges were brought against human rights defenders, including Indigenous leaders. Human rights violations committed by security forces remained unresolved. Women living in poverty continued to lack access to good quality and culturally appropriate health services.

Background

There were mass demonstrations, many led by Indigenous Peoples' organizations, against government policies and legislation on issues such as natural resources; land; education; public services; and the lack of a clear process to guarantee the right of Indigenous Peoples to free, prior and informed consent on development projects and policies or legislation affecting them.

In February, Indigenous Peoples' organizations withdrew from discussions with the government over legislation on mining, water, land, education and the environment, because they believed the government was failing to engage meaningfully with their concerns.

In September, hundreds of police officers demonstrated against what they considered cuts in their pay and benefits. This was regarded by the government as an attempted coup. At least eight people, including two police officers, died during the protests and scores were injured, including the President who was hospitalized for the effects of tear gas. By the end of the year, scores of police officers were under investigation for a range of offences.

In June, Ecuador became the first country to ratify the Optional Protocol to the International Covenant on Economic, Social and Cultural Rights.

Human rights defenders

Charges of sabotage and terrorism were brought against human rights defenders, including Indigenous leaders, in an attempt to silence their opposition to government policies.

■ In June, investigations were opened against three Indigenous leaders – Marlon Santi, President of the Confederation of Indigenous Peoples of Ecuador; Delfin Tenesaca, leader of the Kichwa Confederation of Ecuador; and Marco Guatemal, President of the Indigenous and Peasant Federation of Imbabura – for terrorism and sabotage. The investigation was linked to their participation in a demonstration in Otavalo in protest at their exclusion from a summit of ALBA (Bolivarian Alliance for the Peoples of Our America) countries. The investigation was continuing at the end of the year.

■ In May, charges of sabotage and terrorism were brought against community leaders, Carlos Pérez and Federico Guzmán and three inhabitants of Victoria del Portete, Azuay province. The charges were connected to their involvement in a road blockade to protest against a draft law on water. The charges were dismissed by the courts in August.

Impunity – police and security forces

Further human rights violations by members of the National Police group in charge of organized crime (Grupo de Apoyo Operacional, GAO) were reported. The group has been linked to scores of cases of torture and other ill-treatment and possible extrajudicial executions since its formation in 1996.

In July, the UN Special Rapporteur on extrajudicial executions raised concerns that the vast majority of alleged killings, including killings by police, remained unresolved due to a lack of thorough and independent investigations, inadequate victim and witness support and protection, and delays and corruption in the justice system.

■ At the end of the year, 14 police officers from the GAO were detained awaiting trial, and another three were under investigation, for the torture of Fabricio Colón Pico Suárez, Jenny Karina Pico Suárez and Javier Universi Pico Suárez, and the disappearance of Georgy Hernán Cedeño, in September 2009.

■ The torture and killing of Yandry Javier Vélez Moreira and Juan Miguel Vélez Cedeño in December 2008 and the threats against their sister Leidy Johanna Vélez Moreira, allegedly committed by members of the GAO, remained unresolved.

The Truth Commission in charge of investigating human rights violations between 1984 and 2008 published its final report in June. The Commission documented 118 cases, affecting 456 victims of arbitrary detention, torture, sexual violence, enforced disappearances and killings. The police were implicated in most of these crimes. The government made a commitment to bring the perpetrators to justice and to establish 12 special prosecutors to investigate these crimes. A draft law guaranteeing the right to reparation to victims of these violations was under discussion at the end of the year.

Indigenous Peoples' rights

In September, the UN Special Rapporteur on indigenous people urged the government not to grant concessions for the extraction of natural resources, without a prior, broad and legitimate process of consultation and participation with the Indigenous communities affected.

In April, the Inter-American Commission on Human Rights filed an application with the Inter-American Court of Human Rights on the case of members of the Kichwa Peoples of the Sarayaku community, in Pastaza province. The case related to oil extraction on community land without the Kichwa's prior consultation, as well as to threats and intimidation against members of the community.

Right to health

In January, the Committee on the Rights of the Child (CRC) reported that many communities living in poverty still lacked access to good quality and culturally appropriate health services, despite efforts to extend access.

Sexual and reproductive rights

The CRC also raised concerns about the lack of

access to information on sexual and reproductive health and the prohibition of emergency contraception.

Maternal mortality

Progress was made in reducing maternal mortality, according to official state figures. Other reports also indicated that Ecuador was making progress in reducing infant mortality. However, statistics continued to show great disparities between infant mortality in rural and urban areas and among Indigenous children.

EGYPT

ARAB REPUBLIC OF EGYPT

Head of state:	Muhammad Hosni Mubarak
Head of government:	Ahmed Nazif
Death penalty:	retentionist
Population:	84.5 million
Life expectancy:	70.5 years
Under-5 mortality (m/f):	42/39 per 1,000
Adult literacy:	66.4 per cent

The authorities continued to use state of emergency powers to target government critics, opposition political activists and people suspected of security-related offences, despite a presidential decree in May limiting the application of the Emergency Law. Some were held in administrative detention without charge or trial, others were tried before emergency or military courts whose procedures did not satisfy international standards for fair trial. Journalists and other government critics continued to be prosecuted under criminal defamation legislation. The authorities maintained strict controls on freedom of expression, association and assembly. Torture and other ill-treatment remained common and widespread, and in most cases were committed with impunity. Several deaths as a result of torture or other abuses by police were reported. Several hundred administrative detainees were released but thousands of others, including long-term detainees, continued to be held despite court orders for their release; the government did not disclose the number of those detained. Forced evictions in Cairo, Port Said and Aswan affected thousands of slum-dwellers

who lived in dangerous conditions because of an acute shortage of affordable and adequate housing. Border security forces shot dead at least 30 people, mostly migrants from other African countries, who were seeking to cross the border into Israel. At least 185 people were sentenced to death and at least four were executed.

Background

The government accepted many recommendations made during the UN Human Rights Council's Universal Periodic Review of Egypt in February, but rejected others and deferred a recommendation to allow the UN Special Rapporteur on torture to visit Egypt.

In May, the state of emergency in force since 1981 was renewed for a further two years, but a presidential decree issued at the same time limited the application of the Emergency Law to cases involving "terrorism" and drugs trafficking.

Workers staged many protests against rising living costs and to demand better wages and working conditions. The authorities failed to implement an administrative court ruling to establish a minimum wage commensurate with the average cost of living.

Political activists, including members of the banned Muslim Brotherhood and other political opposition groups such as the National Association for Change, the 6 April Movement and the Egyptian Movement for Change (Kefaya), demonstrated against the state of emergency and police abuses. Many were arrested, beaten and taken to remote locations and dumped after their mobile phones, money and shoes were confiscated. Others were detained and charged with assaulting police officers, tried and sentenced to prison terms.

Elections for the Shura, the upper house of parliament, in June and for the People's Assembly in November and December resulted in large majorities for the ruling National Democratic Party, but were marred by serious allegations of fraud, vote-rigging and violence, which left at least eight people dead. The leading opposition parties formally withdrew from the People's Assembly elections after the first and main round of voting in November.

At least 1,200 supporters and candidates associated with the Muslim Brotherhood were detained after it announced in October that it intended to put up many of its supporters as candidates for election. According to the official results, none of them was elected, eliminating the

E

Muslim Brotherhood from the lower house of parliament in which they had previously formed the main opposition bloc.

Counter-terror and security

The authorities used their state of emergency powers to detain people suspected of security-related offences. Detainees were held incommunicado, often for several weeks. Many alleged that they were tortured or otherwise ill-treated by State Security Investigations (SSI) officials and forced to make "confessions" that they later repudiated when brought to trial. Other security suspects were deported.

■ Husam Radhwan el-Mar'i, a Syrian resident of Yemen, was detained for 38 days after he was arrested at Cairo airport in April. He was held incommunicado and, he alleged, beaten, whipped and tortured with electric shocks because he was suspected of belonging to a "terrorist group". He was released without charge on 19 May and deported to Yemen.

■ In April, an (Emergency) Supreme State Security Court sentenced 26 alleged members of the so-called Hizbullah Cell to prison terms ranging from six months to life after convicting them of planning to attack tourist sites, possessing explosives and passing information to Hizbullah in Lebanon. Four of the defendants were tried in their absence. The 22 who appeared before the court had been detained incommunicado for months at an undisclosed location by order of the Interior Minister after they were arrested in 2008 and 2009. They were convicted on the basis of "confessions" they repudiated and said had been extracted using torture. The court failed to adequately examine their allegations.

Detention without trial – administrative detention

Despite the May presidential decree limiting the use of the Emergency Law, in practice the authorities continued to use emergency powers to detain opposition activists and to curb freedom of expression. The authorities said that hundreds of administrative detainees were released in accordance with the presidential decree, including detainees held in connection with bomb attacks at Taba in 2004, but disclosed no details about those who continued to be detained. Thousands remained in detention without charge or trial despite court orders for their release; in practice, the Interior Ministry circumvented release orders by issuing new detention orders, undermining judicial scrutiny and oversight.

■ Mohamed Farouq El-Sayyed, a Shi'a Muslim, and seven others arrested with him, remained in administrative detention without charge or trial at Damanhour Prison although courts had ordered his release at least seven times. He and 11 others had been arrested in April/May 2009; all were suspected of trying to set up an organization to promote Shi'a Islam in a manner deemed to be threatening to Islam and the Sunni Muslim community. The prosecution released all 12, but they were detained by the Interior Ministry. Four were subsequently released.

Torture and other ill-treatment

Torture and other ill-treatment of security detainees and criminal suspects were systematic in police stations, prisons and SSI detention centres and, for the most part, committed with impunity. In some instances, police assaulted suspects openly and in public as if unconcerned about possible consequences. In other instances, police were reported to have threatened victims against lodging complaints. In April, the Interior Ministry agreed to pay a total of 10 million Egyptian pounds (US$1.76 million) as compensation to 840 members of Gamaa Islamiya, an Islamist group, who had been tortured; however, no action is known to have been taken against those responsible for their torture.

In rare cases, the authorities prosecuted police alleged to have committed assaults, although generally these were cases that had received wide publicity. Those convicted tended to receive lenient sentences.

■ Taha Abdel Tawwab Mohamed, a medical doctor, said he was stripped and beaten by SSI officers in Fayoum on 7 March because of his public support for Mohamed ElBaradei, the former head of the International Atomic Energy Agency, who the authorities consider a government critic. He was released the next day. His lawyer filed a complaint but no action was known to have been taken.

Deaths in custody

At least four people were alleged to have died in custody as a result of torture or other ill-treatment.

■ Khaled Said was severely assaulted by two police officers in plain clothes in front of witnesses at an internet café in Alexandria on 6 June, apparently causing his death. The case provoked a public outcry and two police officers from Sidi Gaber police station were charged with unlawfully arresting and torturing him, although not with direct responsibility for his death. Their trial, sessions of which were attended by Amnesty International observers, was continuing at the end of 2010.

■ In November, the family of Ahmed Shaaban, aged 19, accused police at Sidi Gaber police station of torturing him to death and then dumping his corpse in a canal to suggest that he had committed suicide. The prosecuting authorities closed the case on grounds of insufficient evidence and an autopsy report that stated that he had died of asphyxiation.

Freedom of expression

The authorities maintained curbs on freedom of expression and the media. Politically sensitive reports were suppressed. Candidates for parliamentary elections using slogans deemed to be religious were disqualified. Government critics faced prosecution on criminal defamation charges. Independent TV channels and programmes that criticized the authorities were taken off the air or suspended. Books and foreign newspapers were censored if they commented on issues that the authorities considered sensitive or threatening to national security.

In October, the National Telecommunications Regulatory Authority (NTRA) told organizations using SMS services to send bulk messages to their subscribers that they must obtain a broadcasting licence. The authorities said this was necessary to "better regulate" the service but their action was widely interpreted as intended to curtail the use of mass messaging by government opponents in the lead-up to the November elections. A day before the election, an administrative court annulled the NTRA's order.

■ Hamdi Kandil, spokesperson for the National Association for Change, a grouping of people calling for constitutional and political reform, was charged with criminal defamation in May after he criticized the Minister of Foreign Affairs in an article in *Al-Chorouk* newspaper. He was referred to the Giza Criminal Court for trial, accused of insulting and libelling a public servant. His trial began in November.

Freedom of assembly and association

The authorities maintained legal restrictions and other controls on political parties, NGOs, professional associations and trade unions. Some were denied legal registration. The Muslim Brotherhood remained outlawed but operated openly. Police disrupted and violently dispersed campaign rallies by the Muslim Brotherhood and other opposition parties and

arrested many of their members and supporters, particularly in the run-up to elections.

The One Homeland for Development and Freedoms NGO was denied legal registration and several charitable organizations in Beni Souef were accused of breaching the restrictive NGO law and closed down.

In March, the government said that a new draft NGO law had been devised to replace Law No. 84 of 2002; if implemented, this will further restrict NGOs, including by making them answerable to a new umbrella organization partly comprising presidential nominees.

Discrimination against women

Women continued to suffer from discrimination, violence and sexual harassment. In slums, women were also discriminated against in the allocation of alternative housing during evictions; when a male spouse was absent, local authorities required women to produce proof of their marital status or face possible homelessness.

In its concluding observations in February, the CEDAW Committee urged the government to lift its reservations to Articles 2 and 16 of the Convention, to review and promptly reform laws that discriminate against women, and to strengthen the legal complaints system to allow women effective access to justice. The Committee also urged the government to adopt a comprehensive law criminalizing all forms of violence against women, including domestic violence, marital rape and crimes committed in the name of "honour". However, no steps to implement these recommendations were taken.

Right to adequate housing – forced evictions

The trial of officials in relation to the fatal 2008 rockslide at Al-Duwayqa, an informal settlement in Cairo, concluded in September. Cairo's deputy governor was acquitted but six other officials were convicted of negligence and sentenced to one-year prison terms. At least 119 people were killed and more than 50 injured by the rockslide.

Residents of many other areas officially designated as "unsafe" in informal settlements continued to live in grossly inadequate conditions and were at risk from fire, flooding and other threats.

■ In January, flash floods killed at least six people and displaced thousands of residents from their homes in the Sinai Peninsula and in Aswan, including in "unsafe areas". The authorities' response in providing shelter and support to those affected was inadequate and slow.

■ In August, a fire burned down some 50 shack homes in Zerzara informal settlement in Port Said, leaving residents homeless. The authorities failed to provide shelter or alternative housing.

Up to 12,000 families in the large informal settlement of Manshiyet Nasser in east Cairo were still living amid unstable rocks and cliffs because they could not afford homes elsewhere. The Cairo Governorate allocated more that 5,000 alternative housing units to Manshiyet Nasser residents, but most were located far from their sources of livelihood and affordable services. Those evicted on safety grounds were not consulted about proposed conditions of resettlement nor formally notified of their eviction even if the areas in which they lived had been designated as "unsafe" months earlier. Many did not know whether they would be rehoused. Forced evictions were also carried out in Establ Antar and Ezbet Khayrallah informal settlements in Old Cairo. Many families were made homeless as a result of forced evictions.

The authorities continued to devise and began implementing development plans for some of the 404 officially designated "unsafe areas" throughout Egypt, home to an estimated 850,000 people, without adequately consulting the affected residents. Official plans to clear 33 "shack areas" in Greater Cairo by 2015 include Ezbet Abu Qarn, Ramlet Bulaq and parts of Ezbet Khayrallah and Ezbet Al-Haggana. The residents would be relocated, possibly unwillingly, to housing in two distant locations, 6 October City, south-west of Giza, and 15 May City, south of Cairo.

Migrants, refugees and asylum-seekers

Border security forces continued to use lethal force against foreign migrants who attempted to leave Egypt and cross the border into Israel; at least 30 were reported to have been shot dead. No official investigations were carried out into the circumstances in which lethal force was used. Others seeking to cross the border illegally were arrested and detained.

■ In July, an administrative court annulled a deportation order issued by the Interior Minister against Mohamed Adam Abdallah Yahya and Ishaq Fadlallah Ahmed Dafaallah, two asylum-seekers from Darfur who were facing forcible return to Sudan where they would be at risk of serious human rights abuses.

Death penalty

At least 185 death sentences were imposed and at least four prisoners were executed.

■ Jihan Mohammed Ali and Atef Rohyum Abd El Al Rohyum were hanged on successive days in March; they had been convicted of murdering Jihan Mohammed Ali's husband. She was reported to have said in prison that she alone was responsible for her husband's death; he was executed despite his request for a retrial. Their families were not notified in advance of the executions.

In December, Egypt was one of a minority of states that voted against a UN General Assembly resolution calling for a worldwide moratorium on executions.

Amnesty International visits/reports

🚌 Amnesty International delegates visited Egypt several times in 2010 to conduct research and attend conferences and workshops.

▤ Egyptian authorities failing to protect religious minorities (MDE 12/001/2010)

▤ Egypt: Sweeping reform needed to protect workers' rights (MDE 12/020/2010)

▤ Egypt: Threat of forcible eviction of Greater Cairo's "shack" dwellers (MDE 12/031/2010)

▤ Egypt: "Shouting slogans into the wind" – human rights concerns ahead of the parliamentary elections (MDE 12/032/2010)

▤ Egypt: Release blogger prosecuted by military court, 5 March 2010

▤ Egypt: Halt execution of man accused of murder, 11 March 2010

▤ Egypt: Brutal police killing of young man must be investigated, 14 June 2010

▤ Egypt urged to protect slum-dwellers after rockslide official acquitted, 22 September 2010

▤ Egypt must investigate torture allegations made by freed blogger, 18 November 2010

E

EL SALVADOR

REPUBLIC OF EL SALVADOR

Head of state and government:	Carlos Mauricio Funes Cartagena
Death penalty:	abolitionist for ordinary crimes
Population:	6.2 million
Life expectancy:	72 years
Under-5 mortality (m/f):	29/23 per 1,000
Adult literacy:	84 per cent

Impunity for past human rights violations continued, despite some positive developments. Violence against women and girls, including violations of their sexual and reproductive rights, remained a concern. The government deployed the armed forces in response to a rise in gang violence in the street and unrest in prisons. Indigenous Peoples continued to call for their human rights to be recognized in law and in practice.

Background

The country was gripped by high levels of gang violence and disturbances in prisons. Calls from some members of Congress to reinstate the death penalty in response to the high levels of violence were quashed by the executive.

In February, El Salvador's human rights record was assessed under the UN Universal Periodic Review and the Salvadoran authorities took the positive step of extending an open invitation to the UN and Inter-American special experts on human rights. The UN Human Rights Council urged El Salvador to improve public security, eradicate violence against women and ensure justice and reparation for victims of the internal armed conflict.

Impunity

In January, President Funes signed into law an Executive Decree creating a new National Search Commission for Disappeared Children to look for children who were forcibly disappeared during the armed conflict (1980-1992). The Decree was a response to a 2005 Inter-American Court of Human Rights' order in the case of the Serrano Cruz sisters. The two girls were last seen in 1982, aged seven and three, when they were captured by the military. By the end of the year, however, the new Commission was still not operational and the whereabouts of hundreds of disappeared children remained unknown.

The 1993 Amnesty Law, which obstructs efforts to bring to justice those responsible for human rights violations during the internal armed conflict, remained in place, despite public commitments by the government to take steps towards its repeal.

Violence against women and girls

High numbers of women and girls were abducted and killed. Many were raped and their bodies mutilated. According to the statistics of the National Police, some 477 women and girls were murdered between January and October, a rise of 224 compared with the same period in 2008. In November, thousands of women and girls took to the streets to protest at the failure to bring those responsible for such crimes to justice and to demand that the authorities develop and implement measures to prevent and punish violence against women and girls.

In October, the UN Human Rights Committee called on El Salvador to take action to prevent violence against women and girls and ensure justice for such crimes. The Committee also found that the total ban on abortion, including when pregnancy is a result of rape or endangering the life of women or girls, breached El Salvador's legal obligations to protect women and girls' human rights.

Indigenous Peoples' rights

The government failed to fulfil a pre-election commitment to recognize Indigenous Peoples' rights in law. By the end of the year, El Salvador had not recognized Indigenous Peoples' rights in its Constitution and had still not signed the ILO Convention No. 169.

In July, the Secretary for Social Inclusion announced that a memorandum of understanding had been signed by several government departments to work towards better protection of the rights of Indigenous Peoples. Indigenous groups acknowledged that the memorandum was potentially positive, but reiterated the urgent need for their rights to be recognized in law.

Public security

In June, 17 people were killed when the bus they were in was set alight during gang violence in the city of San Salvador. In response to gang violence and disturbances in several prisons during June, the government deployed military personnel in several prisons and certain districts of San Salvador.

E

Membership of a gang was made a criminal offence in September. There were serious concerns about how the law would be implemented, including fears that it could be used to persecute former gang members, those working to rehabilitate them or people associated with members or former members of gangs.

EQUATORIAL GUINEA

REPUBLIC OF EQUATORIAL GUINEA

Head of state:	Teodoro Obiang Nguema Mbasogo
Head of government:	Ignacio Milán Tang
Death penalty:	retentionist
Population:	0.7 million
Life expectancy:	51 years
Under-5 mortality (m/f):	177/160 per 1,000
Adult literacy:	93 per cent

Four people abducted from Benin by Equatorial Guinean security personnel were executed immediately after being sentenced to death by a military court in August. The same court sentenced two prisoners of conscience to long prison terms, although a civilian court had already acquitted them of the charges. Prisoners of conscience were convicted after unfair trials; several were released in a presidential pardon. There were further reports of politically motivated arrests and harassment of political opponents. Soldiers and other security personnel unlawfully killed, tortured and ill-treated detainees and others with impunity. Freedom of expression and the press remained restricted.

Background

In March, when Equatorial Guinea's report under the UN Universal Periodic Review was adopted by the UN Human Rights Council, the government rejected all recommendations related to the abolition of the death penalty and ratification of the Rome Statute of the International Criminal Court.

Also in March, the Extractive Industries Transparency Initiative (EITI), an international voluntary initiative seeking to promote transparency in oil, gas and mining, rejected Equatorial Guinea's candidacy. The country had failed to comply with requirements, including participation in the EITI process by independent civil society groups and submission of an oil revenue report.

In June, President Obiang publicly pledged to improve human rights, expand press freedom, ensure judicial credibility and introduce transparency and accountability in the oil industry. None of these pledges was implemented by the end of the year.

In July, President Obiang decreed Portuguese as the country's third official language to support its bid for full membership of the Community of Portuguese Speaking Countries (CPLP), but the CPLP postponed making a decision.

In August, the UN Working Group on the use of mercenaries visited the country at the invitation of the government. However, they were not allowed to visit prisons.

In October, UNESCO suspended indefinitely the awarding of the UNESCO-Obiang international prize for the Study of Life Sciences. The award had been postponed in March and in June following worldwide opposition by NGOs and individuals.

Arbitrary arrests and detentions

Despite repeated promises to improve respect for human rights, the authorities arbitrarily arrested and detained dozens of political opponents. Most were released without charge but some were still held at the end of the year.

■ Marcos Manuel Ndong, a former prisoner of conscience and leading member of the opposition party, the Convergence for Social Democracy, was arbitrarily arrested in October. He had been summoned to Malabo Central Police Station by telephone and was arrested for possessing a confidential memorandum. He had been given the inter-ministerial memorandum and added it to his documents in support of an application to set up a savings bank. Apparently, under Equatorial Guinean law it is not illegal to possess a confidential document given by a third party. He was held at the police station for two weeks before being transferred to Malabo's Black Beach prison where he remained until his release without charge or trial on 7 December. The Malabo Court of Investigation and First Instance ignored a writ of habeas corpus lodged by his wife on 14 October.

Unfair trials

In March, prisoners of conscience Marcelino Nguema and Santiago Asumu, both members of the opposition

E

party People's Union (UP), and seven Nigerian nationals were unfairly tried by the Malabo Appeal Court – a court of first instance. The eight men and one woman were charged with attempting to assassinate President Obiang, in connection with an alleged attack on the presidential palace in February 2009. Eight other UP members had the charges against them dropped at the start of the trial. In April, the court acquitted Marcelino Nguema and Santiago Asumu while convicting and sentencing the seven Nigerians to 12 years' imprisonment each. The Nigerians, who were traders and fishermen, had been arrested at sea and were accused of taking part in the attack on the palace.

Despite being acquitted, Marcelino Nguema and Santiago Asumu remained in prison. In August they were tried again on the same charges by a military court which sentenced them to 20 years' imprisonment. Four others tried with them were sentenced to death (see below). None of the six defendants was informed about their trial until they arrived in court. None of them was interviewed by a judge or formally charged. Instead they were interrogated by high-ranking security personnel who were also involved in their torture.

Death penalty

José Abeso Nsue and Manuel Ndong Anseme, both former military officers, Jacinto Michá Obiang, a border guard, and Alipio Ndong Asumu, a civilian, were executed in Malabo on 21 August, within an hour of being sentenced to death by a military court using summary proceedings. They were convicted of attempting to assassinate President Obiang, treason and terrorism. Their trial was unfair and no evidence was presented in court to substantiate the charges other than confessions extracted under torture. They had no access to a defence lawyer. Two military officers with no legal training were allocated to them minutes before the trial started. The speedy execution denied them their right to appeal against their conviction and seek clemency. They were also denied the right to say goodbye to their families. A week later, President Obiang justified the speedy executions saying that the men presented an imminent threat to his life.

The four had been abducted by Equatorial Guinean security officers in January from Benin, where they had lived as refugees for several years. They were taken to Black Beach prison where they were secretly held until their trial in August. The Equatorial Guinean authorities had refused to acknowledge their detention.

Torture and other ill-treatment

Soldiers and police officers tortured and ill-treated detainees and others with impunity, particularly in Bata, despite a law prohibiting torture. At least two people reportedly died as a result of torture. The four men abducted from Benin and later executed were repeatedly tortured during their detention.

■ Manuel Napo Pelico died in July in Basakato de la Sagrada Familia, Bioko Island. Soldiers went to his house to arrest him for refusing to take part in the collective cleaning of the village. They reportedly hit him on the head with the butt of a gun, then dragged him to the military barracks where they left him unconscious and bleeding. When they realized he was dying, they took him back to his home where he died soon after. By the end of the year, his death had not been investigated and those responsible had not been brought to justice.

Prisoners of conscience – releases

Marcelino Nguema, Santiago Asumu and seven Nigerian nationals were released in October following a presidential pardon on the anniversary of independence. Five other prisoners of conscience serving long prison sentences for an alleged attack on Corisco Island in 2004 were released in August. The circumstances of their release were not clear.

Unlawful killings

Soldiers and police were reportedly responsible for unlawful killings.

■ Luis Ondo Mozuy and a friend were arrested on 13 March in Bata's Ncolombong neighbourhood. They had been involved in an argument with a group of youths who fled when a military patrol arrived. The two were taken to Bata police station. While his friend was put in a cell, Luis Ondo was taken out of the police station. A few hours later, soldiers took Luis Ondo's body to the morgue at Bata hospital and forced the official on duty to accept it without following established procedures. There was no investigation into this incident during the year.

Freedom of expression – journalists

Press freedom remained severely restricted with most media outlets controlled by the state. Journalists who asserted their independence faced harassment, dismissal and arrest.

■ Radio Bata journalist Pedro Luis Esono Edu was arrested without a warrant in February, immediately after

E

he reported the discovery of seven bodies, presumed victims of human trafficking, in a rubbish tip in the outskirts of Bata. He was held at Bata police station for three days before being released without charge.

■ In April, Samuel Obiang Mbani, correspondent of African Press Agency and Agence France-Presse in Equatorial Guinea, was arrested at Malabo airport. He was there to cover the arrival of heads of state from the Economic and Monetary Community of Central Africa. He was held at Malabo police station for five hours before being released.

Forced evictions

The government still did not provide compensation or alternative accommodation for the hundreds of families forcibly evicted from their homes in recent years. Residents of Bata remained at risk of being forcibly evicted from their homes to make way for urban development projects.

ERITREA

STATE OF ERITREA

Head of state and government:	Isaias Afewerki
Death penalty:	abolitionist in practice
Population:	5.2 million
Life expectancy:	60.4 years
Under-5 mortality (m/f):	78/71 per 1,000
Adult literacy:	65.3 per cent

Widespread human rights violations were routine. The government severely restricted freedom of expression and freedom of religion. No opposition parties, independent journalism or civil society organizations, or unregistered faith groups were allowed. The authorities used arbitrary arrests, detentions and torture to stifle opposition, holding thousands of political prisoners in dire conditions, many in secret detention. Military conscription was compulsory and deserters, draft evaders and their families were harassed, imprisoned and ill-treated. A "shoot to kill" policy against anyone attempting to flee across the border remained in place.

Background

President Isaias Afewerki and the ruling People's Front for Democracy and Justice, the only permitted political party, exerted complete control over the state without a hint of indefinitely delayed elections. There was no independent judiciary.

Eritrean society remained highly militarized. All adults faced compulsory national service which was frequently extended indefinitely.

The costs of mass military conscription contributed to a crippling of the national economy. Food shortages increased. The UN estimated that as many as two in every three Eritreans were malnourished, but the government restricted food aid and humanitarian access, apparently as a way of controlling and punishing the population, and limiting external influence.

Large numbers of mainly young Eritreans fled the country. The government continued to implement a "shoot to kill" policy for those caught trying to cross the border.

The UN Security Council continued to apply sanctions against Eritrea, including an arms embargo, on the grounds that it was supporting Somali armed groups and for failing to resolve a border dispute with Djibouti.

For the first half of the year Eritrea maintained a troop presence in the disputed Ras Doumeira area and Doumeira island of Djibouti, despite a Security Council resolution calling for Eritrean withdrawal. In June, Eritrea agreed to withdraw its troops and resolve the dispute with Djibouti through mediation by Qatar.

The Eritrea-Ethiopia Boundary Commission decision of 2002 requiring Ethiopia's withdrawal from the border village of Badme was not enforced; and the damages set out by the 2009 Claims Commission to be paid by both sides were not paid. The government used the pretext of the border dispute, and possible threat of future conflict, as justification for the severe curtailment of civil and political rights.

Freedom of religion

Only members of permitted faiths – the Eritrean Orthodox Church, the Roman Catholic and Lutheran churches, and Islam – were allowed to practise their religion. Members of banned minority faiths faced harassment, arrest, incommunicado detention and torture. Many were arrested while worshipping clandestinely in private homes or at weddings or funerals.

Up to 3,000 Christians from unregistered church groups were held in detention during the year, including 60 Jehovah's Witnesses who were known to be in detention in May. Among the 60 were Paulos Eyassu, Isaac Mogos and Negede Teklemariam, detained since 1994 without trial.

A clampdown on Evangelical Christians, in particular the Full Gospel Church, in the Southern Zone (province) was reported in October. Up to 40 men and women were arrested and detained incommunicado, reportedly on the orders of the governor of the Southern Zone.

■ Senait Oqbazgi Habta, a 28-year-old woman, reportedly died in April at the Sawa Military Training Centre. She had been detained for approximately two years for attending a Bible study group. She was detained in a shipping container and denied medication for malaria and anaemia.

Prisoners of conscience and other political prisoners

Large numbers of political prisoners and prisoners of conscience continued to be detained indefinitely without charge, trial or access to legal counsel. They included suspected critics of the government, political activists, journalists, religious practitioners, draft evaders, military deserters and failed asylum-seekers forcibly returned to Eritrea. Many were held in incommunicado detention for long periods, including political prisoners detained since a government clampdown in 2001. The whereabouts and health status of most remained unknown. Prisoners' families faced reprisals for inquiring about them.

■ The G-15 group, prisoners of conscience detained without charge or trial since 2001, continued to be held in secret detention. During 2010 the government again did not respond to allegations that nine of the G-15 had died in detention.

■ Prisoner of conscience Dawit Isaak, a journalist detained in the 2001 clampdown, remained in detention, allegedly in Eiraeiro Prison. He was reportedly in poor mental and physical health.

Freedom of expression – journalists

The government tightly controlled all media and reacted with hostility to any perceived criticism. All independent journalism has been effectively banned since 2001. Numerous journalists remained in incommunicado detention without charge or trial. In many cases the government refused to confirm their location or health status.

■ Yirgalem Fisseha Mebrahtu, a Radio Bana journalist arrested in February 2009 when the authorities closed the station, was reportedly placed in solitary confinement in Mai Swra Prison in May.

Eritrean journalists in the US-based diaspora community reported government surveillance and harassment by Eritrean-government supporters within the USA.

Refugees and asylum-seekers

Many Eritreans fled the country. Families of refugees faced severe reprisals for the flight of their relatives, including fines and prison sentences.

The guidelines issued by UNHCR, the UN refugee agency, in 2009, recommending that states refrain from forcibly returning rejected Eritrean asylum-seekers to Eritrea, remained in force. As of January 2010, 223,562 Eritrean refugees and asylum-seekers were living abroad, according to official figures.

■ In June, Eritrean detainees at the Misratah detention centre in Libya were forced by officials to be photographed and to complete bio-data forms provided by the Eritrean embassy.

■ Yonas Mehari and Petros Mulugeta returned to Germany and were granted asylum in 2010. The two men were asylum-seekers forcibly deported by the German authorities to Eritrea in 2008. They were detained after their return, Yonas Mehari in an overcrowded underground cell and Petros Mulugeta in a shipping container. Both men recounted inhumane conditions, including disease, insanity and death among fellow detainees.

Military conscription

A significant proportion of the population was engaged in compulsory national service, which was mandatory for men and women over the age of 18. An initial period of 18 months' service includes six months' military service and 12 months' deployment in military or government service. This often involves forced labour in state projects. Conscripts perform construction labour on government projects such as road building, work in the civil service or work for companies owned and operated by the military or ruling party elites. Conscripts are paid minimal salaries that do not meet the basic needs of their families. National service can be extended indefinitely and is also followed by reserve duties.

Penalties for desertion and draft evasion were harsh, and included torture and detention without trial.

E

Torture and other ill-treatment

The use of torture in detention facilities was widespread. Detainees, including prisoners of conscience, were often tortured and ill-treated. The most frequent forms of torture reported were whippings, beatings and being tied with ropes in painful positions for prolonged periods.

Prison conditions were extremely harsh, with many prisoners held in overcrowded, unhygienic and damp conditions. Large numbers of detainees were held in underground cells and others were locked in metal shipping containers, many in desert locations creating extreme temperatures. Prisoners were given inadequate food and unclean drinking water. Almost no medical assistance was available. Various prisoners of conscience and political prisoners were reported to have died in detention, but most reports were not confirmed by the authorities.

■ Hana Hagos Asgedom, a Christian imprisoned for nearly four years for her religious beliefs, died in January. She was reportedly beaten with an iron rod for refusing the sexual advances of an officer at the Alla Military Camp and died from a heart attack soon after.

ETHIOPIA

FEDERAL DEMOCRATIC REPUBLIC OF ETHIOPIA

Head of state:	Girma Wolde-Giorgis
Head of government:	Meles Zenawi
Death penalty:	retentionist
Population:	85 million
Life expectancy:	56.1 years
Under-5 mortality (m/f):	138/124 per 1,000
Adult literacy:	35.9 per cent

The ruling Ethiopian People's Revolutionary Democratic Front (EPRDF) won the parliamentary elections in May, which took place in a context of intimidation, harassment and restrictions on freedom of association and assembly. Legislation that severely limits human rights activities came into force. The independent press was severely restricted. State resources, assistance and opportunities were broadly used to control the population.

Background

Parliamentary and State Council elections took place in May. The EPRDF and a small coalition of affiliated parties won 99.6 per cent of parliamentary seats. An opposition coalition, Medrek, the Forum for Democratic Dialogue in Ethiopia, accused the government of electoral fraud and called for a rerun. The National Electoral Board rejected the call and a subsequent appeal to the Federal Supreme Court was dismissed.

The final report of the EU Election Observation Mission stated that the elections fell short of international commitments. The findings highlighted the lack of a level playing field for all contesting parties; violations of freedom of expression, assembly and movement of opposition party members; misuse of state resources by the ruling party; and a lack of independent media coverage. The Prime Minister described the report as "useless trash" and the Chief EU Observer was not granted access to Ethiopia to present the final report.

Ethiopia was considered to have one of the fastest growing economies in Africa. The government received praise from the UN for being on track to halve its poverty rate by 2015. However, the UN also stated that increasing inequality in urban areas and poor education standards were obstacles to development and that Ethiopia was not making sufficient progress on gender equality and maternal mortality.

Pre-election violence and repression

State resources, assistance and opportunities were used repeatedly before May's elections as leverage to pressure citizens to leave opposition parties. Education opportunities, civil service jobs and food assistance were often contingent on membership of the ruling party. Immediately prior to the election, voters in Addis Ababa were reportedly threatened with the withdrawal of state assistance if they did not vote for the EPRDF.

The build-up to the elections was punctuated by incidents of political violence.

■ Aregawi Gebreyohannes, a candidate for Arena-Tigray, one of the opposition parties forming Medrek, was stabbed to death by six unidentified men in Tigray on 2 March. The government rejected opposition claims that the attack was politically motivated and said it had been a "personal quarrel" in a bar. A man was tried and sentenced to 15 years' imprisonment. The opposition said that the trial was "arranged and orchestrated" and that Aregawi Gebreyohannes had previously been subjected to government harassment.

Other killings were also reported. The Oromo Federalist Congress party reported that Biyansa Daba, an opposition activist, was beaten to death on 7 April because of his political activities. In May, the government announced that a policeman had been stabbed to death by two opposition members who had confessed and were carrying Medrek identity cards. Their trial and conviction reportedly took place within one week. On 23 and 24 May, two members of the Oromo People's Congress party were shot in Oromia. The opposition stated that the government's aim was to stop protests; the government stated that the men had been trying to storm a ballot collection office.

Medrek reported in February that armed men were preventing its members from registering as candidates.

Opposition parties said that their members were harassed, beaten and detained by the EPRDF in the build-up to the elections. Hundreds of people were allegedly arrested arbitrarily in the Oromia region, often on the grounds of supporting the Oromo Liberation Front (OLF), an armed group. Detention without trial, torture and killings of Oromos were reported. On 7 February, Dr Merera Gudina, leader of the Oromo People's Congress party and the Chairman of Medrek, told the media that at least 150 Oromo opposition officials had been arrested in less than five months.

Freedom of expression – journalists

Ethiopia's independent press was barely able to function. Journalists worked in a climate of fear because of the threat of state harassment and prosecution. Information was closely controlled by state bodies including the Radio and Television Agency (ERTA) and Ethiopian Press, the state publisher.

■ In January, Ezeden Muhammad, editor and publisher of Ethiopia's largest Islamic weekly, *Hakima*, was sentenced to one year's imprisonment for "incitement" in connection with a 2008 column criticizing comments made by the Prime Minister. In September, Ezeden Muhammad was released, but his 17-year-old son Akram Ezeden, who had been acting as editor during his father's detention, was arrested on the same day. He was later released and the case against him dropped.
■ On 4 March, Voice of America reported that its Amharic-language broadcasts were being jammed. On 19 March, the Prime Minister declared that the radio station had been broadcasting "destabilizing

propaganda" and compared it to Radio Mille Collines, a Rwandan radio station that incited ethnic hatred before and during the 1994 Rwandan genocide.
■ In May, Woubshet Taye, editor-in-chief of the *Awramba Times*, resigned following a warning from the Ethiopian Broadcasting Authority that he would be "responsible for any bloodshed that may occur in connection with the coming election". The *Awramba Times* had featured an article the week before about a pro-democracy demonstration during the 2005 election period.

In March, the Supreme Court reinstated fines imposed in 2007 on four independent publishing companies in the wake of a post-election crackdown in 2005, but overturned by a presidential pardon the same year. The publishers could not pay the re-imposed fines. The High Court was asked by the government to freeze the assets of the publishers and their spouses.

Internet content was censored by the state and some websites were blocked. The National Electoral Board introduced a press code which restricted journalistic activities during the elections, including a ban on interviews with voters, candidates and observers on election day.

The Mass Media and Freedom of Information Proclamation remained in force, giving the government disproportionate power to launch defamation cases, issue financial penalties and refuse media registrations and licences.

Human rights defenders

The Charities and Societies Proclamation, passed in 2009, took effect. The legislation imposed strict controls on civil society organizations and provided for criminal penalties, including fines and imprisonment. Local NGOs were barred from working on issues of human rights and democracy if more than 10 per cent of their income came from foreign sources. The law made human rights defenders fearful of working and led to self-censorship.

Some organizations significantly altered their mandates and ceased their work on human rights. Several human rights defenders fled abroad fearing government harassment following the implementation of the law.

A small number of organizations continued working on human rights and democracy issues, including the Ethiopian Human Rights Council (EHRCO) and the Ethiopian Women Lawyers Association (EWLA), although both were forced to reduce staff numbers and close offices due to the new funding rules. At

E

the end of the year, EHRCO had only three offices (compared to 12 previously). Despite successfully re-registering with the Charities and Societies Agency, the enforcing body, the bank accounts of EHRCO and EWLA were frozen in late 2009 and remained frozen at the end of 2010.

Counter-terror and security

The Anti-Terrorism Proclamation, whose broad definition of terrorism appears to criminalize freedom of expression and peaceful assembly, remained in place. The threat of prosecution contributed to a climate of self-censorship including among journalists, who can be prosecuted for publishing articles referring to individuals or groups deemed to be "terrorists".

Prisoners of conscience and political prisoners

A large number of political prisoners and possible prisoners of conscience remained in detention.

The government continued to imprison numerous ethnic Oromos on accusations of supporting the OLF. These charges often appeared to be politically motivated.

■ In March, 15 Oromo men and women were convicted of membership of the OLF in a group trial and given sentences ranging from 10 years' imprisonment to death. The 15 – arrested in 2008 along with other Oromos who were subsequently released – came from a variety of professions, and many did not know each other before being arrested and tried as a group. There were concerns that the trial fell short of international standards and was politically motivated in the run-up to the elections. Many of the detainees reported that they had been tortured. Two male detainees who were released before the trial died immediately after their release, reportedly as a result of their treatment in detention.

■ Prisoner of conscience Birtukan Mideksa, leader of the Unity for Democracy and Justice Party, was released in October. She had been detained since December 2008 following a previous two-year imprisonment.

Conflicts in the Somali and Oromia regions

Low-level conflict continued between the OLF and government forces. Ethiopian refugee children reported that they had been forcibly recruited by the OLF in Kenya and trafficked back to Ethiopia to serve as porters and cooks.

Clashes continued in the Somali region in the long-running conflict between the Ogaden National Liberation Front (ONLF) and government forces. The ONLF published a statement on 4 February calling on the AU to investigate human rights violations, in particular alleged war crimes by government forces in the region. Access to the Somali region for international journalists and certain humanitarian organizations was restricted by the government and it remained largely inaccessible. A Voice of America journalist was expelled from Ethiopia in June after reporting on clashes between the government and the ONLF.

On 12 October, a peace deal was reportedly signed between a breakaway faction of the ONLF and the government. It was reported that under the agreement, members of the faction received immunity from prosecution and prisoners taken by the government would be released. The main ONLF group reportedly dismissed the deal as "irrelevant".

In November, reports were received that over 100 civilians had been detained in the town of Degeh Bur and transferred to a military prison in Jijiga. In December, it was reported that Ethiopian troops had burnt a village in the Qorahey zone, resulting in the deaths of three civilians.

Death penalty

Death sentences were imposed but no executions were reported.

■ A former regional official, Jemua Ruphael, was sentenced to death in June for murder and supporting an Eritrean-backed armed group.

■ Hassan Mohammed Mahmoud, a former member of the armed Somali group Al-Itihad Al-Islamiya, was found guilty in March of committing terrorist acts in the 1990s and sentenced to death.

Amnesty International visits/reports

▨ Ethiopia: Amnesty International calls on the Government of Ethiopia not to execute Melaku Tefera (AFR 25/001/2010)
▨ Ethiopia releases opposition leader, 6 October 2010

FIJI

REPUBLIC OF THE FIJI ISLANDS

Head of state:	Ratu Epeli Nailatikau
Head of government:	Josaia Voreqe Bainimarama
Death penalty:	abolitionist for ordinary crimes
Population:	0.9 million
Life expectancy:	69.2 years
Under-5 mortality (m/f):	25/24 per 1,000

The military-led government continued to rule without a constitution, and repressive Public Emergency Regulations (PER) remained in place. The government continued to restrict freedom of expression; critics of the government, including members of the Methodist Church, were among those targeted. A new law was passed, stifling media freedom. Human rights defenders were intimidated and persecuted through the courts or directly through the use of the PER. A new decree addressing violence against women had yet to be implemented by the courts and the police.

Freedom of expression

In January, a senior military officer announced that anyone critical of the government would face reprisals from the military. That same month, officials from the Prime Minister's office indefinitely suspended 20 workers of the Suva City Council, alleging that they were anti-government bloggers. The authorities warned the workers that they would be persecuted by the security forces if they took action in the courts. A nine-month investigation revealed no evidence against the workers. They remained suspended with little or no recourse to justice.

Dozens of pensioners said to be critical of the regime had their pensions suspended under the Pensions and Retirement Allowances Decree which came into force in January. However, the government repealed the decree in May.

In June, the Media Industry Development (MID) Decree was passed establishing the Fiji Media Industry Development Authority. The Authority ensures that local media do not publish material deemed to threaten public interest or order. It has wide powers of investigation over journalists and media outlets, including powers of search and seizure. The Media Tribunal, established under the MID Decree, will decide on complaints referred by the

Authority and can impose jail terms and large fines. Despite these extensive punitive powers, the tribunal will not be bound by formal rules of evidence.

■ In August, a journalist who published an article alleging that the Commissioner of Police had been sacked by the government was detained, questioned and threatened by the security forces, and forced to reveal his source for the story.

■ In October, a television journalist was detained and threatened with prosecution under the PER for reporting on the arrest and detention of former Prime Minister Mahendra Chaudhry.

Freedom of association

The Prime Minister continued to ban the Methodist Church from holding its annual conference. He accused church ministers of spying on the military for the government ousted in a 2006 coup.

In October, former Prime Minister Mahendra Chaudhry and five of his associates were detained in the town of Rakiraki for more than 48 hours and charged with breaching the PER by attending a public meeting with three or more people without the approval of the authorities.

Human rights defenders

In January, prominent human rights lawyer Imrana Jalal and her husband were investigated by the Fiji Independent Commission Against Corruption and charged with seven misdemeanour offences relating to the Public Health (Hotels, Restaurant and Refreshment Bars) Regulations, the Food Safety Act and the Penal Code. The charges were politically motivated.

Imrana Jalal had spoken out against human rights violations committed by the military when it overthrew the Laisenia Qarase-led government in December 2006. In July, the court ruled that there had been an abuse of due process and all charges against her were dismissed. Her husband continued to face charges on a related matter concerning his employment in a government-owned company.

■ In January, army officers threatened and intimidated trade unionist Pramod Rae to prevent him from organizing a strike at his workplace, the Bank of Baroda.

■ In February, the Prime Minister warned two human rights defenders that they could be detained at the army barracks because of statements they made on the country's judiciary at Fiji's Universal Periodic Review in Geneva.

F

■ In February, trade unionist Attar Singh was taken from his office to the army barracks in Suva, threatened and then released. In 2007, he had been detained in the same barracks where the military assaulted and threatened to kill him.

Violence against women and girls

High levels of physical and sexual violence against women and girls continued to be reported in the media and by women's organizations. Despite government announcements declaring that the Domestic Violence Decree 2009 had come into force, activists continued to assert that the Decree had not been implemented and that stakeholders, including police, were still not aware of its provisions or how to implement them.

FINLAND

REPUBLIC OF FINLAND

Head of state:	Tarja Halonen
Head of government:	Mari Kiviniemi (replaced Matti Vanhanen in June)
Death penalty:	abolitionist for all crimes
Population:	5.3 million
Life expectancy:	80.1 years
Under-5 mortality (m/f):	5/4 per 1,000

Women were not sufficiently protected in law or in practice against violence. Unaccompanied children seeking asylum were detained. Conscientious objectors to military service were imprisoned.

Violence against women and girls

In May, the Ministry of Justice recommended amendments to the Penal Code regarding rape and sexual abuse, including that sexual intercourse when the victim is incapable of giving genuine consent, for instance because of illness or intoxication, should be categorized as rape. Despite these recommendations, rape continued to be categorized in law according to the degree of violence used or threatened by the perpetrator, and some acts of sexual violence were still only investigated and prosecuted if requested by the victim. Women, therefore, remained inadequately protected from rape and other forms of sexual violence.

In August, the CEDAW Committee reiterated its concerns regarding the use of mediation procedures in domestic violence cases. It noted that such procedures could potentially lead to the re-victimization of women who have suffered violence and that insufficient research had been carried out on the effects of mediation on domestic violence court proceedings.

In September, the government adopted the National Action Plan 2010-2015 to reduce violence against women. However, no additional state funding was granted to implement the plan, raising concerns that it would not be adequately resourced.

Refugees and asylum-seekers

The Asylum Act continued to provide for an accelerated asylum procedure, which allows for the expulsion of an asylum-seeker while their appeal is pending. Consequently, a number of asylum-seekers were denied effective appeal.

Finnish law continued to allow for the detention of children seeking asylum, including unaccompanied children. In 2010, at least 17 children, four of whom were unaccompanied, were held in detention. Due to the lack of facilities, a number of asylum-seekers were detained in unsuitable facilities, including police stations and prisons.

Justice for crimes under international law

In June, François Bazaramba, a Rwandan national residing in Finland, was sentenced to life imprisonment by the District Court of Itä-Uusimaa for committing genocide in Rwanda in 1994. During the proceedings, allegations were made that several witness testimonies had been obtained directly as a result of torture by the Rwandan authorities. The Court determined that, to ensure a fair trial, it would disregard the testimony of two witnesses, after finding that it was likely that their evidence had been obtained through torture or other ill-treatment. The judgement was appealed and proceedings were ongoing at the end of the year.

Prisoners of conscience

Conscientious objectors to military service continued to be imprisoned for refusing the alternative civilian service due to its punitive and discriminatory length. The length of alternative civilian service remained at 362 days, more than double the most common military service period of 180 days.

FRANCE

FRENCH REPUBLIC
Head of state:	**Nicolas Sarkozy**
Head of government:	**François Fillon**
Death penalty:	**abolitionist for all crimes**
Population:	**62.6 million**
Life expectancy:	**81.6 years**
Under-5 mortality (m/f):	**5/4 per 1,000**

Allegations of police ill-treatment continued, and investigations into such allegations were slow to progress. A draft law on migration and asylum was incompatible with the right to seek asylum. The Constitutional Council found that the rules on pre-charge detention for ordinary criminal offences were unconstitutional. Roma and Travellers were stigmatized and targeted for forced evictions and expulsions.

Torture and other ill-treatment

In its concluding observations of 14 May 2010, the UN Committee against Torture expressed concern at the persistent allegations of ill-treatment by French law enforcement officials, and urged the authorities to carry out prompt, transparent and independent investigations into such allegations, and ensure adequate punishment for perpetrators.

■ On 4 November, the European Court of Human Rights found that France had violated the European Convention on Human Rights' prohibition of torture and other ill-treatment in the case *Darraj v. France*. In July 2001, Yassine Darraj, a 16-year-old French national, was taken for an identity check to a police station, where police officers handcuffed him and used force which required an emergency operation and resulted in his unfitness for work for 21 days. The Court ruled that the 800 euro fine for "involuntary injuries", to which two of the police officers were sentenced on appeal, was inadequate.

Deaths in custody

Investigations into deaths in custody appeared to lack independence and impartiality and were slow to progress.

■ On 17 May, the National Commission on Security Ethics (CNDS) called for disciplinary proceedings against the police officers who had allegedly used disproportionate force against Ali Ziri, a 69-year-old Algerian, following his arrest in Argenteuil on 9 June 2009. Ali Ziri had been travelling in his friend Arezki Kerfali's car when they were stopped by police. Arezki Kerfali said the police beat them, and both men were taken to hospital, where Ali Ziri died. Arezki Kerfali was charged with insulting a police officer and the hearing was scheduled to be held on 24 June, but was postponed pending a ruling on the case of Ali Ziri.

■ In March, the judge investigating the death of Abou Bakari Tandia, who died in January 2005 from injuries sustained in police custody, questioned three forensic doctors who issued a report in July 2009 which contradicted the police's version of events. The doctors found that there had been a row between Abou Bakari Tandia and the police officers involved in his detention, which further put into question their claim that his injuries were caused by him throwing himself against his cell wall. In November the judge questioned the police officers as witnesses to the events.

■ In September, the Aix-en-Provence Court of Appeal quashed the decision by the investigating judges to close the investigation against two police officers suspected of the involuntary homicide of Abdelhakim Ajimi, who died after being restrained by police during his arrest in May 2008. In April, the CNDS had recommended disciplinary proceedings against the police officers for disproportionate and unnecessary use of force.

■ Over a year after the launch of a criminal investigation into the "involuntary homicide" of Mohamed Boukrourou, the police officers involved in his arrest had not been questioned, and no disciplinary proceedings against them had been started. On 12 November 2009, four police officers had arrested Mohamed Boukrourou following an argument at his local pharmacy, handcuffed him and asked him to follow them. Witnesses stated that when he refused, the officers dragged him out and threw him into their van where he was beaten and kicked. Less than two hours later, he was dead. His family said that when they saw his body, his face was covered in bruises, his lip was split and his cheek was torn. Two forensic reports, one carried out at the request of the public prosecutor in November 2009 and a second one at the request of his family in June 2010, noted injuries on his body that could have been caused by blows and stated heart failure as the probable cause of death. Both requested further medical examinations to clarify the circumstances of his death, the results of which were pending at the end of the year. The CNDS and the

F

National Police General Inspectorate had also opened investigations in November 2009 and December 2009 respectively, both ongoing.

Guantánamo Bay detainees

■ On 26 February, the Cassation Court ordered the retrial for terrorism-related offences of five French nationals who had been detained in Guantánamo Bay and transferred to France in 2004 and 2005. In February 2009, the Paris Court of Appeal overturned a conviction by the Paris Criminal Court for "criminal association in relation to a terrorist enterprise" because it had illegally used information – provided by the French intelligence services – obtained during interrogation while the men were detained at Guantánamo Bay.

Refugees and asylum-seekers

In July, the Council of State partly annulled the decision by the Board of the Office for the Protection of Refugees and Stateless Persons which qualified 17 countries as "safe" when examining asylum applications. Claims submitted by asylum-seekers from "safe" countries are examined under an accelerated procedure, under which asylum-seekers can be forcibly returned without their appeal being examined. The Council of State decided that Armenia, Madagascar and Turkey did not fulfil the necessary human rights criteria to be on the list of "safe" countries, and considered Mali to be safe for men but not for women.

A draft law on migration and asylum under discussion in the parliament since September would be incompatible with international human rights standards. Under the law, if a group of 10 or more irregular migrants were intercepted near the French border, they would be kept in a "holding area" between the place of arrest and the border. Their applications to enter the rest of France to apply for asylum would be examined; if these were considered "manifestly unfounded" they would be returned to their country of origin, and would have only 48 hours to challenge the decision.

Legal, constitutional or institutional developments

In June, the Senate started examining the draft law on the mandate and powers of the new Defender of Rights institution, which is to merge the CNDS, the Defender of Children, the Ombudsperson, the Equal Opportunities and Anti-Discrimination Commission and the General Inspector of all Places of Deprivation of Liberty. There were fears that this would result in a loss of those institutions' expertise and independence.

On 30 July, the Constitutional Council ruled that the law regarding pre-charge detention (*garde à vue*) was unconstitutional because it did not guarantee detainees' rights of defence, such as effective assistance from a lawyer and being informed of the right to remain silent. However, the ruling stated that the law would remain in force until 1 July 2011. Even more restrictive rules, applicable to people suspected of involvement in terrorism-related activities, serious organized crime or drug trafficking, were not examined by the Council.

A subsequent proposal to modify the regime of pre-charge detention, that failed to meet all human rights concerns, was adopted by the government in October. A few days later, the Cassation Court ruled that the entire system of pre-charge detention was unlawful, including the provisions applicable to people suspected of involvement in terrorism-related activities, serious organized crime or drug trafficking.

Racism and discrimination

Roma and Travellers were stigmatized by government officials. During a ministerial meeting in July to discuss "the problems related to the behaviour of certain Roma and Travellers", President Nicolas Sarkozy referred to "illegal camps" inhabited by Roma as sources of criminality, calling on the government to dismantle those camps within three months. On 5 August, the Ministry of the Interior instructed prefects to systematically dismantle "illegal camps", explicitly prioritizing those inhabited by Roma, and to conduct "the immediate removal of foreigners in an irregular situation". Following its publication by the media, the order was removed and replaced on 13 September by one which referred to "any illegal settlement, whoever inhabits it". However, concerns remained that Roma were being marginalized and targeted for forced evictions and expulsions. In September, the government presented before the parliament a legislative proposal to facilitate the removal of foreigners, including EU nationals, who "abuse their right to a short stay" by repeatedly leaving and entering France.

In August, the CERD Committee expressed concern about discriminatory political speeches. The Committee was also concerned about the increase of racist violence against Roma, and about the difficulties faced by Travellers in exercising their rights to freedom of movement and to vote, and in their access to education and adequate housing.

In October, the Constitutional Council ruled that a law adopted by parliament in September, banning the wearing of clothing intended to cover the face in public, did not disproportionately restrict individual rights. However, it ruled that the ban could not be applied in public places of worship. The law gave rise to concerns that the ban would violate the freedoms of expression and religion of women who choose to wear the burqa or niqab as an expression of their identity or beliefs.

Amnesty International visits/reports

🚍 Amnesty International delegates visited France in September and October.

📰 France: Briefing to the UN Committee against Torture, April 2010 (EUR 21/002/2010)

GAMBIA

REPUBLIC OF THE GAMBIA

Head of state and government:	Yahya Jammeh
Death penalty:	abolitionist in practice
Population:	1.8 million
Life expectancy:	56.6 years
Under-5 mortality (m/f):	123/109 per 1,000
Adult literacy:	45.3 per cent

The government continued to restrict political freedom, stifle freedom of expression and commit human rights violations with impunity. Members of the National Intelligence Agency (NIA), army, police, and shadowy militias close to the President – known as ninjas, drug boys and jugglers – arbitrarily arrested and detained government opponents, human rights defenders, journalists and former security personnel. Torture and other ill-treatment in custody were reported. A second wave of mass arrests took place, culminating in the treason trial of eight prominent men, who were sentenced to death after a grossly unfair trial.

Arbitrary arrests and detentions

In a wave of arrests in March, which followed an earlier wave in November 2009, former government officials were accused of treason or attempts to destabilize the government. In all, several hundred former officials, military officers and civilians were detained. The detainees were overwhelmingly denied access to lawyers and relatives and held in conditions so harsh that they amounted to cruel, inhuman and degrading treatment.

The police, NIA and army continued to unlawfully arrest and detain people in violation of national law. Detainees were held in overcrowded and insanitary conditions in official places of detention such as the Mile 2 Central Prison, the NIA headquarters and police detention centres. They were also held in secret detention centres, including military barracks, secret quarters in police stations, police stations in remote areas and warehouses.

Death penalty

At least 20 people were believed to be on death row at the end of the year. No executions were reported; the last known execution was in the 1980s. In October the authorities increased the penalty for possession of more than 250g of cocaine or heroin to the death penalty.

Eight of the men arrested in March were convicted of treason and sentenced to death in July after a grossly unfair trial during which indictees and witnesses were tortured. The men were accused of procuring arms, ammunitions, equipment and mercenaries from Guinea to stage a coup. They included: former army chief Lang Tombong Tamba; former intelligence chief Lamin Bo Badjie; former deputy chief of police Modou Gaye; Brigadier General Omar Bun Mbaye; former NIA agent and then deputy Gambian Ambassador to Guinea-Bissau Gibril Ngorr Secka; former Kanilai Camp Commander Lieutenant Colonel Kawsu Camara; and two civilians – Abdoulie Joof and Yousef Ezziden.

Freedom of expression – journalists

Freedom of expression continued to be severely limited. Journalists faced threats and harassment if they wrote stories deemed unfavourable to the authorities or if they were believed to have provided such information to media outlets.

■ The regional ECOWAS Community Court in Abuja, Nigeria, heard the case of Musa Saidykhan, former

G

editor-in-chief of *The Independent*, a Banjul-based newspaper which was banned in 2006. Musa Saidykhan alleged that he was tortured after state security agents raided the newspaper in 2006, shut it down and imprisoned its staff. After his release, Musa Saidykhan fled to Senegal. In 2009, the Court had ruled against the Gambian government's objection to it hearing the case.

■ Journalist Ebrima Manneh of the *Daily Observer*, who was arrested in 2006, remained subjected to enforced disappearance despite a 2008 ruling by the ECOWAS Community Court of Justice demanding his release and damages for his family. The government and police officials continued to deny that he is in custody.

Human rights defenders

The climate of fear generated by the President's threats against human rights defenders in 2009 persisted.

■ Nigerian Edwin Nebolisa Nwakaeme, director of a Gambian human rights organization, Africa in Democracy and Good Governance, was arrested on 22 February by the Immigration Department, released three days later, then rearrested on 1 March. He was taken to court in March and charged with giving "false information". In September he was sentenced to six months' imprisonment with hard labour.

■ Two women, Dr Isatou Touray and Amie Bojang Sissoho, were arrested on Monday 11 October 2010 by Gambian security personnel, charged with theft, and sent to Mile 2 Central Prison, notorious for its ill-treatment of inmates and appalling prison conditions. Both women work for the Gambia Committee on Traditional Practices Affecting the Health of Women and Children (GAMCOTRAP), and their organization has faced harassment in the past.

Amnesty International visits/reports

📖 Gambia: human rights defender detained in Gambia (AFR 27/002/2010)

📖 Gambia: Amnesty International calls for investigation of human rights violations committed by security forces and for freedom of expression to be guaranteed (AFR 27/003/2010)

📖 Gambia: "Freedom Day" in The Gambia is a travesty (AFR 27/005/2010)

GEORGIA

GEORGIA
Head of state:	Mikheil Saakashvili
Head of government:	Nikoloz Gilauri
Death penalty:	abolitionist for all crimes
Population:	4.2 million
Life expectancy:	72 years
Under-5 mortality (m/f):	39/33 per 1,000
Adult literacy:	99.7 per cent

Concerns continued over the progress of investigations into crimes under international law during the war between Georgia and Russia in August 2008 and in its immediate aftermath. Despite some progress, solutions for the housing and integration of internally displaced people remained insufficient.

Background

The May municipal elections, while assessed favourably by international observers, were accompanied by reports of harassment and intimidation of some opposition candidates. In October, amendments to the Constitution due to enter into force in 2013 were made which will significantly reduce the presidential powers, and increase the powers of the Prime Minister and the government.

The situation remained tense in and around Abkhazia and South Ossetia, regions of Georgia which had declared themselves independent in 2008 following the war between Russia and Georgia. Discussions in Geneva which began that year as part of the ceasefire agreement remained largely deadlocked.

Civilians also continued to suffer from harassment and insecurity in the Gali region of Abkhazia, where shoot-outs, killings and acts of arson were reported in June.

Aftermath of armed conflict

There was no significant progress in investigating violations of international human rights and humanitarian law during the war in August 2008 and in its immediate aftermath, or in bringing the perpetrators to justice. In September the Council of Europe (CoE) Human Rights Commissioner reported "serious shortcomings" by all sides in the process of clarifying the fate of people missing since the war. The report also criticized the Georgian authorities' apparent failure to effectively investigate the fate of three Ossetian men who allegedly disappeared in Georgian-controlled territory in October 2008.

■ Six Ossetian men, held by the Georgian authorities following the war, were released in March, followed by the release of six people by the de facto authorities in South Ossetia in May. The CoE Human Rights Commissioner called for the release of the remaining people detained in Tskhinvali during and after the conflict in South Ossetia as their health was reportedly deteriorating.

■ On 26 July, prominent journalist and civil society activist Timur Tskhovrebov was attacked in Tskhinvali, South Ossetia, by a group of up to 10 people, leaving him with a knife wound to the neck, a broken finger and other injuries to his face and body. Four days earlier, Boris Chochiev, a senior official in the de facto South Ossetian administration, had condemned the Georgian-Ossetian Civic Forum in the Netherlands, which Timur Tskhovrebov attended, as traitorous and harmful to South Ossetian interests. By the end of the year, no effective investigation had been carried out into the attack.

■ Civilians continued to be detained and arrested in Georgia and South Ossetia for "illegal crossing" of the Administrative Boundary Line (the de facto border between Georgia and South Ossetia created as a result of the war). Incidents of prolonged detention became less frequent during the second part of the year.

The EU Monitoring Mission, the only international monitor with a conflict-related mandate, was denied access to Abkhazia and South Ossetia by the de facto authorities.

Internally displaced people

The government took steps to improve the living conditions of displaced people, for example by renovating some of the poorest accommodation and transferring the ownership to displaced people. However, some of the refurbished collective centres and newly built settlements did not meet international standards of adequate housing, due to insufficient access to water, sanitation and other essential services. Integration of displaced people remained slow; many continue to face obstacles in accessing employment, health care and social security.

Around 500 displaced people in Tbilisi faced forced evictions in June, July and August. The evictions breached international standards, and in several instances the authorities failed to provide

people with any alternative shelter or compensation. In August, the government halted all further evictions pending the adoption of new guidelines on housing which were finalized in October.

Police and security forces

In September, the European Committee for the Prevention of Torture reported some progress in preventing ill-treatment of people by police during pre-trial detention, but concerns remained regarding ill-treatment on arrest and in police stations.

New stop-and-search powers for the police were adopted on 24 September. Several local human rights organizations expressed concerns as the law failed to specify either the exact circumstances in which the police could use these powers, or the length of the time a person could be held under them.

Investigations stalled on the reported incidents of harassment, intimidation and beating of protesters by police and unknown masked men during demonstrations against the President between April and July 2009.

■ The government failed to effectively investigate and bring to justice police officers who had, according to reports, recklessly fired impact projectiles at demonstrators on 6 May 2009, injuring several people.

■ Details of an internal investigation by the Ministry of Interior into the alleged excessive use of force by police officers during the dispersal of peaceful demonstrators outside the Tbilisi police headquarters on 15 June 2009 were not publicly disclosed.

Violence against women and girls

The first state-funded shelters for victims of domestic violence were opened in Tbilisi and Gori. In March 2010, the Parliament adopted the "Law on Gender Equality", to address discrimination in employment, education, health and social services and family relations.

Amnesty International visits/reports

🚍 Amnesty International delegates visited Georgia in May and August.

▨ In the waiting room: Internally displaced people in Georgia (EUR 56/002/2010)

▨ Georgia: Civil society activists at risk in South Ossetia (EUR 56/004/2010)

▨ Thousands forcibly evicted in Georgia (EUR 56/005/2010)

▨ Adequate housing for internally displaced remains a concern (EUR 56/006/2010)

G

GERMANY

FEDERAL REPUBLIC OF GERMANY
Head of state: Christian Wulff (replaced Horst Köhler in July)
Head of government: Angela Merkel
Death penalty: abolitionist for all crimes
Population: 82.1 million
Life expectancy: 80.2 years
Under-5 mortality (m/f):   5/5 per 1,000

Responses to allegations of ill-treatment remained inadequate. Several federal states continued to forcibly return Roma to Kosovo despite their need for international protection.

International scrutiny

In February, the UN Special Rapporteur on racism recommended strengthening the mandate and increasing the resources of the Federal Anti-Discrimination Agency; including an explicit reference to racism as an aggravating circumstance in the criminal code; developing specific training for police officers, prosecutors and judges on the identification of hate crimes; and adopting special measures to ensure adequate representation of people with a migration background in state institutions.

Torture and other ill-treatment

The authorities' failure to ensure that human rights violations by the police were adequately investigated, insufficient information about procedures to file criminal complaints, and difficulties in the identification of police officers may have led to impunity for the perpetrators and jeopardized victims' access to justice and redress.

Allegations of ill-treatment continued and independent police complaints bodies mandated to investigate allegations of human rights violations by law enforcement officials were not established. Only a few federal states provided information on their websites about how to complain about police misconduct.

■ On 3 March, the Public Prosecutor's General Office terminated investigations in the alleged ill-treatment by police officers of a photojournalist during the 2007 Rostock G8 summit, claiming that it was impossible to identify them with sufficient certainty. Berlin was the only federal state to introduce compulsory individual identification for uniformed police – to be implemented in January 2011. No obligation for police officers to wear identity badges was in place in the rest of the country.

■ In the criminal proceedings into the death of Oury Jalloh, who died in 2005 of heat inhalation following a fire in his cell while in police custody in Dessau, the Federal Court of Justice overruled the acquittal of one police officer on 7 January and ordered a retrial. The first instance proceedings, concluded in 2008, had highlighted serious shortcomings in the thoroughness of the early stage of the investigations.

■ According to protesters, the police, deployed to protect a large infrastructure project in Stuttgart, used excessive force during a demonstration on 30 September. On 27 October, the regional parliament of Baden-Württemberg set up a commission of inquiry into the police operation. The Public Prosecutor was investigating the allegations at the end of the year.

Refugees and asylum-seekers

Several federal states continued to forcibly return Roma, Ashkali and Egyptians to Kosovo despite the risk of persecution, and discrimination resulting in lack of access to education, health care, housing and social benefits on their return. However, North Rhine-Westphalia issued a decree on 21 September requiring an individual risk assessment to precede forcible returns of Roma, Ashkali and Egyptians to Kosovo and on 1 December introduced a four-month moratorium on forced returns due to the cold of the Kosovan winter.

During the year, 55 asylum-seekers were transferred to Greece under the Dublin II Regulation, despite the lack of a functioning asylum system in that country. In several cases the Constitutional Court suspended transfers, pending a final decision.

On 15 July, the government informed the UN Secretary-General that it had withdrawn its reservations on the UN Convention on the Rights of the Child, insisting that no changes were required in its asylum legislation. As a result, children aged 16 and 17 continued to go through asylum procedures as adults, without the assistance of a guardian.

■ Khaled Kenjo, a Syrian Kurd who was forcibly returned to Syria in 2009 and subsequently detained and sentenced to a short prison term for "spreading abroad false information that could harm the reputation of the [Syrian] state", was allowed to return to Germany in July and was granted refugee status.

■ Eritrean nationals Yonas Haile Mehari and Petros Aforki Mulugeta, who had been forcibly returned to Eritrea in 2008, returned to Germany in April and June respectively after they had been granted refugee status in 2009 in their absence.

Counter-terror and security

In February, a UN study on secret detention concluded that Germany was complicit in the secret detention of German-Syrian national Muhammad Zammar, who was unlawfully transferred to Syria in December 2001. Evidence before a parliamentary inquiry held from 2006 to 2009 confirmed that German agents had interrogated him in Syria in November 2002 and had also sent questions to the Syrian authorities for use in his interrogation. However, the June 2009 parliamentary inquiry report concluded that the German authorities were not complicit in any human rights violations related to this case. The authorities have since refused to commit to a new investigation into their role in renditions.

The government confirmed that it would continue to rely on "diplomatic assurances" to allegedly mitigate the danger of torture and other ill-treatment when returning people to their country of origin.

■ In May, the High Administrative Court in North Rhine-Westphalia confirmed the 2009 decision of the Administrative Court in Düsseldorf that, in the case of a Tunisian national suspected of terrorism-related activities, the use of "diplomatic assurances" undermined the absolute ban on torture. As a result, his forcible return to Tunisia was not allowed.

■ On 16 September, a stateless Palestinian and a Syrian national, both released from Guantánamo Bay, received protection in the Hamburg and the Rhineland-Palatinate federal states respectively. The Federal Minister of the Interior announced that no more former detainees from Guantánamo Bay would be given protection by Germany.

■ On 7 December, the Cologne Administrative Court dismissed a case brought by German national Khaled El-Masri. He had called on Germany to reconsider its decision not to pursue the extradition of 13 US nationals suspected of transferring him illegally to Afghanistan in 2004. The Court argued that the government acted lawfully, since Khaled El-Masri's request was assessed against Germany's national security and foreign policy interests. Khaled El-Masri appealed against the verdict.

Amnesty International visits/reports

📕 Unknown assailant: Insufficient investigation into alleged ill-treatment by police in Germany (EUR 23/002/2010)

📕 Open secret: Mounting evidence of Europe's complicity in rendition and secret detention (EUR 01/023/2010)

GHANA

REPUBLIC OF GHANA

Head of state and government:	John Evans Atta Mills
Death penalty:	abolitionist in practice
Population:	24.3 million
Life expectancy:	57.1 years
Under-5 mortality (m/f):	119/115 per 1,000
Adult literacy:	65.8 per cent

Threats to freedom of expression grew. Thousands of people were forcibly evicted and thousands remained under threat of forced eviction. The criminal justice system remained slow, and prisons were overcrowded and poorly resourced. Violence against women continued to be pervasive.

Background

A Constitution Review Commission was inaugurated by President Mills in January to conduct public consultations on the 1992 Constitution. It received over 60,000 submissions during the year.

In February, March and April, intra-communal violence in the Bunkpurugu/Yunyoo District of the Northern Region left at least five dead and over 300 houses burned down. Thousands of people fled their homes, some crossing into Togo. At least five people were killed and several houses burned down in May in renewed inter-communal violence in Bawku in the Upper East Region. The ongoing violence prevented local residents from carrying out normal farming and trading activities, resulting in food shortages and leaving approximately 2,000 families in need of food aid.

Freedom of expression

Threats to freedom of expression grew. At least six people were arrested, detained or prosecuted for "causing fear and panic".

■ In October, Amina Mohammad was arrested after saying on a local radio station in Tema that there had been an armed robbery and rape on a bus. She was charged with "causing fear and panic", denied bail by the Accra Circuit Court and remanded in police custody. She was eventually granted bail by a Human Rights Court in Accra in November and her case was adjourned until 2011.

Police and security forces

Individuals were regularly detained in police custody for longer than allowed by law. Police cells were

G

overcrowded and insanitary, and detainees often relied on family members for food and water.

■ In February, two people died in a police cell in Ashiamang, a suburb of Tema. Fifty-two people were being held in a cell built for 20.

■ In September, at least two people were killed and 15 seriously injured in Tema when combined troops of the military and police used live and rubber bullets and tear gas against people protesting against the demolition of their businesses. No investigation was carried out.

■ In October, approximately 19 homes and businesses in Nankpanduri village in the Northern Region were burned down by military and police officers and several people were injured when they were shot or beaten by security forces, who were searching for an escaped prisoner who had killed two police officers.

Justice system

Access to legal aid was inadequate and some prisoners spent over 10 years awaiting trial, although the proportion of remand prisoners began to fall. Prisons were overcrowded and under-resourced.

Death penalty

Seventeen people were sentenced to death by hanging, all for murder. At the end of the year, 123 people were on death row, including three women. No executions were carried out.

Housing rights

Thousands of people were forcibly evicted from their homes. Evictions were carried out without adequate prior consultation, adequate notice and compensation or alternative accommodation. Thousands remained under threat of forced eviction.

■ In May up to 2,000 people were forcibly evicted from their homes in "Abinkyi slum" in Kumasi. Residents were given just two weeks' notice and were not offered any alternative accommodation or compensation.

■ In July, scores of people were forcibly evicted from their homes in "Abuja slum" in Accra. Residents were informed about the demolition only two days before and they were not offered any compensation or alternative accommodation.

Amnesty International visits/reports

🚗 Amnesty International delegates visited Ghana in November.
📄 Thousands facing forced eviction in Ghana (AFR 28/006/2010)

GREECE

HELLENIC REPUBLIC

Head of state:	Karolos Papoulias
Head of government:	George Papandreou
Death penalty:	abolitionist for all crimes
Population:	11.2 million
Life expectancy:	79.7 years
Under-5 mortality (m/f):	5/4 per 1,000
Adult literacy:	97 per cent

Reports of excessive use of force and ill-treatment by law enforcement officials continued. Greece continued to lack a functioning asylum system. Substandard detention conditions at border guard stations and immigration detention centres remained a concern. Incidents of racial violence against migrants and asylum-seekers increased.

Background

The serious financial crisis in Greece led to the country requesting and agreeing a rescue package with the EU, the International Monetary Fund and the European Central Bank. The severe budget cuts adopted by the Parliament in May led to a series of demonstrations by trade unions before and after their adoption. On 5 May, three bank workers died during a demonstration in Athens against the austerity measures after some unidentified assailants threw a petrol bomb at the bank.

Armed opposition groups continued to carry out bomb attacks. In June, a parcel bomb explosion at the Ministry of Citizens' Protection in Athens killed the Minister's aide. Also in June, a Greek journalist was killed by armed attackers in Athens. In November, a series of parcel bombs, addressed to foreign embassies in Greece, the Parliament, international organizations and some heads of EU States were detected and destroyed by the authorities.

In March, new legislation entered into force which would allow migrant children to acquire citizenship if they met certain requirements.

Torture and other ill-treatment

There were reports of indiscriminate and excessive use of tear gas and other chemicals and excessive use of force against protesters during demonstrations.

■ Excessive use of force against peaceful protesters was reported during the commemorative

G

demonstration of the second anniversary of the death of Alexandros Gregoropoulos on 6 December. As a result, a number of protesters reportedly sought hospital treatment, including around 45 with head and other injuries, and around 30 as a result of the excessive use of tear gas and other chemicals. According to reports, some riot police officers beat and injured a photojournalist and a photographer covering the events.

Reports of ill-treatment by law enforcement officials persisted, including against members of vulnerable groups such.as detained asylum-seekers and irregular migrants.

■ Allegations were made regarding the severe beating of several irregular migrants and asylum-seekers detained at the border guard station of Soufli on 16 August. The detainees had protested over their poor detention conditions. Two days later, three of them were allegedly beaten severely following a hunger strike started by the detainees on the day after the first incident of ill-treatment.

■ In October, a special guard was convicted of culpable homicide for shooting 15-year-old Alexandros Gregoropoulos dead in December 2008, and sentenced to life imprisonment. A second special guard was convicted of complicity in culpable homicide and sentenced to 10 years' imprisonment.

At the end of his visit in October, the UN Special Rapporteur on torture called for the ratification of the Optional Protocol to the UN Convention against Torture and the establishment of an independent and effective police complaints mechanism. In December, a Draft Law provided for the establishment of a bureau dealing with incidents of arbitrary behaviour by law enforcement officials. Concerns remained over the independence and effectiveness of the proposed bureau.

Refugees and migrants

Substandard detention conditions in border guard stations and immigration detention centres remained a cause of concern, including overcrowding, prolonged detention in facilities not designed for long-term stay, lack of hygiene, lack of exercise and lack or limited access to medical care.

There was a significant increase in the number of irregular migrants and asylum-seekers arriving in Greece through the Greek-Turkish land border in Evros. In October, UNHCR, the UN refugee agency, called on the government to take urgent measures to address the humanitarian needs in the Evros region, including the deployment of sufficient personnel and immediate measures to ensure basic standards of human dignity in detention centres. Concerns were expressed at the deployment by Frontex, the European external borders agency, of a rapid border intervention team on 2 November to the region.

Greece continued to lack a functioning asylum system and much delayed reforms were in the process of being adopted by the end of the year. In September, UNHCR, the UN refugee agency, called the asylum situation in Greece a "humanitarian crisis" and urged the Greek authorities to speed up the asylum system reforms. European states participating in the Dublin II Regulation continued to exacerbate Greece's humanitarian crisis by insisting on returning asylum-seekers to the country.

The transitional Presidential Decree on asylum determination procedures (Presidential Decree 114/2010) entered into force in November. It reintroduced first instance appeals in asylum and other international protection cases and introduced transitional provisions for dealing with the heavy backlog of pending asylum appeals which reportedly were close to 47,000. The Decree retained the police as the competent authority for the initial examination of asylum claims. Free legal assistance continued to be available only to asylum-seekers who filed an appeal to the Council of State.

In December, a draft law providing for the creation of a new asylum determination authority, staffed entirely by civilian personnel, was laid before the Parliament. The law also provided for the creation of first-reception centres and sought to transpose the EU Returns Directive into Greek legislation. Concerns existed among other issues about the maximum length of pre-removal detention provided for in the draft law.

Long delays in the processing of their asylum claims prompted several asylum-seekers in Athens to go on hunger strike.

Discrimination

Incidents of racial violence against migrants and asylum-seekers reportedly increased, particularly in Athens. It was alleged that the police did not protect victims in the area of Aghios Panteleimon in Athens against such attacks.

Roma

In a decision made public in May, the European Committee of Social Rights found Greece in violation of Article 16 of the European Social Charter, assessing

G

that a significant number of Roma families continued to live in conditions that failed to meet minimum standards. The Committee also held that Roma continued to face forced evictions and legal remedies were not sufficiently accessible to them.

■ In September, in the case of *Georgopoulos et al v. Greece*, the UN Human Rights Committee found Greece in violation of the International Covenant on Civil and Political Rights with regard to demolishing a Romani family's home in 2006 and preventing the construction of a new home in the Roma Riganokampos settlement in the municipality of Patras.

NGOs expressed concerns over the failure of the Greek authorities to implement the 2008 judgement of the European Court of Human Rights in the case of *Sampanis v. Greece*. Romani children, including the applicants in the case, reportedly remained segregated in education and no effective efforts had been made to improve enrolment rates of Romani children or to ensure their education was fully integrated.

Prison conditions

Poor detention conditions and overcrowding continued to be reported in many prisons throughout the year. In December, around 8,000 prisoners around Greece reportedly refused meals and around 1,200 went on hunger strike and called for improvements in overcrowding and detention conditions, among other things.

Conscientious objectors

In September, new legislation on the right to conscientious objection was enacted, by which the length of alternative service was slightly decreased and reserve obligations for conscientious objectors were abolished. However, the maximum length of the alternative service in law remained effectively punitive, at twice the length of normal military service. The reduced length of alternative service, applied at the discretion of the Minister for National Defence, is still likely to be punitive in nature for the vast majority of conscripts.

The repeated persecution of conscientious objectors continued.

■ In February, the Military Appeal Court of Athens upheld the conviction for desertion of professional soldier Giorgos Monastiriotis by the Naval Court of Piraeus and handed down a five months' suspended

prison sentence. In 2003, Giorgos Monastiriotis had refused, citing reasons of conscience, to follow his unit when it was sent to the Iraq war.

Trafficking in human beings

In August, Law 3875/2010 implementing, among others, the 2000 UN Palermo Protocol to Prevent, Suppress and Punish Trafficking in Persons was introduced. It included positive amendments including rendering the protection and support to victims of trafficking independent of their co-operation regarding the prosecution of alleged traffickers following the fulfilment of certain requirements.

Despite the government's announcement regarding the establishment of further shelters for women victims of trafficking and domestic violence in 2009, only two state-run shelters for 38 beneficiaries were reported as operational, while only one NGO-run shelter for women victims of trafficking remained, due to lack of funding.

Workers' rights

Concerns over the thoroughness of the criminal investigation into the attack against Konstantina Kuneva remained and the case was again at risk of being permanently closed. Following an order by the prosecutor at the end of the year, the investigation into the attack was joined to the investigation about the working conditions in cleaning companies, which meant the case would continue. Konstantina Kuneva, a trade union leader, was severely injured in Athens on 22 December 2008, when she was attacked with sulphuric acid by unknown men.

Amnesty International visits/reports

🚐 An Amnesty International delegate visited Greece in April and October.

📃 The Dublin II Trap: Transfers of asylum-seekers to Greece (EUR 25/001/2010)

📃 Stop forced evictions of Roma in Europe (EUR 01/005/2010)

📃 Greece: Irregular migrants and asylum seekers routinely detained in substandard conditions (EUR 25/002/2010)

GUATEMALA

REPUBLIC OF GUATEMALA
Head of state and government: **Álvaro Colom Caballeros**
Death penalty: **retentionist**
Population: **14.4 million**
Life expectancy: **70.8 years**
Under-5 mortality (m/f):   **45/34 per 1,000**
Adult literacy: **73.8 per cent**

Violence against women remained widespread. The authorities failed to uphold the rights of Indigenous Peoples. Justice remained elusive for the vast majority of the 200,000 victims of the 1960-1996 internal armed conflict. Human rights defenders continued to be intimidated.

Background

Violent crime was widespread, affecting most communities. In June, decapitated heads, reportedly placed by street gangs, appeared in the grounds of the Congress building and other landmarks in the capital.

Congress passed a law in October which could have led to the resumption of the use of the death penalty. However, the President vetoed it and in December Guatemala voted in favour of the UN General Assembly resolution calling for a moratorium on the use of the death penalty.

Corruption remained pervasive. Institutions remained fragile and vulnerable to organized crime. In June, Carlos Castresana, the head of the UN-sponsored International Commission against Impunity in Guatemala (Comisión Internacional Contra la Impunidad en Guatemala, CICIG) resigned his post in response to the appointment of an Attorney General with alleged links to organized crime. Three days later, the Constitutional Court annulled the selection process and an interim Attorney General was appointed, pending a new selection process.

Violence against women and girls

According to the Guatemalan Human Rights Ombudsman's Office, 695 women were killed in 2010, bringing the total number of women killed since 2004 to at least 4,400. In September, special courts created by the 2008 Law Against Femicide began to operate in Guatemala City.

In October, the Inter-American Commission on Human Rights (IACHR) agreed to hear the case of Claudina Velásquez, a 19-year-old law student killed in 2005. Five years after her death, nobody has been held to account and serious concerns remained about the effectiveness of the investigation into her death.

Indigenous Peoples' rights

In May, the UN Committee on the Elimination of Racial Discrimination recommended that legislation be introduced to ensure the free, prior and informed consent of Indigenous Peoples for proposed development projects that could affect their lives and livelihoods.

Also in May, the IACHR asked Guatemala to suspend operations at the Marlin 1 gold mine in San Marcos department, decontaminate water sources, begin a health care programme, and guarantee the life and physical security of 18 Mayan communities. Despite a commitment by the President to comply with the decision, at the end of the year the mine was still operating.

In June the UN Special Rapporteur on indigenous people concluded that lack of consultation with communities affected by mining and the lack of security around land tenure were at the heart of disputes between mining companies and Indigenous communities.

Public security

Violent crime and gang violence continued to be widespread. According to the Guatemalan Human Rights Ombudsman's Office, 5,960 people were killed as the result of crime throughout the year.

In August, the Public Prosecutor's Office, supported by CICIG, obtained arrest warrants for 19 individuals, including a former Minister of the Interior and a former Director of Police, in connection with the extrajudicial execution of prisoners in 2005 and 2006. By the end of the year, nine had been arrested and four, who were abroad, were the subjects of extradition or judicial proceedings.

Impunity

The vast majority of the thousands of documented human rights violations dating from the 1960-1996 internal armed conflict remained unresolved. The President's 2008 commitment to declassify and make public all military archives relating to the conflict was not fulfilled.

G

■ The case against former President General Ríos Montt and other military and police leaders of the early 1980s for grave human rights violations remained stalled because the Ministry of Defence failed to hand over documents, despite being ordered to do so by a Guatemalan court.

■ In May, Gilberto Jordán, a former Guatemalan special forces soldier, was arrested in the USA. According to the US Department of Justice, he confessed to taking part in the 1982 Dos Erres massacre in which 250 Indigenous men, women and children were killed, and stated that the first person he killed was a baby, whom he murdered by throwing into the village well. In September he was sentenced to 10 years' imprisonment for concealing his participation in the massacre in his citizenship application.

■ In October, Héctor Roderico Ramírez Ríos and Abraham Lancerio Gómez, two former police officers, were each sentenced to 40 years' imprisonment for the 1984 enforced disappearance of trade unionist Fernando García.

Human rights defenders

During the year, human rights organizations documented 305 incidents of intimidation, threats and attacks against human rights defenders, including eight killings. The authorities failed to hold anybody to account for the vast majority of these and previous crimes.

■ Members of staff at UDEFEGUA, a human rights NGO based in Guatemala City, were subjected to a series of attacks, intimidation and threats. In February, a car of a staff member was tampered with, resulting in temporary loss of control of her car.

Amnesty International visits/reports

🚌 Amnesty International delegates visited Guatemala in July.

GUINEA

REPUBLIC OF GUINEA

Head of state:	Alpha Condé (replaced Sékouba Konaté in December)
Head of government:	Mohamed Saïd Fofana (replaced Jean Marie Doré in December, who replaced Kabiné Komara in January)
Death penalty:	retentionist
Population:	10.3 million
Life expectancy:	58.9 years
Under-5 mortality (m/f):	157/138 per 1,000

Allegations of torture and other ill-treatment by the security forces continued. Dozens of Guineans were arbitrarily arrested and detained. Some of them were prisoners of conscience. No one was prosecuted for crimes against humanity committed in September 2009. Violence broke out late in the year as election results were disputed.

Background

President Sékouba Konaté, appointed interim president in December 2009, gained support from the international community, which pressed the authorities to organize a presidential election. Jean Marie Doré, a civilian, was chosen as Prime Minister in January and a new government was appointed in February. In May, a new Constitution was adopted by presidential decree.

After the first round of the presidential election in June, political and ethnic tensions rose amid accusations of bias within the National Independent Electoral Commission. After three postponements, the second round was held in November. Opposition leader Alpha Condé won the poll, but the defeated candidate, Cellou Dalein Diallo, declared that the election had been rigged and violent clashes broke out between his supporters and the security forces. A state of emergency was declared on 17 November, imposing a curfew and granting the security forces extra powers.

In October, the EU prolonged its sanctions against Guinea. As well as an arms embargo, there was a ban on entry visas for individuals linked to the repression of September 2009.

Crimes under international law – September 2009

The National Commission of Inquiry established to investigate the events of 28 September 2009 submitted its conclusions in February 2010. The Commission acknowledged that demonstrators had faced violent repression by members of the security forces, but blamed the "excited crowd" as well as the lack of equipment and co-ordination of security forces. It accused civil society organizations of spreading "far-fetched figures regarding the number of deaths, rapes and disappearances". Regarding sexual violence, the report noted that no female victim of rape came to testify before the Commission, and that it therefore relied only on medical records. The Commission named Lieutenant Aboubacar "Toumba" Diakite, the man who allegedly attempted to kill President Camara, and his unit of "red berets", as responsible for the violence. It called for them to be tried before Guinean courts. The Commission recommended a general amnesty for misconduct by leaders of the former opposition, now in government.

The Commission stated that political leaders, in refusing to cancel the demonstration after it had been forbidden by the authorities, shared some responsibility for the events. It also stated that demonstrators committed acts of robbery, looting, and destruction of public and private property.

In February, the Deputy Prosecutor of the International Criminal Court (ICC) said that those bearing responsibility for the crimes committed in Guinea should not go unpunished and that the violators should be tried either by the Guinean authorities or by the ICC. She added that crimes against humanity were committed on 28 September 2009 and in its aftermath and that the ICC should continue with its preliminary investigation.

The Guinean authorities took no steps to suspend or prosecute violators of human rights. The government appointed in February included members of the military junta who had served in the previous government. Two former ministers who had been named by the UN International Commission of Inquiry into the events of September 2009 were appointed to the presidential cabinet. The Commission of Inquiry reported to the UN Secretary-General in December 2009 but its report had not been officially made public by the end of 2010.

International scrutiny

Guinea's human rights record was assessed in May under the UN Universal Periodic Review. During the review process, Guinea accepted more than 100 recommendations. It agreed to: bring to justice all alleged perpetrators of extrajudicial executions, acts of torture, ill-treatment, rape and other grave human rights violations; ensure that victims of these violations benefit from full reparation and that families of those who died receive adequate compensation; and reinforce the protection of vulnerable groups, particularly women. Guinea expressed reservations over nine recommendations, including one on the abolition of the death penalty.

Torture and other ill-treatment

Allegations of torture and other ill-treatment by the security forces continued. Most people arrested arbitrarily were beaten at the time of their arrests either on the streets or in their homes. Some were also beaten at the gendarmerie headquarters and in police stations.

■ In October, the security forces ransacked several areas of Conakry, the capital, including Bambeto, Koza and Hamdallaye. Five people, including Mamadou Adama Diallo, were beaten and taken to the police station. They were later released without charge.

■ Aliou Barry, president of the National Observatory for the Defence of Human Rights, was beaten in October when he tried to protect a group of people in Hamdallaye from assault by members of the security forces. His left arm was broken and he was taken to the gendarmerie headquarters and held for a few hours before being released without charge.

Arbitrary arrests and detentions

After the first and second rounds of the presidential election in June and November, dozens of Guineans, including prisoners of conscience, were arrested and detained in military barracks and police stations. Most were denied access to legal representation; many were also denied access to their families and to medical care. Some of them were freed within days or weeks.

Excessive use of force

During protests and political meetings, security forces used unnecessary or excessive force against peaceful demonstrators. At least 10 Guineans were killed in the streets in November. They were shot by the security forces in the head, the abdomen, the thorax and the back of the head.

■ Mamadou Macka Diallo, an 18-year-old student in Conakry, was killed by a policeman in Conakry in November. Abdoulaye Ba, a 16-year-old student was

G

shot dead by a member of the security forces while entering his home in Koza, Conakry. Abdoulaye Boubacar Diallo, a docker, was killed by a member of the security forces as he ran away when he saw the security forces shooting at people.

In September and October, after the postponement of the election, security forces used excessive force to break up demonstrations by supporters of rival political parties. The security forces fired indiscriminately at unarmed civilians, beat protesters and ransacked homes. In October, more than 60 people were injured and at least 15 had bullet wounds. One person, Ibrahim Khalil Bangourah, died as a result of his injuries.

Amnesty International visits/reports

📄 Guinea: "You did not want the military, so now we are going to teach you a lesson" (AFR 29/001/2010)

📄 Guinea: "They ripped off my clothes with their knives and left me completely naked" (AFR 29/002/2010)

📄 Guinea: Amnesty International defends Guinea research against French Government criticism (AFR 29/004/2010)

📄 Guinea: Four soldiers released: Colonel Soryba Yansané, Lieutenant Colonel David Syllah, Commander Pathio Bangourah and Sergeant Moussa Sylla (AFR 29/008/2010)

📄 Guinée: Les autorités doivent mettre un terme au règne de l'impunité – Déclaration commune, ACAT / Amnesty International (AFR 29/011/2010)

📄 Guinée-Conakry: la société civile guinéenne et internationale interpelle les acteurs de la crise et les appelle à la retenue: Communiqué de Presse Conjoint (AFR 29/012/2010)

📄 Guinea: Reform of security forces must deliver justice for Bloody Monday massacre, 23 February 2010

📄 Guinea security forces used excessive force in election protests, 24 October 2010

📄 Guinea authorities must stop arbitrary arrests and killings, 18 November 2010

GUINEA-BISSAU

REPUBLIC OF GUINEA-BISSAU

Head of state:	Malam Bacai Sanhá
Head of government:	Carlos Gomes Júnior
Death penalty:	abolitionist for all crimes
Population:	1.6 million
Life expectancy:	48.6 years
Under-5 mortality (m/f):	207/186 per 1,000
Adult literacy:	51 per cent

The political situation remained fragile as conflict between political and military authorities continued. Divisions within civilian authorities, as well as military in-fighting, exacerbated instability. Tension increased in April following a military rebellion. The armed forces were responsible for human rights violations, including torture and arbitrary arrest and detention. No one was brought to justice for political killings and torture which took place in 2009.

Background

In January, the government signed an agreement with the USA to allow a US prosecutor to work alongside Guinea-Bissau's Attorney General to fight drug trafficking and other crimes. However, the US prosecutor had not been deployed by the end of 2010.

In February, a former Minister of Fisheries and three ministry officials were charged with embezzlement. Their case had not been adjudicated by the end of the year. The National Assembly was apparently reluctant to lift the parliamentary immunity of one of the accused.

In April, the deputy Chief of Staff of the Armed Forces, General António Indjai, deposed and arrested the Chief of Staff, Admiral Zamora Induta. General António Indjai briefly detained the Prime Minister, Carlos Gomes Júnior, and threatened to kill him if demonstrators, who took to the streets in support of the Prime Minister, persisted with their protest. At the same time soldiers acting on the General's orders stormed the UN headquarters in the capital, Bissau and "liberated" the former Chief of Staff of the navy, Vice-Admiral Bubo Na Tchuto. He had taken refuge in the UN building after voluntarily returning to Bissau in December 2009 from Gambia, where he had fled in 2008 after being accused of plotting a coup. He was reinstated as the navy's Chief of Staff in October. In June, President Sanhá removed Admiral Zamora

Induta as Chief of Staff of the armed forces and appointed General António Indjai in his place. His appointment and the reinstatement of Vice-Admiral Bubo Na Tchuto as head of the navy in October were widely criticized inside and outside the country.

In May, Guinea-Bissau's human rights record was assessed under the UN Universal Periodic Review. The UN Human Rights Council's final report was adopted in September. The government rejected five recommendations, including those related to ending impunity of the armed forces for human rights violations. Among those it supported was a commitment to the eventual criminalization of female genital mutilation, but only after a public education campaign.

The National Assembly approved a package of laws in May including amendments to the organic law of the armed forces and laws on the National Guard, Public Order Police and the State Security Information Services.

In September, the EU ended its security sector reform mission to the country, which started in 2008, on grounds of political instability and lack of respect for the rule of law.

In November, Guinea-Bissau ratified the International Convention on the Elimination of All Forms of Racial Discrimination and the International Covenant on Civil and Political Rights. They were to enter into force on 1 December 2010 and 1 February 2011 respectively.

Impunity

Investigations into political killings in March and June 2009 stalled, apparently for lack of resources to question some witnesses outside the country. The armed forces continued to commit human rights violations with impunity.

Arbitrary arrests and detentions

Six military officers, including one woman, arrested in connection with the killing in March 2009 of former Chief of Staff General Tagme na Waie remained in incommunicado detention without charge for 20 months. They were released in December pending formal charges and trial, and were reportedly not allowed to leave the country.

In April, General António Indjai arrested Admiral Zamora Induta, Chief of Staff of the armed forces and accused him of involvement in the disappearance of drugs seized during a raid. However, other reports indicated that the arrest was linked to an investigation

Admiral Zamora Induta had launched in March into the involvement of high-ranking military officers in drug trafficking. General António Indjai also arrested Colonel Samba Djaló, head of the military intelligence service, and accused him of interfering in the activities of political parties. The two arrested men were reportedly tortured in detention at Mansôa military barracks. The Supreme Military Court ordered their conditional release in September, but they remained in detention until mid-December, when they were released without charge, pending further investigations. Apparently, the only restrictions imposed were that they were not allowed to leave the country.

Torture and other ill-treatment

In July, Fernando Té died in hospital a few days after being arrested and beaten by police officers stationed at the 5th police station in Bissau. According to reports, he was arrested following a dispute with a shopkeeper and taken to the police station, where he was beaten before being released without charge a few hours later. Two days after his death, the police officers involved were arrested. However, by the end of the year they had not apparently been charged or tried.

Violence against women and girls

Violence against women and girls, including forced and early marriages, was widespread.

■ A 15-year-old girl was beaten to death in April for refusing to marry a much older man. Women in a village in the southern region of Tombali beat the girl, who had previously run away to avoid being married, during the wedding ceremony. Although the case was referred to the Attorney General's Office, no one was arrested.

■ In March, members of the Evangelical Church in Tombali region were beaten by villagers for sheltering about 20 girls aged between 14 and 16 who had run away to avoid forced marriages to older men.

■ In August, a girl and two of her female relatives were beaten by male relatives in another village in Tombali region. The girl had been given in marriage to an older man, but her female relatives objected to the wedding on grounds that the girl was under age. Although a complaint was lodged with the police, no action was taken.

Amnesty International visits/reports

🚗 Amnesty International visited Guinea-Bissau in March and October to carry out research.

G

GUYANA

REPUBLIC OF GUYANA
Head of state and government: **Bharrat Jagdeo**
Death penalty: **retentionist**
Population: **0.8 million**
Life expectancy: **67.9 years**
Under-5 mortality (m/f):   **66/47 per 1,000**

At least one person was shot by police in circumstances suggesting it may have been an unlawful killing. Indigenous Peoples continued to face obstacles to realizing their land rights. At least one person was sentenced to death; no executions were carried out.

Background

Guyana's human rights record was assessed under the UN Universal Periodic Review in September. The authorities supported a number of recommendations, but rejected a wide range of others. For example, they did not commit to set up an independent inquiry into the deaths of more than 200 people allegedly killed by "death squads" between 2002 and 2006.

Torture and other ill-treatment

Judicial proceedings against three police officers charged in connection with the torture and ill-treatment in October 2009 of three people, including a 15-year-old boy, in Leonora police station stalled in the courts. One of the victims was reported to have accepted a compensation payment and the relative of another victim stated that the case had been "settled". The three officers accused in the case remained on active duty at the end of the year.

Unlawful killings

In June, 16-year-old Kelvin Fraser was fatally wounded by police on the Patentia estate in Essequibo Islands-West Demerara. According to reports, Kelvin Fraser and three youths fled from police investigating complaints that the boys were harassing girl students from the Patentia Secondary School. An officer caught Kelvin Fraser and shot him in the chest while attempting to arrest him. An investigation into the shooting was continuing at the end of the year.

Indigenous Peoples' rights

In September, members were appointed to the newly created Indigenous Peoples' Commission. The Commission's primary functions include promoting and protecting the rights of Indigenous Peoples and making recommendations on economic and education policies to advance their interests.

Indigenous land claims continued to be addressed under the 2006 Amerindian Act. However, Indigenous Peoples alleged that poor demarcation processes were allowing the government to take over traditional lands and that in some areas demarcation had taken place without the free, prior and informed consent of the communities affected.

Violence against women and girls

Levels of violence against women and girls remained high. According to UNIFEM, one in four women in Guyana has been physically abused in a relationship.

In April, the Sexual Offences Act was passed by the National Assembly. The Act, which includes provisions widening the definition of rape and criminalizing rape within marriage, was welcomed as an important step in the eradication of sexual violence.

A Task Force, set up to develop and co-ordinate implementation of the National Plan for the Prevention of Sexual Offences, met for the first time in October.

Rights of lesbian, gay, bisexual and transgender people

Sex between men remained a criminal offence punishable by lengthy prison terms. Laws dating from the former colonial administration continued to be used to discriminate against transgender people.

Right to health – HIV/AIDS

Stigma and discrimination towards people living with HIV/AIDS remained a barrier to the successful implementation of treatment.

Death penalty

At least one person was sentenced to death in 2010. More than 30 people remained on death row at the end of the year. There were no executions during 2010; the last execution took place in 1997.

An amendment to the Criminal Law (Offences) Act, which abolishes mandatory death sentences for murder, passed into law in October. However, the government rejected calls for a moratorium on executions with a view to abolishing the death penalty.

HAITI

REPUBLIC OF HAITI

Head of state:	René García Préval
Head of government:	Jean-Max Bellerive
Death penalty:	abolitionist for all crimes
Population:	10.2 million
Life expectancy:	61.7 years
Under-5 mortality (m/f):	90/80 per 1,000
Adult literacy:	61 per cent

January's earthquake left nearly 2 million people homeless and triggered an unprecedented humanitarian crisis. At the end of 2010, more than a million people remained displaced in makeshift camps where violence against women and girls was increasing. The large number of unaccompanied and orphaned children provoked fears that many were being trafficked to the neighbouring Dominican Republic or other countries. The destruction and depletion of state institutions meant there was virtually no access to justice or remedy for abuses. Haitian police shot dead 12 prisoners in Les Cayes during an attempted prison breakout in January.

Background

On 12 January, an earthquake destroyed large swathes of Port-au-Prince, Haiti's capital, as well as towns and outlying areas in the south of the country, triggering an unprecedented humanitarian crisis. Government estimates put the number of dead at more than 230,000, with a further 300,000 people injured. Public institutions and offices were severely affected: 15 out of 17 ministry buildings, 1,500 schools and 50 hospitals and clinics were destroyed. UN mission headquarters were also destroyed. The international community and humanitarian agencies responded promptly with emergency humanitarian aid, but this was slow to arrive in some of the worst affected communities.

In March, more than 150 donor countries and international organizations met in New York and pledged US$5.3 billion over 18 months to finance Haiti's post-earthquake reconstruction. However, the clearing of rubble and construction of temporary shelters for earthquake survivors progressed slowly. At the end of the year, more than a million people were still living in some 1,110 formal and informal camps, often in dire conditions. A hurricane in October caused further damage to shelters in the camps.

In September, a cholera epidemic broke out in communities along the Artibonite River and spread rapidly to other parts of the country. The UN set up an independent panel of experts to investigate the origin of the outbreak. By December, more than 100,000 cases of cholera had been reported and the death toll had exceeded 2,400.

The first round of general elections to elect Haiti's president, parliament and senate, took place on 28 November. Irregularities and alleged fraud by the Provisional Electoral Council led to demonstrations across the country. National electoral observers expressed concern at the publication of partial results disqualifying Michel Martelly from the presidential run-off scheduled for January 2011 in favour of the ruling party candidate.

Violence against women and girls

Violence against women and girls was pervasive in and around formal and informal camps. Lack of security and effective protection mechanisms increased the risks of rape and other forms of sexual violence. Impunity for these crimes remained a source of concern as very few cases were investigated or prosecuted. Many rape survivors had to overcome fear, discrimination and a lack of financial resources in order to get access to medical care. The National Association for the Protection of Haitian Women and Children, a women's rights organization working with sex workers in Port-au-Prince, reported an increase in the number of girls involved in sex work since the onset of the humanitarian crisis.

■ KOFAVIV, a grassroots organization of rape survivors, documented more than 250 cases of sexual violence in 15 camps during the first five months following the earthquake. The organization also reported sexual abuse of unaccompanied girls in exchange for food or shelter in camps.

Internally displaced people

At the end of the year, more than a million people were still living in appalling conditions in both formal and informal camps. The vast majority of displaced people did not have access to adequate shelter. Construction of transitional shelters was slow, hampered by the fact that suitable land was not made available by the authorities. There was a lack of clear information on the government's plans and policies for the relocation of displaced people into adequate longer-term housing.

H

Forced evictions

Displaced people occupying private land were forcibly evicted by landowners, on most occasions with the assistance of the police or armed men. In April, the government announced a six-week freeze on forced evictions of displaced people, but it lacked the capacity to enforce the measure.

■ In March, nearly 10,000 displaced people were evicted from Sylvio Cator stadium by Haitian police officers. The expulsion took place without a court order and without any information or alternatives being offered to the earthquake survivors. Police officers entered the stadium at night and started pulling down shelters and forced survivors to leave the premises.

Children's rights – trafficking in human beings

Trafficking of children remained a source of concern and efforts to prevent it were stepped up. The Minors Protection Brigade, a specialized Haitian police unit, deployed officers at crossing points with the Dominican Republic to prevent children being trafficked.

The Haitian government increased scrutiny of international adoption applications as a measure to prevent trafficking.

■ In January, 33 children aged between two months and 12 years were intercepted at the border by Haitian authorities. A group of missionaries was attempting to take the children into the Dominican Republic without documentation. The missionaries were charged with "kidnapping" the children and "association to commit a crime"; the crime of trafficking is not on Haiti's statute books. The 10 missionaries were released in February and allowed to leave the country pending investigation.

Extrajudicial execution of prisoners

■ On 19 January, an uprising and breakout took place in Les Cayes prison, and Haitian National Police officers were called to assist prison guards. The operation resulted in the killing of 12 unarmed inmates; 14 others were injured. A joint Haitian-UN investigation panel into the incident was reported to have concluded that most of the dead were "summarily executed" and that police officers opened fire "deliberately and without justification". Fourteen police officers and prison officers were detained pending investigation. At the end of the year, no further information was available on the investigation.

Amnesty International visits/reports

🚌 Amnesty International delegates visited Haiti in March and June.

▨ Human rights must be at the core of relief efforts and the reconstruction of Haiti (AMR 36/001/2010)

▨ Haiti: After the earthquake – initial mission findings (AMR 36/004/2010)

HOLY SEE

HOLY SEE
Head of state and government: Pope Benedict XVI
Death penalty: abolitionist for all crimes

The Holy See did not sufficiently comply with its international obligations relating to the protection of children.

International scrutiny

In May, the Holy See submitted its initial reports on the optional protocols to the UN Convention on the Rights of the Child which at the end of the year had yet to be considered by the UN Committee on the Rights of the Child.

However, by the year's end the Holy See had again failed to submit its second periodic report on the UN Convention on the Rights of the Child, due in 1997, and the initial report on the UN Convention against Torture, due in 2003.

Children's rights – response to child abuse

Increasing evidence of widespread child sexual abuse committed by members of the clergy over the past decades, and of the enduring failure of the Catholic Church to address these crimes properly, continued to emerge in various countries. Such failures included not removing alleged perpetrators from their posts pending proper investigations, not co-operating with judicial authorities to bring them to justice and not ensuring proper reparation to victims.

The Pope acknowledged the abuses during visits to countries where they had been reported, such as Ireland, Malta and the UK, and expressed regret. He affirmed that "just penalties" should be imposed to exclude perpetrators from access to young people and stressed that to prevent abuses education and selection of candidates for priesthood should be improved.

H

In March, in a letter to the Catholics of Ireland, the Pope admitted that "a misplaced concern for the reputation of the Church and the avoidance of scandals" had resulted in the "failure to apply existing canonical penalties and to safeguard the dignity of every person". He exhorted bishops to fully implement the norms of canon law when addressing child abuse and "to continue to cooperate with the civil authorities in their area of competence".

Amendments to the canon law promulgated in May introduced the "delicts" of paedophile pornography and abuse of mentally disabled people; the maximum punishment for these "delicts" is dismissal or deposition. Canon law does not include an obligation for Church authorities to report cases to civil authorities for criminal investigation. Secrecy is mandatory throughout the proceedings.

In November, Holy See representatives conducted an "apostolic visitation" to Ireland, to verify "the effectiveness of processes used in responding to cases of abuse and of forms of assistance provided to the victims". Results of the visit were due to be announced in 2011.

HONDURAS

REPUBLIC OF HONDURAS

Head of state and government:	**Porfirio Lobo Sosa**
Death penalty:	**abolitionist for all crimes**
Population:	**7.6 million**
Life expectancy:	**72.6 years**
Under-5 mortality (m/f):	**44/35 per 1,000**
Adult literacy:	**83.6 per cent**

Freedom of expression came under attack. Little progress was made in repairing the damage to human rights protection and the rule of law that followed the 2009 coup. Impunity for human rights violations by military and police officers persisted. Human rights defenders were subject to intimidation.

Background

Porfirio Lobo of the National Party became President in January. The new government faced criticism for the lack of accountability for human rights violations perpetrated during the de facto government of Roberto Micheletti (June 2009 to January 2010). Few investigations were carried out into police officers and military personnel who arbitrarily detained and ill-treated hundreds of protesters and bystanders during that period.

Military personnel were deployed to the Aguán region at various times throughout the year after land disputes between hundreds of peasant farmers and various companies and private farmers erupted into violence. There were concerns that the military may have used excessive force.

In May, four judges – Tirza del Carmen Flores Lanza, Ramón Enrique Barrios, Luis Alonso Chévez de la Rocha, Guillermo López Lone – and Public Attorney Osmán Fajardo Morel, were arbitrarily removed from their posts for peacefully taking part in demonstrations against the 2009 coup. They had not been reinstated by the end of the year. Judges and court officials who participated in demonstrations in favour of the coup remained in post.

In November, Honduras' human rights record was assessed under the Universal Periodic Review and the Honduran authorities extended an open invitation to UN and Inter-American special experts on human rights.

By the end of the year Honduras had still not been readmitted to the OAS following the June 2009 coup.

International justice

In November, the International Criminal Court Chief Prosecutor announced that preliminary investigations would be opened into reports of widespread and systematic human rights violations under the de facto government.

Human rights defenders

Representatives of human rights organizations were threatened and harassed as they carried out their work.

■ In October, a lawyer from the Association for a more Just Society (ASJ) was forced into a taxi by two unidentified men, one of whom was armed, and asked about her work for the ASJ. When she refused to answer, one of the men said to the other "You know we were paid to execute her… we have to carry out the plan". Half an hour later, the lawyer was ordered to get out of the car and left in the street. A police investigation into the incident was continuing at the end of the year.

H

Freedom of expression and association

At least 10 journalists were murdered between January and December. Joseph Hernández, David Meza Montesinos, Nahúm Palacios, José Bayardo Mairena and Manuel Juárez were all killed in March. Jorge Alberto (Georgino) Orellana, Luis Antonio Chévez, Luis Arturo Mondragón and Israel Zelaya Díaz were killed between April and August, and in December Henry Suazo Santos became the 10th Honduran journalist to be murdered. By the end of the year nobody had been brought to justice for these crimes and no fully resourced and effective programme of protection for journalists at risk had been put in place.

■ In March, Nahúm Palacios Arteaga – a 34-year-old reporter, news director for the TV Channel 5 in Aguán and host of a news programme on Radio Tocoa – was killed as he drove home through the Los Pinos district of Tocoa City, Colón department. Two unidentified men drove up alongside his car firing AK47 automatic weapons. Nahúm Palacios was shot up to 30 times; two people travelling with him in the car were injured. Nahúm Palacios was a prominent public critic of the coup. In July 2009, the Inter-American Commission on Human Rights had granted Nahúm Palacios precautionary measures and requested that the Honduran state immediately adopt measures to protect him. These measures were never implemented.

Violence against women and girls

According to the Public Attorney's Office, 282 women were murdered between January and October. This figure was questioned by women's rights organizations who claimed the true figure was higher.

A decree by the de facto authorities criminalizing the use of emergency contraception remained in place, despite its negative impact on women and girls whose contraceptive method failed or who were at risk of pregnancy resulting from sexual coercion.

Rights of lesbian, gay, bisexual and transgender people

In October, the LGBT community expressed concern to the Inter-American Commission on Human Rights that they continued to be threatened and attacked. Attacks were rarely thoroughly investigated and lack of protection for those who came forward to report these crimes remained a concern.

■ Nohelia Flores Álvarez, a transsexual, pressed charges against a policeman who had stabbed her 17 times in December 2008 after she turned down his request for sexual services. During the investigation and trial Nohelia Flores Álvarez, witnesses, investigators, prosecutors and supporters were repeatedly harassed and threatened, culminating in August with the murder of one of her friends as they walked together; the intended target of the attack was Nohelia Flores Álvarez. In September, the police officer was found guilty of the stabbing, and sentenced to a minimum of 10 years' imprisonment. However, by the end of the year, no one had been brought to justice for the intimidation, threats and killing of those associated with Nohelia Flores Álvarez.

Amnesty International visits/reports

📄 Recommendations to the new Honduran government following the coup of June 2009 (AMR 37/003/2010)

📄 Honduras: Submission to the UN Universal Periodic Review, November 2010 (AMR 37/005/2010)

HUNGARY

REPUBLIC OF HUNGARY

Head of state:	Pál Schmitt (replaced László Sólyom in August)
Head of government:	Viktor Orbán (replaced Gordon Bajnai in May)
Death penalty:	abolitionist for all crimes
Population:	10 million
Life expectancy:	73.9 years
Under-5 mortality (m/f):	9/8 per 1,000
Adult literacy:	99 per cent

Roma continued to face violent attacks and discrimination and lived in a climate of fear. The police completed the investigation into a series of attacks against Roma in 2008 and 2009 and four suspects were charged. International human rights monitoring bodies raised concerns over structural shortcomings of the Hungarian criminal justice system's response to hate crimes. Romani children were segregated in primary school.

Background

The coalition of the Alliance of Young Democrats (Fidesz) and the Christian-Democratic People's Party won the parliamentary elections convincingly in April.

An extreme right-wing political party Movement for a Better Hungary (Jobbik) gained seats in parliament for the first time.

Members of the banned group the Hungarian Guard (Magyar Gárda) reportedly continued their activities under another name, the New Hungarian Guard. In September, the prosecutor pressed charges against three of its leaders for incitement against the decree of an authority and abuse of freedom of assembly.

Racism

After a series of violent attacks against Romani communities which left six people dead in 2008 and 2009, Hungarian NGOs reported further attacks against Roma and criticized the lack of procedures within the criminal justice system to effectively address hate crimes (see Justice system below). In June, the OSCE noted that Roma were more susceptible to being made "scapegoats", blamed for the country's existing socio-economic problems, as a larger percentage of them depended on state support.

■ In June, the police completed the investigation into the series of attacks against Roma in 2008 and 2009. It concluded that four suspects should be charged with multiple co-ordinated homicide. In September, the Pest County Prosecutor submitted the indictment: three men were charged with multiple homicides for "base motivation" (as there is no specific provision in the criminal code for racially motivated crime) and the fourth with abetting the crime of pre-meditated multiple homicides.

In September, the Council of Europe's Advisory Committee on the Framework Convention for the Protection of National Minorities expressed concerns about violent attacks against Roma, and noted that despite the arrests of the alleged perpetrators, there was still "a climate of fear". The Committee further expressed concerns that "intolerance and prejudice towards Roma are being fanned by the statements of certain extreme right-wing politicians." According to local NGOs, such statements were not firmly condemned by the government.

In the run-up to the municipal elections in October, national public radio and television refused to air a party-political advert by the Jobbik party, which referred to so-called "Gypsy crime" and claimed a link between crime and ethnicity. The National Elections Committee ruled that both media had violated electoral principles of equality of political parties and

that the advert had complied with free speech regulations. In September, the Supreme Court upheld the decision.

Justice system

Structural shortcomings of the Hungarian criminal justice system's response to hate crimes were revealed by international and local NGOs and international human rights monitoring bodies. These shortcomings included a lack of capacity to recognize and investigate hate crimes; no specialized training or specific guidelines for police and investigators; inadequate support to victims of hate crimes; and no effective measures to map the nature and scale of the issue, partly because of a lack of data which hampered the authorities' ability to identify trends and prepare relevant policy responses.

There were several documented cases which illustrated that law enforcement authorities often failed to recognize the racial motivation in crimes. In their submission to the UN Universal Periodic Review, Hungarian NGOs also expressed concerns in November over a tendency to classify crimes as "common" crimes rather than hate crimes with a racially aggravated motive. As a result, reliable statistics were not publicly available on the real number of racially motivated crimes in Hungary. Hatred as an aggravated motive was also reportedly ignored in crimes committed against LGBT people or Jewish people.

Discrimination – Roma

The UN Human Rights Committee raised concerns about discrimination against Roma in education, housing, health and political participation and the lack of regulated data collection disaggregated by ethnicity.

■ For the first time, the Supreme Court awarded compensation to victims of anti-Roma school segregation. The Court found in June that five Romani children had been segregated during their primary schooling in the town of Miskolc. The Court held that segregation on the basis of ethnic origin amounts to unequal treatment prohibited by law, and awarded compensation to the victims.

Housing rights

A draft law on construction procedures, submitted to parliament in September by the Minister of Interior, included a provision that would allow local authorities

H

to ban certain behaviour – including rough sleeping – in public spaces. According to NGOs working with homeless people, the sanctions would include fines, evictions or imprisonment. They raised concern that the proposal was an example of penalizing poverty.

Freedom of expression

Despite protests, the parliament adopted two new media acts in September and December. The new legislation was criticized by local NGOs, media and the international community over its possible implications, including restrictions on media content, the lack of clear guidelines for journalists and editors and the strong powers of the new regulatory body, which all risk unfairly restricting freedom of expression. The National Media and Communications Authority was created, which can impose heavy fines on broadcast media for content it considers to run counter to the "public interest", "common morality" and "national order". Fines can also be imposed for "unbalanced" news reporting.

Rights of lesbian, gay, bisexual and transgender people

The organizers of the LGBT pride march in Budapest alleged the police initially refused to use protective cordons to secure the march held on 16 July. Two participants were reportedly beaten after the march.

Amnesty International visits/reports

- Amnesty International delegates visited Hungary in January, February, March and November.
- Violent attacks against Roma in Hungary: Time to investigate racial motivation (EUR 27/001/2010)

INDIA

REPUBLIC OF INDIA

Head of state:	**Pratibha Patil**
Head of government:	**Manmohan Singh**
Death penalty:	**retentionist**
Population:	**1,214.5 million**
Life expectancy:	**64.4 years**
Under-5 mortality (m/f):	**77/86 per 1,000**
Adult literacy:	**62.8 per cent**

Ongoing clashes between armed Maoists and state security forces escalated in Chhattisgarh, Jharkhand and West Bengal. More than 350 people were killed in bomb attacks in those states and in ethnically motivated attacks in Assam and other states. Protests by Adivasis (Indigenous communities) and other marginalized communities against moves to acquire their lands and natural resources without proper consultation or consent resulted in the suspension of key corporate-led projects. Human rights defenders in these cases were attacked by state or private agents, with politically motivated charges, including sedition, being brought against some. More than 100 people, mostly youth protesters, were killed in the Kashmir valley during protests between June and September. Torture and other ill-treatment, extrajudicial executions, deaths in custody and administrative detentions remained rife. Institutional mechanisms meant to protect human rights and human rights defenders remained weak and judicial processes failed to ensure justice for many victims of past violations and abuses. At least 105 people were sentenced to death but, for the sixth successive year, no executions took place.

Background

India's rapid economic growth was limited to key urban and suburban areas; large parts of rural India continued to experience grinding poverty, aggravated by an agricultural crisis and declining food availability for those living in poverty. According to official estimates, about 30 to 50 per cent of the population were living in poverty. Of these, people living in rural areas were guaranteed at least 100 days of work per year, but the authorities continued to pay them below the national minimum wage.

US President Barack Obama's November visit to India underscored the country's growing international and regional status. However, India routinely put economic and strategic interests above human rights considerations. The Indian authorities did not speak out against gross human rights violations committed by the authorities in neighbouring Myanmar, and remained silent on demands for the Sri Lankan government to be held accountable for human rights violations committed at the end of that country's war in 2009.

Relations between India and Pakistan remained fragile following Pakistan's ongoing failure to adequately address the November 2008 Mumbai attacks. Relations were also undermined by a rise in pro-independence protests in Indian-administered Kashmir.

Violence between security forces, militia and Maoists

In Chhattisgarh, clashes escalated between armed Maoists and state forces supported by the Salwa Judum militia, widely believed to be state-sponsored. In November, during a hearing at the Supreme Court on petitions filed against impunity, the state authorities claimed that this militia was no longer active. However, human rights organizations said it had been reconstituted as a local "peace force".

Similar clashes and bomb attacks took place in Adivasi areas of Jharkhand and West Bengal. Both sides routinely targeted civilians, mainly Adivasis, who reported killings and abductions. Around 30,000 Adivasis continued to be internally displaced in Chhattisgarh alone, of whom 10,000 lived in camps and 20,000 were dispersed in neighbouring Andhra Pradesh and Orissa.

■ In May, at least 144 passengers were killed and 200 others injured when an express train derailed reportedly after an explosion on the track in West Medhinipur district. The area routinely saw violence between armed Maoists on the one hand and on the other, the ruling Communist Party of India (Marxist) (CPI-M) and the central paramilitary forces. In August, one of the people accused in the explosion case, Umakanta Mahato, an Adivasi leader of the People's Committee against Police Atrocities (PCPA), was extrajudicially executed after a round of political violence in which three CPI-M supporters were killed by the PCPA.

■ In September, security forces engaged in anti-Maoist operations in Chhattisgarh illegally detained 40 Adivasis, stripped and tortured them. They detained 17 other people, two of whom were 16 years old, and sexually assaulted two of the women. The authorities failed to pursue the findings of an initial inquiry which held security force personnel responsible for the violations.

■ Peace activists belonging to Vanvasi Chetna Ashram (VCA), a Gandhian NGO, were forced to stop working in the conflict areas of Chhattisgarh. VCA founder Himanshu Kumar could not return to Dantewada town which he had fled in 2009 following persistent harassment and intimidation by Salwa Judum, the state police and paramilitary forces.

■ In September, the Chhattisgarh police accused Adivasi leader and prisoner of conscience Kartam Joga, whose petition against impunity was being heard by the Supreme Court, of collaborating with armed Maoists.

■ In December, a local court in Chhattisgarh convicted human rights defender, medical practitioner and prisoner of conscience Binayak Sen of collaborating with Maoists and sentenced him to life imprisonment.

Corporate accountability

Both the authorities and companies failed to ensure adequate consultation with and protection of the rights of local marginalized communities affected by mining, irrigation and other corporate projects. In several states, Adivasi and other marginalized local communities staged protests – some of them successful – against the authorities' failure to respect their claims, guaranteed by the Constitution and recent legislation, over lands which were threatened by corporate ventures.

■ In a landmark victory for Adivasi rights, the Indian government rejected plans to mine bauxite in the Niyamgiri Hills, Orissa, and to expand an alumina refinery in nearby Lanjigarh. The plans were proposed by a subsidiary of UK-based Vedanta Resources and the state-owned Orissa Mining Corporation. The authorities found that both projects violated forest and environmental laws and would perpetrate abuses against the Dongria Kondh and other Adivasi communities.

■ In June, a Bhopal court sentenced eight Indian executives at Union Carbide to two years' imprisonment for their role in the 1984 Bhopal gas tragedy. The gas leak killed between 7,000 and 10,000 people in its immediate aftermath, and a further 15,000 over the next 20 years. The case was reopened by the Supreme Court in August, following public anger at what were widely viewed as excessively lenient sentences.

Excessive use of force

The police used excessive force to quell protests by local communities against forced evictions and the acquisition of their lands for corporate projects. The police failed to protect protesters when private militias, reportedly allied with ruling political parties, violently suppressed protests. The authorities did not carry out impartial and timely inquiries into most of these incidents.

■ In May, Adivasi leader Laxman Jamuda was killed when police fired at people protesting against the acquisition of Adivasi lands for a proposed Tata Steel project in Kalinganagar, Orissa. Nineteen people were injured, 10 sustaining bullet wounds. One thousand police officers cordoned off the villages while 200 private militia members forced their way in and demolished some houses.

■ In May, at least 20 protesters were injured when police used tear gas and batons to disperse about 1,000 farmers demonstrating against the takeover of their farmlands and village common land for South Korean Pohong Steel Company's (POSCO) proposed steel project in Jagatsinghpur district, Orissa.

■ In July, two fishermen were killed when police fired at a protest against the government's takeover of land for a thermal power project promoted by Nagarjuna Construction Company in Sompeta town, Andhra Pradesh. Five people sustained bullet wounds, and 350 people, including 60 police officers, were injured as police, assisted by a private militia, dispersed protesters from 10 villages. The next day, the authorities cancelled the environmental clearance given for the project.

Continuing protests forced the authorities to reconsider existing land acquisition laws. In September, the Federal authorities proposed new legislation for the extractive sector with benefit-sharing arrangements for local communities along with new frameworks for free, prior and informed consent for Adivasis and consultation for other marginalized communities. New legislation containing improvements in land acquisition procedures and rehabilitation and resettlement policies was pending before parliament.

Human rights defenders

People defending the land rights of Adivasis and other marginalized communities, in some cases by using recent legislation to obtain information to protect their rights, continued to face serious threats and violent attacks from private militias.

■ In January, Sadhu Singh Takhtupura was killed in Amritsar district, Punjab, after he led local farmers to resist land grabs allegedly by an alliance of local political leaders, contractors and corrupt officials. In October, another peasant leader, Pirthipal Singh

Alishar, was shot dead by assailants after he led a campaign against usury by money lenders. In both cases, local communities alleged that the police failed to investigate and bring those responsible to justice.

■ In January, Satish Shetty was murdered after refusing to stop exposing land grabs in Pune city using new Right to Information legislation.

■ In July, Amit Jethwa, who had campaigned against illegal mining in the Gir forest of Gujarat, was shot dead outside the high court complex in Ahmedabad.

Campaigners against human rights violations faced harassment, intimidation and arrests on false and politically motivated charges.

■ Between March and June, the Gujarat police detained 13 activists, including Adivasi labour activist Avinash Kulkarni. They faced trial on charges of collaborating with armed Maoists.

Impunity

Impunity for abuses and violations remained widespread; despite ongoing protests in the north-east, the authorities remained unwilling to repeal the Armed Forces Special Powers Act, 1958, which facilitates impunity. Perpetrators of enforced disappearances, extrajudicial executions and other human rights violations in Punjab between 1984 and 1994, and Assam between 1998 and 2001, continued to evade justice. Members of Dalit communities in several states faced attacks and discrimination. The authorities failed to use existing special laws enacted to prosecute perpetrators of such violence.

1984 massacre

In September, the Supreme Court directed the trial of Congress Party leader Sajjan Kumar to proceed. The case against another former Congress Party leader, Jagdish Tytler, was closed in April by a Delhi court. Both men were accused of inciting their supporters to commit the Delhi massacre, in which thousands of Sikhs were killed, following the assassination of then Prime Minister Indira Gandhi in 1984.

Communal violence

Cases against some of those responsible for the 2002 attacks against Muslim minorities in Gujarat, in which about 2,000 people were killed, made little progress. Proceedings were marred by the authorities' openly hostile attitude towards witnesses, the investigating agencies' refusal to examine crucial evidence including official telephone records, and the destruction of evidence linking key political leaders to the violence.

In December, Teesta Setalvad of the Centre for Justice and Peace and a team of lawyers defending victims' rights were harassed by Gujarat police who charged them with concocting evidence.

Jammu and Kashmir

Impunity for past violations in Kashmir, including the disappearance of thousands of people since 1989 during the armed conflict in Kashmir, continued. Official inquiries into some of the violations made slow or little progress.

■ Between June and September, the police and security forces fired at protesters during pro-Independence protests demanding accountability for past violations in the Kashmir valley. More than 100 people, mostly youths, were killed and 800 others, including media workers, were injured. An inquiry, instituted by the state authorities, covered 17 of the 100 deaths, despite demands by Amnesty International and other organizations for an independent, impartial and thorough investigation into all the deaths. The inquiry made little progress.

The authorities made widespread use of administrative detentions, detaining 322 people between January and September. Following the protests, on the basis of recommendations by a government-appointed team of interlocutors who visited the valley, the authorities released two separatist leaders, Shabir Shah and Mohammad Nayeem Khan.

■ Fourteen-year-old Mushtaq Ahmad Sheikh was charged with taking part in violent protests and detained in Srinigar in April. He was later transferred to jails in Udhampur and Jammu where he remained.

Extrajudicial executions

Recent data disclosed by the National Human Rights Commission (NHRC) on people killed in clashes with the police between 1993 and 2008, showed that of the 2,560 deaths reported, 1,224 occurred in "faked encounters" implying they were extrajudicial executions. By the end of the year, the NHRC had awarded compensation to the relatives of 16 victims. Convictions of those responsible for extrajudicial executions were exceptionally rare and proceedings in such cases remained slow.

■ In January, the Supreme Court ordered a Central Bureau of Investigation probe into the 2005 killings, allegedly by the Gujarat police, of Sohrabuddin, his wife Kausar Bi and accomplice Tulsiram Prajapati, after finding the state police investigation shoddy.

■ In November, the Gujarat government constituted a new special police team to investigate the killings of Ishrat Jahan and three others at the hands of the Gujarat police in 2004.

Arbitrary arrests and detentions

More than 100 people were detained without charge, for periods ranging from one week to a month in connection with bomb attacks in several states, including Delhi, Uttar Pradesh and Rajasthan. Reports of torture and other ill-treatment of suspects led to protests by both Muslim and Hindu organizations. Security legislation, tightened after the November 2008 attacks in Mumbai, was used to detain suspects. Despite ongoing protests, the authorities refused to repeal the Armed Forces Special Powers Act 1958, which grants security forces in specified areas or states the power to shoot to kill in circumstances where they are not necessarily at imminent risk.

Death penalty

In December, India voted against a UN General Assembly resolution calling for a worldwide moratorium on executions. At least 105 people, including Ajmal Kasab, the sole surviving Pakistani man accused of involvement in the 2008 Mumbai attacks, were sentenced to death. However, for the sixth successive year, no executions took place and the death sentences of 13 people were commuted to life imprisonment. Amendments to the law extended the death penalty to hijackers. Under new legislation, 16 states published death row figures, but at least five others refused to do so.

Amnesty International visits/reports

Amnesty International delegates visited India in February, May/June and December.

Don't mine us out of existence: Bauxite mine and refinery devastate lives in India (ASA 20/001/2010)

India: Chhattisgarh authorities must immediately release witness to extrajudicial executions (ASA 20/002/2010)

India: Government of Manipur must release Irom Sharmila Chanu (ASA 20/003/2010)

India's relations with Myanmar fail to address human rights concerns in run-up to elections (ASA 20/016/2010)

India: Urgent need for Government to act as death toll rises in Kashmir (ASA 20/027/2010)

India: Briefing on the Prevention of Torture Bill (ASA 20/030/2010)

INDONESIA

REPUBLIC OF INDONESIA

Head of state and government:	Susilo Bambang Yudhoyono
Death penalty:	retentionist
Population:	232.5 million
Life expectancy:	71.5 years
Under-5 mortality (m/f):	37/27 per 1,000
Adult literacy:	92 per cent

The security forces tortured and otherwise ill-treated detainees, and used excessive force against protesters, sometimes leading to death. No adequate accountability mechanisms were in place to ensure justice or act as an effective deterrent against police abuses. The criminal justice system remained unable to address ongoing impunity for current and past human rights violations. Restrictions on freedom of expression were severe in areas such as Papua and Maluku. Religious minorities and lesbian, gay, bisexual and transgender groups faced violent attacks and discrimination. The maternal mortality ratio remained among the highest in the East Asia and Pacific region. No one was executed during the year.

Torture and other ill-treatment

The security forces tortured and otherwise ill-treated detainees, particularly criminal suspects from poor and marginalized communities, and those suspected of pro-independence activities in Papua and Maluku provinces. Accountability mechanisms put in place to deal with violations remained inadequate.

■ Two videos emerged during the year showing members of the police and military torturing and otherwise ill-treating Papuan men. The first video showed Yawan Wayeni, a Papuan political activist, just before his death in August 2009. Despite severe abdominal injuries, he was denied medical assistance by the police, who accused him of being an insurgent. He had been arrested earlier by members of the Police Mobile Brigade at his house in Yapen Island, Papua. The second video published online in October showed Papuans being kicked and otherwise physically abused by members of the Indonesian military, and two Papuan men being tortured during interrogation. Indonesian officials confirmed the authenticity of both videos.

■ Yusuf Sapakoly, 52, died of kidney failure in a hospital in Ambon, Maluku province, after being refused access to adequate medical assistance by

prison authorities. The father of four was arrested in 2007 for assisting a group of peaceful political activists who unfurled the "Benang Raja" flag, a symbol of South Maluku independence, in front of the Indonesian President. Yusuf Sapakoly required dialysis for kidney failure but was consistently denied treatment by authorities at Nania prison. He also said he did not receive adequate treatment for rib injuries he had suffered in detention.

Excessive use of force

The police used excessive force during arrests and to quell demonstrations, sometimes killing people.

■ In August, police opened fire on protesters, killing seven and injuring 20, at the Biau sectoral police station in Central Sulawesi province. The protesters had raided the police station, attacking police officers and burning motorcycles parked outside, in response to the death in custody of Kasmir Timumun. Several police officers were injured during the incident. According to local sources, Kasmir Timumun, aged 19, was found hanging in his cell on 30 August after being held for allegedly speeding and injuring a police officer. The police claimed that he had committed suicide, but his family alleged that there were signs of torture or other ill-treatment including bruises on parts of his body and neck. The family were denied access to his autopsy report.

There were concerns that counter-terrorism operations by the police that led to the deaths of at least 24 suspects did not meet national and international standards on the use of force.

Freedom of expression

Freedom of expression continued to be suppressed in some cases, with human rights defenders, journalists and other activists intimidated, harassed and sometimes killed.

■ In July, Tama Satrya Langkun, a Jakarta-based anti-corruption activist, was severely beaten by unknown persons in an apparent move to silence him. That same month, Ardiansyah Matra, a journalist covering corruption and illegal logging in Papua, was found dead in the province.

■ At least 100 political activists were in prison for peacefully expressing their views in areas seeking independence such as Maluku and Papua.

■ Prisoner of conscience Yusak Pakage, sentenced to 10 years' imprisonment, was released in July following a Presidential Decree. However, Filep Karma who was arrested at the same time and sentenced to 15 years' imprisonment, remained in prison. The two men were convicted in 2005 for raising the "Morning Star" flag.

■ In August, 23 men were arrested in Maluku province for their peaceful political activities. At the end of the year, 21 remained detained. They were facing trial on charges of rebellion which carries the threat of life imprisonment.

Discrimination

Religious minorities and lesbian, gay, bisexual and transgender (LGBT) groups faced violent attacks and discrimination. The police failed to take adequate measures to guarantee their security. An LGBT regional conference due to be held in Surabaya in March was cancelled after threats of violent reprisals by radical Islamist groups. The Ahmadiyya community were targeted for abuse and discrimination. In August, the Minister of Religion called for the community to be disbanded. An estimated 90 Ahmadis displaced in 2006 after arson attacks on their homes, continued living in temporary housing in Mataram, Lombok. At least 30 churches were attacked or forced to close down during the year. In April, the Constitutional Court upheld legal provisions criminalizing blasphemy. At least 14 people were in prison on blasphemy charges by the end of the year.

Sexual and reproductive rights

Laws restricting sexual and reproductive rights hampered the government's efforts to tackle maternal mortality. These included laws that support gender stereotyped roles, particularly regarding marriage and childbearing, and laws that criminalize certain types of consensual sex and the provision of information on sexuality and reproduction. Some laws and policies denied unmarried women and girls full access to reproductive health services. It was illegal for married women and girls to access certain reproductive health services without their husband's consent. Abortion was criminalized in all cases except when the health of the mother or foetus is endangered, or in the case of rape victims.

Many women and girls were at risk of unwanted pregnancies, which left them vulnerable to a range of health problems and human rights abuses, including being forced to marry young or drop out of school. Some sought an abortion, often in unsafe conditions.

According to official government figures, unsafe abortions accounted for between five and 11 per cent of maternal deaths in Indonesia. The maternal mortality ratio remained among the highest in the East Asia and Pacific region, with an estimated 228 maternal deaths per 100,000 live births.

Domestic workers

Domestic workers – an estimated 2.6 million people – the vast majority of whom were women and girls, were denied the full range of legal protection available to other workers under the Manpower Act. A bill on domestic workers was discussed within the Parliamentary Commission on Manpower, Transmigration, Population Affairs and Health. However, the law had yet to be passed by the end of the year.

■ In December 2009, Lenny, a 14-year-old girl from Java, was tricked by a recruitment agent who, instead of employing her as a domestic worker, brought her to his home and "sold" her to her new employers for 100,000 Indonesian rupiah (US$11). Lenny was drugged and taken hundreds of miles away to Aceh. She spent three months working from 4am to 11pm each day, without pay. During that time, she suffered multiple forms of physical and psychological abuse. Lenny finally managed to escape in February, and brought a case against her employers that same month. The case was ongoing at the end of the year.

Impunity

Impunity for past gross human rights violations in Aceh, Papua, Timor-Leste and elsewhere continued. The government continued to promote reconciliation with Timor-Leste at the expense of justice for crimes during the Indonesian occupation of East Timor (1975-1999). Most past human rights violations against human rights defenders, including torture, murder and enforced disappearances, remained unsolved and those responsible were not brought to justice. In September, the government signed the International Convention against enforced disappearance.

■ In 2009, Parliament recommended that an ad hoc human rights court be created to try those responsible for enforced disappearances in 1997-1998. However, the government had not acted on the recommendations by the end of the year.

■ Although two people were convicted of involvement in the 2004 murder of prominent activist Munir Said Thalib (known as "Munir"), credible allegations were made that those responsible for ordering his murder were still at large.

I

Death penalty

No executions were reported. However, at least 120 people remained under sentence of death.

Amnesty International visits/reports

🚍 Amnesty International delegates visited Indonesia in February, March, October and November.

📄 Displaced and forgotten: Ahmadiyya in Indonesia (ASA 21/006/2010)

📄 Indonesia: Left without a choice – barriers to reproductive health (ASA 21/013/2010)

IRAN

ISLAMIC REPUBLIC OF IRAN

Head of state:	Leader of the Islamic Republic of Iran: Ayatollah Sayed 'Ali Khamenei
Head of government:	President: Dr Mahmoud Ahmadinejad
Death penalty:	retentionist
Population:	75.1 million
Life expectancy:	71.9 years
Under-5 mortality (m/f):	33/35 per 1,000
Adult literacy:	82.3 per cent

The authorities maintained severe restrictions on freedom of expression, association and assembly. Sweeping controls on domestic and international media aimed at reducing Iranians' contact with the outside world were imposed. Individuals and groups risked arrest, torture and imprisonment if perceived as co-operating with human rights and foreign-based Persian-language media organizations. Political dissidents, women's and minority rights activists and other human rights defenders, lawyers, journalists and students were rounded up in mass and other arrests and hundreds were imprisoned. Torture and other ill-treatment of detainees were routine and committed with impunity. Women continued to face discrimination under the law and in practice. The authorities acknowledged 252 executions, but there were credible reports of more than 300 other executions. The true total could be even higher. At least one juvenile offender was executed. Sentences of death by stoning continued to be passed, but no stonings were known to have been carried out. Floggings and an increased number of amputations were carried out.

Background

Iran's human rights record was assessed under the UN Universal Periodic Review in February; the government subsequently accepted all general recommendations but rejected those calling for specific reforms to end religious and gender discrimination and the application of the death penalty, especially against juvenile offenders. The government also rejected recommendations that it co-operate with certain UN human rights bodies.

In April, Iran was elected to the UN Commission on the Status of Women. In August, the CERD Committee expressed concern at the "limited enjoyment of political, economic, social and cultural rights" by various minority communities, in particular with regard to housing, education, freedom of expression and religion, health and employment. In September, the UN Secretary-General highlighted "many areas of continuing concern with respect to human rights" in a report to the General Assembly. In December, the UN General Assembly passed a resolution expressing concern about human rights in Iran and called for government action to end violations.

Scores if not hundreds of Iranians continued to flee the country in fear for their safety because of the high levels of repression by the authorities.

International tension persisted over Iran's nuclear enrichment programme. In June, the UN Security Council imposed further sanctions on Iran over concerns that it was developing nuclear weapons.

Armed groups killed civilians in bomb attacks. For example, an attack in July on a mosque at Zahedan killed 21 people, including worshippers, and injured hundreds of others. Another, near a mosque in Chabahar, killed at least 38 people and injured over 50. The People's Resistance Movement of Iran (PRMI), an armed group also known as Jondallah, claimed responsibility for both. In September, a bomb attack in Mahabad killed at least 10 people and injured over 80, including children, following which Iranian security forces were reported to have crossed into Iraq and killed at least 30 people. Kurdish groups denied responsibility for the attack.

Freedom of expression, association and assembly

The government entrenched the severe curbs on freedom of expression, association and assembly it had imposed in 2009. The security forces were deployed in force to deter or disperse further public protests. Scores if not hundreds of people arrested in connection with the mass protests in 2009 continued to be held, most of them serving prison terms, although others were released. Scores more were arrested throughout 2010.

Mir Hossein Mousavi and Mehdi Karroubi, who had stood against President Ahmadinejad in the June 2009 presidential election, continued to face severe restrictions on their freedom of movement. Government supporters attacked them or their families, and newspapers were instructed not to report about them or about former president Mohammad Khatami. Two major political parties opposed to the government were banned while others remained prohibited.

The government purged universities of "secular" teaching staff and imposed education bans on students engaged in campus protests.

The authorities continued to restrict access to outside sources of information such as the internet. International radio and television broadcasts were jammed. In January, the authorities banned contact by Iranians with some 60 news outlets and foreign-based organizations. Those willing to speak to the few large Persian-language media outlets on human rights issues were threatened or harassed by security officials. Many Iranians turned to social networking websites to express their views.

The authorities banned newspapers and student journals and prosecuted journalists whose reporting they deemed "against the system". Wiretapping and intercepting of SMS and email communications were routine. A shadowy "cyber army", reportedly linked to the Revolutionary Guards, organized attacks on domestic and foreign internet sites deemed to be anti-government, while other sites, including some associated with religious leaders, were filtered.

Arbitrary arrests and detentions

Security officials, generally in plain clothes and without showing identification or arrest warrants, continued to arrest arbitrarily government opponents and people seen to be dissenting from officially approved values on account of their views or lifestyle. Among those arrested were human rights activists, independent trade unionists, students and political dissidents.

Those arrested were often held for long periods during which they were denied contact with their lawyers or families, tortured or otherwise ill-treated, and denied access to medical care. Some were

sentenced to prison terms after unfair trials. Others sentenced after unfair trials in previous years remained in jail.

■ In February, the UN Working Group on Arbitrary Detention declared that three US nationals detained in July 2009 while hiking near the Iraq-Iran border were held arbitrarily. In August, it concluded that Isa Saharkhiz, a journalist and member of Iran's Committee to Protect Freedom of the Press, held since July 2009 and sentenced in September 2010 to three years' imprisonment for "insulting the country's leadership" and "propaganda against the system", was also being arbitrarily detained and should be released.

■ Human rights lawyer Nasrin Sotoudeh was arrested on 4 September. She remained held at the end of 2010, on trial on security charges relating to her peaceful human rights activities and defence of her clients.

Unfair trials

The year saw a further degradation of the criminal justice system, which offered little protection of human rights. Political suspects received grossly unfair trials in which they often faced vaguely worded charges that did not amount to recognizably criminal offences. Frequently, they were convicted in the absence of defence lawyers on the basis of "confessions" or other information allegedly obtained under torture in pre-trial detention. Courts accepted such "confessions" as evidence without investigating how they were obtained.

■ Blogger Hossein Ronaghi-Maleki, arrested in December 2009, was sentenced to 15 years in prison on national security charges. When he complained that he had been tortured, the judge told him he "deserved it".

Torture and other ill-treatment

Torture and other ill-treatment in pre-trial detention remained common, facilitated by the routine denial of access to lawyers and continuing impunity for perpetrators. Methods reported included severe beatings; forcing detainees' heads into toilets to make them ingest human excrement; mock executions; confinement in very small, cramped spaces; deprivation of light, food and water; and denial of medical treatment. In one case, a male detainee was reported to have been raped; others were threatened with rape.

■ In August, Gholam-Reza Bayat, a Kurdish youth, was reported to have died from internal bleeding after he was beaten in custody in Kamyaran.

Details of torture in 2009 continued to emerge. In February, a former member of the volunteer paramilitary Basij force described how tens of boys had been rounded up in Shiraz, thrown into shipping containers and systematically raped. After expressing concerns to a Basij leader, he and others were detained for 100 days without access to their families and beaten. He also alleged that he faced a mock execution.

Impunity

Members of the security forces continued to violate human rights with near-total impunity.

The prosecution of 12 men, including 11 officials accused of committing serious abuses at Kahrizak prison before it was closed in July 2009, appeared to scapegoat low-ranking officials for only some of the serious abuses that took place after the June 2009 election, which in several cases had led to the death of detainees. Two of the 12 were sentenced to death but then pardoned by their victims' families, as permitted under Iranian law. Nine others received prison terms.

Judicial proceedings were initiated during 2010 against at least 50 individuals in relation to abuses at a Tehran University dormitory immediately after the 2009 election.

Human rights defenders

Human rights defenders were subject to serious human rights violations as they continued to press for greater respect for the rights of women and ethnic minorities and for an end to executions of juvenile offenders and stoning executions. Women's rights activists, lawyers, trade unionists, ethnic minority rights activists, students and others campaigning for human rights, unfairly tried and imprisoned in previous years, continued to be held. Others faced arbitrary arrest, harassment, prosecution and unfair trials. Some were prisoners of conscience; others were banned from travelling abroad. The ban on independent trade unions was maintained.

■ Emadeddin Baghi, a journalist, author and head of a banned NGO that advocated prisoners' rights who was detained between December 2009 and June 2010, began serving a seven-year prison sentence in December; he had been prosecuted for his peaceful human rights and journalistic activities.

The authorities harassed and, in some cases, arrested members of grassroots human rights organizations, including the Committee of Human Rights Reporters (CHRR) and Human Rights Activists of Iran (HRAI).

■ Shiva Nazar Ahari, a CHRR member arrested in December 2009, was released on bail in September, just before receiving a six-year prison term. She remained free pending the outcome of her appeal against the sentence, more than half of which is to be served in "exile".

Discrimination against women

Women faced continuing discrimination in law and practice; those campaigning for women's rights were targeted for state repression. Parliament debated draft legislation on family protection whose controversial provisions, if enacted, would further erode women's rights. Women's rights activists, including those mounting the One Million Signatures Campaign to demand legal equality for women, continued to face pressure.

■ Mahboubeh Karami, a member of the One Million Signatures Campaign, was detained for the fifth time in March and held until 18 August. In September, she was sentenced to four years' imprisonment for membership of the HRAI, "propaganda against the state" and "conspiring against the state". She remained free pending appeal.

■ Two women, Fatemeh Masjedi and Maryam Bigdeli, who had been convicted on charges relating to their peaceful collection of signatures for the One Million Signatures Campaign, were facing six months' imprisonment at the end of the year after an appeal court upheld the convictions.

In April, the Supreme Leader called for renewed attention to enforcing the state-imposed obligatory dress code. In May, a "chastity and modesty" campaign based on a 2005 law was launched, targeting those who do not comply with the dress · code in public, including on university campuses. In September, reports suggested that women's enrolment in universities had dropped substantially.

Discrimination – ethnic minorities

Iran's ethnic minority communities, including Ahwazi Arabs, Azerbaijanis, Baluch, Kurds and Turkmen, suffered ongoing systematic discrimination in law and practice. The use of minority languages in schools and government offices continued to be prohibited. Those who campaigned for greater political participation or recognition of minorities' economic, social and cultural rights faced systematic threats, arrest and imprisonment.

In September, four Ahwazi Arabs held since June 2009 were reported to have been sentenced to death on charges including "enmity against God and corruption on earth".

Around 20 Azerbaijani activists arrested in May around the anniversary of mass demonstrations in 2006 against a cartoon in a state-run newspaper which many Azerbaijanis found insulting were released in November. Akbar Azad, a writer, remained held as his family could not meet the high bail set.

Mohammad Saber Malek Raisi, a Baluch youth aged 15 from Sarbaz, was reported in July to have been held without charge or trial since September 2009, possibly to force his elder brother to surrender to the authorities. In December, 11 Baluch men convicted after unfair trials were executed in Zahedan, apparently in retaliation for the PRMI bomb attack five days earlier.

Kaveh Ghasemi Kermanshahi, a Kurdish human rights activist and member of the One Million Signatures Campaign, was held between February and May, including 80 days in solitary confinement. His trial on national security charges began in October.

In October, Arash Saghar, a Turkmen activist in the election campaign of Mir Hossein Mousavi, was sentenced to eight years in prison after being convicted of "spying for Turkmenistan".

Freedom of religion

Members of religious minorities, including Christian converts, Sunni Muslims, dissident Shi'a clerics, and the Ahl-e Haq and Dervish communities, continued to suffer discrimination, harassment, arbitrary detention, and attacks on community property. Members of the Baha'i community, who remained unable to access higher education, faced increased persecution.

Dissident Shi'a cleric Ayatollah Kazemeyni Boroujerdi remained imprisoned following an unfair trial in 2007. Seven of his followers were arrested in December.

Seven Baha'i leaders arrested in 2008 were sentenced in August to 20 years' imprisonment following grossly unfair proceedings. They were convicted of espionage and engaging in propaganda against Islam. In September, the sentences were reportedly halved on appeal.

In May, 24 Dervishes were sentenced to prison terms, internal exile and flogging for taking part in a 2009 demonstration in Gonabad, north-eastern Iran.

Yousef Naderkhani, a Christian convert and member of the Church of Iran in Rasht, was sentenced to death in October after being convicted of apostasy.

Cruel, inhuman and degrading punishments

Sentences of flogging and amputation continued to be imposed and increasingly carried out, although it was not possible to ascertain the real total. Speaking before the UN Human Rights Council in April and June, Mohammad Javad Larijani, head of Iran's official human rights body, insisted that the government did not consider such punishments as forms of torture.

In April, journalist and filmmaker Mohammad Nourizad was sentenced to three and a half years in prison and 50 lashes for "propaganda against the system" and "insulting officials". He said in November that he and others had been tortured. He began a hunger strike in December.

Death penalty

The authorities acknowledged 252 executions, including of five women and one juvenile offender. There were also credible reports of more than 300 other executions that were not officially acknowledged, mostly in Vakilabad Prison in Mashhad. At least 143 juvenile offenders remained on death row. The actual totals were likely to have been higher as the authorities restricted reporting on the death penalty.

Death sentences were imposed for drug smuggling, armed robbery, murder, espionage, political violence and sexual offences. The authorities imposed the death penalty and used execution as a political tool.

In January, two men sentenced to death for their alleged membership in a monarchist organization in connection with the post-election unrest were hanged without warning.

In May, four Kurds convicted for their alleged links with Kurdish opposition groups were executed.

No stonings were reported, but at least 15 prisoners, mostly women, remained at risk of stoning.

Sakineh Mohammadi Ashtiani, a woman whose 2006 sentence of death by stoning was under review, attracted global attention when it appeared likely that she would be executed. Those campaigning on her behalf faced harassment or arrest.

In December, an amended anti-narcotics law was published, extending the death penalty to offences involving synthetic drugs. The same month, Iran was one of the minority of states that voted against a UN General Assembly resolution calling for a worldwide moratorium on executions.

Amnesty International visits/reports

🚌 The authorities did not reply to letters sent by Amnesty International and continued to deny the organization access to Iran, maintaining a block on the organization's ability to conduct in-country fact-finding on human rights that has been in force since 1979.

📄 Iran: Amnesty International's comments on the national report presented by the Islamic Republic of Iran for the Universal Periodic Review (MDE 13/021/2010)

📄 From protest to prison: Iran one year after the election (MDE 13/062/2010)

📄 Sakineh Mohammadi Ashtiani: A life in the balance (MDE 13/089/2010)

📄 Iran: Executions by stoning (MDE 13/095/2010)

IRAQ

REPUBLIC OF IRAQ

Head of state:	Jalal Talabani
Head of government:	Nuri al-Maliki
Death penalty:	retentionist
Population:	31.5 million
Life expectancy:	68.5 years
Under-5 mortality (m/f):	43/38 per 1,000
Adult literacy:	77.6 per cent

Armed groups opposed to the government carried out numerous suicide bomb and other attacks, killing hundreds of civilians. Militia groups also carried out targeted killings. Serious human rights violations were committed by Iraqi security forces and US troops: thousands of people were detained without charge or trial, including some held for several years, although many others were released. All prisons formerly controlled by US forces were transferred to Iraqi administration by mid-July together with all but some 200 detainees who remained in US custody in Iraq. Torture and other ill-treatment of detainees by Iraqi security forces were endemic; some detainees were tortured in secret prisons and several others died in custody in suspicious circumstances. The courts handed down death sentences after unfair trials and at least 1,300 prisoners were reported to be on death row. One execution was reported, although the real total was believed to be much higher. Around 3 million Iraqis were either internally displaced within Iraq or refugees abroad. Women continued to face discrimination and violence.

Background

Parliamentary elections in March resulted in a stalemate until November, when a new government was agreed headed by the incumbent Prime Minister, Nuri al-Maliki. Armed groups opposed to the government stepped up suicide bomb and other attacks in the interim period, killing and injuring hundreds of civilians.

The USA withdrew its last combat troops from Iraq in mid-August, although around 50,000 US troops remained reportedly in a support and training role.

In July, US forces in Iraq (USF-I) completed their handover of detainees and prisons to the Iraqi government as required by the 2008 Status of Forces Agreement (SOFA) between the USA and Iraq. Several thousand detainees were transferred to Iraqi custody. Around 200 detainees, mostly leaders of armed groups and former senior members of the Ba'ath administration under Saddam Hussein, remained in USF-I detention, in a section of Camp Cropper (renamed al-Karkh Prison by the Iraqi government in July), apparently at the request of the Iraqi authorities. The SOFA contained no human rights safeguards despite the well-established record of torture and other ill-treatment of detainees by Iraqi security forces.

Most Iraqis continued to live in poverty. Shortages of water and electricity supplies were chronic, and unemployment was above 50 per cent. The continuing high level of insecurity deterred foreign investment, and corruption in government institutions was rife. In July, a US official audit concluded that the Pentagon could not account for over 95 per cent of US$9.1 billion intended for Iraqi reconstruction that it had been given to manage.

In February, Iraq's human rights record was assessed under the UN Universal Periodic Review.

In August, the UN Security Council unanimously adopted resolution 1936, extending the mandate of the United Nations Assistance Mission for Iraq (UNAMI) for another year.

In November, Iraq ratified the International Convention against enforced disappearance, although it entered reservations concerning individual claims.

Abuses by armed groups

Armed groups opposed to the government and the presence of US forces committed gross human rights abuses, including kidnapping, torture and murder. They carried out suicide bombings in public places and other large-scale indiscriminate attacks against civilians, and assassinated individuals. Many attacks were carried out by al-Qa'ida in Iraq, two of whose leaders were killed in April in a raid by US and Iraqi forces, and its allies among Sunni armed groups.

In October, it was reported that many former members of Awakening Councils, Sunni militia recruited to assist US forces fighting al-Qa'ida in Iraq, had gone over to al-Qa'ida under threat and out of disillusion with what they saw as their abandonment by the USF-I.

Shi'a militia, in particular members of 'Asa'ib Ahl al-Haq (the League of the Righteous), a Mahdi Army splinter group, also committed gross human rights abuses, including kidnapping and murder.

Many victims of attacks were civilians, including members of ethnic and religious minorities, local authority officials, lawyers and judges, journalists and other professionals. Women and children were among those killed.

■ On 25 January, three co-ordinated suicide car bombs exploded in quick succession in central Baghdad, killing at least 41 people and injuring more than 75 others. The Islamic State of Iraq, a front for al-Qa'ida in Iraq, claimed responsibility.

■ On 2 February, a woman walking with Shi'a pilgrims in Baghdad detonated an explosive belt killing at least 54 people and injuring more than 100 others.

■ On 14 May, three suicide bombers killed around 25 people and injured more than 100 at a football field in a Shi'a neighbourhood of Tal-'Afar, a Turkomen town between Mosul and the Syrian border.

■ On 31 October, more than 40 worshippers were killed in a Catholic church in Baghdad following an attack claimed by the Islamic State of Iraq, during which about 100 worshippers were taken hostage. Following a three-hour stand-off, Iraqi security forces stormed the church and the hostage-takers reportedly used grenades and detonated suicide belts to kill hostages.

Detention without trial

Thousands of people continued to be held without charge or trial. Some were held by the USF-I and transferred to Iraqi custody by mid-July, when the last US-run prison, Camp Cropper, was handed to Iraqi control. Many detainees had no access to lawyers and their families, and some were held in secret prisons operated by the Ministries of Interior and Defence where torture and other ill-treatment were rife. Most detainees were Sunni Muslims suspected of

supporting Sunni armed groups. Many had been held for several years.

■ Qusay 'Abdel-Razaq Zabib, a police officer, remained held without charge or trial. He was arrested by US soldiers at the police station where he worked, near Tikrit, on 17 July 2008, apparently because he was suspected of supporting armed groups. He was held at a succession of US-run prisons and was at Camp Taji when he and the prison were transferred to Iraqi control. In mid-November he was transferred from prison to a police station in Tikrit, from where he was released on 30 December.

Torture and other ill-treatment

Torture and other ill-treatment of detainees were rife in Iraqi prisons, especially those controlled by the Ministries of Defence and Interior. Detainees were beaten with cables and hosepipes, suspended by their limbs for long periods, given electric shocks, had their limbs broken, were asphyxiated with plastic bags, and raped or threatened with rape. Torture was used to extract information from detainees and "confessions" that could be used as evidence against them in court. USF-I secret files published by the Wikileaks organization in October showed that US soldiers had many times reported evidence of torture by Iraqi security forces to their superiors up to the end of 2009; such reporting apparently did not prompt investigations.

■ In April, a secret detention facility was reported to have been uncovered at the former Muthanna airport in central Baghdad in which more than 400 detainees were being held, mostly Sunni Arabs who had been detained in Mosul in late 2009. The secret prison, most of whose inmates said they had been tortured, was reported to be controlled by the office of Prime Minister Nuri al-Maliki. The government released about 95 of the detainees and moved others to al-Rusafa Prison in Baghdad. It denied that the prison was secret but closed it down, arresting three officers of the military unit that had run it.

Deaths in custody

Several detainees died in custody possibly as a result of torture or other ill-treatment.

■ Riyadh Mohammad Saleh al-'Uqaibi, a former army officer, died on 12 or 13 February at the Muthanna airport prison. Arrested in late September 2009, he was alleged to have been beaten so severely under interrogation that he sustained broken ribs, liver damage and internal bleeding. His body was returned to his family weeks later with a death certificate giving heart failure as the cause of death.

■ Two unnamed detainees died in US custody at Camp Cropper on 27 March and 12 April, before it was transferred to the Iraqi government. The USF-I announced that autopsies were being conducted but in both cases the cause and circumstances of death had not been disclosed by the end of 2010.

Trials of former Ba'ath party officials

The Supreme Iraqi Criminal Tribunal (SICT) continued to try former senior members of the Ba'ath party as well as military and other officials in the government of Saddam Hussain, toppled in 2003, who were accused of war crimes, crimes against humanity and other grave offences. Trials failed to meet international fair trial standards; the SICT lacked independence and was said by lawyers and judges to be influenced by political interference.

■ In October, two former government ministers – 74-year-old Tareq 'Aziz, the former Foreign Affairs Minister; and Sa'doun Shakir, former Interior Minister – as well as 'Abed Hamoud, Saddam Hussain's private secretary, were sentenced to death by the SICT after being convicted of participating in the elimination of Shi'a religious parties.

Human rights violations by US forces

US forces in Iraq committed serious human rights violations, including killings of civilians.

■ 'Omar 'Abdullah and his wife were killed on 10 March when US troops opened fire on their car in Baghdad's al-Iskan neighbourhood. A US military statement was reported to have said that the couple were killed during a joint US-Iraqi security operation and that there would be a joint investigation; no further information was released.

Thousands of classified files were published by Wikileaks. These showed, among other things, that US troops manning security roadblocks had shot dead many Iraqi civilians in previous years and that, contrary to their denials, the US military authorities had sought to keep a count of the number of Iraqi civilians killed in the conflict in Iraq. Revised estimates put the total number of civilian casualties in the conflict in Iraq between 2004 and 2009 at 66,081.

Violence against women and girls

Women were targeted for violence by armed groups, and women who did not adhere to a strict dress code were under threat. Women also suffered violence within the family and were inadequately protected under Iraqi law and in practice. Many women and girls were subject to harmful practices, including forced and early marriage.

In October, the Human Rights Ministry reported that at least 84 women had been killed in "honour killings" in 2009 – not including the Kurdistan region. It reiterated its call for legal changes, including amendments to Article 409 of the Penal Code, which provides that any man who kills his wife or female relative for surprising her in the act of adultery should receive no more than a three-year prison term. No change to the law was made.

Refugees and internally displaced people

Around 1.5 million displaced Iraqis were said to be living as refugees in Syria, Jordan, Lebanon, Turkey and other countries in the region. At least 1.5 million others were internally displaced, including about 500,000 homeless people living in settlements or camps in extremely harsh conditions. Thousands of internally displaced people returned to their homes in the belief that security conditions had improved, but they faced many problems. Several European countries forcibly returned failed Iraqi asylum-seekers to Iraq, in direct breach of advice from UNHCR, the UN refugee agency.

Death penalty

At least 279 people were sentenced to death and at least 1,300 prisoners were said to be on death row, although the authorities generally did not disclose information about the death penalty. One execution was made public, but it appeared that the total number of executions was considerably higher.

Most death sentences were passed by the Central Criminal Court of Iraq against defendants convicted of involvement in armed attacks. Trials consistently failed to satisfy international standards for fair trial; defendants frequently alleged that they had been forced to sign "confessions" under torture or other duress while held incommunicado in pre-trial detention and were unable to choose their own defence lawyers. Death sentences were also passed by the SICT.

■ 'Ali Hassan al-Majid, a cousin of and former senior official under Saddam Hussain, was executed on 25

January. He had been sentenced to death four times, the last of which was on 17 January.

In December, Iraq was one of a minority of states that voted against a UN General Assembly resolution calling for a worldwide moratorium on executions.

Kurdistan region of Iraq

The Kurdistan region remained largely unaffected by the political violence seen in other parts of Iraq. Human rights conditions continued generally to improve, although many abuses were reported.

In May, legislation was passed to create a human rights commission for the Kurdistan region. In June, the Kurdistan parliament extended the application of the 2006 anti-terrorism law for a further two years. In November a law restricting demonstrations was passed.

In November, on the occasion of the holy 'Eid al-Adha festival, the President of the Kurdistan Regional Government (KRG) issued an amnesty under which 207 prisoners were said to have been released. Among those freed were a few people who had been serving prison terms for "honour crimes"; women's rights activists criticized these releases.

Attacks on opposition activists

Members and supporters of political opposition groups were threatened, harassed, attacked or arrested.

■ On 14 February, unidentified gunmen attacked the office of the Kurdistan Islamic Union (KIU) party in Sulaimaniya, but caused no casualties. Four days later, the KRG authorities detained several KIU members in Dohuk.

■ On 16 February, armed men reportedly linked to the Patriotic Union of Kurdistan (PUK), one of the parties forming the KRG, violently disrupted a meeting of the opposition Goran Movement in Sulaimaniya; the authorities arrested 11 Goran Movement activists but took no action against those who broke up the meeting.

Freedom of expression

Several independent journalists were attacked.

■ On 4 May, Sardasht Osman, a student and journalist, was abducted in Erbil by unidentified armed men. Two days later, his body was found in Mosul, outside the area administered by the KRG. He was reported to have received anonymous threats because of articles criticizing senior Kurdish political leaders. However, a KRG-appointed investigative committee reported on 15 September that he had been killed by Ansar al-Islam, a Kurdish Sunni armed group. The authorities said one of the alleged perpetrators had been arrested. Sardasht Osman's family rejected the investigative committee's findings.

Violence against women

Women continued to suffer discrimination and violence. Incidents of men killing female relatives were reported, and scores of women died reportedly as a result of self-inflicted burns. Female genital mutilation was reported to be widely practised. According to Kurdish official records, in the first half of 2010 at least 671 women suffered "serious domestic violence" and at least 63 women were sexually abused.

Amnesty International visits/reports

🚗 Amnesty International visited the Kurdistan region of Iraq in May/June for human rights research and government meetings; they met the Minister of Interior and other senior officials and were allowed access to a number of detainees. Access to other parts of Iraq was considered unsafe.

▨ Iraq: Civilians under fire (MDE 14/002/2010)

▨ Iraq: Human rights briefing (MDE 14/004/2010)

▨ New order, same abuses: Unlawful detentions and torture in Iraq (MDE 14/006/2010)

IRELAND

REPUBLIC OF IRELAND

Head of state:	Mary McAleese
Head of government:	Brian Cowen
Death penalty:	abolitionist for all crimes
Population:	4.6 million
Life expectancy:	80.3 years
Under-5 mortality (m/f):	6/6 per 1,000

Child protection standards were inadequate in both law and practice. Prison conditions fell below required standards. There was a shortfall in mental health services.

Background

The Council of Europe's Committee for the Prevention of Torture visited Ireland at the beginning of the year, focusing on prison conditions and the care afforded to patients in psychiatric institutions. The Council of Europe Convention on Action against Trafficking in Human Beings was ratified in July.

Children's rights

The government failed to implement a number of commitments it made in 2009 following the report of the Commission to Inquire into Child Abuse. This included a failure to introduce draft legislation to give child protection guidelines a statutory basis.

In February, the all-party Oireachtas (parliament) Joint Committee on the Constitutional Amendment on Children proposed a new constitutional provision on children's rights. However, the government did not schedule the required referendum in 2010 as promised.

There were serious concerns about the lack of adequate investigation and transparent reporting by the Health Service Executive on deaths of children in state child protection services. In March, the government established an Independent Child Death Review Group to review the Executive's investigations into the deaths of children in care.

Discrimination – lesbian, gay, bisexual and transgender people

The Civil Partnership Act 2010 was passed in July, providing for the registration of civil partnerships, including by same-sex couples, to come into force in 2011. However, it fell short of providing an equal right of same-sex couples to civil marriage, and inequality in the legal situation of children of same-sex couples also remained unresolved.

Following the withdrawal of its appeal in the case of *Foy v. An t-Ard Chláraitheoir & Ors* in June, the government promised to introduce legislation recognizing the gender identity of transgendered people.

Prison conditions

Prison conditions did not meet required standards. An October report by the Inspector of Prisons found serious overcrowding in prisons and described violence between prisoners in Mountjoy Prison as endemic. The report also described the practice of "slopping out", where prisoners urinate and defecate into a small pot in their cell, in Mountjoy, Cork and Limerick prisons as "inhumane and degrading".

Refugees and asylum-seekers

A report published by the Free Legal Advice Centres in February criticized the living conditions of asylum-seekers under the government's "direct provision and dispersal system", which places individuals in various accommodation centres around the country where they are expected to stay while awaiting a determination on their status. The report found that

the system "does not provide an environment conducive to the enjoyment or fulfillment of the most basic human rights, including the rights to health, food, housing and family life".

In light of the concerns about asylum determination procedures in Greece, the High Court decided to refer to the Court of Justice of the European Union to determine whether Ireland should be required to take responsibility for processing the asylum claims of those who passed through Greece. At the end of the year, transfers to Greece under the Dublin II Regulation were effectively suspended.

Right to health – mental health

In July, the annual report of the Inspector of Mental Health Services highlighted poor conditions in a number of in-patient centres, describing some as "entirely unacceptable and inhumane". It pointed out that significant staffing cuts were affecting progressive community mental health services, "causing reversion to a more custodial form of mental health service".

Women's rights

In December, in *A, B, and C v. Ireland*, the European Court of Human Rights found a violation of Article 8 of the convention in the case of one of the three applicants, C, because she had no effective or accessible procedure to establish her constitutional right to a lawful abortion where her life was at risk.

ISRAEL AND THE OCCUPIED PALESTINIAN TERRITORIES

STATE OF ISRAEL

Head of state:	Shimon Peres
Head of government:	Benjamin Netanyahu
Death penalty:	abolitionist for ordinary crimes
Population:	7.3 million (Israel); 4.4 million (OPT)
Life expectancy:	80.3 years (Israel); 72.9 years (OPT)
Under-5 mortality (m/f):	6/5 per 1,000 (Israel); 23/18 per 1,000 (OPT)

A ceasefire between Israeli forces and Palestinian armed groups agreed in January 2009 was generally respected. The Israeli army maintained draconian controls on the movement of Palestinians in the Occupied Palestinian Territories (OPT), including a blockade on the Gaza Strip that deepened hardship and virtually imprisoned the entire population of 1.5 million. The Israeli authorities rejected or delayed applications for permits to leave Gaza submitted by hundreds of Palestinians requiring specialist medical treatment; a few died as a result. Most of Gaza's inhabitants depended on international aid, which was severely hampered by the blockade. In May, Israeli forces killed nine men aboard an aid flotilla in international waters that was aiming to breach the blockade. In the West Bank, the movement of Palestinians was severely curtailed by hundreds of Israeli checkpoints and barriers, and by the 700km fence/wall that Israel continued to build mostly inside the West Bank. There was a substantial increase in the number of demolitions by Israeli authorities of Palestinian homes, water cisterns and other structures in the West Bank, affecting thousands of people. Israeli authorities also destroyed homes in Bedouin villages in the south of Israel. The expansion of illegal Israeli settlements on seized Palestinian land, partially frozen until 26 September, resumed. Israel still did not conduct adequate investigations into alleged war crimes and other serious violations of international law by its forces during Operation "Cast Lead", the 22-day offensive in Gaza in December 2008/January 2009,

during which nearly 1,400 Palestinians, including more than 300 children, were killed. Israeli soldiers and settlers who committed serious abuses against Palestinians, including unlawful killings, assaults and attacks against property, were generally not held to account for their crimes. Israeli military forces killed 33 Palestinian civilians in the OPT, including eight children. Hundreds of Palestinians were arrested and detained by Israeli forces; at least 264 were held without charge or trial under administrative detention orders, some had been held for over two years. Reports of torture and other ill-treatment were frequent, but investigations were rare. Around 6,000 Palestinians remained in Israeli prisons, many after unfair military trials. Israeli conscientious objectors to military service continued to be imprisoned.

Background

The border area between Israel and Lebanon remained tense. On 3 August, an exchange of fire between Israeli and Lebanese soldiers resulted in the deaths of at least three soldiers and a Lebanese journalist.

While the ceasefire between Israeli forces and Palestinian armed groups was largely maintained, the latter periodically fired indiscriminate rockets and mortars into southern Israel (see Palestinian Authority entry), although at a lower rate than in previous years, and Israeli forces attacked and killed Palestinians they said were responsible. On 31 August, four Israeli settlers were shot dead in the West Bank; the attack was claimed by the Izz al-Din al-Qassam Brigades, the military wing of Hamas, the Palestinian group that won elections in 2006 and administers Gaza.

Negotiations between Israel and the Palestinian Authority (PA), but excluding Hamas, were convened by the US government in September. However, they were soon suspended when Israel's 10-month partial moratorium on new settlement-building in the OPT ended on 26 September, prompting the PA's withdrawal from direct talks. The moratorium had excluded East Jerusalem and its surrounding area, and in the West Bank construction for "security needs" and of public buildings had continued unabated.

Gaza blockade and humanitarian crisis

The blockade of the Gaza Strip, in force since June 2007, suffocated the economy and drove people

I

there further into poverty. Amid continuing health and sanitation problems, poverty and malnutrition, some 80 per cent of Gazans were forced to depend on international humanitarian aid, the flow of which was impeded by the blockade. Severe shortages fuelled high prices. Most UN reconstruction projects to provide clinics and schools had to be delayed; as a result, some 40,000 Palestinian children eligible to enrol in UN schools in September had to be turned away.

Virtually all Gazans were effectively trapped in the small enclave, including seriously ill patients who needed treatment elsewhere and many students and workers wishing to study or take up jobs abroad. Only relatively few were allowed to exit Gaza.

In May, Israeli troops forcibly intercepted an international aid flotilla aiming to break the blockade. They killed nine of those aboard and injured more than 50, some seriously. Several Israeli soldiers were injured. Several inquiries were established into the attack, including two by the UN. In September, the investigative body appointed by the UN Human Rights Council concluded that "lethal force was employed by the Israeli soldiers in a widespread and arbitrary manner which caused an unnecessarily large number of persons to be killed or seriously injured." An Israeli government-appointed commission of inquiry lacked independence and transparency.

Following international criticism of the attack, the government announced a partial easing of the blockade, although insufficient to markedly improve conditions in Gaza. Israel continued to ban all export of goods from Gaza until 8 December, and the announced easing of restrictions on exports had not been implemented by the end of the year. Amnesty International considered the blockade to constitute collective punishment in breach of international humanitarian law and called repeatedly for it to be lifted.

Restrictions in the West Bank

Hundreds of Israeli military checkpoints and barriers restricted the movement of Palestinians in the West Bank, hindering or blocking access to workplaces, education and health facilities, and other services.

By the end of 2010, the construction of around 60 per cent of the planned 700km fence/wall had been completed; more than 85 per cent of its entire route is on Palestinian land inside the West Bank. The fence/wall separated thousands of Palestinians from

their farmland and water sources, while access to East Jerusalem by West Bank Palestinians possessing entry permits was possible through only three of 16 checkpoints at the fence/wall. This had particularly serious consequences for patients and medical staff trying to reach the six specialist Palestinian hospitals in East Jerusalem.

Palestinians continued to be denied access to large swathes of land near to Israeli settlements established and maintained in breach of international law; the settler population in the West Bank, including East Jerusalem, reached over half a million. Palestinians were also barred from or had restricted access to around 300km of "by-pass" roads used by Israeli settlers. However, travel time for Palestinians between most towns, particularly in the north, was reduced in 2010 by Israel's removal of some barriers and by some improvements to the road network for cars with Palestinian licence plates, although journeys remained slow and arduous.

Right to adequate housing – forced eviction

Palestinians living in the West Bank, including East Jerusalem, faced such tight restrictions on what they could build that their right to adequate housing was violated. Forced evictions were carried out in the West Bank, including East Jerusalem, on the grounds that the houses had been built without permits; such permits are almost impossible for Palestinians to obtain from the Israeli authorities. Demolition crews, accompanied by security officials, generally arrived without notice and gave families little opportunity to remove their possessions. Under Israeli military law, applied to Palestinians in most of the West Bank, there is no requirement for evicted families to be re-housed or compensated. Palestinians in East Jerusalem fared little better under the Israeli civil authorities. In 2010, Israeli authorities demolished 431 structures in East Jerusalem and the West Bank, a 59 per cent increase over 2009. At least 594 Palestinians – half of them children – were displaced after their homes were demolished by order of the Israeli authorities, while more than 14,000 Palestinians were affected by demolitions of water cisterns, wells and structures relating to their livelihoods.

■ Israeli forces twice demolished homes and structures in Khirbet Tana, a West Bank village just west of the Jordan Valley in an area declared a "closed military zone". On 10 January, they demolished the homes of 100 residents, the village school and 12 animal pens; and on 8 December, they demolished 10 homes, 17 animal shelters and the rebuilt school. The village had previously been demolished in 2005. Village residents have been denied building permits by the Israeli authorities since the 1970s, while the nearby settlements of Mekhora and Itamar have been established.

Inside Israel there was a marked increase in the demolition of Bedouin homes in the Negev (or Naqab) area in the south. Dozens of villages, home to tens of thousands of Bedouin who are Israeli citizens, are not formally recognized by the Israeli authorities. These villages lack basic services, and residents are under constant threat of destruction of their homes and eviction from the land.

■ The "unrecognized" Negev village of al-'Araqib, home to around 250 Bedouin, was destroyed eight times between 27 July and 23 December by the Israel Land Administration and police forces. After each demolition, villagers rebuilt makeshift shelters.

Excessive use of force

Israeli security forces used excessive force against Palestinian civilians, including non-violent demonstrators in the West Bank and Gaza, as well as farmers, fishermen and others working in the Israeli-declared "exclusion zone" inside Gaza or its coastal waters. According to the UN Office for the Coordination of Humanitarian Affairs, 33 Palestinian civilians in the OPT, including eight children, were killed by Israeli military forces during 2010. Fifteen Palestinian civilians, including four children, were killed and more than 100 injured by Israeli forces enforcing the 1,500m-wide "exclusion zone" inside Gaza's northern and eastern borders and the maritime restrictions.

■ Two Palestinian teenagers died after Israeli security forces shot them with live ammunition following a demonstration on 20 March in the West Bank village of Iraq Burin. Muhammed Qadus was shot in the chest; Usaid Qadus was shot in the head. In April, following an Israeli military police investigation, two senior Israeli officers were reprimanded over the killings.

■ In September, three Palestinian shepherds – Ibrahim Abu Said, aged 91, his 16-year-old grandson Hosam Abu Sa'id, and 17-year-old Isma'il Abu 'Oda – were killed by Israeli tank shells while grazing their sheep inside the Gaza "exclusion zone" near Beit Hanoun. The authorities later admitted that the three victims were civilians, not "terrorists" as they had initially stated, and announced an investigation into the incident. Its outcome was not known by the end of 2010.

Impunity

Israeli soldiers, members of the security forces and settlers continued to enjoy impunity for human rights abuses committed against Palestinians, including unlawful killings. Settler violence included shooting at Palestinians and destruction of Palestinian property. In only extremely rare cases were the perpetrators held to account for their actions.

According to a detailed report on impunity published by the Israeli human rights organization B'Tselem in October, the Israeli military killed 1,510 Palestinians in 2006-09, excluding those killed during Operation "Cast Lead". Of these, 617, including 104 children aged under 18, were not taking part in any hostilities when they were killed. B'Tselem called for an investigation into 288 of the killings committed in 148 incidents, most in the Gaza Strip; investigations were opened in only 22 incidents, most in the West Bank. B'Tselem reported that only four investigations were opened within a month of the incident. In two investigations, the case was closed without any prosecution of the soldiers involved.

Operation 'Cast Lead'

Although some Israeli military investigations into specific incidents were ongoing, the Israeli authorities still failed to conduct independent investigations into alleged war crimes and other serious violations of international law by Israeli forces during Operation "Cast Lead" that conform with international standards. The UN-mandated Fact-Finding Mission on the conflict (the Goldstone report) found in 2009 that Israeli forces and Palestinian armed groups had both committed war crimes and possibly crimes against humanity.

By the end of 2010, only three Israeli soldiers had been convicted in connection with Operation "Cast Lead". Two of them were found guilty of "unauthorized conduct" for ordering a nine-year-old Palestinian boy, Majed R., to act as a "human shield" by opening bags they believed were booby-trapped. In November, they were demoted and given suspended three-month prison sentences.

Due to the failure of both sides to conduct adequate investigations, Amnesty International urged that the matter be addressed through international justice mechanisms.

Israel paid US$10.5 million compensation to the UN in January for UN buildings damaged during Operation "Cast Lead". However, no compensation was paid to or on behalf of any of the victims of the attacks. The UN said the payment concluded the financial issues relating to the Operation, even though the Goldstone report had specifically recommended that the UN seek compensation not only for UN personnel and civilians killed or injured in attacks on UN premises, but also for civilian victims of other attacks during the Operation.

Justice system
Detention without trial
Israel continued to impose a system of administrative detention whereby Palestinians are held for prolonged periods without charge or trial. At least 264 Palestinians were subject to administrative detention orders in 2010. Some had been held for more than two years.

■ Moatasem Nazzal, a 16-year-old student from Qalandiya refugee camp near Ramallah, was arrested without explanation at his home on 20 March. He was interrogated while shackled. He was given three successive administrative detention orders, keeping him in prison until 26 December 2010.

Prison conditions – denial of family visits
Around 680 Palestinian prisoners continued to be denied family visits, some for a third year, because Palestinians in Gaza remained barred from travelling into Israel, where the prisoners are held, since the imposition of the Gaza blockade.

Unfair trials
Palestinians in the OPT subject to Israel's military justice system continued to face a wide range of abuses of their right to a fair trial. They are routinely interrogated without a lawyer and, although they are civilians, are tried before military not ordinary courts.

Torture and other ill-treatment
Consistent allegations of torture and other ill-treatment, including of children, were frequently reported. Among the most commonly cited methods were beatings, threats to the detainee or their family, sleep deprivation, and being subjected to painful stress positions for long periods. Confessions allegedly obtained under duress were accepted as evidence in Israeli military and civilian courts.

■ A.M., a 15-year-old Palestinian from Beit Ummar village near Hebron, was arrested on 26 May, held in Gush Etzion detention centre, interrogated for six days allegedly using torture, then released after he "confessed" to throwing stones. He said security officials attached an electric cable to his genitals and threatened to give him electric shocks. In August, two NGOs, one Palestinian and the other Israeli, filed complaints to the Israeli police and army about his alleged torture. The police complaint was closed on the ground of "insufficient evidence", while the army was still reviewing the complaint at the end of 2010.

Freedom of expression and association
There was an increase in the number of arrests, trials and imprisonment of people engaged in non-violent protests against the fence/wall. Frequently, the authorities resorted to Military Order 101, which forbids a gathering of 10 or more people "for a political purpose or for a matter that could be interpreted as political" unless a permit is first obtained from an Israeli military commander.

■ In October, an Israeli military court sentenced Abdallah Abu Rahma to one year in prison. A teacher and head of the Popular Committee Against the Wall in the West Bank village of Bil'in, he was found guilty of "organizing and participating in an illegal demonstration" and "incitement". He was acquitted of "stone-throwing" and "possession of arms". He was a prisoner of conscience.

■ Former nuclear technician Mordechai Vanunu was returned to prison in May for three months on charges of having had contact with a foreign national. Almost immediately, he was put in solitary confinement. He was a prisoner of conscience. He had previously spent 18 years in jail for revealing Israel's nuclear capability to a British newspaper. Since his release in 2004, he has been subject to police supervision under the terms of a military order, renewed every six months. Among other things, the order bans him from communicating with foreigners or leaving the country. In October 2010, the Israeli Supreme Court rejected a petition to overturn the restrictions.

Prisoners of conscience – Israeli conscientious objectors
At least 12 Israeli conscientious objectors to military service were imprisoned.

■ Shir Regev, from Tuval village in northern Israel, was imprisoned three times for a total of 64 days for refusing to perform military service as he opposes Israel's military occupation of the Palestinian Territories.

Amnesty International visits/reports

🚌 Amnesty International delegates visited Israel and the OPT in April and May.

📄 Israel and Occupied Palestinian Territories: As safe as houses? Israel's demolition of Palestinian homes (MDE 15/006/2010)

📄 Israel/Occupied Palestinian Territories: Amnesty International's assessment of Israeli and Palestinian investigations into Gaza conflict (MDE 15/022/2010)

📄 Israel/Occupied Palestinian Territories: Human Rights Council fails victims of Gaza conflict (MDE 15/023/2010)

📄 Israel: End arbitrary restrictions on Vanunu (MDE 15/024/2010)

ITALY

ITALIAN REPUBLIC

Head of state:	**Giorgio Napolitano**
Head of government:	**Silvio Berlusconi**
Death penalty:	**abolitionist for all crimes**
Population:	**60.1 million**
Life expectancy:	**81.4 years**
Under-5 mortality (m/f):	**5/4 per 1,000**
Adult literacy:	**98.8 per cent**

Roma rights continued to be violated and forced evictions contributed to driving those affected deeper into poverty and marginalization. Derogatory and discriminatory remarks by politicians against Roma, migrants and lesbian, gay, bisexual and transgender people promoted a climate of rising intolerance. Violent homophobic attacks continued. Asylum-seekers were unable to access effective procedures to seek international protection. Reports of ill-treatment by law enforcement officials continued. Concerns persisted about the thoroughness of investigations into deaths in custody and alleged ill-treatment. Italy refused to introduce the crime of torture into domestic legislation.

International scrutiny

The UN High Commissioner for Human Rights visited Italy for the first time in March. Among other things, she was concerned that Italian authorities were treating Roma and migrants as "security problems" rather than looking at ways to include them in society.

In April, the Council of Europe Committee for the Prevention of Torture published reports on the periodic visits to Italy of September 2008 and July 2009, highlighting, among other things, the lack of a torture provision in the criminal code and the overcrowding of prison facilities. The 2009 report also condemned the policy of intercepting migrants at sea and forcing them to return to Libya or other non-European countries as a violation of the principle of non-refoulement (prohibition on returning individuals to countries where they would risk serious human rights violations).

On 25 June, the European Committee of Social Rights found that Italy discriminated against Roma and Sinti in the enjoyment of several rights, including their right to housing and protection against poverty and social exclusion, and the right of migrant workers and their families to protection and assistance.

In February, Italy's human rights record was assessed under the UN Universal Periodic Review. In May, the government responded by rejecting 12 of the 92 recommendations received. Of particular concern was the refusal to introduce the crime of torture into domestic legislation and to abolish the crime of irregular migration.

Discrimination

Roma continued to face discrimination in the enjoyment of their rights to education, housing, health care and employment. Derogatory remarks by some politicians and representatives of various authorities helped foster a climate of intolerance towards Roma, migrants and lesbian, gay, bisexual and transgender people.

In August, the Observatory for Security Against Discriminatory Acts set up by police authorities became operational; this mechanism aims to encourage and make it simpler for victims to submit complaints against discriminatory attacks.

Roma – forced evictions

Forced evictions of Roma continued throughout the country. Some families were subjected to repeated forced evictions, which disrupted their communities, their access to work and made it impossible for some children to attend school.

■ In January, Rome local authorities started to implement the "Nomad Plan", following the declaration in 2008 by the central government of the "Nomad emergency", which authorizes prefects to derogate from a number of laws when dealing with people who are deemed to be "nomads". The Plan proposed the eviction of thousands of Roma and their partial resettlement into refurbished or new camps. Its implementation perpetuated a policy of segregation and resulted in poorer living conditions for many, due to delays in the building of new camps or in the adaptation of existing ones. Despite some improvements, the level of consultation by the authorities with the affected families remained inadequate.

■ In Milan, local authorities pursued forced evictions relentlessly and without a strategy in place to offer alternative accommodation to those affected. Some Romani families were assigned social housing pending their eviction. The allocation, initially withdrawn by local authorities due to political considerations, was confirmed by a court decision in December which also found the conduct of the authorities discriminatory. An appeal against it was pending at the end of the year.

Rights of lesbian, gay, bisexual and transgender people

Violent homophobic attacks continued. Due to a gap in the law, victims of crimes motivated by discrimination on grounds of sexual orientation and gender identity were not given the same protection as victims of crimes motivated by other sorts of discrimination.

Asylum-seekers' and migrants' rights

Asylum-seekers and migrants continued to be denied their rights, particularly regarding access to a fair and satisfactory asylum procedure. The authorities failed to adequately protect them from racially motivated violence and, by making unsubstantiated links between migrants and crime, some politicians and government representatives fostered a climate of intolerance and xenophobia.

UNHCR, the UN refugee agency, and NGOs continued to express concern that the agreements between Italy, Libya and other countries to control migration flows were leading to hundreds of asylum-seekers, including many children, being denied access to procedures to claim international protection. Asylum applications in Italy continued to fall dramatically.

■ In October, 68 people rescued at sea were forcibly returned to Egypt within 48 hours, allegedly without having been given the opportunity to apply for international protection. The 68 people were on a boat carrying 131 people that was intercepted by the Italian authorities near the coast of Sicily. The total number included 44 minors, and 19 people who were arrested for abetting illegal migration.

In January, two days of violent clashes between migrant workers, local residents and the police in the town of Rosarno led to over 1,000 migrants (most of whom had permits) fleeing or being removed from the area by law enforcement agencies. The clashes started after a migrant worker was injured by gunshots from a moving car, as he and others were walking home after working in the fields. In April, a judicial inquiry into the causes of the riots led to over 30 people – Italian and foreign nationals – being arrested for the exploitation and enslavement of the migrant workers employed in the agricultural sector in the area. The inquiry was still ongoing at the end of the year.

Counter-terror and security
Renditions

In December, the 2009 convictions of 25 US and Italian officials involved in the abduction of Abu Omar from a Milan street in 2003 were upheld by the Milan Court of Appeal. The 23 convicted US officials were tried in their absence. The Court sentenced the accused to up to nine years' imprisonment. After his kidnapping, Abu Omar was unlawfully transferred by the CIA from Italy to Egypt where he was held in secret detention and allegedly tortured. The Court confirmed the dismissal of charges against five high-level officials of the Italian intelligence agency, based on reasons of state secrecy.

Guantánamo detainees

The criminal proceedings concerning terrorism-related charges against Adel Ben Mabrouk and Rihad Nasseri, two Tunisian nationals transferred from detention in Guantánamo Bay to Italy in 2009, were ongoing. There were concerns that the accused would be deported to Tunisia in violation of the principle of *non-refoulement*.

Deaths in custody

There were continued reports of ill-treatment by law enforcement officials. Concerns persisted about the independence and impartiality of investigations and about the thoroughness of the collection and preservation of evidence in cases of deaths in custody and alleged ill-treatment, which often led to impunity. Repeated petitions to the authorities from the victims and their families remained essential to ensure thorough investigations and bring the perpetrators to justice.

■ The appeals against their convictions by four police officers, who in July 2009 had been sentenced to three years and six months in prison for the unlawful killing of

18-year-old Federico Aldrovandi, remained pending at the end of the year. Federico Aldrovandi died in 2005 after being stopped by police officers in Ferrara. In March, three police officers, accused of helping their colleagues to hide and forge evidence of the case, were sentenced to prison terms of eight, 10 and 12 months respectively. In October, Federico Aldrovandi's parents accepted the sum of 2 million euros in reparation for their son's death, on condition they renounced the suit for damages in the pending proceedings.

■ Proceedings against a prison guard for failing to assist Aldo Bianzino were pending. Aldo Bianzino died in prison in Perugia in 2007 two days after his arrest. Proceedings for homicide against unidentified perpetrators were closed in 2009.

■ Attempts to clarify circumstances and determine any responsibilities in the death of Stefano Cucchi were ongoing. Stefano Cucchi died in October 2009 in a hospital's prison wing in Rome several days after his arrest. His relatives believed that his death had been caused by the ill-treatment he allegedly suffered before reaching the hospital.

■ In December, a doctor was charged with the manslaughter of Giuseppe Uva who died in June 2008 in a hospital in Varese, allegedly due to the wrong medical treatment. Investigations into the ill-treatment allegedly suffered by Giuseppe Uva while in police custody hours before his death were ongoing.

Torture and other ill-treatment

In March and May, the Genoa Court of Appeal issued second instance verdicts in the trials on the torture and other ill-treatment perpetrated by law enforcement officials against G8 protesters in 2001. The opportunity to file appeals with the Court of Cassation was still open at the end of the year.

In March, the Court recognized that most of the crimes that had taken place at the temporary detention centre of Bolzaneto, including grievous bodily harm and arbitrary inspections and searches, had expired due to the statute of limitations, but still ordered all of the 42 accused to pay civil damages to the victims. The Court also imposed prison sentences of up to three years and two months on eight of the accused.

In May, the same Court found 25 of the 28 people accused of similar abuses at the Armando Diaz School guilty, including all high-ranking police officers present at the time of the events, and imposed prison sentences of up to five years. Many of the charges were dropped due to the statute of limitations.

If Italy had introduced torture as a specific crime in its criminal code, however, the statute of limitations would not have applied.

Amnesty International visits/reports

🚍 Amnesty International delegates visited Italy in March and July.

▣ The wrong answer: Italy's "Nomad Plan" violates the housing rights of Roma in Rome (EUR 30/001/2010)

▣ Dangerous Deals: Europe's reliance on "diplomatic assurances" against torture (EUR 01/012/2010)

▣ Open secret: Mounting evidence of Europe's complicity in rendition and secret detention (EUR 01/023/2010)

JAMAICA

JAMAICA	
Head of state:	Queen Elizabeth II, represented by Patrick Linton Allen
Head of government:	Bruce Golding
Death penalty:	retentionist
Population:	2.7 million
Life expectancy:	72.3 years
Under-5 mortality (m/f):	28/28 per 1,000
Adult literacy:	85.9 per cent

J

Hundreds of people in inner-city communities were the victims of gang murders or police killings. At least 43 reports of extrajudicial executions were received during a two-month state of emergency. Children were detained in conditions that breached human rights standards. At least four people were sentenced to death; there were no executions.

Background

The number of people murdered, mainly in the context of gang violence in marginalized inner-city communities, remained high. A state of emergency was declared in May in Kingston and St Andrew. This followed an outbreak of gang violence as armed supporters of Christopher "Dudus" Coke protested against his extradition to the USA on drug-related charges. The state of emergency remained in force until 22 July.

On 23 July, six anti-crime bills entered into force. Some of their provisions are in breach of human rights principles and standards.

Jamaica's human rights record was assessed under the UN Universal Periodic Review (UPR) in November.

Police and security forces

The number of people reportedly killed by the police reached a record high. Evidence suggested that some of the killings may have been unlawful killings, including extrajudicial executions.

Following a visit to Jamaica in February, the UN Special Rapporteur on torture reported that many people had been beaten in detention by police. He recommended, among other things, that Jamaica ratify the UN Convention against Torture.

At least 4,000 people were detained during the state of emergency and 76 people were killed, including three members of the security forces. The Office of the Public Defender received at least 43 complaints of extrajudicial executions.

■ Sheldon Davis, a physically disabled man, was killed in Tivoli Gardens on 30 May. According to Sheldon Davis' mother, around 30 law enforcement officers came to their house and started interrogating him. They accused him of being involved in gang violence, which he denied. He was taken into custody, and several days later his family found out that he had been killed. The security forces reported that he was killed after attempting to grab a soldier's gun. An investigation was ongoing at the end of the year.

The Office of the Public Defender initiated an independent investigation into complaints received about the conduct of the security forces during the state of emergency. At the end of the year, ballistic tests had still not started. Jamaican human rights NGOs expressed concern at the failure to preserve crime scenes and to ensure accountability for the use of firearms by members of the security forces.

In August, the Independent Commission of Investigations, which is tasked with investigating abuses by the security forces, formally began its operations. However, at the end of the year, it was still engaged in recruiting and training staff, and mainly supervised investigations carried out by the police Bureau of Special Investigation.

Justice system

Although during the UPR the government stated that reforms to the justice system were being implemented, considerable delays continued to be reported in the delivery of justice. By the end of the year, the Office of the Special Coroner, which is supposed to examine fatal shootings by police, had still not been established.

Children's rights

The UN Special Rapporteur on torture reported that children continued to be held together with adults in police detention and in some correctional centres. He also noted that children and adolescents in need of care and protection, children with learning difficulties, and those in conflict with the law were often held together.

In March, the Armadale Inquiry investigating the deaths of seven girls in the Armadale Juvenile Correctional Centre on 22 May 2009, reported that practices found at the Centre contravened the UN Standard Minimum Rules for the Administration Chrlotteof Juvenile Justice. In response, the government announced that it would implement a number of measures, including the separation of children on remand from those under correctional orders. However, in October, the Children's Advocate disclosed that more than 100 children were still held in police lockups together with adults.

Violence against women and girls

Sexual violence remained widespread and reports of sexual abuse of children rose compared to 2009, according to police statistics published in September.

Rights of lesbian, gay, bisexual and transgender people

Scores of homophobic attacks, harassment and threats against of lesbian, gay, bisexual and transgender (LGBT) people were reported to LGBT organizations, including at least three cases of "corrective" rapes of lesbians.

■ On 3 September, a woman was raped by a gang of six men who had previously verbally abused her. She also suffered genital mutilation after the rape.

A survey of 11 lesbian, bisexual and transgender women victims of violence found that only one had reported the rape to the police and after two years she was still waiting for the court hearing. The others had not reported the crime because they feared being criminalized on account of their sexual orientation.

Death penalty

At least four people were sentenced to death; no executions were carried out. There were seven people on death row at the end of the year.

In September, the government announced that it was considering submitting to the Parliament an amended version of the Charter of Rights. The amendment would reverse a 1993 ruling by the Judicial Committee of the Privy Council, the highest court of appeal, that execution after five years on death row was inhuman and degrading punishment.

Amnesty International visits/reports

Jamaica: Submission to the UN Universal Periodic Review (AMR 38/001/2010)

Jamaica violence investigation must be thorough, 26 May 2010

JAPAN

JAPAN
Head of government: **Naoto Kan (replaced Hatoyama Yukio in June)**
Death penalty: **retentionist**
Population: **127 million**
Life expectancy: **83.2 years**
Under-5 mortality (m/f):   **5/4 per 1,000**

The *daiyo kangoku* pre-trial detention system persisted, increasing the risk of abusive interrogation practices. The comfort women reparations movement gathered further momentum, with several Japanese cities urging the central government to compensate and issue apologies to survivors of the comfort women system. The Minister of Justice set up a working group on capital punishment in July; that same month, two people were executed. Refugees and asylum-seekers remained vulnerable to abuses; one man was killed while being deported and two immigration detainees committed suicide.

Background

In May, the UN High Commissioner for Human Rights visited Japan and called on the government to establish a national human rights institution, abolish the death penalty and resolve the "comfort women" issue. In June, Naoto Kan became Prime Minister following Hatoyama Yukio's resignation nine months into the job. The Social Democratic Party withdrew from the ruling coalition over failure to renegotiate the relocation of the US marine air base in Futenma,

Okinawa. After the July elections, the ruling coalition lost control of the Upper House to the Liberal Democratic Party.

Justice system

The *daiyo kangoku* system continued to facilitate torture and other ill-treatment aimed at extracting confessions during interrogation. Under the *daiyo kangoku* system, the police can detain suspects for up to 23 days.

■ Sugaya Toshikazu was exonerated of murder in March after just over 17 years in prison. He was granted a retrial after it was shown that DNA evidence used in his first trial was faulty and his confession coerced during pre-trial detention.

■ The Supreme Court rejected a Nagoya High Court ruling in the case of Okunishi Masaru, ordering it to reconsider a retrial appeal. This was the first time in 34 years that the Supreme Court had revoked a lower court ruling involving a retrial appeal for death row inmates. In his first trial, Okunishi Masaru said he had been forced to confess. He was acquitted for lack of evidence. The Nagoya High Court then reversed his acquittal and he was sentenced to death in 1969.

Violence against women and girls

In May, the UN Special Rapporteur on violence against women noted that survivors of sexual crimes "do not want to receive economic compensation without an official apology and official recognition of State responsibility". She considered the "comfort women" reparation movement one of the most organized and well documented. Councils in 21 Japanese cities or towns adopted resolutions advocating apology and compensation for survivors of the "comfort women" system.

Death penalty

Two people were executed in July, exactly one year since the last executions. At least 111 prisoners, including several mentally ill prisoners, remained on death row in harsh conditions. Executions are typically carried out in secret by hanging. Prisoners are usually notified only a few hours before their execution if at all. Family members are informed only after the execution.

In March, the Japanese Diet (parliament) approved a bill to abolish the statute of limitations on murder cases subject to capital punishment. In July, the Minister of Justice established a working group within the Ministry to study capital punishment. It held hearings in August, September and October without releasing conclusions.

■ In November, the first death sentence was handed down under the *saiban-in* (lay judge) system at the Yokohama District Court for murder.

Refugees and asylum-seekers

Claims for refugee status continued to be subject to lengthy delays, with some claims taking up to a decade to be finalized. Asylum decisions remained beyond the purview of judicial or other independent review. As of December an estimated 1,000 individuals had filed asylum claims and approximately 30 individuals were granted refugee status. Under the Immigration Control and Refugee Recognition Act, irregular migrants and asylum-seekers, including children, were detained for indefinite periods without recourse to independent review of the necessity of their detention. Japan became the first Asian state to resettle refugees processed outside the country, accepting 27 refugees from Myanmar who had been processed in Thailand.

■ In March, Ghanaian national Abubakar Awudu Suraj died while being escorted by Japanese immigration officers onto a plane for deportation. The investigation was completed but no arrests were made by the end of the year.

■ Two detainees at the East Japan Immigration Centre committed suicide. Detainees at the West Japan and East Japan Immigration Centres went on hunger strike in February and May respectively, demanding that those detained for long periods, minors and sick people be released from detention and that detention conditions, including access to medical treatment, be improved.

Amnesty International visits/reports

🚌 Amnesty International delegates visited Japan in November.

JORDAN

HASHEMITE KINGDOM OF JORDAN

Head of state:	King Abdullah II bin al-Hussein
Head of government:	Samir Rifai
Death penalty:	retentionist
Population:	6.5 million
Life expectancy:	72.4 years
Under-5 mortality (m/f):	24/19 per 1,000
Adult literacy:	91.1 per cent

Reports of torture and other ill-treatment persisted and members of the security forces continued to enjoy impunity. Trials before the State Security Court (SSC) continued to breach international fair trial standards. Dozens of people were arrested for security offences and thousands of others were held without charge or prospect of trial. Freedoms of expression, association and assembly continued to be restricted. The authorities arbitrarily withdrew Jordanian nationality from some citizens of Palestinian origin. Migrant domestic workers continued to be exploited and abused. Women faced legal and other discrimination and, despite a legal change to protect them from violence, at least 15 women were reported to have been victims of so-called honour killings. Nine people were sentenced to death; no executions were carried out.

Background

The government passed temporary laws in the absence of parliament which remained suspended by order of the King until new elections were held on 9 November. These were boycotted by several political parties, including the main opposition Islamic Action Front, who complained that the electoral system was insufficiently representative and was weighted in favour of rural areas compared to the cities where citizens of Palestinian origin predominate. Most of the seats in the parliament inaugurated on 29 November were held by members of tribes loyal to the King.

Torture and other ill-treatment

Reports of torture and other ill-treatment of security detainees and criminal suspects continued. The authorities failed to institute adequate legal and other safeguards against such abuses.

In May, the UN Committee against Torture reiterated long-standing concerns at Jordan's failure to investigate and prosecute allegations of torture, to provide adequate protection against torture, and to prosecute perpetrators in accordance with the seriousness of the crime. It noted the "numerous, consistent and credible allegations of a widespread and routine practice of torture and ill-treatment" including in General Intelligence Department (GID) and Criminal Investigations Department detention. The government did not respond to the Committee's recommendations.

■ Charges against a police officer relating to an apparently unlawful killing were dropped when the victim's family agreed not to pursue the case. Fakhri Anani Kreishan, who died in November 2009 after being attacked by police officers in Ma'an, was found at autopsy to have sustained a lethal head injury caused by a hard object. The police officer alleged to have delivered the blow remained on active duty.

Unfair trials – State Security Court
Dozens of people accused of state security offences faced unfair trials before the SSC. In October the UN Human Rights Committee reiterated its recommendation that the authorities consider abolishing the SSC.

■ In March, the SSC disregarded a 2009 Court of Cassation finding which led it to overturn life sentences against eight men convicted by the SSC of planning a "terrorist attack" in 2004. The Cassation Court's decision was based on grounds including that the "confessions" were "extracted under coercion" and so were "invalid". The SSC referred the case to the Public Prosecutor for a fresh investigation and the men remained in prison. It appeared that no official investigation was conducted into allegations that the "confessions" were obtained under duress.

Detention without trial
According to the Jordanian National Centre for Human Rights, during the first six months of 2010, 6,965 people were held under the 1954 Law on Crime Prevention, which provides provincial governors with powers to detain indefinitely without charge anyone suspected of committing a crime or considered a "danger to society".

■ 'Isam al-'Utaibi, also known as Sheikh Abu Muhammad al-Maqdisi, was held without charge for over two months by the GID in Amman before being referred for trial to the SSC and transferred to prison on charges including recruiting members to "terrorist

organizations". Two years earlier he had spent three years in GID detention without charge.

Freedom of expression, association and assembly
Journalists and others who criticized the government or participated in peaceful protests were arrested and, in some case, prosecuted. Arrests increased in the run-up to the parliamentary elections in November when tens of people were briefly detained for objecting to the electoral system.

■ Workers' rights activist Muhammad al-Sneid was arrested on 10 May and held for around 10 days after he participated in a peaceful protest in Ma'daba town against a Ministry of Agriculture decision to dismiss him and other public service workers. In July, the SSC sentenced him to three months' imprisonment for holding an "unlawful gathering".

Discrimination – Jordanian citizens of Palestinian origin
The authorities continued arbitrarily to withdraw Jordanian nationality from citizens of Palestinian descent. Hundreds of thousands of people of Palestinian origin are recognized as Jordanian citizens. Those whose nationality was withdrawn had few means to challenge the decision and were effectively made stateless and denied access to health care and education facilities.

Migrants' rights – domestic workers
Regulations introduced in 2009 to protect migrant domestic workers from exploitation and physical and psychological abuse in the workplace were, in the main, not implemented. TAMKEEN, an organization offering legal assistance to domestic migrant workers, reported in May that it had received 290 complaints of unpaid salaries, passport confiscation and poor working conditions from "guest workers" in the previous 12 months.

Violence and discrimination against women and girls
Women continued to be victims of "honour" killings, with at least 15 such cases reported. The government introduced temporary amendments to the Penal Code to prevent leniency in sentencing men convicted of killing female relatives in the name of family "honour", including to Article 98 which allows reduced sentences for those who kill in a "fit of rage caused by

an unlawful or dangerous act on the part of the victim". However, the Court of Cassation sent two such cases back to the Criminal Court for it to consider reducing the sentences in accordance with Article 98.

Temporary amendments to the Personal Status Law failed to address adequately discrimination against women, including by failing to ensure sex-equality in joint financial or property settlements following divorce. The amendments raised the minimum marriage age for girls to 18, but allow exceptions so that in some cases girls as young as 15 can marry.

Death penalty

Nine people were sentenced to death in 2010, according to Amnesty International's sources; the Justice Minister said the total was six. Amendments to the Penal Code reduced the number of capital offences. In March, the Justice Minister announced that the crime of rape may cease to be a capital offence. No executions were carried out.

In December, Jordan abstained on a UN General Assembly resolution calling for a worldwide moratorium on executions.

KAZAKHSTAN

REPUBLIC OF KAZAKHSTAN

Head of state:	Nursultan Nazarbaev
Head of government:	Karim Massimov
Death penalty:	abolitionist for ordinary crimes
Population:	15.8 million
Life expectancy:	65.4 years
Under-5 mortality (m/f):	34/26 per 1,000
Adult literacy:	99.7 per cent

Reports of torture or other ill-treatment remained widespread, despite government promises to adopt a zero tolerance policy toward its practice. Impunity for such human rights violations persisted. The authorities stepped up efforts to forcibly return asylum-seekers and refugees to China and Uzbekistan under national security and counter-terrorism measures.

Background

In January, Kazakhstan assumed chairmanship of the OSCE, making counter-terror and security measures in Europe and Central Asia the OSCE's priority. Human rights commitments did not figure prominently in the chairmanship's agenda.

In May, parliament approved a constitutional amendment that made President Nursultan Nazarbaev "leader of the nation", thereby granting him and his immediate family permanent immunity from prosecution. The amendment also gave him the lifelong right to make final decisions on foreign and security policy matters. Defacing pictures of the "leader of the nation" and misrepresenting his biography were made criminal offences. In September, President Nazarbaev indicated that he would run for another term in office in 2012.

Torture and other ill-treatment

The authorities introduced a number of measures intended to prevent torture, including widening access to places of detention to independent public monitors and committing publicly to a policy of zero tolerance on torture.

Kazakhstan's human rights record was assessed under the UN Universal Periodic Review in February. In its presentation, the government delegation reiterated that the Kazakhstani authorities were committed to a policy of zero tolerance on torture, and that they "would not rest until all vestiges of torture had been fully and totally eliminated".

In February, the government postponed the creation of an independent detention monitoring mechanism, the National Preventive Mechanism (NPM), for up to three years. However, in line with their obligations under the Optional Protocol to the UN Convention against Torture, the authorities continued to develop a legal framework for the NPM in close co-operation with domestic and international NGOs and intergovernmental organizations.

In April, the Prosecutor General's Office told Amnesty International that members of Independent Public Monitoring Commissions had been given unprecedented access to pre-trial detention centres of the National Security Service (NSS); four visits had been carried out in 2009 and eight in 2010.

Despite these measures, people in police custody reported that they were frequently subjected to torture and other ill-treatment, both before and after the formal registration of their detention at a police station. Law enforcement officials often failed to respect the existing law on detention, which requires that they register detainees within three hours of their arrest.

In October, the UN Special Rapporteur on torture criticized Kazakhstan for continuing to conceal the full extent of torture and other ill-treatment in its detention and prison system.

Impunity

Impunity for such human rights violations remained fundamentally unchallenged. The authorities failed to fully and effectively implement Kazakhstan's obligations under the UN Convention against Torture. They also failed to implement the recommendations of the UN Committee against Torture and other UN treaty bodies and special procedures, especially with regard to initiating prompt, thorough, independent and impartial investigations into allegations of torture or other ill-treatment.

In April, the Prosecutor General's Office informed Amnesty International that in 2009 only two allegations of torture by security officers had been confirmed and that criminal cases had been opened against the offending officers. It dismissed as unfounded all allegations of torture by security officers raised by a number of people whose cases had been taken up by Amnesty International, other human rights organizations and the UN Special Rapporteur on torture.

■ In April, Alexander Gerasimov filed the first individual complaint against Kazakhstan with the UN Committee against Torture since the country's ratification of the Optional Protocol to the UN Convention against Torture in 2008. Alexander Gerasimov alleged that at least five police officers tortured him in 2007. Using a technique called "dry submarino," the officers tied his hands behind his back, pushed him face down on the floor, put a plastic bag over his head and held him down while one officer repeatedly jammed a knee into his back. The officers also delivered severe blows to his kidneys and threatened him with sexual violence. He was hospitalized for 13 days as a result of his injuries, and spent more than one month in intensive psychiatric care for post-traumatic stress disorder. In his complaint to the Committee, Alexander Gerasimov alleged that his case was not thoroughly or independently investigated and that no one was held accountable for these violations of his human rights.

Refugees and asylum-seekers

A new law on refugees, which came into force on 1 January, excluded certain categories of asylum-seekers from qualifying for refugee status in Kazakhstan. These included people charged in their country of origin with membership of illegal, unregistered or banned political or religious parties or movements. In practice, this exclusion particularly affected Muslims from Uzbekistan who worshipped in mosques which were not under state control or who were members or suspected members of Islamist parties or Islamic movements banned in Uzbekistan, and who had fled the country, fearing persecution for their religious beliefs. The exclusion also affected people of Uighur origin from the Xinjiang Uighur Autonomous Region of China who were charged with or suspected of belonging to separatist movements or parties.

The newly formed State Migration Committee, under the Ministry of Labour, began a review of all cases of those granted refugee status by UNHCR, the UN refugee agency, prior to the State Migration Committee's inception. It revoked the refugee status of many people from Uzbekistan and China, most of whom were awaiting resettlement to a third country.

Growing numbers of these individuals, as well as other asylum-seekers from Uzbekistan and China, were stopped by police or NSS officers for document checks and arbitrarily detained either for short periods in pre-charge detention facilities or indefinitely in NSS detention facilities pending forcible return to their countries of origin. They had no or limited access to lawyers, UNHCR or their families. Many complained about torture or other ill-treatment in detention.

■ In June 2010, NSS officers detained 30 Uzbekistani refugees and asylum-seekers in the city of Almaty with a view to forcibly deporting them to Uzbekistan. All 30 men had fled Uzbekistan due to fear of persecution for their affiliation to religious groups banned there. Detainees' wives were told that their husbands faced extradition to Uzbekistan on charges of membership of illegal religious or extremist organizations and charges of attempting to overthrow the state.

On 8 September one of the men, Nigmatulla Nabiev, was granted asylum for one year. However, on 13 September, the Almaty deputy prosecutor announced that the Prosecutor General's Office had decided to extradite the remaining 29 men. At least two of the 29 were said to have been extradited to

K

Uzbekistan in September before their appeals against their detentions and the decisions to extradite them had been heard. By the end of December the majority of the 29 men's appeals had been turned down. At least two other Uzbekistani asylum-seekers were extradited in October and November.

Amnesty International visits/reports

📕 Kazakhstan: No effective safeguards against torture (EUR 57/001/2010)

📕 Uzbekistani asylum-seekers at risk of extradition from Ukraine and Kazakhstan (EUR 04/002/2010)

KENYA

REPUBLIC OF KENYA

Head of state and government:	Mwai Kibaki
Death penalty:	abolitionist in practice
Population:	40.9 million
Life expectancy:	55.6 years
Under-5 mortality (m/f):	112/95 per 1,000
Adult literacy:	86.5 per cent

A new Constitution was passed providing a more comprehensive basis for the protection and fulfilment of human rights. The Constitution also offered a framework for addressing much needed political, judicial and other reforms. The government introduced a number of laws aimed at giving effect to the provisions of the new Constitution. However, impunity for past and current human rights violations continued to prevail, including for crimes committed during the post-elections violence of 2007/8 and for endemic violence against women.

Background

On 4 August, a significant majority (nearly two-thirds) of voters in a public referendum voted to adopt a new Constitution. The Constitution came into effect on 27 August.

Campaigns for the referendum and the conduct of the referendum itself were relatively peaceful but there were some reports of violence. These included three grenade attacks in June at a rally opposing the proposed Constitution at Uhuru Park in Nairobi, the capital. Six people were killed and over 100 injured

in the explosions and ensuing stampede. The government announced investigations into the attacks but no progress was reported by the end of 2010.

In June, three Members of Parliament and one political activist were arrested and charged over remarks that implied that certain communities would have to leave their homes if the Constitution was ratified. Their trial was pending at the end of the year.

The official anti-corruption authority filed various cases in court against high-profile public officials. Proceedings continued at the end of the year. In line with the new Constitution, a cabinet minister accused of corruption in a pending court case was suspended.

Impunity

No measures were implemented to ensure accountability for human rights violations, including possible crimes against humanity, committed in the post-election violence in 2007/8. A private members' bill seeking to establish a special tribunal to investigate and prosecute these crimes stalled in Parliament.

■ There was no progress in the investigations into the killings of Oscar Kingara and Paul Oulu, two human rights activists killed in 2009.

■ By the end of the year the killers of Francis Kainda Nyaruri, a freelance journalist murdered in 2009, had not been brought to justice.

Impunity – police and security forces

The government announced that it was finalizing three proposed laws on police reforms – the Independent Policing Oversight Authority Bill (establishing a police oversight authority), the National Police Service Bill (providing a new legal framework for policing) and the National Police Service Commission Bill (establishing a police service commission). The Bills had not been submitted to Parliament by the end of the year.

There were cases of unlawful killings and other human rights violations by the police and other security personnel. In March, eyewitnesses reported that seven men were shot dead by a group of administration police during a police operation in Kawangware, an informal settlement in Nairobi. Police officers claimed the men were part of a criminal gang, but witnesses said they were taxi drivers. The trial of seven police officers charged with the men's killings was pending in court by the end of the year.

K

No individual police officers or security personnel were brought to justice for unlawful killings and other human rights violations committed during the year and in the recent past.

International justice

In March, the International Criminal Court (ICC) decided to investigate crimes against humanity allegedly committed during the post-election violence of 2007/8. In December the ICC Prosecutor requested the Court to issue summonses against six individuals for crimes against humanity alleged to have been committed during the post-election violence. Parliament passed a motion in December calling for the executive arm of government to initiate Kenya's withdrawal from the Rome Statute establishing the ICC and for the repeal of the International Crimes Act which incorporates the statute into Kenyan law. The government's formal reaction to the motion was pending at the end of the year.

Although Kenya is obliged to arrest and surrender to the ICC anyone named in an arrest warrant, in August during celebrations to mark the new Constitution the government hosted Sudanese President Omar Al Bashir, against whom the ICC issued arrest warrants in March 2009 and July 2010.

Truth, Justice and Reconciliation Commission

The Truth, Justice and Reconciliation Commission (TJRC) established in the wake of the post-election violence started its operations. By the end of the year the TJRC was engaged in a country-wide process of taking statements from possible witnesses. However, its work was constrained by questions over the credibility of the chairperson and lack of funding. In April, the Commission vice-chair resigned, citing allegations that the chairperson had been involved in human rights violations and other issues that might be the subject of the TJRC's inquiry. Following a petition in April by eight of the nine TJRC Commissioners, in October the Chief Justice appointed a tribunal to investigate the issue. In November the TJRC chair stepped aside pending the tribunal's report, which was due within six months.

Witness protection

In June the Witness Protection (Amendment) Act became law, expanding the definition of a witness in need of protection and establishing an independent witness protection agency.

Up to 22 witnesses who testified before a 2008 official inquiry into the post-election violence, who might be called to testify in future ICC or other trials, were reported to be living in fear. An unknown number fled the country because of threats.

Violence against women and girls

Sexual and other forms of gender-based violence remained rampant throughout the country. The official Demographic and Health Survey 2008-2009 found that spousal violence was widespread, in particular marital rape which is not criminalized under Kenyan law. The Survey also found that female genital mutilation was still practised by a number of communities. The social stigma attached to victims of sexual violence means that most incidents of sexual and gender-based violence are never reported.

In July Parliament passed the Counter Trafficking in Persons Act, penalizing human trafficking, including trafficking of children. The President assented to the law in October.

Housing rights

The government failed to enforce existing laws and standards on sanitation in slums and informal settlements, leaving millions of people without access to toilets and private washing facilities. The lack of access to facilities in the immediate household vicinity, combined with an absence of effective police presence in the slums and settlements, placed women at risk of sexual violence, particularly at night.

Forced evictions

More than 50,000 people living alongside railway lines remained under the threat of forced evictions after the state-owned Kenya Railways Corporation issued a 30-day notice to quit in March. The Corporation announced that the evictions related to an upgrading project. Although the evictions were not carried out by the end of the year, the Corporation had not formally withdrawn the threat of evictions. Most of the people likely to be affected had been living and working on these lands for years and a 30-day notice period was wholly inadequate. No comprehensive resettlement or compensation plan was announced and the government did not make provision for those who would lose their homes, livelihoods, possessions and social networks as a result of the project.

K

In July, bulldozers from Nairobi City Council demolished around 100 homes and 470 market stalls in Kabete, Nairobi. No official notice was given to those affected. Angry residents clashed with armed police in the following days as tensions flared in the settlement. A 74-year-old man who tried to complain about the police beating a woman was shot dead by police at close range. By the end of the year the police officer responsible for the shooting had not been brought to justice. The evictions left hundreds of people, mainly women and children, without shelter. Many slept outdoors without blankets or warm clothes and had no money to buy food or other essentials.

The government repeatedly announced plans to continue evicting thousands of people from the Mau Forest Complex. Hundreds of households evicted from the Complex in 2009 remained in makeshift displacement camps without proper access to emergency shelter and other services.

By the end of the year the government had not fulfilled its 2006 pledge to release national guidelines on evictions.

Internally displaced people

Thousands of people remained displaced as a result of the post-election violence of 2007/8. By September the government had provided resettlement land only for a few hundred households. Following evictions from the Mau Forest Complex, some 30,000 people remained displaced in a dozen makeshift camps.

Refugees and asylum-seekers

The continued closure of the Kenya/Somali border hindered the ability of the government, UNHCR (the UN refugee agency) and other organizations to address the needs of Somali asylum-seekers and refugees (see Somalia entry). The Kenyan authorities continued to prevent some Somali asylum-seekers from entering the country and to forcibly return some who crossed the border.

Overcrowding in the three Dadaab refugee camps, which host thousands of Somali refugees, continued to impede the refugees' access to shelter, water, sanitation and other essential services. The government agreed that one of the camps in Dadaab could be extended and a fourth camp established.

The Kenyan authorities continued to deny reports that they were involved in the forcible recruitment of refugees as soldiers in support of the Transitional Federal Government of Somalia in 2009. Some of

those recruited from the camps in Dadaab were less than 18 years old.

Unlawful transfers of suspects

Between July and September up to 12 people suspected of involvement in bomb attacks in Kampala were arrested and transferred from Kenya to Uganda outside established legal procedures. These include extradition procedures which require reciprocal arrest warrants in both countries and judicial hearings. Kenyan authorities also ignored habeas corpus applications for some of the suspects who were unlawfully transferred to Uganda and charged with terrorism and murder (see Uganda entry).

Death penalty

Courts continued to impose the death penalty, although no executions were reported. The death penalty was retained in the new Constitution.

In July, the Court of Appeal, Kenya's highest court, declared that the mandatory application of the death penalty for the crime of murder is unconstitutional as it is "antithetical to the Constitutional provisions on the protection against inhuman or degrading punishment or treatment and fair trial". The Court expressly stated that the reasoning behind its rejection of the mandatory death penalty for the crime of murder might also apply to other capital crimes such as treason, robbery with violence and attempted robbery with violence. However, the Court ruled that the death penalty itself is constitutional.

Amnesty International visits/reports

📧 Amnesty International delegates visited Kenya in February, March, June, July, August, November and December.
📖 Insecurity and indignity: Women's experiences in the slums of Nairobi, Kenya (AFR 32/002/2010)
📖 Kenya: More than 50,000 face forced eviction (AFR 32/004/2010)
📖 Risking rape to reach a toilet: Women's experiences in the slums of Nairobi, Kenya (AFR 32/006/2010)
📖 Kenya: New Constitution offers a basis for better protection and fulfillment of human rights but measures to end impunity still needed (AFR 32/011/2010)
📖 Kenya: Important judgment highlights unfairness and cruelty of the death penalty in the country (AFR 32/012/2010)
📖 From life without peace to peace without life: The treatment of Somali refugees and asylum-seekers in Kenya (AFR 32/015/2010)
📖 Kenyan investigations into alleged police killings must be impartial, 12 March 2010

K

KOREA

(DEMOCRATIC PEOPLE'S REPUBLIC OF)

DEMOCRATIC PEOPLE'S REPUBLIC OF KOREA
Head of state:	Kim Jong-il
Head of government:	Choe Yong-rim (replaced Kim Yong-il in June)
Death penalty:	retentionist
Population:	24 million
Life expectancy:	67.7 years
Under-5 mortality (m/f):	63/63 per 1,000

Widespread violations of human rights continued, including severe restrictions on freedom of association, expression and movement, arbitrary detention, torture and other ill-treatment resulting in death, and executions. The authorities quashed dissent of any kind; the media was strictly controlled. Detainees were subjected to forced labour and dire conditions. A combination of poor economic policies and management, adverse weather conditions, and reduced international aid left millions of people without sufficient access to food. Essential medicines remained beyond the reach of millions of people. Thousands crossed the border into China in search of food and economic opportunity; many were arrested by the Chinese authorities and forcibly repatriated to North Korea where they faced detention, interrogation and torture.

Background

North Korea appeared to be preparing for a leadership change: Kim Jong-un, the third son of leader Kim Jong-il, was made a four-star general in September, suggesting that he was the anointed successor.

The Korean peninsula witnessed heightened tension after North Korea shelled Yeonpyeong island near the disputed sea border known as the Northern Limit Line in November. Two South Korean marines and two civilians were killed; it was the first time civilians had been killed as a result of cross-border military hostilities since the 1950-53 Korean War. In March, South Korea accused North Korea of sinking a South Korean naval ship, the *Cheonan*, resulting in the death of 46 naval personnel. In December, the prosecutor of the International Criminal Court, Luis Moreno-Ocampo, announced that he had opened a preliminary investigation into possible war crimes by North Korea linked to its recent clashes with South Korea.

Food crisis, malnutrition and health

In July, Amnesty International reported that the government's delayed and inadequate response to the continuing food crisis was having a devastating impact on the population's health. It called on the government to seek international humanitarian assistance and not impede its effective distribution. Donor governments were urged to provide assistance through the UN on the basis of need, not political considerations.

UNICEF said that each year some 40,000 children under five became "acutely malnourished" in North Korea, with 25,000 needing hospital treatment. A survey carried out by the government with UN support showed that about one third of the population suffered from stunting – below normal body growth. In some regions the figure was 45 per cent.

In October, UN Secretary-General Ban Ki-moon expressed concern "that the acute humanitarian needs" of at least 3.5 million women and children in North Korea would worsen because of food shortages.

Detention conditions

The government operated at least six facilities housing thousands of political prisoners. People were arbitrarily detained, or held for indeterminate periods without charge or trial. Detainees faced serious, systematic and sustained violations of their human rights, including extrajudicial executions, torture and other ill-treatment and forced labour. Torture appeared to be widespread in prison camps. Many detainees died due to strenuous, and often hazardous, forced labour with little rest and inadequate access to food or medical care. Many were executed for minor infractions and others were forced to witness the public executions.

■ In February, Jeong Sang-un, an 84-year-old former prisoner of war who had fought for South Korea during the 1950-53 Korean War, was believed to be held in a political prison camp in North Korea after he was forcibly returned by the Chinese authorities. He appears to have been one among thousands of people who left North Korea for China in search of food. Shortly after he arrived in China, he was arrested by authorities in Jilin province, and detained until he was forcibly returned to North Korea in February. At the time of his return, he was very frail, and needed help to walk. Jeong Sang-un did not face any trial in North Korea, and was sent directly to Yodok political prison camp (or *kwanliso*) in South Hamkyung province.

K

- In February, Robert Park, a 28-year-old US missionary and human rights activist, was released after 43 days in a detention facility in Pyongyang. He had been arrested after entering North Korea on 25 December 2009 with the apparent intention of highlighting the plight of political prisoners in the country.
- In August, following a visit by former US President Jimmy Carter, 31-year-old Aijalon Gomes, another US national, was freed. A friend of Robert Park, he had entered North Korea illegally in January, and had been sentenced to eight years' hard labour and fined approximately US$600,000.

Freedom of expression, association and movement

The authorities imposed severe restrictions on freedom of speech and assembly, despite constitutional guarantees of these rights. Criticism of the government and its leaders was strictly curtailed, punishable by arrest and incarceration in a prison camp. The government distributed all radio and television sets; citizens were forbidden to alter them to make it possible to receive broadcasts from other nations. Those caught listening to foreign broadcasts were detained and sentenced to long prison terms.

North Korean citizens faced restrictions on travel both within the country and abroad. Thousands of North Korean nationals who fled to China in search of food and employment were often forcibly repatriated to North Korea by the Chinese authorities. They were routinely beaten and sent to detention facilities on return. Those suspected of being in touch with South Korean NGOs or attempting to escape to South Korea were more severely punished.

Death penalty

North Korea continued to carry out executions, some in public and others in secret. At least 60 people were reportedly executed publicly.
- Chong, an armaments factory worker, was reportedly executed publicly in the eastern coastal city of Hamhung in late January. He had been charged with divulging – via an illegal Chinese mobile phone – the price of rice and other information on living conditions to a friend who had defected to South Korea years ago.

International scrutiny

In March, North Korea responded to the report arising from the UN Universal Periodic Review's (UPR) 2009 assessment of its human rights record. However, in

stating that it had simply "taken note" of recommendations made during the UPR, North Korea became the first country to refuse to expressly accept any of the recommendations emerging from the process. This contradicted earlier state promises to co-operate with the UPR process. In June, Marzuki Darusman, an Indonesian national, was appointed as the new UN Special Rapporteur on human rights in North Korea.

Amnesty International visits/reports

- The crumbling state of health care in North Korea (ASA 24/001/2010)

KOREA
(REPUBLIC OF)

REPUBLIC OF KOREA

Head of state:	Lee Myung-bak
Head of government:	Kim Hwang-Sik (replaced Yoon Jeung-hyun in October, who replaced Chung Un-chan in August)
Death penalty:	abolitionist in practice
Population:	48.5 million
Life expectancy:	79.8 years
Under-5 mortality (m/f):	6/6 per 1,000

The government increasingly used vaguely worded national security, defamation and other laws to harass and suppress its critics. In February, the Constitutional Court ruled that the death penalty did not violate the Constitution. In October and November, the Court conducted hearings on whether restrictions on migrant workers' labour mobility, and military conscription without options for conscientious objection, constituted violations of fundamental rights.

Background

Tensions between South and North Korea were exacerbated by several incidents in the West Sea (Yellow Sea) (see North Korea entry). The National Human Rights Commission of Korea was accused of losing independence and authority under its present leadership after failing to speak out or act on some significant human rights issues. Commissioners and experts resigned and new appointments appeared to be politically motivated.

Freedom of expression and association

Vaguely worded clauses of the 1948 National Security Law (NSL, last amended 1997) were increasingly used to silence dissent and arbitrarily prosecute individuals peacefully exercising their rights to freedom of expression and association. According to the National Police Agency, as of August,106 people were charged and 13 detained under the NSL. By the end of the year, at least seven people were incarcerated for peacefully exercising their right to freedom of expression.

The authorities continued to use Article 7 (praising or sympathizing with anti-state groups) of the NSL to suppress publication or distribution of material deemed to "benefit" North Korea.

■ In June, prosecutors began investigating staff at the People's Solidarity for Participatory Democracy (PSPD) NGO under charges of criminal defamation, "obstruction of performance of official duties" and Article 7 of the NSL. The charges were linked to a letter sent by the PSPD to the UN Security Council expressing doubts over South Korea's investigation report on the sinking in March of the naval ship, the *Cheonan* (see North Korea entry).

■ In September, the Seoul Central District Court ruled in favour of defendant Park Won-soon, activist and director of the Hope Institute. In 2009, the National Intelligence Service sued him for damages of US$176,000 for allegedly defaming the "nation" by stating in an interview that the National Intelligence Service was pressuring corporations not to financially support civil society groups.

■ In December, prosecutors demanded a seven-year sentence under the NSL for Professor Oh Se-chul of the Socialist Workers League of Korea. In August 2008, he and six members of the group were charged with violating NSL Article 7. Attempts to detain them under the NSL in 2008 had twice been rejected by Seoul Central District Court.

■ In December, the Seoul Central District Court acquitted four producers and one scriptwriter of Munhwa Broadcasting Corporation (MBC). They had been charged with defaming the former Agriculture Minister and negotiator on US beef imports.

In June 2009, prosecutors accused the MBC staff of distorting facts, deliberately mistranslating and exaggerating the dangers of US beef in an episode of the investigative documentary series *PD Notebook*, which aired in April 2008. The government blamed the programme for sparking candlelight protests against US beef imports. The Prosecutor's Office appealed the decision, and the case was pending before the Supreme Court. This followed an earlier acquittal of the five by the same court in January, which the Prosecutor's Office also appealed against.

Freedom of assembly

The authorities continued to curb people's right to demonstrate peacefully. A new law, introduced on 1 October in the run-up to the G20 summit, banned demonstrations in "places of security and safety". Riot police, mostly conscript soldiers, were deployed in large numbers prior to the summit. On 7 November, capsaicin liquid, which causes a burning sensation on contact, was used to control one anti-G20 demonstration.

■ In November, seven Filipino activists travelling to Seoul to attend non-governmental preparations for the G20 summit, were barred from entering South Korea and forcibly deported. While detained at Incheon International Airport, immigration officers told them they were on a government blacklist.

■ In November, prosecutors demanded that Park Rae-gun be sentenced to five years and four months' imprisonment and Lee Jong-hoe to four years' imprisonment for "hosting an illegal protest" and "blocking traffic". The protests were calling for justice for those killed in the January 2009 police action against rooftop protests by evicted tenants at a building in the Yongsan district of Seoul. The trial, due in December, was postponed to January 2011.

Conscientious objectors

In November, the Constitutional Court heard oral arguments as they deliberated whether fundamental rights are violated when criminal punishment is imposed on those who, on grounds of conscience, refuse military conscription or reserve force training. They also considered whether failure to provide alternative service options for such conscientious objectors violated their fundamental right to freedom of conscience. As of November, 965 such prisoners of conscience remained in detention.

Migrants' rights

In October, the Constitutional Court heard oral arguments as part of their deliberations on whether it is

K

constitutional to limit job changes for migrant workers under the Employment Permit System. Thousands of migrant workers continued to be deported.

■ In November, Trinh Cong Quan, a 35-year-old undocumented migrant worker from Viet Nam, died after attempting to escape from immigration officers by jumping from the factory building where he was working. Immigration authorities had raided the factory without seeking the employer's permission, as part of a government crackdown on undocumented workers. Trinh Cong Quan had a wife and child in South Korea.

Death penalty

In a five to four ruling, the Constitutional Court in February stated that capital punishment did not violate "human dignity and worth" protected in the Constitution. Three death penalty abolition bills were pending before the National Assembly, one introduced in 2010. Death sentences were imposed, but there were no executions. Sixty-three prisoners were under sentence of death, three of whom were in the process of appeal.

KUWAIT

STATE OF KUWAIT

Head of state:	al-Shaikh Sabah al-Ahmad al-Jaber al-Sabah
Head of government:	al-Shaikh Nasser Mohammad al-Ahmad al-Sabah
Death penalty:	retentionist
Population:	3.1 million
Life expectancy:	77.9 years
Under-5 mortality (m/f):	11/9 per 1,000
Adult literacy:	94.5 per cent

Critics of the Prime Minister were harassed and prosecuted. Foreign migrant workers were exploited and abused by employers. Thousands of Bidun resident in Kuwait remained stateless, impeding their access to health, education and other rights. At least three people were sentenced to death; no executions were reported.

Background

Kuwait's human rights record was assessed under the UN Universal Periodic Review in May. In September, the government accepted 114 recommendations,

including to improve conditions for foreign migrant workers, and rejected 25 recommendations, including to establish a moratorium on executions.

Freedom of expression and association

Two critics of the Prime Minister continued to face harassment and prosecution.

■ Muhammad 'Abd al-Qader al-Jasem, a journalist and critic of the Prime Minister, was arrested on 11 May and charged with undermining the status of the Amir of Kuwait by writing articles in his blog. He was released on bail on 28 June. On 22 November, he was sentenced by the Criminal Court to a one-year prison term and immediately detained to start serving the sentence. He lodged an appeal. He faced several other lawsuits filed against him by the Prime Minister.

■ Khaled al-Fadala, Secretary General of the National Democratic Alliance, a grouping of liberal political organizations, was sentenced to three months' imprisonment and a fine on 30 June after he was convicted of insulting the Prime Minister in a speech criticizing corruption in Kuwait. He began serving his sentence on 2 July but was released 10 days later. The Court of Cassation found that there had been procedural irregularities and ordered his retrial.

■ Thirty-three Egyptian nationals who met at a restaurant in Kuwait to express support for a potential candidate in Egypt's 2011 presidential election were arrested on 9 April; 25 of them were then summarily deported and the other eight are believed to have been released.

■ On 8 December, the police forcibly dispersed a public gathering at the house of Jama'an al-Harbash, a member of parliament (MP), and reportedly assaulted several MPs and others who then required hospital treatment. One of them, human rights defender Dr 'Obaid al-Wasmi, filed a formal complaint the next day against the Interior Ministry and the police officers he alleged had assaulted him; two days later, he was arrested. On 20 December, he appeared before the Criminal Court to face six charges, including spreading false information abroad, taking part in a public gathering with criminal intent, and insulting the Amir.

Counter-terror and security

Two Kuwaiti nationals, Fawzi al-Odah and Faiz al-Kandari, continued to be detained by the US authorities at Guantánamo Bay, Cuba. In September, a US judge denied a habeas corpus petition brought on behalf of Faiz al-Kandari, effectively consigning him to indefinite detention.

K

In April, the government refused appeals by the US authorities to confiscate the passports and impose other restrictions on two former Guantánamo detainees, Khaled al-Mutairi and Fouad al-Rabia.

In May, eight men accused of belonging to al-Qa'ida and planning to attack a US base in Kuwait were acquitted by a criminal court; the acquittals were confirmed by the Court of Appeal on 28 October. In December 2009, a court had accepted that the accused were ill-treated in pre-trial detention; no action was known to have been taken against those allegedly responsible for their ill-treatment.

Women's rights

Women continued to face discrimination in law and practice. However, the government enacted new legislation to make Kuwaiti women eligible to receive the state social allowance if their husbands do not receive it and to provide for paid maternity leave for women employed by the state.

■ In April, a court banned women from being hired as prosecutors, rejecting a petition by Shurouk Al-Failakawi, a law graduate, against the head of the Supreme Judicial Council, in which she sought appointment as a prosecutor. The case was referred for appeal.

Discrimination – the Bidun

In November, the government announced what it called a comprehensive plan to resolve the problems facing the Bidun community, indicating that many would be accorded Kuwaiti nationality although more than half would not and so would remain stateless. Thousands of Bidun long resident in Kuwait have continued to be denied Kuwaiti nationality and are currently stateless. As such, they are denied access to health, education, employment and social services on an equitable basis with Kuwaiti citizens.

Migrants' rights

Foreign migrant workers were inadequately protected by law and in practice, so continued to be exploited and abused by employers. Suicide rates among such workers were reported to be high.

New labour legislation relating largely to the private sector came into force on 20 February. It prohibits the employment of minors aged under 15 and requires that a public authority be established to oversee the recruitment and employment of foreign migrant workers.

Death penalty

At least two men and one woman were sentenced to death for murder. One death sentence was reported to have been commuted on appeal. No executions were reported.

■ In January, the death sentence against a Filipina domestic worker, Jakatia Pawa, was upheld by the Court of Cassation. She was sentenced to death in 2008 for the murder of her employer's 22-year-old daughter.

In December, Kuwait was one of the minority of states that voted against a UN General Assembly resolution calling for a worldwide moratorium on executions.

KYRGYZSTAN

KYRGYZ REPUBLIC
Head of state: **Roza Otunbaeva (replaced Kurmanbek Bakiev in July following his resignation in April)**
Head of government: **Almaz Atambaev (replaced interim head Roza Otunbaeva in December, who had replaced Daniar Usenov in April)**
Death penalty: **abolitionist**
Population: **5.6 million**
Life expectancy: **68.4 years**
Under-5 mortality (m/f): **49/42 per 1,000**
Adult literacy: **99.3 per cent**

K

Four days of violence in June between ethnic Kyrgyz and ethnic Uzbeks left hundreds dead and forced hundreds of thousands to flee their homes. Serious human rights violations marred the efforts to restore order to the region, including widespread reports of the use of excessive force by security forces, arbitrary detentions, and torture and other ill-treatment during transfer and in custody. Attempts to establish the truth about what happened were undermined by apparent ethnic bias. At least 271 people were remanded in custody charged with participation in the June violence, the majority ethnic Uzbeks. Human rights defenders, civil society activists and lawyers were beaten and detained; some were held on serious criminal charges and tortured to extract confessions.

Background

Rising tensions between the government of President Kurmanbek Bakiev and the opposition escalated in early April, resulting in violent clashes between security forces and demonstrators on 7 April in the capital, Bishkek. Eighty-seven people were killed and hundreds wounded, including police officers, armed men and unarmed civilians. Shortly afterwards, the opposition dissolved the parliament and the constitutional court and formed an interim government, led by Roza Otunbaeva. President Bakiev resigned on 15 April and fled the country. In the weeks that followed, ethnic Kyrgyz mobs attacked Kurdish, Meskhetian Turk and Russian villages across the country, killing villagers, looting and destroying properties and livestock. In May, violent clashes between mainly Kyrgyz supporters of ousted President Bakiev and Uzbeks in Jalal-Abad city left at least five people dead and dozens injured.

On 10 June, clashes between gangs of mostly ethnic Kyrgyz and Uzbek young people in Osh city rapidly escalated. Over the next four days, large-scale arson, looting and violent attacks, including killings and sexual violence, swept through Osh and Jalal-Abad regions, disproportionately affecting Uzbek-populated areas. Official statistics released in October provisionally placed the number of dead at 408, although the final number, which had not been published by the end of year, was likely to be higher. At least 1,900 were severely injured. The violence was followed by heavy-handed search operations by security forces as well as criminal investigations and prosecutions, largely perceived to be flawed and biased.

Satellite imagery revealed that 1,807 buildings in Osh city alone were totally destroyed. Some 400,000 people, both Kyrgyz and Uzbek, fled their homes. Up to 100,000 refugees, mostly Uzbek women and children and the elderly, fled across the border to Uzbekistan, although almost all had returned by the end of June. Thousands remained internally displaced living in temporary, mostly inadequate, accommodation with relatives, host families, or in public buildings, tents and camps.

The facts and causes of the June violence continued to be hotly contested by the ethnic communities. There were several credible independent reports of the complicity of Kyrgyzstani officials and security forces in the attacks.

The authorities recognized the need to ensure an independent investigation into the June events and mandated two commissions of inquiry: one national, one international. In addition, the Kyrgyzstani national Ombudsman announced that he would conduct his own inquiry. By the end of the year no reports had been published.

A referendum on 27 June approved a new Constitution which introduced parliamentary democracy, limited the length of the presidential time in office to one six-year term and confirmed Roza Otunbaeva as President until December 2011. Parliamentary elections on 10 October returned five parties to parliament, but the first attempt to form a coalition government failed in November. A coalition government was finally formed at the end of December.

Torture and other ill-treatment

Reports of torture or other ill-treatment in the aftermath of the June violence were widespread. Beatings by law enforcement officers appeared to continue to be routine: in the street during apprehension, during transfer to detention centres, during initial interrogation, and in pre-charge detention facilities. Search operations by security forces, ostensibly to seize weapons and detain suspects, were reportedly carried out using excessive force. There were serious concerns that the law enforcement operations and criminal investigations in the aftermath of the June violence disproportionately targeted Uzbeks and Uzbek neighbourhoods, while failing to identify and investigate alleged Kyrgyz perpetrators. Hundreds of men, the majority Uzbek, were arbitrarily detained and allegedly beaten during raids and later tortured or otherwise ill-treated in detention. In August, President Otunbaeva reportedly said she was aware that human rights violations had been committed by security forces during the June events and their aftermath, but that she had effectively no control over law enforcement in the south of the country.

■ Early on 21 June, security forces entered the Uzbek village of Nariman in Osh region, reportedly beat people with rifle butts and destroyed personal documents during house searches. A spokesperson for the Ministry of Internal Affairs claimed that the operation was intended to dismantle the barricades which had been erected, arrest suspects and seize weapons. Reportedly, one man was shot and died on the way to hospital, another was beaten to death and many more were injured. Several men were detained.

Unfair trials

Trials continued to fall short of international standards.

Following unfair trials, courts handed down at least 24 life sentences and six long-term sentences of between 15 and 25 years' imprisonment for murder and mass disturbances in relation to the June unrest. Allegations of forced confessions were not investigated, defence witnesses were not interviewed, and lawyers were threatened and physically attacked.

■ In September, the trial of prominent human rights defender Azimzhan Askarov and seven co-defendants, accused of the murder of a Kyrgyz police officer during violence in Bazar-Korgan, was marred by repeated acts of violence against Azimzhan Askarov's family and lawyers both inside and outside the courtroom. Court officials, including the judge, reportedly intervened only sporadically to stop the violence and restore order. The defendants' lawyers were not given the opportunity to question witnesses or submit petitions, or to call defence witnesses as the authorities were not able to guarantee their safety. When the lawyers expressed concern that they would not be able to defend their clients under these conditions, the judge reportedly threatened to have their licences to practise revoked. The defendants denied their guilt and maintained in court that they had been forced to confess under duress. Their allegations were not investigated and five of them, including Azimzhan Askarov, were sentenced to life imprisonment. The Jalal-Abad regional court which heard the appeal case did not examine any of the defendants' allegations of forced confessions or order an investigation into these allegations. Defence lawyers were not able to call witnesses, and relatives and colleagues of the murdered police officer continued to threaten the lawyers. The appeal court upheld the sentences imposed by the court of first instance. An appeal to the Supreme Court was pending at the end of the year. As the director of the NGO Vozdukh (Air), Azimzhan Askarov had been working on cases of torture in the region for many years.

■ In November, former President Bakiev, some of his relatives and members of his administration, as well as members of the elite Special Forces unit Alfa went on trial in Bishkek on charges relating to the April violence. President Bakiev was tried in his absence for authorizing the use of force. The members of the Alfa unit were accused of carrying out the order to shoot to kill. During the mass trial, which started in a covered sports stadium in Bishkek, relatives of those killed shouted racist abuse at the ethnic Russian lawyers and defendants and threatened to kill them if they did not leave the country. The trial was suspended on 30 November after a small device exploded outside the stadium.

Impunity

In November, President Otunbaeva told prosecutors that she was concerned about the number of complaints she had received of torture and other ill-treatment by security forces in relation to the June events which apparently had not been properly investigated. By the end of December no prosecution for ill-treatment in police custody appeared to have taken place. The deputy prosecutor for Osh region stated that his office had received very few complaints of torture in detention. This contrasted starkly with the allegations raised by human rights organizations and defence lawyers of widespread beatings or other ill-treatment of Uzbek detainees.

The first deputy Minister of Internal Affairs stated in September that there had been isolated cases of torture and ill-treatment of detained Uzbek suspects and that the Ministry had ordered investigations into the most serious of these cases. In some instances, the deputy Minister had conducted investigations personally. He had interviewed Azimzhan Askarov, who, when asked directly, had denied outright any torture or other ill-treatment by police officers. This brief interview in the presence of local police officers constituted the extent of the investigation to date into the torture allegations repeatedly raised by Azimzhan Askarov's lawyer, in spite of previously documented evidence, including photographs, of injuries sustained whilst in custody.

Ethnic bias

There were concerns over ethnic bias in the attitudes of the authorities following the June events. Groups of Kyrgyz civilians, often women, assaulted the relatives of victims and detainees outside police stations or the prosecutor's offices, effectively obstructing their attempts to submit complaints about allegations of torture to police and prosecutors. Groups of Kyrgyz women also assaulted ethnic Kyrgyz, Uzbek and Russian lawyers defending Uzbek suspects on court premises and inside police compounds, mostly in the presence of police officers who did not intervene to stop the assaults. By the end of the year, no investigations had reportedly been opened into offences by these groups.

■ On 5 November, a court in Jalal-Abad convicted two Kyrgyz men of murdering three Uzbek civilians on 13 June and sentenced them to 25 and 20 years in prison. This was the only conviction of the year of ethnic Kyrgyz for a serious criminal offence committed in the course of the June violence. The Jalal-Abad prosecutor's office

K

stated that 88 people faced charges in relation to the June violence, and that 26 were ethnic Kyrgyz.

By 10 November 2010, official figures revealed that 271 individuals had been arrested in relation to the June violence. Human rights defenders and lawyers maintained that the majority of those arrested were ethnic Uzbeks.

Repression of dissent

In April the interim government revoked the entry ban on several foreign human rights defenders which had been imposed by the government of ousted President Bakiev.

However, in a climate of ethnic tensions and growing nationalist discourse, human rights defenders found themselves in the difficult position of having to justify their work protecting different ethnic communities. Those who documented the June events were targeted by the authorities, who attempted to confiscate their material and obstruct their work. Uzbek human rights defenders and lawyers were particularly at risk of violence and were threatened, beaten, and, in some cases, detained, tortured and sentenced to life imprisonment after an unfair trial. Their Kyrgyz colleagues and those of other ethnic origins also came under increasing pressure and were threatened and assaulted by Kyrgyz civilians for defending the rights of Uzbek suspects.

■ Lawyer Tair Asanov was attacked in court after calling for an investigation into police ill-treatment against his client and nine other men during their trial in Osh. Tair Asanov's client was accused of crimes ranging from involvement in the death of the Kara Suu District Police Chief and his driver, to taking part in riots. After he requested an investigation into the beatings, Tair Asanov was attacked by relatives of the murdered police chief, who were present in the courtroom. After the hearing ended, relatives followed Tair Asanov outside the courtroom and attacked him again. Police were present while he was being beaten but did not intervene.

Amnesty International visits /reports

🚌 Amnesty International delegates visited Kyrgyzstan in September.

📖 Partial truth and selective justice: The aftermath of the June 2010 violence in Kyrgyzstan (EUR 58/022/2010)

LAOS

LAO PEOPLE'S DEMOCRATIC REPUBLIC

Head of state:	Choummaly Sayasone
Head of government:	Thongsing Thammavong (replaced Bouasone Bouphavanh in December)
Death penalty:	abolitionist in practice
Population:	6.4 million
Life expectancy:	65.9 years
Under-5 mortality (m/f):	68/61 per 1,000
Adult literacy:	72.7 per cent

Lao authorities denied independent monitors unfettered access to more than 4,500 Lao Hmong asylum-seekers and refugees, who had been forcibly returned from Thailand in 2009 and placed in resettlement sites. Restrictions on freedom of expression, association and assembly continued. Prisoners of conscience and political prisoners remained imprisoned. At least four people were sentenced to death for drug trafficking, despite a de facto moratorium on executions. No official statistics on death sentences were made public.

Background

Laos rejected recommendations made by the Universal Periodic Review Working Group in May to abolish the death penalty. It signed the UN Convention against Torture in September. In November, the first meeting of states parties to the Convention on Cluster Munitions was held in the capital, Vientiane. In December, Laos abstained on a UN General Assembly resolution calling for a worldwide moratorium on executions.

The INGO Network, a group of international non-governmental organizations, voiced concerns about the negative impact of the rapid increase in large foreign investment projects, such as mining and hydropower. The INGO Network also highlighted the need to address social development, disparities in income and access to health and education services.

Land conflicts comprised the highest number of cases in the courts. The authorities cited gaps in laws and regulations, biased judges and a lack of transparency by justice and law enforcement officials as complicating factors.

Refugees and asylum-seekers

Laos denied independent monitors unfettered access to resettlement sites at Phonkham in Borikhamsay province, and Phalak and Nongsan in Vientiane province. This hampered proper assessment of the situation of some 4,500 Hmong forcibly returned from Thailand in December 2009. The remote Phonkham site housed around 3,500 returnees, including more than 1,000 young children. It had no electricity until June, and lacked adequate health care and education facilities. Despite official assurances, identity papers and travel documents were not issued to residents.

The authorities considered all the returnees as "illegal migrants".

Prisoners of conscience/political prisoners

Lack of transparency about the fate and whereabouts of prisoners of conscience and political prisoners continued.

■ The authorities rejected a Universal Periodic Review Working Group recommendation to release prisoners of conscience Bouavanh Chanhmanivong, Seng-Aloun Phengphanh and Thongpaseuth Keuakoun, arrested in October 1999 while attempting to stage a peaceful protest. They remained in prison despite having completed their 10-year sentences.

■ The fate and whereabouts of nine people, arrested in November 2009 for planning to petition the authorities about loss of land and lack of social and economic support, remained unknown.

■ No news emerged about Thao Moua and Pa Fue Khang, two Hmong arrested in 2003 and sentenced to 12 and 15 years' imprisonment respectively after a politically motivated unfair trial. They were last known to be held at Samkhe prison in Vientiane.

Freedom of religion

In the provinces, a small number of Christians were harassed in attempts to make them recant their faith.

■ In January in Katin village, Saravan province, police and local officials forced dozens of Christians to leave a religious service at gunpoint. When they refused to recant their faith, they were forcibly taken out of the village on foot and left on the side of the road several miles away, without their belongings.

LEBANON

LEBANESE REPUBLIC

Head of state:	Michel Suleiman
Head of government:	Saad Hariri
Death penalty:	retentionist
Population:	4.3 million
Life expectancy:	72.4 years
Under-5 mortality (m/f):	31/21 per 1,000
Adult literacy:	89.6 per cent

Palestinian refugees continued to face discrimination, which impeded their access to work, health, education and adequate housing. At least 23 recognized Iraqi refugees were reported to have been deported while scores of other refugees and asylum-seekers were detained in what may amount to arbitrary detention. At least 19 people were convicted following unfair trials of collaboration with or spying for Israel; 12 of them were reported to have been sentenced to death. Reports continued of torture in detention. Migrant domestic workers continued to suffer widespread discrimination and abuse. Few official steps were taken to investigate the fate of thousands of individuals missing since the 1975-90 civil war.

Background

Tension increased within the fragile unity government and in the country amid reports that Hizbullah members were to be indicted by the Special Tribunal for Lebanon (STL) in connection with the 2005 assassination of former Prime Minister Rafic Hariri. Hizbullah called for a boycott of the STL and accused it of being politicized and failing to investigate earlier allegations that had led to four former Lebanese security and intelligence heads being detained without charge for nearly four years. In September, Prime Minister Saad Hariri said that it had been a mistake to accuse the Syrian government of responsibility for his father's assassination.

At least seven civilians were among 16 individuals killed in political violence or by the security forces. In a possible case of excessive use of force, two civilians were shot dead by border police in November near the northern village of Wadi Khaled; according to reports, they were on a motorcycle and failed to stop. Two other civilians were then shot dead by border police during a protest against the killings.

L

Tension remained high along the southern border with Israel. Israeli airforce jets repeatedly violated Lebanese airspace and Israeli forces continued to occupy part of Ghajar village. In August, at least two Lebanese soldiers, a Lebanese journalist and an Israeli soldier were killed in a cross-border clash.

At least two people were killed and others injured by Israeli cluster bomb units and landmines left in southern Lebanon in previous years.

Lebanon's parliamentary Human Rights Committee continued drafting a National Human Rights Action Plan.

In November, Lebanon's human rights record was assessed under the UN Universal Periodic Review, and Lebanon agreed to take all necessary measures to stop torture and cruel, inhuman or degrading treatment.

Unfair trials

At least 20 individuals were tried for security offences before courts whose procedures were unfair.

More than 120 individuals suspected of involvement with the Fatah al-Islam armed group, detained without charge since 2007, continued to await trial before the Judicial Council. Most were allegedly tortured. The Judicial Council, widely believed to lack independence, fails to provide for the right to appeal, even in death penalty cases. Defendants often wait for long periods for trial without being formally charged.

Scores of people were detained on suspicion of collaborating with or spying for Israel. At least 19 were sentenced to prison terms or death after trials before military courts. Trials before military courts are unfair as judges are predominantly serving military officers. In addition, civilians should not be tried under military jurisdiction.

■ The trial began of Maher Sukkar, a Palestinian refugee, and 10 others before a military court on security-related offences including "forming an armed gang to commit crimes against people and property". No investigation was carried out into his allegation that he "confessed" under torture in April while held incommunicado.

■ The trial continued before the Judicial Council of Kamal al-Na'san, Mustafa Sayw and others suspected of involvement in the 2007 'Ayn 'Alaq bus bombings which killed three people. Kamal al-Na'san and Mustafa Sayw were arrested in early 2007, held for nine and 26 months respectively in solitary confinement at the Information Branch of the Internal Security Forces (ISF) in Beirut, and reportedly tortured and otherwise ill-treated. Kamal

al-Na'san retracted part of his statement in court, saying it had been coerced. No investigations were known to have been carried out into the torture allegations.

Torture and other ill-treatment

Reports continued of torture and other ill-treatment of detainees and few steps were taken to improve the situation. However, the authorities did permit a visit of the UN Subcommittee on Prevention of Torture to the country in May, and in November announced that they would criminalize all forms of torture and ill-treatment. Detainees continued to be held incommunicado, allegations of torture were not investigated and "confessions" allegedly given under duress were accepted as evidence in trials. The government failed for a further year to submit its first report under the UN Convention against Torture, which Lebanon ratified in 2000. It also failed to establish an independent body empowered to inspect detention centres, as required by the Optional Protocol to the Convention against Torture to which Lebanon became party in 2008.

■ Mohammad Osman Zayat was reported to have been severely beaten during arrest by plain-clothed members of the ISF on 24 June. While detained at the ISF's Information Branch in Beirut, he was repeatedly forced to stand in stress positions, beaten and given electric shocks to sensitive parts of his body. As a result, he signed "confessions" that were expected to be used against him in trial.

Discrimination – Palestinian refugees

Two amendments to the Labour and Social Security laws were approved in August but did little to diminish the discriminatory laws and regulations faced by some 300,000 Palestinian refugees who are denied basic rights, including the right to inherit property and to work in around 20 professions. One amendment cancelled the fees payable by Palestinian refugees for work permits, but administrative and other difficulties in obtaining the permits continued and few if any new ones were issued. The other amendment gave Palestinians access to pensions, but only when provided by a yet-to-be-established employers' fund. It did not give Palestinians access to sickness and other benefits.

Violence and discrimination against women

In May, the Appeals Court overturned a lower court ruling that would have given Lebanese women the right to pass on their nationality to their children. Samira Soueidan had obtained the earlier court decision in June 2009 but the Minister of Justice appealed. Under Lebanese law, nationality is passed on through the father only.

Women migrant domestic workers continued to face exploitation and physical, sexual and psychological abuse at work. It was reported in June that, in a rare prosecution, a Lebanese woman was sentenced to one month's imprisonment and fined for beating and mistreating a Sri Lankan woman she employed as a housemaid.

Refugees and asylum-seekers

Scores of refugees and asylum-seekers, mostly Iraqis and Sudanese, were detained beyond the expiry of sentences imposed for irregular entry into Lebanon or despite having been cleared of an offence. Many were held in poor conditions at an underground facility at 'Adliyeh in Beirut and were forced to decide between remaining in indefinite detention or returning "voluntarily" to their countries of origin. At least 23 recognized Iraqi refugees were reported to have been deported in clear violation of international law.

■ On 10 November, 'Alaa al-Sayad, an Iraqi refugee, was taken from detention at the 'Adliyeh facility and was reported to have been beaten severely to force him to board a plane on which he was then forcibly returned to Iraq.

Some 20,000 Palestinian refugees, who had been forced to flee the Nahr al-Bared refugee camp area in 2007 during a 15-week battle between the Lebanese Army and Fatah al-Islam, remained displaced due to the devastation and delays in reconstruction. Around 11,000 had been able to return to live in areas close to the camp.

Enforced disappearances and abductions

The government took few steps to investigate the fate of thousands of people who went missing during the 1975-90 civil war despite continuous campaigning by relatives seeking the truth. However, senior government leaders boycotted the Arab Summit held in Libya in March in protest at Libyan leader Mu'ammar al-Gaddafi's alleged involvement in the abduction and enforced disappearance of a senior Shi'a Imam, Musa al-Sadr, and two companions in 1978.

The Council of Ministers provided a short document about mass graves to a court that was hearing a lawsuit filed by two NGOs. The NGOs were working on behalf of people whose relatives had disappeared or been abducted, and who hope to protect and identify the bodies buried in three mass graves cited in an official 2000 report.

Death penalty

At least 12 people were reported to have been sentenced to death, including five in their absence, after being convicted of collaborating with or spying for Israel. In June, President Suleiman said he would be prepared to sign execution warrants of those sentenced to death for acting as agents for Israel. Tens of other prisoners continued to be held on death row. There were no executions, maintaining the de facto moratorium in force since 2004.

■ On 18 February, Mahmoud Rafeh was sentenced to death by a military court for "collaboration and espionage on behalf of the enemy". He said he was tortured to make him "confess", an allegation that was not investigated by the court.

Amnesty International visits/reports

🚗 An Amnesty International delegate visited Lebanon in October to conduct human rights research.

LIBERIA

L

REPUBLIC OF LIBERIA

Head of state and government:	Ellen Johnson-Sirleaf
Death penalty:	abolitionist in practice
Population:	4.1 million
Life expectancy:	59.1 years
Under-5 mortality (m/f):	144/136 per 1,000
Adult literacy:	58.1 per cent

Although the government made some institutional progress towards improving the human rights situation, levels of violent crime, including rape and other forms of sexual violence against women and girls, remained high. There were serious problems within the criminal justice system, with allegations of police inefficiency, brutality and corruption, and long delays in the judicial system leading to overcrowded prisons full of untried detainees. After substantial delays, the Independent National Human Rights Commission was established; its Commissioners were confirmed by the Senate in September 2010.

Background

Complete impunity prevailed for perpetrators of crimes against humanity during the recent civil war. Widespread unemployment, including among former combatants, remained a threat to peace and security. Crises in neighbouring Guinea and Côte d'Ivoire, with refugees, arms and fighters easily crossing the borders, contributed to fears of instability. Nearly 30,000 Ivorian refugees arrived late in the year. Mob and vigilante justice remained high, as did violent land disputes, violent crime, sexual and domestic violence, child abuse, female genital mutilation, and the worst forms of child labour. The global economic depression and depreciation of the Liberian dollar contributed to high food prices, widespread hunger and an alarming food security situation, all compounded by dire poverty.

The Access to Information Act increased freedom of the press but some restrictions remained in place. Three parliamentary bills tabled in 2007 to reform the media made no progress. Physical intimidation, deterrent lawsuits and administrative interference limited the ability of journalists to carry out their work.

The government took some steps to build the domestic institutional framework to address human rights issues. It established the Constitutional Review Task Force, the Law Reform Commission and the Land Commission. The government made institutional progress to address rape and other forms of sexual violence against women and girls, and to improve the administration of justice.

Impunity

Crimes committed during the civil war

Little progress was made in bringing to justice people responsible for gross human rights violations during the conflict in Liberia in 1989-1996 and 1999-2003. The recommendation of the Truth and Reconciliation Commission (TRC) that a criminal tribunal be established to prosecute people identified as responsible for crimes under international law was not implemented, nor were most TRC recommendations on legal and other institutional reforms, accountability, and reparations.

In April, the Justice Minister publicly expressed interest in trying perpetrators of the worst crimes committed during the civil war. A committee was established, which included the Justice Minister, to review the TRC's report, which was published in December 2009, and give advice on whether prosecutions should go ahead. No individuals were tried in the domestic justice system. Some former warlords named in the TRC report maintained seats in the Senate and other positions of power.

The trial of former Liberian President Charles Taylor continued at the Special Court for Sierra Leone in The Hague. He was facing charges of war crimes, but only for his alleged involvement in the war in Sierra Leone. He was not charged with crimes under international law committed in Liberia.

Recent human rights violations

Impunity for human rights violations committed since the end of the civil war remained a serious concern. Senators, Deputy Ministers, police officials, Special Security Service agents and Liberia National Police officers were allegedly engaged in or ordered beatings, looting, arbitrary arrests, abductions, shootings, ritualistic killings and other abuses. In most cases, no investigations were carried out and no action was taken against alleged perpetrators.

Justice system

Despite efforts to improve institutional protection of human rights in the criminal justice system and to address capacity and resource constraints, serious challenges remained. The police, judiciary, and penal sector were inadequate, corrupt, and abusive.

Law enforcement forces were reported to have unlawfully arrested and detained people and to have used torture and other ill-treatment, including during attempts to extort money on the streets. Many Liberia National Police officers were poorly equipped, poorly paid, corrupt and slow to respond to criminal activity. Conditions in police lock-ups were appalling, with juveniles and adults routinely held together. Detainees were often subject to abuse by police and other detainees.

The formal justice system often failed to deliver fair trials and due process. Lengthy pre-trial detention beyond that allowed by law was the norm, with roughly 90 per cent of prisoners being pre-trial detainees. As well as corruption and inefficiency, the system suffered from lack of transport, court facilities, lawyers and qualified judges.

Conditions in the country's 14 prison facilities were harsh. Prisons were understaffed, overcrowded, without enough food, water, sanitation or medical services. Security was inadequate, resulting in prisoner escapes and rampant inmate-on-inmate violence, including beatings and rape. Half the country's prisoners were held at Monrovia Central Prison, which typically housed between 800 and 1,000 inmates – four times its capacity. Pre-trial detainees were often mixed in with convicted prisoners.

In the parallel traditional justice system, the operation of customary courts failed to meet standards of due process, gender equality, and separation of powers. Trial by ordeal continued, whereby the guilt or innocence of the accused can be determined in an arbitrary manner involving torture and sometimes death.

Death penalty

No steps were taken to abolish the death penalty after its reintroduction in 2008 in violation of the Second Optional Protocol of the International Covenant on Civil and Political Rights, to which Liberia acceded in 2005. Several people were sentenced to death in 2010.

Women's rights

Rape and other forms of sexual violence against women and girls remained widespread, as did domestic violence and forced and underage marriage. The majority of reported cases of rape involved girls under the age of 16. It was difficult to estimate the number of rapes, because of stigmatization and rejection by the families and communities of the survivors.

By March, the Sexual and Gender Based Violent Crimes Unit, established in the Ministry of Justice in February 2009 to deal exclusively with issues relating to prosecutions of gender-based crimes, had conducted seven trials, four of which resulted in convictions. The cases were heard before a special court, Criminal Court E, set up as mandated by the 2008 Gender and Sexually-Based Violence Bill to deal with violent gender-based crimes, with exclusive original jurisdiction over cases of sexual assault.

Women's participation in politics and public life increased as a result of President Johnson-Sirleaf's efforts to obtain greater gender parity in ministries, on the Supreme Court and within local government.

The maternal mortality ratio remained among the highest in the world in spite of government efforts to address the problem. Women continued to die in high numbers primarily because of an acute shortage of skilled medical personnel, inadequate emergency obstetric care, inefficient referral systems, poor nutritional status of pregnant women, and extremely high numbers of teenage pregnancies.

Children's rights

Widespread child abuse, including sexual violence, continued. Female genital mutilation (FGM) was widely performed particularly in rural areas. Liberian law did not specifically prohibit FGM.

Many children lived on the streets, especially in Monrovia, including former combatants and unaccompanied internally displaced people. Orphanages faced major challenges in providing basic sanitation, adequate medical care and appropriate diet. Many orphans lived outside these institutions.

Although the law prohibited the employment of children under the age of 16 during school hours, child labour was widespread, including the worst forms of child labour, such as hazardous labour in the alluvial diamond industry, rock breaking for construction, and child prostitution and trafficking. The Ministry of Labour's Child Labour Commission responsible for enforcing child labour laws and policies was largely ineffective.

Cases of children in conflict with the law continued to be addressed inappropriately due to the absence of a functional juvenile justice system.

Resettlement and land disputes

A large number of internally displaced people and refugees were in need of adequate resettlement. Between 2004 and late 2010, more than 168,000 Liberians returned home out of a total registered refugee population of 233,264. Unofficial returns were uncounted. The arrival of close to 30,000 Ivorian refugees in Liberia created a crisis, putting added pressure on strained and impoverished communities. Ivorian and other refugees in Liberia were often in desperate straits, with little access to food, water, shelter, jobs, education, or much-needed medical care.

Many former Liberian refugees who returned home faced destitution, with scarce job opportunities, lack of access to land, shelter and water in addition to lack of basic services, such as health care and education. Some returned refugees became internally displaced because their property had been appropriated by others. Violent land disputes often arose between returning land owners who fled the war and internally displaced people who took over their land; these conflicts were often exacerbated by unclear land titles and the lack of government action to address the problem. Land disputes heightened ethnic tensions between the

L

Krahn and the Sarpo, between the Krahn and the Gio, between the Mandingo and Gio/Mano, and between the Kissi and the Gbandi.

Inter-ethnic and religious violence

Despite frequent interaction between the Christian majority and the Muslim minority, some tensions existed, occasionally leading to killings, burning, looting, and damaging of Catholic and Muslim religious edifices by rival ethnic and religious groups. One particularly serious instance of mass inter-ethnic, religious violence occurred in Voinjama and Konia, in Lofa County in February.

Amnesty International visits/reports

🚌 Amnesty International delegates visited Liberia in April and October/November.

📋 Liberia: Submission to the UN Universal Periodic Review, November 2010 (AFR 34/001/2010)

📋 Liberia: President should act on rights commission – delays are impeding efforts to promote and protect human rights (AFR 34/002/2010)

LIBYA

SOCIALIST PEOPLE'S LIBYAN ARAB JAMAHIRIYA

Head of state:	Mu'ammar al-Gaddafi
Head of government:	al-Baghdadi Ali al-Mahmoudi
Death penalty:	retentionist
Population:	6.5 million
Life expectancy:	74.5 years
Under-5 mortality (m/f):	20/19 per 1,000
Adult literacy:	88.4 per cent

The authorities restricted rights to freedom of expression, association and assembly and repressed virtually all dissent. Hundreds of prisoners continued to be arbitrarily detained on security grounds, including some who had been acquitted by courts or had completed prison sentences, although releases were reported. Foreign nationals suspected of entering Libya irregularly were subject to indefinite detention and ill-treatment; they included refugees and asylum-seekers. At least 18 executions were reported. The government failed to disclose the findings of an investigation into an incident at Abu Salim Prison in 1996 when hundreds of inmates were alleged to have

been killed by security forces, and took no action to provide justice for victims of gross human rights violations committed in the 1970s-1990s.

Background

In May, Libya was elected to the UN Human Rights Council and in November to the board of a new UN body established to promote the rights of women. Also in November, Libya's human rights record was assessed under the UN Universal Periodic Review; the government rejected recommendations calling for the death penalty not to be applicable to "offences" related to freedom of expression, and to disclose the names of victims killed in Abu Salim Prison in Tripoli. A planned visit to Libya by the UN Working Group on Arbitrary Detention did not take place and the government did not accede to a request to visit by the UN Special Rapporteur on torture.

Negotiations between the EU and Libya on a Framework Agreement continued. Following a visit by EU Commissioners in October, the EU and Libya agreed a joint "co-operation agenda" on controlling migration.

Swiss businessmen Rachid Hamdani and Max Goeldi were released in February and June respectively and permitted to leave Libya. Both had been detained on politically motivated charges and banned from travel following a diplomatic row between Libya and Switzerland over the arrest in Geneva in 2008 of a son of Libyan leader Mu'ammar al-Gaddafi.

In December, the Gaddafi Development Foundation, headed by Saif al-Islam al-Gaddafi, a son of the Libyan leader, announced that it will no longer address human rights concerns.

Repression of dissent

The government maintained strict curbs on freedom of expression, association and assembly, and government critics faced arrest and risked prosecution under laws criminalizing peaceful dissent, including the Penal Code and Law 71 of 1972. These prescribe severe punishments – including the death penalty – for activities that amount to no more than the peaceful exercise of freedom of expression and association. Some prisoners were released.

■ On 8 March, Abdelnasser al-Rabbasi was released early from a 15-year prison sentence imposed for "undermining the prestige of the Leader of the

Revolution" after he sent an email to the *Arab Times* newspaper held to be critical of the Libyan leader. He had been held since January 2003.

■ On 14 April, Jamal el-Haji was released after the State Security Court acquitted him of insulting the judiciary. He had been arrested in December 2009 after making an official complaint about ill-treatment when he was detained from February 2007 to March 2009.

The media was heavily restricted and largely state-controlled, although privately owned newspapers associated with Saif al-Islam al-Gaddafi continued to express some criticism of state corruption and inefficiency.

On 21 January, the privately owned daily newspapers *Oea* and *Cyrene* announced that they would only publish online. *Oea* later reported that the suspension of its print version was a result of "a story which later proved to be true". While *Oea*'s weekly supplement went back to print in July, the Secretary of the General People's Committee (the Prime Minister) ordered its suspension in November following the publication of an opinion piece alleging government incompetence and corruption.

■ On 16 February, four employees of the "Good Evening Benghazi" radio programme were arrested, a day after the show was cancelled. Muftah al-Kibaili, Suleiman al-Kibaili, Khaled Ali and Ahmed Al-Maksabi were released the next day. The programme had a reputation for reporting on "sensitive" political issues.

In September, the authorities announced that associations that were not compliant with Law 19 of 1369 (Islamic calendar year) would be closed. The law gives the authorities extensive power over the establishment, activities and dissolution of any association.

■ On 6 November, 22 journalists of the Libya Press Agency, affiliated with Saif al-Islam al-Gaddafi, were arrested several days after the authorities suspended *Oea*'s weekly supplement; they were quickly released following the intervention of the Libyan leader.

In December, the Libya Press Agency announced its decision to close its offices in Libya due to "security harassment".

Counter-terror and security

In January, the Secretary of the General People's Committee for Justice told the General People's Congress that over 300 individuals remained imprisoned without any legal basis. In response,

Mu'ammar al-Gaddafi described them as "terrorists" and said they should not be released, but two months later over 200 prisoners were freed under a framework of "reconciliation" between the state and those suspected of security-related offences. They were said to have included 80 detainees who had been cleared by the courts or completed their sentences. On 31 August, 37 more prisoners were released, including members of the Libyan Islamic Fighting Group (LIFG) and Abu Sufian Ibrahim Ahmed Hamuda, a former Guantánamo Bay detainee returned to Libya by the US authorities in 2007. The government said it would compensate financially those who had been detained without any legal basis, but offered no other forms of redress.

■ In August, the authorities released Mahmoud Mohamed Aboushima; he had spent over five years in detention although the High Court cleared him of charges of belonging to the LIFG in July 2007.

More than 200 people continued to be arbitrarily detained, including suspected members of armed Islamist groups and others suspected of committing "offences against the state". Some had been cleared by the courts or had completed their prison sentences; others were serving prison terms imposed after unfair trials.

■ Mahmud Hamed Matar continued to serve a sentence of life imprisonment imposed after an unfair trial. He had been detained for 12 years before being tried and sentenced in February 2002 on security-related charges. Although a civilian, he was tried before a military court.

■ Jalal al-Din 'Uthman Bashir remained in Abu Salim Prison. He was arrested in September 1995 and held incommunicado until 1999, when he was tried before the People's Court, convicted of supporting the LIFG and sentenced to life imprisonment. His case was reviewed in 2006 after the abolition of the notoriously unfair People's Court and his sentence was reduced to 10 years' imprisonment. 2010 was his 15th year in detention.

Impunity

The government disclosed no information about the official investigation said to have been held into the Abu Salim Prison killings in June 1996, when the security forces allegedly killed up to 1,200 inmates. In Benghazi, victims' families continued to be pressured by the authorities to accept financial compensation and renounce their rights to truth or judicial redress.

L

In October, the Organizing Committee of the Families of Victims of Abu Salim in Benghazi suspended their weekly public protests after security officials undertook to address their health, housing and socio-economic concerns.

The authorities took no steps to investigate past gross human rights violations or bring to justice those responsible.

■ No investigation was held into the enforced disappearance of Jaballah Hamed Matar (brother of Mahmud Hamed Matar) and 'Ezzat Youssef al-Maqrif, prominent members of the National Front for the Salvation of Libya, a banned political opposition group, who are believed to have been detained by Egyptian security officials in Cairo and handed to the Libyan authorities in March 1990.

Refugees, asylum-seekers and migrants

In June, Law No. 19 of 2010 on Combating Irregular Migration was passed. This provides for indefinite detention followed by deportation of those believed to be irregular migrants, and allows no right of appeal.

On 8 June, UNHCR, the UN refugee agency, disclosed that the Libyan government had ordered it to cease operation; it was subsequently permitted to partially resume its work but was no longer allowed to process new refugee cases or visit detention centres.

Thousands of suspected irregular migrants, including refugees and asylum-seekers, were held in severely overcrowded conditions in detention centres until July, when the authorities released over 4,000 of them and granted them three months' temporary residence.

Suspected irregular migrants faced habitual verbal abuse, beatings and other ill-treatment, in some cases amounting to torture, while detained. In early July, the Libyan leader called for an investigation into reports that about 200 Eritrean nationals had been beaten by security officials at Misratah Detention Centre on 30 June and during their forcible transfer to Al-Birak Detention Centre. By the end of the year, no information had been disclosed about the outcome of the investigation.

Women's rights

The law continued to discriminate against women, notably in relation to marriage, divorce and inheritance, and polygamy remained allowed for men.

In January, a new nationality law was adopted to permit Libyan women married to foreign spouses the right to pass on Libyan nationality to their children on a similar basis as permitted for Libyan men married to foreign spouses.

Discrimination – members of the Tabu community

Members of the Tabu community in south-eastern Libya faced discriminatory measures. The authorities refused to renew or issue passports, birth certificates and other identification documents, and schools in Kufra municipality refused to enrol some Tabu students.

Forced evictions of members of the Tabu community continued in Kufra until early April; families told Amnesty International that those evicted were neither consulted about the evictions nor provided with alternative housing.

Death penalty

At least 18 prisoners, possibly more, were reported to have been executed, many of them foreign nationals. In May, a newspaper close to Saif al-Islam al-Gaddafi reported that over 200 people were on death row.

In December, Libya was one of the minority of states that voted against the UN General Assembly resolution calling for a moratorium on the death penalty.

Amnesty International visits/reports

🚍 The authorities publicly invited Amnesty International to visit Libya in response to a report published by the organization in June but did not permit such a visit to take place in 2010.

📑 "Libya of tomorrow": What hope for human rights? (MDE 19/007/2010)

📑 Seeking safety, finding fear: Refugees, asylum-seekers and migrants in Libya and Malta (REG 01/004/2010)

LITHUANIA

REPUBLIC OF LITHUANIA
Head of state: **Dalia Grybauskaitė**
Head of government: **Andrius Kubilius**
Death penalty: **abolitionist for all crimes**
Population: **3.3 million**
Life expectancy: **72.1 years**
Under-5 mortality (m/f): **14/9 per 1,000**
Adult literacy: **99.7 per cent**

Legal provisions entered into force that discriminated against gay and lesbian people. A criminal investigation into complicity in the CIA-led rendition and secret detention programme was threatened with closure.

Counter-terror and security

In January, following the recommendation of a 2009 parliamentary inquiry, the Prosecutor's Office opened an investigation into abuse of power by intelligence officials over the creation of secret detention sites used in the CIA-led rendition and secret detention programme. The inquiry report concluded that secret prisons had existed on Lithuanian territory.

In February, a UN study on secret detention practices confirmed that flights operating under the rendition programme had landed in Lithuania, some under the cover of CIA "dummy" flight plans.

In June, the European Committee for the Prevention of Torture inspected the former CIA detention centres.

In November, concerns arose that the investigation by the Prosecutor's Office into secret detention sites would be closed prematurely.

Discrimination – lesbian, gay, bisexual and transgender people

In February, the authorities informed the Council of Europe that Lithuania did not plan to sign Protocol 12 to the European Convention on Human Rights, which protects against discrimination in respect of all rights.

In March, amendments to the Law on the Protection of Minors against the Detrimental Effect of Public Information entered into force. The new law classifies any information which "denigrates family values", or which encourages a concept of marriage other than the union of a man and a woman, as detrimental to children and bans such information from public places accessible to minors.

The first Baltic Pride march to be held in Lithuania took place in Vilnius on 8 May, after attempts by certain authorities to ban it failed. In October, the parliament rejected a request by the Prosecutor's Office to lift the immunity of two of its members who had allegedly behaved violently during the march.

Adoption by the parliament of amendments to the Administrative Code, introducing fines for the "promotion of homosexual relations", was pending at the end of the year.

Amnesty International visits/reports

- Amnesty International delegates visited Lithuania in November.
- *Open secret: Mounting evidence of Europe's complicity in rendition and secret detention* (EUR 01/023/2010)
- *Lithuania: Amnesty International condemns MPs' call to use recently adopted homophobic legislation to ban the Baltic Pride* (EUR 53/002/2010)
- *Lithuania: Baltic Pride is under threat!* (EUR 53/004/2010)
- *Lithuania: New move towards penalizing homosexuality* (EUR 53/008/2010)

MACEDONIA

THE FORMER YUGOSLAV REPUBLIC OF MACEDONIA
Head of state: **Gjorge Ivanov**
Head of government: **Nikola Gruevski**
Death penalty: **abolitionist for all crimes**
Population: **2 million**
Life expectancy: **74.5 years**
Under-5 mortality (m/f): **17/16 per 1,000**
Adult literacy: **97 per cent**

Progress was slow in war crimes prosecutions. Anti-discrimination legislation failed to meet international standards. Freedom of the media declined.

Background

The dispute with Greece over the name "Macedonia" continued to dominate international relations and domestic politics. In November the European Commission criticized Macedonia's uneven progress towards EU accession, highlighting concerns about independence of the judiciary and media freedom, but recommended that accession talks should be opened, pending resolution of the country's name.

L

Relations deteriorated between the Macedonian majority government and ethnic Albanian political parties, including within the governing coalition. Divisions arose over war crimes proceedings, the proposed 2011 census – which ethnic Albanians alleged would be discriminatory – and government expenditure on monuments to Macedonia's history.

Justice system

Reforms required by the European Commission partially addressed concerns about the independence of the judiciary, but in November the Commission remained concerned about executive interference and political control by the Ministry of Justice. According to the Ombudsperson, 20 per cent of complaints received in 2009 related to the judiciary.

War crimes

In May the Appeals Chamber of the International Criminal Tribunal for the former Yugoslavia (Tribunal) upheld the 2008 conviction of Johan Tarčulovski, who was sentenced to 12 years' imprisonment for his involvement in war crimes committed by the Macedonian police in Ljuboten during the 2001 conflict. An appeal against the acquittal of former Macedonian Interior Minister Ljube Boškoski was dismissed.

Little progress was made in the four war crimes cases returned to Macedonia for prosecution from the Tribunal in February 2008. Proceedings in the "Mavrovo" road workers case, which opened in September 2008, were repeatedly adjourned including in February, when the accused were not provided with Albanian-language documentation. The prosecution commenced in April against 11 of the 23 accused, one of whom, Sulejman Rushiti, committed suicide in Izdrovo prison in May. The Macedonian road workers were allegedly abducted in August 2001 by the ethnic Albanian National Liberation Army and ill-treated, sexually violated and threatened with death before being released.

According to the government the three other cases were under investigation, but no further progress was reported. Ethnic Albanian political parties argued for the cases to be dropped under the 2002 Amnesty Law, which granted amnesty to those involved in the 2001 armed conflict, except in cases taken under the jurisdiction of the Tribunal. As the cases were investigated but not prosecuted by the Tribunal, they argued that the Amnesty Law should apply.

Impunity continued for the enforced disappearance in 2001 of six ethnic Albanians and the abduction of 13 ethnic Macedonians and one Bulgarian.

Torture and other ill-treatment

In March the Macedonian Helsinki Committee reported that serious shortcomings in psychiatric hospitals often amounted to violations of patients' rights. Living conditions were described by the Ombudsperson in September as "catastrophic". In September the European Committee for the Prevention of Torture carried out a visit to places of detention, including social care homes and psychiatric hospitals.

Reports of ill-treatment by police continued.

■ Roma alleged excessive use of force when 200 riot police took part in shutting down an unofficial market in the Skopje suburb of Šuto Orizari in April. Among those reportedly injured were 17 police officers and, according to the Mayor, more than 40 Romani people. However, NGOs reported that Roma did not complain for fear of retribution. An internal inquiry concluded that the police "had acted within the limits of their competences".

■ The government agreed a friendly settlement with Jasmina Sulja following her application to the European Court of Human Rights. She claimed that she had been denied an effective remedy as a result of the authorities' failure to investigate the death of her partner, Sabri Asani, an ethnic Albanian, who died after allegedly being beaten in police custody in January 2000.

Counter-terror and security

■ In October the European Court of Human Rights sent a communication to the Macedonian authorities following an application by Khaled el-Masri against Macedonia for its role in his unlawful abduction, detention and ill-treatment for 23 days in Skopje in 2003. Following his detention, he was transferred to the custody of US authorities and flown to Afghanistan, where he was allegedly subjected to torture and other ill-treatment.

Freedom of expression

Investigative journalists alleged government interference in their work, including through threats to their lives, intimidation and defamation cases brought by government officials.

■ In February, three students were acquitted on charges of failing to protect public safety during a demonstration in March 2009 against the government's building programme, when the police failed to protect them from attack by counter-demonstrators.

M

Discrimination

In April the parliament adopted an Anti-Discrimination Law, which failed to meet EU standards, including by failing to protect lesbian, gay, bisexual and transgender people from discrimination.

Roma

In June the UN Committee on the Rights of the Child (CRC) raised concerns that Roma and refugee children remained without registration and identity documents, and highlighted discrimination against minority children, especially Roma, including street children and disabled children. In March the Ombudsperson reported that Romani children were over-represented in schools for children with mental disabilities.

Macedonia's failure to fund and implement National Action Plans for the Decade of Roma Inclusion, including a strategy to improve the status of Romani women, was criticized in June by the European Commission against Racism and Intolerance.

The UN Development Fund for Women published research in January by Romani women documenting the disproportionate barriers they faced in reporting domestic violence. In February a second report revealed that 75 per cent of Romani women experienced discrimination by public officials when accessing services.

Some 320,000 people, including Roma, continued to live in informal settlements, many without potable water or sanitation.

■ A Roma family forcibly evicted in Skopje's Aerodrom municipality in April were reportedly beaten by police in May, when they attempted to rebuild their home on the same site.

Refugees and asylum-seekers

Some 1,542 Roma and Ashkali refugees from Kosovo remained in Macedonia. Few were granted asylum; the majority were transferred to a local integration programme under the Ministry of Labour and Social Welfare. Roma protested in March, April and October to UNHCR, the UN refugee agency, that the Ministry had failed to pay their monthly allowances, so that they were unable to pay rent and utility bills; as a result some families had reportedly become homeless. UNHCR made disbursments to bridge the gap between payments.

Following liberalization of the EU visa regime, ethnic Albanians and Roma from northern Macedonia travelled to EU member states, apparently seeking asylum. More than 400 were summarily returned to Macedonia from Belgium in March. In October the EU Commissioner for Home Affairs reportedly threatened to withdraw the visa agreement.

Women's rights

Following the introduction of free legal aid in December 2009, women's organizations sought to provide legal assistance to women in cases of domestic violence. The CRC noted a high rate of teenage births and abortions amongst Roma and other minority girls, and a lack of reproductive health care in rural areas.

Amnesty International visits/reports

▤ Former Yugoslav Republic of Macedonia: Amnesty International's follow-up information to the concluding observations of the Committee against Torture (Index: EUR 65/002/2010)

▤ Europe: Open secret – mounting evidence of Europe's complicity in rendition and secret detention (EUR 01/023/2010)

MADAGASCAR

REPUBLIC OF MADAGASCAR

Head of state:	Andry Nirina Rajoelina
Head of government:	Camille Albert Vital
Death penalty:	abolitionist in practice
Population:	20.1 million
Life expectancy:	61.2 years
Under-5 mortality (m/f):	105/95 per 1,000
Adult literacy:	70.7 per cent

M

Human rights violations were committed with almost total impunity by the security forces, including unlawful arrests and detentions, excessive use of force against demonstrators and attacks on journalists and opposition leaders. Political opponents of the government were denied fair trials.

Background

The political situation remained unstable and the international community was unable to resolve the political crisis that began in December 2008. Negotiations in Pretoria failed in May. Madagascar continued to be suspended from regional and international organizations.

Several ministers were dismissed by Andry Nirina Rajoelina, head of state and of the High Transitional Authority (HAT). Tensions remained high within the army. In May, at least four security personnel were shot dead in clashes in the Fort Duchesne military camp. Some senior officers and at least 22 gendarmes were detained following this incident. On 17 November, a mutiny erupted on the day of a national referendum and some military officers announced the creation of a "military council for the welfare of people". They later surrendered to the HAT authorities.

Explosions occurred in various places including the Ministry of Foreign Affairs in October.

A National Electoral Commission was installed in March and a national referendum and local elections took place in November and December; presidential elections were planned for 2011. The authorities banned any public demonstration during electoral periods.

Excessive use of force and unlawful killings

Regular public demonstrations organized by the opposition were violently dispersed by the security forces, resulting in deaths and injuries. Those responsible enjoyed impunity.

■ At least one student protestor at Antananarivo University in Antsiranana was shot dead by a member of the security forces in April. No independent investigation was conducted.

Arbitrary arrests and detentions

Political opponents of the HAT and supporters of former President Marc Ravalomanana were arbitrarily arrested and detained by the security forces. Some people arrested in 2009 were still detained. At least 18 detainees went on hunger strike.

■ Ralitera Andriamalala Andrianandraina, former Director of Security at the High Constitutional Court of Madagascar who was arrested in April 2009, remained in custody in Antanimora prison. In August, he was sentenced by an Antananarivo criminal court to a suspended two-year prison term on charges including endangering state security. He was not released because he was accused by the authorities of involvement in the killing of a bookshop employee at Ambohijavoto in April 2009. His new trial had not been scheduled by the end of the year. His health deteriorated in prison and he was admitted to hospital in mid-January 2010.

■ In May, a group of HAT officers arrested and beat Ambroise Ravonison and Harison Razafindrakoto, two members of the opposition who were participating in a radio broadcast in Antananarivo. Ambroise Ravonison was accused of insulting the president of the HAT. He was detained at Antanimora prison for two weeks and then sentenced to eight months' suspended imprisonment. Harison Razafindrakoto was released.

■ On 8 October, Jaky Ernest Rabehaja, one of the leaders of a strike by magistrates in October, was arrested and forced to board a security force vehicle. He was later released on the outskirts of Antananarivo.

Freedom of expression – journalists

Journalists continued to be victims of harassment and intimidation. Private media outlets and those believed to have links with the opposition were targeted and at least three radio stations were closed down.

■ On 6 October, officials from the Ministry of Communication closed down the Fototra radio station owned by Saraha Georget Rabeharisoa, leader of the Green Party, who had recently announced that she was a presidential candidate.

■ Ten employees of Radio Fahazavàna, owned by the reformed Protestant church of Madagascar (FJKM), were arrested and detained in May and the radio station was closed down by the Ministry of Communication. They were conditionally released in September but the radio station remained closed at the end of the year.

Unfair trials

The trial of those accused of unlawful killings at Ambohitsorohitra presidential palace on 7 February 2009 started in June. At least 19 people were sentenced to various prison terms. The trial did not meet international standards of fairness. The right to defence, the right to challenge the lawfulness of detention, the right to a fair hearing and the right to defend oneself in person or through a lawyer were denied to some of the defendants.

■ On 28 August, an Antananarivo court condemned former president Marc Ravalomanana and eight other people to lifelong hard labour for their alleged involvement in the unlawful killings on 7 February 2009 in Antananarivo. An arrest warrant was issued against Marc Ravalomanana who was sentenced in his absence. The trial was criticized by members of the Malagasy Bar Association.

Amnesty International visits/reports

▢ Madagascar: Urgent need for justice – human rights violations during the political crisis (AFR 35/001/2010)

▢ Madagascar: Amnesty International urges release of political prisoners – investigation into excessive use of force against demonstrators and freedom of the media (AFR 35/003/2010)

MALAWI

REPUBLIC OF MALAWI

Head of state and government:	Bingu wa Mutharika
Death penalty:	abolitionist in practice
Population:	15.7 million
Life expectancy:	54.6 years
Under-5 mortality (m/f):	125/117 per 1,000
Adult literacy:	72.8 per cent

A same-sex couple were sentenced to 14 years' imprisonment and then pardoned. Prisons were overcrowded and lacked adequate facilities.

Background

Malawi's human rights record was assessed under the UN Universal Periodic Review, during which officials stated that an independent police complaints commission had been established to investigate police brutality.

Up to 1.1 million Malawians were in need of food aid despite five consecutive years of maize production surpluses.

Prison conditions

Prisons were overcrowded: the prison system, with a capacity of 6,000, was holding around 13,000 prisoners. Prison congestion was exacerbated by prolonged pre-trial detention, with pre-trial detainees forming up to 20 per cent of the prison population. Overcrowding, poor nutrition, poor sanitation and inadequate health facilities contributed to the spread of infections including tuberculosis and measles. Many prisoners relied on families and charities for supplementary food.

■ In Chichiri prison in June, prisoners were locked in overcrowded communal cells with poor ventilation and had to sleep sitting up. Up to 200 prisoners shared one toilet. One inmate, Alex Mkula, had been held for nine years without trial: he was later released on bail. The female section of Chichiri prison was similarly congested. Eight of the 55 female prisoners were mothers with babies.

In its Universal Periodic Review, Malawi stated it had ended mandatory pre-trial detention to prevent prison overcrowding.

Rights of lesbian, gay, bisexual and transgender people

On 18 May, two prisoners of conscience, Steven Monjeza and Tiwonge Chimbalanga, were convicted on charges of "gross indecency" and "unnatural acts" after holding a same-sex engagement party in December 2009. Both were sentenced to 14 years with hard labour. On 29 May they were pardoned by President Mutharika, following a visit to Malawi by UN Secretary-General Ban Ki-moon. However, Tiwonge Chimbalanga went into hiding in fear of hate attacks.

In its Universal Periodic Review, Malawi stated that it had no plans to legalize homosexuality.

Freedom of expression – journalists

In February the Journalists Union of Malawi expressed concern about a government directive advising officials that they should not advertise in newspapers published by Nation Publications Limited, including The Nation, Weekend Nation and Nation on Sunday, after they had published articles considered critical of the government.

Trial of former opposition politician

The long-running trial of Malawi's former President Bakili Muluzi continued at the High Court in Blantyre but was delayed by his health problems. He was arrested in 2005 on corruption charges, but alleged the charges were politically motivated.

Amnesty International visits/reports
🚌 Amnesty International delegates visited Malawi in June.

M

MALAYSIA

MALAYSIA
Head of state:	King Sultan Mizan Zainal Abidin
Head of government:	Najib Tun Razak
Death penalty:	retentionist
Population:	27.9 million
Life expectancy:	74.7 years
Under-5 mortality (m/f):	12/10 per 1,000
Adult literacy:	92.1 per cent

The government restricted freedom of expression in electronic and print media. Detention without charge or trial continued as the Internal Security Act (ISA) entered its 50th year. Refugees, migrants and Malaysian nationals were subjected to judicial caning for criminal offences, including immigration violations. Under Shari'a law, three women were caned for the first time. Malaysia was elected to the UN Human Rights Council in May.

Background

Najib Tun Razak served his second year as Prime Minister after ousting Abdullah Badawi. He had until March 2013 to call parliamentary elections. The trial of opposition leader Anwar Ibrahim on politically motivated criminal charges of sodomy for the second time in 12 years continued. If convicted, Anwar Ibrahim faced imprisonment and a ban from political office for five years. In announcing a new multi-year economic policy in March, Najib Tun Razak called for the reform of Malaysia's positive discrimination policy which favours Bumiputeras (a legal status which comprises ethnic Malays and Indigenous people in eastern Malaysia).

Freedom of expression

The authorities restricted freedom of expression by requiring government licences for publications and imposing criminal penalties under the Sedition Act on those speaking out against the government.

■ In June, the Home Affairs Ministry suspended distribution of *Suara Keadilan*, the newspaper of the main opposition party, the People's Justice Party (PKR), by refusing to renew the required licence for its publication. In July, the government restricted distribution of another opposition paper, *Harakah*, run by the Malaysian Islamic Party (PAS).

■ The blogger Irwan Abdul Rahman, also known as Hassan Skodeng, was arrested in August after he posted a satire of the chairman of Malaysia's largest utility company challenging an energy-conservation campaign. Irwan Abdul Rahman was released on bail and charged under the Communications and Multimedia Act 1998 with improper use of the internet by posting false or offensive content with malicious intent. If convicted, he faced up to one year in prison and a fine of 50,000 Malaysian ringgit (US$15,500).

■ The authorities pressured a Chinese-language radio station to sack host Jamaluddin Ibrahim after his programme criticized the government's positive discrimination policy. In August, the Malaysian Communications and Multimedia Commission sent a letter to the station, reportedly alleging that the programme threatened national security and compromised race relations.

■ Police arrested political cartoonist Zunar in September before the launch of his book *Cartoon-o-phobia* and confiscated copies. He was charged under the Sedition Act and faced up to three years in prison. In June, the Home Affairs Ministry banned three of the cartoonist's earlier books and magazines as being "detrimental to public order" under the Printing Press and Publications Act 1984. Under this law, printing and distributing these cartoons were punishable by up to three years' imprisonment or fines of up to 20,000 Malaysian ringgit (US$6,200). Zunar was released on bail.

Arbitrary arrests and detentions

■ In January, police raided a private Islamic religious class near Kuala Lumpur, and detained 50 people under the ISA. Most of the detainees were soon released, but the government summarily deported several of the foreign detainees to countries, including Syria, where they faced risk of torture for suspected involvement in political Islamic groups.

■ At a peaceful protest in August marking the ISA's 50th anniversary, police arrested 30 out of an estimated 300 demonstrators in Petaling Jaya town. All those detained were subsequently released. Malaysian law severely restricts public protest and freedom of assembly by banning public gatherings of more than five people without a permit.

■ In July, Mohamad Fadzullah Bin Abdul Razak, a Malaysian national aged 28, was arrested under the ISA upon his return from Thailand. The government alleged that he was involved in an international terrorist network. The authorities gave him a two-year detention order under the ISA, which provides for indefinite detention without charge or trial.

Refugees and migrants

The detention of refugees in Malaysia was "systematic", according to the UN Working Group on Arbitrary Detention, which visited in June. In addition to detention for immigration offences, migrant workers commonly faced abusive labour conditions.

■ In August, the government announced that it would nearly double the size of RELA (Ikatan Relawan Rakyat), a civilian-volunteer force which used its policing power to arrest migrants and refugees for immigration offences. RELA officers often extorted money from migrants and refugees, and sometimes beat them. The government also reinstated RELA officers in immigration detention facilities, after withdrawing them in 2009.

■ Conditions in immigration detention centres remained poor. In response to a recurrent lack of water at the Lenggeng Immigration Detention Centre, an estimated 500 Burmese asylum-seekers protested in June by going on hunger strike.

■ In October, seven immigration officers and two foreign nationals were reportedly arrested for alleged involvement in human trafficking. However, no criminal procedures were initiated; instead they were detained without trial under the ISA.

Torture and other ill-treatment

■ The authorities regularly caned people for a host of offences, including immigration violations. Caning was provided for more than 60 criminal offences. In one week alone, scores of migrant workers were deported to Indonesia after being caned for immigration offences.

■ In February, three women were caned, for the first time in Malaysia's history. The women, all Muslims, were convicted of extramarital sex and caned under Shari'a provisions, near Kuala Lumpur. In April, the first woman sentenced to caning, Kartika Sari Dewi Shukarno, had her 2009 sentence of six strokes commuted to community service.

Death penalty

Courts sentenced at least 114 people to "hang by the neck until dead", according to reports in the state-owned news agency Bernama and other Malaysian media. The authorities did not disclose the number of executions carried out.

More than half of known death sentences were for possession of illegal drugs above certain specified quantities, an offence which carried the mandatory death penalty. Defendants in such cases faced charges of drug trafficking. Under the drug laws, they were presumed guilty unless they could prove their innocence, which contravened international fair trial standards.

Citizens of other ASEAN nations accounted for one in six known death sentences. This included seven from Indonesia, three each from Myanmar, Singapore and Thailand, and two from the Philippines.

Amnesty International visits/reports

🚗 Amnesty International delegates visited Malaysia in March/April and November/December.

📑 Trapped: The exploitation of migrant workers in Malaysia (ASA 28/002/2010)

📑 A blow to humanity: Torture by judicial caning in Malaysia (ASA 28/013/2010)

MALDIVES

REPUBLIC OF MALDIVES

Head of state and government:	Mohamed Nasheed
Death penalty:	abolitionist in practice
Population:	0.3 million
Life expectancy:	72.3 years
Under-5 mortality (m/f):	31/26 per 1,000
Adult literacy:	98.4 per cent

The political divide between the President and the opposition-dominated parliament reached crisis proportions in June, and at least four members of parliament were detained in July. After intense negotiations, parliament approved the establishment of a permanent Supreme Court in August. The International Commission of Jurists visited the Maldives in September to assess how the judicial system should be reformed.

Background

The government claimed that the opposition was using their majority in parliament to block government efforts to improve public services. The opposition said they were exercising their parliamentary rights, as set out in the Constitution, to ensure government accountability. In June, cabinet ministers resigned over the stalemate but were later reinstated. The President reinstated the 12 ministers, but Parliament

M

did not approve seven of them, including the Foreign Minister and leading human rights defender Dr Ahmed Shaheed.

Unresolved differences between the government and its opposition sparked protests. Clashes occurred between supporters of the governing and opposition parties in mid-July. About a dozen people were injured on all sides, including several police personnel. In late July, all sides accepted offers of help from international bodies, including a visiting US State Department official, to facilitate dialogue. Street violence subsided in August, when all parties in parliament agreed to set up the Maldives' permanent Supreme Court, which had been functioning on an interim basis since 2008.

During the UN Universal Periodic Review of the Maldives in November, more than 10 states called on the government to take measures to ensure equality between men and women.

Rising sea levels continued to threaten the future of the archipelago.

Arbitrary arrests and detentions

At least four members of parliament (MPs) were detained in July for up to nine days. Three were opposition MPs. They claimed the government had detained them to force them to comply with its political agenda.

■ Opposition MP Abdullah Yameen was detained by the Maldives National Defence Force on 15 July. The authorities failed to respect a court order to produce him before a judge, or charge him with a recognizable criminal offence. Instead, they said he had been detained to protect him against threats from political mobs. Abdullah Yameen said the crowd of people who attacked his home on 14 July were government activists. He was released on 23 July.

Justice system

Fundamental flaws in the criminal justice system continued to lead to unfair trials. There is no unified definition of a criminal offence in Maldivian law, and many judges have no formal legal training. Under a partnership programme with the government, the International Commission of Jurists visited the Maldives in September. They noted that: "Reform measures still pending include the Judicature Bill, the Penal Code, a Criminal Procedure Code, and the Evidence Bill."

Amnesty International visits/reports

▯ Release of Maldives opposition leader is chance for political resolution (ASA 29/001/2010)

▯ Suggested recommendations to States considered in the ninth round of the Universal Periodic Review, November 2010 (IOR 41/023/2010)

MALI

REPUBLIC OF MALI

Head of state:	Amadou Toumani Touré
Head of government:	Modibo Sidibé
Death penalty:	abolitionist in practice
Population:	13.3 million
Life expectancy:	49.2 years
Under-5 mortality (m/f):	193/188 per 1,000
Adult literacy:	26.2 per cent

Al-Qa'ida in the Islamic Maghreb (AQIM) held a number of hostages in northern Mali. The group killed some hostages and released others. There was no progress in passing laws to give women equal rights or to abolish the death penalty. Thirteen people were sentenced to death, but no executions were reported.

Background

AQIM intensified its activities in some sub-Saharan countries including Mali throughout the year. In September, when two Malian civilians were killed by the Mauritanian air force shelling an AQIM base, Mauritania apologized to Mali. In October, President Amadou Toumani Touré asked Saharan countries to strengthen co-operation in the fight against AQIM.

The Bill for Persons and Family Code, which grants equal rights to women and sparked controversy in 2009, was again debated by sub-committees at the National Assembly. A vote on the Bill did not take place before the end of the year.

Abuses by armed groups

Seven hostages captured by AQIM in Mauritania and Niger and held in Mali were released during 2010.

■ AQIM threatened to kill Pierre Camatte, a French hostage abducted in November 2009, if four al-Qa'ida prisoners held in Mali were not released. In February, around the same time as Pierre Camatte was released by AQIM, the four prisoners were set free; the Malian authorities declared that they had served their prison sentences.

■ Michel Germaneau, a French humanitarian aid worker captured in northern Niger in April and taken to northern Mali, was killed by AQIM in July. A few days earlier, the Mauritanian army had launched a failed attempt with French support to release him.

■ In August, two Malians were abducted by AQIM in Kidal. One, a member of the security forces, was released a few days later. Sidi Mohamed Ag Chérif, known as Merzuk, a guide working for the customs office, was killed two days after his abduction.

■ In September, seven people including nationals from France, Togo and Madagascar working for AREVA and Satom, two French companies, were abducted in Arlit, northern Niger and held by AQIM in northern Mali. AQIM later demanded a large ransom and the repeal of a French law (banning the Islamic veil) to secure their release.

Death penalty

There was no progress towards the abolition of the death penalty. A draft bill to abolish the death penalty proposed by the government in 2007 was again postponed by the National Assembly. Thirteen people were sentenced to death during the year, although no executions were reported.

■ In May, two brothers, Siaka and Kassoum Diallo, were sentenced to death for murder by the Bamako Assize Court.

Amnesty International visits/reports

📓 Mali - Mauritania - Niger: Amnesty International calls for the release of all hostages held by Al Qa'ida in the Islamic Maghreb (AFR 05/004/2010)

MALTA

REPUBLIC OF MALTA
Head of state:	George Abela
Head of government:	Lawrence Gonzi
Death penalty:	abolitionist for all crimes
Population:	0.4 million
Life expectancy:	80 years
Under-5 mortality (m/f):	7/7 per 1,000
Adult literacy:	92.4 per cent

The authorities failed to provide international protection to a group of Somali nationals rescued at sea. Migrants and asylum-seekers were routinely detained, and remedies to challenge rejections of asylum claims remained flawed. Abortion was still illegal in all cases.

Refugees and asylum-seekers

The authorities failed to provide international protection to people rescued at sea, in breach of their obligation not to return individuals to a country where they are at risk of torture or other ill-treatment. The authorities also failed to ensure access to a fair and satisfactory asylum procedure.

■ On 17 July, 55 Somali nationals travelling from Libya were intercepted at sea by a Maltese military vessel. Twenty-eight were allowed on board, transferred to Malta and eventually granted asylum; the remaining 27 boarded another ship, believing they would be taken to Italy, but were returned to Libya. They were reportedly detained for days or weeks without access to asylum procedures and remained at risk of being returned to Somalia where they could face persecution. All of the males were reportedly beaten with batons, and some were tortured with electric shocks during interrogation.

Malta maintained its system of mandatory detention of all asylum-seekers, refugees and migrants it considered had landed or remained in the island unlawfully.

In July, in the case *Louled Massoud v. Malta*, the European Court of Human Rights found Malta in breach of the right to liberty, as domestic law did not provide the applicant with an effective and speedy remedy for challenging the lawfulness of his detention.

In January, the UN Working Group on Arbitrary Detention issued a report on Malta following its 2009 visit there, reiterating its criticism of the mandatory

M

detention regime for irregular migrants and asylum-seekers, the lack of a clearly defined time limit for detention under Maltese law and of genuine and effective judicial remedies to challenge the detention.

Concerns remained about the right of rejected asylum-seekers to appeal effectively against adverse decisions, due to the lack of independence of the Refugee Appeals Board, the limited expertise of its members, and the fact that its sessions were held behind closed doors.

Conditions in detention and in open centres – and support to vulnerable groups including people with mental illness – remained poor, despite the authorities' commitment to improve living conditions and recruit more social workers.

Women's rights – sexual and reproductive rights

In November, the CEDAW Committee adopted its Concluding Observations on Malta. The Committee criticized the complete ban on and the criminalization of abortion, urging Malta to introduce exceptions for cases of therapeutic abortion and when pregnancy is the result of rape or incest. The Committee also expressed concern at the prevalence of violence against women.

Amnesty International visits/reports

🚗 Amnesty International delegates visited Malta in September.

📗 Seeking safety, finding fear: Refugees, asylum-seekers and migrants in Libya and Malta (REG 01/004/2010)

M

MAURITANIA

ISLAMIC REPUBLIC OF MAURITANIA

Head of state:	General Mohamed Ould Abdel Aziz
Head of government:	Moulaye Ould Mohamed Laghdaf
Death penalty:	abolitionist in practice
Population:	3.4 million
Life expectancy:	57.3 years
Under-5 mortality (m/f):	128/112 per 1,000
Adult literacy:	56.8 per cent

Torture and other ill-treatment were widespread and prison conditions remained harsh. Dozens of people were arbitrarily arrested and detained for days or weeks. People suspected of belonging to armed groups were detained without trial for long periods. The practice of slavery continued. At least 16 people were sentenced to death.

Background

Mauritania and neighbouring countries agreed to strengthen their co-operation and co-ordinate their response to armed groups that crossed their borders, following increased activities by al-Qa'ida in the Islamic Maghreb (AQIM), including hostage taking and armed attacks. In July, Mauritania adopted a new anti-terrorism law; an earlier version of the law adopted in January was declared unconstitutional by the Constitutional Council. The new law gave additional powers to the security forces to fight against AQIM.

In September, the former Commissioner for Human Rights, Lemine Ould Dadde, who had had ministerial rank, was arrested and charged with embezzlement.

Mauritania was elected to serve on the UN Human Rights Council in May, and in November the country's human rights record was assessed under the UN Universal Periodic Review.

Arbitrary arrests and detentions

In May, at least 50 warehouse workers who were seeking a pay rise were arrested arbitrarily in Tevragh Zeina, Nouakchott. Forty were released after more than seven days and the others were kept in detention for more than 15 days. Mohamed Abdallaye Ould Diaby and Bounah Ould Alayah spent more than 18 days in detention before being released without charge or trial.

■ In October, Abdelkerim Verag El Baraoui, a Tunisian national, was released after more than three years in detention, following a trial in which he was acquitted of belonging to a banned movement. Three other people tried in the same case were sentenced to death; others were sentenced to prison terms. Immediately after his release he was unlawfully arrested by the state security police. The prosecution authorities told his defence lawyers that they were not aware of his arrest. It was reported that Abdelkerim Verag El Baraoui was sent to Senegal.

Counter-terror and security

In February, two Malians were killed and many more injured during a military operation in Lemzeirib, 650km east of Zouérate, close to the Malian border.

At least 20 Malians were arrested and held without charge or trial for six months. The Mauritanian authorities accused the two people killed of belonging to a group of drug traffickers close to AQIM. In September, two Malian civilians were killed in the region of Tombouctou when the Mauritanian air force shelled an AQIM base. Mauritania apologized to Mali.

Throughout the year at least 10 people, including nationals from neighbouring countries, were arrested and accused of links with al-Qa'ida or other armed groups. Others were arrested in the context of counter-terror measures. A few were suspected of having participated directly or indirectly in terrorist acts. Several were held without trial throughout the year. Many detainees, including those accused of belonging to AQIM, were held in incommunicado detention for prolonged periods, exceeding the 15 days allowed by law. The security forces and prison officers refused to allow family visits.

■ Malick Kraina, a Tunisian national arrested in May in Nouakchott, spent more than 26 days in incommunicado detention before being charged with joining AQIM.

■ Mohamed Lemine Ag Maleck, a Malian history student, was arrested in July in Oualata, 1,200km south of Nouakchott. He was held for more than 20 days at the police station before being charged with giving information to a foreign power. The accusation was based on his possession of a GPS device and a camera, equipment he was using to take photos and design itineraries for a tourism agency.

Torture and other ill-treatment

Police officers, military personnel and prison guards used torture and other ill-treatment against men and women detained for political reasons or on suspicion of criminal offences. Torture was generally inflicted immediately after arrest in detention centres including the first police brigade and the gendarmerie barracks.

Despite denials by the Mauritanian authorities that torture was still practised, scores of people alleged that they were tortured or ill-treated during the year, including detainees at Dar Naïm prison, Nouakchott central prison and Nouadhibou prison. During a trial held in July and August, although the detainees alleged that they had been tortured, the judge did not order any inquiry.

■ Most, if not all, of the 20 or more Malians arrested in Lemzeirib in February were allegedly tortured by the army. Some were stabbed by soldiers at the time of their arrest and some were burned with cigarettes.

Deaths in custody

At least 12 detainees died during the year in Dar Naïm prison alone, apparently as a result of inadequate food and lack of medical care. No investigation was known to have been carried out.

■ It emerged during the year that Ousseyni Wellé, a Senegalese national sentenced to death in 2008, had died in 2009 in Dar Naïm prison, allegedly as a result of torture. No investigation was known to have been carried out.

Prison conditions

Hundreds of detainees were held in overcrowded prisons with inadequate sanitation and health care, and poor quality food. The conditions in some prisons amounted to cruel, inhuman or degrading treatment.

Detainees in the prisons of Nouadhibou and Dar Naïm, near Nouakchott, were held in cramped conditions in stifling heat and rarely allowed to leave their cells or breathe fresh air. More than 1,000 people were held in Dar Naïm, built to house 350.

Prison officials acknowledged to Amnesty International that the prisons in Dar Naïm and in Nouadhibou did not meet national standards, and referred to lack of medical care and inadequacies in the water disposal system, dampness and lack of ventilation in cells.

Migrants' rights

More than 250 people, mostly from sub-Saharan Africa, in particular Mali, Senegal and Guinea, were arbitrarily arrested and held at a detention centre in Nouadhibou for a few days on suspicion of trying to reach Europe. Despite promises to refurbish the detention centre, the authorities did nothing to improve the harsh detention conditions.

Slavery

Although slavery was abolished in 1981 and has been a criminal offence since 2007, the practice persisted. There have been no judicial proceedings against slave owners.

Two families were freed from slavery during the year with the help of two human rights organizations, SOS Esclaves and L'Initiative pour la Résurgence du Mouvement Abolitionniste en Mauritanie (IRA Mauritanie).

■ Moulkheir Mint Yarba was born into slavery, as were other members of her family. In February, she was freed with her four children. In December 2007, she

M

had been freed for the first time, but she was recaptured by another slave owner two months later. During her slavery, she was occasionally beaten and deprived of food.

■ Aichetou Mint M'Bareck was held in slavery since her birth in 1975. In October, together with her seven children, she managed to escape from captivity. During her slavery, she was separated from her children, she was beaten and her children were not able to attend school.

Human rights defenders

Human rights defenders were arrested and one was beaten at the time of arrest and at a police station in Nouakchott.

■ Eight anti-slavery activists were arrested and detained in December in Nouakchott after raising the case of two young girls who they believed were held in slavery. They were members of the Initiative pour la Résurgence du Mouvement Abolitionniste en Mauritanie (IRA, Initiative for the Resurgence of the Abolitionist Movement in Mauritania) and were charged with assaulting police officers and obstructing public order. The authorities did not recognize the IRA, although it had applied for registration. Amnesty International considered the eight detainees to be prisoners of conscience.

Death penalty

Although no executions have taken place since 1987, the number of death sentences passed by the courts rose sharply in 2010. At least 16 people were sentenced to death following trials before the Nouadhibou and the Nouakchott tribunals, despite allegations in court that some had been tortured. The tribunals took no steps to investigate these allegations. Three people, including Sidi Ould Sidna who had been sentenced to death in May for murder, were again sentenced to death on charges of belonging to a banned organization in October.

Amnesty International visits/reports

🚗 Amnesty International delegates visited Mauritania in September and October.

📄 Mauritania: Submission to the UN Universal Periodic Review, November 2010 (AFR 38/001/2010)

📄 Mauritania: The Human Rights Council cannot ignore the systematic use of torture (AFR 38/003/2010)

MEXICO

UNITED MEXICAN STATES

Head of state and government:	Felipe Calderón Hinojosa
Death penalty:	abolitionist for all crimes
Population:	110.6 million
Life expectancy:	76.7 years
Under-5 mortality (m/f):	22/18 per 1,000
Adult literacy:	92.9 per cent

Thousands of people were abducted and killed by criminal gangs. Police and military forces deployed to combat gangs were responsible for grave human rights violations. Serious deficiencies in the judicial system and oversight mechanisms persisted and impunity for human rights violations was the norm. Several human rights defenders and journalists were killed, threatened and harassed. Promised protection measures and new procedures to investigate attacks were still pending at the end of the year. Irregular migrants were routinely targeted for abduction, rape and murder; the mass killing of 72 migrants revealed the scale and systematic nature of the abuses committed against them. Legislative measures were insufficient to prevent and punish widespread violence against women. The National Supreme Court (Suprema Corte de Justicia de la Nación, SCJN) issued several landmark rulings on human rights cases. The Inter-American Court of Human Rights (Inter-American Court) issued judgements against Mexico for grave human rights violations committed by the armed forces. There were no advances in ending impunity for past human rights violations committed during Mexico's "dirty war" (1964-1982). Many Indigenous communities continued to have limited access to basic services. Five prisoners of conscience were released.

Background

The government recorded more than 15,000 gang-related killings, particularly in the northern states. The majority of these occurred in conflicts between drug cartels and other criminal gangs, but an unknown number also resulted from clashes with police and security forces. In Ciudad Juárez, nearly 3,000 people were killed, including several mass killings of young people. Drug rehabilitation centres were targeted and scores of patients were killed in different states. More than 50 soldiers and 600 police officers were killed in gang-related violence. Police were suspected of widespread involvement with criminal gangs. Passers-by and other members of the public were also killed, forcing thousands to flee their homes. Violence spread to new regions of the country. Prosecutions of those responsible for the killings were rare.

The US government continued to provide security and other transfers to Mexico as part of the Merida Initiative, a three-year regional co-operation and security agreement. However, the State Department recommended that Congress withhold approval of a small proportion of funds as the Mexican government had failed to meet human rights conditions.

A number of legal reforms affecting the constitutional recognition of international human rights treaties, the National Human Rights Commission (Comisión Nacional de Derechos Humanos, CNDH), the criminal justice system, policing, national security, and the role of the military in law enforcement and military jurisdiction were still pending before Congress at the end of the year. The Office of the UN High Commissioner for Human Rights issued a report on the situation of human rights defenders. The SCJN dismissed legal challenges to Mexico City's legalization of same-sex marriages and adoption.

Police and security forces
The military
There were further reports of unlawful killings, enforced disappearances, torture and arbitrary detention by members of the military. The CNDH registered 1,163 complaints of abuses by the military and in November reported ongoing investigations into more than 100 complaints of unlawful killings by the armed forces in the 18 months to November 2010.

The military justice system continued to claim jurisdiction in such cases, while the civilian judicial authorities refused to investigate. Little information was available on progress of military prosecutions, but no serving military official was known to have been convicted of human rights violations during the year. Government proposals for limited legislative reform to military jurisdiction did not guarantee that human rights violations would be excluded from the military justice system.

■ On 19 March, Javier Francisco Arredondo and Jorge Antonio Mercado Alonso, two students at a private university in Monterrey, were killed when the military opened fire on suspected members of a criminal gang. A CNDH investigation into the case

showed that the military planted guns on the students and destroyed crime scene evidence to falsely accuse the victims of belonging to a criminal gang. There were no further advances reported in the investigation by the end of the year.

■ On 3 April, two brothers aged five and nine – Bryan and Martín Almanza – were shot and killed by the army, according to eyewitnesses, while travelling by car with their family in Tamaulipas state. Military and civilian authorities denied military responsibility, but the CNDH demonstrated that the crime scenes had been altered and evidence ignored. No information was available on progress in the investigation, which remained under military jurisdiction at the end of the year.

Police forces
Reports of arbitrary detention, torture, excessive use of force and enforced disappearance by municipal, state and federal police forces continued. Attempts to reform the police were undermined by the failure to establish credible oversight controls or conduct effective criminal investigations into human rights abuses.

■ In May, six municipal police officers were detained in Cárdenas, Tabasco state, by members of the organized crime unit of the Federal Attorney General's Office. They were reportedly nearly asphyxiated with plastic bags, subjected to electric shocks and beaten during interrogation. No information was available at the end of the year on the investigation into the allegations of torture.

Irregular migrants
Tens of thousands of migrants heading for the USA faced abduction, rape and murder by criminal gangs as they travelled through Mexico. Often these crimes were carried out with the knowledge, complicity or acquiescence of federal, state or municipal police. Those responsible for the abuses were rarely held to account. The appointment of a special prosecutor in Chiapas state was one of the few successful initiatives to investigate abuses against migrants. The government announced improved co-ordination of federal and state agencies to tackle the issue. Some migration legislation was reformed to allow migrants to file criminal complaints and receive emergency medical care.

■ In August, 72 mainly Central American migrants were killed by a criminal gang in Tamaulipas state. Eight suspects were later arrested in connection with the killings.

Staff and volunteers at church-based shelters providing humanitarian assistance to migrants faced intimidation and threats.

M

Freedom of expression – journalists

Threats and attacks on journalists and media outlets continued. At least six journalists were killed. Criminal gangs particularly targeted journalists covering crime issues. In some states, local media outlets self-censored, avoiding coverage of such stories. The Federal Attorney General's Office renewed commitments to investigate these offences. However, the vast majority remained unresolved. A government protection programme for journalists was agreed but not operational by the end of the year.

■ In June, two journalists – Juan Francisco Rodríguez Ríos and his wife, María Elvira Hernández Galeana – were shot and killed in Coyuca de Benítez, Guerrero state. He was a trade union representative and had called for an end to impunity for those responsible for attacks on journalists. There were no advances in the investigation into the couple's killing by the end of the year.

Human rights defenders

Human rights defenders in many parts of the country were attacked and harassed. Despite government commitments to respect their work and guarantee their safety, some government officials made statements questioning the legitimacy of some defenders and official protection measures were often poorly applied. A protection programme and new procedures for investigations into attacks against defenders had not been finalized by the end of the year.

■ In August, after intense national and international campaigning, Indigenous rights activist and prisoner of conscience Raúl Hernández was acquitted and was released from jail in Guerrero state. He had spent more than two years in custody on fabricated murder charges. After his release, he and other members of the Me'phaa Indigenous People's Organization faced threats and intimidation.

■ In April, two human rights defenders, Alberta Cariño and Jyri Antero Jaakkola, a Finnish citizen, were shot and killed by armed men belonging to the Social Welfare Union of the Triqui region (Unión del Bienestar Social de la Región Triqui, UBISORT), linked to the then Oaxaca state government. The two defenders were participating in a humanitarian convoy to take food, water and medical supplies to the Indigenous Triqui community of San Juan Copala, which was under siege by UBISORT and another armed group. Those responsible for the shooting remained at large at the end of the year.

Unfair trials

The criminal justice system often fell short of international fair trial standards, facilitating politically motivated prosecutions, unsound convictions and the widespread use of pre-charge detention orders (*arraigo*). In those cases where national and international attention highlighted injustices, federal legal remedies sometimes secured releases. However, those responsible for the misuse of the criminal justice system were not held to account.

■ In June, the SCJN ordered the release of 12 activists of the Peoples' Front for the Defence of Land in San Salvador Atenco, Mexico state, after concluding that their conviction for kidnapping was unsound. No official has been held to account for the torture and other ill-treatment of more than 200 detainees, including sexual assault of women prisoners, during the police operation which resulted in their detention.

■ In June, prisoners of conscience Sara López, Joaquín Aguilar and Guadalupe Borja were released on bail after a federal review court reduced the charges against them. In December, they were convicted of a lesser charge but not imprisoned. An appeal was pending at the end of the year. The three community leaders had been detained in July 2009 and falsely accused of kidnapping officials during protests against high electricity bills in the community of Candelaria, Campeche state.

Violence against women and girls, and sexual and reproductive rights

Violence against women remained widespread. Hundreds of women were killed in the home and community during the year. Legislative measures introduced in recent years to improve protection were often not applied in practice or were ineffective in protecting women or ensuring perpetrators were held to account.

Despite the 2009 judgement by the Inter-American Court, the government failed to take effective measures to investigate and bring to justice those responsible for the abduction and killing of three women in Ciudad Juárez in 2001 (the Cotton Field case) or to combat the ongoing pattern of violence against women and discrimination in the city. More than 300 women were killed during the year. The bodies of at least 30 victims bore injuries suggesting that they had suffered sexual violence and torture. Few perpetrators were held to account. In December, Marisela Escobedo was shot and killed by a gunman outside the governor's palace in Chihuahua City during a protest to demand justice for her daughter who was murdered in Ciudad Juárez in 2008.

An SCJN ruling was pending on suits challenging the constitutionality of amendments to 17 state constitutions guaranteeing the legal right to life from the moment of conception. In another case, the SCJN ruled that state governments were obliged to comply with national health professional procedures when providing services to women victims of violence, including the provision of emergency contraception.

Indigenous Peoples' rights

Indigenous communities continued to have unequal access to justice, health, education and other rights and services. Government authorities failed to engage effectively with Indigenous communities to improve the protection of their rights and access to services. Despite government commitments to reduce maternal mortality, inadequate health services continued to contribute to disproportionately high levels of maternal deaths among Indigenous women in southern states.

■ In April, prisoners of conscience Alberta Alcántara and Teresa González were released from prison after the SCJN ruled that their conviction was unsafe. The two Indigenous women, both from Santiago Mexquititlán, Querétaro state, had spent three years in prison falsely accused of kidnapping federal police officers.

■ The local government failed to prevent armed groups laying siege to San Juan Copala in the Indigenous Triqui region of Oaxaca state. As a result, sections of the community were denied access to basic heath care, food, water and education services for several months.

International scrutiny

The Inter-American Court of Human Rights issued judgements against Mexico for grave human rights violations in the cases of Inés Fernández and Valentina Rosendo, two Indigenous women raped by soldiers in 2002, and Rodolfo Montiel and Teodoro Cabrera, two environmentalists tortured in 1999 by the army in Guerrero state and imprisoned and convicted of spurious criminal charges. The Court ordered Mexico to recognize its responsibility, provide reparations to the victims, and ensure effective investigation of those responsible by the civilian authorities. The Mexican government promised to comply, but at the end of the year these judgements – and two others from 2009 – remained largely unimplemented.

In March, the UN Human Rights Committee issued a series of recommendations to the Mexican government after reviewing its compliance with the International Covenant on Civil and Political Rights.

There were visits by the UN Special Rapporteurs on education and on the independence of judges and lawyers, and a joint visit by the UN and OAS Special Rapporteurs on freedom of expression. In May, the government was forced to make public a 2008 report by the UN Subcommittee on the Prevention of Torture.

Amnesty International visits/reports

🚗 Amnesty International delegates visited Mexico on three occasions during the year.

📄 Standing up for justice and dignity: Human rights defenders in Mexico (AMR 41/032/2009)

📄 Invisible victims: Migrants on the move in Mexico (AMR 41/014/2010)

📄 Memorandum to the Government of Mexico and the Congress of the Union: Reforms to respect and ensure international human rights law and restrict military jurisdiction (AMR 41/070/2010)

📄 The invisibles – a film (amnesty.org/en/theinvisibles)

MOLDOVA

REPUBLIC OF MOLDOVA

Head of state:	Mihai Ghimpu (acting)
Head of government:	Vladimir Filat
Death penalty:	abolitionist for all crimes
Population:	3.6 million
Life expectancy:	68.9 years
Under-5 mortality (m/f):	26/21 per 1,000
Adult literacy:	98.3 per cent

Torture and other ill-treatment in police detention remained widespread; the state failed to carry out prompt and impartial investigations and police officers sometimes evaded penalties. Lesbian, gay, bisexual and transgender (LGBT) activists were again denied the right to demonstrate. Fair trial standards were not upheld in the self-proclaimed territory of Transdniestria.

Torture and other ill-treatment

In March the UN Committee against Torture published its concluding observations on Moldova's second periodic report. The Committee expressed concern at the "numerous and consistent allegations

M

of widespread use of torture and other forms of ill-treatment in police custody" and called on the authorities to publicly and unambiguously condemn torture. It also expressed concern that pre-trial temporary isolation facilities continued to fall under police jurisdiction despite the fact that plans to build new detention centres and transfer management to the Ministry of Justice were part of the Moldova National Human Rights Action Plan in 2005. Ensuring the separation of the authorities responsible for interrogation and those in charge of detention is an important safeguard against torture and other ill-treatment in detention.

Impunity

In November the Prosecutor General's office announced that the system of specialized prosecutors for the investigation of torture allegations, which had been in operation since 2007 in Bălţi, Cahul and the capital, Chişinău, would be extended to the whole country. However, there were continuing problems of impunity for torture and other ill-treatment. The state failed to carry out prompt, thorough and independent investigations into torture allegations. Witnesses were put at risk by the failure to suspend from active duty police officers who were under investigation for torture or other ill-treatment for the duration of the official investigation. In some cases police officers had evaded sanctions altogether.

■ By the end of the year two police officers who had been sentenced to six years' imprisonment in November 2007 for torturing Viorica Plate were still at liberty, living openly in Moldova and had yet to serve their sentences. In February 2008, Viorica Plate informed Amnesty International that she and her lawyer had been harassed by the police officers who had tortured her in May 2007. In March 2008, Amnesty International was informed by the Prosecutor General's office that the police officers could not be placed in custody because they had appealed their convictions. In September 2008 the Supreme Court had turned down their appeal.

At the end of the year trials were continuing against police officers accused of torture and other ill-treatment as a result of the large number of detentions during and after the violent demonstrations against the April 2009 parliamentary election results. Lawyers and NGOs reported delays and withholding of evidence by the authorities. In August, members of the National Commission, set up in October 2009 to investigate and report on the events, stated that the

Ministry of Internal Affairs had withheld video evidence taken by their street operatives during the demonstrations. This came to light when the Prosecutor General's office showed a video which they stated had been filmed by Ministry of Internal Affairs operatives and which had not previously been made available to the National Commission.

■ In May, an investigation into the beating of Damian Hîncu by police officers during the April 2009 protests was suspended, on the grounds that he could not identify the policemen because they had forced him to lie with his face on the ground at the time. Shortly after the case was suspended, CCTV footage came to light showing Damian Hîncu being beaten by somebody who very closely resembled the Chişinău Chief of Police. A new case was begun against the Chief of Police, who later resigned.

Freedom of expression – Lesbian, gay, bisexual and transgender rights

On 28 April, the Chişinău Court of Appeal ruled that a pro-equality march planned by LGBT rights activists for 2 May in the city centre should be relocated to an unfrequented area in the city, due to "security and public morality concerns". The organization, Information Centre GenderDoc-M, applied to Chişinău City Hall in March to hold a demonstration in the Grand National Assembly Square in the city centre, anticipating approximately 50 participants. The organization did not receive a response to its application, but Chişinău City Hall sent a request to the Chişinău Court of Appeal to have the march banned from the city centre. The activists refused to hold the march in the authorized location in protest against the decision. Chişinău city authorities applied for the march to be banned in response to numerous petitions from a range of religious and other anti-LGBT rights groups. The counter-demonstration organized by those groups was allowed to take place in the city centre on the same day.

International justice

On 12 October, Moldova ratified the Rome Statute of the International Criminal Court, with effect from 1 January 2011.

Unfair trials

Transdniestrian Republic

■ Ernest Vardanean, a journalist working in Transdniestria, was detained outside his home in

M

Tiraspol in the self-proclaimed Transdniestrian Republic on 7 April on charges of "treason in the form of espionage". The offence carries a sentence of between 12 and 20 years' imprisonment. On 11 May, before the trial began, a video was broadcast by Transdniestria's main television station, which showed Transdniestria's de facto Minister of State Security stating that Ernest Vardanean was guilty of the offence he had been charged with. Ernest Vardanean also appeared in the video apparently corroborating the claims of the Minister and expressing his regret over the "terrible error." The video subsequently became available on the internet. Ernest Vardanean had almost no contact with the outside world during the 42 days between his initial detention and the broadcasting of the video. He was reportedly in pre-trial detention in the National Security Service headquarters in Tiraspol at the end of the year.

MONGOLIA

MONGOLIA

Head of state:	Tsakhia Elbegdorj
Head of government:	Batbold Sukhbaatar
Death penalty:	retentionist
Population:	2.7 million
Life expectancy:	67.3 years
Under-5 mortality (m/f):	49/40 per 1,000
Adult literacy:	97.3 per cent

The President announced a moratorium on the death penalty in January. Law enforcement officials continued to commit human rights abuses with impunity. Impunity for torture and other ill-treatment remained widespread.

Background

In November, Mongolia's human rights record was assessed under the UN Universal Periodic Review. The UN Committee against Torture held its initial review of Mongolia since ratifying the Convention in 2000.

Mongolia's Working Group of the Parliament Sub-committee on Human Rights, which was set up in 2009 to investigate allegations that law enforcement officials subjected people to torture and other ill-treatment, unfair trials and illegal detention during the

1 July 2008 riot, made no further progress and did not meet in 2010.

Impunity

Complaints against law enforcement officials rarely resulted in prosecution or criminal convictions. The government stated that 108 complaints of torture or other ill-treatment were made to the Prosecutor's Office, of which 38 were investigated. The authorities failed to prevent, investigate and punish attacks against lesbian, gay, bisexual and transgender people.

Two years after the 2008 riot, the Prosecutor's Office confirmed that they would not prosecute four senior police officials and 10 police officers accused of authorizing and using live ammunition which killed four people. The decision failed to uphold Mongolia's obligations under human rights law – to ensure that arbitrary or excessive use of force, including lethal force, is punished as a criminal offence.

■ In October, Bat Khurts, Chief Executive of Mongolia's National Security Council, was arrested at Heathrow Airport in London, UK, on a European arrest warrant. Bat Khurts was wanted in connection with the kidnapping in France of Mongolian national Enkhbat Damiran. Enkhbat Damiran was abducted in 2003 and taken via Germany to Mongolia where he was tortured. Bat Khurts was being held in a UK prison, awaiting extradition to Germany. Following news of his arrest, people believed to be his supporters carried out retaliatory attacks against Enkhbat Damiran's brother, and threatened journalists reporting on the story.

Death penalty

On 14 January, the President announced a moratorium on the death penalty, commuting all death sentences of those who appealed for clemency to 30-year prison terms. Information on the government's use of the death penalty remained a state secret. A bill to ratify the Second Optional Protocol to the International Covenant on Civil and Political Rights, aimed at abolishing the death penalty, was submitted to Parliament in October. In December, Mongolia voted in favour of a UN General Assembly resolution calling for a worldwide moratorium on executions.

Torture and other ill-treatment

The Special Investigation Unit charged with investigating complaints against public officials lacked resources and funding to fulfil its mandate. In November, the UN Committee against Torture urged

M

the authorities to amend the Criminal Code in line with international standards. It called for the introduction of systematic video and audio recording of all interrogations, in places where torture and other ill-treatment were likely to occur. The Committee also urged the authorities to ensure that alleged perpetrators of acts of torture are investigated and, if appropriate, prosecuted, convicted and punished.

Housing rights

The *ger* districts (informal settlements) in Mongolia suffered from a lack of access to basic services, including adequate housing, infrastructure, sanitation and drainage. Air and soil pollution caused by coal-burning stoves for heating and inadequate services, including waste management, contributed to serious health risks, such as respiratory disease and hepatitis.

Legal developments

In July, Mongolia became the second state to ratify the Optional Protocol to the Covenant on Economic, Social and Cultural Rights.

Amnesty International visits/reports

- Mongolia: Submission to the UN Universal Periodic Review, November-December 2010 (ASA 30/001/2010)
- Mongolia: Submission to the UN Human Rights Committee for the Pre-Sessional Meeting of the Country Report Taskforce (ASA 30/005/2010)
- Mongolia: Briefing to the UN Committee against Torture (ASA 30/007/2010)

MONTENEGRO

REPUBLIC OF MONTENEGRO
Head of state: Filip Vujanović
Head of government: **Igor Lukšić (replaced Milo Đukanović in December)**
Death penalty: **abolitionist for all crimes**
Population: **0.6 million**
Life expectancy: **74.6 years**
Under-5 mortality (m/f):   **11/9 per 1,000**

War crimes prosecutions continued. Journalists and some NGOs were subject to intimidation. Roma continued to be denied social and economic rights.

Background

Although the European Commission in November had highlighted the continued need for the country to combat organized crime, improve the situation of displaced people, and ensure freedom of expression, Montenegro was granted EU candidate country status in December. Also in December, Prime Minister Milo Đukanović resigned. Except between late 2006 and early 2008, he had held power as Prime Minister, or as President, since 1992.

International justice

While war crimes prosecutions against low-ranking military personnel or police officials continued, senior officials were rarely indicted. Under an extradition agreement signed with Serbia in October, 11 people wanted in Montenegro were arrested in Serbia including five men suspected of committing war crimes in Dubrovnik, Croatia.

- Proceedings continued against nine former police officers and officials, five in their absence, for the enforced disappearance in 1992 of Bosniak refugees, who were handed over to the de facto Bosnian Serb authorities. In November the authorities granted former President Momir Bulatović permission to divulge state secrets when he appeared as a witness in this case.
- Six former members of the Yugoslav People's Army convicted in May for war crimes were found guilty of torture and inhumane treatment of 169 Croatian prisoners of war and civilians at Morinj camp near Kotor in 1992. They were sentenced to less than the statutory minimum of five years' imprisonment, on the grounds that they had not previously been convicted of any offence.
- Proceedings opened in June against seven former members of the Yugoslav Army (which succeeded the Yugoslav People's Army) for crimes against humanity against Bosniak civilians in Bukovica in 1992-3. In related civil proceedings in April, Šaban and Arifa Rizvanović were each awarded 10,000 euros compensation for torture inflicted by Yugoslav Army reservists in 1993.

Torture and other ill-treatment

The Ombudsperson's Office was established as a National Prevention Mechanism in line with the Optional Protocol to the UN Convention against Torture, empowered to conduct unannounced visits to places of detention. In March, the European Committee for the Prevention of Torture reported on its 2008 visit,

M

concluding that investigations into alleged ill-treatment needed to be more effective. In October, the NGO Youth Initiative for Human Rights reported that the Ministry of the Interior had started responding more promptly to allegations reported by the NGO, and that some police officers had subsequently been disciplined or charged.

■ In January, Dalibor Nikezić and Igor Milić, detainees at Spuž prison, filed a new complaint against prison guards, alleging they had been ill-treated and threatened to force them to withdraw a previous complaint. Their first complaint was rejected by the State Prosecutor in February. Despite viewing a prison surveillance video (showing the men being dragged from their cells and beaten), she found no basis for a criminal prosecution.

Freedom of expression

Journalists and some NGOs continued to be threatened and intimidated. Public officials brought defamation proceedings against journalists, resulting in heavy fines, sometimes exceeding the 14,000 euros set out in law. NGOs and journalists considered that amendments to the Law on Freedom of Information proposed in June restricted freedom of expression and access to information. In October, the State Prosecutor refused to provide the NGO Human Rights Action with information on the progress of 14 criminal proceedings in which they had an interest, including the 2007 threats to the life of Aleksandar Zeković, member of the Committee for Civic Control of Police.

Discrimination

An Anti-Discrimination Law, including provisions protecting lesbian, gay, bisexual and transgender people, was adopted in July, despite homophobic remarks by the Minister of Human and Minority Rights during the parliamentary debate. The law was not implemented by the end of the year as amendments to the Law on the Ombudsperson, empowering the Ombudsperson's Office to receive complaints of discrimination, had not been adopted. Roma continued to be denied social and economic rights. In the absence of adequate housing, many lived in unsafe conditions: in October, two Romani children died in an unofficial settlement on a garbage dump at Lovanja after their home, built of tar paper, caught fire.

Refugees and asylum-seekers

More than 24,000 displaced people remained in Montenegro, including 3,192 Roma, Ashkali and Egyptians from Kosovo. New legislation and reduced fees enabled some refugees and displaced people to apply for permanent or temporary residence. By December, only 880 people had applied for permanent and 40 for temporary residency, reflecting continued problems in obtaining the necessary documentation. People displaced from Kosovo feared they would be returned after the Podgorica city authorities announced that they would dismantle the Konik camp, where they had lived since 1999.

MOROCCO/ WESTERN SAHARA

KINGDOM OF MOROCCO

Head of state:	King Mohamed VI
Head of government:	Abbas El Fassi
Death penalty:	abolitionist in practice
Population:	32.4 million
Life expectancy:	71.8 years
Under-5 mortality (m/f):	43/29 per 1,000
Adult literacy:	56.4 per cent

Restrictions on freedom of expression, association and assembly continued, particularly on issues considered politically sensitive such as the status of Western Sahara. Human rights activists, journalists, members of the unauthorized political group Al-Adl wal-Ihsan, and Sahrawi activists continued to face harassment and politically motivated charges. Dozens of people were detained on suspicion of security-related offences; some were held incommunicado and allegedly tortured or otherwise ill-treated. Security forces forcibly removed thousands of Sahrawis from a protest camp amid clashes resulting in deaths and injuries. Arrests and collective expulsions of foreign nationals continued. Death sentences were passed; no executions were carried out. No steps were taken to bring perpetrators of past gross human rights violations to justice, and little progress was made in introducing long-promised judicial and institutional reforms.

Background

The stalemate over the status of Western Sahara continued between Morocco, which annexed the

M

territory in 1975, and the Polisario Front, which calls for its independence and runs a self-proclaimed government in exile. In April, the UN Security Council renewed the mandate of the UN Mission for the Referendum in Western Sahara without including a human rights monitoring component.

In October and December, the UN Secretary-General's Personal Envoy for the Western Sahara visited and subsequently convened informal talks between Morocco, the Polisario Front and the governments of Algeria and Mauritania.

Also in October, thousands of Sahrawis set up a camp in Gdim Izik, a few kilometres from Laayoune, to protest against their perceived marginalization and lack of jobs and housing. On 8 November, security forces dismantled the camp and forcibly removed several thousand Sahrawis, sparking violence in the camp. Many protesters were beaten and had their property destroyed. Shortly after, communal violence broke out in Laayoune, resulting in injuries and damage to property. A total of 13 people, including 11 members of the security forces, died in connection with the events. The authorities arrested around 200 people, many of whom alleged they were tortured or otherwise ill-treated in detention. At least 145 were facing trial on public order and other charges, including 20 civilians who were transferred to the Military Court in the capital, Rabat.

In July, the Salé Court of Appeal upheld the convictions in the so-called Belliraj Affair, a highly politicized case marred by allegations of torture and procedural irregularities, but reduced some of the sentences.

Transitional justice
The Advisory Council for Human Rights, mandated to follow up on the recommendations of the Equity and Reconciliation Commission, published a report in January. The report covered the period since the Commission, which had investigated enforced disappearances and other human rights violations between 1956 and 1999, ended its work in 2005. The report failed to provide a comprehensive list of those who had disappeared or any detailed findings on individual cases or whether they had been referred for further investigation. The overdue list of 938 victims of enforced disappearance and other human rights violations was published on 14 December as an annexe to the initial report. Little and vague information, if any, was added on individual cases. Six pending cases were listed and referred for further investigation.

Victims and survivors continued to have no effective access to justice, and none of those who perpetrated the gross violations were investigated or brought to account.

By the end of 2010, the authorities had still not taken any concrete measures to implement recommendations for judicial and institutional reform made by the Equity and Reconciliation Commission, including reform of the judiciary and security forces. The EU provided 20 million euros to assist the government to introduce legal reforms and 8 million euros towards preserving the memory and archives of the gross human rights violations between 1956 and 1999.

Freedom of expression
Human rights defenders, journalists and others were penalized for commenting on issues that the authorities considered politically sensitive, including the monarchy, and for criticizing state officials or institutions.

■ Taoufik Bouachrine, a journalist and publisher of the daily *Akhbar al-Youm Al-Maghribya* newspaper, was sentenced to six months' imprisonment and a fine on 10 June after he was convicted of fraud by the Court of First Instance of Rabat. He appealed. He had previously been acquitted in 2009 but the case was reopened by the prosecuting authorities, possibly for political reasons on account of his writings criticizing the monarchy and the government.

■ Chekib El Khiari, a human rights defender and a journalist, continued serving a three-year prison sentence. He was convicted in June 2009 on charges of undermining or insulting public institutions after he alleged that high-ranking state officials were involved in drug trafficking and corruption.

■ Kaddour Terhzaz, a 73-year-old retired senior military officer, remained in solitary confinement at Salé Prison serving a 12-year sentence imposed for "divulging military secrets". He had written a letter to the King to ask that better provision be made for former air force pilots previously held captive by the Polisario Front; in the letter he had criticized the leadership of Morocco's armed forces.

Attacks on independent media continued. In July, the Minister of Communication declared that all TV networks must obtain official authorization before undertaking assignments outside the capital – a stipulation that appeared intended to curtail freedom of expression and restrict media coverage of social protests.

M

In July, the independent weekly *Nichane* was forced to cease publication, reportedly due to loss of income. It was subject to an advertising boycott after it published an opinion poll about the King in August 2009.

In October, the Ministry of Communication suspended the Al Jazeera bureau in Rabat after it accused the station of damaging "the image of Morocco and its superior interests, notably the issue of territorial integrity" in reference to the status of Western Sahara.

In November, the authorities were reported to have prevented several Moroccan and foreign journalists from travelling to Laayoune to report on events related to the forced removal of Sahrawis from the protest camp.

Repression of dissent – Sahrawi activists

The authorities continued to restrict the peaceful exercise of freedom of expression, association and assembly by Sahrawis advocating self-determination for the people of Western Sahara. Sahrawi human rights defenders and activists faced harassment, surveillance by security officials and politically motivated prosecutions. Sahrawi human rights organizations continued to be blocked from obtaining official registration.

■ Ahmed Alansari, Brahim Dahane and Ali Salem Tamek continued to be detained, although four other Sahrawi activists arrested with them in October 2009 were freed pending trial. The seven, who were arrested on their return from Algeria after visiting the Tindouf camps administered by the Polisario Front, were charged with "undermining internal security". Their case was sent to the Permanent Military Court but then referred back to a regular court. The trial began before a Casablanca court on 15 October and was continuing at the end of 2010.

Torture and other ill-treatment

There were new reports of torture and other ill-treatment, notably by the Directorate for Surveillance of the Territory (DST) and, in some instances, the National Brigade of the Judicial Police, in most cases apparently committed with impunity. The most frequently reported methods included beatings, electric shocks and threats of rape. The victims included security suspects held by the DST and other criminal suspects.

■ Mohamed Sleimani, Abdalla Balla, Bouali M'naouar, Hicham el-Hawari, Izaddine Sleimani, Hicham Sabbah and Tarek Mahla, all members of Al-Adl wal-Ihsan, were reported to have been tortured and otherwise ill-treated by National Brigade of the Judicial Police officers over three days following their arrest on 28 June. At least five of the seven alleged that they had been raped. No investigation was known to have been conducted by the authorities. The seven were held incommunicado for longer than the maximum allowed by law, during which they said they were forced to sign incriminating statements under torture. They were charged with kidnapping and assaulting a former member of Al-Adl wal-Ihsan. On 21 December, all of the defendants were acquitted and released. The former member of Al-Adl wal-Ihsan appealed against the acquittals.

■ Fodail Aberkane was reported to have died on 18 September as a result of internal bleeding caused when he was beaten by a group of seven or eight police officers at Salé police station. His family lodged a complaint. An investigation led to the arrest of several policemen believed to be responsible.

Counter-terror and security

The authorities announced that they had dismantled several "terrorist networks" and arrested dozens of people. Detainees were held incommunicado, often in excess of the maximum 12 days permitted by law, at an unrecognized detention centre, believed to be at Témara, where they faced torture and other ill-treatment.

■ Youssef al-Taba'i was reported to have been held in extremely cold conditions, beaten, deprived of sleep and food, and had freezing water poured over him when he was held for more than three weeks at the Témara detention centre following his arrest on 28 March in Casablanca. He was charged with terrorism-related offences.

Defendants charged with terrorism-related offences faced unfair trials. Some were convicted on the basis of confessions that they alleged were extracted under duress; the courts did not conduct adequate investigations into their complaints.

Detainees awaiting trial on terrorism-related charges staged hunger strikes to protest against their alleged torture and conditions of imprisonment. Hunger strikes were also staged by prisoners serving sentences, including Islamists convicted in connection with bomb attacks in 2003 in Casablanca. The government failed to take adequate steps to ensure that all detainees, particularly those held on security-related grounds, were protected against torture or other ill-treatment, and to investigate allegations of such abuses.

M

Migrants' rights

In August and September, the authorities cracked down on foreign migrants who they said had entered or were living in Morocco without proper authorization. They arrested 600 to 700 people, including children, in Oujda, Rabat, Tangier and other cities. During some raids, security forces used bulldozers to destroy migrants' dwellings and were reported to have beaten people. Those arrested were transported to the desert area near the Algerian border and left there without adequate food and water and without recourse to appeal.

Freedom of religion

The authorities summarily expelled 130 foreign Christians, including teachers and aid workers, during 2010, apparently because they were suspected of proselytizing although none was charged with this. Proselytizing is a criminal offence under Article 220 of the Penal Code.

Death penalty

At least four people were sentenced to death; the government maintained the de facto moratorium on executions in place since 1993.

In December, Morocco abstained on a 2010 UN General Assembly resolution calling for a worldwide moratorium on executions.

Polisario camps

Polisario Front officials detained Mostafa Salma Sidi Mouloud, a former Polisario Front police officer, on 21 September after he publicly expressed support for the autonomy of Western Sahara under Moroccan administration. He was detained at the border post leading to the Polisario Front-controlled Tindouf camps in the Mhiriz region. After international criticism, the Polisario Front said on 6 October that he had been released. However, he remained held and denied contact with his family until 1 December, when he was transferred to the UNHCR, the UN refugee agency, in Mauritania.

No steps were known to have been taken by the Polisario Front to address the impunity of those accused of committing human rights abuses in the camps in the 1970s and 1980s.

Amnesty International visits/reports

In November, Amnesty International delegates conducted a fact-finding visit in Morocco and Western Sahara following the events at the protest camp and in Laayoune, and met government officials and others.

Morocco/Western Sahara: Broken promises – the Equity and Reconciliation Commission and its follow-up (MDE 29/001/2010)

Morocco/Western Sahara: Rights trampled – protests, violence and repression in Western Sahara (MDE 29/019/2010)

MOZAMBIQUE

REPUBLIC OF MOZAMBIQUE

Head of state:	Armando Guebuza
Head of government:	Aires Bonifacio Baptista Ali (replaced Luísa Días Diogo in January)
Death penalty:	abolitionist for all crimes
Population:	23.4 million
Life expectancy:	48.4 years
Under-5 mortality (m/f):	162/144 per 1,000
Adult literacy:	54 per cent

The police committed human rights violations including extrajudicial executions and arbitrary arrests. Police used live ammunition during protests, killing 14 people and injuring more than 400. There were reports of torture and other ill-treatment in prisons.

Background

In January, President Armando Guebuza was sworn in for a second term. In the same month he replaced Prime Minister Luísa Días Diogo with Aires Bonifacio Baptista Ali.

At least 10 people were killed during lynchings by community members that occurred throughout the country in 2010. Scores of others were seriously injured during attempted lynchings. The majority of these incidents occurred in Sofala province.

A number of prison escapes occurred. In January, 51 prisoners escaped from a prison in Nampula, of whom seven were recaptured. In March, three prisoners escaped from the maximum security prison in Maputo and in October a further 17 prisoners escaped from a prison in Nampula. Seven guards were arrested in connection with the Maputo escape.

Hundreds of undocumented migrants, some of them refugees, were arrested. The majority were allegedly attempting to enter South Africa irregularly. In June, nine people drowned and more than 40 went missing after a boat carrying scores of undocumented migrants sank off the coast of Cabo Delgado province.

M

In October, the government publicly declared its commitment to ensuring reform of the prison system and particularly to reducing overcrowding in prisons. Discussions started on a Bill on alternatives to prison sentences.

Also in October, the Interior Minister was removed from his post and made Minister of Agriculture. This move followed protests in Maputo and Manica provinces where police used live ammunition to control the crowds, killing 14 people.

In November Mozambique ratified the UN Convention on the Rights of Persons with Disabilities and its Optional Protocol.

Police

Police were convicted of criminal activities including assault, robbery, extortion and murder. There were a number of cases of police being killed or seriously injured by alleged criminals, apparently sometimes because of links between police officers and criminal gangs.

Excessive use of force

Police continued to use excessive force during demonstrations and to stop alleged criminals. In May, the body of Agostinho Chaúque – whom the authorities had called "public enemy number one" – was found in Matola city near his family home. Police claimed he was killed in an exchange of fire in Maputo city.

■ In September, police fired live ammunition at crowds in Maputo and Manica provinces who were demonstrating against the rising price of bread and basic commodities, including by burning tyres and blocking roads. At least 14 people were killed and more than 400 injured. The police said they used live ammunition because they had run out of rubber bullets. More than 140 people were arrested for instigating the violence. Most of these had charges against them dropped by the courts due to lack of evidence. Although several criminal proceedings related to the demonstrations were under way at the end of the year, none appeared to relate to the use of firearms by the police. Furthermore, no one had as yet been held responsible for similar lethal use of firearms during demonstrations in 2008.

■ In September, police shot and killed a man known as Walter M.K. in Maputo city. According to police, when police asked to see his identification he pulled out a gun and opened fire. The police also said Walter

M.K. had been wanted in connection with the murder of two police officers and armed bank robbery. No inquiry or investigation is known to have been carried out into his death.

Arbitrary arrests and detentions

In addition to the mass arrests following the protests in September, there were reports of arbitrary arrests and detentions by police.

■ On 10 August, Hermínio dos Santos, Chairperson of Mozambique's Forum of War Veterans (FDGM), was arrested, apparently because he was planning to organize a demonstration. Members of the Rapid Intervention Force (FIR) were stationed outside his home for four days before his arrest and he was arrested by members of the Public Order Police and FIR, apparently because he failed to respond to a summons. However, according to reports, he had not personally been served the summons. He was charged with disobedience, tried and acquitted by the Machava Judicial Court in Maputo on 30 August.

Torture and other ill-treatment

There were reports of cruel, inhuman and degrading treatment in prisons. In April, at least seven inmates at the Brigada Operacional's Maximum Security Prison in Maputo told the Justice Minister during her visit to the prison that they had been beaten, kicked, whipped and tied up by prison guards. One reported that the guards had allowed other inmates to beat him and had joined in the beatings. Five of the prisoners were apparently ill-treated as a disciplinary measure for being in possession of mobile phones; another was ill-treated for returning late to his cell, while the seventh was not aware of the reason for this treatment. The Director of the prison and other prison guards were suspended but no information was available regarding criminal proceedings against them by the end of the year.

Amnesty International visits/reports

Mozambique: Submission to the UN Universal Periodic Review, January 2011 (AFR 41/002/2010)

M

MYANMAR

UNION OF MYANMAR

Head of state:	Senior General Than Shwe
Head of government:	General Thein Sein
Death penalty:	abolitionist in practice
Population:	50.5 million
Life expectancy:	62.7 years
Under-5 mortality (m/f):	120/102 per 1,000
Adult literacy:	91.9 per cent

Elections in Myanmar were carried out amid severe restrictions on freedoms of expression, peaceful assembly, and association. The authorities arrested government critics and ethnic minority activists for political activities. Some 2,200 political prisoners remained in detention, many suffering from ill-health. The government forcibly displaced residents of villages, or in some cases entire areas, to facilitate government-run or supported development and infrastructure projects.

Background

In November, Myanmar carried out its first national elections in two decades amid credible reports of widespread fraud and irregularities. The election process was designed to maintain the military's grasp on authority, and many ranking officers resigned from the military in order to contest the polls and participate in the new government as civilians. A government-sponsored party reportedly won an overwhelming majority of the vote.

The winner of the 1990 elections, the National League for Democracy (NLD) led by Daw Aung San Suu Kyi, boycotted the polls. A week after the elections, the government released Aung San Suu Kyi after seven and a half years under house arrest.

Throughout August the government continued to pressure ethnic minority armed groups that had previously agreed to ceasefires, to become Border Guard Forces. Sporadic battles before and after the elections displaced people internally and forced some to seek refuge across the Thai border.

Throughout the year, there were growing calls for an international Commission of Inquiry to investigate allegations of crimes against humanity and war crimes in Myanmar.

Elections-related violations

Electoral laws promulgated in March and further directives later in the year violated the rights to freedom of expression, peaceful assembly, and association. They disenfranchised or otherwise excluded many individuals and groups, including Aung San Suu Kyi and all other political prisoners, by prohibiting them from joining political parties, voting or contesting the elections. Campaign speeches broadcast on state media were prevented from criticizing the government or mentioning any of the country's problems. Authorities arrested some individuals who spoke out on elections-related issues or criticized the government, both before and after the polls.

■ On 27 September, authorities sentenced Ashin Okkanta, an ethnic Mon monk arrested in January, to 15 years' imprisonment for campaigning against elections and calling for the release of all political prisoners in Myanmar.

■ During the final two weeks of September, authorities arrested 11 students in Yangon for handing out leaflets urging people not to vote, six of whom remained in detention.

Repression of ethnic minority activists

The government continued to repress ethnic minorities protesting in relation to the elections as well as those who peacefully opposed the impact of development and infrastructure projects on the environment. Authorities also persecuted ethnic minorities for their real or suspected support of armed groups.

■ In April, soldiers arrested two men in Pa Laai village, Nam-Zarng township, Shan state, accusing them of supporting armed Shan rebels. The soldiers beat one of the men to death, while the fate and whereabouts of the other are unknown.

■ In June, Zaw Wine, 40, escaped from soldiers who had ordered him to go to Par Pra village in Kayin state to acquire intelligence about the Karen National Liberation Army (KNLA). He had also been told to put on the group's uniform and pose for a photograph – a tactic previously used by soldiers in order to frame and then kill villagers for being part of the armed opposition group.

■ In September, 11 people from Rakhine state were given prison sentences of between three and nine years for, among other offences, alleged links to the banned All Arakan Students' and Youths' Congress (AASYC).

■ In September, authorities arrested U Pyinnya Sara, a Rakhine monk and cultural historian, and sentenced him to eight years and three months in prison on charges including handling obscene materials, insulting religion, criminal breach of trust and possession of foreign currency.

■ In October, a closed court in Yangon's Insein Prison sentenced Nyi Nyi Tun, of joint Mon and Burman ethnicity, Editor of *Kantarawaddy News Journal*, to 13 years in prison, on charges including contacting an exile news agency and using electronic media without permission.

Political prisoners

The number of political prisoners in Myanmar reached an estimated 2,200 during 2010, and was likely to have been significantly higher on account of ethnic minority prisoners whose names and cases were unknown. Most were prisoners of conscience. At least 64 political activists were sentenced to prison terms. This number included some of the 49 arrested during the year, and 38 were transferred between prisons, including to those in remote areas. Torture and other ill-treatment continued to be reported during pre-trial detention and in prisons.

Thirty-eight political prisoners were released, including NLD spokesperson U Win Htein, released two months after the expiry of his prison sentence, and Deputy NLD Chairperson U Tin Oo, released after seven years of house arrest. On 13 November, Aung San Suu Kyi was released without conditions from house arrest after the expiry of her sentence. Myint Maung and Thura Aung, imprisoned in 2008 and 2009 for helping farmers file legal cases against illegal confiscation of their land, were released in August after their sentences were reduced on appeal.

Prisoners of conscience who remained in prison included:

■ Min Ko Naing, former student leader and veteran political activist who is serving a 65-year prison sentence for organizing a demonstration in 2007, remained in solitary confinement, having previously been held in solitary confinement for long periods during 16 years' imprisonment between 1988 and 2004.

■ Naw Ohn Hla Hla, Cho Cho Lwin, Cho Cho Aye and San San Myint were sentenced to two years' imprisonment with hard labour in February for holding weekly prayers for the release of Aung San Suu Kyi and other political prisoners at Yangon's Shwedagon Pagoda.

■ Ngwe Soe Lin, 28, a reporter for the overseas media organization the Democratic Voice of Burma, was sentenced in January to 13 years for filming without permission.

Lack or refusal of adequate medical treatment in prisons continued to be reported, with many prisons having no medical facilities. Many political prisoners, particularly those held in remote prisons where medical treatment was often denied them, suffered from ill-health. These included a group of Shan politicians, all prisoners of conscience, sentenced in 2005 for criticizing the National Convention and denied adequate medical attention in prison:

■ Khun Htun Oo, 67, Chairman of the Shan Nationalities League for Democracy (SNLD), serving a 93-year prison sentence in Puta-O prison, suffered from diabetes.

■ Sai Hla Aung, 66, an SNLD official serving a 79-year prison sentence in Kyaukphyu prison, suffered from a skin disease.

■ General Hso Ten, 74, serving a 106-year sentence in Sittwe prison, was transferred between three different prisons in one week in August, and dislocated his arm when shackled during the journey. He had heart diseases, cataracts and diabetes.

■ Mya Aye, 44, had angina, high blood pressure and gastric problems in Taunggyi prison.

Forced displacement

The army continued to forcibly displace residents of entire villages, primarily those populated by ethnic minorities, adding to the country's roughly 500,000 internally displaced people.

■ In January, following the establishment of an army camp in northern Kayin state, government troops raided 10 villages, killing four people and causing at least 1,000 more to flee their homes.

■ In mid-February, troops in Bago Division burned dozens of houses and a clinic, and forced around 2,000 villagers to flee their homes.

■ In July, around 500 people were forced to flee their homes after troops shelled Dutado village in Hpapun township, Kayin state, in an attack apparently aimed at the KNLA. The army then entered the village and burned to the ground around 70 houses, the village school and a church.

■ In November, battles between a breakaway faction of the Democratic Karen Buddhist Army (DKBA) and the Myanmar army in Myawaddy, and further attacks by the army against other ethnic minority armed groups near Three Pagodas Pass, resulted in over 20,000 refugees fleeing Myanmar temporarily and thousands more being internally displaced.

M

Development-related violations

The army committed human rights violations in connection with oil, gas, mining and hydropower development projects, including forced labour, killings, beatings and land confiscation. The authorities continued to target villagers suspected of opposing or questioning the projects.

■ In late May and early June, authorities began forcibly relocating several villages in Kachin state as part of the ongoing Ayerarwaddy Myitsone Dam project.

■ The authorities confiscated land without compensation and forcibly displaced villagers in Rakhine state as construction of the Shwe gas and oil transport pipelines began.

■ Battalions providing security for the Yadana, Yetagun and Kanbauk-Myaing Kalay natural gas pipelines in Tanintharyi Division and Kayin state forced civilians to work on barracks, roads and miscellaneous projects, and committed at least two extrajudicial executions.

International scrutiny

In February, the UN Special Rapporteur on human rights in Myanmar visited the country for five days – his third since his appointment in 2008. In March, his report to the UN Human Rights Council (HRC) in Geneva emphasized that human rights violations resulted from state policy "that involves authorities in the executive, military and judiciary at all levels". Pointing out that some of these violations may constitute crimes against humanity or war crimes under international law, he called for a UN commission of inquiry. The HRC adopted resolution 13/25 on Myanmar in March calling on the government to ensure free and transparent elections and to release all prisoners of conscience. By year's end, 14 countries publicly backed the Special Rapporteur's call for a commission of inquiry: Australia, Canada, Czech Republic, Estonia, France, Greece, Hungary, Ireland, Lithuania, Netherlands, New Zealand, Slovakia, UK and USA. In July the Special Rapporteur was denied a visa for his fourth visit to Myanmar.

Also in March, in response to the promulgation of electoral laws, the UN Secretary-General wrote a letter to Senior General Than Shwe urging the release of all political prisoners prior to elections.

In April, the EU extended its sanctions regime against Myanmar for a further year.

In May, the USA also extended sanctions, and in July renewed its ban on imports from Myanmar, while defending its policy of engagement with the Myanmar authorities.

In May, the UN Working Group on Arbitrary Detention also ruled that the detention of Aung San Suu Kyi was arbitrary and in contravention of articles 9, 10, 19 and 20 of the Universal Declaration of Human Rights, which forbid arbitrary arrest and provide for the rights to a fair and public hearing, and freedom of expression and assembly.

In September, the UN Secretary-General released his own report on the human rights situation in Myanmar, expressing grave concern at the continued detention of political prisoners and calling for a credible and inclusive electoral process. The Secretary-General's Special Adviser was permitted to visit the country in late November after the elections. He recommended that the political transition include those who did not or could not participate in the elections, and again called for the release of political prisoners.

Throughout the year, public statements by ASEAN on the elections and human rights were muted, restricted to calls for a credible, inclusive, "free and fair" process, although a joint EU-ASEAN ministerial statement in May stated that the early release of detainees would help make elections more inclusive and aid a peaceful political transition. This statement was reiterated in the Chair's Statement of the 8th Asia-Europe Meeting (ASEM) in October.

In December the UN General Assembly adopted its 20th resolution on Myanmar, strongly regretting that the government did not hold free, fair, transparent and inclusive elections. The resolution called for an inclusive post-election phase and the release of all prisoners of conscience.

Amnesty International visits/reports

▥ Myanmar: End repression of ethnic minorities (ASA 16/003/2010)
▥ Myanmar's 2010 elections: A human rights perspective (ASA 16/007/2010)
▥ Myanmar elections will test ASEAN's credibility (ASA 16/010/2010)
▥ India's relations with Myanmar fail to address human rights concerns in run up to elections (ASA 20/016/2010)
▥ Myanmar opposition must be free to fight elections, 10 March 2010
▥ ASEAN leaders should act over Myanmar's appalling rights record, 6 April 2010
▥ Myanmar: Political prisoners must be freed, 26 September 2010
▥ Myanmar government attacks on freedoms compromise elections, 5 November
▥ Myanmar should free all prisoners of conscience following Aung San Suu Kyi release, 13 November 2010

NAMIBIA

REPUBLIC OF NAMIBIA
Head of state and government: Hifikepunye Pohamba
Death penalty: abolitionist for all crimes
Population: 2.2 million
Life expectancy: 62.1 years
Under-5 mortality (m/f):   58/45 per 1,000
Adult literacy: 88.2 per cent

The long-running treason trial of Caprivi detainees entered its 11th year. Another detainee died in custody, bringing the total number of Caprivi detainees who have died in custody to 21. Human rights defenders, journalists and civil society organizations critical of government and the ruling South West African People's Organization (SWAPO) party were targeted by government officials and SWAPO supporters.

Background
Opposition political parties petitioned the High Court to nullify the results of the National Assembly elections that were held in November 2009.

Caprivi detainees' trial
The Caprivi high treason trial, the biggest and longest criminal trial in Namibia's history, continued. The accused were charged with involvement in attacks carried out in the Caprivi Strip in 1999 by the Caprivi Liberation Army. At the start of the trial in October 2003, there were 132 people on trial. By the end of 2010, 21 of them had died in custody, including Ritual Mukungu Matengu who died on 28 May.

Saviour Ndala Tutalife, Postrick Mwinga and Britian Simisho Lielezo, three Caprivi detainees who lodged compensation claims for torture against the Minister of Home Affairs and the Minister of Defence, had their cases dismissed by the High Court. The judgement in Britian Simisho Lielezo's case was handed down in January and that of Saviour Ndala Tutalife and Postrick Mwinga in July.

Freedom of expression
Media organizations and journalists critical of the government and members of the ruling SWAPO party were targeted by the authorities and their supporters. Also targeted were human rights defenders and organizations critical of the government. The government maintained a ban imposed in 2000 stopping government departments placing advertisements in the Namibian newspaper, an independent paper seen as critical of the government and SWAPO.

■ On 8 January, John Grobler, a freelance journalist, was attacked by four men, allegedly for publishing an article in the Namibian in September 2009 in which he pointed out the lack of transparency in a business deal involving prominent members of SWAPO.

■ In January, senior government officials ordered the Konrad Adenauer Stiftung foundation to leave the country for reporting that the 2009 elections were relatively free but not fair and organizing meetings attended by opposition political parties.

■ On 28 October, the National Council, Namibia's parliament, decided to discuss action that should be taken against Phil ya Nangoloh, director of Namibian Rights and Responsibilities Inc (NamRights Inc), formerly the National Society for Human Rights in Namibia. Phil ya Nangoloh had issued a statement accusing former President Sam Nujoma of inciting violence. The National Council called on the judiciary and law enforcement agencies to take action against Phil ya Nangoloh, and he received death threats.

Violence against women and girls
Rape, attempted rape and murder of women were reported throughout the year.

■ Magdalena Stoffels, a 17-year-old high-school pupil, was raped and murdered in Windhoek in July. A suspect was arrested and held in custody.

NEPAL

FEDERAL DEMOCRATIC REPUBLIC OF NEPAL
Head of state: Ram Baran Yadav
Head of government: Madhav Kumar Nepal
                                        (interim since June)
Death penalty: abolitionist for all crimes
Population: 29.9 million
Life expectancy: 67.5 years
Under-5 mortality (m/f):   52/55 per 1,000
Adult literacy: 57.9 per cent

Nepal made little progress in ending impunity, accounting for past violations or ensuring respect for human rights. Officials actively obstructed accountability mechanisms, and commitments made by political leaders as part of the peace process were not fulfilled in practice. Torture and other ill-treatment in police custody remained widespread. Ethnic, religious and gender discrimination went largely unchallenged. Violence against women and girls persisted.

Background

Under the 2006 Peace Accord, the Constituent Assembly was tasked with writing a new Constitution addressing human rights issues at the core of Nepal's political conflict. However, the Constituent Assembly's term expired on 28 May without completing a draft. Nepal failed to elect a Prime Minister after voting numerous times; the country was governed by the caretaker government of Prime Minister Madhav Kumar Nepal. Under the Public Security Act, police arrested and detained people, including peaceful Tibetan demonstrators, without any formal procedures.

Transitional justice

A long-delayed draft bill to establish a Truth and Reconciliation Commission, a requirement of the Peace Accord, was tabled in parliament in April but had not been ratified. The draft had notable shortcomings, including the proposed Commission's lack of independence from political influence and a proposal to grant it the power to recommend amnesty for perpetrators of serious human rights violations.

Enforced disappearances

A draft bill criminalizing enforced disappearances and establishing a Commission of Inquiry was pending. It incorporated proposed amendments to address some of the serious shortcomings of previous drafts. The amendments included defining enforced disappearances in certain circumstances as a crime against humanity and ensuring that punishments were proportionate to the extreme seriousness of the offence. However, families of the disappeared were dissatisfied with the draft and claimed that it was prepared without adequate consultation.
■ In July, lawyers and human rights defenders working on the case of Arjun Bahadur Lama, a teacher who was abducted and killed by Maoists during the armed conflict, were threatened by Maoist supporters after a suspect in the case was refused a visa by the US embassy.
■ In September, a team led by Nepal's Human Rights Commission (NHRC), including foreign forensic experts and UN observers, exhumed the remains of four bodies thought to be those of a group of men abducted by the security forces in Janakpur in October 2003. Positive identification of the remains was pending. Despite the exhumation, investigation into the case made little progress and no one was arrested.

Impunity

Impunity persisted for perpetrators of human rights abuses during the conflict. The authorities failed to implement court-ordered arrests of military personnel accused of offences involving human rights violations; police refused to file complaints or investigate such cases.
■ The Nepal Army refused to hand over Major Niranjan Basnet, charged with the torture and murder of 15-year-old Maina Sunuwar in 2004, despite a court order. Niranjan Basnet was repatriated from a UN Mission in December 2009. The army failed to hand him over to the police upon his return and in a letter to the Defence Ministry requested that the case be withdrawn. In mid-July, an internal inquiry by the Nepal Army declared Niranjan Basnet "innocent" of the charges.

Excessive use of force

Excessive use of force by the police and military, and killings of people suspected of affiliation with armed groups in faked "encounters" were reported.
■ On 13 June, 20-year-old Advesh Kumar Mandal of Janakpur was shot dead by the police. He was alleged to be a member of Janatantrik Terai Mukti Morcha (JTMM), a Terai-based armed group.

Torture and other ill-treatment

Torture and other ill-treatment of detainees by police persisted. National laws providing safeguards against torture fell short of international standards, and remained inadequately implemented.
■ On 25 May, Sanu Sunar, a Dalit aged 46, died from injuries sustained in police custody at the Kalimati Police Station after he was arrested for theft. The NHRC said Sanu Sunar died as a result of police torture and recommended legal action. On 24 June, the Kathmandu District Court ordered the detention of three policemen suspected of abuses against Sanu Sunar, but investigations made little progress.

Abuses by armed groups

Over 100 mainly Terai-based armed groups continued to commit human rights abuses, including abductions, assaults and killings. Some groups had identifiable political or religious orientations, others functioned as criminal gangs.

■ JTMM-Rajan Mukti members shot and killed Lal Kishor Jha, aged 50, an employee of the Mahottari District Education Office on 28 October in Janakinagar as he left his home. He was shot, twice from behind, for his alleged involvement in the sale of Guthi land (land given as a religious endowment) and financial irregularities at the District Education Office.

Discrimination

Dalits, Indigenous Peoples, disabled people, religious and sexual minorities suffered social exclusion, despite legal recognition of their equal rights. Legislative efforts to combat gender inequality did little to curtail discrimination against women in public and private life. Women, particularly Dalit women, faced obstacles in relation to access to justice, asset and property ownership, inheritance, income and employment conditions, and political representation.

There was some progress in the courts' approach to caste discrimination. In August, the Kanchanpur Appellate Court upheld two separate district court convictions, made in January and March respectively, of two men for attacks against Dalits that were motivated by caste discrimination.

Violence against women and girls

Nepal's quest to "end violence against women in 2010" had little visible impact. In the first half of the year, over 300 domestic violence cases were reported to police in the Kathmandu valley alone; many more went unreported. Women accused of witchcraft (typically poor, isolated or Dalit) were assaulted and tortured by community members. Legislative weakness and inadequate policing obstructed prosecution of domestic and sexual violence cases.

■ In early 2010, men from a village in Siraha district where a rape had occurred prevented staff members of the Women's Rehabilitation Centre accompanying women witnesses from reaching the court to testify; the accused was found not guilty.

Young Nepalese women sought economic opportunities abroad. Poor regulation, poor implementation of existing laws and corruption all contributed to the exploitation of those travelling abroad for work.

NETHERLANDS

KINGDOM OF THE NETHERLANDS

Head of state:	Queen Beatrix
Head of government:	Mark Rutte (replaced Jan Peter Balkenende in October)
Death penalty:	abolitionist for all crimes
Population:	16.7 million
Life expectancy:	80.3 years
Under-5 mortality (m/f):	6/5 per 1,000

Iraqis were forcibly returned to Iraq in contravention of UNHCR guidelines. The introduction of new accelerated asylum-determination procedures and the detention of asylum-seekers and irregular migrants gave rise to concern.

Discrimination

In September, following criticism by international and national human rights bodies and organizations, the interim government put forward an action plan to combat discrimination before parliament. However, there were concerns that the plan lacked measures to adequately address discriminatory government policies and practices, such as ethnic profiling by law enforcement officials.

In October, in its coalition agreement, the new government announced its intention to introduce legislation that would ban the wearing in public of clothing that is intended to conceal the face. This raised concerns that the prohibition would violate the freedom of expression and religion of women who choose to wear the burqa or niqab as an expression of their identity or beliefs.

Refugees, asylum-seekers and migrants

At least 75 Iraqis were forcibly returned to Baghdad, in contravention of UNHCR, the UN refugee agency, guidelines. Following a letter from the European Court of Human Rights on 22 October asking the authorities to refrain from returning to Baghdad any Iraqi who challenged his or her return until further notice, the forcible return of a number of Iraqis was deferred.

On 24 November, the government announced that returns would be resumed.

In October, the government announced that returns to Somalia of individuals from Mogadishu had been temporarily suspended because of the security situation in Mogadishu. However, returns of individuals from other parts of Somalia to Mogadishu were still planned.

Despite the lack of a functioning asylum system and concerns, among other things, about detention conditions in Greece, transfers of asylum-seekers to the country under the Dublin II Regulation continued. In October, the Minister of Justice announced that transfers would be temporarily suspended pending outcomes in cases before the European Court of Human Rights and the Court of Justice of the European Union regarding the lawfulness of transfers to Greece.

From 1 July, most asylum claims were processed in a new eight-day asylum procedure, with a possible extension to 14 days in some cases. There was concern that this procedure may impede asylum-seekers from substantiating their claims and result in the rejection of well-founded claims for protection.

According to government figures, 3,980 irregular migrants and asylum-seekers were subject to administrative detention in the first six months of the year. They were held in detention centres under a regime designed for remand prisoners; alternatives to detention were used infrequently. In March, the CERD Committee expressed concern at the practice of detaining families with children and unaccompanied children seeking asylum upon their arrival in the Netherlands.

Amnesty International visits/reports

🔲 Netherlands: Stop forcible returns to Iraq (EUR 35/001/2010)

🔲 European states must stop forced returns to Iraq (EUR 01/028/2010)

N

NEW ZEALAND

NEW ZEALAND

Head of state:	Queen Elizabeth II represented by Anand Satyanand
Head of government:	John Key
Death penalty:	abolitionist for all crimes
Population:	4.3 million
Life expectancy:	80.6 years
Under-5 mortality (m/f):	6/5 per 1,000

Indigenous Peoples' property rights were recognized by the Marine and Coastal Area Bill. The New Zealand Human Rights Commission called for a review of the Immigration Act which continued to put asylum-seekers at risk of persecution because of the passenger screening process.

Indigenous Peoples' rights

In April, the Government announced its support for the UN Declaration on the Rights of Indigenous Peoples.

In September, the Marine and Coastal Area (Takutai Moana) Bill was introduced which aims to repeal the Foreshore and Seabed Act 2004 that discriminated against Maori property claims. However, the Bill did not afford Indigenous Peoples the right to exclusive occupation or the right to register a claim for property already in private ownership. The Bill was pending before parliament at the end of the year.

Counter-terror and security

In August, the Minister of Defence confirmed that detainees arrested by the Afghan Crisis Response Unit, which the New Zealand Special Air Service has worked with, had been transferred to the National Directorate of Security, Afghanistan's Intelligence Service, where they were at grave risk of torture and other ill-treatment.

Refugees and asylum-seekers

In May, the New Zealand Human Rights Commission called for a review of the Immigration Act 2009. The Act allowed the detention period for refugees and asylum-seekers to be extended without warrant to up to 96 hours and lacked an explicit guarantee against the detention of children and young people. The Act empowered the chief executive of the Immigration Department to refuse a person permission to board an aircraft to travel to New Zealand without providing a reason. This could expose asylum-seekers to harm if they were at risk of torture or other serious human rights violations in their own countries. The Act also denied asylum applicants access to judicial review.

Legal, constitutional or institutional developments

The Immigration Act 2009 allows schools to provide education to children who are unlawfully in New Zealand, partly remedying New Zealand's General Reservation to the UN Convention on the Rights of the Child.

The government continued to refuse to legally entrench the New Zealand Bill of Rights Act 1990, allowing for the possible enactment of legislation that could be inconsistent with its provisions.

Police and security forces

In March, a High Court judge found that police in Whakatane had subjected a detainee to excessive use of force. The detainee had been held in a cell for over seven hours and repeatedly squirted with pepper spray and hit with a baton.

An investigation into complaints against three police officers for the ill-treatment of detainees was ongoing at the end of year.

In October, two off duty policemen in Manukau were convicted of assaulting a group of students.

NICARAGUA

REPUBLIC OF NICARAGUA

Head of state and government:	**Daniel Ortega Saavedra**
Death penalty:	**abolitionist for all crimes**
Population:	**5.8 million**
Life expectancy:	**73.8 years**
Under-5 mortality (m/f):	**29/22 per 1,000**
Adult literacy:	**78 per cent**

Rape and sexual abuse remained widespread and more than two thirds of reported cases between January and September involved girls under the age of 17. The total ban on all forms of abortion remained in force. The independence of the judiciary was called into question.

Background

A health emergency was announced following flooding in August and September and the subsequent outbreak of Leptospirosis which left scores dead.

A new Ombudswoman on sexual diversity, a post specifically designed to protect the rights of lesbian, gay, bisexual and transgender people, was appointed. In May Nicaragua ratified ILO Convention No. 169. However, by the end of the year it had still not ratified the Rome Statute of the International Criminal Court.

Concern about the independence of the judiciary increased following months of turmoil in the Supreme Court. The crisis started in January when President Ortega issued a decree that effectively ended the tenure of eight of the 16 judges who were allied to the opposition Constitutional Liberal Party, and a Supreme Court ruling that this decree was legal and

binding in July. The new Supreme Court ruled in September that limiting the presidential term of office to two non-consecutive terms was not applicable, a ruling widely regarded as paving the way for the current President Daniel Ortega – who was President from 1985 to 1990 – to run for re-election.

Violence against women and girls

Rape and sexual abuse remained pervasive. Statistics from the Police Unit for Women and Children stated that of the rapes reported between January and August, two thirds involved girls under the age of 17. Official efforts to combat sexual violence against women and girls were ineffective. The government failed to put in place any integrated plan of action to eradicate sexual violence, protect survivors or ensure they had access to comprehensive psychosocial support services for their recovery. In October, the UN Committee on the Rights of the Child requested that the Nicaraguan authorities take urgent action to eradicate sexual violence against children.

■ In April, 15-year-old Lucía was kidnapped and sexually abused by a neighbour. She was not found until July and there were concerns that delays in finding her were the result of lack of police resources and capacity. Lucía's kidnapper remained at large after she returned home and she and her guardian reported to the police that they had been intimidated and harassed by him. By the end of the year, nobody had been brought to justice for the kidnapping and sexual abuse, nor had Lucía been given adequate protection.

Sexual and reproductive rights

The total ban on all forms of abortion remained in force. The law allowed for no exceptions and women and girls pregnant as a result of rape or whose life or health was threatened by continued pregnancy were denied the right to seek safe and legal abortion services. All abortion remained a criminal offence and anyone seeking, or assisting someone seeking, an abortion risked prosecution.

In February, Nicaragua's human rights record was assessed under the UN Universal Periodic Review and 12 member states recommended that the abortion ban be repealed. In September, the UN Committee on the Rights of the Child asked the state to decriminalize abortion. It was the fifth UN expert committee to recommend reforming the laws on the total ban on abortion and end this grave violation of the human rights of women and girls.

In September, on the Latin American and Caribbean day for the decriminalization of abortion, human rights activists, including health professionals, called on President Daniel Ortega to ensure the provision of safe and legal abortion services to women and girls when their life or health is at risk or as an option for survivors of rape who are pregnant.

Despite the urgency of the situation, the Supreme Court of Justice failed to rule on an appeal lodged on the constitutionality of the law banning all abortion, despite having committed itself to do so by May 2009.

Amnesty International visits/reports

🚗 Amnesty International delegates visited Nicaragua in March.

📄 Amnesty International Briefing on Nicaragua to the United Nations Committee on the Rights of the Child (AMR 43/004/2010)

📄 Listen to their voices and act: Stop rape and sexual abuse of girls in Nicaragua (AMR 43/008/2010)

NIGER

REPUBLIC OF NIGER

Head of state :	**Major Salou Djibo (replaced Mamadou Tandja in February)**
Head of government:	**Mahamadou Danda (replaced Ali Badjo Gamatié in February)**
Death penalty:	**abolitionist in practice**
Population:	**15.9 million**
Life expectancy:	**52.5 years**
Under-5 mortality (m/f):	**171/173 per 1,000**
Adult literacy:	**28.7 per cent**

Human rights activists continued to be targeted until the overthrow of President Mamadou Tandja in February. The ousted President and other political and military officials were held without charge or trial. Several foreign nationals were taken hostage by al-Qa'ida in the Islamic Maghreb (AQIM), one of whom reportedly died in captivity.

Background

In February, President Mamadou Tandja was overthrown by a military junta that suspended the Constitution and dissolved all state institutions. The Supreme Council for the Restoration of Democracy (CSRD) appointed Major Salou Djibo as Niger's interim president. The military leadership promised a new Constitution and a rapid return to democracy.

In May, a new electoral code was promulgated. In October, a national pact paving the way towards democracy was signed in Rome by the CSRD, the government, the transitional parliament, major political parties and civil society groups. A new Constitution was adopted in October and parliamentary elections were scheduled for January 2011.

In March, AQIM raided a military outpost in western Niger, killing at least five soldiers.

As a result of widespread crop failure and high food prices, the country faced a severe food crisis with more than half the population short of food. This situation worsened in August after heavy rainfall and localized flooding.

Detention without trial

Several political leaders were arrested and detained after the military coup. Most were released a few days later, but some were detained without charge or trial.

■ In February, ousted President Mamadou Tandja and Minister of Interior Albadé Abouba were placed under house arrest. By the end of 2010, they were still detained in Niamey, the capital, outside any legal process. In November, the Court of Justice of ECOWAS ordered the authorities of Niger to release former President Tandja.

■ In October, Colonel Abdoulaye Badié, second-in-command of the ruling junta, and three other senior military officers were arrested and accused of plotting to destabilize the regime. They were detained at the headquarters of the National Gendarmerie in Niamey and had not been charged or tried by the end of the year.

Human rights defenders

Human rights activists were targeted early in the year.

■ In January, Marou Amadou, President of the United Front for the Protection of Democratic Assets (FUSAD), who had been detained for one month in 2009, was given a three-month suspended sentence for "regionalist propaganda" after calling for protests against the government of Mamadou Tandja.

■ In February, Abdoul-Aziz Ladan, President of the Mouvement nigérien pour la sauvegarde de la démocratie (MOSADEM), was charged with "complicity in defamation" for criticizing official policy. The charges were dropped after the overthrow of President Tandja.

Hostage-taking

Several foreign nationals were taken hostage by AQIM.

■ In April, Michel Germaneau, a 78-year-old French

national doing voluntary humanitarian work, was abducted by AQIM, which demanded the release of AQIM members held in neighboring countries. His death was announced by AQIM in July, a few days after the Mauritanian army launched a rescue attempt in Mali, with the co-operation of the French authorities.

■ In September, seven people – five French nationals, one Togolese and one Malagasy – were abducted by AQIM in Arlit, northern Niger. Two were working for a French company exploiting uranium mines in the area. The hostages were reportedly held in north-western Mali. In October, AQIM reportedly demanded for their release the repeal of France's ban on Muslim face veils, the release of members of their organization and about 7 million euros.

Death penalty

Following the execution in Libya in May of 18 Africans including three nationals of Niger, the President of Niger met Libyan leader Mu'ammar al-Gaddafi, who reportedly agreed to stop executions of nationals of Niger. The two also discussed the commutation of the sentences of 22 nationals of Niger sentenced to death in Libya to life imprisonment, and their repatriation to Niger to serve their sentences.

Amnesty International visits/reports

⬜ Niger: Submission to the UN Universal Periodic Review, January 2011 (AFR 43/001/2010)

⬜ Mali-Mauritania-Niger: Amnesty International calls for the release of all hostages held by Al Qa'ida in the Islamic Maghreb (AFR 05/004/2010)

⬜ Niger: Une opportunité historique pour abolir la peine de mort (AFR 43/002/2010)

NIGERIA

FEDERAL REPUBLIC OF NIGERIA

Head of state and government:	Goodluck Jonathan (replaced Umaru Musa Yar'Adua in February)
Death penalty:	retentionist
Population:	158.3 million
Life expectancy:	48.4 years
Under-5 mortality (m/f):	190/184 per 1,000
Adult literacy:	60.1 per cent

The police continued to commit human rights violations, including unlawful killings, torture and other ill-treatment, and enforced disappearances. The justice system was under-resourced and riddled with delays. Prisons were overcrowded; the majority of inmates were pre-trial detainees, some held for many years. Approximately 920 people were on death row, many sentenced after unfair trials. No executions were reported. The security situation in the Niger Delta deteriorated during the year. Human rights defenders and journalists continued to face intimidation and harassment. Violence against women remained widespread and the government failed to protect the rights of children. Forced evictions continued across the country.

Background

President Umaru Musa Yar'Adua died in May following a long illness, and was replaced by Goodluck Jonathan, the Vice President, who had been acting President since February.

The Chairman of the Independent National Electoral Commission was removed in April and replaced in June. Elections were scheduled for January 2011, then postponed to April 2011.

Widespread political violence linked to the 2011 elections led to the deaths of dozens of people. Among those killed were candidates, their family members, and supporters.

On 31 December, at least 13 people were killed and many more injured when a bomb exploded inside the Sani Abacha military barracks in Abuja, the capital.

Plateau state

Between 17 and 20 January, more than 300 people were killed in religious and ethnic violence in and around the city of Jos, Plateau state; over 10,000 people were displaced and thousands of shops and homes were destroyed. On 7 March more than 200 men, women and children were killed by armed men when the villages of Dogo Nahawa, Zot, and Ratsat were attacked. Homes and property were burned, and thousands of people were displaced.

At least three bombs exploded in and around Jos on 24 December, killing 80 and injuring many more. The bombings triggered further violence in and around the city, leaving dozens dead and many more injured. Several buildings were also burned down.

A Presidential Advisory Committee established in February to investigate the violence reported to President Jonathan in August. He pledged to

N

implement the Committee's recommendations, but the report was not made public. The findings of earlier investigations into violence in 2008 had not been published by the end of 2010.

Boko Haram

Between July and December, more than 30 people were killed in Borno state by people believed to be members of the religious sect commonly known as Boko Haram. Many of the attacks targeted the police. Six people were killed on 24 December when suspected Boko Haram members attacked two churches in Maiduguri.

Hundreds of soldiers were deployed to Borno state in October. On 22 November, a police spokesperson announced that more than 170 people had been arrested by the police in the preceding six weeks. Many were transferred to Abuja; by the end of the year most remained in police detention and had yet to be produced in court.

On 31 December, the police announced they had arrested a further 92 suspected members of Boko Haram.

Suspected members of Boko Haram also carried out attacks in Bauchi and Yobe states, killing at least five policemen. In September a group of suspected Boko Haram members attacked Bauchi Federal Prison and freed over 700 inmates, including approximately 123 members of Boko Haram.

A committee set up in August 2009 to investigate the Boko Haram crisis in July 2009 in which over 700 people died did not make their findings public during 2010. In April, the High Court, Borno state ordered the police to pay compensation in the case of Alhaji Baba Fugu, who was extrajudicially executed in police custody during the 2009 crisis. An appeal by the police against the decision had not been heard by the end of the year.

Abia state

Criminal gangs kidnapped scores of people, including children, in Abia state, sometimes for as little as 10,000 Naira (US$65). According to the Nigerian Medical Association, 21 doctors were kidnapped. On 29 September, the army was deployed to Abia state. On 12 October, the Joint Task Force (JTF), which combined troops of the army, navy, air force and the mobile police, announced that they had killed 172 suspected members of kidnapping gangs in shoot-outs, and arrested 237. NGOs estimated that hundreds of people were killed by security forces in Abia state in 2010.

Unlawful killings and enforced disappearances

In February, senior government ministers called for reform of the Nigeria Police Force and an improved complaints mechanism. However, no further action was taken.

Widespread disregard for human rights and due process within the police force continued. Hundreds of people were killed by the police in 2010. Many were unlawfully killed before or during arrest in the street or at roadblocks, or subsequently in police detention. Many other people disappeared after arrest. A large proportion of these unlawful killings appeared to be extrajudicial executions. Most perpetrators remained unpunished. In May, the NGO LEDAP (Legal Defence and Assistance Project) estimated that in 2009 at least 1,049 people had been killed by the police.

■ Police at a checkpoint in Ilorin, Kwara state, shot and killed a nursing mother and her eight-month-old baby in January. Four police officers were arrested.

■ In April, police opened fire at protesters in Ajegunle, Lagos, killing four people. They had been protesting at the death of Charles Okafor who died after police beat him during a raid on a viewing centre where he had been watching a football match.

■ In June, Assistant Superintendent of Police Boniface Ukwa was shot dead by policemen at a roadblock in Enugu. He was off duty and not in uniform. The police subsequently claimed that he was killed in a shoot-out with kidnappers.

The police were ordered to pay compensation in some cases, including that of Kausarat Saliu, a three-year-old girl shot dead in April 2009 at a roadblock in Lagos, while travelling with her parents on a commercial bus.

Torture and other ill-treatment

Police routinely tortured suspects, including children. In March, the then Attorney General and Minister of Justice of the Federation formally accepted the draft National Anti-Torture Policy. No further action was taken.

Detainees were regularly held by the police for longer than the constitutionally guaranteed 48 hours before being brought before a judge, often for weeks and even months.

■ Shete Obusoh and Chijioke Olemeforo were arrested by police officers from the Special Anti-Robbery Squad on 4 October and spent 17 days in police detention before being taken to court and remanded in prison on

21 October. They said that during this time they were hung from the ceiling in the police station and beaten with gun butts and machetes.

Justice system

Seventy per cent of Nigeria's nearly 48,000 prison inmates were pre-trial detainees. Many had been held for years awaiting trial in appalling conditions. Few could afford a lawyer and the government-funded Legal Aid Council had only 122 lawyers for the whole country.

At the end of 2010, most justice sector reform bills were still pending before the National Assembly. A Bill strengthening the National Human Rights Commission made progress but had not been sent for presidential assent by the end of the year.

The courts continued to be riddled with delays.

■ In August, the Federal High Court in Port Harcourt ordered the police to produce Chika Ibeku, declaring his detention without charge or bail unlawful. It took a further three months before the court issued the order and began serving the named police officials. The habeas corpus application had been filed by the Nigeria Bar Association Human Rights Institute in May 2009.

Death penalty

Approximately 920 people were on death row, including eight women, 10 prisoners over the age of 70, and more than 20 who were under 18 at the time of the offence. No executions were reported. Many death row inmates were sentenced to death following blatantly unfair trials or after spending more than a decade in prison awaiting trial.

Following meetings of the Council of States and the National Economic Council in April and June, chaired by the President and Vice President respectively, state governors announced their intention to review all cases of death row inmates and to sign execution warrants in order to reduce prison congestion.

Niger Delta

The improved security situation brought about by the presidential amnesty granted to members of armed groups in 2009 had deteriorated by the end of 2010. Armed groups and gangs kidnapped dozens of oil workers and their relatives, including children, and attacked several oil installations. The security forces, including the military, continued to commit human rights violations in the Niger Delta, including extrajudicial executions, torture and other ill-treatment, and destruction of homes.

On 1 December, following fighting between the JTF and an armed group in Delta state, the JTF razed the nearby community of Ayokoromo. At least 120 homes were burned down. The JTF claimed nine villagers were killed but community leaders and NGOs put the death toll at 51, including women and children. In January, the Movement for the Emancipation of the Niger Delta (MEND) called off its ceasefire, which had been in place since October 2009. In March, two bombs exploded in Warri, Delta state, killing at least one person. In October, three car bombs exploded in Abuja, disrupting Nigeria's independence celebrations and killing 12 people. MEND claimed responsibility.

■ In January, two workers at Chevron's gas plant, Escravos, in Delta state, were shot dead. Members of the JTF, who had been guarding the facility, allegedly drove past and opened fire as the workers were leaving the plant. Chevron paid the families of the two men compensation, but did not accept any responsibility for the killings.

Pollution and environmental damage caused by the oil industry continued to have a serious impact on people living in the Niger Delta. Laws and regulations to protect the environment were poorly enforced. Government agencies responsible for enforcement were ineffective and, in some cases, compromised by conflicts of interest. Communities in the Niger Delta frequently had no access to vital information about the impact of the oil industry on their lives.

■ On 1 May, crude oil from a leaking pipe from an offshore platform of ExxonMobil's Qua Iboe oilfield reached the shores of the Ibeno community, Akwa Ibom state.

Violence against women

Violence against women remained pervasive, including domestic violence, rape and other forms of sexual violence by state officials and private individuals. The authorities consistently failed to exercise due diligence in preventing and addressing sexual violence by both state and non-state actors, leading to an entrenched culture of impunity.

■ Maryam Mohammed Bello and Halima Abdu were presented in court in February and remanded in prison after spending one year in police detention in Maiduguri, where they said they were repeatedly raped. Both women became pregnant while in police custody. The women were eventually bailed in October.

Children's rights

By the end of the year, 12 of Nigeria's 36 states still had not passed the Child Rights Act. Children were routinely detained with adults in police and prison cells. Only one of the country's three remand homes was functioning. It was overcrowded, with approximately 600 children held in facilities designed for 200.

Government provision for homeless and vulnerable children remained inadequate with over 1 million street children across the country.

By the end of 2010, no investigation had been carried out into the violent clash involving the Kala-Kato Islamic sect on 29 December 2009 in Bauchi, which left at least 38 people dead, 22 of them children. Many were reportedly shot by the police.

Freedom of expression

Human rights defenders and journalists continued to face intimidation and harassment. Several human rights defenders and journalists were threatened and beaten by police and security forces, and at least two were killed in suspicious circumstances. By the end of 2010, the Freedom of Information Bill, first presented in 1999, had not been passed by the National Assembly.

■ In March, the Shari'a Court in Magajin Gari, Kaduna, ordered the Civil Rights Congress (CRC) to stop its online forum from debating the amputation of the right hand of Mallam Bello Jangebe 10 years earlier.

■ On 24 April, Edo Sule Ugbagwu, a senior judiciary correspondent with *The Nation* newspaper, was killed in Lagos by unknown gunmen. By the end of the year no one had been brought to justice for his killing.

■ On 29 December, human rights activist Chidi Nwosu was shot dead by unknown gunmen in his house in Abia state. He was President of the Human Rights, Justice and Peace Foundation and was known for his work against corruption and human rights abuses.

Forced evictions

Forced evictions continued throughout Nigeria. They were carried out without genuine consultation, adequate notice and compensation or alternative accommodation. More than 200,000 people remained at risk of forced eviction in Port Harcourt, Rivers state, as a result of the state government's plans to demolish the city's waterfront communities.

■ On 23 December, at least one person died and several others were injured when armed police officers opened fire during a forced eviction in Makoko

community in Lagos. The police were accompanying Lagos state's Environmental Task Force, the Kick Against Indiscipline (KAI) Brigade, to demolish structures in the area. This was the second time in 2010 that Makoko residents faced eviction from their homes. In April, the KAI had forcibly evicted hundreds of people from their homes in Makoko.

Amnesty International visits/reports

🚗 Amnesty International delegates visited Nigeria in March, April and October.

📄 Nigeria: Amnesty International condemns ban on internet debate (AFR 44/002/2010)

📄 Provisions of the "Prevention of Terrorism Bill 2009" are incompatible with Nigeria's human rights obligations: Briefing to the National Assembly (AFR 44/005/2010)

📄 Amnesty International, Human Rights Watch and Nigerian civil society groups call on state governments not to resume the execution of prisoners (AFR 44/010/2010)

📄 "Just move them": forced evictions in Port Harcourt, Nigeria (AFR 44/017/2010)

📄 Nigeria: 50 years of independence – making human rights a reality (AFR 44/021/2010)

📄 Nigeria: Port Harcourt demolitions – excessive use of force against demonstrators (AFR 44/022/2010)

📄 Nigeria: Police must immediately account for disappeared detainee (AFR 44/029/2010)

📄 Nigeria: Activists assaulted and illegally detained by Nigerian police, 8 April 2010

📄 Nigeria: Governor "threatens to execute inmates" to ease prison congestion, 21 April 2010

NORWAY

KINGDOM OF NORWAY

Head of state:	King Harald V
Head of government:	Jens Stoltenberg
Death penalty:	abolitionist for all crimes
Population:	4.9 million
Life expectancy:	81 years
Under-5 mortality (m/f):	5/4 per 1,000

Asylum-seekers were forcibly returned to Greece under the Dublin II Regulation and to Iraq. Protection for women survivors of sexual violence remained inadequate.

Refugees, migrants and asylum-seekers

Despite serious concerns about inadequate asylum determination procedures and poor detention conditions in Greece, 277 asylum-seekers had been transferred there under the Dublin II Regulation by 30 September. In October, the immigration authorities suspended Dublin II transfers to Greece and started substantively examining these asylum applications.

Contrary to guidelines by UNHCR, the UN refugee agency, 140 Iraqis were forcibly returned from Norway to Iraq, including on charter flights organized jointly with other European states.

In October, the Ministry of Justice invited NGO input into policy proposals being drafted to improve the situation of asylum-seeking children. In the same month, the Minister of Justice announced planned improvements to the asylum procedure and reception conditions for asylum-seeking families with children. In December, the Directorate of Immigration announced the closure of places for up to 292 asylum-seeking children in various reception centres.

In April, the government signed a three-party agreement with Afghan authorities and UNHCR on the return of asylum-seekers to Afghanistan, including plans for a reception centre for asylum-seeking children returned to Afghanistan.

■ In August, a Syrian Kurd rejected asylum-seeker, Abd al-Karim Hussein, was forcibly returned to Syria, where he was held in incommunicado detention for 15 days, during which time he said he was tortured. He was released without charge and subsequently fled Syria.

Violence against women

Protection and access to justice for survivors of rape and other sexual violence remained inadequate in law and practice. The definition of rape in the General Civil Penal Code continued to link rape with the use or threat of physical violence by the perpetrator. Prosecution and conviction rates for rape remained low and national statistics on rape were not maintained.

International justice

In March, the Borgarting Court of Appeal found Mirsad Repak, a naturalized Norwegian citizen who served in the Croatian Defence Forces, guilty of war crimes and crimes against humanity committed in 1992 at Dretelj detention camp, during the war in Bosnia and Herzegovina. In December, the Supreme Court quashed the Court of Appeal's decision to convict Mirsad Repak on charges related to war crimes and crimes against humanity, on the basis that these crimes were not part of the Norwegian Penal Code at the time they were committed. The Supreme Court's decision on the charge of "deprivation of liberty" was expected in 2011.

Legal, constitutional or institutional developments

By the end of the year, Norway had not signed the Optional Protocol to the International Covenant on Economic, Social and Cultural Rights and continued to delay ratification of the Optional Protocol to the Convention against Torture.

Amnesty International visits/reports

▤ Case closed: Rape and human rights in the Nordic countries – summary report (ACT 77/001/2010)

▤ European states must stop forced returns to Iraq (EUR 01/028/2010)

OMAN

SULTANATE OF OMAN

Head of state and government:	Sultan Qaboos bin Said
Death penalty:	retentionist
Population:	2.9 million
Life expectancy:	76.1 years
Under-5 mortality (m/f):	14/13 per 1,000
Adult literacy:	86.7 per cent

Several bloggers who criticized the government were assaulted or detained. The State Security Court was abolished and a new law against financing terrorism took effect. No death sentences or executions were reported.

Background

In January, the Sultan appointed the 14 members of the National Human Rights Committee, created by decree in 2008. The Committee is affiliated to the Majlis al-Dawla, the upper legislative house, but is mandated to function independently.

In December, Oman abstained in a UN General Assembly resolution calling for a worldwide moratorium on executions.

Freedom of expression

The government maintained strict curbs on freedom of expression. Several bloggers appeared to have been targeted after criticizing the government. However, in January legal proceedings against A'sim al-Sheedi, a journalist accused of defamation after he published an article in December 2009 alleging police corruption, were indefinitely suspended.

■ Abdul Khaleq al-M'amari, a lawyer and blogger, was found unconscious in his home in Muscat in September. He was reported to have been beaten and to have sustained injuries that left him unable to speak for several days. He was attacked the day after he criticized government spending plans for Oman's national day. No official investigation was known to have been carried out.

■ 'Abdullah al-'Aisari, a blogger, was arrested on around 17 November and, according to reports, detained incommunicado. He had criticized on his blog the government's decision to change the date of Eid al-Adha, which falls during the Muslim holy pilgrimage to Mecca, to bring it into line with the date set by the Saudi Arabian authorities. He was released without charge on 24 November.

Counter-terror and security

The Law on Combating Money Laundering and Financing of Terrorism was enacted in June. It defines the offence of financing terrorism in very broad terms as the financing of "terrorism, terrorist crimes or terrorist organizations" as well as "the commission of any action regarded as a crime within any of the relevant treaties and conventions" to which Oman is party. However, it does not list these treaties and conventions. The law also requires lawyers to disclose to the authorities information about their clients if they suspect their clients have committed offences under this law, so breaching the principle of lawyer-client confidentiality.

Discrimination – Aal Tawayya and Aal Khalifaya tribes

At least five people belonging to Aal Tawayya and Aal Khalifaya tribes continued to be denied equitable access to their economic and social rights as a consequence of a 2006 Interior Ministry decision to rename their tribes "Awlad Tawayya" and "Awlad Khalifayn", affiliating them to the al-Harithi tribe. This reduced their status to that of "*akhdam*", effectively servants of the al-Harithi tribe. The government said it had addressed the tribes' grievance. However, some members of the tribes were reported to still face difficulties in renewing their identity cards, which are needed to register businesses, obtain travel documents, and arrange matters such as divorce and inheritance.

PAKISTAN

ISLAMIC REPUBLIC OF PAKISTAN

Head of state:	Asif Ali Zardari
Head of government:	Yousuf Raza Gilani
Death penalty:	retentionist
Population:	184.8 million
Life expectancy:	67.2 years
Under-5 mortality (m/f):	85/94 per 1,000
Adult literacy:	53.7 per cent

Massive floods displaced millions of Pakistanis, leaving them in need of food, health care and shelter. Insurgent groups unlawfully killed people in Pakistan's conflict-ridden Northwest and Balochistan. They inflicted cruel punishments on the civilian population and launched deadly suicide attacks in the major cities, causing hundreds of civilian deaths and injuries. More than 2 million people were displaced by the conflict in north-west Pakistan. Torture, deaths in custody, "honour killings" and domestic violence persisted, despite new international commitments to safeguard rights. Members of the armed forces continued to arbitrarily arrest civilians, subjecting some to extrajudicial executions. New cases of enforced disappearance soared, particularly in Balochistan, where many victims were found dead. Old cases of enforced disappearance remained unresolved. Violence against religious minorities intensified with the government failing to prevent or punish the perpetrators. An informal moratorium on executions remained, but over 300 people were sentenced to death.

Background

Floods, which began in north-western Pakistan in July, killed almost 2,000 people and directly affected more than 20 million. This acute humanitarian crisis added to the existing misery of those already displaced by the conflict. The Pakistani army pushed Taleban forces out of the Swat Valley and South Waziristan in 2009, and out of the Bajaur and Orakzai agencies in 2010. Despite successes on the battlefield, military and civilian authorities failed to address the underlying causes of the conflict. They did nothing to improve the area's significant underdevelopment, failing to re-build basic infrastructure, including schools, and neglecting to restore businesses. Humanitarian relief for the displaced remained inadequate. Humanitarian organizations and independent monitors were barred from effectively operating in conflict areas.

US drone strikes targeting suspected al-Qa'ida and Taleban insurgents in Pakistan's border regions more than doubled to a reported 118 strikes in 2010, fuelling anti-American sentiment among the population.

On 24 March, Pakistan ratified the International Covenant on Civil and Political Rights and the UN Convention against Torture, with sweeping reservations. No steps were taken to incorporate these international commitments into domestic law.

In April, the 18th constitutional amendment ended the President's power to dissolve Parliament, introduced citizens' right to freedom of information, enhanced provincial autonomy, and obliged provinces to provide free education to all children.

In October, Asma Jahangir, a prominent human rights advocate, was elected the first woman President of the Supreme Court Bar Association.

Violations by security forces

Hundreds of civilians were killed in army operations against insurgents in the Northwest. Dozens of suspected insurgents were killed by *lashkars* (tribal militias) sponsored by the army but lacking proper training or monitoring.

■ On 8 March, a *lashkar* set fire to 130 homes of suspected Taleban members in Bajaur agency.

Extrajudicial executions

Security forces reportedly killed suspected members of armed groups in the Northwest and Balochistan, mostly with impunity. The Human Rights Commission of Pakistan (HRCP), an NGO, recorded 282 bodies of suspected insurgents found between the end of military operations in Swat Valley in July 2009 and May. Local people attributed these killings to the security forces. Several activists campaigning against enforced disappearance in Balochistan disappeared themselves and were killed.

■ On 14 July, Supreme Court lawyer and former senator Habib Jalil Baloch was shot dead in Quetta district. The

Baloch Armed Defence Group, allegedly sponsored by Pakistani security forces, claimed responsibility.

■ In late October, Mohammad Khan Zohaib and Abdul Majeed, both aged 14, were found shot dead after reportedly being detained by Frontier Corps personnel in October and July respectively in Khuzdar town, Balochistan.

■ Faqir Mohammad Baloch, a member of the Voice for Baloch Missing Persons, was abducted on 23 September. His body, bearing a bullet wound and signs of torture, was found in Mastung district on 21 October.

■ The mutilated body of 38-year-old lawyer Zaman Marri was found on 5 September in Mastung. He had gone missing on 19 August in Quetta. Zaman Marri had represented his cousin Ali Ahmed Marri, who was taken by men in plain clothes on 7 April. His body was found on 11 September in the same area.

Abuses by armed groups

Armed groups in the Northwest inflicted cruel and inhuman punishments, attacked civilians and destroyed civilian structures, including schools.

■ On 19 February, the Pakistani Taleban publicly amputated the hands of five men they had accused of theft in Dabori town, Orakzai.

■ In May, the Taleban publicly executed a man in Miramshah town, North Waziristan, after accusing him of murdering two brothers. The Taleban "sentenced" him unlawfully in a makeshift tribunal.

■ In late October, the Taleban publicly flogged 65 alleged drug dealers in Mamozai town, Orakzai agency.

Anti-government armed groups killed or injured thousands of civilians in suicide bombings and targeted attacks.

■ On 17 April, suicide bombers killed 41 displaced people queuing for relief supplies in Kohat town in Khyber Pakhtunkhwa province.

■ On 20 May, the Taleban in North Waziristan strapped explosives on two men suspected of passing information to the USA and publicly blew them up.

■ On 14 August, 17 Punjabis were killed in Quetta district. The Balochistan Liberation Army declared the attack retribution for the disappearance and murder of people in Balochistan.

■ On 2 October, Mohammad Farooq Khan, a doctor, religious scholar and educator, and his associate, were shot dead in Mardan city. The Taleban claimed responsibility for the killing. Mohammad Farooq Khan had publicly declared suicide bombing un-Islamic.

P

Arbitrary arrests and detentions

According to the HRCP, between 1,000 and 2,600 people, including children related to suspected insurgents, continued to be held in military custody after search and military operations in Swat, Khyber Pakhtunkhwa province.

■ A local *jirga* (council of tribal elders) demanded that families of Taleban members in Swat surrender them by 20 May or face expulsion. As a result, 130 relatives of suspected Taleban members were taken into "protective custody" in a camp guarded by the army at Palai area, Swat.

Torture and other ill-treatment

Police tortured and otherwise ill-treated detainees in their custody. They failed to take sufficient measures to protect people from mob violence and in some instances appeared to have colluded in it.

■ On 1 March, two men accused of robbery were filmed being held down and whipped by police in a police station in Chiniot city, Punjab province. Following broadcast of the film on national television, five police officers were arrested. Their cases were pending.

■ On 15 August, two brothers accused of robbery, 17-year-old Hafiz Mohammad Mughees Sajjad and Mohammad Muneeb Sajjad, aged 15, were beaten to death by a mob in Sialkot city, Punjab. The incident was caught on film. A judicial inquiry found that the boys had been innocent of the charges and that police officers present at the scene of the lynching had failed to stop the attack.

Enforced disappearances

In March, a three-member panel constituted by the Supreme Court began to review cases of enforced disappearance. Its mandate included recording evidence of released people and investigating the role of the intelligence agencies. The Judicial Commission reached its conclusion on 31 December and submitted its findings and recommendations to the Federal government for review. The Commission's report remained classified at the end of the year.

Hundreds of people went missing, apparently after being held by the intelligence services or the army. The majority of cases were in Balochistan. Hundreds of habeas corpus petitions remained pending in provincial High Courts but the intelligence services refused to respond to court directions. Families of the disappeared were threatened for speaking out about their missing loved ones.

■ The whereabouts of two members of the Baloch National Front, Mahboob Ali Wadela and Mir Bohair Bangulzai, remained unknown. Mahboob Ali Wadela was taken by Maripur police from a bus in Yousuf Goth neighbourhood, Karachi city, on 2 April; Mir Bohair Bangulzai was taken by uniformed police from his car in Quetta on 1 April. Maripur and Quetta police refused to register a complaint by the men's relatives.

Freedom of expression

Journalists were harassed, ill-treated and killed by state agents and members of anti-government armed groups. State agents failed to protect journalists from attacks by armed groups; 19 media workers were killed, making Pakistan the most dangerous country for media workers in 2010, according to the Pakistan Federal Union of Journalists and the Committee to Protect Journalists. The authorities blocked some online news sites.

■ Umar Cheema, journalist with *The News*, reported that he had been abducted and held for six hours on 4 September. He was taken blindfolded to the outskirts of the capital, Islamabad, stripped naked, hung upside down and beaten by people who warned him about criticizing the government. Prime Minister Gilani ordered a judicial inquiry and the Lahore High Court took notice of the case of its own accord but by the end of the year, no one was held to account.

■ Misri Khan Orakzai, aged 50, of the *Daily Ausaf* in Hangu city, Khyber Pakhtunkhwa province, was shot dead by unidentified gunmen on 13 September after receiving several death threats from insurgents.

■ On 8 November, access to the online news site *Baloch Hal* was blocked by the Pakistan Telecommunication Authority for allegedly publishing "anti-Pakistan" material. The site covered human rights violations including enforced disappearances.

■ On 18 November, the bodies of 24-year-old Abdul Hameed Hayatan, a journalist at *Daily Karachi* and *Tawar,* and Hamid Ismail were found in Turbat city, Balochistan. The whereabouts of the two men had remained unknown after their arrest at a security forces checkpoint near Gwadar city on 25 October. Their bodies bore torture marks. Nearby a message was found, saying: "Eid present for the Baloch people."

Discrimination – religious minorities

The state failed to prevent and prosecute discrimination, harassment and violence against religious minorities and, increasingly, moderate Sunni Muslims. Ahmadis,

Shi'as and Christians were attacked and killed in apparent sectarian violence. Sectarian groups reportedly linked to the Taleban attacked Shi'as, Ahmadis and Sufis with impunity. Blasphemy laws continued to be misused against Ahmadis and Christians, as well as Shi'a muslims and Sunnis.

■ On 28 May, 93 members of the Ahmadiyya community were killed and 150 injured in attacks on two Ahmadiyya mosques in Lahore after the provincial government ignored requests for improved security following threats from armed groups. On 31 May, gunmen stormed the hospital where victims were undergoing treatment and killed six more people, including hospital staff.

■ On 1 July, 42 people were killed and 175 others injured in a suicide bomb attack on the Data Darbar Sufi shrine in the city of Lahore.

■ On 1 September, at least 54 Shi'a worshippers were killed and some 280 others injured when suicide bombers attacked a procession in Lahore.

■ On 3 September, a suicide attack killed at least 65 people in a Shi'a gathering in Quetta and injured another 150; the Taleban claimed responsibility for the attack.

Abuse of blasphemy laws persisted. At least 67 Ahmadis, 17 Christians, eight Muslims and six Hindus were charged with blasphemy and several cases were dismissed following dubious accusations or improper investigations by the authorities, according to the National Commission for Justice and Peace.

■ On 8 November, 45-year-old Aasia Bibi, a Christian mother of five, was charged with blasphemy and sentenced to death after an unfair trial. Following an altercation with local women who regarded a bowl of water she brought as "unclean", Aasia Bibi had been saved by police from the ensuing mob violence but was arrested on 19 June 2009. An appeal was pending.

The state failed to protect several of those charged with blasphemy from subsequent attacks.

■ On 19 July, two Christian brothers, 32-year-old Rashid, a pastor, and Sajid Emanuel, aged 27, were shot dead in front of a court in Faisalabad city after they had been charged with blasphemy. The police did not adequately protect the brothers despite credible death threats.

■ On 11 November, Imran Latif, aged 22, was shot dead in Lahore after being released on bail on 3 November. The court had found little evidence to substantiate a blasphemy charge brought against him five years earlier.

Violence against women and girls

Gender-based violence, including rape, forced marriages, "honour killings", acid attacks and other forms of domestic violence, was committed with impunity as police were reluctant to register and investigate complaints. According to the women's helpline Madadgaar, 1,195 women had been murdered as of late November. Of these, 98 had been raped before they were killed. Madadgaar figures showed a total of 321 women raped, and 194 gang-raped.

On 22 December the Federal Shariat Court ruled to reverse several provisions of the 2006 Women's Protection Act. The verdict sought to reinstate certain provisions of the 1979 Hudood Ordinance which were extremely discriminatory against women.

■ On 29 April, three sisters, Fatima, aged 20, Sakeena, aged 14 and Saima, aged 8, were disfigured by acid thrown at them in Kalat town, Balochistan, apparently for violating a ban on leaving the house without a male guardian.

Death penalty

An informal moratorium on executions, begun in late 2008, continued. However, the death penalty was imposed on 356 people, including one juvenile, mostly for murder. Some 8,000 prisoners remained on death row, according to the Human Rights Commission of Pakistan.

Amnesty International visits/reports

🚗 Amnesty International delegates visited Pakistan in June. Amnesty International consultants maintained a continuous presence in the country.

📄 'As if hell fell on me': The human rights crisis in northwest Pakistan (ASA 33/004/2010)

P

PALESTINIAN AUTHORITY

PALESTINIAN AUTHORITY
Head of Palestinian Authority:	Mahmoud Abbas
Head of government:	Salam Fayyad
Death penalty:	retentionist
Population:	4.4 million
Life expectancy:	73.9 years
Under-5 mortality (m/f):	23/18 per 1,000
Adult literacy:	94.1 per cent

In the West Bank, the security forces of the Fatah-controlled Palestinian Authority (PA) arbitrarily detained people connected with Hamas, while in the Gaza Strip the Hamas de facto administration arbitrarily detained people connected with Fatah. In both areas, detainees were tortured and otherwise ill-treated with virtual impunity. Both the PA and Hamas restricted freedom of expression and association. In Gaza, at least 11 people were sentenced to death and five executions were carried out, the first since 2005. The humanitarian crisis for the Gaza Strip's 1.5 million residents deepened as Israel's military blockade of the territory, as well as sanctions on the de facto Hamas authorities imposed by other states, were maintained.

Background

The West Bank, including East Jerusalem, and the Gaza Strip remained under Israeli occupation, although two separate non-state Palestinian authorities operated with limited powers – the Fatah-led caretaker PA government in the West Bank headed by Prime Minister Salam Fayyad; and the Hamas de facto administration in Gaza headed by former PA Prime Minister Isma'il Haniyeh. Tension between Fatah and Hamas remained high.

Hamas and its affiliated armed groups largely maintained the unofficial ceasefire with Israel in force since January 2009, but other Palestinian armed groups sporadically fired indiscriminate rockets and mortars from Gaza into southern Israel.

The PA continued to be recognized internationally as the sole representative of Palestinians and participated in new negotiations for a political settlement with Israel convened by the US government in September. The talks broke down when Israel refused to extend a partial moratorium on construction in Israeli settlements in the West Bank, excluding East Jerusalem. Hamas was excluded from any formal involvement in the negotiations.

Israel maintained control of Gaza's borders and airspace, and imposed extensive restrictions on movement throughout the West Bank. Israel's continuing military blockade of Gaza severely affected living conditions for inhabitants, exacerbating the humanitarian crisis there. Some 80 per cent of Gazans were reliant on international humanitarian relief. Movement of people into and out of Gaza was strictly controlled and limited, even for those seriously ill and in need of specialist medical treatment not available in Gaza. The continuing ban by Israel on a wide range of imports, despite some "easing" announced in June and December, had a severely negative impact on food security, health and local infrastructure. The blockade constituted collective punishment, a breach of international humanitarian law. Some 46 Palestinians were killed and 89 others were injured in underground tunnels used for smuggling basic goods into Gaza from Egypt; they died or were injured as a result of Israeli air strikes, tunnel collapses and other accidents.

Several Latin American states formally recognized Palestine as an independent state on the basis of its 1967 borders.

The Hamas authorities failed to investigate alleged war crimes and possible crimes against humanity committed by Hamas' military wing and other Palestinian armed groups during Operation "Cast Lead", the 22-day military offensive launched by Israel that ended on 18 January 2009. In September 2009, the UN Fact Finding Mission's report had recommended that both Israel and the relevant Palestinian authorities be given six months to investigate and prosecute those responsible for war crimes committed during the conflict. The Hamas de facto administration, in a report submitted to the UN in February, denied that Palestinian armed groups had targeted civilians. A committee appointed by Hamas stated in another report published in July that there was no "credible testimony" to charge individuals with intentionally targeting Israeli civilians.

Hamas continued to deny Gilad Shalit, an Israeli soldier taken captive in June 2006, access to the ICRC or visits from his family.

Arbitrary arrests and detentions

PA security forces in the West Bank arbitrarily arrested and detained suspected Hamas supporters, and Hamas security forces in Gaza arbitrarily arrested and detained suspected Fatah supporters. In both areas, the authorities gave the security forces wide powers of discretion, including to arrest and detain suspects in breach of the law and to torture and otherwise ill-treat them with impunity. The Independent Commission for Human Rights (ICHR) reported receiving complaints of more than 1,400 arbitrary arrests in the West Bank and more than 300 in Gaza.

Torture and other ill-treatment

Torture and other ill-treatment of detainees by security and police forces were reported – by the PA's Preventive Security force and the General Intelligence Service in the West Bank; and by Internal Security in Gaza. The ICHR said it had received over 150 complaints of torture or other ill-treatment by the PA in the West Bank and over 200 by Hamas in Gaza. New reports emerged of cases from 2009.

In both areas, torture and other ill-treatment were committed with impunity. In a rare prosecution, five members of the PA's General Intelligence Service were tried during 2010 in connection with the death in custody of Haitham Amr in June 2009, but were acquitted by a military court.

■ Mohammed Baraka Abdel-Aziz Abu-Moailek was reported to have been tortured by Internal Security officials in Gaza. He was held incommunicado for more than 50 days after his arrest in April 2009 on suspicion of "collaboration" with Israel. He said he was tortured with electric shocks, beaten on the soles of his feet (the falaqa method), burned with cigarettes and threatened with death to force him to confess. He remained on trial and in detention at the end of 2010.

■ Ahmed Salhab, a mechanic, was reported to have been tortured following arrest in September by PA security officials, allegedly for suspected association with Hamas. He said he was tied tightly in stress positions for long periods (the shabeh method). This exacerbated a serious back injury caused by previous torture by PA security officials. He was released without charge in October.

One death in custody following an assault by police was reported in Gaza.

■ Nazira Jaddou'a al-Sweirki died on 1 January shortly after she was hit on the back and otherwise assaulted by police in Gaza. Three of her adult sons were beaten and two were detained on suspicion of supporting Fatah.

Justice system

In the West Bank, the security authorities failed to comply with many court orders to release detainees. The PA continued to prohibit former members of the judiciary and police from working for the Hamas de facto administration in Gaza. In Gaza, the Hamas administration continued to use alternative prosecutors and judges who lacked appropriate training, qualifications and independence.

Death penalty

In Gaza, military and criminal courts sentenced at least 11 people to death. Five men were executed after trials that failed to meet international fair trial standards – two in April who had been convicted of "collaboration" with Israel; and three in May who had been convicted of murder.

Freedom of expression and association

Both the PA in the West Bank and the Hamas de facto administration in Gaza maintained tight controls on freedom of expression, and harassed and prosecuted journalists, bloggers and other critics.

■ Walid al-Husayin, a blogger, was detained by the General Intelligence Service on 31 October in the West Bank town of Qalqilya. He was suspected of posting comments on his blog advocating atheism and criticizing Islam and other religions. He remained held at the end of the year.

■ Paul Martin, a British journalist, was arrested in February by the Hamas authorities in Gaza after he tried to help a man accused of "collaboration" with Israel. Paul Martin was initially accused of spying for Israel but was released after 25 days in custody without charge.

The PA and Hamas authorities restricted freedom of association. Both prevented the Islamist organization Hizb ut-Tahrir from holding meetings, forcibly dispersed peaceful protests, and restricted the activities of other political parties and NGOs.

■ On 25 August in Ramallah, PA security officials forcibly dispersed a peaceful protest against the PA's agreement to participate in new peace talks with Israel. Journalists, photographers and human rights monitors were among those assaulted.

■ The South Society for Women's Health, an NGO providing family planning advice to women in Rafah, was reported to have been forced to close for three

P

weeks from 31 May by the Hamas authorities and then only allowed to reopen under Interior Ministry supervision. Two other women's NGOs in Rafah were also closed on 31 May.

■ The Sharek Youth Forum, an NGO funded by the UN Development Programme and operating in both the West Bank and Gaza Strip, was issued with a temporary closure notice in Gaza on 30 November, following several months of harassment by the Hamas authorities. Its Gaza offices remained closed at the end of 2010.

Abuses by armed groups

Palestinian armed groups associated with Fatah, Islamic Jihad and the Popular Front for the Liberation of Palestine fired indiscriminate rockets and mortars into southern Israel, killing one civilian, a migrant worker from Thailand, on 18 March, and endangering the lives of others. The scale of rocket fire was much reduced compared to previous years. Israeli forces launched attacks on those they held responsible.

In May and June, unidentified Palestinian gunmen burned facilities in Gaza used by the United Nations Relief and Works Agency for Palestine Refugees in the Near East (UNRWA) for its summer games programme for children.

In the West Bank, four Israelis, including a pregnant woman, were killed on 31 August near the Kiryat Arba Israeli settlement as new US-sponsored negotiations between Israel and the PA were about to begin. The following day, two other Israelis were shot and wounded near another settlement, Kochav Hashachar. The Izz al-Din al-Qassam brigades, the military wing of Hamas, claimed responsibility for both attacks.

Amnesty International visits/reports

🚌 Amnesty International delegates visited the West Bank in April and May.

📄 Palestinian Authority: Hamas fails to mount credible investigations into Gaza conflict violations (MDE 21/001/2010)

📄 Hamas must prevent further attacks on Israeli civilians (MDE 21/002/2010)

📄 Israel/Occupied Palestinian Territories: Amnesty International's assessment of Israeli and Palestinian investigations into Gaza conflict (MDE 15/022/2010)

📄 Israel/Occupied Palestinian Territories: Human Rights Council fails victims of Gaza conflict (MDE 15/023/2010)

PANAMA

REPUBLIC OF PANAMA

Head of state and government:	Ricardo Martinelli
Death penalty:	abolitionist
Population:	3.5 million
Life expectancy:	76 years
Under-5 mortality (m/f):	27/20 per 1,000
Adult literacy:	93.5 per cent

There were concerns about violence against women and discrimination against Indigenous Peoples and Afro-Panamanians. Four people died in clashes between protesters and police.

Background

Panama's human rights record was assessed under the Universal Periodic Review in November. Some of the concerns raised centred on violence against women and freedom of expression.

Freedom of assembly

In July, there were protests in Bocas del Toro province against proposed changes to the labour laws, which were seen as anti-union and increased tensions between workers and the main employer, a banana company. The protests lasted approximately two weeks, ending in violence between police and protesters. Four protesters were killed and hundreds of people injured.

A special commission set up by presidential decree to investigate these incidents concluded in October that more than 56 police officers and 700 protesters had been injured; 55 suffered permanent damage to their eyes as the result of use of tear gas by the police. The commission also concluded that of the four protesters killed, two died from gunshot wounds and two from injuries related to the use of tear gas. The commission recommended that the UN Basic Principles on the Use of Force and Firearms by Law Enforcement Officials be incorporated into national guidelines. It also recommended that the authorities drop charges of "crimes against the internal security of the State" levied against some 350 protesters, but that there should be no impunity for acts of violence. No one had been charged in connection with the deaths of the four protesters by the end of the year.

Violence against women and girls

In February the CEDAW Committee welcomed a government plan to address violence against women, in place since 2004, and some modifications to laws aimed at increasing protection for victims of domestic violence. However, the Committee noted its concern at the high prevalence of violence against women and the lack of adequate protection and support for victims as well as the absence of awareness campaigns. In a report provided to the Committee, the government noted that between 2005 and 2009 the Panama City special prosecution services had registered 17,067 complaints of violence against women and 1,198 of violence against girls.

Indigenous Peoples' rights

In May, the UN Committee on the Elimination of Racial Discrimination expressed concern about continuing racial discrimination and the marginalization, impoverishment and vulnerability of Afro-Panamanians and Indigenous Peoples. Among other recommendations, the Committee called for appropriate mechanisms to ensure the free, prior and informed consent of Indigenous Peoples affected by development projects; for an end to forced removals of such communities; and for legislation prohibiting racial discrimination.

■ In June, the Naso people, a 4,500-strong community in the Bocas del Toro province, filed a petition with the Inter-American Commission on Human Rights alleging, among other things, that the state had failed to afford them proper recognition and had supported cattle ranchers who had carried out forced evictions in 2009 in a continuing dispute over land.

PAPUA NEW GUINEA

PAPUA NEW GUINEA
Head of state: Queen Elizabeth II represented by Paulias Matane
Head of government: Sam Abal (replaced Michael Somare in December)
Death penalty: abolitionist in practice
Population: 6.9 million
Life expectancy: 61.6 years
Under-5 mortality (m/f): 70/68 per 1,000
Adult literacy: 59.6 per cent

Violence against women and sorcery-related killings continued to be widespread but the government did little to address them. Torture and ill-treatment of detainees and prisoners were prevalent. Police often beat detainees with gun butts and knives, and raped or sexually abused women detainees.

Violence against women and girls

Violence against women continued to be widespread, perpetuated by women's low status in society and traditional practices such as polygamy and bride price. A culture of silence and impunity prevailed, and women remained fearful of reporting sexual and physical violence to the authorities.

In April, a clinic in Lae reported that it received between 200 and 300 new patients a month, most of them women who had been raped, beaten or attacked with knives.

In May, the UN Special Rapporteur on torture visited the country and found that women were at a very high risk of abuse in the private and public spheres. During arrest and detention, police officers tortured and ill-treated women, subjecting them to sexual abuse – it appeared that police frequently arrested women for minor offences with the intention of sexually attacking them. Police punished women detainees by placing them, or threatening to place them, in cells with male detainees, where many were gang-raped.

In July, while reviewing Papua New Guinea's CEDAW obligations, the CEDAW Committee expressed its deep concern at the persistence of sexual violence at domestic and community levels and at the lack of data on its nature, extent and causes. A government

P

representative promised the Committee that the government would legislate against domestic violence.

Sorcery-related killings

■ In September in the Western Highlands, a mother of four was tied up, interrogated, tortured and then burnt alive after being accused of being a witch. Her husband and children escaped to live with relatives, fearing to return to their family home.

■ In October in Chimbu Province, four people accused of witchcraft, including an elderly couple, were tortured and thrown into a fast-flowing river.

Torture and other ill-treatment

In February, police refused to investigate allegations that members of the police mobile squad had beaten and forcibly evicted people living near the Porgera mine area in 2009.

In May, the UN Special Rapporteur on torture found that torture and other ill-treatment were widespread in prisons and police stations. Detainees who tried to escape were often brutally beaten with bush knives and gun butts; some were shot at close range, or had their tendons cut with axes and bush knives. Police often punished detainees by beating them, and many juveniles were held with adult prisoners.

■ In September in the Northern Province, a policeman who apprehended a robbery suspect shot him in the leg and left him to bleed until another policeman helped the man to hospital.

■ In October, a policeman who had been drinking alcohol killed a 15-year-old boy being held in a police cell by opening fire at him at point-blank range.

■ In November, prison wardens shot dead five prisoners trying to escape from jail. Another five prisoners were wounded during the shooting.

PARAGUAY

REPUBLIC OF PARAGUAY

Head of state and government:	Fernando Lugo
Death penalty:	abolitionist for all crimes
Population:	6.5 million
Life expectancy:	72.3 years
Under-5 mortality (m/f):	44/32 per 1,000
Adult literacy:	94.6 per cent

Indigenous Peoples continued to be denied their right to their traditional lands. Mistreatment and torture by police of members of organized social movements and *campesino* (peasant farmer) leaders were reported. There were growing concerns at attacks on human rights defenders.

Background

A number of violent incidents, including kidnapping and unlawful killings, were reported throughout the year, some of which allegedly involved the Paraguayan People's Army (Ejército del Pueblo Paraguayo, EPP), an armed opposition group. In response, a 30-day state of exception was declared in April, covering approximately half of the country. NGOs criticized the vague definition of "terrorism" contained in new anti-terrorism legislation introduced during the state of exception.

In August, Paraguay ratified the International Convention against enforced disappearance. In March, the UN Special Rapporteur on the right to education expressed concerns regarding the poor quality of education, lack of resources, inadequate infrastructure, and the lack of viable options for rural populations seeking higher education in Paraguay.

Indigenous Peoples' rights

A public policy proposal for social development promoted by the Executive's Social Cabinet and published in February put forward Indigenous Peoples' rights and the need to safeguard their traditional lands as an "emblematic focus" of policy. The proposal cited figures showing that since 2008 Indigenous Peoples had been given title to only 26,119 hectares of land, taking the total expanse of titled territory to 55,970 hectares; the target set by the authorities was to recognize Indigenous title to 279,850 hectares of land by 2013.

In June, the Ministry of Health set up a new Indigenous health directorate. As an important first

P

step, the directorate included ethnicity in forms used across the public health system as a means to monitor the implementation and effectiveness of policies.

With the publication of the Inter-American Court of Human Rights' judgement in the Xákmok Kásek case in August, Paraguay became the only state under the competence of the Court to have three separate judgements condemning its violation of Indigenous Peoples' rights.

■ There was still no resolution to the Yakye Axa and Sawhoyamaxa land claims, despite Inter-American Court of Human Rights orders dating from.2005 and 2006. A proposal to provide the Yakye Axa community with alternative lands to those of their initial claim was rejected following procedural delays. In September, direct negotiations began between high-ranking government officials and the current owners of the lands claimed by both communities.

■ In the context of a visit to the Puerto Colón area by the Inter-American Commission on Human Rights Rapporteur on Indigenous Peoples in September, two community leaders from the Kelyenmagategma community received death threats.

■ A scientific expedition organized by the UK-based Natural History Museum, in co-ordination with a Paraguayan environmental NGO and the government Environmental Secretariat, but planned without consultation with Indigenous authorities and representatives, was cancelled in November after concerns were raised that the visit could have a detrimental and irreversible impact on the livelihoods of uncontacted Ayoreo Indigenous Peoples.

■ Investigations into the alleged aerial fumigation of Indigenous communities in Itakyry in 2009 had not yielded results by the end of the year.

Police and security forces and the justice system

There were serious concerns about torture and other ill-treatment, excessive use of force and procedural irregularities by police during raids and detentions, particularly in the context of security operations related to the EPP and the ensuing judicial processes. NGOs presented concerns regarding 12 emblematic cases, also involving violence committed by private individuals, in a closed hearing of the Inter-American Commission on Human Rights in October.

The declaration of the state of exception in April was based on the justification that "internal upheaval caused by criminal groups operating in the area, [is]

placing the normal functioning of constitutional bodies at imminent risk", but the law passed contained many flaws including lack of clarity regarding the rights that would be restricted.

■ In June, two police officers died in Kuruzú de Hierro, Horqueta district, in a reported clash with alleged members of the EPP. Shortly after the incident, special police forces (Fuerza Operativa de la Policía Especializada, FOPE) raided the homes of a number of local residents, provoking allegations of excessive use of force and ill-treatment. There were concerns regarding the pace of investigation into the allegations.

Sexual and reproductive rights

In September, a Guiding Framework on Sexual Education developed in co-ordination with various government departments, civil society and UN agencies was published by the Education Ministry. The Framework would bring education programmes into line with international standards regarding sexual and reproductive rights, with a view to tackling prevalent problems such as sexual abuse and violence.

Violence against women and girls

In September, a child pornography ring operating inside Tacumbú National Penitentiary was discovered, only days after a visit from the UN Subcommittee on the Prevention of Torture visited to update recommendations it made in 2009 on prison conditions. It was understood that prisoners invited young girls into the prison, forced them to perform sexual acts which were filmed and later sold. Some prison officials, including the prison director and pastors working within the prison, were alleged to have been involved in the abuse. Investigations were continuing; the prosecutor's findings had not been published by the end of the year.

Human rights defenders

Statements made during the year demonstrated a serious deterioration in respect for the legitimacy of the role and rights of human rights defenders. Government officials called into question the role of human rights defenders and organizations working on cases related to abuses committed during security operations. This contributed to the wider misrepresentation of the role and work of defenders which was prevalent in the media.

In December, a raid was carried out on the offices of the NGO Iniciativa Amotocodie, weeks after their

P

national and international campaign to stop a scientific expedition to an area where uncontacted tribes were present. The warrant for the raid and the actions of prosecutors implementing it, including the confiscation of documents not related to the charges, broke many procedural guarantees, and appeared to be in reprisal for the organization's work denouncing the expedition.

Amnesty International visits/reports

🚌 An Amnesty International delegate visited Paraguay in November.

📄 Paraguay: Submission to the UN Universal Periodic Review, July 2010 (AMR 45/003/2010)

PERU

REPUBLIC OF PERU

Head of state and government:	Alan García Pérez
Death penalty:	abolitionist for ordinary crimes
Population:	29.5 million
Life expectancy:	73.7 years
Under-5 mortality (m/f):	38/27 per 1,000
Adult literacy:	89.6 per cent

Indigenous Peoples continued to be denied their right to free, prior and informed consent to development projects affecting them. The authorities failed to ensure justice for the victims of Bagua in 2009. Impunity for past human rights violations persisted, despite some progress. Women, especially Indigenous women and those on low incomes, continued to be denied their sexual and reproductive rights.

Background

There were widespread protests against the social and environmental impacts of large-scale development projects. These included protests in June at an oil spill into the Marañón River in the Peruvian Amazon and of toxic waste into the Escalera River in Huancavelica province, as well as demonstrations in September over concerns that the building of a dam would affect the right to water of the population of Espinar district in Cusco. In response, President Alan García passed a decree law in September allowing the military to be deployed to deal with civil protests, raising concerns of increasing incidents of excessive use of force by the security forces.

There were reports of armed confrontations in the Andean region between members of the armed opposition group Shining Path (Sendero Luminoso), and the military and police.

Indigenous Peoples' rights

In June, President García refused to promulgate the Law on the Right of Indigenous People to Prior Consultation. This landmark law was drawn up with the participation of Indigenous communities and passed by Congress in May. The authorities also failed to comply with a Constitutional Court ruling issued in June calling for the establishment of a framework to ensure the consultation of Indigenous Peoples affected by development projects, in accordance with ILO Convention No. 169. Scores of new concessions were granted to companies for oil exploration without the free, prior and informed consent of affected communities.

Impunity

Hundreds of people injured and the families of the 33 people killed, including 23 police officers, in confrontations at the road blockade in Bagua in the Amazon region in 2009 were still awaiting justice. Charges were brought against 109 civilians, mainly Indigenous people, and at least 18 police officers. By the end of the year, judges had yet to rule on whether there was sufficient evidence to initiate proceedings against the officers.

■ Indigenous leader Segundo Alberto Pizango Chota, who faced charges related to the Bagua protest, was detained for a day on his return from exile in May and then released on bail. At the end of the year criminal charges against him and four other Indigenous leaders remained pending.

■ Two foreign priests faced expulsion because of their work defending the rights of local communities in the face of large-scale economic projects. One of the priests, Father Bartolini, who was accused of public security offences, was acquitted in December. In the same trial, five Indigenous and community leaders were convicted and given suspended sentences of four years' imprisonment. All the charges appeared to have been brought in order to hinder the human rights work of the accused. Appeals against the convictions were pending at the end of the year.

Workers' rights

Trade unionists Pedro Condori Laurente and Claudio Boza Huanhayo were conditionally released in July after being held in prison for seven months awaiting trial on apparently unsubstantiated charges of killing a police officer during a miners' strike in 2008 in Huarochiri province. An appeal against the decision to release them was pending at the end of the year.

Excessive use of force

In April, five protesters were killed in Chala, Caraveli province, Arequipa department, during a police operation to control a demonstration against legislative measures on informal mining that they claimed would restrict their activities. Charges were filed against the officer in charge of the operation.

Sexual and reproductive rights

Women, particularly Indigenous women and women on low incomes living in rural areas, continued to face obstacles in accessing their sexual and reproductive rights.

Although the Ministry of Health challenged the 2009 Constitutional Tribunal ruling that the morning-after pill should not be provided by the state, provision of the pill did not resume. The authorities failed to issue a protocol for health professionals on therapeutic abortion, which is legal when the life or health of a woman is at risk.

The Inter-American Commission on Human Rights condemned the state's failure to implement a 2003 agreement to ensure truth, justice and reparation for over 2,000 women who were forcibly sterilized under the government of former President Alberto Fujimori (1990-2000).

Maternal mortality

The National Institute of Statistics reported a significant decrease in the maternal mortality ratio, previously one of the highest in the region. However, there were concerns that the ratio had not decreased in rural areas. Official figures also showed that there had been no improvement in the situation of women in rural areas facing transport difficulties in getting to distant health facilities.

Impunity – past human rights violations

In September, a series of decree laws were issued effectively rolling back advances in tackling impunity over the previous 10 years. Congress voted to revoke Decree Law 1097, which effectively granted amnesty to perpetrators of human rights violations. However, two further decrees allowing members of the armed forces accused of human

rights violations to be tried under military courts remained in place.

Seven years after the Truth and Reconciliation Committee's report was finalized, progress was slow in ensuring truth, justice and reparation, despite some advances. Individual reparations, including formalizing ownership of land granted to relatives and victims, a priority agreed by the government in 2003 before the Inter-American Commission on Human Rights, remained pending at the end of the year. In January, the Supreme Court upheld the sentence passed on former President Alberto Fujimori in 2009. In October, members of the "Colina group" death squad and former high-ranking officials in the government of Alberto Fujimori, were convicted of the killing of 15 people in 1991 and of the enforced disappearance of nine villagers in Santa province in the Ancash region and of Pedro Yauri in Huaura province in the region of Lima in 1992. However, thousands of other cases remained unresolved.

In November, trials began of soldiers accused of killing 69 villagers in 1985 in Accomarca, Vilcashuamán province. A new grave was discovered in the grounds of the Cabitos barracks in Huamanga province, and excavations began of mass graves in Huanta province on the site of the Christmas 1984 massacre of 25 members of the Indigenous community of Putka.

Prison conditions

Challapalca prison in Puno province, which is 4,600m above sea level and was closed between 2005 and 2007, remained open. Despite assurances from the authorities that the prison would be closed, 131 prisoners were still held there in October. The prison's inaccessibility limits prisoners' ability to exercise their right to visits from lawyers and doctors.

Amnesty International visits/reports

🚗 In October an Amnesty International delegation headed by the Secretary General visited Peru and met with officials of the Ministries of Health, Justice and Foreign Affairs as well as with Congress.

📄 Bagua: Consultation promised but justice not delivered (AMR 46/010/2010)

P

PHILIPPINES

REPUBLIC OF THE PHILIPPINES
Head of state and government: Benigno S. Aquino III
(replaced Gloria Macapagal-Arroyo in June)
Death penalty: abolitionist for all crimes
Population: 93.6 million
Life expectancy: 72.3 years
Under-5 mortality (m/f):   32/21 per 1,000
Adult literacy: 93.6 per cent

More than 200 cases of enforced disappearances recorded in the last decade remained unresolved, as did at least 305 cases of extrajudicial execution (with some estimates ranging as high as 1,200). Almost no perpetrators of these crimes have been brought to justice. Private armed groups continued to operate throughout the country, despite government commitments to disband and disarm them. Despite its 2010 deadline, the previous administration failed to "crush" the communist insurgency, and in August the new Aquino administration announced that counter-insurgency operations would be extended. Tens of thousands reportedly remained displaced in Mindanao two years after the end of the internal armed conflict, although the actual number was not known.

Background

National elections were held in May and local elections in October. Both were marred by politically motivated killings. In May Benigno Aquino III, son of former President Corazon Aquino and assassinated senator Benigno Aquino Jr., was elected President.

The resumption of peace talks between the government and the Moro Islamic Liberation Front (MILF) remained delayed. However, in July, the government named its negotiating panel. In September, the MILF said it was ready to begin peace talks and named its peace negotiators.

Peace talks remained elusive between the government and the communist New People's Army (NPA).

Unlawful killings

During both the May and October elections, the number of political killings increased. Political party supporters faced intimidation and violence, including grenade attacks.

Hundreds of cases of extrajudicial executions and enforced disappearances from the last decade remained unresolved and perpetrators were not brought to justice. Almost none of the victims' families received reparations. At least 38 alleged political killings were reported during the year.

At least six journalists were reportedly killed in 2010. In the course of a single week in June, radio reporters Desiderio Camangyan (Mati City, southern Philippines) and Joselito Agustin (Laoag City, northern Philippines), and print journalist Nestor Bedolido (Digos City, southern Philippines) were shot dead.

In September, the trial of the suspected perpetrators of the 2009 Maguindanao massacre began after significant delays. Fifty-seven people, including 32 journalists, were killed in the massacre, which took place in the run-up to national elections. At least 83 suspects were arrested and charged, including at least 16 policemen and members of the powerful political Ampatuan family. One hundred and thirteen suspects in the massacre remained at large.

■ Suwaid Upham, who was allegedly one of the gunmen during the massacre, came forward in March and was willing to testify in court as a possible witness. However, in June he was shot dead. Reportedly, despite efforts on his part, he had been unable to enrol in the Witness Protection Programme. Two suspects were arrested in connection with his murder.

The Philippine National Police reported that there were 117 private armed groups in February. In May, the Independent Commission Against Private Armies reported that there were at least 72 active private armed groups in the country, and that another 35 had already been dismantled by the police and military.

Many members of government-established, armed "force multipliers" – including Civilian Volunteer Organizations (CVOs), police auxiliary units, and the Citizens' Armed Forces Geographical Unit (CAFGU) – were also members of private armed groups. A former army general and member of the Independent Commission Against Private Armies told the media that local officials often used these volunteer groups and auxiliary units as private armies.

In November, the President vowed that he would disband and disarm identified private armed groups, but refused to abolish CVOs, the CAFGU and police auxiliary units, saying that they needed to be professionalized instead. The Armed Forces stated that it needed to increase the number of CAFGUs. In the wake of the Maguindanao massacre, the police said it had suspended recruitment for police auxiliary units.

In February, the Commission on Human Rights of the Philippines announced that it had recorded 777 cases of extrajudicial executions and 251 cases of enforced disappearance since 2001. In September, human rights group Karapatan recorded 1,206 extrajudicial executions and 206 victims of enforced disappearance during the same period. A report published in September, commissioned by the United States Agency for International Development and NGO the Asia Foundation recorded 305 cases of extrajudicial executions with 390 victims from 2001 to 2010. The same report stated that only 1 per cent of reported cases resulted in a conviction, and that members of the armed forces were implicated in 20 per cent of cases.

Civilians continued to be killed as the military's counter-insurgency plan failed to differentiate between civilians and members of the NPA. In some cases, the police or the military claimed that the deaths occurred during "legitimate encounters".

■ In November, botanist Leonardo Co and two other members of his team were shot dead in Leyte province, central Philippines, while collecting indigenous tree species. Military officials claimed that they were caught in the crossfire between the army and the NPA. However, a surviving member of the botanist's team denied this.

Torture and other ill-treatment

■ In August, Philippine media broadcast a video of a plain-clothes police officer in a Manila police station torturing Darius Evangelista, a suspect apparently held for petty theft, while uniformed police officers looked on. The footage showed the suspect naked, being yanked by a cord attached to his genitals and whipped with a rope. The video prompted the authorities to suspend all 11 police officers involved. Darius Evangelista was arrested by policemen in March, but has not been seen since. There were no records of his arrest in the police logs. Darius Evangelista's wife filed a formal complaint against nine police officers stating that his case was a violation of the Anti-Torture Act of 2009.

■ In January, 40-year-old Ambrosio Derejeno was reportedly subjected to enforced disappearance. A family member last saw him in the custody of CAFGU members in Samar province. He was tied up and surrounded by men in camouflage uniform pointing their guns at him. Under the Anti-Torture Act of 2009,

the act of using firearms to threaten someone who is restrained constitutes torture.

In December, the President signed the Implementing Rules and regulations for the Anti-Torture Act.

Indigenous Peoples' rights

In June, members of an Indigenous Dumagat community from Rizal province, northern Philippines, were reportedly driven from their homes by the military. One of the community members said that the soldiers tied up the men and abducted at least one of them. Three members of the community, who were reportedly members of a left-leaning Indigenous Peoples' party, were killed by unknown perpetrators in July.

According to a media report, the Army revived the vigilante group *Alsa Lumad* (Rise, Indigenous Peoples) in September in its campaign against the NPA. The report further stated that the government had resorted to arming Indigenous Peoples as part of its counter-insurgency operations against the NPA.

Sexual and reproductive rights

In September, the President stated that "the government is obligated to inform everybody of their responsibilities and their choices," and announced that the authorities would provide contraceptives to poor couples who requested it. The influential Catholic Church expressed its strong opposition to the move.

In August the Centre for Reproductive Rights issued a report which found that more than 560,000 women terminated their pregnancies each year and about 1,000 of them died annually after clandestine illegal abortions.

P

Amnesty International visits/reports

Amnesty International visited the Philippines in January and November-December.

POLAND

REPUBLIC OF POLAND

Head of state:	**Bronisław Komorowski (replaced Lech Kaczyński in August)**
Head of government:	**Donald Tusk**
Death penalty:	**abolitionist for all crimes**
Population:	**38 million**
Life expectancy:	**76 years**
Under-5 mortality (m/f):	**9/7 per 1,000**
Adult literacy:	**99.5 per cent**

In October, Poland became the first European country to acknowledge a rendition victim's claims when a Saudi national allegedly held in a secret detention centre in Poland was granted "victim" status. The UN Special Rapporteur on the right to health noted that restrictive legislation had resulted in an increase of unsafe, clandestine abortions.

Background

Presidential elections were held in two rounds in June and July following a plane crash in April, in which President Lech Kaczyński and other senior public officials died. As a result of the elections, Bronisław Komorowski – who had been serving as interim President – was sworn in on 6 August.

Counter-terror and security

A criminal investigation by the Appellate Prosecution Authority in Warsaw into Poland's complicity in the CIA-led rendition and secret detention programme continued. The Polish Air Navigation Services Agency released information in December 2009 indicating that flights operating under the rendition programme had landed in Poland – mainly at Szymany Airport, near the alleged site of a secret detention facility at Stare Kiejkuty.

Documents released by the Polish Border Guard Office in July confirmed that seven planes operating under the CIA-led rendition programme landed at Szymany airport between December 2002 and September 2003. Passengers, in addition to crew, were aboard at landing and/or departure.

■ In September, the Prosecutor's Office confirmed that it was investigating claims by Abd al-Rahim al-Nashiri, a Saudi national currently held at Guantánamo Bay, that he was held in a secret detention centre in Poland. In October, he was granted "victim" status, the first rendition claim to be acknowledged by any European authority.

■ In December, international lawyers co-operating with the NGOs Reprieve and Interights filed an application for Abu Zubaydah for crimes allegedly committed against him while he was held by the CIA in Poland. The application included a request for Abu Zubaydah to be formally recognized as a victim of torture and unlawful detention. Following the recognition of their victim status, Abd al-Nashiri, Abu Zubaydah and their lawyers were given access to the Prosecutor's investigation files and allowed to take part in the investigation.

In October, the UN Human Rights Committee called on the Polish authorities to ensure that the inquiry into allegations of the involvement of officials in renditions and secret detentions had full investigative powers to call witnesses and compel the production of documents.

■ On 17 September, acting on an international arrest warrant issued by the Russian authorities, police in Warsaw arrested Chechen figurehead Akhmed Zakayev. Following the arrest, Russia demanded Akhmed Zakayev's extradition, alleging his involvement in terrorism-related activities. On 18 September, Warsaw District Court ordered his release on the grounds of his asylum status in the UK. The District Prosecutor appealed the decision. In October, an Appeal Court upheld the decision to release Akhmed Zakayev, who returned to the UK. On 23 December, the District Court in Warsaw discontinued the extradition proceedings on the grounds that Akhmed Zakayev was no longer in Poland.

Discrimination

Following several years of preparatory work, the parliament adopted anti-discrimination legislation in December. NGOs criticized its limited scope, however, as the grounds on which discrimination is prohibited do not include gender identity, political opinion, or other status such as marital. They also voiced concern that instead of creating a new independent office to monitor and promote the new legislation, the institution responsible for this would be the Ombudsperson.

Sexual and reproductive rights

The UN Special Rapporteur on the right to health highlighted in May that the Act on Family Planning, which revoked economic and social reasons as grounds for lawful termination of pregnancies, had

P

resulted in an increase of unsafe, clandestine abortions. In October, the UN Human Rights Committee expressed concern that many women were denied access to reproductive health services, including lawful termination of pregnancy.

Human rights monitoring bodies have further identified a conscientious objection clause in the Act, which allows medical personnel to refuse to perform certain procedures, as an obstacle to accessing reproductive rights. According to a report adopted by the Council of Europe's Social, Health and Family Affairs Committee of the Parliamentary Assembly in September, health care institutions in Poland lacked a formal policy on conscientious objection. The report raised concern over the misuse of this clause by hospital management, who had frequently adopted an unwritten policy of banning some interventions, including abortions.

■ The case of a pregnant woman who died of septic shock after being refused diagnostic care and treatment in several hospitals for fear of risking the life of the foetus was pending before the European Court of Human Rights.

Excessive use of force

In October, the UN Human Rights Committee expressed concerns about reports of excessive use of force by law enforcement officials. It also noted that incidents of police violence were not always reported due to victims' fear of being prosecuted.

■ On 23 May, at a market in Warsaw's Praga district, a police officer shot a 36-year-old Nigerian trader who died on the spot. The incident happened during a police action which reportedly involved a licence check of the market traders. The Prosecutor General's Office started an investigation on 24 May into two cases: excessive use of force by a state agent and bodily harm causing death; and an attack against a public official.

■ One of the leaders of the Campaign Against Homophobia, Robert Biedroń, was arrested and allegedly beaten by the police on 11 November. The incident happened after an anti-fascist demonstration against a march by extreme right groups in Warsaw. Robert Biedroń filed a complaint citing excessive use of force by the police that resulted in a spine injury, bruising and chafing. He was detained for 20 hours and alleged that he had been denied contact with his family and lawyer. The police reportedly accused him of attacking a public official.

Refugees and asylum-seekers

The refugee centre in the town of Łomża was closed in November following a campaign by a Member of Parliament and a petition by 800 citizens of Łomża. During the campaign, the mostly Chechen refugees were labelled as criminals by some media. Various national NGOs protested against the closure during the school year. After the closure, the refugees had to either look for rental housing or another refugee centre with places available.

Rights of lesbian, gay, bisexual and transgender people

A significant rise in hate speech and intolerance against lesbian, gay, bisexual and transgender people was noted by the UN Human Rights Committee in October.

Amnesty International visits/reports

⬛ Open secret: Mounting evidence of Europe's complicity in rendition and secret detention (EUR 01/023/2010)

PORTUGAL

PORTUGUESE REPUBLIC
Head of state:	Aníbal António Cavaco Silva
Head of government:	José Sócrates Carvalho Pinto de Sousa
Death penalty:	abolitionist for all crimes
Population:	10.7 million
Life expectancy:	79.1 years
Under-5 mortality (m/f):	6/5 per 1,000
Adult literacy:	94.6 per cent

There were continued failures to ensure prompt, thorough and impartial investigations into reports of ill-treatment by law enforcement officials. Reports of domestic violence decreased slightly. Roma families living in Beja did not have access to adequate housing.

Torture and other ill-treatment

Following the adoption of the report by the Working Group on the Universal Periodic Review, Portugal made a commitment to increase efforts to ensure prompt, thorough and impartial investigations into allegations of ill-treatment or excessive use of force by law enforcement officials. In at least two cases, there was little or no progress in investigations into such allegations, several years after their occurrence.

■ Leonor Cipriano's appeal against the ruling by the Criminal Court of Faro to acquit the three police officers involved in her detention in 2004 was still pending. The Court had found on 22 May 2009 that she had been tortured in police custody, but claimed it was not able to identify those responsible.

■ Hearings in the trial of three judicial police officers accused of torturing Virgolino Borges in police custody in March 2000 were scheduled but then postponed until the end of the year. The investigation had been closed in 2005 by the Criminal Investigating Court on the grounds that the injuries could have been self-inflicted. Virgolino Borges challenged this decision and in November 2005 the Appeals Court (Tribunal da Relação) ordered the case to go to court.

Violence against women and girls

New regulations to protect women from domestic violence were adopted in April, including provisions recognizing the right of victims to receive information, protection, shelter and financial and other assistance. The number of reports of domestic violence decreased slightly in comparison to 2009; the NGO Association for Victim Support registered 15,236 complaints of domestic violence in 2010 compared with 15,904 in 2009. However, the NGO União de Mulheres Alternativa e Resposta registered 43 murders in 2010, compared with 29 in 2009.

Right to adequate housing – Roma

■ Around 50 Roma families continued to live in the Quinta das Pedreiras neighbourhood in the town of Beja, where they were resettled in 2006 following their eviction from the neighbourhood of Bairro da Esperança. There were continued concerns that the houses in Quinta das Pedreiras did not meet minimum standards of health, sanitation and security. On 29 April, the European Roma Rights Centre filed a complaint with the European Committee for Social Rights, claiming that Portugal had violated the right to housing of the Roma living in Quinta das Pedreiras.

PUERTO RICO

COMMONWEALTH OF PUERTO RICO

Head of state:	Barack H. Obama
Head of government:	Luis Fortuño
Death penalty:	abolitionist for all crimes
Population:	4 million
Life expectancy:	79 years
Under-5 mortality (m/f):	9/8 per 1,000

There were reports of police ill-treatment of students during a demonstration. The living conditions of residents of an informal settlement under a government eviction order remained a concern.

Excessive use of force

In May, during a two-month strike by university students in San Juan, a number of incidents of excessive use of force by officers from the Puerto Rican Police Department were reported.

These incidents included the indiscriminate use of batons and pepper-spray against non-violent protesters during a demonstration by striking students at the Sheraton Hotel on 20 May. Video footage showed police officers shocking a student with a Taser during the demonstration while he was being restrained on the ground by three officers.

Right to adequate housing

In November, the community of Villas de Sol in Toa Baja signed an agreement to form a co-operative on land given to them by the municipality of Toa Baja in exchange for a parcel of land donated to the residents by Doctor Eduardo Ibarra, President of the College of Surgeons. However, at the end of the year the community remained under a government eviction order, which was extended to 31 December 2010, and without permanent access to water and electrical supplies. Amnesty International called on the federal authorities to extend the eviction deadline to 2011 to allow the community sufficient time to build adequate alternative housing on the new land, as well as to allow municipal authorities to ensure adequate housing services, including water, sanitation and electricity were available at the new site.

Amnesty International visits/reports

🔲 Puerto Rico: Amnesty International calls for police restraint as student strike continues (AMR 47/001/2010)

🔲 Puerto Rico: Amnesty International calls for eviction notice for residents of Villas del Sol to be extended into 2011 (AMR 51/108/2010)

QATAR

STATE OF QATAR
Head of state:	Shaikh Hamad bin Khalifa al-Thani
Head of government:	Shaikh Hamad bin Jassim bin Jabr al-Thani
Death penalty:	retentionist
Population:	1.5 million
Life expectancy:	76 years
Under-5 mortality (m/f):	10/10 per 1,000
Adult literacy:	93.1 per cent

Women continued to face discrimination and violence. Migrant workers were exploited and abused, and inadequately protected under the law. Around 100 people remained arbitrarily deprived of their nationality. Sentences of flogging were passed. Death sentences continued to be upheld, although no executions were carried out.

Background

In June, a woman was appointed as a judge, for the first time in Qatar, to the Court of First Instance.

Qatar's human rights record was assessed under the UN Universal Periodic Review in June. Qatar was urged to fulfil its human rights obligations, including by reviewing and repealing laws that discriminate against women. In May, Qatar was re-elected to the UN Human Rights Council.

The Penal Code was amended in June to extensively define torture and intimidation; however, it retains the death penalty as a possible punishment in cases where torture leads to death.

Discrimination and violence against women

Women continued to face discrimination in law and practice and were inadequately protected against violence within the family.

Freedom of expression

At least six foreign nationals were convicted of blasphemy, four of whom received maximum seven-year prison sentences. In July, for example, the Doha Court of First Instance sentenced a Lebanese man to seven years' imprisonment for blasphemy; he was reported to have "uttered blasphemous words" while being carried on a stretcher to an ambulance. It was not clear whether the prison sentence was enforced in this and other cases.

At least 90 people, mostly foreign nationals, were convicted of charges relating to "illicit sexual relations" and either deported or sentenced to imprisonment followed in some cases by deportation. Two men were convicted of sodomy and two other men had their sentences for the same "offence" upheld.

A draft press and publications law to replace Law No 8 of 1979 was approved by the Cabinet but had not been enacted by the end of the year.

Migrants' rights

Migrant workers, who make up more than 80 per cent of Qatar's population, continued to be exposed to abuses and exploitation by employers, despite recent amendments to labour laws. In November, the Prime Minister announced that the sponsorship system was being reviewed and may be amended.

Discrimination – denial of nationality

The government continued to deny Qatari nationality to around 100 people, most of them members of al-Murra tribe that was partly blamed for a coup attempt in 1996. They were consequently denied employment opportunities, social security and health care, or denied entry to the country, and had no means of remedy before the courts.

Freedom of movement

■ Rashid al-Amoodi was informed that he was banned from travelling on 4 July 2009 when he sought to travel from Doha to Dubai. His travel ban was still in force at the end of 2010, although he was not formally informed of it by the authorities or given any opportunity to challenge it. The government gave no reason for the ban.

Detention without charge or trial

Criminal suspects were reported to have been detained without charge or trial.
■ Mohamed Farouk El Mahdy, a UK citizen, was arrested on 15 October 2009 and held without charge or trial until his release on bail on 14 September 2010. He was held in connection with a client of his former employer who was alleged to have defaulted on a loan.

Cruel, inhuman and degrading punishments

At least 21 people, mostly foreign nationals, were sentenced to floggings of between 30 and 100 lashes for offences related to "illicit sexual relations" or alcohol consumption. Only Muslims considered

Q

medically fit were liable to have such sentences carried out. It was not known if any of the sentences were implemented.

Death penalty

The appeal court confirmed at least three death sentences. At least 17 people were believed to be under sentence of death at the end of the year, including at least seven sentenced to death in 2001 for involvement in the 1996 coup attempt. No executions were reported.

In December, Qatar was one of the minority of states that voted against a UN General Assembly resolution calling for a worldwide moratorium on executions.

ROMANIA

ROMANIA

Head of state:	Traian Băsescu
Head of government:	Emil Boc
Death penalty:	abolitionist for all crimes
Population:	21.2 million
Life expectancy:	73.2 years
Under-5 mortality (m/f):	20/15 per 1,000

Roma continued to be victims of ethnic stereotyping and discrimination in access to education, housing and employment. Racist and discriminatory remarks against Roma were reported from senior government figures and continued to be challenged by NGOs. The European Court of Human Rights found that Romania had violated the prohibition of torture and other ill-treatment. Despite new evidence of Romanian participation in the CIA's rendition and secret detention programme, the government continued to deny any involvement.

Background

On 19 May, some 40,000 people attended what was reportedly the largest demonstration since the fall of Nicolae Ceauşescu in 1989. Public sector employees, including teachers and health care workers, as well as pensioners and mothers, protested against the austerity programme agreed to by the government, the International Monetary Fund and the EU to address the economic crisis. The programme stipulated a 25 per cent cut in salaries in the public sector, a 15 per cent cut in pensions, reduction of family benefits and cuts in welfare programmes. In July, the government reduced the capacity of or dissolved several agencies entrusted with promotion of equal opportunities and protection from discrimination. In August, the CERD Committee warned that the austerity measures might have a negative impact on the situation of the most vulnerable groups, and called for the adoption of measures that would ensure protection of such groups from the effects of the crisis.

An unauthorized protest by police officers over wage cuts led to the resignation of the Minister of Interior in September. In October, the government won a vote of no confidence for the second time in four months.

Discrimination – Roma

In spite of protests by NGOs, Roma continued to be victims of negative ethnic stereotyping, including at the highest levels of political discourse. The Minister of Foreign Affairs spoke about "links between criminality and the Romani community" and referred to a "natural" rate of delinquency among Roma. In November, during his visit to Slovenia, the President also referred to Roma as "delinquents" and spoke of them as "difficult to integrate" and "unwilling to work". In December the government submitted a legislative proposal to parliament to change the official name of Roma as a minority to "Ţigan". NGOs protested, given that the name "Ţigan" has pejorative connotations and stigmatizes the community.

In terms of wider society, an opinion poll on the public perception of Roma carried out by the Romanian Institute for Evaluation and Strategy in October showed that 67 per cent of Romanians would not accept a member of the Romani community in their family.

In August, the CERD Committee raised concerns that Roma continued to be victims of racial stereotyping and discrimination in access to quality education, housing, health care services and employment. Romania was criticized for a failure to adopt legislation required to turn previous commitments with regard to the situation of Roma into practice. The NGO Decade Watch concluded in April that this failure resulted from a lack of political will. The NGO Agentia de Dezvoltare Comunitară Împreună had reported in February that implementation of the National Roma Strategy was inadequate due to lack of funding of measures at the county level and lack of indicators to allow monitoring of the different bodies involved.

Right to education

In a response to complaints against segregation of Romani pupils in schools, the Ministry of Education issued an internal guideline in March. This targeted school inspectorates, kindergartens, school principals and teachers and imposed a set of rules for the prevention and elimination of segregation of Romani pupils in the educational system.

■ In May, the Court of Appeal in Craiova upheld the decision of the lower court that a Romani pupil had faced discrimination from her teacher and raised damages awarded from 360 to 10,000 euros. In 2007, the teacher had refused to let the Romani girl attend classes. After several weeks, an intervention by the local school inspectorate and pressure from local media allowed the girl to return to school.

Housing rights

In August, the CERD Committee called on Romania to facilitate access of Roma to housing and to avoid unlawful expropriation and forced evictions without offering alternative accommodation.

■ Approximately 75 Roma, including families with children, who had been forcibly evicted by the local authorities in Miercurea Ciuc in 2004, continued to live in metal mobile cabins next to a sewage treatment plant on the outskirts of the town. The cabins were overcrowded, and sanitation facilities were woefully inadequate, with only four toilet cubicles for the entire community. Despite promises at the time that the cabins would be temporary, by the end of the year the local authorities had still not provided adequate alternative accommodation.

■ On 10 June, the Deputy Mayor of the town of Baia Mare announced a plan to evict approximately 200 Romani families from the Craica area of the town and demolish their homes. According to local NGOs, some of the families received notification of the eviction in February, but it was not carried out due to weather conditions. Individuals and families not originally from Baia Mare were reportedly to be sent back to their original place of residence.

■ On 17 December, 56 Roma families were forcibly evicted from Coastei Street in the city of Cluj. About 40 families were relocated to housing units that did not meet the criteria for adequate housing, and the remaining families were made homeless by the eviction.

Torture and other ill-treatment

Concerns of inadequate implementation of the prohibition of torture and other ill-treatment persisted, in particular with regard to the failure to prohibit the use of evidence gathered under torture or other ill-treatment in the criminal code, despite amendments in May.

In August, the CERD Committee noted excessive use of force and ill-treatment by law enforcement officials against minorities, and Roma in particular. Local NGOs also expressed concerns about continuing reports of torture and other ill-treatment in detention, and an ongoing climate of impunity in some cases.

■ In June, the European Court of Human Rights found Romania in breach of the prohibition of torture and other ill-treatment in the case of Dragoş Ciupercescu represented by the Romanian Helsinki Committee (APADOR-CH). In 2003 while in pre-trial detention, Dragoş Ciupercescu had been subjected to strip-searches carried out by masked wardens, and held in a nine-bed cell together with 19 other prisoners where each of them had $0.75m^2$ of living space.

■ In July, the European Court of Human Rights held that Romania had violated the prohibition of torture and failed to carry out an effective investigation into a death, thereby also violating the right to a remedy. The case involved Gabriel Carabulea, a Romani man who died in police custody in May 1996. In an investigation into the case, the military prosecutor had determined in 1998 that the man had died of heart disease. The European Court concluded that his death resulted from a blunt force trauma which he suffered after the arrest and that the injuries appeared to have been inflicted upon him intentionally.

Counter-terror and security

In February, a UN Study on secret detention concluded that a plane operating within the CIA's rendition programme flew from Poland to Romania on 22 September 2003. In response, the Romanian authorities acknowledged that several planes leased by the CIA made stopovers in Romania, but denied that the planes had carried detainees or that the country had hosted a secret detention site.

In July, the Polish Border Guard Office released information about the flight on 22 September 2003 which loaded passengers in Poland and flew to Romania. The government continued to deny any involvement in the CIA's rendition and secret detention programme.

R

Amnesty International visits/reports

🚌 Amnesty International delegates visited Romania in August and December.

📄 Treated like waste: Roma homes destroyed, and health at risk, in Romania (EUR 39/001/2010)

📄 Romania: Stop forced eviction of Romani settlement in Craica, Baia Mare (EUR 39/002/2010)

📄 Romania: Roma in Miercurea Ciuc continue to suffer violations of their right to adequate housing EUR (39/005/2010)

📄 Open secret: Mounting evidence of Europe's complicity in rendition and secret detention (EUR 01/023/2010)

RUSSIAN FEDERATION

RUSSIAN FEDERATION

Head of state:	Dmitry Medvedev
Head of government:	Vladimir Putin
Death penalty:	abolitionist in practice
Population:	140.4 million
Life expectancy:	67.2 years
Under-5 mortality (m/f):	18/14 per 1,000
Adult literacy:	99.5 per cent

Human rights defenders and independent journalists continued to face threats, harassment and attacks, and investigations yielded few concrete results. Freedom of assembly and expression continued to come under attack, including through the banning of demonstrations, their violent dispersal and the prosecution of individuals under anti-extremism legislation. The security situation in the North Caucasus remained volatile. Attacks by armed groups and persistent human rights violations, including killings, enforced disappearances and torture, continued to affect the region. Across Russia, there were frequent reports of torture and other ill-treatment by law enforcement officials.

Background

At the end of the year, Russia seemed to have weathered the economic crisis without major social, economic or political upheaval. There was some improvement in relations with a number of neighbouring and western countries.

The leadership continued to stress its commitment to modernization, including by strengthening the rule of law and reforming the justice system. However, pervasive corruption and the ineffective separation of powers were widely perceived as obstructing this agenda.

The year was marked by the activities of various social movements across the country, often at a very local level, on a range of issues including violations of civil and political rights, environmental concerns and pressing social needs. Protests in Moscow, St Petersburg and elsewhere were mostly peaceful, though several unauthorized actions were dispersed by law enforcement officials using excessive force.

There were concerns about the strong political bias in the broadcast and printed media, but electronic media displayed more pluralism. Digital video and online social networks were used creatively to mobilize social activism and expose human rights violations. State media, in particular television, was frequently employed as a vehicle for discrediting opposition politicians, neighbouring leaders and civil society activists.

The Russian authorities failed to further investigate human rights violations carried out by armed forces in the August 2008 conflict with Georgia. Russia and the de facto authorities in South Ossetia failed to co-operate with investigations by the Council of Europe into the fate of missing people, or to provide access for the EU Monitoring Mission to the conflict-affected areas in South Ossetia.

Torture and other ill-treatment

Reports of torture and other ill-treatment by law enforcement officials, often allegedly with the purpose of extracting confessions or money, remained widespread. Corruption and collusion between the police, investigators and prosecutors were widely perceived as undermining the effectiveness of investigations and obstructing prosecutions. Detainees frequently reported unlawful disciplinary punishments and the denial of necessary medical care.

■ On the night of 31 August, 17-year-old Nikita Kaftasyev and a friend were stopped by the police in Kstovo in the Nizhnii Novgorod region. Nikita Kaftasyev alleged that he and his friend were beaten by the police. They were held overnight at the police station, where the beatings continued. Nikita Kaftasyev suffered serious injuries to his genitals. The next morning he reported that the police took him home, and then tried to make his mother sign a statement that she had no claims against the police.

Justice system

Judicial reform continued to be presented as a government priority. However, reforms remained piecemeal and had only a limited impact on the underlying structural deficiencies. Major causes of these were the widespread corruption within, and political influence on, the justice system.

Following widespread criticism of police abuse, including from within the law enforcement agencies, the government presented a new draft law on police. Human rights organizations expressed concern that the proposal failed to introduce effective mechanisms to make law enforcement officials accountable for abuses and human rights violations.

In a move intended to increase the independence of criminal investigations, the government announced in September that the Investigative Committee would be transformed, as of 2011, into an independent investigative body. It would be answerable directly to the President and removed from the control of the Prosecutor General's Office. The Committee had been originally created in 2007 in order to separate investigative and prosecutorial functions.

Widespread concern over deaths in custody resulting from the denial of adequate medical care led to changes in the law governing pre-trial detention. House arrest and restrictions on the use of pre-trial detention were introduced for people suspected of economic crimes. The Prosecutor General's Office concluded that inadequate medical treatment had caused the death in custody of lawyer Sergei Magnitskii in November 2009, though no one was prosecuted for this.

Concerns over the independence of prosecutors and the judiciary grew in the course of the second trial of Mikhail Khodorkovsky and Platon Lebedev on charges relating to the theft of oil produced by YUKOS. The charges appeared to be politically motivated. On 30 December they were each sentenced to a total of 14 years' imprisonment following an unfair trial that was marred by procedural violations, including the harassment of witnesses and the court's refusal to hear key defence witnesses. The two men would therefore be due for release in 2017, taking account of time already spent in detention.

Freedom of assembly

The clampdown on social activism continued, especially on those groups which raised controversial issues, were capable of mobilizing public dissent or were funded from abroad. Organizers often faced harassment and intimidation, including from law enforcement officials and members of pro-government organizations. Several peaceful demonstrations in Moscow and St. Petersburg were declared unauthorized and forcibly dispersed resulting in scores of demonstrators being held for several hours in police custody. Some demonstrators were sentenced to several days of detention solely for exercising their right to freedom of assembly.

In October, activists united in the "Strategy 31" movement were finally allowed to organize a peaceful demonstration in support of freedom of assembly in Triumfalnaya Square in Moscow. Since May 2009, the movement had been denied permission to assemble in the square on at least 10 occasions.

Widespread public protests against the planned construction of a highway through Khimki forest near Moscow led to the project being halted for a few months while at the same time activists faced intimidation and harassment. Konstantin Fetisov, a peaceful protester against the project, was assaulted in November by unknown men and seriously injured.

In an unprecedented decision in October, a court in St Petersburg declared the banning of a parade by LGBT rights activists by the city council had been unlawful. Later that month, the European Court of Human Rights ruled that the banning of Pride marches by the Moscow city authorities in 2006, 2007 and 2008 had violated the right to freedom of peaceful assembly and that the organizers had been discriminated against on the grounds of their sexual orientation.

Freedom of expression

Journalists, ecological activists, members of the political opposition and human rights defenders faced harassment, intimidation and attacks. The authorities continued to send out mixed messages on freedom of expression. They promised greater respect and protection for journalists and civil society activists, while at the same time launching, or failing to curb, smear campaigns against prominent government critics.

In November, journalist Oleg Kashin was violently attacked in Moscow. The attack sparked widespread outrage and a promise from President Medvedev that the attack would be diligently investigated.

Investigations into attacks on, and the murders of, other prominent human rights defenders and journalists produced few results. The Investigative Committee continued to name the same men as

R

suspects in the murder of journalist and human rights defender Anna Politkovskaya, shot in October 2006, although they had been acquitted on the grounds of insufficient evidence.

Vague definitions in the law on combating extremism were frequently exploited to restrict freedom of expression.

■ In January the Supreme Court of Tatarstan confirmed the sentence of Irek Murtazin, the former press officer of the President of Tatarstan, who was sentenced in 2009 to 18 months' imprisonment in an open colony for inciting hatred against the government. He had published a book criticizing the Tatarstan authorities.

■ In July, Andrei Yerofeev and Yuri Samodurov were convicted and fined for inciting hatred against the Orthodox Church. In 2007, they had organized an exhibition entitled "Forbidden Art 2006", which displayed contemporary art that had previously been removed from museums and exhibitions on account of its controversial content.

■ A member of the Jehovah's Witnesses faced trial at the end of the year in the Gorny-Altai region on charges of inciting hatred after he distributed leaflets of his religious denomination.

Human rights defenders

The environment for human rights defenders and independent NGOs remained difficult. Threats, assaults, administrative harassment and public attacks on their character and integrity continued, with the intention of impeding their work and undermining their credibility with the public.

■ In April, the Investigative Committee announced that it had identified the murderer of Natalia Estemirova, a human rights defender from Chechnya who was killed on 15 July 2009. According to the Investigative Committee, her murderers were members of an armed group, an explanation which was widely doubted.

■ In May, human rights defender Aleksei Sokolov was sentenced to five years' imprisonment for theft and robbery. There were reports at the time that the trial procedures were unfair. In August the sentence was reduced to three years. Aleksei Sokolov was transferred from his native Sverdlovsk Region to Krasnoyarsk in Siberia to serve his sentence. Reportedly, he was beaten and ill-treated on the journey to Krasnoyarsk. Friends and colleagues remained concerned that the case against him had been fabricated in order to stop his activities for the protection of detainees.

■ In September, the criminal trial of Oleg Orlov, head of

the human rights centre Memorial, started. He faced charges of defamation following his remarks about the responsibility of the Chechen President for the murder of his colleague Natalia Estemirova in July 2009.

Racism

Racially motivated violence remained a serious problem. According to preliminary data from the SOVA Center for Information and Analysis, 37 people died as a result of hate crimes. In April, Moscow judge Eduard Chuvashov was killed, reportedly by members of a far-right group, after he had sentenced several perpetrators of hate crimes to long-term imprisonment. In October, 22-year-old Vasilii Krivets was sentenced to life imprisonment for the murder of 15 people of non-Slavic appearance. The detention of two suspects in the murder of lawyer Stanislav Markelov and journalist Anastasia Baburova in January 2009 was extended until the end of the year. The investigation announced that the two suspects belonged to a right-wing group and had planned to kill Stanislav Markelov following his representation of the family of a murdered anti-fascist campaigner.

Insecurity in the North Caucasus

The security situation in the North Caucasus remained volatile, with violence continuing to spread beyond Chechnya to the neighbouring regions of Dagestan, Ingushetia, Kabardino-Balkaria and North Ossetia. Government authorities publicly acknowledged that measures to combat armed violence were not effective. High numbers of law enforcement officials were killed in attacks by armed groups, who also targeted civilians indiscriminately in suicide bombings. In September, a car bomb in Vladikavkaz, North Ossetia-Alania, reportedly killed at least 17 people and left over 100 injured.

Across the North Caucasus, law enforcement officials were accused of human rights violations. Accusations included unlawful detention, torture and, in some cases, extrajudicial execution of people suspected of belonging to armed groups. There was a complete lack of effective investigations into these human rights violations and subsequent accountability. Journalists and human rights activists who reported on such violations faced intimidation and harassment.

In its June session, the Parliamentary Assembly of the Council of Europe discussed the effectiveness of legal mechanisms in addressing human rights violations in the North Caucasus. It called on the Russian authorities to implement the decisions of the European Court of Human Rights and abstain from unlawful measures in its fight against armed groups and terrorism.

Chechnya

The relatives of suspected armed fighters continued to allege that they were being targeted. Journalists and civil society organizations faced strict controls and intimidation from the authorities. Government officials hampered investigations into enforced disappearances, torture and unlawful detention when they refused to co-operate with investigative bodies.

■ In February, at least four Chechen civilians were reportedly deliberately killed by law enforcement agencies when picking wild garlic at the border between Chechnya and Ingushetia. The authorities claimed they had killed armed fighters in an operation in a sealed-off territory, but survivors of the group of garlic pickers gave a different account. At least one of the victims was knifed; others were shot at point blank range.

■ In April, Islam Umarpashaev from Grozny was released after being held incommunicado and chained to a radiator since December 2009 in an unknown location by men believed to be members of law enforcement bodies. He was not charged with any crime. His family filed a complaint with the authorities and the European Court of Human Rights regarding his unlawful detention. Islam Umarpashaev, who went into hiding after his release, and his family were put under severe pressure to withdraw their complaints.

In a further sign of increasing restrictions on the freedom of expression of Chechen women, there were several reported instances of women being shot at with paint ball guns apparently for failing to wear headscarves.

Dagestan

According to the authorities, the number of attacks on police and government officials rose by 20 per cent, while Russian human rights organizations reported an increase in arbitrary detentions and enforced disappearances. Lawyers, journalists and human rights defenders faced increased attacks and harassment.

■ In June, lawyer Sapiyat Magomedova, was reportedly severely beaten by police officers while visiting a client who was detained at a police station in the city of Khasavyurt. She was subsequently charged with insulting public officials.

■ In July, another lawyer, Dzhamilya Tagirova, was reportedly assaulted by an investigator inside a police station in the capital Makhachkala, when she objected to the misrepresentation of her client's statements in the interview record drawn up by the officer.

Two more female lawyers from Dagestan were reportedly assaulted by law enforcement officers in the course of fulfilling their duties as legal representatives.

■ On 3 June 2010, the Supreme Court of Dagestan sentenced Rasil Mamedrizaev to 15 years' imprisonment for the murder of Farid Babaev, head of the Dagestan branch of the party "Yabloko". Farid Babaev, who had highlighted many human rights violations in Dagestan and had stood for election to the Russian parliament, was shot in November 2007.

■ In July, 14-year-old Makhmud Akhmedov was detained by police. He stated he had been held overnight in police custody and was tortured and otherwise ill-treated in order to extract a confession of having stolen an electric drill. A criminal investigation was opened, and four police officers charged in December.

Ingushetia

Despite efforts by the President of Ingushetia to promote dialogue with independent human rights organizations, serious human rights violations continued and journalists and human rights activists continued to face threats and attacks.

■ In June, brothers Beslan and Adam Tsechoev were detained by a group of masked police officers at their home, and then ill-treated and held incommunicado for six days at the Malgobek District Police Department. Beslan Tsechoev remained in detention at the end of the year. Despite the well-documented nature of his injuries, including by the Human Rights Commissioner of Ingushetia, the Prosecutor's Office refused to open a criminal investigation.

■ In July, Mustafa Mutsolgov and Vakha Sapraliev were allegedly extrajudicially executed by law enforcement officers, who reportedly took them out of the car they were driving and handcuffed them before shooting them at close range. In August, masked law enforcement officers reportedly beat and ill-treated Mutstafa Mutsolgov's father, Alikhan Mutsolgov, and took his 15-year-old brother Magomed away and subjected him to torture and other ill-treatment, forcing him to implicate his deceased brother in illegal activities. By the end of the year, family members were yet to receive confirmation that their complaints were being investigated.

Amnesty International visits/reports

🚃 Amnesty International delegates visited Ingushetia in November.

📃 Russian Federation: Briefing to the UN Committee on the Elimination of Discrimination against Women (EUR 46/022/2010)

R

RWANDA

REPUBLIC OF RWANDA

Head of state:	Paul Kagame
Head of government:	Bernard Makuza
Death penalty:	abolitionist for all crimes
Population:	10.3 million
Life expectancy:	51.1 years
Under-5 mortality (m/f):	167/143 per 1,000
Adult literacy:	70.3 per cent

The authorities restricted freedom of expression and association before presidential elections in August. Media outlets that criticized the government were closed down and editors fled Rwanda. Human rights defenders faced intimidation. Investigations into killings were inadequate. High-ranking military officers were detained without trial. Some improvements in the justice system were offset by laws criminalizing dissent. No country extradited genocide suspects to Rwanda.

Background

A clampdown on freedom of expression and association before August's presidential elections prevented new opposition parties from fielding candidates. President Paul Kagame was re-elected with 93 per cent of the vote.

Growing splits emerged within the ruling party, the Rwandan Patriotic Front (RPF). The former head of the army, Faustin Kayumba Nyamwasa, fled to South Africa. Some senior military officers were arrested and held incommunicado. Others fled to neighbouring countries.

Tension grew between the government and supporters of Laurent Nkunda, the former leader of the Congolese armed group the National Congress for the Defence of the People (CNDP). Arrested in January 2009, he remained under house arrest in Rwanda without charge or trial.

Grenade attacks in Rwanda's capital, Kigali, led to heightened security concerns.

Rwanda's hostile response to a UN mapping report on human rights violations in the Democratic Republic of Congo (DRC) between 1993 and 2003 drew attention to impunity for past abuses by the Rwandan Patriotic Army.

International donors grew increasingly concerned about the deteriorating human rights situation. The EU, France, Spain, the UN and the USA publicly expressed concern before the elections.

Freedom of expression

Freedom of expression was further restricted. The RPF became increasingly sensitive to criticism in advance of the presidential elections.

Laws on 'genocide ideology' and 'sectarianism'

The authorities continued to misuse broad and ill-defined laws on "genocide ideology" and "sectarianism". The laws prohibit hate speech, but also criminalize legitimate criticism of the government.

In April, the government announced a review of the "genocide ideology" law, and indicated that the "sectarianism" law might also be reviewed. However, the government continued to use these laws and the timeframe for review remained unclear.

■ Bernard Ntaganda, the leader of an opposition party, PS-Imberakuri, was arrested in June and remained in detention in December. Charges against him included inciting ethnic division in relation to statements criticizing government policies.

■ Victoire Ingabire, the leader of FDU-Inkingi, an opposition party seeking registration, was arrested in April and rearrested in October. Charges against her included "genocide ideology" and were based, in part, on her public call for the prosecution of RPF war crimes.

Journalists

The government used regulatory sanctions, restrictive laws and criminal defamation cases to close down media outlets critical of the government. In July, the government began to enforce certain aspects of a 2009 media law which maintains defamation as a criminal offence. Some leading editors and journalists fled the country after facing threats and harassment.

■ The Rwandan Media High Council (MHC), a regulatory body close to the ruling party, suspended two private Kinyarwanda newspapers, Umuseso and Umuvugizi, from April to October. The MHC alleged that the newspapers had insulted the President and caused trouble in the army.

■ Jean-Léonard Rugambage, a journalist working for Umuvugizi, was shot dead on 24 June outside his home in Kigali. He had been investigating the shooting in South Africa of Kayumba Nyamwasa, and his newspaper published a story alleging that Rwandan intelligence was involved. In October, two men were convicted of Jean-Léonard Rugambage's murder and sentenced to life imprisonment. The convicted men claimed that Jean-Léonard Rugambage had killed a member of one of their families during the 1994 genocide, although he had previously been acquitted in gacaca proceedings.

- Jean-Bosco Gasasira, editor of *Umuvugizi* and Didas Gasana, editor of *Umuseso*, fled Rwanda in April and May respectively after receiving threats.

Human rights defenders

Human rights defenders faced renewed threats, including from government representatives. They self-censored their work to avoid confrontation with the authorities.

The government expelled a staff member of Human Rights Watch from Rwanda. Other international NGOs reported increased constraints on their work. International human rights groups, including Amnesty International, were attacked in speeches by senior government officials.

A Rwandan government representative criticized Rwandan human rights organizations at the African Commission on Human and Peoples' Rights in May.

Freedom of association

Restrictions on freedom of association prevented new opposition parties from contesting the elections. FDU-Inkingi and the Democratic Green Party were unable to obtain security clearance to organize meetings needed for their registration. The only new party to secure registration, PS-Imberakuri, was infiltrated by dissident members and decided not to stand.

Opposition politicians were harassed and threatened. Investigations into threats were cursory and did not lead to prosecutions.

Prisoner of conscience

Charles Ntakirutinka, a former government minister, remained in Kigali Central Prison, serving a 10-year sentence due to end in 2012. He had been convicted, in an unfair trial, of inciting civil disobedience and association with criminal elements.

Justice system

Witness protection staff received training and kept better records. Concerns remained about the willingness of witnesses to testify, given restrictions on freedom of expression through laws on "genocide ideology" and "sectarianism".

In October, Rwanda promulgated a law on "life imprisonment with special provisions", the sentence which replaced the death penalty. The law requires prisoners to be kept in individual cells for up to 20 years, which could constitute prolonged solitary confinement for those whose family members are unwilling or unable to visit. Such prisoners would only have the right to communicate with a lawyer in the presence of a prison guard, violating their defence rights during appeal hearings and possibly preventing prisoners from reporting abuse. The sentence was not applied due to a lack of individual cells.

Prison overcrowding continued to be a problem.

The deadline to complete gacaca trials of genocide cases was postponed indefinitely in September.

Enforced disappearances

At least four individuals disappeared between March and May. Some were close to Laurent Nkunda's wing of the CNDP or had past links to armed groups in the DRC. Their whereabouts remained unknown at the end of the year. At least one of these individuals, Robert Ndengeye Urayeneza, was believed to have been subjected to enforced disappearance and detained in Rwandan military custody.

Ill-treatment by police

Some members of PS-Imberakuri and FDU-Inkingi arrested in June and July were ill-treated by the police. They were beaten and were handcuffed to other prisoners, including while going to the toilet.

Military justice

Several high-ranking military officials were arrested and detained without charge. They were denied access to legal counsel and held under house arrest or incommunicado in military detention for several months.
- Lt. Col. Rugigana Ngabo, the younger brother of Kayumba Nyamwasa, was arrested in August on allegations of destabilizing national security. He was held incommunicado without charge.

International justice

International Criminal Tribunal for Rwanda

The mandate of the International Criminal Tribunal for Rwanda (ICTR) was extended until the end of 2011 for first-instance trials and to the end of 2012 for appeals. Ten suspects subject to arrest warrants by the ICTR remained at large. The ICTR Prosecutor made new applications in November to transfer cases to Rwanda. Past applications failed after Trial Chambers decided that the accused would not receive fair trials.

Universal jurisdiction – genocide suspects living abroad

Judicial proceedings against genocide suspects took place in Belgium, Finland, Netherlands, Spain,

R

Switzerland, and the USA. Sweden consented to extradition in 2009, but the case has yet to be decided before the European Court of Human Rights. No country extradited genocide suspects to Rwanda due to fair trial concerns.

International Criminal Court

The Rwandan executive secretary of the Democratic Forces for the Liberation of Rwanda (FDLR), Callixte Mbarushimana, was arrested in October in France after an arrest warrant was issued by the International Criminal Court (ICC) for war crimes and crimes against humanity committed in eastern DRC in 2009. France had granted him refugee status in 2003 and French prosecuting authorities had declined to open criminal investigations into earlier allegations of his involvement in the Rwandan genocide. In November, his surrender to the ICC was ordered by the Paris Appeal Court.

Impunity for war crimes and crimes against humanity

■ A Spanish judge requested the extradition of Kayumba Nyamwasa from South Africa, where he fled from Rwanda in February. He was indicted by Spain in 2008 on charges of war crimes and crimes against humanity committed in 1994, as well as the murder of three Spanish aid workers in 1997 in Rwanda. Rwanda also requested his extradition on charges of threatening state security. South Africa had not acted on either request by the end of the year.

■ French magistrates conducted investigations in Rwanda in September into the shooting down of the plane in April 1994 which killed Rwandan President Juvénal Habyarimana and sparked the genocide. It was the first time that French magistrates had visited Rwanda as part of their investigations. French judges dropped international arrest warrants issued in November 2006 against nine senior RPF members for shooting down the plane, in which French nationals were also killed, and instead placed some of these individuals under investigation.

Failure to investigate and prosecute killings

Rwandan authorities failed to adequately investigate and prosecute killings before the elections.

■ André Kagwa Rwisereka, Vice President of the opposition Democratic Green Party, was found dead in Butare on 14 July. André Rwisereka, who left the RPF to create the Democratic Green Party, had been concerned for his security in the weeks before his murder. The police opened investigations, but the prosecution claimed to have insufficient evidence to press charges.

■ Denis Ntare Semadwinga was stabbed to death at his home in Gisenyi on 20 June. Before his murder, he had been questioned by Rwandan security services about his relationship with Laurent Nkunda.

Refugees and asylum-seekers

The government exerted pressure on neighbouring countries to repatriate refugees. UNHCR, the UN refugee agency, announced that a cessation clause for Rwandan refugees in the Great Lakes region could be invoked by the end of December 2011, meaning that they would lose their refugee status, but only if certain indicators of progress were attained.

On 14 and 15 July, a joint operation between the Ugandan and Rwandan authorities forcibly returned around 1,700 failed asylum-seekers and some refugees from Nakivale and Kyaka II camps in south-western Uganda. The operation violated international refugee and human rights law. Rwandans, including a number of recognized refugees, were forced onto trucks at gunpoint. Several were injured, including pregnant women. At least one man died after jumping off a truck.

Amnesty International visits/reports

🚙 Amnesty International delegates visited Rwanda in March and September.

📑 Rwanda: Politician charged, was not ill-treated (AFR 47/002/2010)

📑 Rwanda: End human rights clampdown before presidential elections (AFR 47/003/2010)

📑 Investigate murder of Rwandan journalist, Jean-Léonard Rugambage (AFR 47/004/2010)

📑 Completing the work of the International Criminal Tribunals for the former Yugoslavia and Rwanda (REG 01/005/2010)

📑 Safer to stay silent: The chilling effect of Rwanda's laws on "genocide ideology" and "sectarianism" (AFR 47/005/2010)

📑 Rwanda: Pre-election attacks on Rwandan politicians and journalists condemned, 4 August 2010

📑 Rwanda: Opposition leader must receive fair trial (PRE 01/139/2010)

📑 Rwanda: Intimidation of opposition parties must end (PRE 01/058/2010)

R

SAUDI ARABIA

KINGDOM OF SAUDI ARABIA
Head of state and government: **King Abdullah bin 'Abdul 'Aziz Al-Saud**
Death penalty: **retentionist**
Population: **26.2 million**
Life expectancy: **73.3 years**
Under-5 mortality (m/f): **26/17 per 1,000**
Adult literacy: **85.5 per cent**

Over 100 suspects in security-related offences were detained in 2010. The legal status and conditions of imprisonment of thousands of security detainees arrested in previous years, including prisoners of conscience, remained shrouded in secrecy. At least two detainees died in custody, possibly as a result of torture, and new information came to light about methods of torture and other ill-treatment used against security detainees. Cruel, inhuman and degrading punishments, particularly flogging, continued to be imposed and carried out. Women and girls remained subject to discrimination and violence, with some cases receiving wide media attention. Both Christians and Muslims were arrested for expressing their religious beliefs. Saudi Arabian forces involved in a conflict in northern Yemen carried out attacks that appeared to be indiscriminate or disproportionate and to have caused civilian deaths and injuries in violation of international humanitarian law. Foreign migrant workers were exploited and abused by their employers. The authorities violated the rights of refugees and asylum-seekers. At least 27 prisoners were executed, markedly fewer than in the two preceding years.

Background

In February, the Minister of Justice said that Saudi Arabia aimed to build a justice system incorporating the best of other states' judicial systems, inc11luding to provide an effective legal framework against terrorism and to allow women lawyers to represent clients in courts dealing with domestic disputes. However, at the end of 2010 the justice system remained largely secret. A *fatwa* (No. 239 of 12 April 2010), criminalizing the "financing of terrorism", was issued by the Council of Senior 'Ulema. It provided judges with discretion to impose any sentence, including the death penalty.

In May, the King ordered the formation of a committee to streamline procedures based on Shari'a (Islamic law) and to limit corporal punishment; this was expected to limit floggings to 100 lashes, so ending judges' discretion that in some cases had led to sentences of tens of thousands of lashes. The reform had not been introduced by the end of 2010.

Counter-terror and security

Over 100 people were detained for suspected security-related offences, and the legal status of thousands of others arrested in previous years remained unclear and secret.

■ In March, the authorities said they had detained 113 such suspects in recent months: 58 Saudi Arabians, 52 Yemenis, one Somali, one Bangladeshi and one Eritrean national. One of the 58 Saudi Arabians, a woman named as Haylah al-Qassir, was reported to have been arrested in February in Buraidah. The 113 were said by the authorities to have comprised three armed cells and to have been planning violent attacks; they were said to have been uncovered after two suspected al-Qa'ida members were killed by security forces in October 2009 in Jizan province. No further information was disclosed.

■ Dr Ahmad 'Abbas Ahmad Muhammad, an Egyptian national, continued to be held at al-Hair prison in Riyadh. His legal status was unclear. He was arrested shortly after a suicide bombing in May 2003 in Riyadh which killed 35 people. He had reportedly travelled to Saudi Arabia from Egypt to take a job at a health centre.

At least 12 suspects detained in previous years were released in July apparently after the authorities decided that they no longer posed a threat after they attended a "rehabilitation programme". Ten others, all reported to be former Guantánamo Bay detainees returned to Saudi Arabia by the US authorities, received suspended prison sentences in March ranging from 3 to 13 years and were banned from travelling outside Saudi Arabia for five years. No details were available about their trial or the charges they faced. Some 15 other Saudi Arabians remained in US detention at Guantánamo Bay.

In June, the Deputy Minister of Interior told *Okaz* newspaper that a large number of detainees were being tried and that each would "get what he deserves", but gave no details. In September, press reports suggested that courts comprising three judges were being established to try defendants facing capital charges, while single-judge courts would try other defendants. The reports suggested

S

that these courts were about to begin operation in Jeddah and then move to Riyadh. The first trial of 16 defendants opened in October in a prison in Jeddah; among the defendants were seven advocates of peaceful political reform who had been detained since February 2007. The trial was held in camera and the authorities did not disclose the precise charges; the defendants were not permitted access to lawyers.

■ Sulaiman al-Rashudi, a former judge in his seventies, was arrested on 2 February 2007 in Jeddah along with other advocates of reform and was among the 16 defendants brought to trial in October. In August 2009, human rights activists had petitioned the Board of Grievances, an administrative court, to order the Ministry of Interior to release him. The Ministry declared that the administrative court was not competent to hear the case because Sulaiman al-Rashudi had been charged and his case had been referred to the Special Criminal Court.

Freedom of religion

Scores of Muslims and Christians were arrested in connection with their religious beliefs or expression of those beliefs. Members of the Shi'a Muslim community were targeted for holding collective prayer meetings, celebrating Shi'a religious festivals and on suspicion of breaching restrictions on building Shi'a mosques and religious schools.

■ Turki Haydar Muhammad al-'Ali and five other people, mostly students, were arrested in January after posters of an al-Hussainiya (Shi'a religious centre) were displayed on the occasion of their holy day of 'Ashura in December 2009. They were detained without charge or trial at al-Ihsa prison and all were believed to be still held at the end of 2010.

■ Makhlaf Daham al-Shammari, a human rights activist and a Sunni Muslim, was arrested on 15 June after he published an article criticizing what he said was prejudice by Sunni religious scholars against members of the Shi'a community and their beliefs. He was still held at Dammam General Prison at the end of 2010; an appeal against his arbitrary detention submitted to the Board of Grievances had not been heard by the end of the year.

■ In October, 12 Filipinos and a Roman Catholic priest were arrested in Riyadh by religious police who raided a religious service being held in secret; they appeared to be accused of proselytizing. They were released on bail the following day.

Torture and other ill-treatment

The authorities maintained a high degree of secrecy about detainees and their detention conditions and treatment, but reports emerged of at least two deaths in custody, possibly as a result of torture or other ill-treatment.

■ Dr Muhammad Amin al-Namrat, a Jordanian, died in January in the General Intelligence prison in 'Asir province. An Arabic teacher, he was reported to have been sentenced to two years in prison in 2007 for urging his students to take up arms against US forces in Iraq. He appeared to have been detained beyond the expiry of his sentence. No official investigation into his death was reported.

■ Mohammed Farhan died in September while detained at a police station in Jubail. A medical report was said to have referred to marks of strangulation on his neck. No investigation into his death was reported to have taken place by the end of the year.

A former detainee who had been held in Riyadh's 'Ulaysha prison as a security suspect in 2007 and 2008 told Amnesty International that he had been kept handcuffed and shackled for 27 days following his arrest before the handcuffs were removed and he was allowed to take a shower for the first time. He said that he had been interrogated during the night for more than a month and that this was routine for security suspects.

Cruel, inhuman and degrading punishments

Corporal punishment, particularly flogging, was routinely imposed as a sentence by the courts and carried out as the main or as an additional punishment.

■ In January, a court in Jubail sentenced a 13-year-old school girl to 90 lashes, to be carried out in front of her classmates, after it convicted her of assaulting a teacher. She was also sentenced to two months' imprisonment. Further details were not known and it was not clear whether the flogging was carried out or not.

■ In November, a man was reported to have been sentenced to 500 lashes and five years' imprisonment by a court in Jeddah for homosexuality, among other charges.

Women's rights

Women continued to face discrimination in law and in practice and to be subjected to domestic and other violence. The law does not give women equal status with men, and rules on male guardianship subordinate women to men in relation to marriage,

S

divorce, child custody and freedom of movement. This leaves women vulnerable to violence within the home, which may be committed by men with impunity.

■ The case of a 12-year-old girl whose father had forcibly married her to an 80-year-old man for money was widely publicized in Saudi Arabia and abroad. Legal action by local human rights activists highlighted the case and resulted in the girl obtaining a divorce in February.

■ In February, the Supreme Judicial Council overturned a lower court decision in 2006 requiring a married couple, Fatima al-Azzaz and Mansur al-Taimani, to divorce against their wishes. The earlier case had been brought by the brother of Fatima al-Azzaz on the ground that her husband was from a tribe of lower social status and therefore did not satisfy the rule of parity of status, which provides that spouses must be of equal social status or the marriage will be invalid.

In November, Saudi Arabia was elected to the board of a new UN body established to promote women's rights.

Migrants' rights

The sponsorship system governing employment of foreign nationals continued to expose them to exploitation and abuse by private and government employers, and allowed them little or no redress. Typical abuses included long working hours, non-payment of salaries, being refused permission to return home after completing their contracts and violence, particularly against women domestic workers.

■ Yahya Mokhtar, a Sudanese medical doctor who had been stranded with his family since 2008 because his former employer refused to allow him to leave Saudi Arabia, was allowed to return to Sudan in May.

■ L.P. Ariyawathie, a Sri Lankan employed as a domestic worker, was found to have 24 nails and a needle driven into her hands, leg and forehead when she returned to Sri Lanka in August. She said that the injuries had been inflicted by her employer when she complained about her heavy workload. It was unclear whether the Saudi Arabian authorities were investigating the matter.

■ An Indonesian domestic worker, Sumiati Binti Salan Mustapa, was hospitalized in Madina following reports that her employers cut her face with scissors, burned her with an iron and beat her. The mutilated body of another Indonesian worker, Kikim Komalasari, was found in a skip in Abha. The Saudi Arabian and Indonesian authorities were said to be investigating the cases.

Air strikes and killings of civilians in northern Yemen

In November 2009, Saudi Arabian forces became involved in the conflict between Yemeni government forces and Huthi rebels in the Sa'dah area of Yemen (see Yemen entry). Saudi Arabian forces clashed with armed Huthis and carried out air strikes against towns and villages in Sa'dah. Some of these attacks appeared to be indiscriminate or disproportionate and to have caused civilian deaths and injuries in violation of international humanitarian law. They ceased when the Yemeni government and Huthi rebels agreed a ceasefire in February.

Refugees and asylum-seekers

In June and July, the authorities forcibly returned some 2,000 Somali nationals to Somalia, despite the continuing armed conflict there and appeals from UNHCR, the UN refugee agency. Most of those returned were women.

■ Twenty-eight Eritreans continued to be restricted to a camp near Jizan city; they were believed to have been there since 2005.

Death penalty

The recorded number of executions fell for a second year running. At least 27 people were executed, a marked reduction on the 69 recorded in 2009 and 102 recorded in 2008. Six foreign nationals were among those executed.

At least 140 prisoners were under sentence of death, including some sentenced for offences not involving violence, such as apostasy and sorcery.

■ 'Ali Hussain Sibat, a Lebanese national, and 'Abdul Hamid bin Hussain bin Moustafa al-Fakki, a Sudanese national, were under sentence of death having been convicted in separate trials of committing sorcery. In both cases, their trials were unfair; they were tried in secret and without access to defence lawyers.

In December, Saudi Arabia was one of the minority of states that voted against a UN General Assembly resolution calling for a worldwide moratorium on executions.

SENEGAL

REPUBLIC OF SENEGAL

Head of state:	Abdoulaye Wade
Head of government:	Souleymane Ndéné Ndiaye
Death penalty:	abolitionist for all crimes
Population:	12.9 million
Life expectancy:	56.2 years
Under-5 mortality (m/f):	125/114 per 1,000
Adult literacy:	41.9 per cent

In southern Casamance clashes between the army and an armed group increased during the first half of the year; civilians were abducted and killed. Torture was regularly used by the police and condoned by the judiciary and led to the death of at least one detainee. Despite renewed promises by the government, the trial of former Chadian President Hissène Habré did not begin.

Background

The conflict between the army and the Democratic Forces of Casamance Movement (Mouvement des forces démocratiques de Casamance, MFDC) intensified. In March, the army shelled MFDC positions in villages around Ziguinchor (the main city of Casamance) after continuous sporadic attacks by MFDC members against military and civilian targets. Despite the consequent rise in tension, which further undermined the 2004 peace agreement, both parties continued to declare officially that they were ready to engage in talks. These had not started by the end of 2010.

In July and August, thousands of demonstrators took to the streets of Dakar, the capital, to protest against recurrent power cuts.

Arrests of armed group leaders

The army briefly detained several MFDC leaders and reportedly ill-treated some of them.

■ In March, two leaders of the armed branch of the MFDC, Bourama Sambou and Boubacar Coly, were arrested in the village of Belaye. They were held for four days without charge and reportedly ill-treated at the gendarmerie of Ziguinchor.

■ In May, four MFDC leaders, Mamadou Teuw Sambou, Pape Tamsir Badji, Joseph Diatta and Ansoumana Diédhiou, were detained in Dakar after being returned from Gambia where they had spent four years in prison. They were released two weeks later without charge.

Abuses by armed groups

Several civilians, including young girls, were abducted; some were reportedly sexually abused by members of the MFDC. Soldiers were also arbitrarily killed by alleged members of the MFDC.

■ In January, Didier Coly, a former army corporal, was shot dead in the village of Bourafaye Bainouk by alleged members of the MFDC who reportedly suspected him of being an army informer.

■ In September, MFDC fighters abducted four young girls in the village of Waniak. The girls were released some days later and were reportedly sexually abused.

Torture and other ill-treatment

The police regularly tortured suspects.

■ In July, Abdoulaye Wade Yinghou, aged 29, was arrested as he walked past a demonstration in a Dakar suburb. Witnesses saw police beat him with rifle butts during his arrest and at the police station. The following day, his family were told by police officers that he had died following a seizure or illness. An autopsy revealed facial injuries and broken ribs. An inquiry was opened but its findings had not been made public by the end of the year.

Impunity

Despite official promises, most of the officials responsible for acts of torture and other crimes under international law continued to enjoy impunity. Torture was condoned by the judiciary, with prosecutors refusing to open inquiries into allegations of torture and judges sentencing people on the basis of information extracted under torture.

Impunity was facilitated by the fact that judicial proceedings against members of the security forces could only take place with the authorization of the Minister of the Interior (police officers) or the Ministry of Defence (gendarmes and military personnel).

Moreover, despite a law passed in 2009 that created a National Inspector of Places of Deprivation of Liberty, a key measure to prevent torture in detention, by the end of 2010 nobody had been appointed to this position.

International justice – Hissène Habré

Ten years after some victims of Chad's former President Hissène Habré lodged a complaint against him in Senegal, no criminal proceeding had been opened by the Senegalese judiciary. The authorities continued to claim that the only obstacle was financial and that the international community should find a solution.

In July 2010, following a joint AU-EU mission, a

round table was announced to finalize the financial terms of Hissène Habré's trial. The round table was held in November, and European and African donors agreed to contribute to financing the trial. However, despite a promise to an Amnesty International delegation in Dakar in October that criminal proceedings would start very soon, there was no progress by the end of the year.

Hissène Habré and his lawyers continued to challenge Senegal's jurisdiction. In May, the Community Court of Justice of ECOWAS declared Hissène Habré's 2009 complaint against Senegal admissible. The complaint claimed that the prosecution violated the prohibition of retroactive criminal law in the African Charter on Human and Peoples' Rights, even though the crimes alleged were all violations of international law when they were committed. In November, the ECOWAS Court ruled that Senegal could only try Hissène Habré if ad hoc or special jurisdictions were put in place.

Amnesty International visits/reports

🚗 In September, an Amnesty International delegation visited Senegal to publish a report on impunity and meet the authorities.

📓 Senegal: Land of impunity (AFR 49/001/2010)

SERBIA

REPUBLIC OF SERBIA, INCLUDING KOSOVO

Head of state:	Boris Tadić
Head of government:	Mirko Cvetković
Death penalty:	abolitionist for all crimes
Population:	9.9 million
Life expectancy:	74.4 years
Under-5 mortality (m/f):	15/13 per 1,000

War crimes prosecutions continued in Serbia, but little progress was made in establishing the fate of those missing since the 1999 war. Discrimination against minorities continued in both Serbia and Kosovo, where serious inter-ethnic violence occurred in the north. Roma were forcibly returned to Kosovo from EU member states.

Background

In July, the International Court of Justice (ICJ) issued an advisory opinion that Kosovo's 2008 declaration of independence did not violate applicable international law. In September the UN General Assembly adopted a resolution on Kosovo, which envisaged the resumption of talks between Serbia and Kosovo, facilitated by the EU.

Serbia moved closer to EU membership in November when the European Commission sent the government a questionnaire to assess Serbia's readiness for EU candidate status. Progress remained conditional on Serbia's continued co-operation with the International Criminal Tribunal for the former Yugoslavia (Tribunal). Also in November, the Chief Prosecutor of the Tribunal urged Serbia to take more proactive measures to arrest former Bosnian-Serb General Ratko Mladić and former Croatian Serb leader Goran Hadžić.

International justice

In March, the Serbian parliament narrowly adopted the "Srebrenica Resolution", which condemned crimes committed against the Bosniak (Bosnian Muslim) population of Srebrenica in July 1995, and apologized to the families of the victims, but failed to refer to genocide, as required by the 2007 ICJ decision in a case brought by Bosnia and Herzegovina (BiH) against Serbia.

Following Croatia's 2008 claim against Serbia, in January Serbia filed a counterclaim at the ICJ, alleging that Croatia had committed genocide against Croatian Serbs.

Closing arguments were heard in July at the Tribunal against former Assistant Interior Minister Vlastimir Đorđević, indicted for crimes against humanity and war crimes in Kosovo. He was charged with crimes leading to the deportation of 800,000 Albanian civilians, the enforced disappearance of more than 800 ethnic Albanians, and leading a conspiracy to conceal their bodies by transporting them to Serbia for reburial.

In the same month, the Tribunal Appeals Chamber ordered the partial retrial of Ramush Haradinaj, former commander of the Kosovo Liberation Army (KLA) and later Prime Minister of Kosovo, and two other KLA commanders. The Appeals Chamber judgement highlighted "the gravity [that] the threat of witness intimidation posed to the trial's integrity". In 2008, the accused were acquitted of joint criminal enterprise in the persecution and abduction of civilians suspected of collaborating with Serbian forces in 1998. A revised indictment issued in November focused on the alleged murders of Serbs, Roma and Ashkali.

S

Also in July, a UK court dismissed Serbia's extradition request for former Bosnian Presidency member, Ejup Ganić, on the basis of insufficient evidence. Ejup Ganić had been arrested in London on an indictment alleging his involvement in an attack on a Yugoslav National Army column in Sarajevo in May 1992.

Serbia

Justice system

The Belgrade Special War Crimes Chamber continued to try cases arising from the wars in BiH, Croatia and Kosovo.

The trial of the ethnic Albanian "Gnjilane/Gjilan Group" continued. The group was accused of the imprisonment, torture and abuse, including rape, of 153 civilians, and the murder of at least 80 of them in 1999. Eight of the accused were tried in their absence.

In September, nine members of the Jackals paramilitary unit were charged with war crimes for killing at least 43 ethnic Albanian civilians on 14 May 1999 in Cuška/Çyshk village in Peć/Peja in Kosovo.

■ In October, the Serbian and BiH Government Commissions for Missing Persons reported that the remains of around 97 individuals, the majority of them Bosnian Muslims, had been recovered from the banks of Lake Perućac. The remains of six ethnic Albanians abducted in Đakovica/Gjakovë by Serb forces in 1999 were reportedly suspected to be among them.

Torture and other ill-treatment

The European Commission expressed concern about continued impunity for torture and other ill-treatment in November. Serbia had not established a National Preventive Mechanism as required by the Optional Protocol to the UN Convention against Torture, nor adopted a 2009 by-law on the internal oversight of prisons.

■ The Požarevac Public Prosecutor rejected a complaint by "JD", that he was tortured by five guards at Zabela prison on 18 May; the incident had been recorded by surveillance cameras.

■ Five Leskovac prison staff, arrested in November 2009 on suspicion of abusing and torturing detainees, returned to work in 2010. In November, in the absence of a response from the prosecutor, the Leskovac Committee for Human Rights filed a complaint to the Constitutional Court on behalf of "DB", who alleged that his arm had been broken by prison guards.

Rights of lesbian, gay, bisexual and transgender people

The first Belgrade Pride since 2001 took place in October. More than 5,000 police officers were deployed to protect 1,000 Pride participants from around 6,500 counter-demonstrators, who attacked the police and political party offices and caused more than a million euros' worth of damage. Some 124 police officers were injured by counter-demonstrators, of whom 249 were arrested, and 131 detained for further questioning under a hastily amended article of the Criminal Code increasing the period of detention from eight to 30 days. In December, 83 people were charged with causing violence. No one was arrested for attacks on activists which had taken place before and after the march.

Discrimination

The parliament selected the Commissioner for Equality as envisaged in the 2009 Anti-Discrimination Law. Following a disputed nomination procedure, a lawyer supported by the ruling party was elected in May and had received around 119 complaints of discrimination by the end of the year.

Forced evictions

Forced evictions of Romani people from informal settlements continued across Belgrade. Several other Roma communities remained at risk of forced eviction, including in Belvil, where infrastructure developments funded by European financial institutions are planned.

■ In April, 38 Romani families were forcibly evicted from an informal settlement in Čukarica municipality. The majority were sent back to southern Serbia from where they originated.

■ In October, 36 Roma, including 17 children, were evicted from 25 Vojvodjanska Street, Belgrade. Five of the families were subsequently rehoused in containers, which did not meet international standards for adequate housing.

Refugees and migrants

Following the liberalization of EU visa arrangements, Roma, ethnic Albanians from southern Serbia (and ethnic Albanians from Kosovo who had illegally obtained Serbian registration documents) travelled to EU member states, reportedly seeking international protection; many were summarily returned. In October, the government strengthened border controls after intervention by the EU. Roma families threatened with forced eviction from a settlement at Vidikovac were among those who left the country.

Human rights defenders

Human rights defenders and journalists continued to be subject to threats, attacks and hate speech. The authorities failed to respond to death threats made in April against Marko Karadžić, then State Secretary for Human Rights and Minorities.

In July, Teofil Pančić, a journalist for the weekly magazine *Vreme*, was attacked with metal bars by two men who were later arrested.

Violence against women and girls

The 2009 Law on Domestic Violence and Strategy for Gender Equality was not fully implemented, placing women and children at risk of domestic violence.

Kosovo

In September, President Sejdiu resigned after the Constitutional Court found that his leadership of the Democratic League of Kosovo (LDK) was incompatible with holding public office. In October, the government fell following a no-confidence vote in the Assembly. In December the Democratic Party of Kosovo (PDK) won parliamentary elections, which were marred by allegations of fraud, but with an insufficient majority to form a government.

In November, the European Commission expressed concern about corruption and organized crime, Kosovo's weak judiciary, and the lack of media freedom.

In December, a report for the Council of Europe alleged that Prime Minister Hashim Thaçi and other members of the KLA were complicit in the abduction, torture and other ill-treatment and murder of Serb and Albanian civilians transferred to prison camps in Albania in 1999. In one of the camps, detainees were allegedly murdered and their organs removed for trafficking.

Justice system

The EU-led police and justice mission in Kosovo (EULEX) reported that the domestic justice system remained weak and subject to political interference. Judges and witnesses received threats, and protection mechanisms were rarely invoked.

EULEX restarted proceedings against Albin Kurti, leader of the NGO Vetëvendosje! (Self-determination!), which had been abandoned by the UN Interim Administration Mission in Kosovo (UNMIK) in 2008. He was convicted in June of obstructing officials during a demonstration on 10 February 2007 and sentenced to nine months' imprisonment, but released immediately. Other charges were dropped.

Crimes under international law

In May, EULEX announced that only 60 of the 900 war crimes cases inherited from UNMIK were under investigation. Investigations into the abduction of non-Albanians after June 1999 were transferred to the

local Special Prosecutor, on the basis that EULEX did not consider them war crimes.

Further arrests were made in January and July based on the testimony of Nazim Bllaca, who had been arrested in 2009. He claimed that he had participated between 1999 and 2003 in 17 cases of murder and attempted murder ordered by the Kosovo Information Service.

■ In May, former KLA commander Sabit Geçi was arrested on suspicion of involvement in war crimes committed in 1999 in Drenica. According to media reports, he was also allegedly involved in the torture of ethnic Albanians and Kosovo Serbs at a detention facility in Kukës in Albania.

After his extradition from Norway in July, a Kosovo Serb, Vukmir Cvetković, was convicted of war crimes by Peć/Peja Court in November, and sentenced to seven years' imprisonment for driving ethnic Albanians from their homes in Klina/ë.

Enforced disappearances

A draft Law on Missing Persons failed to include provisions for reparation, including compensation, to relatives of the disappeared. Around 1822 people were considered missing at the end of the year.

The Office of Missing Persons and Forensics (OMPF) was transferred from EULEX to the Kosovo Ministry of Justice in August. In September, the OMPF and Serbian Commission for Missing Persons visited potential mass graves at Rudnica in Serbia and Belaćevac in Kosovo. During 2010, OMPF exhumed the bodies of 34 individuals; identified 57 mortal remains and returned 103 bodies to families for burial. Some three wrongly identified bodies were re-identified by the International Commission on Missing Persons.

Torture and other ill-treatment

The European Committee for the Prevention of Torture visited places of detention in Kosovo in June. In the same month several Vetëvendosje! activists were ill-treated and some hospitalized during a police operation to arrest Albin Kurti (see Justice system, above). The Kosovo Centre for the Rehabilitation of Torture Victims reported some improvements in prison conditions, but noted that prisoners alleged that corruption among prison staff often led to unfair disciplinary measures.

Inter-ethnic violence

Violent incidents between Kosovo Serbs and ethnic Albanians continued in the predominantly Serbian northern municipalities, often fuelled by political developments.

S

In May, the Kosovo Police used tear gas to separate Serbs and Albanians during a protest by ethnic Albanians against the participation of Kosovo Serbs in Serbian local elections. On 2 July, 1,500 Serbs protested against the opening of a civil registration office in Bosnjačka Mahala, an ethnically mixed area of north Mitrovica/ë. An explosive device killed a Bosniak paediatrician and 11 Serbian protesters were injured. On 5 July, a Kosovo-Serb member of the Kosovo Assembly was shot and wounded in both legs in front of his house in north Mitrovica/ë.

Tension increased following the ICJ ruling on Kosovo's 2008 declaration of independence. In September, ethnic Albanians in north Mitrovica/ë requested additional police protection following several grenade attacks and the killing of Hakif Mehmeti on 7 September. A Serbian Kosovo Police officer was arrested three days later. On 12 September, Kosovo Force (KFOR) troops and EULEX police were deployed following Turkey's victory over Serbia in basketball, and Albanians from south Mitrovica/ë clashed with Serbs on the bridge over the river Ibar, separating the Serb and Albanian parts of the town. Two KFOR officers, a police officer and five civilians were injured. In the same month an ethnic Albanian baker in Zvečan was physically attacked three times, and his shop damaged by an explosive device.

Accountability

In March, the Human Rights Advisory Panel declared inadmissible a complaint by the families of Mon Balaj and Arben Xheladini, killed by Romanian police, and by Zenel Zeneli and Mustafë Nerjovaj who were seriously injured, during a demonstration on 10 February 2007. The Panel's decision followed a 2009 Administrative Directive issued by UNMIK which effectively rendered inadmissible applications by plaintiffs who had been offered financial compensation under a UN third party claims process.

On similar grounds, the Panel declared inadmissible a complaint by 143 internally displaced Roma and Ashkali residents of UNMIK-administered camps in northern Mitrovicë/a that they had suffered lead poisoning and other health problems due to contamination of the camps where they had lived since 1999. Their third-party claim against the UN had been pending since February 2006.

■ The Panel continued to consider complaints against UNMIK for failing to investigate the post-war abduction of Serbs.

Discrimination

Discrimination remained pervasive against non-Albanian minorities, women and lesbian, gay, bisexual and transgender people. Roma, Ashkali and Egyptians experienced cumulative discrimination, including in access to education, health care and employment and few enjoyed the right to adequate housing. Many remained without personal documents which would enable them to register citizenship and access basic services.

■ In October, the lead-contaminated camp at Česmin Lug was closed and some Roma, Ashkali and Egyptian inhabitants were resettled in the Roma neighbourhood in south Mitrovica/ë. In November, NGOs began to administer medical treatment for lead poisoning, as specified by the World Health Organization.

Refugees and migrants

Roma, Ashkali and Egyptians were forcibly returned to Kosovo from the EU and Switzerland, even though a revised return and reintegration strategy, published by the Ministry of Interior in April, had not been fully implemented. Many of those returned were denied basic rights and were at risk of cumulative discrimination amounting to persecution. Those without documentation were effectively stateless. In October, Roma attempting to return to Suvi do/Suhadol were reportedly threatened by Albanians, and refused to return on security grounds.

According to UNHCR, the UN refugee agency, 2,253 people from minority communities voluntarily returned to Kosovo in 2010, and 48 Kosovo Albanians, 77 Kosovo Serbs and 386 Roma, Ashkali and Egyptians, considered to be in need of continued international protection, were forcibly returned from western Europe.

Violence against women

Protection orders in domestic violence cases failed to provide adequate protection or were not issued. Violations of such orders were rarely prosecuted.

The NGO Medica Kosovo sought to amend the Law on Civilian Victims of War, to ensure that women raped during the war were given civilian victim status and eligible for compensation.

Amnesty International visits/reports

🚌 Amnesty International delegates visited Kosovo in May/June and Serbia in June and October.

▯ Serbia: Stop forced evictions of Roma in Serbia (EUR 70/007/2010)

▯ Not welcome anywhere: Stop the forced return of Roma to Kosovo (EUR 70/011/2010)

▯ Serbia: Briefing to the UN Committee on the Elimination of Racial Discrimination (EUR 70/016/2010)

SIERRA LEONE

REPUBLIC OF SIERRA LEONE
Head of state and government:	**Ernest Bai Koroma**
Death penalty:	**retentionist**
Population:	**5.8 million**
Life expectancy:	**48.2 years**
Under-5 mortality (m/f):	**160/136 per 1,000**
Adult literacy:	**39.8 per cent**

The government continued to rebuild institutions and infrastructure in the wake of the civil war, promoting development and providing basic health and education. In an effort to reduce the high rate of maternal mortality, the government introduced a free health care policy for pregnant and lactating women and for children under five. Despite some progress however, the country continued to suffer from widespread poverty-related violations of socio-economic rights; a high incidence of sexual and gender-based violence; violations of children's rights; impunity for past crimes against humanity; justice system weaknesses; non-implementation of crucial Truth and Reconciliation Commission (TRC) recommendations; prevalent corruption; and the looming threat of ethnic violence.

Background

Sierra Leone continued to move beyond the legacy of its 11-year civil war (1991-2002), which resulted in economic devastation, infrastructure collapse, mass displacement, and atrocities including sexual slavery, forced recruitment of child soldiers and amputations. There was progress on the legal front with some implementation of recent legislation such as the Chieftaincy Act, Child Rights Act, Domestic Violence Act and Registration of Customary Marriage and Divorce Act.

In October, Sierra Leone ratified the Convention on the Rights of Persons with Disabilities.

Despite the work of the Anti-Corruption Commission, which obtained a number of successful prosecutions, corruption remained a persistent problem.

Justice system

The justice sector remained beset by major challenges. The law reform process, including a constitutional review, made little progress.

The criminal justice system continued to suffer from an acute shortage of magistrates, lengthy delays in proceedings, overloaded public lawyers, inadequate prosecutorial capacity, delays in the appointment of local court chairs, capacity constraints and corruption, all of which directly impeded Sierra Leoneans' access to justice.

Despite improvements in prison conditions, prisons were overcrowded and had inadequate medical supplies and food. Many detainees were held in prolonged pre-trial detention, and juveniles were detained together with adults. These and other problems combined to make detention in Sierra Leone dangerous and occasionally lethal; conditions were often so harsh that they constituted cruel, inhuman or degrading treatment or punishment.

Police and security forces

Police brutality, corruption, excessive use of force, poor conditions in police detention cells, and unlawfully prolonged detention without charge were commonplace. Police were also often ineffective in maintaining law and order. There were no effective police investigations into ritual murders and few investigations into sexual and gender-based violence.

■ In February, police were sent to quell disturbances by school pupils at the national stadium and injured many children, some as young as six years old.

■ No police were held accountable for the unresolved extrajudicial killings by police in Lungi in September 2009, where three people were shot dead and at least 13 others were injured.

Freedom of expression – journalists

Despite improvements in media freedom since the war, the government failed to abolish the provisions of the Public Order Act of 1965 on seditious libel, which placed undue restrictions on freedom of expression. A petition filed by the Sierra Leone Association of Journalists challenging the constitutionality of the Act was quashed by the Supreme Court in November 2009. No reform initiative took place in 2010, although the President had promised in 2009 that the government would review the Act.

Concerns were raised by journalists that some of the provisions of the Sierra Leone Broadcasting Corporation Act passed in 2009 could undermine the independence of the broadcasting corporation.

Children's rights

Children faced serious violations of their rights in many domains. The government failed to uphold and enforce its

S

domestic legislation and to respect its international treaty obligations to protect children and guarantee their rights.

Thousands of children endured the worst forms of child labour in diamond mines and other ultra-hazardous sectors. Sierra Leone's thousands of child miners experienced gross violations of their basic rights. Denied education, health care and basic protections, they endured gruelling and dangerous work. Some died in collapsing pits or mining accidents. Others were scarred for life from the back-breaking work and from exposure to disease.

Few government programmes adequately addressed the continuing special needs of war-affected children and young people – orphans, unaccompanied internally displaced people and former child soldiers. Street children were vulnerable to a wide range of abuses, with little or no protection.

Violence against women and girls

Domestic violence remained widespread. Few cases were reported to the authorities and these were overwhelmingly characterized by inadequate investigation, few prosecutions, out-of-court settlements and interference by traditional leaders. By the end of 2010, only one case had been prosecuted under the Domestic Violence Act 2007. Women's lack of access to the police, exorbitant fees charged by medical officers and pressure to make out-of-court settlements all contributed to impunity and state inaction.

Discriminatory customs continued, such as female genital mutilation (FGM) and forced or early marriage. NGOs made some gains in campaigns to stop FGM among girls but the prevalence was still estimated at around 90 per cent. Laws passed in 2007 – the Child Rights Act and the Registration of Customary Marriage and Divorce Act – prohibited marriage before the age of 18 but were widely ignored. Girls as young as 10 were often married.

Rape of girls by close relatives, schoolteachers and security personnel continued, as did teenage pregnancies, child trafficking, sexual exploitation, and gender discrimination in education.

Maternal mortality

President Ernest Koroma launched on 27 April a "Free Health Care Service" for pregnant women, lactating mothers and children under five. The new programme to abolish health care user fees reportedly cost US$90m and was expected to cover 230,000 pregnant women and around one million children under five in 2010 alone. Mothers and children were supposed to access a package of medical care that included all treatment and medicines at no cost, ensuring minimal essential care for all. This constituted a leap forward for a country with some of the worst maternal and child mortality rates in the world.

However, the launch of free care was rushed and ill-prepared. Requisition and distribution systems were inadequate, monitoring and accountability mechanisms were largely absent, so many women and children still had to pay for some or all medicines.

Many factors that contribute to maternal mortality remained unaddressed, such as unsafe abortions, female genital mutilation, early marriage and the lack of sexual and reproductive education.

International justice

The trial of former Liberian President Charles Taylor before the Special Court for Sierra Leone (SCSL) in The Hague continued in 2010.

Since 2002 the Court had sentenced eight men to prison terms: Moinina Fofana; Allieu Kondewa; Issa Sesay; Morris Kallon; Augustine Gbao; Alex Brima; Ibrahim Kamara; and Santigie Kanu. Sam Hinga Norman died of natural causes in 2007 as did Foday Sankoh in 2003. Sam Bockarie was killed in Liberia in 2003 and Johnny Paul Koroma remained at large.

The few trials before the Court contributed to partial disclosure of the truth about the serious crimes committed in Sierra Leone's armed conflict since 1996. The convictions of the Revolutionary United Front (RUF) leaders Issa Sesay, Morris Kallon and Augustine Gbao were the first for attacks on UN peacekeepers as a violation of international humanitarian law and for forced marriage as an inhumane act constituting a crime against humanity.

However, fewer than a dozen of those responsible for hundreds of thousands of crimes under international law were held to account by the SCSL, and most perpetrators went unpunished. The Lomé Accord of 1999 contains an amnesty provision for those responsible for crimes under international law committed in Sierra Leone. This is not a bar to prosecution before the SCSL, but prevails under Sierra Leonean law, so no investigations or trials for crimes committed in the civil war took place before national courts in Sierra Leone.

Concerns also remained regarding the SCSL's inaccessibility to the public, its cost management and slowness, selective justice, inadequate legacy programmes (to rebuild the local justice system and strengthen local institutions), and failure to prosecute corporate actors such as diamond dealers. In 2010, as the SCSL was establishing a policy on access to its archives, concerns were raised that the policy could be overly restrictive and might not allow prosecutors to use the archives to pursue war criminals in other jurisdictions such as Liberia.

Political violence

The threat of political and ethnic violence between supporters of the two main political parties, the Sierra Leone People's Party (SLPP) and the All People's Congress (APC), grew ahead of elections in 2012. Violence and human rights abuses that occurred during the previous election in 2007, and after the APC victory in 2007, still had not been prosecuted or punished, although a judicial commission found that abuses did take place. Youth supporting the SLPP, the People's Movement for Democratic Change (PMDC) and the APC clashed throughout 2009 and again in mid-2010.

A 2010 initiative by the government to launch a Commission of Inquiry into the alleged extrajudicial execution of 26 people by the government in 1992 increased divisions along political and ethnic lines, as did the gradual replacement of roughly 200 high-level government professionals from the southern and eastern provinces with primarily northern APC supporters. With some major political parties adopting regional and ethnic opinions in their campaigns, 2010 saw a resurgence in identity politics and the sharpening of ethnic and party divisions along APC and SLPP lines.

Perceived ethnic and political biases in the police and army also increased mistrust and hostility. Doubts were raised about the independence of the army and tensions were reported in the ranks. In addition, the ruling APC co-opted "youth leaders" and recruited a number of ex-militia combatants – some implicated in serious attacks on political opponents – to join the Operational Support Division (OSD) of the police. Fears rose that if this practice continued, the opposition might similarly recruit from among the thousands of resettled former fighters, posing a grave threat to the country's medium and long-term security.

Death penalty

Sierra Leone was reviewing its Constitution, and the latest draft apparently retained the death penalty. A new death sentence was passed in the High Court in Kenema in November. A member of the military convicted In August 2009 after a court martial for a killing was sentenced to death by firing squad but the President had not signed the death sentence by the end of the year. Ten men and three women remained on death row.

Amnesty International visits/reports

🚗 Amnesty International delegates visited Sierra Leone in April and October.

📰 Sierra Leone: Government launches free maternal health care (AFR 51/003/2010)

📰 UN Secretary-General Ban Ki-moon must encourage the government of Sierra Leone to do better on maternal mortality (AFR 51/004/2010)

📰 Sierra Leone: Inquest or commission of inquiry into 1992 extra-judicial executions must form part of a comprehensive plan to end impunity (AFR 51/007/2010)

SINGAPORE

REPUBLIC OF SINGAPORE

Head of state:	S.R. Nathan
Head of government:	Lee Hsien Loong
Death penalty:	retentionist
Population:	4.8 million
Life expectancy:	80.7 years
Under 5-mortality (m/f):	4/4 per 1,000
Adult literacy:	94.5 per cent

Government critics and human rights defenders continued to be penalized for exercising their right to freedom of expression. The media continued to be tightly controlled through restrictive censorship laws and legal actions against publishers. Arbitrary detention, judicial caning and the death penalty were retained.

Freedom of expression and assembly

Opposition party leader Chee Soon Juan remained bankrupt following defamation suits by current and former ministers, and was thus barred from seeking public office and from leaving Singapore. He and his colleagues faced fines and possible imprisonment for public speaking without a permit and holding illegal assemblies. Appeals against their convictions were ongoing and they remained free on bail at the end of the year.

S

- In March, the *International Herald Tribune* newspaper apologized and paid fines for a defamation claim in relation to an article on political dynasties which included the names of former Prime Minister Lee Kwan Yew and Prime Minister Lee Hsien Loong in a list of families occupying high positions in Asia.
- In July, police arrested British journalist Alan Shadrake after he published a book on executions in Singapore. He was charged with contempt of court for statements in his book that allegedly impugned the judiciary's independence. He was convicted in November, and sentenced to six weeks' imprisonment and a fine of S$20,000.

Detention without trial

An unknown number of suspected Islamic militants were held under the Internal Security Act (ISA), which provided for detention without trial. One further arrest was known to have been made. Seven who had been held for up to nine years were released.

Death penalty

At least eight people were sentenced to death. No official information on executions was available.
- Tens of thousands of Malaysians campaigned to have the sentence of Malaysian Yong Vui Kong commuted and the Malaysian government appealed to the Singapore authorities. He was sentenced to death in 2009 for trafficking drugs, a crime which carries a mandatory death sentence. Yong Vui Kong's lawyer appealed on the grounds that the mandatory death penalty was unconstitutional. The Court of Appeal rejected the appeal. Yong Vui Kong's lawyer also filed a petition for a judicial review of the clemency process.

Torture and other ill-treatment

Caning was imposed for some 30 offences, including vandalism and immigration violations.
- In April, a man from Cameroon was caned for overstaying his visa.
- In June, a Swiss man was caned for vandalizing a train carriage.

International scrutiny

The UN Special Rapporteur on racism visited Singapore in April. His recommendations included the need for action to protect migrant workers and steps to create a legal and institutional framework to fight racism. He stated that it was time to allow Singaporeans to share their views on ethnicity and work together to find solutions.

Prisoners of conscience

For the first time several former prisoners of conscience made public their experiences, including Teo Soh Lung who published a book about her two detentions under the ISA, in 1987 and again in 1990.

SLOVAKIA

SLOVAK REPUBLIC

Head of state:	Ivan Gašparovič
Head of government:	Iveta Radičová (replaced Robert Fico in July)
Death penalty:	abolitionist for all crimes
Population:	5.4 million
Life expectancy:	75.1 years
Under-5 mortality (m/f):	9/8 per 1,000

Commitments were made to eliminate segregation in education on grounds of ethnic origin, but Roma continued to face discrimination in education, housing and health care. Slovakia ignored rulings from the European Court of Human Rights and returned an asylum-seeker to Algeria.

Background

A new centre-right coalition government came to power in July. The government programme adopted in August included the commitment to implement measures to eliminate segregation in education on the basis of ethnic origin.

Discrimination – Roma

Discrimination against Roma continued at several levels. The Ministry of the Interior reportedly announced that it had started working on a system of collection of data on crimes committed by people living in Romani settlements. In September, the Minister stated that "municipalities in the proximity of segregated settlements belong to areas with higher criminality".

In October, the Regional Court in Košice ruled that Roma were discriminated against on the ground of their ethnic origin when they were prevented from entering one of the cafés in the town of Michalovce; it was one of the first rulings of this kind. However, the Court refused to grant any compensation to the victims.

Right to education

The CERD Committee published its concluding observations on Slovakia in March. It reiterated its concerns about the de facto segregation of Romani children in education. The Committee urged Slovakia to end and prevent such discrimination and to take into account its close link to discrimination in housing and employment.

In August, the new government acknowledged the existence of ethnic segregation in education as a systemic problem. However, in September the Ministry of Education denied that segregation of Romani children was a serious issue, and alleged there had been only a few complaints against this form of discrimination.

■ In November, the NGO Centre for Civil and Human Rights made a complaint to the Office of the Regional Prosecutor regarding an order issued by the municipality of Prešov in 2008, which allegedly breached the Anti-discrimination Act. The order established catchment areas for the town's seven elementary schools. The NGO claimed that the municipality designated streets, in some cases even house numbers, in such a way that streets primarily or exclusively inhabited by Roma fell under the catchment area of one particular school, and as a result the school became progressively a Roma-only school.

Housing rights

Several municipalities either adopted a decision to build or started building walls to separate the areas where Roma live from the non-Roma parts of towns or villages.

■ Following the construction of a wall separating a Romani settlement from the rest of the village of Ostrovany in 2009, the Slovak National Centre for Human Rights stated that, while the construction did not amount to a discriminatory action, the municipality had not sufficiently fulfilled their obligation to prevent discrimination. The Centre also highlighted that the construction of walls represents social separation.

■ In August, the municipality of the town of Michalovce finished building a wall to separate the Romani settlement and a non-Roma residential area of the town. Romani inhabitants of the settlement referred to the barrier as the "Berlin Wall" and expressed discontent about the separation. In September, the Ombudsperson held that the building of the wall did not violate basic rights and freedoms.

■ In September, the municipality of Prešov erected a wall that separates the predominantly Roma housing estate from the town. The mayor of Prešov allegedly stated that this was how the municipality reacted to

complaints about vandalism. The Slovak National Centre for Human Rights held that the construction constituted an affirmation of inequality.

■ Nearly 90 Romani families in Plavecký Štvrtok, a village approximately 20km north of Bratislava, were at risk of forced eviction from their homes. Since January, the municipality had issued notices to 18 families asking them to demolish their homes themselves, arguing that the families had failed to provide documents to prove the houses were constructed in compliance with the law.

Enforced sterilization of Romani women

In March, the CERD Committee urged the authorities to establish clear guidelines to ensure patients are fully informed before giving consent to sterilization and to ensure that practitioners, as well as Romani women, are familiar with such guidelines. Five cases involving allegations of enforced sterilizations of Romani women were pending before the European Court of Human Rights. In two cases, the Court declared the case applications admissible.

Torture and other ill-treatment

■ In November, the District Court in Košice held the first hearing in the case of the ill-treatment by police of six Romani boys in April 2009. The Prosecutor General charged 10 police officers with abuse of powers, including racial motivation. Four of the accused police officers faced charges of lack of due diligence, as they allegedly witnessed the abuse without intervening. All of the accused police officers reportedly pleaded not guilty and refused to testify at the court hearing. Three of them continued to work for the police.

Counter-terror and security

The authorities returned an individual to a country where he might have been at risk of torture and other ill-treatment.

■ In April, the Ministry of Interior forcibly returned an asylum-seeker, Mustafa Labsi, to Algeria, despite a 2008 ruling of the Constitutional Court that had halted an extradition attempt on human rights grounds, particularly due to the risk of torture. Algeria had requested Mustafa Labsi's extradition in 2007, after convicting him in his absence in 2005 for crimes of terrorism, and sentencing him to life imprisonment in 2008. The European Court of Human Rights had also issued an order for interim measures in August 2008 requiring the authorities not to extradite, until the appeals on his asylum claim had been completed. Before his extradition in April, Mustafa Labsi had been held in detention since 2007; in October, the

S

Constitutional Court found that the detention violated his right to freedom and security. At the end of the year, he was being held in El Harrach prison in Algeria, awaiting trial on charges of belonging to a "terrorist group abroad".

Refugees and asylum-seekers
Guantánamo detainees
The government agreed to accept three men formerly held in US custody at Guantánamo Bay, and they were transferred to Slovakia on 5 January. The three were detained at Medveďov centre for illegal migrants on their arrival. In June and July they went on hunger strike to protest against their detention and poor living conditions. In July, the government issued the three men with residence permits valid for five years.

Right to health – reproductive rights
According to the Slovak Family Planning Association, the top management of hospitals often abused the right of conscientious objection in relation to abortion. As a result, it was alleged that only one of the five public hospitals in Bratislava carried out abortions because of the decisions of the hospital management. Despite recommendations by the CEDAW Committee in 2008, the authorities had not issued regulations on invoking conscientious objection as grounds for refusal to perform certain health procedures.

Rights of lesbian, gay, bisexual and transgender people
The organizers of Bratislava Pride had to change the route of the first LGBT Pride march on 22 May after the police announced that they would not be able to protect the participants from attacks by counter-demonstrators. The march was reportedly marked by violence and intimidation due to the failure of authorities to ensure adequate security. According to the organizers, at least two men who were carrying the rainbow flag were injured by counter-demonstrators before the rally started.

Amnesty International visits/reports
Amnesty International delegates visited Slovakia in March, April and September.
Unlock their future: End the segregation of Romani children in Slovakia's schools (EUR 72/004/2010)
Steps to end segregation in education: Briefing to the government of Slovakia (EUR 72/009/2010)
Romani children continue to be trapped in separate and unequal education, despite judgments by the European Court of Human Rights (EUR 01/029/2010)

SLOVENIA

REPUBLIC OF SLOVENIA
Head of state:	Danilo Türk
Head of government:	Borut Pahor
Death penalty:	abolitionist for all crimes
Population:	2 million
Life expectancy:	78.8 years
Under-5 mortality (m/f):	5/4 per 1,000
Adult literacy:	99.7 per cent

Despite some efforts, the authorities continued to fail to restore the rights of people whose permanent residency status was unlawfully revoked in 1992 (known as the "erased"); they also failed to grant reparations to those affected. Discrimination against Roma continued.

Discrimination
The 'erased'
The authorities continued to fail to guarantee the rights of former permanent residents of Slovenia originating from other former Yugoslav republics. Their legal status had been unlawfully revoked in 1992, resulting in violations of their economic and social rights. Some of them were also forcibly removed from the country.

On 8 March, the National Assembly passed a law which aimed at retroactively reinstating permanent residency status to the "erased". The parliamentary and public discussion prior to the adoption of the law was marred by xenophobic statements by several parliamentarians.

On 12 March, the right wing parties filed a proposal with the Parliament to organize a referendum on the adoption of the new law. However, the proposal was eventually rejected by the Constitutional Court in June.

In July, the European Court of Human Rights ruled that the authorities had violated the right to private and family life of eight applicants whose permanent residency permit had been revoked in 1992. The Court also found a violation of the right to an effective remedy, as the authorities had failed to implement two separate decisions of the Constitutional Court, issued in 1999 and 2003, related to the rights of the "erased".

In August, the CERD Committee recommended, among other things, that the authorities grant full reparation, including restitution, satisfaction, compensation, rehabilitation and guarantees of non-repetition, to all people affected by the revocation of their permanent residency status.

Roma

Many Roma experienced inadequate housing conditions, including lack of access to water, sanitation facilities and electricity. Romani settlements were very often isolated and segregated. Roma families were excluded from access to social housing programmes and faced discrimination when trying to buy property. Cases of verbal and physical intimidation and hate speech against Roma were common in local communities and they remained largely unaddressed by the relevant authorities. Remedies to challenge the discriminatory practices were inadequate and often unavailable.

In May, the UN Expert on Human Rights, Water and Sanitation concluded upon her visit to Slovenia that at least 21 Roma settlements did not have access to water and warned of the devastating consequences for these communities. She urged the authorities to undertake urgent steps to address the situation.

Similarly, in August the CERD Committee urged the authorities to challenge discrimination against Roma in different aspects of social life, including in the fields of education, housing, health and employment. It also recommended that the authorities undertake measures to completely eradicate the practice of segregating Roma pupils in the education system.

Amnesty International visits/reports

🚍 Amnesty International delegates visited Slovenia in November.

SOLOMON ISLANDS

SOLOMON ISLANDS
Head of state:	Queen Elizabeth II, represented by Sir Frank Kabui
Head of government:	Danny Philip (replaced Derek Sikua in August)
Death penalty:	abolitionist for all crimes
Population:	0.5 million
Life expectancy:	67 years
Under-5 mortality (m/f):	56/57 per 1,000
Adult literacy:	76.6 per cent

Violence against women and girls persisted with government efforts to combat the issue yielding little impact. Access to clean water and sanitation remained out of reach for many inhabitants of informal settlements in the capital, Honiara.

Violence against women and girls

Women continued to be attacked and killed with impunity. Survivors of such attacks reported that the Public Solicitors office (legal aid) refused to represent them in applying for injunction orders from the courts unless they had visible injuries.

In March, a woman was killed in Western Province by her partner. That same month, a woman who had been beaten and knifed by her husband spoke of her ordeal at a public rally celebrating International Women's Day in Honiara while still bearing visible signs of the attack she had sustained a few days earlier. She was the first survivor of such violence to speak publicly about her experience, raising awareness about the issue, particularly among government officials.

The government launched a national gender policy in March, which set out plans to address gender-based violence. These included a review of laws addressing violence against women and girls, increasing the capacity of the police to investigate and prosecute perpetrators of family violence and more support for the provision of services, such as counselling and safe houses, for survivors of violence. The government also established a task force to look at legal reforms to better combat violence against women.

■ In August, a woman was attacked by her partner in the centre of Honiara, in plain view of police officers who did not stop the beating or arrest the man.

Right to adequate housing – lack of access to water and sanitation

Thousands of people in several informal settlements in Honiara continued to have no access to clean piped water and sanitation.

In Kobito 1, 2, 3 and 4 settlements, many families had to walk a round-trip of more than 1km to collect drinking water from the community pipe. Other families had little or no choice but to use contaminated creeks for washing, bathing and drinking. In other settlements around Honiara town, one toilet was normally shared between five to six households; toilets were often unsanitary.

Death penalty

In December, Solomon Islands abstained from voting on a UN General Assembly resolution calling for a worldwide moratorium on executions despite the country being abolitionist for all crimes.

S

SOMALIA

SOMALI REPUBLIC

Head of state of Transitional Federal Government:	Sheikh Sharif Sheikh Ahmed
Head of government of Transitional Federal Government:	Mohamed Abdullahi Mohamed Farmajo (replaced Omar Abdirashid Ali Sharmarke in November)
Head of Somaliland Republic:	Ahmed Mohamed Mahamoud Silanyo (replaced Dahir Riyale Kahin in July)
Death penalty:	retentionist
Population:	9.4 million
Life expectancy:	50.4 years
Under-5 mortality (m/f):	186/174 per 1,000

Armed conflict between armed Islamist groups and pro-government forces continued in southern and central Somalia. Thousands of civilians were killed or injured as a result of indiscriminate attacks and generalized violence, and at least 300,000 were displaced during the year. Access by aid agencies to civilians and the displaced was further restricted by armed groups and insecurity. Humanitarian workers, journalists and human rights activists remained at risk of killings and abductions. Armed groups controlled most of southern and central Somalia and they increasingly carried out unlawful killings, torture and forced recruitment. The Transitional Federal Government (TFG) controlled only part of the capital Mogadishu and there was no effective justice system. Serious human rights abuses, including war crimes, remained unpunished. In semi-autonomous Puntland, there were clashes with an armed group. In Somaliland, a new government was appointed following presidential elections.

Background

The TFG struggled to extend control over Mogadishu, faced with persistent attacks by the armed Islamist groups al-Shabab and Hizbul Islam, and internal divisions. On 15 March, the TFG signed a framework agreement with Ahlu Sunna Wal Jamaa (ASWJ), a Sufi armed group, formalizing a military alliance and recognizing the group's control of parts of central Somalia. However, an ASWJ faction later denounced the TFG's failure to implement the agreement. In May, tensions surfaced between the TFG President and the Prime Minister, who resigned in September. Mohamed Abdullahi Mohamed Farmajo became the new TFG Prime Minister on 1 November. Consultations over a draft constitution started in July.

Al-Shabab claimed responsibility for suicide attacks, including at the Muna hotel in Mogadishu in August, which killed 33 people. The armed group also claimed responsibility for bombings in Kampala, Uganda in July (see Uganda entry), saying they were in revenge for civilian casualties caused by the African Union Mission in Somalia (AMISOM).

AMISOM, mandated to protect TFG institutions, increased its troops, composed of Ugandan and Burundian soldiers, to 8,000, partly in response to the Kampala bombings. AMISOM denied accusations that they responded to armed groups' attacks in Mogadishu with indiscriminate shelling and shooting, resulting in civilian deaths. However, AMISOM apologized for the killing of two civilians on 23 November in Mogadishu, saying it had opened an investigation and had arrested soldiers involved in the incident. On 22 December, the UN Security Council extended AMISOM's authorized troop strength from 8,000 to 12,000.

International support for TFG security forces continued, despite concerns about their lack of accountability. In May, the EU started training 1,000 TFG soldiers in Uganda. The UN Monitoring Group highlighted continuous violations of the arms embargo on Somalia. In April, the UN Security Council imposed a travel ban, an assets freeze and a targeted arms embargo against nine individuals and entities in relation to Somalia.

In August, the new UN Special Representative for Somalia announced that the UN presence in Somalia would increase. The human rights situation was raised in reports by the UN Secretary-General, the UN Independent Expert on Human Rights and in a special session on Somalia at the UN Human Rights Council in September. However, despite continuing calls for an end to impunity for crimes under international law, no mechanism to investigate such crimes was established by the end of the year.

The international community co-ordinated further military responses and explored legal options to address piracy off Somalia's coast, as hijacking of ships and kidnapping of maritime crews expanded in the Indian Ocean. The Puntland government reportedly approved an anti-terrorism law in July.

Indiscriminate attacks

All parties to the conflict continued to use mortars and heavy weapons in areas populated or frequented by civilians, killing and injuring thousands of people. In Mogadishu, armed groups launched attacks from residential areas, and AMISOM and the TFG reportedly fired indiscriminately in response. From 4 January to 19 November, two hospitals in Mogadishu received 4,030 war-related casualties, 18 per cent of them children under five. Medical records from another hospital in Mogadishu between January and June showed that almost half of its patients were suffering war-related injuries and of these, 38 per cent were women and children under 14.

■ On 29 January, as a result of fighting between armed groups and the TFG and AMISOM, 19 civilians were killed and more than 100 injured. One hospital in Mogadishu supported by Médecins Sans Frontières admitted 89 people injured by shelling between 29 January and 2 February, including 52 women and children.

■ In July, some 170 people were killed and 700 injured by fighting in Mogadishu, according to ambulance services. Between 18 and 21 July, more than 50 people were reportedly killed, including 10 children, and dozens more injured by shelling between armed Islamist groups and TFG and AMISOM troops in districts of Mogadishu such as Hamar Weyne and Bakara market.

■ An offensive launched during Ramadan by al-Shabab against the TFG and AMISOM triggered intense fighting in Mogadishu between late August and early September. Some 230 civilians were killed and another 400 wounded, according to the UN. On 24 August, two al-Shabab suicide bombers wearing government uniforms stormed the Muna hotel in TFG-controlled Mogadishu, killing at least 33 people, including hotel staff and guests, members of parliament and TFG security forces.

Displacement

Fighting, insecurity and poverty displaced some 300,000 people during the year. According to UNHCR, the UN refugee agency, 1.5 million Somalis were internally displaced in the country at the end of the year.

In January, fighting between al-Shabab and Hizbul Islam on the one hand, and Ahlu Sunna Waal Jamaa on the other, in the city of Dhusamareb in central Somalia and the city of Beletweyne in the Hiran region caused the displacement of tens of thousands of civilians.

In Mogadishu, some 23,000 people were displaced within two weeks as a result of the Ramadan offensive. Many joined settlements for displaced people along the Afgoye corridor outside Mogadishu, which hosted about 410,000 people with little or no access to humanitarian aid. From September onwards, thousands of displaced people in Afgoye were reported to have been forcibly evicted following acquisition of land by businessmen.

On 19 and 20 July, the Puntland authorities forcibly removed some 900 internally displaced people mainly from southern and central Somalia to the Galgadud region.

Civilians continued to flee to neighbouring countries. Despite the risks related to conflict and violence, Somalis were deported back to southern and central Somalia by Kenya, Saudi Arabia, and European countries, including the Netherlands, Sweden and the UK. In October, fighting between pro-TFG forces and al-Shabab in Belet Hawo, on the border with Kenya, displaced some 60,000 people. Between 1 and 2 November, 8,000 civilians who had fled into Kenya near the town of Mandera were ordered to return to Somalia by the Kenyan authorities. On 4 November, Kenyan police moved them further inside Somalia.

Restrictions on humanitarian aid

Some 2 million people were in need of humanitarian support by the end of 2010 because of armed conflict and displacement, despite good harvests during the year. Humanitarian operations were impeded by fighting and insecurity, killings and abductions of humanitarian workers and restrictions on aid agencies' access to populations in need. At least two humanitarian workers were killed. In March, the UN Monitoring Group on the arms embargo on Somalia stated that a large part of World Food Programme (WFP) aid to Somalia was diverted to contractors and armed groups. The UN Security Council requested the UN humanitarian co-ordinator for Somalia to report to it every 120 days.

■ In January, WFP suspended its work in southern Somalia due to insecurity and growing threats by armed groups. On 28 February, al-Shabab announced that it was banning WFP from areas under its control,

S

claiming that food distribution undermined local farmers and that WFP had a political agenda. The ban, which remained in place at the end of the year, threatened up to one million people in need of food aid in southern Somalia, despite good rains and harvests in some regions.

■ On 15 January, Nur Hassan Bare "Boolis", a security staff member of SAACID, an aid organization running a feeding programme in Mogadishu, and four other men were abducted by al-Shabab. He was found dead the next day with his hands bound. The other men were released days later, including another SAACID employee who was reportedly tortured.

■ On 29 June 2010, a shell hit Keysaney hospital in northern Mogadishu, killing a patient; two more shells hit the same hospital in the following days, despite the ICRC urging parties to the conflict to spare medical facilities.

■ In August, al-Shabab banned three humanitarian organizations from areas under its control, claiming that they were spreading Christianity. In September, it banned three more aid organizations, accusing them of links with the USA.

Freedom of expression – journalists and civil society

Intimidation of Somali journalists and civil society organizations by armed groups continued. The threat of killings and abductions forced more Somali activists to flee the country. Armed groups also closed or took over radio stations and banned certain topics from being reported. At least three journalists were killed during the year. Foreign observers only visited AMISOM bases in Mogadishu in southern Somalia. In Puntland, the government restricted media reports on its conflict with a local militia.

■ On 21 February, Ali Yusuf Adan, a correspondent for the media outlet Somaliweyn, was captured by al-Shabab in the city of Wanleweyn, apparently after a report alleging the group had killed a man in the area. He was freed unharmed on 2 March.

■ On 4 May, journalist Nur Mohamed Abkey of Radio Mogadishu, a TFG-owned station, was abducted by gunmen in southern Mogadishu and shot in the head. His body was dumped in an alleyway and reportedly bore traces of torture. His Radio Mogadishu colleagues received a phone call from alleged al-Shabab members claiming responsibility for the killing.

■ On 3 April, the armed group Hizbul Islam ordered radio stations to stop broadcasting music within 10 days, claiming it was un-Islamic. On 9 April, al-Shabab banned the BBC and Voice of America from broadcasting in areas under its control. They also seized the BBC's satellite dishes and FM transmitters.

■ On 13 August, Abdifatah Jama, deputy director of the radio station Horseed FM, was sentenced to six years' imprisonment on charges related to an interview with Sheikh Mohamed Said Atom, leader of an armed group in Puntland. He was tried and convicted the day after his arrest, reportedly under Puntland's new anti-terror legislation. Puntland's Information Minister then threatened journalists with punishment should they interview Sheikh Mohamed Said Atom's forces. Abdifatah Jama appealed against his conviction and was pardoned by the Puntland President and released in November.

Child soldiers

Armed Islamist groups, in particular al-Shabab, increased their forced recruitment of boys as young as nine years old, alongside young men, into their forces. Girls were sometimes reportedly recruited to cook and clean for al-Shabab forces or forced to marry al-Shabab members.

In June, the TFG President ordered the Army Chief to investigate media reports that child soldiers were used in TFG forces. The findings of the investigation were not made available by the end of the year. In November, the new TFG Prime Minister pledged to the UN Special Representative on children and armed conflict to work towards an action plan to end the recruitment and use of child soldiers.

Abuses by armed groups

Armed Islamist groups continued to unlawfully kill and torture people they accused of spying or not conforming to their own interpretation of Islamic law. They killed people in public, including by stoning them to death, and carried out amputations and floggings. They also imposed restrictive dress codes, flogging women who did not wear the hijab and forcing men to wear trousers no longer than the ankle.

■ In January, a man accused of rape was reportedly stoned to death by members of al-Shabab in the city of Barawe, Lower Shabelle.

■ In April, the bodies of five beheaded men were found in Mogadishu. It was alleged that al-Shabab had beheaded them because they were involved in building a new Parliament.

■ Two men reportedly had their hands amputated by members of al-Shabab in July in the town of Balad, north of Mogadishu, on accusations of theft.

■ On 27 October, two young women were reportedly

shot dead by al-Shabab members in a public killing in Beletweyne. They were reportedly accused of spying. The town had recently been the scene of fighting between al-Shabab and pro-TFG forces.

Somaliland

Presidential elections were held on 26 June in the Republic of Somaliland. Ahmed Mohamed Mahamoud Silanyo, a former opposition politician, was declared the new President in July. According to independent observers, the elections were generally free, fair and peaceful. However, media freedom organizations reported some instances of restrictions on journalists in the lead-up to the elections.

Tensions flared in the border areas of Sool and Sanaag claimed by Puntland. A new armed group clashed with Somaliland security forces from May onwards. Thousands of people were reportedly displaced by the clashes.

Displaced people from southern and central Somalia continued to live in difficult conditions.

Minority groups continued to suffer discrimination.
■ In September, two women from a Gaboye minority clan who had been acquitted by a court in Aynabo, Saraar region, were attacked by local people and kept in prison for their own protection. They were also allegedly attacked by prison inmates. They were subsequently released.

Death penalty

In December, the TFG carried out its first execution since 2007. In Puntland, at least six people were sentenced to death and at least seven were reportedly executed. In Somaliland, two people were reportedly sentenced to death.
■ On 7 December, Nur Ahmed Shire was executed by TFG forces in the district of Hamar Weyne in Mogadishu. A former TFG soldier, he had reportedly been convicted of killing another TFG soldier.

Amnesty International visits/reports

📄 Somalia: International military and policing assistance should be reviewed (AFR 52/001/2010)

📄 No end in sight: The ongoing suffering of Somalia's civilians (AFR 52/003/2010)

📄 Hard news: journalists' lives in danger in Somalia (AFR 52/009/2010)

📄 Amnesty International's human rights concerns in southern and central Somalia (AFR 52/013/2010)

📄 From life without peace to peace without life: The treatment of Somali refugees and asylum-seekers in Kenya (AFR 32/015/2010)

SOUTH AFRICA

REPUBLIC OF SOUTH AFRICA

Head of state and government:	Jacob G. Zuma
Death penalty:	abolitionist for all crimes
Population:	50.5 million
Life expectancy:	52 years
Under-5 mortality (m/f):	79/64 per 1,000
Adult literacy:	89 per cent

Incidents of torture and extrajudicial executions by police were reported. High levels of violence against women and girls continued, and there were indications of an increase in harmful practices affecting their rights. Serious incidents of violence against lesbian women, targeted for their sexuality, continued to be reported. There were some improvements in access to health services for people living with HIV, but poverty remained an important barrier especially in rural areas. Refugees and migrants continued to suffer discrimination and displacement in large-scale incidents of violence. There were further threats to the work of human rights defenders.

Background

Political tensions continued over the direction of economic policy and appropriate solutions to poverty, inequality and unemployment, with prolonged public sector workers' strikes and numerous protests in poor urban communities. In April, President Zuma appointed a 20-member National Planning Commission, chaired by the former Finance Minister Trevor Manuel, to produce a national development plan and longer-term vision for the country. The high levels of poverty and income inequality, with persistent racial and gender disparities, were acknowledged in the Millennium Development Goals country report in September. In October, trade unions and civil society organizations (CSOs) launched a campaign for economic policies promoting social justice and protection of socio-economic rights.

Torture and other ill-treatment

Incidents of torture and other ill-treatment by police of detained crime suspects were reported. Corroborated methods included severe beatings, electric shocks and suffocation torture while the person was shackled or hooded, and death threats.

S

The police oversight body, the Independent Complaints Directorate (ICD), reported that from April 2009 to March 2010 it had received five direct complaints of torture and 920 complaints of assault with intent to cause grievous bodily harm, some of which were being investigated for evidence of torture. Seven of the 294 deaths in custody were linked to torture and 90 others to "injuries sustained in custody". The ICD also investigated 24 complaints of rape by police officers.

A draft law establishing the ICD on an independent statutory basis, separate from police legislation, was still being considered by Parliament at the end of the year. In parliamentary hearings in August, CSOs called for the inclusion of explicit obligations to investigate complaints of torture and rape in custody and for mandatory reporting by police with knowledge of these offences. Their recommendations were included in a revised bill.

Despite continuing efforts by the South African Human Rights Commission and CSOs, South Africa did not ratify the Optional Protocol to the Convention against Torture. A new version of the draft law to make torture a criminal offence was circulated for comment, but had not been presented in Parliament before the end of the year.

■ In May, a police officer, Vinod Maharaj, was arrested and allegedly tortured by members of the Organized Crime Unit and the special police unit, the Hawks. He was allegedly subjected to electric shocks, beatings, removal of a fingernail and suffocation torture. Four days after his arrest he was brought to court on weapons and murder charges. Although the court ordered the police to ensure his access to medical treatment, he was denied this. Four days later he was taken to hospital for emergency surgery. He was in remand custody with no trial date set at the end of the year.

■ In June, a lawyer consulting with his client at Protea Police Station in Soweto heard screaming from an adjacent office where a man was apparently being electrocuted. When he attempted to persuade police officers to intervene, he was verbally abused, threatened with violence and told to leave the police station. Lawyers managed later to trace the man who was being tortured and a second detainee who had also been assaulted; they were being held under police guard in Leratong Hospital. Access to them was denied. Four days later they were removed from hospital by members of the Organized Crime Unit and allegedly subjected to further torture, before being

transferred to remand custody on murder and robbery charges. One was later released.

■ Three suspected illegal immigrants arrested near the border with Lesotho were detained and assaulted at Ladybrand police station. On 14 June, their lawyer observed that they had facial injuries and blood on their clothes and one required urgent medical attention. The following day immigration officials authorized their release. When they attempted to complain of assault by the police, the lawyer and one of the detainees were verbally abused, pushed and threatened with violence by a police officer at the station. When the lawyer attempted to obtain the medico-legal reporting form, the same officer allegedly assaulted him repeatedly and forced him out of the police station. In September the Director of Public Prosecutions decided to prosecute two police officers on assault charges, following a prompt ICD investigation into the allegations.

■ Following an ICD investigation and police disciplinary hearing, the station commander of Sasolburg police station was dismissed from service for raping a woman volunteer in his office on 5 February. His criminal trial had not concluded by the end of the year.

The Judicial Inspectorate for Correctional Services received over 2,000 complaints of assaults against prisoners by prison warders between April 2009 and March 2010. Overcrowding remained a serious problem, with 19 of 239 facilities having occupancy rates of over 200 per cent capacity and conditions described as "shockingly inhumane".

Extrajudicial executions

In September, Cabinet approved a bill to amend Section 49 of the Criminal Procedure Act governing the use of force during arrest. The proposals in the bill raised public concern as they would allow "arrestors" to use deadly force against a suspect resisting or fleeing arrest where they believed there was a substantial risk of "future death" if the arrest was delayed. The draft provisions would allow members of the public as well as police officers to use deadly force in circumstances beyond those allowed by international human rights standards.

In November, the ICD reported a six per cent decline, to 860, in deaths in custody and "as a result of police action" between April 2009 and March 2010. However, in KwaZulu-Natal province, there was a year-on-year increase from 258 to 270 deaths. The National Commissioner of Police, General Bheki Cele, told Parliament in October that the increase in shootings by police was due to the dangers they faced and inexperience.

Violence against women and girls

High levels of violence against women and girls continued to be reported and to cause national concern. Over 63,500 cases of sexual offences, including rape, against women and children were reported to the police between April 2009 and March 2010.

The report of a parliamentary committee, tabled in Parliament in February, recommended substantial changes to the Domestic Violence Act (DVA) and in policies and practices used by police, justice and social support agencies. The recommendations followed wide-ranging hearings with CSOs on failures in implementation which left many victims without access to effective remedies. The ICD reported to Parliament in November that only a quarter of the 522 police stations they inspected in the previous year were fully compliant with their obligations under the DVA. Police lack of understanding of the requirements of the law, a reluctance to discipline members who did not implement the law and failure to arrest violent abusers were the main problems reported by the ICD.

Abductions and forced marriages of girls apparently increased, particularly in rural areas of Eastern Cape Province, linked to a traditional practice, *ukuthwala*.
■ In August a magistrate's court in Willowvale, Eastern Cape, dismissed the claim of a husband for the return of his 17-year-old wife or the recovery of the *lobola* (bride price). The young woman, who was defended by the Women's Legal Centre, was 14 years old when she underwent a customary marriage.

In response to large-scale virginity testing events, some financially supported by state-funded traditional leaders in KwaZulu-Natal Province, the Commission on Gender Equality and some CSOs condemned virginity testing as violations of the right to equality, dignity, privacy and the rights of the child.

In March, the Equality Court in Johannesburg ruled, in a case brought by the NGO Sonke Gender Justice, that the African National Congress (ANC) Youth League president, Julius Malema, had infringed women's right to dignity and that his comments at a public meeting about women who reported rape amounted to hate speech. He was ordered to issue a public apology and to pay a contribution to an organization assisting survivors of gender-based

violence, but he did not do so. In October, he applied for leave to appeal the ruling.

Draft anti-trafficking legislation was introduced in Parliament but had not been passed by the end of the year.

Rights of lesbian, gay, bisexual and transgender people

Serious incidents of violence against lesbian women or women believed to be lesbian, targeted for their sexuality, continued to be reported. It was not clear at the end of the year if proposed draft legislation to criminalize hate crimes included victims targeted on grounds of sexual orientation, which CSOs had recommended. In December, South Africa supported an amendment to restore a reference to sexual orientation in a UN resolution calling on states to investigate discrimination-related killings.

Right to health – people living with HIV/AIDS

An estimated 5.7 million people were living with HIV, according to UNAIDS. By the end of the year the number of AIDS patients receiving antiretroviral treatment (ART) had increased to over 971,500, according to the World Health Organization. More than a third were in KwaZulu-Natal, the province worst affected by the epidemic and with the highest infection rates among pregnant women. The government agreed to new treatment guidelines in March which increased earlier access to ART for pregnant women and people co-infected with HIV and tuberculosis. Access to treatment also improved in a number of provinces when the Department of Health, in partnership with NGOs and donors, strengthened the capacity of clinics outside hospitals to provide comprehensive treatment and care. However, poverty, inadequate daily food, unreliable and costly transport systems and the shortage of health care workers in rural areas remained major barriers to access.

In March, the government launched a drive to scale-up voluntary HIV testing and, in KwaZulu-Natal, it promoted medical male circumcision to reduce HIV infection rates. Both programmes were criticized for over-focusing on numerical targets. In some cases, informed consent and adequate counselling were absent. The South African National AIDS Council was accused of lack of leadership in monitoring the implementation of the national strategic plan on HIV and AIDS.

S

Refugees and migrants

Refugees and migrants continued to suffer violations of the right to life and to physical integrity. In the first six months of the year at least 14 incidents involving violent attacks and looting of shops, particularly of Somali and Ethiopian nationals, were recorded in five provinces. Large-scale displacements of non-national communities occurred in a number of areas, including Siyathemba/Balfour, Sasolburg and Middelburg. Police protection was often slow or inadequate and victims faced difficulties in getting justice and compensation. In some areas in Gauteng Province, co-operation between senior police officers and UN agency and civil society monitors prevented violence from escalating.

In May, migrants and refugees received written and verbal threats of violence if they failed to close their businesses or leave by the end of the 2010 World Cup. In June, an Inter-Ministerial Committee (IMC) was established to co-ordinate the official response to incidents of violence. Despite increased security force deployment after 11 July, at least 15 attacks on property and individuals occurred in Western Cape and Gauteng provinces, including in Philippi East, Khayelitsha, Wallacedene and Kya Sands, and hundreds of people were displaced. Members of the IMC publicly denied that the incidents were xenophobic, but in September the deputy Minister for Social Development acknowledged that refugees and migrants were victims of "hate crimes".

A High Court ruling in November ordering banks to accept documentation from refugees and asylum-seekers to enable them to open bank accounts was welcomed by refugee rights organizations.

On at least two occasions, in cases brought by Lawyers for Human Rights, the courts ordered the release of Zimbabwean and Somali nationals held unlawfully in custody and at risk of forcible return. The Ministry of Home Affairs' scheme announced in September to regularize the status of thousands of Zimbabweans living in South Africa and lift the moratorium against their deportation raised fears of future mass deportations due to the practical challenges of receiving and processing applications within the time frame. In December, the Minister stated that Zimbabweans who had entered the permit application process by 31 December would not be deported. According to official figures over 250,000 had applied by the cut-off date. Security personnel reportedly used excessive force against Zimbabweans

waiting to make applications at the Cape Town Department of Home Affairs office.

Human rights defenders

■ The trial of 12 supporters of the housing rights movement, Abahlali baseMjondolo, on charges relating to violence in the Kennedy Road informal settlement in September 2009 started in November. One state witness, who repudiated her earlier statement to the police as coerced, received death threats several days after her name was published by the media. The trial was postponed until May 2011. All the accused were out on bail.

■ In January, members of a community affected by mining operations and police repression of their protests in Limpopo province applied to the High Court for judicial review of an officially approved lease granted to Anglo-Platinum mining company. The applicants sought an order declaring that the agreement was not based on informed consent and the community's right to just and adequate compensation. The case had not been heard by the end of the year.

■ In August, members of the Hawks unlawfully arrested a *Sunday Times* investigative journalist, Mzilikazi wa Afrika, apparently in connection with his reporting on an alleged hit squad linked to senior members of the Mpumalanga provincial government. They seized his notebooks and held him at various locations for 24 hours before he was allowed access to his lawyer. Following an urgent court application, the Pretoria High Court ordered his immediate release. The incident occurred at a time of increased pressure from the ruling ANC and the government for stricter control of the media and freedom of expression through a proposed Media Appeals Tribunal and draconian Protection of Information law. CSOs launched a Right2Know campaign in opposition to these developments.

Amnesty International visits/reports

🚗 Amnesty International representatives visited the country in March, August and November.

📰 South Africa: police negligence in xenophobic attack (AFR 53/003/2010)

📰 South Africa: grave concern at continuing violence against refugees and migrants (AFR 53/004/2010)

📰 Human rights concerns in South Africa during the World Cup (AFR 53/007/2010)

SPAIN

KINGDOM OF SPAIN

Head of state:	King Juan Carlos I de Borbón
Head of government:	José Luis Rodríguez Zapatero
Death penalty:	abolitionist for all crimes
Population:	45.3 million
Life expectancy:	81.3 years
Under-5 mortality (m/f):	5/5 per 1,000
Adult literacy:	97.6 per cent

Allegations of torture and ill-treatment by law enforcement officials persisted, and investigations into such allegations continued to be inadequate. Spain refused to abolish incommunicado detention despite repeated recommendations by international human rights bodies. A man suspected of terrorism was extradited to Morocco despite risks of torture and unfair trial. The armed group Euskadi Ta Askatasuna (ETA) announced a ceasefire. Former detainees from Guantánamo Bay were granted international protection. Reports of violence against women and girls increased. An investigating judge was suspended for launching an investigation into international crimes committed during the Spanish Civil War and the Franco regime.

Torture and other ill-treatment

Allegations of torture and other ill-treatment by law enforcement officials continued. No measures were taken to compile and publish data on cases which may have involved violations of the human rights of people in police custody, as provided by the Human Rights Action Plan adopted by the government in 2008.

In June, the reform of the criminal code did not amend the definition of torture, despite recommendations by the UN Committee against Torture to bring it in line with international human rights standards. The criminal code continued to distinguish between "serious" infringements of the article prohibiting torture and infringements "which are not".

■ The trial of two police officers charged with killing Osamuyia Akpitaye while he was being forcibly deported from Spain in June 2007 was set for 16 and 17 March 2011.

Counter-terror and security

The authorities continued to hold in incommunicado detention people suspected of terrorism-related activities. People can be held for up to 13 days during which time they cannot appoint their own lawyer or consult their duty lawyer in private, do not have access to a doctor of their own choice and cannot let their family know of their whereabouts. In May, the government rejected recommendations from the UN Universal Periodic Review to abolish this form of detention.

■ Following a formal complaint by Mohammed Fahsi's lawyer, in January Investigating Court No. 23 of Madrid agreed to examine his allegations of torture, but in April it had closed the investigation. Mohammed Fahsi had alleged he had been tortured during his incommunicado detention following his arrest by the Civil Guard in January 2006. His complaint was initially rejected by the Public Prosecutor and investigating judge. The Investigating Court reasoned that the complaint had been filed more than three years after the events and that Mohammed Fahsi had told the forensic doctor that the treatment he received was "normal". An appeal against the court's decision was pending at the end of the year. In January, Mohammed Fahsi had been sentenced to seven years' imprisonment for belonging to a terrorist organization; he had already spent four years in pre-trial detention. He had appealed that decision before the Supreme Court and was released pending the ruling.

■ On 25 June, Investigating Court No. 1 of Madrid dismissed the complaint by Maria Mercedes Alcocer of torture, injury and serious threats by members of the Civil Guard while she was held incommunicado from 10 to 13 December 2008. A forensic report, dated 12 December 2008, documented bruises and traces of kicks and blows. However, in its decision to close the case the court stated that none of the forensic reports revealed any external sign of violence against Maria Mercedes Alcocer and implied that the complaint's only aim was to identify the members of the Civil Guard who had been involved in her detention. Her appeal against the decision was pending at the end of the year. In May, Maria Mercedes Alcocer had been charged before the National High Court for collaborating with an armed group. The verdict was pending at the end of the year.

■ On 28 September, the European Court of Human Rights found that Spain had violated the prohibition of torture and other ill-treatment. The authorities had failed to investigate allegations of torture by Mikel San Argimiro Isasa during the five days he spent in incommunicado detention at the Directorate-General of the Civil Guard in Madrid in May 2002.

■ On 30 December, the Criminal Court of Guipúzcoa convicted four civil guards of torturing Igor Portu and

Mattin Sarasola while they were in police custody on the morning of 6 January 2008. The court ruled that the fact that the two men had been convicted of belonging to the armed group ETA and committing serious terrorism offences did not make their statements unreliable. However, their allegations of ill-treatment during their subsequent detention and transportation were rejected for lack of proof. The 11 other civil guards on trial were acquitted.

Extradition

■ On 14 December, the Spanish authorities extradited Ali Aarrass, a dual Moroccan-Belgian national accused of terrorism-related offences, to Morocco. By doing so the Spanish authorities breached interim measures ordered by the UN Human Rights Committee calling on Spain not to enforce the extradition until the Committee had taken a decision on his case.

Abuses by armed groups

In March, a French police officer was killed by members of the armed group ETA in a shoot-out in Dammarie-lès-Lys, near Paris. On 5 September, ETA announced that it would not carry out any "offensive armed actions".

Refugees and migrants

According to the Ministry of the Interior, 3,632 irregular migrants arrived on Spanish coasts, which was 50 per cent less than in 2009 and the lowest number for the decade. The decrease was due in part to the continued policies of interception of migrants and asylum-seekers at sea, and readmission agreements signed with countries of origin and transit.

In September, the government rejected the recommendation by the Universal Periodic Review working group to sign and ratify the UN Migrant Workers Convention.

Guantánamo Bay detainees

In February, the then Foreign Minister confirmed that Spain was willing to provide five former detainees from Guantánamo with international protection. The announcement was followed by the arrival of a Palestinian man on 24 February, a Yemeni man on 4 May and an Afghan man on 21 July, all of whom had been held in US custody at Guantánamo Bay.

Trafficking in human beings

In June, the government amended the definition of human trafficking in the criminal code and brought it into line with the Council of Europe Convention on Action against Trafficking in Human Beings. However, there were concerns that the right to a recovery and reflection period for foreign nationals in an irregular situation who are believed to be victims of human trafficking was not always respected in practice. Such a period is enshrined in the Law on Foreign Nationals for a minimum of 30 days during which expulsion proceedings should be suspended. At the end of the year no measures had been taken to instruct the relevant authorities on how to identify victims of trafficking according to the law.

■ On 17 March, Gladys John, a Nigerian citizen who was two months pregnant, was expelled to Nigeria despite concerns of the UN refugee agency, UNHCR, that she could be a victim of human trafficking. On 10 March, the Central Court for Administrative Litigation No. 6 in Madrid had rejected her asylum application and refused to recognize her as a victim of human trafficking.

Children's rights

Allegations of corporal punishment, isolation, abusive prescription of drugs and inadequate health care in centres for minors with behavioural or social problems persisted. In September, the UN Committee on the Rights of the Child expressed concern that those centres might constitute a form of deprivation of liberty. The Committee recommended that Spain should ensure that legislation and administrative regulations in all autonomous communities conform fully to the Convention on the Rights of the Child.

Violence against women

According to the Ministry of Health, Social Policy and Equality, the number of women killed at the hands of their partners or former partners increased to 73, of whom 27 were migrant women.

Migrant women in an irregular situation who were victims of domestic or gender-based violence continued to fear registering a complaint with the police due to the risk of expulsion following such a complaint. An amendment to the Law on Foreign Nationals in December 2009 included expulsion proceedings to be initiated when migrant women in an irregular situation register a complaint of gender-based violence.

Victims of gender-based violence also continued to encounter many obstacles to fair and timely reparation.

■ In July, 10 years after the events, Ascensión Anguita received compensation from her ex-husband for the serious physical and mental effects he caused by stabbing her 15 times. She was unable to work and suffered from post-traumatic stress disorder, and had been living on a monthly disability allowance.

Racism and discrimination

The authorities failed to take steps to combat discrimination against foreign nationals and to support freedom of expression and religion.

■ In January, a circular issued by the General Directorate of the Police and Civil Guard allowed for the preventive detention of foreign nationals who do not produce identity documents during identity checks. Police unions were concerned that this could lead to unlawful detentions, and called for the immediate' withdrawal of the circular.

■ In May, the government supported the recommendations by the UN Universal Periodic Review working group to collect and publish statistics on racially motivated crimes and to develop a national plan of action against racism and xenophobia. However, at the end of the year no further steps had been taken. The provision by the Human Rights Plan of 2008 to establish a National Strategy to Combat Racism had still not been implemented.

■ Several municipalities passed regulations banning the wearing of full-face veils in municipal buildings. The Senate approved a motion in June urging the government to ban the use of full-face veils "in public spaces and events". There were concerns that a wide-ranging ban would violate the rights to freedom of expression and religion of women who choose to wear a full-face veil as an expression of their identity or beliefs.

Enforced disappearances

Although amendments were made to the criminal code in June, the government failed to introduce a definition of crimes under international law such as enforced disappearances and extrajudicial executions.

■ In April, the Supreme Court accused investigating judge Baltasar Garzón of breaking the 1977 Amnesty law. Baltasar Garzón had initiated Spain's first ever investigation into crimes committed during the Spanish Civil War and the Franco regime, involving the enforced disappearance of over 114,000 individuals between 1936 and 1951. Subsequently, in May the General Judicial Council suspended him from duty for the duration of his trial before the Supreme Court. Amnesty laws and statutes of limitation for enforced disappearance, torture or crimes against humanity are inconsistent with international law, and in 2008, the UN Human Rights Committee had called on Spain to consider repealing the 1977 Amnesty law. However, it still remained in force at the end of the year.

International justice

In September and November, the National Criminal Court closed investigations into crimes committed in Myanmar and Tibet. The decisions were taken following the limitation of universal jurisdiction by an amendment to the Law on the Judiciary in October 2009. Since the amendment, domestic courts were no longer able to prosecute cases unless the victims were Spanish citizens, the alleged perpetrator was in Spain, or there was another "relevant connecting link" with Spain and only if there was no effective investigation or prosecution already in another country or international court.

■ In September, the government requested the extradition of Faustin Kayumba Nyamwasa, head of the Rwandan army, from South Africa. In 2008, the National Criminal Court had charged him with genocide and crimes against humanity in Rwanda.

Amnesty International visits/reports

▤ Dangerous deals: Diplomatic assurances in Europe (EUR 01/012/2010)
▤ Spain: Follow-up information to the Concluding Observations of the Committee against Torture (EUR 41/003/2010)

SRI LANKA

DEMOCRATIC SOCIALIST REPUBLIC OF SRI LANKA

Head of state and government:	Mahinda Rajapaksa
Death penalty:	abolitionist in practice
Population:	20.4 million
Life expectancy:	74.4 years
Under-5 mortality (m/f):	21/18 per 1,000
Adult literacy:	90.6 per cent

The Sri Lankan government failed to effectively address impunity for past human rights violations, and continued to subject people to enforced disappearances and torture and other ill-treatment. The authorities imposed severe restrictions on freedom of expression, assembly and association. Thousands of Tamil people suspected of ties with the Liberation Tigers of Tamil Eelam (LTTE) remained detained without charge. Both sides in the conflict that ended in May 2009 have been accused of war crimes; Amnesty International called for an independent international investigation.

S

Background

President Mahinda Rajapaksa was elected to a second term in January in the first peace time election in 26 years. His main opponent, former Army Chief of Staff Sarath Fonseka, was arrested after the election and charged with engaging in politics while in military service and corrupt arms procurement, for which he received a 30-month prison sentence in September. Sarath Fonseka also faced criminal charges, including that he made false accusations in a local newspaper that Sri Lanka's Defence Secretary had ordered the killing of surrendered LTTE members in May 2009. Journalists and trade unionists suspected of supporting the opposition were victims of a post-election crackdown.

In March, UN Secretary-General Ban Ki-moon announced plans to establish a Panel of Experts to advise him on accountability issues in Sri Lanka. President Rajapaksa protested against the announcement and appointed an ad hoc Lessons Learnt and Reconciliation Commission (LLRC) to examine the failure of the 2002 ceasefire, but its terms of reference made no mention of seeking accountability for violations of human rights or humanitarian law. Sri Lanka lost its preferential access to the EU market in August because it failed to respond to a set of conditions laid down by the European Commission to address shortcomings in its implementation of three UN human rights conventions.

The outcome of the April parliamentary elections, subsequent cabinet appointments, and new legislation consolidated power in the immediate Rajapaksa family, which controlled five key ministries and more than 90 state institutions. A Constitutional amendment in September removed the two-term limit on the presidency and gave the President direct control of appointments to institutions important to human rights protection, including the National Police Commission, the Human Rights Commission and the Judicial Services Commission.

The authorities continued to deny access to human rights organizations and other independent observers to visit the country to conduct research. In October, Amnesty International, Human Rights Watch and the International Crisis Group declined an invitation to testify before the LLRC, noting its severe shortcomings, including the Commission's inadequate mandate, insufficient guarantees of independence, and lack of witness protection.

Internally displaced people

About 20,000 of some 300,000 people who were displaced by armed conflict in 2009 remained in government displacement camps in the north; shelters and health facilities continued to deteriorate. Sri Lanka's Defence Ministry continued to control humanitarian access to these camps and to places of resettlement. Many families who left the camps still lived in unsettled conditions and continued to depend on food aid. Tens of thousands remained with host families and some 1,400 remained at transit sites.

Violations by government-allied armed groups

Armed Tamil groups aligned with the government continued to operate in Sri Lanka and commit abuses and violations, including attacks on critics, abductions for ransom, enforced disappearances and killings.

■ In March, former parliamentarian Suresh Premachandran accused members of the Eelam People's Democratic Party (EPDP) in Jaffna of killing 17-year-old Thiruchelvam Kapilthev. Suresh Premachandran said the police ignored statements by friends of the victim that implicated the EPDP, and said they were protecting the killers because of the upcoming parliamentary election.

Enforced disappearances

Enforced disappearances and abductions for ransom carried out by members of the security forces were reported in many parts of the country, particularly in northern and eastern Sri Lanka and in Colombo. Hundreds of LTTE members who reportedly disappeared after they had surrendered to the army in 2009 remained unaccounted for.

■ An eyewitness testifying before the LLRC in August told Commissioners that her family members, including two children, had surrendered to the army in the Vadduvaikkal area in May 2009 and that she had seen those who surrendered being taken away in 16 buses along the Mullaitivu Road. She said she had searched for them at detention centres and prisons but failed to locate them. Two priests who encouraged them to surrender were also missing.

Arbitrary arrests and detentions

The Sri Lankan government continued to rely on the Prevention of Terrorism Act (PTA) and emergency regulations that grant the authorities broad powers to arrest and detain suspects and to circumvent normal

S

procedural safeguards against arbitrary arrest and detention. In April, Amnesty International called on Sri Lanka's new Parliament to lift the State of Emergency, in force almost continuously since 1971, and abolish the PTA and other associated security laws and regulations. In May, the authorities lifted some emergency provisions restricting freedom of expression and association and allowing for household registration, but other laws containing similar provisions remained in effect.

Thousands of people with alleged LTTE links were detained without charge or trial for "rehabilitation" or investigation. About 6,000 of more than 11,000 people arbitrarily detained in 2009 for "rehabilitation" remained in detention camps without access to lawyers, courts or the ICRC; many gained some access to families during the year. There was also evidence of secret detention in the north. Officials said 700 to 800 detainees identified by the state as "hardcore" LTTE members and held separately would be investigated by the authorities for possible prosecution. Hundreds more were held without charge in police lock-ups and southern prisons under the PTA and emergency regulations; some had been detained for years. Most of the detainees were Tamil; some were Sinhalese.

■ In October, a lawyer representing four Sinhalese men accused of supporting the LTTE said his clients had been detained without charge for almost three years. The men were among 25 trade union activists and journalists abducted in February 2007 and later found in the custody of the police's Terrorism Investigation Division (TID); 21 were eventually released by the courts without charge.

Torture and other ill-treatment

Police and army personnel continued to torture or otherwise ill-treat detainees. Victims included detained Tamils suspected of links to the LTTE and individuals arrested for suspected "ordinary" criminal offences. Some people died in custody after being tortured by police.

■ In videotaped testimony made available by Janasansadaya, a Sri Lankan NGO, Samarasinghe Pushpakumara said he was detained on 10 November and tortured by Beruwala police after an officer pretended to hire him as a driver and then arrested him for burglary. Samarasinghe Pushpakumara said he was assaulted, threatened with criminal charges for possession of drugs or bombs, and told he could be killed. He was blindfolded and tied to a bed for two days

before police released him without charge, but with a warning to keep silent about his treatment.

Extrajudicial executions

Police killings of criminal suspects in apparent staged "encounters" or "escape" attempts continued to be reported; police descriptions of the cases were often strikingly similar.

■ The deaths in custody in September of Suresh Kumar of Matale, Ranmukage Ajith Prasanna of Embilipitiya and Dhammala Arachchige Lakshman of Hanwella were all reported by an NGO, the Asian Human Rights Commission. In each case, police claimed that the victim was taken from the police station to identify a weapons cache, attempted to escape, and was shot.

Impunity

Investigations into human rights violations by the military, police and other official bodies and individuals made no apparent progress; court cases did not proceed. Military and civilian officials rejected allegations that Sri Lankan forces had violated international humanitarian law in the final phase of the armed conflict that ended in May 2009 and made repeated public statements claiming that "zero civilian casualties" had occurred.

On 6 July, Minister Wimal Weerawansa led a demonstration that temporarily closed down the UN's Colombo office in an unsuccessful bid to force Secretary-General Ban Ki-moon to withdraw his panel of experts.

Hundreds of people seeking news of relatives who disappeared after arrest by the army attempted to testify before the LLRC when it held sessions in the north and east starting in August. Few were able to speak to the Commissioners, and there were reports that witnesses were photographed and threatened. The Commission's interim report made useful recommendations to safeguard the rights of detainees and address other public grievances, but failed to address the need for accountability.

Suspected perpetrators of human rights violations continued to hold responsible positions in government.

In November, the government investigated claims that the LTTE killed captured soldiers as the army advanced towards Kilinochchi, but continued to reject allegations that its own forces killed civilians and captured combatants during the armed conflict.

S

Human rights defenders

Human rights defenders continued to be arbitrarily arrested, abducted, attacked and threatened.

■ Pattani Razeek, head of the Community Trust Fund, a Sri Lankan NGO, went missing on 11 February when he left Polonnaruwa city to travel to the eastern town of Valaichchenai. His family lodged a complaint with the local police in Puttalam town where he lived, and also reported his enforced disappearance to the Human Rights Commission of Sri Lanka, but his whereabouts have not been traced. A suspect with alleged political links accused of making ransom demands remained at large.

Journalists

Journalists were physically assaulted, abducted, intimidated and harassed by both government personnel and members of government-allied armed groups. Little effort was made to investigate attacks or bring perpetrators to justice.

■ Prageeth Eknaligoda, an outspoken critic of the Sri Lankan government, went missing on 24 January. He had been reporting on the 26 January presidential elections and had completed an analysis that favoured the opposition candidate, Sarath Fonseka. Police said investigations had revealed nothing about his whereabouts or the circumstances of his disappearance, and a habeas corpus petition filed by his family in the Colombo High Court was subjected to repeated delays.

■ In May, Sri Lanka's Minister of External Affairs announced that the government would pardon J.S. Tissainayagam, the first journalist in Sri Lanka to be convicted under the Prevention of Terrorism Act. He was released on bail in January following an appeal. He left Sri Lanka in June.

S

SUDAN

REPUBLIC OF SUDAN
Head of state and government: Omar Hassan Ahmed Al Bashir
Death penalty: retentionist
Population: 43.2 million
Life expectancy: 58.9 years
Under-5 mortality (m/f):   117/104 per 1,000
Adult literacy: 69.3 per cent

In Darfur and south Sudan, hundreds of thousands of civilians continued to suffer the effects of armed conflict and restricted access to humanitarian aid. The conflict in Darfur escalated and included attacks on villages which resulted in thousands of newly displaced people. Sexual violence against women remained rife in and around camps for the internally displaced. Abductions and attacks on humanitarian convoys also increased. Human rights violations, mainly by the National Intelligence and Security Service (NISS), continued to be committed with impunity. Perceived critics of the government were arrested, tortured or ill-treated and prosecuted for exercising their rights to freedom of expression, association and assembly. Death sentences were handed down, including against juveniles. Women, young girls and men were arrested and flogged in the north because of their "dress" or "behaviour" in public places.

Background

Presidential and parliamentary elections took place in April. President Al Bashir was re-elected amidst reports of fraud and vote-rigging, which prompted some of the main opposition parties to withdraw from the elections.

Preparations for the referendum on self-determination for south Sudan, scheduled to take place on 9 January 2011, were marked by disputes between the National Congress Party (NCP) and the Sudan People's Liberation Movement (SPLM). Contentious issues included voter registration and border demarcation, particularly in the area of Abyei, an oil rich region and one of three transitional areas (together with Blue Nile and South Kordofan).

In February, negotiations resumed between the government and a number of Darfuri armed groups in preparation for peace talks in Doha, Qatar, under the auspices of UN-AU joint mediation and the government of Qatar. A Framework Agreement to Resolve the Conflict in Darfur, similar to one signed in 2009, was signed in Doha on 23 February by the government and the armed opposition Justice and Equality Movement (JEM).

On 1 October, the UN Human Rights Council renewed the mandate of the Independent Expert on the situation of human rights in Sudan.

In October, a UN Security Council delegation visited Sudan in connection with preparations for the referendum.

An International Donors and Investors Conference for east Sudan was held in Kuwait in December. East Sudan continued to suffer marginalization, arms proliferation and insecurity. In addition, hundreds of refugees arrived each month from neighbouring countries, namely Eritrea, Ethiopia and Somalia.

International justice

On 8 February, the International Criminal Court (ICC) decided not to confirm the charges against Bahar Idriss Abu Garda, leader of the United Resistance Front, a Darfur-based armed group. Bahar Idriss Abu Garda had been summoned in relation to three war crimes in an attack on Haskanita in 2007 against peacekeepers from the African Union Mission in Sudan (AMIS). He appeared voluntarily before the ICC on 18 May 2009. The pre-trial chamber rejected the ICC Prosecutor's appeal on 23 April 2010 and again refused to confirm the charges.

On 17 June, Abdallah Banda Abbaker Nourein, Commander in Chief of the JEM Collective Leadership, and Saleh Mohammed Jerbo Jamus, former Chief of Staff of the Sudan Liberation Army-Unity who then joined the JEM, appeared before the ICC. The hearing to confirm the charges against them took place on 8 December.

On 12 July, the ICC issued an additional arrest warrant against President Al Bashir for genocide. The pre-trial chamber found there were reasonable grounds to believe that President Al Bashir was responsible for three counts of genocide against the Fur, Massalit and Zaghawa ethnic communities.

The Assembly of the AU reaffirmed in July its decision not to co-operate with the ICC in relation to the arrest and surrender of President Al Bashir. The Assembly asked AU member states to comply with its decision. President Al Bashir visited Chad and Kenya, both states parties to the Rome Statute, in July and August.

The Sudanese government did not co-operate with the ICC. The three people against whom the ICC had issued arrest warrants – President Al Bashir, Ahmed Haroun, governor of South Kordofan since May 2009, and Ali Kushayb, former Janjaweed leader – also remained free from prosecution in Sudan.

Armed conflict – Darfur

In February, as the prospect of a peace agreement was being discussed in Doha by the government and various armed groups from Darfur, the government launched a military campaign in Darfur. Armed clashes between government troops and the Sudan Liberation Army (SLA) Abdel Wahid faction, mainly in the Jebel Marra area in West Darfur, led to the displacement of an estimated 100,000 people between February and June. The joint UN-AU Mission in Darfur (UNAMID) and humanitarian organizations were denied access to the Jebel Marra area for several months. Fighting between various communities also escalated and was exacerbated by divisions within armed groups. Inter-communal fighting and clashes between government troops and the SLA/Abdel Wahid and the JEM led to hundreds of civilian casualties.

The framework agreement signed in Doha included an exchange of prisoners and the government released 57 alleged JEM prisoners in February. Fifty of them had been sentenced to death by special counter-terrorism courts following the JEM attack on Khartoum in May 2008.

The governments of Sudan and Chad formed a joint force to patrol their borders and the government of Chad denied Khalil Ibrahim, leader of the JEM which was mainly based in eastern Chad, access to its territory. While Khalil Ibrahim took refuge in Libya, the JEM re-entered Darfur. The agreement between the JEM and the Sudanese government collapsed, leading to military confrontations including in the Jebel Moon area.

In Kalma camp in South Darfur, armed clashes between supporters and opponents of the Doha peace process led to tens of casualties amongst camp residents in July and forced half the residents out of the camp. The camp's inhabitants were denied access to humanitarian aid by the government for several weeks while those who left the camp were not easily traceable by humanitarian agencies.

In September, the government adopted a new strategy for Darfur to control the conflict, encouraging the "voluntary" return of internally displaced people

S

(IDPs) to their areas of origin, and planning a shift from recovery to development activities. The new strategy was rejected by several armed groups and political parties who alleged that the government was attempting to dismantle the camps and force people to return to their villages while pursuing a military solution to the conflict.

■ In July, the police and the NISS arrested a number of individuals in Kalma camp. At least two were reportedly tortured and remained in incommunicado detention without charge at the end of the year. Following the arrests, six camp residents, one a woman, sought refuge at a UNAMID community policing centre. Although the government reportedly presented UNAMID with arrest warrants for the five men, UNAMID refused to surrender them without guarantees for their safety, including freedom from torture and the death penalty.

■ Four IDPs from Abushok camp in North Darfur who were arrested in August 2009 under the 1997 Emergency and Public Safety Act remained in detention without charge. Thirteen IDPs in total were arrested following the killing of a sheikh in the camp. Seven were released in February and another two in September. While charges against all of them were dropped following early investigations, the detainees were nevertheless transferred to Shalla prison and detained without access to their families or a lawyer. North Darfur has been under a state of emergency since 2006, which gives extraordinary powers to the state governor and other officials to arrest and detain people without charge.

■ On 1 December, a Doha civil society consultation was held at Zalingei University in West Darfur, in the presence of the Qatari mediator and the joint UN-AU chief mediator Djibril Bassolé. Outside the meeting, students calling for accountability for crimes in Darfur clashed with students supporting the NCP. Following the departure of the delegation, the NISS opened fire on the demonstrators. Two men, including one student, were killed and at least nine people were injured.

Armed conflict – south Sudan

The population of south Sudan and the three transitional areas continued to be affected by inter-communal fighting over cattle, land and natural resources, although the scale of the violence decreased over the year. The proliferation of small arms and human rights abuses by various groups, including soldiers of the Sudan People's Liberation Army (SPLA), continued to affect communities and humanitarian workers.

Nevertheless, tens of thousands of IDPs and refugees returned to south Sudan from the north and from neighbouring countries, mainly Uganda.

The Lord's Resistance Army (LRA) attacked villages in south Sudan. According to UNHCR, the UN refugee agency, by August, 25,000 people had fled their homes in Western Equatoria out of fear of LRA attacks. The escalation in LRA attacks limited the population's access to fields and crops and increased food insecurity.

Arbitrary detentions, torture and other ill-treatment

A new National Security Act passed in December 2009 came into force in February. The Act maintained the NISS's extensive powers of arrest and detention without judicial oversight for up to four and a half months.

The NISS continued to arrest and detain political activists and human rights defenders, hold them incommunicado, torture and ill-treat them, and prosecute them for the peaceful exercise of their rights to freedom of expression, assembly and association. NISS agents remained immune from prosecution and disciplinary measures for human rights violations.

As a result of these practices, human rights defenders continued to flee the country and to limit their activities when inside Sudan.

■ Mohammed Moussa Abdallah Bahr El Din, a student at the University of Khartoum's Department of Education, was seized by NISS agents on 10 February. His body was found a day later in Khartoum with signs of torture, reportedly including cuts and burns on his hands and feet. A postmortem confirmed the signs of torture. No independent investigation was initiated into his death.

■ Between 30 October and 3 November, 13 people were arrested by the NISS in Khartoum, including a lawyer, a journalist and a number of youth activists. In December, family members were allowed to visit some of them in prison but the detainees still had no access to lawyers. All were of Darfuri origin.

Freedom of expression – prisoners of conscience

Between May and August, the NISS resumed its pre-print censorship of the press in the north and closed down a number of newspapers. Some were not allowed to go to print for the entire duration of the censorship. Journalists were arrested because of their work.

In south Sudan, journalists also suffered harassment and arbitrary arrest, particularly because of their coverage of the elections. Security forces and SPLA soldiers arrested and used violence against journalists as well as election monitors and members of the opposition. Voters were also harassed and intimidated in voting polls in the south.

■ *Rai Al Shaab*, a newspaper affiliated to the opposition Popular Congress Party, was closed down in May and five staff members were arrested. In July, Abuzar Al Amin, deputy editor-in-chief, was sentenced to five years in prison while Ashraf Abdelaziz, one of the newspaper's editors, and Al Tahir Abu Jawhara, head of the political news desk, were sentenced to two years. The journalists were reportedly tortured or otherwise ill-treated in detention.

■ On 23 April, Bonifacio Taban Kuich, a presenter with the radio station Bentiu FM, was arrested by the security forces in Bentiu hospital. He was reporting on a protest against the results of the local elections in Unity State, during which police reportedly shot into the crowd, killing two people and injuring four. Bonifacio Taban Kuich was allegedly beaten and interrogated about his work. He was released without charge on 6 May.

Cruel, inhuman and degrading punishments

The public order police continued to arrest women, young girls and men in the north, on grounds of "indecent" or "immoral" dress or behaviour, and courts carried out numerous flogging sentences during the year. More restrictions on public behaviour were introduced and the public order police reportedly formed committees to determine criteria for arresting people on the basis of "indecent" public behaviour or dress.

Before the April elections, President Al Bashir reiterated his commitment to the public order regime, the set of laws and structures that allow for detentions and floggings in north Sudan. The public order police continued to blackmail women and sexually harass them during arrest and in detention and to target women from vulnerable backgrounds, including women living in poverty, IDPs and women from Eritrean and Ethiopian communities living in Khartoum.

■ The appeal of Lubna Hussein, a journalist who defied the public order regime by taking her case to an ordinary court and who was convicted in September 2009 for wearing trousers, remained pending before the Constitutional Court.

■ In August, 19 young men were arrested in Khartoum by the public order police for cross-dressing and wearing make-up. The men were denied access to a lawyer, and publicly given 30 lashes before a reported audience of some 200 people.

■ On 14 December, dozens of protestors rallied in Khartoum calling for an investigation into the public flogging of a woman by two members of the public order police in the presence of a judge. The flogging had been filmed and received wide publicity. More than 60 men and women were arrested by the NISS and held until the evening. Many women were beaten during their arrest.

Death penalty

Courts in north and south Sudan continued to pass death sentences, including against juveniles. Although 50 men were released following the signing of the framework agreement for peace negotiations between the JEM and the government in February in Doha, 55 men remained in prison awaiting the results of the appeals against their death sentences. Eight of the 55 were believed to be children and although the government gave assurances that they would not be executed, their sentences had not been commuted by the end of the year.

■ On 14 January, six men were executed for the murder of 13 policemen during clashes in the IDP camp of Soba Aradi, south of Khartoum. Violence erupted after the security forces attempted to forcibly evict the camp residents in May 2005. The six men were only allowed access to a lawyer five months after their arrest. All were reportedly tortured to "confess". The Constitutional Court upheld the death sentences despite the allegations of torture.

■ On 21 October, a special court in Darfur sentenced 10 men to death. Four were reportedly under the age of 18: Idriss Adam Abbaker; Abdallah Abdallah Daoud; Ibrahim Shareef Youssif; and Abdelrazig Daoud Abdessed. They were convicted of involvement in an attack on a government escorted convoy in South Darfur. The trial did not meet international standards of fair trial. Only two of the alleged children were medically examined to determine their age. Idriss Adam Abbaker was confirmed as a child and had his sentence commuted. One medical examination confirmed that

S

Abdallah Abdallah Daoud was a child, but a second examination found that he was over 18 and was taken into account by the court.

Amnesty International visits/reports

- Sudan: Briefing to international election observers (AFR 54/009/2010)
- Agents of fear: The National Security Service in Sudan (AFR 54/010/2010)
- Sudan: Doctors detained, risk of torture (AFR 54/020/2010)
- Sudan: Three journalists sentenced, one acquitted (AFR 54/025/2010)
- The chains remain: Restrictions on freedom of expression in Sudan (AFR 54/028/2010)
- Sudan: Activists held incommunicado in Sudan (AFR 54/036/2010)

SWAZILAND

KINGDOM OF SWAZILAND

Head of state:	King Mswati III
Head of government:	Barnabas Sibusiso Dlamini
Death penalty:	abolitionist in practice
Population:	1.2 million
Life expectancy:	47 years
Under-5 mortality (m/f):	111/92 per 1,000
Adult literacy:	86.5 per cent

Human rights defenders and political activists were subjected to arbitrary detention, ill-treatment and harassment. Sweeping provisions in anti-terrorism legislation were used to detain and charge political opponents. Torture and incidents of unjustified use of lethal force were reported. The Prime Minister appeared to publicly condone the use of torture. Discriminatory laws affecting women's rights were not repealed. Over 41 per cent of women attending antenatal clinics were HIV positive. Access to treatment for AIDS in rural areas was undermined by poverty and shortages of drugs and doctors.

Background

The government continued to exclude governance issues from its dialogue with the trade union movement and civil society. An ILO delegation visited the country in October to investigate complaints of restrictions on freedom of association.

Swaziland's economy continued to decline, with a fall of 62 per cent in revenue from the Southern African Customs Union, and rising levels of unemployment and poverty. Average life expectancy continued to fall due to the twin epidemics of HIV and tuberculosis.

Repression of dissent

Civil society and political activists reported incidents of ill-treatment, house searches and surveillance of communications and meetings. Some planned protests and trade union marches were disrupted during the year, although a large trade union-led march in November proceeded without incident.

- In June and July, armed police conducted raids and prolonged searches in the homes of dozens of high profile human rights defenders, trade unionists and political activists while investigating a spate of petrol bombings. Some of the searches, particularly of political activists, were done without search warrants. Some individuals were taken to police stations and interrogated about their activities and at least two activists reported being subjected to torture by suffocation and beatings.
- On 6 September, in a bid to disrupt planned protest marches, police broke up a peaceful civil society meeting in Manzini. They unlawfully arrested more than 50 people including human rights defenders and foreign trade union officials. Police also seized camera equipment, threatened and detained one journalist and assaulted another. After their release or deportation some of them reported that they had been assaulted at the time of their arrest. The marches, organized by the Swaziland labour federations and the Swaziland Democracy Campaign, went ahead on 7 and 8 September under heavy police and military presence.

On 8 September, the Prime Minister stated at a press conference that torture should be considered as a form of punishment against "interfering foreigners" and dissidents. There was no clear repudiation of his widely reported comments later from his office.

Counter-terror and security

The authorities continued to use the sweeping provisions of the 2008 Suppression of Terrorism Act (STA) to detain and charge political activists. The STA was also used as a basis for search warrants and other measures to intimidate human rights defenders, trade unionists and media workers.

- In June, Zonke Dlamini and Bhekumusa Dlamini, both members of an organization banned under the STA, were arrested separately in connection with police investigations into petrol bombings. They were charged under the STA and denied bail after a High Court hearing. The court was informed during the hearing that they had been subjected to suffocation torture and other ill-treatment in police custody following their arrests. Zonke Dlamini also alleged that his confession, which led to the arrest of Bhekumusa Dlamini, had been extracted under duress. Trial proceedings had not concluded by the end of the year.

Death in custody

■ Political activist Sipho Jele died in Sidwashini Remand Centre several days after being arrested at a May Day workers' rally. On 3 May he was charged in the High Court under the STA, apparently because he was wearing a T-shirt and possessed a membership card of an organization banned under the STA. He was not represented by a lawyer and no record was kept of the proceedings. It later emerged that he asked the court not to remand him back into police custody for fear of being tortured. He was found hanging in his cell block on 4 May. The Prime Minister, in an unusual step, ordered an inquest into his death. A range of witnesses was heard in open court. The coroner had not reported her findings to the Prime Minister by the end of the year. Sipho Jele had been detained previously in 2005 and allegedly tortured before being charged with treason, for which he was never brought to trial.

Freedom of expression

Freedom of expression continued to be restricted by statutory laws affecting the media, sweeping provisions under the STA, and specific threats made by public officials against journalists and editors.
■ In March, Bheki Makhubu, the editor of the independent publication, *The Nation*, appeared in court to answer charges of "criminal contempt of court". The charges arose from two articles expressing concern about the rule of law in Swaziland. The case had not been heard by the end of the year.

Excessive use of force

The misuse of deadly force by the police and other law enforcement officials continued to be reported, with evidence indicating that the victims were not posing a threat to life when they were shot. In January, the then Chairperson of the Human Rights and Public Administration Commission, Rev David Matse, publicly expressed concern that police and soldiers appeared to be using a "shoot-to-kill policy" which violated the right to life.

■ On 3 January, Sicelo Mamba was shot dead, allegedly by security guards protecting a farm and wildlife reserve. He was shot three times with a high velocity rifle, twice in the head. The security guards and their employer, a prominent farmer, appeared to believe that they had immunity from prosecution under the 1997 Game Act. No official investigation had been instituted by the end of the year.
■ On 14 February, Sifiso Nhlabatsi was allegedly shot by police while he was handcuffed and in their custody. He had been removed from Mbabane police station cells and taken to Thembelihle forest where he was interrogated, allegedly assaulted and shot. He required hospital treatment for gunshot injuries to his upper back. The police publicly stated that they had shot him "in the buttocks while trying to escape during his arrest".

Women's rights

Finalization of draft legislation affecting women's right to equality continued to be delayed, despite recognition in Swaziland's MDG Report for 2010 that this was leading to the feminization of poverty. The persistence and scale of gender-based violence was confirmed in the same report as "a major problem". In August, the government approved a National Gender Policy document.

In May, the Supreme Court overturned on technical grounds a High Court decision granting some married women the right to own immovable property. However, the appeal judges agreed that the relevant provision of the Deeds Registry Act of 1968, which denied these women this right, was unconstitutional. The Supreme Court gave parliament a year to amend the provision.

In October, the Sexual Offences and Domestic Violence Bill was introduced in parliament for full debate, more than five years after it was initially drafted. The Bill had not been enacted by the end of the year.

Right to health – poverty and HIV

Swaziland's HIV prevalence rate among adults aged 15-49 years remained the highest in the world. Women remained disproportionately affected by the epidemic, with the majority of new infections continuing to occur in females. In November, the Minister of Health announced a slight decline since 2008 to 41.1 per cent in the HIV prevalence rate among pregnant women attending antenatal clinics. Government officials stated at the UN in October that women were providing 90 per cent of all care for people with AIDS-related illnesses.

S

Just over 50 per cent of people needing antiretroviral therapy (ART) were receiving treatment in 2010. Access and adherence to ART continued to be hampered by shortages of medical staff and drugs. Socio-economic barriers included unaffordable public transport for patients in rural areas. Improved treatment outcomes were reported, however, from a capacity-building project for clinics in the poorest region, Shishelweni, jointly run by Médecins Sans Frontières and the Ministry of Health.

Right to education

In March, the Supreme Court ruled that the right to free primary school education was not a fundamental right. Despite a 2009 High Court ruling affirming this obligation under the Constitution, the Supreme Court stated that the problem was a question of the availability of resources, "not a fastidious insistence on the true and proper interpretation of section 29(6) of the Swazi Constitution". The appeal had been lodged by the Swaziland National Ex-Mineworkers Association after their application for an order to enforce the 2009 ruling had been dismissed in January 2010.

Death penalty

Although the 2006 Constitution permits the use of capital punishment, no executions have been carried out since 1983. No new death sentences were imposed in 2010. Two people remained under sentence of death. Public calls for the resumption of executions were made in response to incidents of violent crime.

Amnesty International visits/reports

🚍 Amnesty International delegates visited Swaziland in March and August.

📄 Swaziland: Amnesty International urges the government to ensure an effective and impartial inquiry into the death in custody of Sipho Jele (AFR 55/001/2010)

📄 Swaziland: Activists at risk in Swazi police crackdown (AFR 55/002/2010)

📄 Swaziland: Security forces commit human rights violations against human rights defenders and demonstrators (AFR 55/004/2010)

📄 Swaziland: Too late, too little: The failure of law reform for women in Swaziland (AFR 55/007/2010)

📄 Swaziland: Arrests of human rights activists in Swaziland condemned, 6 September 2010

SWEDEN

KINGDOM OF SWEDEN

Head of state:	King Carl XVI Gustaf
Head of government:	Fredrik Reinfeldt
Death penalty:	abolitionist for all crimes
Population:	9.3 million
Life expectancy:	81.3 years
Under-5 mortality (m/f):	4/4 per 1,000

The Swedish authorities considered a large number of asylum applications to be "manifestly unfounded". The accelerated asylum-determination procedures applied to these cases did not meet international standards for refugee protection. There were forcible returns to Iraq and Eritrea. Concerns remained about the thoroughness of police investigations into rape cases.

Refugees, asylum-seekers and migrants

Forced returns to Eritrea and Iraq continued despite recommendations to the contrary from UNHCR, the UN refugee agency.

In March the High Court of Migration determined that individuals detained pending transfer to another EU member state under the Dublin II Regulation had the right to legal representation to challenge their detention.

In November, the Swedish Migration Board announced it would no longer transfer asylum-seekers to Greece under the Dublin II Regulation following serious concerns about the inadequacy of asylum-determination procedures and detention conditions in the country. Following a court ruling in December, it was further agreed that all such asylum-seekers would have their claims examined in Sweden.

In contrast to recent years, the Swedish authorities considered a large number of asylum applications to be "manifestly unfounded", the majority of which were Roma applicants from Serbia and Kosovo, according to the Migration Board. The accelerated asylum-determination procedures applied to these cases did not meet international standards for refugee protection; applicants were not given a full asylum interview and were denied access to legal aid. In addition, those whose claims had been rejected could be forcibly returned to their home countries or a third country pending appeal against an initial rejection of their claim.

S

Violence against women

In October, the Sexual Offences Commission reviewing the implementation, efficiency and effectiveness of the 2005 Sexual Crimes Act published its final report. The Commission recommended changes to legislation in order to strengthen the protection of individuals' sexual integrity and autonomy.

The number of reported rapes resulting in a conviction remained low, with the majority of cases being closed in the early stage of the criminal investigation. Concerns continued that investigations into rape cases were inadequate and that police failed to effectively use forensic evidence and to request the right type of forensic legal certificates.

In May, Sweden ratified the Council of Europe Convention on Action against Trafficking in Human Beings.

Torture and other ill-treatment

Sweden refused to exclude reliance on "diplomatic assurances" to facilitate the deportation of individuals to countries where they might face torture or other ill-treatment, and continued to fail to introduce torture as a crime in its penal code.

■ Ahmed Agiza remained in prison in Egypt following an unfair trial by a military court, and concerns remained about his deteriorating physical health. Sweden continued to fail to fully investigate the renditions of Ahmed Agiza and Mohammed El Zari on a CIA-leased plane from Sweden to Egypt in December 2001, where the two men alleged they were tortured and ill-treated in Egyptian custody. Although the men received monetary compensation, Sweden has failed to provide them with full, effective redress.

■ Two further investigations into the death of Johan Liljeqvist, a 24-year-old man who died in April 2008 following his arrest by the police in Gothenburg, were closed in March and November respectively, despite medical evidence indicating that his death was "connected to the intervention of the police".

In December, a report examining police investigations into cases of death in police custody, initiated following the Liljeqvist case, was released. The report heavily criticized the adequacy of police investigations in such cases and recommended immediate changes to improve their independence, impartiality and thoroughness.

Amnesty International visits/reports

⬚ Case closed: Rape and human rights in the Nordic countries - summary Report (ACT 77/001/2010)

⬚ European states must stop forced returns to Iraq (EUR 01/028/2010)

⬚ Europe: Open Secret: Mounting evidence of Europe's complicity in rendition and secret detention (EUR 01/023/2010)

SWITZERLAND

SWISS CONFEDERATION

Head of state and government:	Doris Leuthard
Death penalty:	abolitionist for all crimes
Population:	7.6 million
Life expectancy:	82.2 years
Under-5 mortality (m/f):	6/5 per 1,000

A National Human Rights Institution was established and a National Commission for the Prevention of Torture appointed to monitor detention facilities. A popular referendum amended the constitution to require the immediate deportation of foreign nationals convicted of certain criminal offences. Criminal law continued to lack a definition of torture consistent with international law.

Legal, constitutional and institutional developments

In September, the Federal Council established the Swiss Competence Centre for Human Rights as a national human rights institution, to begin its work in 2011. Human rights organizations welcomed the initiative, but were concerned about its lack of independence, resources and the limited role for cantonal authorities.

On 28 November, a referendum known as the "Deportation Initiative" was held seeking to amend the constitution to allow for the automatic deportation of foreign nationals convicted of specified criminal offences. It passed with a 52.9 per cent vote in favour. If implemented, such deportations, with no provision for the right to appeal, would violate Switzerland's obligations under international law.

On 10 December, Switzerland agreed to sign the International Convention against enforced disappearance.

S

Refugees, asylum-seekers and migrants

From February onwards, the Federal Administrative Court suspended the return of several asylum-seekers to Greece under the Dublin II Regulation pending the Court's judgement in a lead case regarding such transfers. Despite this practice, the Federal Office for Migration transferred 50 asylum-seekers to Greece during the year.

In May, the UN Committee against Torture expressed concern that the Federal Act on Foreign Nationals might violate the principle of *non-refoulement*. The law permits the automatic expulsion of foreign nationals considered to represent a security threat, with no opportunity for appeal. The Committee called for the legislation to be modified.

■ In July, the European Court of Human Rights ruled that Switzerland had violated the right to private and family life of two Ethiopian women asylum-seekers. They had been required to live in reception centres in different cantons from their husbands for five years while awaiting their removal to Ethiopia.

In November, the UN Committee on Economic Social and Cultural Rights raised concerns about the adequacy of reception facilities for asylum-seekers, which included accommodation in underground nuclear bunkers for indefinite periods.

Torture and other ill-treatment

On 1 January, the National Commission for the Prevention of Torture was appointed and started monitoring detention facilities and group deportations.

In May, the UN Committee against Torture noted that, while several acts amounting to torture were criminalized under domestic criminal law, legislation lacked a definition of torture consistent with international law.

Police and security forces

In May, the UN Committee against Torture expressed concern about allegations of excessive use of force by police during questioning, in particular of foreign nationals, and especially those of African origin. The Committee reiterated the need to establish an independent mechanism to investigate such complaints in each canton.

■ The UN Committee against Torture urged Switzerland to open an independent, impartial inquiry into the death of Joseph Ndukaku Chiakwa, a Nigerian national who died at Zurich airport in March during an attempted mass deportation. Eye-witnesses stated that the people facing deportation had been physically restrained, with plastic hand and ankle cuffs, helmets, and straps to secure their knees, waist and arms. A criminal investigation was pending at the end of the year.

Guantánamo Bay detainees

In January and March, the Federal Council confirmed the arrival of former detainees from US custody at Guantánamo Bay. An Uzbekistani man and two ethnic Uighurs from China were accepted by the cantons of Geneva and Jura respectively.

No final decision was taken by the authorities regarding asylum claims issued by three other Guantánamo Bay detainees in 2008. In November, the Federal Administrative Court overruled a decision by the Federal Office for Migration on one of the detainees, stating that the security assessment had been made without considering public documents from the US and without questioning the applicant.

Violence against women

The UN Committee against Torture and the Committee on Economic, Social and Cultural Rights, in May and November respectively, recommended that Switzerland deal with impunity in cases of domestic violence. Recommendations included that the state specifically criminalize domestic violence, ensure that survivors are able to issue complaints without fear of reprisals, investigate allegations and prosecute perpetrators. Both Committees recommended modifying immigration legislation which had led migrant women to remain in abusive relationships due to fear of losing their residence permits.

Amnesty International visits/reports

📰 Switzerland: The "Deportation Initiative" cannot override international human rights obligations (EUR 43/002/2010)

S

SYRIA

SYRIAN ARAB REPUBLIC

Head of state:	Bashar al-Assad
Head of government:	Muhammad Naji al-'Otri
Death penalty:	retentionist
Population:	22.5 million
Life expectancy:	74.6 years
Under-5 mortality (m/f):	21/16 per 1,000
Adult literacy:	83.6 per cent

The authorities remained intolerant of dissent. Those who criticized the government, including human rights defenders, faced arrest and imprisonment after unfair trials, and bans from travelling abroad. Some were prisoners of conscience. Human rights NGOs and opposition political parties were denied legal authorization. State forces and the police continued to commit torture and other ill-treatment with impunity, and there were at least eight suspicious deaths in custody. The government failed to clarify the fate of 49 prisoners missing since a violent incident in 2008 at Saydnaya Military Prison, and took no steps to account for thousands of victims of enforced disappearances in earlier years. Women were subject to discrimination and gender-based violence; at least 22 people, mostly women, were victims of so-called honour killings. Members of the Kurdish minority continued to be denied equal access to economic, social and cultural rights. At least 17 people were executed, including a woman alleged to be a victim of physical and sexual abuse.

Background

Syria remained under a national state of emergency in force continuously since 1963, which provides the authorities with wide powers of arrest and detention.

In January, a progressive law was adopted to prohibit and criminalize the trafficking of people.

In July, the Ministry of Higher Education prohibited women from wearing the *niqab* (face-covering veil) in universities.

In September, the UN Special Rapporteur on the right to food expressed concern that an estimated 2 to 3 million people in Syria were living in "extreme poverty" and urged the government to develop a comprehensive national strategy aimed at realizing the right to adequate food.

In October, arrest warrants were issued against 33

Lebanese and other nationals in response to a case initiated by Jamil al-Sayyed, one of four senior Lebanese officials who were detained without charge or trial in Lebanon for more than three years in connection with the investigation into the assassination of former Lebanese Prime Minister Rafic Hariri in 2005. The four officials had been released by the Lebanese authorities in 2009 after the prosecutor of the Special Tribunal for Lebanon (STL) confirmed that the STL was unable to indict them within the legal timeframe.

A new law apparently intended to tighten controls on internet-based media was reported to be under consideration.

Repression of dissent

The authorities continued to use state of emergency powers to punish and silence their critics, including political activists, human rights defenders, bloggers and Kurdish minority rights activists. Critics were arbitrarily arrested and detained for long periods without trial or imprisoned after unfair trials before the Supreme State Security Court (SSSC) or military or criminal courts. Human rights NGOs could not obtain licences to operate, exposing members who are lawyers to disciplinary action by the government-controlled Bar Association. Hundreds of people considered to be dissidents, including former political prisoners and members of their families, were barred from travelling abroad; some were barred from working in the public sector.

■ Muhannad al-Hassani, a leading human rights lawyer, was sentenced to a three-year prison term in June after the Damascus Criminal Court convicted him of "weakening nationalist sentiment" and disseminating "false news" by publishing information about unfair trials before the SSSC on the internet. He was held at 'Adra prison near Damascus where, in October, he was assaulted by a criminal inmate who had been moved into his cell.

■ Haytham al-Maleh, aged 79, a human rights lawyer and government critic, was sentenced to three years in prison in July after being convicted of "weakening nationalist sentiment" and disseminating "false news" on account of comments he made in a telephone interview with a foreign satellite TV channel in September 2009. He was held at 'Adra prison, prompting concern for his health; he suffers from diabetes and other ailments.

■ Three senior members of the unauthorized Kurdish

S

Yekiti Party continued to be detained incommunicado at 'Adra prison and on trial before the SSSC. Hassan Saleh, Ma'rouf Mulla Ahmed and Muhammad Ahmed Mustafa were charged with "aiming at separating part of the Syrian lands" and "joining a political or social international organization", and faced long jail terms if convicted. They were arrested shortly after they allegedly called for Kurdish areas of Syria to be granted autonomy at a Yekiti Party conference in December 2009.

■ Raghdah Sa'id Hassan, a writer, was arrested in February, detained incommunicado for three months and then charged with "weakening nationalist sentiment" and spreading "false news". At the end of 2010, she remained held at Douma women's prison and on trial before a military criminal court.

■ Radeef Mustafa, a lawyer and leading figure in the unauthorized Kurdish Committee for Human Rights in Syria (RASED), faced disciplinary proceedings by the Syrian Bar Association for engaging in these activities and criticizing the state of emergency in articles he published on the internet; he was at risk of being banned from working as a lawyer.

■ Suhair Atassi, President of the unauthorized Jamal Atassi Forum, a pro-democracy discussion group, was one of at least seven human rights defenders and political activists who were prevented from travelling abroad.

Counter-terror and security

Suspected Islamists and suspected members of the banned Muslim Brotherhood faced arbitrary arrest, prolonged detention, torture and other ill-treatment, and unfair trials, usually before the SSSC which rarely imposes prison sentences of less than five years. Those convicted of belonging to the Muslim Brotherhood were sentenced to death but their sentences were immediately commuted to 12-year prison terms. Hundreds of convicted Islamist prisoners were held at Saydnaya Military Prison, where conditions were harsh.

■ The fate and whereabouts of Nabil Khilioui, a suspected Islamist detained by Military Intelligence officials in August 2008, remained unknown; he was a victim of enforced disappearance.

■ Usra al-Hassani was arrested on 2 January and held incommunicado for several months. She was still held without charge at 'Adra prison at the end of the year. She had previously been detained incommunicado for almost a year prior to July 2009 for contacting an international organization about her husband's

detention by US authorities at Guantánamo Bay.

■ Ziad Ramadan, a former work colleague of a suspect in the 2005 assassination of former Lebanese Prime Minister Rafic Hariri, remained detained since July 2005 without charge and in harsh conditions at the Palestine Branch of Military Intelligence in Damascus, although the STL had informed the Syrian authorities that it saw no grounds for his detention.

Torture and other ill-treatment

Torture and other ill-treatment were used extensively and with impunity in police stations and security agencies' detention centres. According to reports, suspected Islamists and members of the Kurdish minority were subject to particularly harsh abuse. The SSSC and other courts often convicted defendants on the basis of "confessions" alleged to have been extracted under torture or other duress.

■ 'Abdelbaqi Khalaf, a Syrian Kurdish pro-democracy activist detained in September 2008, was reported to have been shackled by his wrists to a wall for eight days, tortured and otherwise ill-treated during more than a year in incommunicado detention. In August 2010 it was reported that he was being tortured to force him to "confess" to killing two members of the security forces. He was held at 'Adra prison.

In May, the UN Committee against Torture expressed concern about "numerous, ongoing and consistent" reports of torture by law enforcement and investigative officials, at their instigation or with their consent, particularly in detention facilities, and criticized the "quasi permanent" status of state of emergency legislation which "allows the suspension of fundamental rights and freedoms". The government did not respond and had not implemented any of the Committee's many recommendations by the end of 2010.

Deaths in custody

Eight deaths in custody possibly as a result of torture were reported; none was known to have been investigated by the authorities.

■ Jalal al-Koubaisi died in Criminal Security custody within days of his arrest on 27 May, apparently for encouraging people to shop at a particular store. He was held incommunicado. On 1 June, his family was told to go to a hospital to collect his body. The body had bruising and other marks indicating that he may have been tortured. No official investigation was known to have been held.

S

Impunity

The authorities took no steps to account for thousands of people, mostly Islamists, who disappeared in the late 1970s and early 1980s, and others abducted in Lebanon by Syrian forces or by pro-Syrian Lebanese and Palestinian militias, who then handed them over to Syrian forces in the years before they withdrew from Lebanon in April 2005. The authorities also failed to disclose what occurred at Saydnaya Military Prison in July 2008, when 17 prisoners and five other people were reported to have been killed and since when there has been no information or known contact with 49 prisoners held there at the time. In May, the UN Committee against Torture urged the government to carry out an independent investigation and to "inform the families of those prisoners if their relatives are alive and still held in prison".

■ Nizar Ristnawi, a prisoner of conscience and one of the 49 Saydnaya prisoners whose fate remained unknown, should have been released on 18 April 2009 when his four-year prison term expired. In March 2009, the UN Working Group on Arbitrary Detention declared his detention to be arbitrary and urged the government "to take the necessary steps to remedy his situation".

Discrimination and violence against women and girls

Women faced discrimination in law and in practice, and high levels of violence, particularly within the family. Laws assigning inferior status to women as compared to men, notably the Personal Status Law governing marriage and its dissolution, inheritance and other matters, remained in force. Such discrimination was reinforced by social customs.

Women and girls were inadequately protected from violence within the family: the Penal Code prescribes lower penalties for murder and other violent crimes committed against women when defence of family "honour" is considered a mitigating factor. At least 16 women, two men and four children under the age of 18 were reported to have been victims of so-called honour killings. In November, a joint study by the government and the UN Population Fund reported that one in three women suffers domestic violence in Syria. The government was reported to be planning to establish a National Family Protection Unit and a National Observatory for Domestic Violence.

Discrimination – Kurdish minority

Kurds, who comprise up to 10 per cent of the population and live mostly in the north-east, continued to experience identity-based discrimination, including restrictions on use of their language and culture. Tens of thousands of Syrian Kurds were effectively stateless, further restricting their access to social and economic rights.

■ Luqman Ibrahim Hussein and three others were detained for 39 days apparently for observing a protest of one minute's silence on 10 September in 'Amudah. They were protesting against Legislative Decree 49 of 2008, which further restricted housing and property rights in border areas, including the predominantly Kurdish-populated north-east border areas. On 9 November, while free on bail, the four were sentenced to one month in prison but were not detained as they had already spent over a month in jail.

Refugees and asylum-seekers

Syria continued to host hundreds of thousands of Iraqi refugees who had access to its education and health infrastructures, but continued to be denied the right to work.

On 1 February, the authorities and UN agencies permanently closed the desolate camp at al-Tanf in the border area between Iraq and Syria, where Palestinian refugees who were long-term residents of Iraq had lived. Out of the 1,300 Palestinian refugees who had lived at different times in the camp, around 1,000 were relocated to third countries while the rest were temporarily moved to al-Hol camp in north-east Syria.

Death penalty

Death sentences continued to be imposed and at least 17 people were executed, although the true number may have been much higher. The authorities rarely disclose information about executions.

■ Eliaza al-Saleh, Ahmed al-'Abbas and Mazen Bassouni were executed on 4 November. All three had been convicted of murdering Eliaza al-Saleh's husband. Evidence that she had suffered years of physical and sexual abuse by her husband was apparently ignored at her trial and appeal. Her family learned of her execution three days after it was carried out.

In December, Syria was one of a minority of states that voted against a UN General Assembly resolution calling for a worldwide moratorium on executions.

S

🚗 An Amnesty International delegation visited Syria in June for research on women's rights; the delegation met the Deputy Minister for Social Welfare.

📄 'Your son is not here', Disappearances from Syria's Saydnaya Military Prison (MDE 24/012/2010)

TAIWAN

TAIWAN
Head of state: **Ma Ying-jeou**
Head of government: **Wu Den-yih**
Death penalty: **retentionist**

Executions resumed. The authorities failed to deliver on promises to amend a law governing freedom of assembly. A corruption scandal affecting the judiciary prompted calls for judicial reform. Migrant workers continued to face multiple abuses of their rights.

Background

The government continued reviewing all laws, regulations and administrative measures for alignment with the International Covenant on Civil and Political Rights and the International Covenant on Economic, Social and Cultural Rights. Local activists questioned whether completion to a high standard was feasible by the December 2011 deadline.

Death penalty

In April, four people were executed, the first executions since 2005. On 28 May, Taiwan's Constitutional Court rejected a petition to halt executions made on behalf of 44 death row inmates, four of whom had been executed in April. Four new death sentences were imposed, bringing the total number of prisoners awaiting execution to more than 70. In October, an expert panel established in the Ministry of Justice recommended abolition of the death penalty.

Freedom of expression

In September, the Taipei District Court suspended prosecution of two academics and leaders of human rights organizations, Lin Chia-fan and Lee Ming-tsung, for leading demonstrations without permits in 2008.

The court submitted Lee Ming-tsung's case for constitutional interpretation of several articles of the Assembly and Parade Law to assess possible infringement of citizens' rights to assembly and free speech. In November, students protested against the government's failure to deliver on its 2009 proposals to amend the law, including removing the requirement for prior police approval of demonstrations.

Justice system

In July, the president of the Judicial Yuan resigned after a major corruption scandal involving high court judges. The crisis prompted demands for effective evaluation of judges and the draft Judges Act, under deliberation for more than 20 years, finally became a priority in the Legislative Yuan.

Migrants' rights

Migrant workers in Taiwan faced multiple abuses of their rights, including the right to transfer between employers and to form unions. Harsh and discriminatory working conditions, and exorbitant brokers' fees contributed to large numbers leaving their original employer and becoming undocumented. Domestic workers are not protected by the Labor Standards Law, and are particularly vulnerable to sexual harassment, inadequately paid overtime and poor living conditions.

TAJIKISTAN

REPUBLIC OF TAJIKISTAN

Head of state:	Emomali Rahmon
Head of government:	Okil Okilov
Death penalty:	abolitionist in practice
Population:	7.1 million
Life expectancy:	67.3 years
Under-5 mortality (m/f):	83/74 per 1,000
Adult literacy:	99.7 per cent

Torture and other ill-treatment continued. Freedom of expression remained restricted. The authorities failed to effectively prevent and prosecute violence against women and to protect survivors.

Torture and other ill-treatment

There were continued reports of torture and other ill-treatment by law enforcement officers. The common police practice of incommunicado detention before formally opening a criminal case increased the risk of torture and other ill-treatment. Confessions extracted under duress continued to be used as evidence in courts. Victims rarely reported physical abuse by law enforcement officers for fear of repercussions, and impunity remained the rule. Tajikistani human rights groups, lawyers and judges called on the government to include a precise definition of torture, in line with international standards, in national legislation.

■ On 26 February, Nematillo Botakozuev, a Kyrgyzstani human rights defender, was detained by police in the Tajikistani capital, Dushanbe, after he had visited the office of the UNHCR, the UN refugee agency, to apply for refugee status. He was wanted by the Kyrgyzstani authorities for his alleged involvement in a demonstration in the town of Nookat in 2008. He was held incommunicado for almost a month and reportedly tortured at the premises of the State Committee for National Security. He was also reportedly denied appropriate medical treatment. On 22 May he was extradited to Kyrgyzstan and released by a court in the city of Osh.

■ Ilhom Ismonov was detained on 3 November in Khujand in Soghd region and charged with "organizing a criminal group". He was not brought before a judge until nine days later on 12 November, in contravention of the Tajikistani Criminal Procedure Code, which states that detainees must be brought before a judge to rule on their continued detention no later than 72 hours

after their arrest. He was also denied access to his lawyer until he appeared in court. He reportedly told the judge that he had been given electric shocks and had boiling water poured over his body while held at the Department for the Fight against Organized Crime (6th Department) of the Ministry of Internal Affairs in Khujand. The judge reportedly did not address the torture allegations. In December, the Prosecutor's office of Soghd region informed Ilhom Ismonov's wife and lawyer that its examination of the case had shown that the allegations of torture were false, that he had not been unlawfully detained, and that there had been no problem with his access to a lawyer. No details were given on how the examination was conducted.

Freedom of expression – journalists

Tajikistani and international human rights groups reported that independent media outlets and journalists continued to face criminal and civil law suits for criticizing the government. Pressure on the media increased particularly in the run-up to the parliamentary elections in February and in the aftermath of the September ambush in Rasht district by alleged Islamist militants and former opposition commanders, in which 28 government troops were killed. In September and October the websites of local news agencies and an opposition blog were allegedly blocked by the authorities, and tax inspections allegedly targeted media outlets that had been critical of the authorities in connection with the Rasht events.

Violence against women

Violence against women remained a serious problem; between one third and half of all women have suffered physical, psychological or sexual violence at the hands of their husbands or other family members at some time during their lives. Despite some initial steps by the government to combat violence against women – such as the establishment of five police stations with specially trained police officers – Tajikistan continued to fall short of its international obligations to protect women from violence in the family. Women's access to the criminal justice system was still very restricted with inadequate police and judicial response, resulting in massive under-reporting. There were insufficient services to protect the survivors of domestic violence, such as shelters and adequate and safe alternative housing. There was still no functioning nationwide cross-referral system between health workers, crisis and legal aid centres, law enforcement agencies and

T

others for survivors of domestic violence. The draft law "Social and legal protection from domestic violence" – in preparation for several years – had still not been presented to parliament.

Amnesty International visits/reports

🚍 Amnesty International delegates visited Tajikistan in March.

TANZANIA

UNITED REPUBLIC OF TANZANIA

Head of state:	Jakaya Kikwete
Head of government:	Mizengo Peter Pinda
Head of Zanzibar government:	Ali Mohamed Shein (replaced Amani Abeid Karume in November)
Death penalty:	abolitionist in practice
Population:	45 million
Life expectancy:	56.9 years
Under-5 mortality (m/f):	112/100 per 1,000
Adult literacy:	72.6 per cent

Government actions undermined freedom of expression. The police and other law enforcement officials accused of committing human rights violations were not brought to justice and impunity for perpetrators of sexual and other forms of gender-based violence continued.

Background

President Kikwete was re-elected for a five-year term in general elections held at the end of October. The main opposition challenger, Willibrod Slaa, and his party, Chama Cha Demokrasia na Maendeleo (CHADEMA), alleged election irregularities and disputed the validity of the presidential result and some of the parliamentary election results.

In July, a public referendum approved the formation of a national government of unity in Zanzibar. The referendum sought to address past political disagreements between the ruling party, Chama Cha Mapinduzi, and the opposition Civic United Front, which had led to violence between their supporters in Zanzibar.

The general elections and the referendum in Zanzibar were generally peaceful. However, delays in announcing some of the election results led to heightened public tension and protests in a number of areas.

Freedom of expression

In the run-up to the general elections the government threatened to either ban or deregister two newspapers – *Mwananchi* and *MwanaHALISI*. Government officials sent letters to the newspapers alleging that they were publishing materials with the intention of "inciting chaos and breaking peace" in the country. The government letters did not specify any particular articles deemed by the government to be offensive. By the end of the year the government had not banned or deregistered either of the two newspapers.

A number of journalists complained of intimidation and harassment by some government and public officials because they had criticized the conduct of these officials or the policies and practices of the government.

Impunity

The government did not institute investigations into alleged human rights abuses committed by police and private company guards in July 2009 in Loliondo, Ngorongoro district, northern Tanzania. According to reports, an unknown number of women were raped by police officers and guards; families were separated and up to 3,000 people from the Maasai pastoralist community were forcibly evicted. These alleged abuses were committed in the context of an operation to evict these people from their homes and grazing land ostensibly in order to conserve a wildlife protection area.

Throughout the year there were reports of unlawful killings, torture and other ill-treatment by the police and other law enforcement officials in the course of security operations in different parts of the country. No investigations into these allegations were carried out, and those responsible were not brought to justice.

Violence against women

Sexual and other forms of gender-based violence remained widespread, particularly domestic violence. Few perpetrators were brought to justice.

Despite a law prohibiting female genital mutilation (FGM), the practice remained prevalent in certain areas such as the Dodoma region in central Tanzania. According to the Legal and Human Rights Centre – a local NGO – implementation of the law prohibiting FGM was hampered by widespread ignorance of the law, enduring traditional beliefs and the lack of public confidence in the criminal justice process.

T

Discrimination – attacks on albino people

There were no reports of albino people being killed for their body parts during the year, although there were up to eight attempted killings, including two mutilations. Some human rights defenders working to promote the human rights of people with albinism reported threats and intimidation from suspected perpetrators of human rights abuses against albino people.

The police were slow to investigate cases of human rights abuses suffered by albino people, and little action was taken in response to the threats to human rights defenders. Overall, the government's efforts to prevent human rights abuses against albino people were inadequate.

Refugees and migrants

As of November, up to 38,000 Burundian refugees remained in Mtabila refugee camp in western Tanzania despite the government's official position that it considered the camp closed. Official efforts to promote voluntary repatriation among the Burundian refugees led to about 6,500 being repatriated from the camp since January 2009. Affected refugees cited possible land disputes in Burundi and fears related to the 2010 election process in the country as reasons for their reluctance to return there. Some stated that they had genuine and well-founded fears of persecution if they were to be returned. There were no procedures in place to assess whether repatriation was a valid option for some of the refugees.

Prison conditions

There were reports of overcrowding and insanitary conditions in a number of prisons. Some prisons were holding twice their capacity. There were also concerns that children were being held with adult inmates.

Death penalty

Courts continued to hand down the death penalty for capital offences. The government did not take formal steps to abolish the death penalty. A court petition filed by three local civil society organizations in 2008 challenging the constitutionality of the death penalty remained pending in the High Court.

Amnesty International visits/reports

- An Amnesty International delegate visited mainland Tanzania in November.

THAILAND

KINGDOM OF THAILAND

Head of state:	**King Bhumibol Adulyadej**
Head of government:	**Abhisit Vejjajiva**
Death penalty:	**retentionist**
Population:	**68.1 million**
Life expectancy:	**69.3 years**
Under-5 mortality (m/f):	**13/8 per 1,000**
Adult literacy:	**93.5 per cent**

Official censorship of websites, radio and television stations, and print publications was tightened as freedom of expression remained restricted. Violence continued in the internal armed conflict in southern Thailand, with security forces subjecting suspects to torture and other ill-treatment, and members of Muslim armed groups attacking civilians, particularly teachers. Anti-government protests in Bangkok and several other provinces were characterized by excessive use of force by security forces, violent acts by some protesters, and the detention of several hundred prisoners. An Emergency Decree containing many provisions that contravened international human rights law and standards was in effect in Bangkok for almost eight months. Migrant workers with irregular status in Thailand faced a range of human rights abuses and, along with refugees, were forcibly returned to Myanmar.

Background

A political crisis polarized Thai society for a fifth consecutive year, spiking sharply after former Prime Minister Thaksin Shinawatra, deposed in a 2006 coup and in self-imposed exile, was convicted in his absence by a court in Bangkok in late February on corruption charges. Mid-March through late May saw increasingly violent anti-government protests by the United Front for Democracy against Dictatorship, partly affiliated with Thaksin Shinawatra. More than 90 people were killed, at least 2,000 others were injured, and 37 buildings in Bangkok were burned down. The government invoked the Internal Security Act in March and the Emergency Decree in April; the latter remained in place in Bangkok and three other provinces until almost the end of the year. In the aftermath of the violence, the government established several bodies for national reform and a Truth for Reconciliation Commission.

The internal armed conflict in southern Thailand continued, reaching a death toll of 4,500 since 2004. In November, Thailand experienced its largest single influx of refugees in 25 years when at least 20,000 refugees fled fighting across the Myanmar border.

Political violence

Between 10 April and 19 May, 74 protesters or passers-by, 11 members of the security forces, four medics and two journalists were killed during sometimes violent anti-government protests in Bangkok and elsewhere. The security forces used excessive force, including lethal use of firearms and "live fire zones", which killed several unarmed protesters and bystanders. Major General Khattiya Sawasdipol, a leader of the demonstrators' defences, was shot and killed by a sniper on 13 May. Some protesters and elements seemingly aligned with them were also armed and used lethal force against the security forces. The government detained over 450 people in the wake of the protests, approximately 180 of whom remained in detention or on bail pending trial at the end of the year. Some were charged with terrorism.

Freedom of expression

The government clamped down on freedom of expression, mainly through the Emergency Decree, the lèse majesté law, and the 2007 Computer-related Crimes Act.

■ In October, Amornwan Charoenkij was arrested under the Emergency Decree in Ayutthaya province – despite the Decree not being in effect there – for selling slippers featuring the Prime Minister's face and a message referring to the 91 dead from the May violence.

The Emergency Decree authorized the newly established Center for the Resolution of the Emergency Situation (CRES) to censor websites, radio and television stations, and printed publications without a court warrant. During each of the last three weeks of May, as violence during anti-government protests peaked, the CRES announced that it had censored 770, 1,150 and 1,900 websites, respectively. The Ministry of Information, Communication and Technology announced in June that it had blocked access in Thailand to 43,908 websites on grounds that they violated the lèse majesté law and national security.

At least five cases were brought under the Computer-related Crimes Act for content deemed offensive to the monarchy and/or a threat to national

security, bringing the total to 15 since the Act was promulgated in 2007.

■ On 29 April, businessman Wipas Raksakulthai was arrested for forwarding a message on the social networking site, Facebook, which allegedly violated the lèse majesté law. A prisoner of conscience, he was refused bail and at the end of the year remained in detention awaiting a trial date.

■ On 24 September, Chiranuch Premchaiporn, director of online newspaper Prachatai, was arrested for comments posted on the website which violated the lèse majesté law. She was released on bail and at year's end was waiting for a referral to the public prosecutor.

Refugees and migrants

Migrant workers who did not register their status before a 28 February deadline were forcibly removed to Myanmar, and were subject to trafficking and extortion by both Thai officials and a Myanmar government-backed ethnic minority militia. In November, Thailand violated the principle of *non-refoulement* by forcing many refugees fleeing from fighting in Myanmar to return there, placing them at risk of serious human rights abuses. A government process with the stated aim of verifying the immigration status of over 1.4 million registered migrant workers was marred by concerns for the safety of Myanmar nationals who had to return to Myanmar to take part; unregulated brokers charging extortionate fees; and insufficient provision of information to those meant to take part. The verification process excluded the roughly 1.4 million other migrant workers who did not register with the immigration authorities before the 28 February deadline.

Irrespective of their immigration status, many foreign nationals – mainly from Asia – continued to face discrimination in access to work, industrial accident compensation, and disability registration, and were subject to restrictions on their movements as well as dangerous and unhealthy working conditions. Alleged instances of extortion, torture and other violence against migrant workers by both employers and officials, including, in particular, law enforcement officers, were either not investigated or not prosecuted.

Following an influx of at least 20,000 refugees in early November, many returned to Myanmar voluntarily, but others were forced to return or were prevented from crossing the border into Thailand. This was also true throughout the rest of the year in relation to smaller groups of refugees escaping sporadic fighting across the border.

■ In Waw Lay village in Phop Phra district in Tak province, Thai authorities forcibly returned 166 Burmese refugees on 25 December, at least 360 on 8 December, roughly 650 on 17 November, and approximately 2,500 on 10 November.

Internal armed conflict

Human rights abuses by all sides continued in the internal armed conflict in Thailand's predominantly Muslim southern provinces, where the Emergency Decree was renewed for the 21st time since July 2005 (it was lifted in one district in late December). The security forces continued to use torture on suspects, leading to several deaths in custody. Armed groups continued to target civilians, both Buddhist and Muslim, and to carry out indiscriminate attacks, particularly during the Ramadan period. Attacks on teachers and schools reached such a level in October that nearly all schools in the south closed for a week. On the sixth anniversary of the deaths of 85 people in Tak Bai, Narathiwat province, and after a 2009 decision not to prosecute the security forces involved, 14 co-ordinated bomb attacks took place, killing two people and injuring 74 others.

The government passed legislation to empower the civilian-led Southern Border Provinces Administrative Centre to operate independently of the military and report directly to the Prime Minister, but impunity continued for the security forces.

■ In August, the police dropped all charges against a former paramilitary ranger alleged to have been involved in a 2009 attack on the Al-Furqan mosque in which 10 Muslims were killed. For the seventh consecutive year, no official was successfully prosecuted for human rights violations in the south.

Death penalty

There were no known executions. As of August, there were 708 people facing the death penalty whose cases were on appeal·or final, 339 of them for drug offences. On 13 January, the Minister of Interior announced a campaign to extend the death penalty for drug offences under three existing laws. These developments contradicted Thailand's Second National Human Rights Plan for 2009 to 2013 which included the intention to abolish the death penalty.

In both April and May, following outbreaks of violence between anti-government protesters and security forces, the government stated that some detainees would be charged with terrorism, which could result in the death penalty.

Death row prisoners continued to be shackled in leg irons upon arrival in prison despite a 2009 court decision (since appealed) declaring it "illegal". The Truth for Reconciliation Commission recommended in July that the practice be stopped immediately.

■ In December, Thailand abstained from a UN General Assembly resolution calling for a worldwide moratorium on executions, having voted against the resolution in 2007-2009.

Amnesty International visits/reports

- Reverse backward slide in freedom of expression (ASA 39/001/2010)
- Accountability must prevail in political crisis (ASA 39/003/2010)
- Open Letter: Call for an independent and impartial investigation (ASA 39/004/2010)
- Demand the release of online news editor: Chiranuch Premchaiporn (ASA 39/005/2010)
- Military must halt reckless use of lethal force, 17 May 2010

TIMOR-LESTE

DEMOCRATIC REPUBLIC OF TIMOR-LESTE
Head of state: José Manuel Ramos-Horta
Head of government: Kay Rala Xanana Gusmão
Death penalty: abolitionist for all crimes
Population: 1.2 million
Life expectancy: 62.1 years
Under-5 mortality: 92/91 per 1,000

Impunity persisted for perpetrators of gross human rights violations committed during Indonesian occupation between 1975 and 1999. The police and military were implicated in alleged ill-treatment and excessive use of force. Despite the enactment of a law against domestic violence, levels of domestic violence remained high.

Background

In February, the mandate of the UN Integrated Mission in Timor-Leste (UNMIT) was extended for another year.

Police and security forces

The resumption of primary policing responsibilities by the Timor-Leste National Police Force (Policia Nacional

Timor-Leste, PNTL) progressed steadily, and PNTL internal disciplinary mechanisms were strengthened. However, reports continued of human rights violations committed by police and military personnel, including ill-treatment and excessive use of force. There were at least 59 allegations of human rights violations by the national police and 13 by the military.

Justice system
Judicial and accountability mechanisms remained weak. Attempts to hold to account those responsible for the violence that erupted in 2006 after one third of the military were dismissed remained slow.

In March, 24 people were convicted of involvement in the February 2008 attacks on the President and Prime Minister. However, in August the President pardoned 23 of them, including ex-insurgent leader Gastão Salsinha. Civil society organizations expressed concern that the pardons called into question the credibility of the justice system.

■ On 26 March, Domingos Noronha (aka Mau Buti), a former Mahidi Militia member, was sentenced to 16 years' imprisonment for serious crimes committed in 1999. He was found guilty on three counts of murder.

Violence against women and girls
In May, the Law Against Domestic Violence was passed, providing a framework for government, police and community responses to domestic violence. The Law defined domestic violence broadly to include physical, sexual, psychological and economic violence, and provided for a range of services to victims. However, many cases of domestic violence continued to be resolved though traditional justice mechanisms which did not provide full redress to victims. Levels of domestic violence remained high.

Impunity
The Timor-Leste Office of the Ombudsman for Human Rights and Justice and the Indonesian National Human Rights Commission signed a memorandum of understanding in January on the implementation of recommendations of the joint Indonesia-Timor-Leste Commission of Truth and Friendship (CTF) and of the Commission for Reception, Truth and Reconciliation (CAVR). The content of the memorandum was not made public.

In early July, two draft laws establishing a National Reparations Programme and an "Institute for Memory", mandated to implement recommendations

of the CTF and CAVR, were presented for public consultation. Parliament was scheduled to debate the laws in late September; however, the debate was delayed until February 2011.

There was very little progress in addressing past serious human rights violations, including crimes against humanity, committed in Timor-Leste during Indonesian occupation (1975-1999). President Ramos-Horta rejected calls from national and international NGOs for an international tribunal for past crimes, although he said he would not oppose it should the UN Security Council decide to establish one. The Serious Crimes Investigation Team continued to investigate serious human rights violations committed in 1999.

Amnesty International visits/reports
Timor-Leste: International Criminal Court – Justice in the shadow (ASA 57/001/2010)

TOGO

TOGOLESE REPUBLIC

Head of state:	Faure Gnassingbé
Head of government:	Gilbert Fossoun Houngbo
Death penalty:	abolitionist for all crimes
Population:	6.8 million
Life expectancy:	63.3 years
Under-5 mortality (m/f):	105/91 per 1,000
Adult literacy:	64.9 per cent

Following presidential elections in March, security forces used violence to repress peaceful demonstrations. Freedom of the press was also undermined, with journalists being attacked while doing their work. Despite the work of the Truth, Justice and Reconciliation Commission (TJRC), impunity remained the rule.

Background
In March, President Faure Gnassingbé claimed victory in presidential elections that were denounced as fraudulent by the opposition. In May, the Union of Forces for Change (UFC), the main opposition party, decided to join the government, leading to a split and the creation in October of a new political party, the National Alliance for Change (ANC).

T

Prisoners of conscience and political prisoners

More than a dozen political activists were arrested, charged with security offences and detained for weeks or months.

■ In March, two members of the UFC, Augustin Glokpon and Jacob Benissan, were arrested as they were taking election campaign materials to the town of Vogan. They were held for a week at the gendarmerie in Lomé, the capital, charged with "an attempt on the security of the state", then sent to Kara prison. Both were prisoners of conscience and were provisionally released on 31 March.

■ In March, four members of a political movement, Citizens' Movement for an Alternative (MCA), Fulbert Attisso, Guillaume Coco, Yaovi Abobi and Eric Solewassi, were arrested in Lomé. They were charged with "an attempt on the security of the state" and provisionally released in September.

Freedom of assembly, excessive use of force

After the election, the opposition organized weekly peaceful gatherings to contest the results. The security forces repeatedly dispersed the demonstrations with tear gas and used excessive force on several occasions.

■ In April, members of the gendarmerie broke up a meeting of the opposition umbrella organization Republican Front for Alternation and Change (FRAC) and arrested more than 70 people. They were detained for a few hours and some alleged they were beaten.

■ In June, a demonstration to protest against rising fuel prices was violently repressed. At least one person, Komassi Koami Dodoè, was shot dead by a military officer in Agoè neighbourhood and two others were severely injured. An inquiry was opened but by the end of the year no findings had been made public.

■ In October, the security forces attacked the home of Jean-Pierre Fabre, an opposition leader. The whole area was surrounded and the security forces fired tear gas grenades and beat protesters.

■ In November, a march organized by several human rights organizations to protest against the repeated violations of the right to peaceful assembly was dispersed by security forces who wounded several people.

Freedom of expression

Several journalists working for international media outlets were denied visas to cover the elections.

■ In August, Didier Agbedivlo alias Didier Ledoux, a journalist with the daily *Liberté,* was assaulted by gendarmes when photographing the Court in Lomé.

■ In November, a cameraman, Tony Sodji, was wounded by plain-clothes gendarmes who shot him with a tear gas grenade at close range while he was filming a demonstration. Earlier, in September, he had been stabbed by gendarmes while covering demonstrations.

Impunity

In August, the TJRC opened regional branches throughout the country to collect testimonies. The TJRC was established in 2009 to shed light on human rights violations committed between 1958 and 2005. By the end of 2010, more than 5,800 people had made statements before the TJRC but most of these cases were from the 1960s to 1980s. No victims of past human rights violations received any reparations.

No progress was made in the investigation of 72 complaints lodged by victims of political repression in 2005.

Amnesty International visits/reports

▤ Togo: Political activists arrested, risk torture (AFR 57/001/2010)

T

TRINIDAD AND TOBAGO

REPUBLIC OF TRINIDAD AND TOBAGO

Head of state:	George Maxwell Richards
Head of government:	Kamla Persad-Bissessar
	(replaced Patrick Manning in May)
Death penalty:	retentionist
Population:	1.3 million
Life expectancy:	69.9 years
Under-5 mortality (m/f):	37/28 per 1,000
Adult literacy:	98.7 per cent

Dozens of people were killed by police, some in circumstances suggesting that the killings may have been unlawful. At least 40 people were on death row; there were no executions.

Background

In April, Prime Minister Patrick Manning called legislative elections, 30 months ahead of schedule, shortly before a vote of no confidence in his administration and amid allegations of corruption. A coalition of five parties, the People's Partnership, won the elections with a political manifesto based on fighting crime, increasing transparency, eradicating poverty and promoting social justice. The newly elected Prime Minister, Kamla Persad-Bissessar, made a commitment to resume public consultation on constitutional reform. The public security situation remained a key political priority, with 472 homicides recorded by the police.

Police and security forces

Dozens of people were killed by the police. In some cases, witness testimonies contradicted claims by the police that they had fired in self-defence.

■ On 3 January, Tristan Cobbler called his mother and told her that he had been shot in the leg by the police and was hiding in a bushy area in Mentor Alley, Laventille. Tristan Cobbler's mother said, she then heard her son say: "Oh God, I can't move. Don't shoot me". She found her son's body where he had indicated he was hiding. The autopsy revealed that he had died of multiple gunshot wounds to the legs, neck, back and chest. The police declared that a gun was found beside the body.

■ Bianca Charles was killed on 16 July by a stray bullet fired by the police in Morvant. According to the police

patrol, suspected criminals, whom they were chasing, opened fire on them. The police said they returned fire and one bullet hit Bianca Charles, who was standing in front of her restaurant. However, according to Bianca Charles' husband, who witnessed the incident, the suspects were not shooting at the police.

Violence against women and girls

According to police statistics, 482 rapes, incest and other sexual offences were reported between January and September 2010; the comparable figure for 2009 was 491 cases. However, women's organizations believed that such crimes were under-reported as police were not adequately trained in how to deal with cases of violence against women. Access to justice for victims of sexual offences remained unsatisfactory. Conviction rates for sexual offences were low. A national policy on gender and development, drafted in 2009, which put forward a number of policy measures to prevent and address gender-based violence, had not been adopted by the end of 2010.

Death penalty

At least 40 people were on death row; no executions took place.

Some ministers in the new government voiced their support for the resumption of hangings as a deterrent against crime. The new Prime Minister said that execution by hanging was "the law of the land" and that her government "will abide by the rule of law and implement the law of Trinidad and Tobago". However, she also stated that the new government was considering proposing an amendment to the law in order to end mandatory death sentences for murder.

TUNISIA

REPUBLIC OF TUNISIA

Head of state:	Zine El 'Abidine Ben 'Ali
Head of government:	Mohamed Ghannouchi
Death penalty:	abolitionist in practice
Population:	10.4 million
Life expectancy:	74.3 years
Under-5 mortality (m/f):	24/21 per 1,000
Adult literacy:	78 per cent

The authorities maintained tight restrictions on freedom of expression, association and assembly, and government critics continued to be harassed, threatened and imprisoned. Former political prisoners were also harassed, intimidated and subject to restrictions. Torture and other ill-treatment in police stations and prisons were reported. People prosecuted under the anti-terrorism law were sentenced to long prison terms after unfair trials. Death sentences continued to be imposed, but the government maintained a moratorium on executions.

Background

Article 61 bis of the Penal Code was amended in June to make it a crime punishable by up to 20 years in prison for anyone to "directly or indirectly, have contacts with agents of a foreign country, foreign institution or organization in order to encourage them to affect the vital interests of Tunisia and its economic security". The amendment was made one month after Tunisian human rights activists met EU officials and parliamentarians in Spain and Belgium to urge the EU to bring pressure on the Tunisian government to uphold its international human rights obligations in the context of negotiations over Tunisia's "advanced status" with the EU. It appeared that the new law was intended to criminalize and deter such lobbying of other states and multilateral institutions in support of human rights in Tunisia.

In June, the UN Committee on the Rights of the Child issued its observations on children's rights in Tunisia, recommending the need to amend the Penal Code to prohibit all forms of corporal punishment against children which remained lawful in the home and alternative care settings.

Anti-government protests

Anti-government protests erupted following the self-immolation of 24-year-old Mohamed Bouazizi on 17 December in the town of Sidi Bouzid in a desperate act of protest after a local official prevented him from selling vegetables and allegedly assaulted him. The security forces used excessive force, including live ammunition, to disperse protests that were largely peaceful – at least two people were killed. Many others were injured by live ammunition, rubber bullets, tear gas or beatings. At the end of the year, the protests were continuing and had spread across the country.

■ Mohamed Ammari and Chaouki Belhoussine El Hadri were shot dead by security forces during a protest on 24 December in Manzel Bouzayane, a small town in Sidi Bouzid province.

Freedom of expression and assembly

The authorities maintained tight control over the media and the internet. Those who openly criticized the government or exposed its human rights violations continued to be harassed, placed under intensive surveillance, unjustly prosecuted, and physically assaulted. Independent human rights organizations faced difficulties in holding public events, renting venues for events, or had their events subjected to a heavy security presence.

■ Fahem Boukadous, a journalist, and Hassan Ben Abdallah, an unemployed graduate, were both serving four-year prison sentences in Gafsa Prison for their alleged participation in popular protests in 2008 against unemployment and high living costs in Gafsa province, south-west Tunisia. Fahem Boukadous was also convicted of "spreading information liable to disrupt public order" for reporting on the protests for a private TV channel. Both men were sentenced after unfair trials. They were first tried and convicted in their absence in 2008 but were retried in January and March after they requested retrials. In October-November, Fahem Boukadous staged a 39-day hunger strike to protest against his imprisonment and harsh conditions; he ended it when the prison authorities undertook to improve his prison conditions.

■ In March, the authorities prevented journalists and human rights activists from attending press conferences in Tunis at which the International Association for the Support of Political Prisoners and Human Rights Watch planned to publish separate reports on harassment of former political prisoners in Tunisia.

T

Restrictions on former political prisoners

Many former political prisoners continued to be under administrative control orders which required them to report frequently to police stations and usually involved oppressive police surveillance and restrictions on the exercise of their civil rights. Some were rearrested or returned to prison for resuming peaceful political activity or publicly criticizing the government; others were denied access to medical care. Most had their freedom of movement restricted within Tunisia and were denied passports. As a result, most were prevented from obtaining paid employment or leading normal lives.

■ Sadok Chourou was released from Nadhour Prison on 30 October. He had been released conditionally in 2008 but returned to prison for a further year after he gave interviews to al-Hiwar satellite TV channel and other internet media in November 2008, a few days after his conditional release. When released on 30 October, officials told him that he should not engage in any media or political activities but provided no official notification of this.

■ Abdellatif Bouhajila continued to be denied a passport to enable him to travel abroad for medical treatment. Conditionally released in 2007 from a 17-year sentence imposed after he was convicted of membership of an Islamist group, al-Ansar (the Partisans) in 2001, he was reported to be in poor health due to ill-treatment in prison and hunger strikes.

Human rights defenders

Human rights defenders faced continuing harassment by the authorities, including heavy surveillance and interference with or blocking of internet and telephone communications. They were also prevented from attending meetings or gatherings that focused on human rights. Some were physically assaulted. Most independent human rights organizations continued to be denied official registration. In February, the UN Special Rapporteur on human rights defenders called on the Tunisian authorities to cease their physical and psychological "campaign of intimidation" against human rights defenders.

■ Ali Ben Salem, aged 78, continued to be harassed and intimidated by the authorities because of his human rights work and as a founding member of several human rights organizations, including the National Council for Liberties in Tunisia and the Association against Torture in Tunisia. He also hosts in his home the Bizerte regional office of the Tunisian

League for Human Rights. State Security officers continued to be permanently posted in front of his house, and his telephone lines and internet access were cut. He was under constant surveillance and physically prevented from attending meetings on human rights. He continued to be denied a free health care card and a passport and so could not receive the medical treatment that he requires for serious back and heart ailments.

■ Human rights activist and journalist Zouheir Makhlouf was released in February; he had been arrested in October 2009 and sentenced in connection with a documentary film about pollution in the Nabeul industrial area in north-east Tunisia. In April, eight police officers visited him and said he was under arrest. They beat him in front of his wife and children when he asked to see the arrest warrant, then detained him for seven hours at a police station. He had bruises and a broken nose when released. He was again beaten in December by a man in plain clothes believed to be a police officer after he left his home to report on unrest in Sidi Bouzid region.

Counter-terror and security

The authorities continued to arrest, detain and try people on security-related charges, including some who were forcibly returned to Tunisia from other states. According to reports, around 2,000 people have been convicted of offences under the anti-terrorism law since 2003, including many who were tried and sentenced in their absence in trials that often failed to meet international fair trial standards. Defendants alleged that they had been forced to "confess" under torture or other duress while held incommunicado in pre-trial detention, but their "confessions" were accepted as evidence by the courts without any or adequate investigation.

In January, during a visit to Tunisia, the UN Special Rapporteur on the promotion and protection of human rights while countering terrorism criticized the Anti-terrorism Law of 2003. He urged the government to amend the law's over-broad definition of "terrorism" and to restrict the law's application so as to exclude those who have been improperly convicted of "terrorism".

■ Seifallah Ben Hassine continued to be held in isolation at Mornaguia Prison near Tunis. He had been held in isolation since 2007, far beyond the 10 days permitted under Tunisian law. He was convicted in 2003 under the Anti-terrorism Law and Military Justice

Code, and was a defendant in six separate trials, including four before the Tunis Military Court. His six sentences totalled 68 years in prison to be served consecutively. He was arrested while travelling in Turkey where he says he was held incommunicado for a month and tortured before being forcibly returned to Tunisia.

Women's rights

The authorities continued to portray Tunisia as a state committed to the promotion and protection of women's rights. However, women journalists who criticized the government and women human rights defenders were subject to harassment and denigrating smear campaigns in the state-controlled media.

■ Faten Hamdi, a reporter with Radio Kalima, unauthorized to broadcast in Tunisia, was attacked in February by two plain-clothes police officers in Tunis. The officers tried to force her into their car and hit her in the face, but she managed to get away.

Women judges who were among the ousted leadership of the Association of Tunisian Judges and had called for the independence of the judiciary faced continued harassment.

■ Kalthoum Kennou was transferred from Kairouan to Tozeur against her will instead of being returned to her home town of Tunis. Other judges faced salary cuts without warning and denial of promotion.

In October, the CEDAW Committee, commenting on women's rights in Tunisia, expressed concern about allegations of "arbitrary arrest and harassment" of NGOs and human rights defenders and the "exclusion of autonomous women's organizations" from participation in the policy-making process and from state funding.

Death penalty

At least 22 people were sentenced to death; there were no executions. The government maintained the de facto moratorium on executions in force since 1991. At least 136 prisoners on death row, including four women, were not permitted contact with their families or lawyers.

Amnesty International visits/reports

📋 Freed but not free: Tunisia's former political prisoners (MDE 30/003/2010)

📋 Independent voices stifled in Tunisia (MDE 30/008/2010)

TURKEY

REPUBLIC OF TURKEY

Head of state:	Abdullah Gül
Head of government:	Recep Tayyip Erdoğan
Death penalty:	abolitionist for all crimes
Population:	75.7 million
Life expectancy:	72.2 years
Under-5 mortality (m/f):	36/27 per 1,000
Adult literacy:	88.7 per cent

Constitutional amendments and revisions to the Anti-Terrorism Law represented a step towards upholding human rights, but fell short of the fundamental change required. Criminal prosecutions violating the right to freedom of expression continued. Proposed independent human rights mechanisms were not established. Reports of torture and other ill-treatment continued, and criminal investigations and prosecutions of law enforcement officials remained ineffective. Numerous unfair trials were held using anti-terrorism legislation. Bomb attacks claimed the lives of civilians. The rights of conscientious objectors, lesbian, gay, bisexual and transgender (LGBT) people and refugees and asylum-seekers remained unsecured in law. Minimal progress was made in preventing violence against women.

Background

Constitutional amendments were approved by Parliament in May and by referendum in September, with an approval rating of nearly 60 per cent. Amendments included changing the composition of the Constitutional Court and the powerful Higher Council of Judges and Prosecutors, allowing military officials to be tried in civilian courts, the establishment of an Ombudsman office and positive measures to combat discrimination.

The Kurdistan Workers' Party (PKK) renewed ceasefire declarations throughout the year but clashes with the Turkish armed forces continued. In November, talks were reported to have taken place between the state and imprisoned PKK leader Abdullah Öcalan.

In October, the trial began of 152 activists and elected officials in Diyarbakır accused of membership of the PKK-linked Kurdistan Communities Union (KCK). Of these defendants, 104 were in pre-trial detention. Concerns were raised that much of the

T

evidence against the defendants was based on their attendance at meetings and demonstrations, and on press releases they had published.

The prosecution in connection with Ergenekon, an alleged ultra-nationalist network with links to state institutions, continued. Progress in investigating the link between the suspects and past human rights violations remained slow.

No progress was made in removing the legal barriers that prevent women wearing the headscarf in universities, although implementation of the ban relaxed during the year.

In May, the UN Human Rights Council considered Turkey's human rights record under the UN Universal Periodic Review. The government committed to complying with many of the recommendations, but notably rejected those calling for the greater recognition of minority rights and those to amend or abolish articles of the Penal Code that limit freedom of expression.

Freedom of expression

There was more open debate regarding previously taboo issues. However, people were prosecuted under different articles of the Penal Code because they had criticized the armed forces, the position of Armenians and Kurds in Turkey, and ongoing criminal prosecutions. In addition, anti-terrorism laws, carrying higher prison sentences and resulting in pre-trial detention orders, were used to stifle legitimate free expression. Kurdish political activists, journalists and human rights defenders were among those most frequently prosecuted. Arbitrary restrictions continued to be imposed, blocking access to websites, and newspapers were issued with temporary closure orders. There were continued threats of violence against outspoken individuals.

■ In April, journalist Veysi Sarısözen was convicted under Article 7/2 of the Anti-Terrorism law for "making propaganda for an illegal organization" and sentenced to 15 months in prison for an article he wrote in *Gündem* newspaper. At the end of the year this was one of four convictions under the Anti-Terrorism Law pending at the Supreme Court of Appeals.

■ *Taraf* journalists continued to face threats and intimidation due to articles they had published in the newspaper. In November, the Justice Ministry permitted the opening of an investigation under Article 301 of the Penal Code, "denigrating the Turkish nation", against Rasim Ozan Kütahyalı for a series of articles criticizing the armed forces. In the same month,

threats of violence against Orhan Miroğlu were posted on a website, HPG online, allegedly controlled by the PKK. Orhan Miroğlu was also being prosecuted under Article 216 of the Penal Code "causing enmity or hatred among the population" following an article he wrote in 2009 regarding the situation of Turkish citizens of Kurdish origin.

■ In November, arrests were made in a police operation targeting the Turkish Revenge Brigades Union, a clandestine group that had previously claimed responsibility for threats and acts of violence against prominent human rights defenders and others.

■ In September, the European Court of Human Rights ruled in the case of *Dink vs. Turkey* that the authorities had failed to take reasonable measures to protect the life of journalist and human rights defender Hrant Dink. They had failed to act on information that could have prevented his murder in January 2007, or to conduct an effective investigation following the murder; in particular the Court noted the failure of the authorities to examine the role of the security services. The Court also concluded that Turkey had violated Hrant Dink's right to freedom of expression in relation to cases brought against him under Article 301 of the Penal Code.

Torture and other ill-treatment

Allegations of torture and other ill-treatment persisted, especially outside places of detention, including during demonstrations, but also in police custody and during transfer to prison. In November, the UN Committee against Torture issued a series of recommendations to the authorities to combat "numerous, ongoing and consistent allegations of torture" for which the Committee expressed grave concern during their review of Turkey.

■ In January, Murat Konuş died after being held in police custody in Istanbul on suspicion of aggravated theft. Video camera footage showed him entering the police station in good health and being carried out three hours later. An official autopsy recorded injuries to his body and found that his death was due to cerebral bleeding. In May seven police officers were charged with causing his death through torture. The trial was ongoing at the end of the year.

■ In June, a landmark judgement saw 19 officials, including police officers and prison guards convicted for their part in the torture that resulted in the death of political activist Engin Çeber in Istanbul in October 2008. Of those convicted, three prison guards and a prison manager were sentenced to life imprisonment following an investigation and prosecution that contrasted starkly with other cases involving alleged torture committed by state officials. The convictions remained pending at the Supreme Court of Appeals at the end of the year.

Impunity

Investigations of alleged human rights abuses by state officials remained flawed and, when opened, criminal cases were routinely drawn out and ineffectual. The losing of evidence by state officials, and counter-charges being issued against those who alleged human rights abuses, contributed to the perpetuation of impunity. Independent human rights mechanisms proposed by the government were not established. For example, civil society was not effectively consulted over the draft law to establish the Human Rights Institution (a body proposed to protect human rights and prevent violations), which failed to provide the necessary guarantees of independence.

■ No progress was made in the prosecution of a police officer for intentional killing following the death in custody of Nigerian asylum-seeker Festus Okey in 2007. Following a flawed investigation, the prosecution remained stalled due to disputes regarding the victim's identity. In November, the presiding judge rejected an application by members of the Migrants' Solidarity Network to intervene in the case and issued a criminal complaint against them on the grounds that their submission to the court amounted to libel.

■ In June, the prosecutor investigating the death in custody of Resul İlçin in October 2009 in the south-eastern province of Şırnak ruled that no officials should face criminal charges. The decision was based on an official autopsy report which found that Resul İlçin's death was due to a heart attack, despite the report also recording severe injuries to the head and other parts of his body. An appeal against the decision to close the case was rejected by the local administrative court in July.

Prison conditions

Allegations of ill-treatment in prisons persisted, especially of remand prisoners directly following transfer. Denial of effective access to medical treatment and arbitrary limitations applied to prisoners' rights to associate with each other continued.

■ In July, leukaemia patient Abdullah Akçay died in prison following the refusal of requests for his transfer from custody on health grounds. The requests were based on medical reports stating that he could not be treated effectively while in prison.

■ In July, the European Committee for the Prevention of Torture published a report based on a visit in January to the high security prison on the island of İmralı where PKK leader Abdullah Öcalan is imprisoned. The report recorded an improvement in some aspects of the prison regime, notably due to the transfer of five prisoners, ending his 10-year isolation. A report concerning another Committee visit to places of detention in 2009 remained unpublished pending government permission.

Unfair trials

Unfair trials under anti-terrorism legislation continued. In such cases, excessive pre-trial detention without consideration of alternatives by the judicial authorities remained routine, and lawyers had no effective mechanism to challenge the lawfulness of the detention in practice.

In July, important legal amendments ended the prosecution of children under anti-terrorism laws solely for their participation in demonstrations. However, the amendments allowed adults to be prosecuted under the unfair laws and failed to address the vague and overly broad definition of terrorist crimes in law.

■ In August, Erdoğan Akhanlı was remanded in custody pending trial under anti-terrorism laws. The prosecution case was primarily based on a statement later retracted by the witness, who alleged that it had been obtained under torture. Defence lawyers' applications for Erdoğan Akhanlı's release were denied by the court on the basis of the weight of the evidence against him. In December, he was released from detention pending the outcome of the trial.

Abuses by armed groups

Bomb attacks resulted in the death and injury of civilians.

■ In July, four activists travelling to the scene of an attack on an oil pipeline were killed when their vehicle hit a mine. A statement made by the PKK indicated that its members were responsible for laying the mine.

■ In September, nine people were killed when a civilian minibus hit a mine while travelling on a road close to the village of Geçitli/Peyanis in the south-eastern province of Hakkari. No group claimed responsibility for the attack. Eyewitnesses claimed that two military bags and munitions were recovered from the scene.

T

Workers' rights

Long-standing demands by trade unions for Istanbul's central Taksim Square to be opened for demonstrations on 1 May were granted for the first time in recent history, and the demonstrations passed peacefully in contrast to previous years. Constitutional amendments granted the right of collective bargaining for public sector employees but the right to strike was still denied to all civil servants. As a result, Turkey failed to comply with ILO conventions to which it is a party.

Children's rights

Following legislative amendments (see Unfair trials above) the vast majority of children prosecuted for their participation in demonstrations were released. However, flaws in the juvenile justice system, notably the absence of Children's Courts in some provinces, were not addressed, nor were steps taken to rehabilitate children previously held in extended detention or to investigate the widespread claims of ill-treatment.

Prisoners of conscience – conscientious objectors

The right to conscientious objection to military service remained unrecognized in domestic law. Conscientious objectors were repeatedly prosecuted for their refusal to perform military service, and those who voiced their public support for this right were subjected to criminal prosecution and conviction.

■ In June, conscientious objector Enver Aydemir was released after six months in military custody. Multiple charges resulting from his refusal to perform military service remained pending at the Military Supreme Court of Appeals. In the same month, human rights defender Halil Savda and three other activists were convicted under Article 318 of the Penal Code for "alienating the public from the institution of military service" following their attendance at a public demonstration in support of Enver Aydemir. The case remained pending at the Supreme Court of Appeals. A prosecution brought following Enver Aydemir's alleged ill-treatment in military custody was also continuing at the end of the year.

■ In August, conscientious objector İnan Süver was detained due to his refusal to perform military service. He was released in December but remained in prison due to previous convictions. His trial for "violation of leave" continued at the end of the year.

Refugees and asylum-seekers

Access to the temporary asylum procedure continued to be arbitrarily denied, resulting in people being forcibly returned to places where they may face persecution. Immigration detention regulations ruled unlawful by the European Court of Human Rights in 2009 remained in force at the end of the year. Civil society organizations were consulted over three new laws relating to asylum but the drafts had not been published by the end of the year.

Rights of lesbian, gay, bisexual and transgender people

Constitutional amendments improving protections against discrimination failed to address discrimination on grounds of sexual orientation and gender identity. Discrimination continued in law and practice.

■ In March, the Minister for Women and the Family stated that homosexuality was a disease and required treatment. The government failed to distance itself from the remarks and no apology was issued.

■ In April, LGBT solidarity organization Black Pink Triangle won its legal battle against closure following a complaint from the İzmir Governor's office that its statute breached "Turkish moral values and family structure".

■ In May, five transgender women, all members of the NGO Pembe Hayat, which supports LGBT people's rights, filed criminal complaints against police officers who had reportedly harassed and assaulted them in Ankara after stopping their car. The police officers filed counter charges, alleging that the activists had resisted arrest. A criminal case was opened but all the activists were acquitted at the first trial hearing. No charges were brought against the police officers.

Violence against women and girls

The government's National Action Plan 2007-10 to combat domestic violence failed to record significant progress, due in part to a lack of co-ordination, insufficient resource allocation and the lack of measurable goals. Critically, the number of shelters for women victims of domestic violence remained far below the number required in domestic law. According to official records, 57 existed in Turkey, an increase of eight over the previous year. In July, the CEDAW Committee issued a series of recommendations including the enactment of comprehensive legislation on violence against women.

T

Amnesty International visits/reports

🚍 Amnesty International delegates visited Turkey in January, February, March, April, May, June, July, September, October and December including to monitor trials.

📄 Turkey: Activist group will not be closed for 'violating Turkish moral values' (EUR 44/009/2010)

📄 Turkey: Conscientious objection is a human right not a personality disorder (EUR 44/013/2010)

📄 Turkey: All children have rights: End unfair prosecutions of children under anti-terrorism legislation in Turkey (EUR 44/011/2010)

📄 Turkey: Peaceful protesters convicted for 'alienating the public from military service' in Turkey (EUR 44/016/2010)

📄 Turkey: Attack on minibus condemned (EUR 44/021/2010)

📄 Turkey: Briefing to the Committee against Torture (EUR 44/023/2010)

📄 Turkey: UN Committee calls on government to act against torture and impunity (EUR 44/025/2010)

TURKMENISTAN

TURKMENISTAN

Head of state and government:	Gurbanguly Berdymukhamedov
Death penalty:	abolitionist for all crimes
Population:	5.2 million
Life expectancy:	65.3 years
Under-5 mortality (m/f):	72/56 per 1,000
Adult literacy:	99.5 per cent

Freedom of expression, association, religion and movement continued to be restricted. Dozens of people imprisoned following unfair trials remained in prison, many held incommunicado. At least eight conscientious objectors served prison terms.

Repression of dissent

The authorities continued to suppress dissent. Journalists working with foreign media outlets known to publish criticism of the authorities faced harassment and intimidation. Independent civil society activists were unable to operate openly in Turkmenistan. Fear for dissidents' safety was heightened after President Berdymukhamedov called on the Ministry of National Security (MNS) in September to fight those who, according to the government website, "defame our democratic law-based secular state and try to destroy the unity and solidarity of our society."

■ Prisoners of conscience Annakurban Amanklychev and Sapardurdy Khadzhiev, associated with the NGO Turkmenistan Helsinki Foundation, continued to serve prison terms for "illegal acquisition, possession or sale of ammunition or firearms", imposed in 2006 following an unfair trial. The UN Working Group on Arbitrary Detention studied the case and concluded in August that the two men were arbitrarily detained to punish them for exercising their rights to freedom of expression and association and for their human rights activities. It stated that the two had been denied a fair trial and called on the authorities to promptly release them and award them appropriate financial compensation.

■ In September, the satellite TV channel K+, which broadcasts to Central Asia, aired an interview with Farid Tukhbatullin, director in exile of the Turkmen Initiative for Human Rights (TIHR). It provided people in Turkmenistan with a rare opportunity to receive information about human rights in their country from a non-governmental source. Subsequently, the TIHR website was disabled by an attack by unknown hackers, until the group moved its site from a Moscow host to one in another country. In October Farid Tukhbatullin received reliable information that MNS officials had discussed "get[ting] rid of [him] quietly", in a way that was hard to trace.

Freedom of religion

Religious activity was strictly controlled. In its January report to the Human Rights Committee, Turkmenistan stated that "[t]he activity of unregistered religious organizations is prohibited". Many religious minorities continued to be denied registration, often without explanation. Lack of registration made them more vulnerable to raids and other harassment by the authorities.

■ In October Protestant Pastor Ilmurad Nurliev was sentenced to four years' imprisonment for "swindling". His supporters believed he was targeted for his religious activity and that the evidence produced against him was fabricated. The court reportedly ordered that he be forced to undergo treatment for alleged drug use, a practice which his supporters denied.

Refusal to serve in the army remained a criminal offence. At least eight Jehovah's Witnesses were serving prison terms for conscientious objection and three more were serving suspended sentences.

■ Dovleet Byashimov was detained in August and sentenced to 18 months' imprisonment by Turkmenabad City Court for his refusal to serve in the

T

army on conscientious grounds. After his arrest, he was reportedly held incommunicado and severely beaten.

Enforced disappearances

The authorities continued to withhold information about the whereabouts of dozens of people arrested and convicted in connection with the alleged assassination attempt on former President Saparmurad Niyazov in 2002. Calls on the authorities to disclose information about those who had died in custody remained unanswered.

Freedom of movement

Dissidents and religious believers were in many cases prevented from travelling abroad on the basis of a "black list".

From July onwards officials prevented scores of dual passport holders from leaving Turkmenistan unless they surrendered one passport and acquired an exit visa if they chose to keep their Turkmenistani citizenship. The attempt to remove citizenship without proper legal procedures and without the possibility of appeal or review by an independent court may amount to a violation of the human right not to be arbitrarily deprived of nationality.

"Propiska" – the system of registering the place of permanent residence – continued to restrict people's rights to freedom of movement within Turkmenistan, and affected access to housing, employment, social benefits, health care and education. The threat of losing a "propiska" was used by the police and security services to prevent people complaining of ill-treatment by police.

Amnesty International visits/reports

▧ Turkmenistan: Severe restrictions on freedom of movement remain (EUR 61/002/2010)

▧ Turkmenistan: Activist at serious risk of harm (EUR 61/003/2010)

UGANDA

REPUBLIC OF UGANDA

Head of state and government:	Yoweri Kaguta Museveni
Death penalty:	retentionist
Population:	33.8 million
Life expectancy:	54.1 years
Under-5 mortality (m/f):	129/116 per 1,000
Adult literacy:	74.6 per cent

Law enforcement officials committed human rights violations, including unlawful killings and torture, and perpetrators were not held to account. There were concerns about electoral violence and human rights abuses ahead of general elections in early 2011. A number of new and proposed laws threatened the rights to freedom of expression and freedom of assembly. Gender-based violence was widespread and was committed with impunity. Lesbian, gay, bisexual and transgender (LGBT) people continued to face discrimination and violence.

Background

In October, eight presidential candidates, including President Museveni, were cleared by the Electoral Commission to run for the presidency in general elections scheduled for February 2011. Fears of electoral violence were raised by lingering perceptions that the electoral body was not impartial and concerns over the transparency of the voter registration process.

A major corruption case in which a former health minister, two deputies and a government official faced criminal charges of embezzlement and abuse of office continued. The charges relate to the management of the Global Fund against HIV/AIDS, Tuberculosis and Malaria.

In a September letter to the UN, Uganda rejected the findings of the UN mapping exercise documenting the most serious violations of human rights and international humanitarian law committed within the Democratic Republic of the Congo between March 1993 and June 2003 by different armed forces and groups including the Ugandan army – the Uganda People's Defence Forces. The government took no action to institute investigations into the allegations of human rights violations and crimes committed by the army.

U

Election-related abuses

Throughout the year, numerous instances of electoral violence and human rights abuses were recorded. These were not investigated and suspected perpetrators were not brought to justice.

■ In January, the police arrested 35 female activists from the Inter-Party Cooperation Coalition – an alliance of opposition parties – who were protesting against the Electoral Commission, accusing it of partiality. The activists complained of ill-treatment by the police – including being forced to undress and being held overnight with men in the same police holding cells – and the use of excessive force. They were subsequently charged with holding an unlawful assembly.

■ In June, the police and a group of men armed with sticks and locally known as "the Kiboko squad" disrupted a rally in Kampala by opposition leader Kizza Besigye and beat him, as well as officials and supporters of his party. The government promised an investigation but no announcement was made of any progress by the end of the year.

Key opposition leaders had public rallies and media events, particularly radio talk shows, cancelled or blocked by the police and government representatives. An opposition leader, Olara Otunnu, faced criminal charges of sectarianism for discussing alleged government complicity in human rights abuses during the war in northern Uganda.

The government proposed a Public Order Management Bill which would, if enacted into law, unduly restrict the rights to peaceful assembly and to freedom of expression. The Bill had not been submitted for debate in Parliament by the end of the year.

Unlawful killings, torture and other ill-treatment

Dozens of people in the north-eastern Karamoja region were reported to have been killed during the year in disputed circumstances by government soldiers engaged in security and disarmament operations. Army personnel were also accused of committing torture and other ill-treatment in the course of these operations. The government did not institute credible investigations into alleged human rights violations and no one was brought to justice.

In October, the Uganda Human Rights Commission reported that torture and ill-treatment by the police, other law-enforcement officials and the military remained widespread.

A number of suspects detained in connection with the July bomb attacks in Kampala (see below) reported that they were tortured and ill-treated by police.

Violence against women and girls

In October, following consideration of Uganda's state report, the UN Committee on the Elimination of Discrimination against Women expressed concern that violence against women and girls remained widespread. The Committee noted the inordinately high prevalence of sexual offences against women and girls. Female victims of rape and other forms of sexual and gender-based violence continued to face economic and social obstacles to justice, including the costs of criminal investigations and discrimination by government officials.

In April, the President gave assent to the Domestic Violence Act, a law specifically criminalizing domestic violence. However, domestic violence remained rampant and perpetrators were rarely brought to justice.

In July, Uganda ratified the Protocol to the African Charter on the Rights of Women in Africa.

Trial of Kizza Besigye

In October, the Constitutional Court declared that charges of treason and murder against Kizza Besigye and others were unconstitutional, mainly on the grounds that the state had failed to uphold the right to a fair trial. The Court noted an incident in 2007 when security personnel re-arrested the accused in the High Court despite a court order granting them bail.

Armed conflict

Northern Uganda was relatively calm; the region had previously been affected by the long-term conflict between the government and the Lord's Resistance Army (LRA). LRA forces in the Central African Republic, the Democratic Republic of Congo and Sudan continued to commit human rights abuses, including unlawful killings and abductions.

U

International justice

In June, the International Crimes Act, 2010, which incorporates the Rome Statute of the International Criminal Court (ICC) into domestic law, came into effect.

Arrest warrants issued in 2005 by the ICC for Joseph Kony, leader of the LRA, and three LRA commanders remained in force, but the men remained at large.

Bomb attacks

In July, at least 76 people were killed and hundreds injured in bomb attacks by unknown people at two different public venues in Kampala. Following criminal investigations, 17 people of different nationalities including Ugandans, Kenyans and Somalis were charged with terrorism and murder and committed to stand trial in November in connection with the attacks. The trial process was continuing at the end of the year.

Up to 12 suspects were transferred from Kenya to Uganda outside established legal processes in both countries (see Kenya entry).

■ In September, Al-Amin Kimathi, head of the Muslim Human Rights Forum, an NGO in Kenya, was arrested in Uganda, along with Kenyan lawyer Mbugua Mureithi. The two had travelled from Kenya to Uganda to observe the trial of six Kenyans charged with terrorism in connection with the bomb attacks. Mbugua Mureithi was held incommunicado for three days then deported to Kenya. Al-Amin Kimathi was held incommunicado for six days and charged with terrorism and murder in connection with the July bomb attacks. The Ugandan authorities gave no details of the allegations against him; he appeared to have been arrested and charged solely for carrying out his legitimate work. He remained in prison at the end of the year.

Freedom of expression

The Regulation of Interception of Communications Act, 2010 became law in September. It gives the government far-reaching discretion in surveillance and interception of all forms of communication. The law lacks adequate safeguards and threatens freedom of expression.

The government proposed a Press and Journalists (Amendment) Bill which would, if enacted, significantly restrict freedom of expression by allowing the authorities to refuse to grant licences to print media outlets on broad and loosely defined grounds such as "national security". The Bill had not been submitted to Parliament by the end of the year.

Dozens of journalists faced various criminal charges related to their media work and materials critical of government policy and practice.

In September, the Constitutional Court declared the offence of sedition in the Penal Code Act to be unconstitutional on the basis of section 29 of the Constitution which guarantees freedom of expression.

Refugees and asylum-seekers

In July, a joint operation between the governments of Uganda and Rwanda resulted in the forcible return to Rwanda of around 1,700 Rwandan asylum-seekers from two refugee settlements in Uganda. Police officers fired shots into the air when some of the asylum-seekers tried to escape. In the ensuing panic and stampede, people were reportedly injured and children separated from their parents. Most of the affected refugees complained that they had not been allowed a fair and satisfactory determination of their applications for refugee status. The operation resulted in the death of at least one man who jumped off a truck en route to Rwanda and injuries to over 20 people.

There were cases of refugees living in settlement camps and urban areas being arbitrarily arrested, unlawfully detained and tortured or ill-treated. Perpetrators, usually the police and other law enforcement officials, were rarely brought to justice.

The authorities threatened to return at least three Somali asylum-seekers to southern and central Somalia despite the risks they would face there.

Discrimination – lesbian, gay, bisexual and transgender people

The Anti-Homosexuality Bill, 2009 which would further entrench discrimination and lead to other human rights violations against LGBT people remained pending in Parliament.

In October and November a local publication, *The Rolling Stone,* published front page articles identifying people it said were homosexuals; one included the words "Hang them". The articles contained names, pictures and in some cases addresses and other details. The people named included activists and human rights defenders. A number of people named in the publication complained of harassment and threats by people known to them. In November, some of the individuals named filed a civil law case in the High Court against the publishers, alleging violation of their rights to life, dignity and privacy. The Court's decision was pending at the end of the year. However, the authorities did not condemn the publication or take any measures to protect the people placed at the risk of violence by the articles.

LGBT individuals and rights activists continued to face arbitrary arrests, unlawful detention, torture and other ill-treatment by the police and other security personnel.

U

Death penalty

Civilian and military courts continued to impose the death penalty for capital offences. There were no executions.

Amnesty International visits/reports

🚌 Amnesty International delegates conducted research and other work in Uganda in April, June, September, November and December. In November, Amnesty International's Secretary General led a high-level mission to Uganda.

📄 "I can't afford justice": Violence against women in Uganda continues unchecked and unpunished (AFR 59/001/2010)

📄 Proposed Ugandan media law threatens the right to freedom of expression (AFR 59/006/2010)

📄 Uganda: Proposed law on the regulation of public meetings by the police threatens human rights (AFR 59/008/2010)

📄 Uganda: Failure to investigate alleged human rights violations in Karamoja region guarantees impunity (AFR 59/013/2010)

📄 Uganda: Amnesty International Memorandum on the Regulation of Interception of Communications Act, 2010 (AFR 59/016/2010)

📄 Deadly Uganda blasts condemned, 11 July 2010

📄 Uganda forcibly returns 1,700 Rwandan asylum-seekers, 15 July 2010

UKRAINE

UKRAINE

Head of state:	**Viktor Yanukovich (replaced Viktor Yushchenko in February)**
Head of government:	**Mykola Azarov (replaced Yuliya Timoshenko in March)**
Death penalty:	**abolitionist for all crimes**
Population:	**45.4 million**
Life expectancy:	**68.6 years**
Under-5 mortality (m/f):	**18/13 per 1,000**
Adult literacy:	**99.7 per cent**

There were reports of torture and other ill-treatment in prisons and police custody. Prisoners and criminal suspects received inadequate medical care. Human rights defenders were physically attacked and faced harassment from law enforcement officers. Refugees and asylum-seekers were threatened with forcible return and other human rights violations. Police discriminated against ethnic minorities and peaceful demonstrators were detained and subjected to violence.

Torture and other ill-treatment

Allegations continued of torture and other ill-treatment in police custody. In March, the Human Rights Department within the Ministry of Internal Affairs, which had monitored police detention, was closed. It was replaced with a smaller division without a monitoring remit.

On 1 July, the European Court of Human Rights ruled that a group of prisoners had been subjected to torture and other ill-treatment when they were beaten in Zamkova Prison in Khmelnitskiy region in two separate incidents in 2001 and 2002. The beatings took place during a training programme for the Rapid Reaction Unit, a special group of prison guards called in to deal with unrest in prisons.

■ On 1 July, prisoners in Vinnytsya Remand Prison No. 1 were reportedly ill-treated by the Rapid Reaction Unit as punishment for protesting against the ill-treatment of a group of prisoners the day before. Prisoners' relatives gave accounts of the events over the two days. On 30 June a group of 15 prisoners were due to be taken to court. The police officers escorting them ordered one of them to strip naked. When he refused to remove his underpants, he was beaten, handcuffed and tied to the wall. Other prisoners were also beaten. When the police convoy arrived to escort prisoners to court the next day, the prisoners refused to leave their cells in protest at the previous beatings. The prison authorities called in the Rapid Reaction Unit, which allegedly beat prisoners indiscriminately.

Deaths in custody

In January, the Deputy Head of the Department for the execution of sentences stated that health facilities in prisons were underfunded. Prisoners were not allowed out of prison for medical treatment outside the prison system.

■ Tamaz Kardava died in hospital on 7 April having been denied vital medical care. A Georgian citizen and a refugee from the conflict in Abkhazia, Tamaz Kardava was already suffering from Hepatitis C when he was detained in Ukraine in August 2008. He was allegedly tortured in Shevchenkovskiy district police station in Kyiv to force him to confess to a burglary. Medical reports confirmed that he had been badly beaten and raped with a police baton. For the last two months of his pre-trial detention he had been denied any specialized medical treatment for his condition, and his health worsened dramatically. On 30 March he spent six hours lying on the floor in the courtroom on a stretcher

U

in Shevchenkovskiy Court in Kyiv. The judge refused his lawyer's request to transfer him immediately to hospital.

Human rights defenders

The work of human rights defenders and human rights NGOs was made more difficult as they faced obstruction in the courts and physical attacks. At least three human rights defenders were targeted in relation to their legitimate human rights work.

■ In May, Andrei Fedosov, the chair of a mental disability rights organization, Uzer, was assaulted by unidentified men following threatening phone calls. Police refused to register his complaint and took no action. In July, he was detained for a day in relation to a crime allegedly committed 10 years before, when he was 15 years old. On 20 September the charges against him were dropped as it was proved that he was in a closed children's hospital at the time and could not have committed the crime.

■ On 29 October, trade union activist Andrei Bondarenko was ordered to undergo a forced psychiatric examination by a court in Vinnytsya. The decision was upheld on appeal in November. Andrei Bondarenko had no record of mental illness and had undergone three psychiatric examinations to prove his sanity, most recently in October. Among the reasons quoted by prosecutors for him to be examined was his "excessive awareness of his own and others' rights and his uncontrollable readiness to defend these rights in unrealistic ways". Andrei Bondarenko had defended the rights of seasonal workers in sugar beet factories in Vinnytsya district and had exposed corruption at high levels.

Refugees, asylum-seekers and migrants

Asylum-seekers in Ukraine continued to be at risk of arbitrary detention, racism and extortion at the hands of the police and return to countries where they would be at risk of serious human rights violations. An inadequate asylum system left them unprotected.

In January, the EU-Ukraine Readmission Agreement came into force for third country nationals. According to the agreement, EU states can return irregular migrants to Ukraine providing they entered the EU via Ukraine. According to the International Organization for Migration, between January and July, 590 people were returned according to the terms of the Readmission Agreement. There were reports of migrants being beaten or otherwise ill-treated while in detention. Furthermore, although the Readmission Agreement is intended to apply to "illegal aliens", asylum-seekers were reportedly among those returned.

■ At the end of the year four asylum-seekers from Uzbekistan – Umid Khamroev, Kosim Dadakhanov, Utkir Akramov and Zikrillo Kholikov – were in detention awaiting extradition to Uzbekistan. All four were wanted in Uzbekistan on charges including membership of an illegal religious or extremist organization, dissemination of materials containing a threat to public security and order, and attempts to overthrow the constitutional order. They would risk torture and other ill-treatment if returned. In July, the European Court of Human Rights made a formal request to the government not to return the asylum-seekers to Uzbekistan until their case had been considered, but withdrew this request upon assurances that the men would not be returned until they had exhausted all stages of the asylum process.

Racism

Police continued to apprehend and detain people because of the colour of their skin.

■ On 29 January, three plain-clothes police officers approached two Somali men, Ismail Abdi Ahmed and Ibrahim Muhammad Abdi, outside their apartment building, and asked them to produce their documents. The police officers then reportedly forced their way into the apartment, searched it without a search warrant, and punched one of the occupants. The police officers removed US$250 from the pocket of a pair of jeans belonging to Ibrahim Muhammad Abdi. Throughout the search, the police officers called the Somali men "pirates". On 13 February, two of the same police officers returned to the apartment. They told the Somali men living there that they wanted to film them retracting the public statements they had made about the search. The Somalis refused to open the door and, after several hours, the officers left.

Freedom of assembly

■ In May and June, peaceful demonstrators protesting the illegal felling of trees in Kharkiv were beaten by members of the "Municipal Guard" (commercial security guards employed by the City Council. Some were later refused medical treatment, including Liubov Melnik who was hospitalized after being beaten by "Municipal Guards". She was reportedly asked by Municipal Guard personnel to deny that she had been beaten by the guards, but had injured herself by falling. The hospital then informed her that there were no more beds and discharged her and, subsequently, three

U

Kharkiv hospitals refused to treat her. On 2 June, demonstrators positioned in the trees were injured when loggers started to cut them down.

Demonstrators described how the police stood by while the guards beat protesters and journalists without intervening. On 28 May, between 10 and 12 people were detained for approximately eight hours by the police before being brought before a judge. Andrei Yevarnitsky and Denis Chernega were sentenced to 15 days' detention on 9 June for "malicious refusal to obey a law enforcement officer", although video footage of the events shows the demonstrators leaving with police officers peacefully.

Amnesty International visits/reports

🚌 Amnesty International delegates visited Ukraine in January, April and November.

📘 "Put deeds before words": Deliver human rights for Ukraine (EUR 50/004/2010)

UNITED ARAB EMIRATES

UNITED ARAB EMIRATES

Head of state:	Shaikh Khalifa bin Zayed Al Nahyan
Head of government:	Shaikh Mohammed bin Rashid Al Maktoum
Death penalty:	retentionist
Population:	4.7 million
Life expectancy:	77.7 years
Under-5 mortality (m/f):	10/12 per 1,000
Adult literacy:	90 per cent

Foreign migrant workers were denied substantive rights and faced exploitation and abuse. Women continued to be discriminated against in both law and practice. At least 28 people were sentenced to death; no executions were reported.

Background

In March, following his visit to the UAE in October 2009, the UN Special Rapporteur on racism urged the government to allow long-term residents of the UAE to apply for citizenship, and resolve equitably the situation of UAE residents who remain stateless,

allowing them to have access to health, education and social services as well as jobs. He also urged the government to take legislative and other measures to protect foreign migrant workers from exploitation.

In April, police in Sharjah were reported to have undertaken door-to-door searches looking for couples living out of wedlock and to have arrested at least one couple.

In August, the Supreme Court ruled that the interests of the child should be considered paramount in child custody cases.

In October, the government announced that it had completed payment of compensation to Bangladeshi nationals formerly employed as child camel jockeys in the UAE.

Women's rights

Women remained subject to discrimination in law and in practice.

In February, the CEDAW Committee urged the government to take comprehensive measures to address domestic and other forms of violence against women, noting that there is no law specifically criminalizing violence against women, and to establish an independent national human rights institution conforming to international standards whose mandate should specifically include promoting gender equality.

In October, the Supreme Court upheld a husband's right to "discipline" his wife and children, provided that it left no mark, effectively sanctioning domestic violence. The ruling stated that the action taken must not exceed limits provided for in Islamic law.

Migrants' rights

Foreign migrant workers, particularly those from poor and developing countries employed in construction and as domestic workers, continued to be bound to their employers under the much-criticized sponsorship system of employment, and faced exploitation and abuse. The government took no effective steps to alleviate this, although some large foreign investors required local employers to improve working conditions as part of contract agreements.

U

Torture and other ill-treatment

In January, a court in Abu Dhabi acquitted Sheikh Issa bin Zayed al-Nahyan of assault and rape-related charges in connection with a 2004 attack on an Afghan merchant with whom he had a business dispute. The court ruled that he had been acting under the influence of drugs administered by associates who wished to film and then blackmail him.

In April, 17 Indian men who had been sentenced to death in March by a lower court in Sharjah told journalists that they had been ill-treated following their arrest in January 2009. No investigation into their allegations was known to have been carried out.

Death penalty

At least 28 people were sentenced to death by lower courts, including the 17 Indian nationals sentenced in March. Lower court cases are referred first to appeal courts and then to the Supreme Court. No executions were recorded.

In December, the UAE abstained when the UN General Assembly voted in favour of a worldwide moratorium on executions.

UNITED KINGDOM

UNITED KINGDOM OF GREAT BRITAIN AND NORTHERN IRELAND

Head of state:	Queen Elizabeth II
Head of government:	David Cameron (replaced Gordon Brown in May)
Death penalty:	abolitionist for all crimes
Population:	61.9 million
Life expectancy:	79.8 years
Under-5 mortality (m/f):	6/6 per 1,000

An inquiry into allegations of UK involvement in torture and other human rights violations of people held overseas was announced. Key counter-terrorism powers were under review. The government continued to rely on diplomatic assurances in its attempts to return individuals to countries where torture is practised. Allegations of human rights abuses by UK soldiers in Iraq continued to emerge. The Bloody Sunday Inquiry concluded that the deaths and injuries caused by British soldiers that day were unjustified. Forced returns to Baghdad continued.

Counter-terror and security
Torture and other ill-treatment

In July, the Prime Minister announced the establishment of an inquiry into UK involvement in the alleged mistreatment of individuals detained abroad by foreign intelligence services, in the context of counter-terrorism operations. The three-person inquiry panel, to be led by the Intelligence Services Commissioner, should begin its work in 2011. Civil society and human rights organizations raised concerns about whether the inquiry would have adequate powers and be sufficiently independent.

On the same date the government published the guidelines issued to intelligence officers and service personnel on the detention and interrogation of detainees overseas, and for sharing intelligence relating to detainees. Human rights organizations stated that the guidance was not compatible with international human rights standards.

In July, the High Court ordered the disclosure of a number of previously secret documents relating to the detention of UK nationals and residents in the custody of US and other overseas intelligence agencies. The documents provided further evidence of UK involvement in and knowledge of human rights violations, up to the highest levels of government.

In November, the Justice Secretary announced financial payments to 16 UK nationals or residents as part of a mediated settlement of civil damages claims brought by individuals detained in Guantánamo Bay. The terms of the settlement remained confidential.

■ On 10 February, the Court of Appeal ordered the disclosure of seven previously redacted paragraphs concerning the treatment in US custody of former Guantánamo detainee Binyam Mohamed. The disclosed paragraphs reaffirmed that UK intelligence officers knew that Binyam Mohamed was subjected to torture and other ill-treatment while in US custody. On 17 November, the Crown Prosecution Service announced that there was insufficient evidence to prosecute a UK security services officer for any criminal offence arising from an interview conducted with Binyam Mohamed while in detention in Pakistan on 17 May 2002.

Wider investigations into allegations of criminal wrongdoing by the UK security services remained open at the end of the year, including in relation to the case of former UK resident Shaker Aamer. At the end of the year he remained detained without charge in Guantánamo Bay, despite public confirmation by the

UK authorities that they would accept him.

Legal and policy developments

On 12 January, the European Court of Human Rights ruled that powers, under Section 44 of the Terrorism Act 2000, permitting the police to stop and search people without reasonable suspicion were unlawful, as they violate the right to respect for private life. The government subsequently announced that individuals would no longer be searched under these powers.

In July, the Home Office announced a "rapid review" of six key counter-terrorism powers: control orders; stop and search powers under Section 44 of the Terrorism Act 2000; the Regulation of Investigatory Powers Act 2000 and access to communications data; deportations with assurances; measures to deal with organizations that promote hatred or violence; and the pre-charge detention of terrorist suspects.

■ In April, the government announced that Lotfi Raissi, wrongly alleged to have participated in the attacks in the USA on 11 September 2001, was eligible for compensation, eight years after the courts found that there was "no evidence whatsoever" to support the allegations.

"Control Orders"

As of 10 December, eight individuals, all British nationals, were under "control orders". The control order regime, under the Prevention of Terrorism Act 2005, allows a government minister, subject to limited judicial scrutiny, to impose severe restrictions on an individual who is suspected of involvement in terrorism-related activity. The regime was renewed by Parliament in March 2010 for one more year.

■ In June, the Supreme Court issued its judgement in the case of "AP", ruling that the term of his control order requiring him to live in a city some 150 miles away from his family, when taken together with the 16-hour curfew restriction and the resultant social isolation, constituted a deprivation of his right to liberty.

The High Court reinforced the importance of family rights in September when it ruled that the forced relocation of "CA" could not be justified as it disproportionately affected his right to family life.

■ On 26 July, the High Court ruled that the government could rely on the same material to impose a control order against "AY" as had been used in a previously unsuccessful prosecution.

Deportations

There were continued attempts to deport individuals alleged to pose a threat to "national security" to countries where they would be at risk of torture and other ill-treatment. In May, the new government stated that it would maintain and extend the use of "diplomatic assurances", arguing they were sufficient to mitigate the risk of torture.

Proceedings by which these deportations could be challenged before the Special Immigration Appeals Commission (SIAC) remained unfair. In particular, they relied on secret material undisclosed to the individuals concerned or the lawyer of their choice.

■ Despite the SIAC determining in 2007 that Mouloud Sihali, an Algerian national, was not a risk to national security, the government continued to seek his deportation to Algeria. In March, the SIAC dismissed his appeal against his deportation, concluding that diplomatic assurances negotiated between the UK and Algeria would be sufficient to mitigate any risk he may face upon his return. The case was pending before the Court of Appeal at the end of the year.

■ In May, the SIAC ruled that the UK could not proceed with deportation in the case of two Pakistani nationals to Pakistan, due to the risk that they would be subject to torture or other ill-treatment on return. It further held that confidential assurances could not be accepted as a sufficient safeguard to mitigate that risk.

■ The first challenge to the Memorandum of Understanding negotiated between the Ethiopian and UK governments failed. In September, the SIAC ruled that "XX", an Ethiopian national who argued that he would be at risk of torture if returned, could be sent back to Ethiopia relying on assurances of humane treatment from the Ethiopian government. The decision was to be appealed.

Justice system

The government continued its attempts to introduce greater secrecy into judicial proceedings. On 4 May, the Court of Appeal ruled that the government could not rely on closed material procedures in the civil lawsuit brought by six former Guantánamo detainees over alleged complicity in torture by UK state actors. The Court stated that permitting such a procedure, which would allow the UK government to present secret material in closed sessions, in the absence of statutory power to do so, would contravene the fundamental principle of fair trial. The case was pending at the Supreme Court.

In July, the UK government announced plans to publish policy proposals for how intelligence material should be treated during judicial proceedings.

■ On 6 October, the inquiry into the death of Azelle Rodney, who was shot dead by Metropolitan Police

U

officers on 30 April 2005, began. Attempts by the government to keep secret key evidence in Azelle Rodney's death led to proposals for "secret inquests" which were twice rejected by Parliament. Concerns remained as to the degree this inquiry would be held in secret.

■ On 3 November, the coroner for the inquest into the deaths resulting from the London bombings on 7 July 2005 ruled that she did not have the power to hold closed hearings which would allow for secret material to be presented by the UK government in the absence of the victim's families. On 22 November, the government's appeal challenging the ruling was rejected.

Armed forces in Iraq

In March, the European Court of Human Rights found that the UK had violated Article 3 of the European Convention on Human Rights in the case of *Al-Saadoon and Mufdhi*. The two Iraqi nationals had been transferred to Iraqi custody despite substantial grounds for believing that they would risk facing the death penalty and execution.

In March, the Ministry of Defence announced the establishment of the Iraq Historic Allegations Team to investigate allegations of criminal wrongdoing in relation to the abuse of Iraqi citizens by UK armed forces. Investigations began in November and were expected to take two years.

The Supreme Court ruled in June that members of the armed forces serving outside UK jurisdiction were not entitled to benefit from the rights guaranteed by the Human Rights Act 1998.

■ Oral hearings before the Baha Mousa inquiry concluded in October. The inquiry examined the circumstances surrounding the death of Baha Mousa at a UK-run detention facility in Iraq in September 2003, after he had been tortured by UK troops over a period of 36 hours. The final report was expected in 2011.

In December, the High Court rejected an application brought by 142 Iraqis seeking a single public inquiry into alleged torture and other ill-treatment in UK military detention and interrogation facilities in southern Iraq between March 2003 and December 2008. The court did not rule out the possibility of such an inquiry in the future. The decision was to be appealed.

International justice

In November, the Home Secretary introduced draft legislation before Parliament containing measures that, if enacted, would make it more difficult for magistrates to issue arrest warrants for suspected war criminals and torturers visiting the UK.

Police and security forces

In July, the Crown Prosecution Service announced that no charges would be brought in relation to the death of Ian Tomlinson. He died in April 2009 during the G-20 demonstrations in London shortly after being struck with a baton on the back of his leg by a police officer who then pushed him to the floor. Prosecutors concluded that there was no realistic prospect of a conviction against the police officer involved following disagreements between the medical experts as to the cause of death.

■ In August, the Crown Prosecution Service announced that four officers of Metropolitan Police Service's Territorial Support Group would be charged with causing actual bodily harm to Babar Ahmad during his arrest on 2 December 2003.

Northern Ireland

In February, it was announced that three paramilitary groups had decommissioned their weapons, including the Irish National Liberation Army. Paramilitary violence, however, continued: there were serious attacks on members of the security forces and other targets by dissident republican groups, and a killing in Belfast in May attributed to a loyalist group.

On 15 June, the Bloody Sunday Inquiry published its findings into the events of 30 January 1972, during which 13 civil rights marchers were killed and as many others wounded by British soldiers in Northern Ireland. The inquiry concluded that none of those killed or injured that day bore any responsibility for the shootings; none of them posed a threat of causing death or serious injury. The report confirmed that several of the victims were shot in the back whilst running away. The inquiry also found that the accounts put forward by many of the soldiers were manifestly and knowingly untrue. Accordingly, the deaths and injuries caused by British soldiers that day were found to be unjustified. In response the Prime Minister gave a public state apology.

In December, the Northern Ireland Executive announced its intention to establish an inquiry into historical institutional child abuse.

■ In September, the final report of an inquiry into the death of Billy Wright in 1997 found no evidence of state collusion in his death, but recommended comprehensive reform of the prison service. Final reports of inquiries into the killings of Robert Hamill and Rosemary Nelson, a human rights lawyer, remained pending.

■ The government continued to renege on its commitment to establish an independent inquiry into state collusion in the death of the prominent human rights lawyer Patrick Finucane in 1989.

Refugees, asylum-seekers and migrants

In July, the Supreme Court held that individuals should not be required to conceal their sexual identity in order to avoid persecution by their country of origin. A previous court decision had found that it was permissible to return asylum-seekers in such a context, provided their situation could be regarded as "reasonably tolerable".

In August, the Court of Appeal of England and Wales referred the compatibility with refugee and human rights law of transferring asylum-seekers to Greece under the Dublin II Regulation to the Court of Justice of the European Union. The UK authorities confirmed in September that transfers to Greece would be halted until the Court of Justice had ruled.

■ Forced returns to Baghdad, Iraq took place, contrary to the advice of UNHCR, the UN refugee agency.

■ On 12 October, Jimmy Mubenga died during an attempt to forcibly return him to Angola. Witnesses stated that prior to his collapse excessive force had been used to restrain him by guards working for a private security firm.

In December the Deputy Prime Minister reaffirmed the coalition government's commitment to ending the detention of children for immigration purposes, setting a deadline of May 2011 to end the practice.

Violence against women

Concerns were raised about the lack of implementation of the European Convention against Trafficking in Human Beings. The government had failed to put the necessary safeguards in place for child victims of trafficking, or to correctly identify victims of trafficking, which resulted in breaches of victims' human rights and undermined prosecutions.

In July, the Home Secretary agreed to extend a pilot project until March 2011, supporting victims of domestic violence who lack access to public funds because of their insecure immigration status, while seeking a permanent solution to ensure their protection.

On 25 November, the government published its new National Action Plan to implement UN Security Council Resolution 1325 on women, peace and security, to ensure a gender perspective in addressing post-conflict situations.

Amnesty International visits/reports

🚌 Amnesty International delegates observed court proceedings in England throughout the year.

📰 Time for an inquiry into the UK's role in human rights violations overseas since 11 September 2001 (EUR 45/001/2010)

📰 Submission to the UK Government Consultation on "A Bill of Rights for Northern Ireland – Next Steps" (EUR 45/002/2010)

📰 United Kingdom: Court of Appeal rules that secret procedures violate fair trial rights in civil proceedings (EUR 45/003/2010)

📰 United Kingdom: Proposed torture inquiry must be independent, impartial and thorough (EUR 45/005/2010)

📰 United Kingdom: Bloody Sunday inquiry vindicates the innocence of victims (EUR 45/008/2010)

📰 United Kingdom: Disclosed documents further demonstrate urgent need for an effective inquiry into the UK's role in the torture and ill-treatment of detainees held in overseas custody (EUR 45/011/2010)

📰 United Kingdom: Five years on: Time to end the control orders regime (EUR 45/012/2010)

📰 United Kingdom: Submission for the review of counter-terrorism and security powers (EUR 45/015/2010)

📰 Open Secret: Mounting evidence of Europe's complicity in rendition and secret detention (EUR 01/023/2010)

U

UNITED STATES OF AMERICA

UNITED STATES OF AMERICA

Head of state and government:	Barack H. Obama
Death penalty:	retentionist
Population:	317.6 million
Life expectancy:	79.6 years
Under-5 mortality (m/f):	7/8 per 1,000

Forty-six people were executed during the year, and reports of excessive use of force and cruel prison conditions continued. Scores of men remained in indefinite military detention in Guantánamo as President Obama's one-year deadline for closure of the facility there came and went. Military commission proceedings were conducted in a handful of cases, and the only Guantánamo detainee so far transferred to the US mainland for prosecution in a federal court was tried and convicted. Hundreds of people remained held in US military custody in the US detention facility on the Bagram airbase in Afghanistan. The US authorities blocked efforts to secure accountability and remedy for crimes under international law committed against detainees previously subjected to the USA's secret detention and rendition programme.

International scrutiny

In November, the USA's human rights record was assessed under the UN Universal Periodic Review. The US delegation stated that the USA would conduct a "considered, interagency examination of all 228 recommendations" that came out of the process and would provide a formal response in March 2011.

Detentions at Guantánamo

On 22 January, President Obama's one-year deadline for closure of the Guantánamo detention facility passed with 198 detainees still held in the base, about half of them Yemeni nationals. By the end of the year, there were still 174 men held there, including three who had been convicted under a military commission system which failed to meet international fair trial standards.

On 5 January, the White House announced that the decision had been taken to suspend transfers of Yemeni detainees from Guantánamo to Yemen,

following an attempted bombing of a commercial airliner over Detroit two weeks earlier in which the suspect had alleged links with militants in Yemen. The suspension remained in force throughout the year.

On 22 January, the Guantánamo Review Task Force issued its final report of an interagency review – ordered as part of President Obama's executive order of 22 January 2009 – of the cases of 240 Guantánamo detainees. The Task Force concluded that 48 detainees could neither be prosecuted nor released by the USA. It also revealed that 36 detainees had been referred for possible prosecution, either in a federal court or by military commission, and approved the transfer or release of 126 detainees "subject to appropriate security measures". The 126 included 29 Yemeni nationals. A further 30 Yemenis were approved for "conditional" detention, a designation which meant they could not be released from Guantánamo unless the "security situation improves in Yemen"; or "an appropriate rehabilitation program becomes available"; or "an appropriate third-country resettlement option becomes available".

Trials of Guantánamo detainees

In April, the Pentagon released the rules governing military commission proceedings. The new manual confirmed that the US administration – like its predecessor – reserved the right to continue to detain individuals indefinitely even if they were acquitted by military commission.

Two Guantánamo detainees were convicted by military commission during the year, bringing to five the total number of people convicted by military commission since 2001, three of whom had pleaded guilty. In July, Sudanese national Ibrahim al-Qosi pleaded guilty to terrorism-related charges and was sentenced the following month to 14 years' imprisonment. In October, Canadian national Omar Khadr, who was 15 years old at the time he was taken into US military custody in Afghanistan in July 2002, pleaded guilty to five "war crimes" charges. He was sentenced to 40 years in prison by a military commission "jury", but under a plea trial agreement this was limited to eight years. The Canadian and US authorities agreed to support his transfer to Canada after he serves one year in US custody.

Five Guantánamo detainees accused of involvement in the attacks of 11 September 2001 – Khalid Sheikh Mohammed, Walid bin Attash, Ramzi bin al-Shibh, 'Ali 'Abd al-'Aziz and Mustafa al

Hawsawi – remained in Guantánamo at the end of the year, 13 and a half months after Attorney General Eric Holder announced that the five would be transferred for prosecution in a federal court in New York. The five detainees had been held incommunicado for up to four years in secret US custody before being transferred to Guantánamo in 2006. They were charged in 2008 for trial by military commission.

By the end of the year, there was still only one Guantánamo detainee who had been transferred to the US mainland for prosecution in a federal court. In November, Tanzanian national Ahmed Ghailani, who had been transferred from Guantánamo in 2009, was convicted by a US District Court in New York of involvement in the bombings of two US embassies in east Africa in 1998. In pre-trial rulings in May and July, the judge had denied defence motions to dismiss the indictment against Ahmed Ghailani on the grounds that he had been tortured in secret CIA custody prior to being transferred to Guantánamo in 2006 or that he had been denied the right to a speedy trial in the five years he had spent in CIA and then military custody prior to being transferred to New York. Ahmed Ghailani was due to be sentenced in January 2011.

US detentions in Afghanistan

Hundreds of detainees were held in the newly constructed US Detention Facility in Parwan (DFIP) on the Bagram air base in Afghanistan; the DFIP replaced the Bagram Theater Internment Facility in late 2009. For example, about 900 detainees were being held in the DFIP in September. Most of them were Afghan nationals, taken into custody by coalition forces in southern and eastern Afghanistan. The US authorities stated that the DFIP would eventually be transferred to the control of the Afghan authorities "for incarceration of criminal defendants and convicts", and that "transitioning operations" would begin in January 2011. The speed of transition, the Pentagon said in October, would depend, among other things, on "operational conditions", Afghan judicial capacity, and whether the Afghan government was "fully trained and equipped to perform its prosecution and incarceration responsibilities in accordance with its international obligations and Afghan law".

Litigation continued in the USA on the question of whether detainees held at Bagram should have access to the US courts to be able to challenge the lawfulness of their detention. In May, the US Court of Appeals overturned a 2009 ruling by a District Court judge that three Bagram detainees – who were not Afghan nationals and were taken into custody outside Afghanistan – could file habeas corpus petitions in his court. After the Court of Appeals refused to reconsider its decision in July 2010, US lawyers for the detainees returned to the District Court to pursue the litigation, which was continuing at the end of the year.

Amnesty International and other organizations wrote to the US Secretary of Defense in June raising concerns about allegations that detainees held in a screening facility at Bagram air base had been subjected to torture or other ill-treatment, including prolonged isolation, sleep deprivation and exposure to extreme temperatures.

Impunity

There continued to be an absence of accountability and remedy for the human rights violations, including the crimes under international law of torture and enforced disappearance, committed as part of the USA's programme of secret detention and rendition (transfer of individuals from the custody of one state to another by means that bypass judicial and administrative due process) operated under the administration of President George W. Bush.

In his memoirs, published in November, and in a pre-publication interview, former President Bush admitted that he had personally authorized "enhanced interrogation techniques" for use by the CIA against detainees held in secret custody. One of the techniques he said he authorized was "water-boarding", a form of torture in which the process of drowning a detainee is begun.

On 9 November, the US Department of Justice announced, without further explanation, that no one would face criminal charges in relation to the destruction in 2005 by the CIA of videotapes made of the interrogations of two detainees – Abu Zubaydah and 'Abd al-Nashiri – held in secret custody in 2002. The 92 tapes depicted evidence of the use of "enhanced interrogation techniques", including "water-boarding", against the two detainees.

The "preliminary review" ordered in August 2009 by Attorney General Eric Holder into some aspects of some interrogations of some detainees held in the secret detention programme was apparently continuing at the end of the year.

U

On 8 September, the full US Court of Appeals for the Ninth Circuit upheld the US administration's invocation of the "state secrets privilege" and agreed to dismiss a lawsuit brought by five men – UK resident Binyam Mohamed; Italian national Abou Elkassim Britel; Egyptian national Ahmed Agiza; Yemeni national Muhammad Faraj Ahmed Bashmilah; and Bisher al-Rawi, an Iraqi national and UK permanent resident – who claimed they were subjected to enforced disappearance, and torture or other cruel, inhuman or degrading treatment at the hands of US personnel and agents of other governments as part of the USA's secret detention and rendition programme operated by the CIA. The six judges in the majority pointed to the possibility that "non-judicial relief" might be open to the plaintiffs, and that action to this end could be taken by the executive or Congress.

There were calls for the USA to investigate how much US officials knew about the torture or other ill-treatment of detainees held by the Iraqi security forces after new evidence emerged in files released by the Wikileaks organization in October. (See Afghanistan, Iraq and Yemen entries.)

Excessive use of force

Fifty-five people died after being struck by police Tasers, bringing to at least 450 the number of such deaths since 2001. Most of the deceased were unarmed and did not appear to present a serious threat when they were shocked, in some cases multiple times. The cases continued to raise concern about the safety and appropriate use of such weapons.

The deaths of two Mexican nationals at the hands of US Customs and Border Patrol police led to calls for a review of the agency's practices.

■ In May, 32-year-old Anastacio Hernández suffered respiratory failure, and later died, when US Border police reportedly hit him with batons and shocked him with a Taser as they tried to deport him to Mexico.

■ In June, 15-year-old Sergio Hernández Güereca died after being shot in the head by a US Border Patrol agent. A Federal Bureau of Investigation (FBI) news release said the officer opened fire after being surrounded by individuals throwing rocks. However, video footage showed that the boy had run back into Mexico when the officer fired his gun several times across the border, striking Sergio Hernández from a distance. An investigation by the US authorities was continuing at the end of the year.

In July, six New Orleans police officers were charged in connection with the police shooting of unarmed civilians on the city's Danziger Bridge in the days after Hurricane Katrina in August 2005. The charges, stemming from a federal investigation, included civil rights violations and conspiracy to cover up the incident, in which a 17-year-old boy and a man with learning difficulties died.

Prison conditions

There were complaints of cruel conditions for prisoners held in long-term isolation in super-maximum security units. Complaints included ill-treatment of prisoners held in the federal system under Special Administrative Measures.

■ Syed Fahad Hashmi, a student, was held for more than three years in pre-trial solitary confinement in the federal Metropolitan Correctional Center, New York. He was confined for 23 or 24 hours a day to a small cell with very little natural light. He had no outdoor exercise and very limited contact with his family. In April, he pleaded guilty to one count of conspiring to help al-Qa'ida. His attorneys had filed unsuccessful applications for alleviation of his pre-trial conditions, citing their effect on his health and ability to assist in his defence. He was sentenced to 15 years' imprisonment in June.

■ Albert Woodfox and Herman Wallace, former Black Panther Party members, remained in solitary confinement in prisons in Louisiana, where they had spent more than 35 years confined to sparse, single cells, with no work or rehabilitation programmes. The conditions were first imposed after the murder of a prison guard in 1972. Appeals challenging the fairness of their convictions for the murder, as well as their cruel conditions of confinement, were pending in the federal courts at the end of the year.

Unfair trials

In June, a new appeal was filed in the case of Gerardo Hernández, one of five men convicted in 2001 of acting as intelligence agents for Cuba and related charges. The appeal was based, in part, on evidence that the US government had secretly paid journalists to write prejudicial articles in the media at the time of trial, thereby undermining the defendants' due process rights. In October, Amnesty International sent a report to the Attorney General outlining the organization's concerns in the case.

U

Violence against women

In July, Congress passed the Tribal Law and Order Act of 2010, which gives Indigenous women who survive rape a better chance of obtaining justice. The law improved co-ordination between federal, state, local and tribal law enforcement agencies in investigating such crimes, and took steps to restore tribal authority and resources to deal with crimes on tribal land. The law was introduced in response to concerns raised by tribal organizations and in Amnesty International's 2007 report *Maze of Injustice*, which exposed the disproportionately high levels of sexual violence against Indigenous women and widespread impunity for perpetrators.

Right to health – maternal mortality

Hundreds of women continued to die from preventable pregnancy-related complications. Wide disparities persisted in access to good quality health care based on race, ethnicity, immigration or Indigenous status, geographical location and income. There were calls for federal and state governments to take all necessary steps to improve maternal health care and outcomes, and eliminate disparities.

A law was passed in March that would expand health care coverage by 2014 to more than 30 million people in the USA who were uninsured. A number of legal challenges to the legislation were pending in US courts at the end of the year.

Children's rights

On 17 May, the US Supreme Court ruled that the imposition of life imprisonment without the possibility of parole for a non-homicidal crime on a perpetrator who was under 18 at the time of the crime violated the constitutional ban on "cruel and unusual" punishment. The majority noted that support for this conclusion came in the fact that the USA was the "only Nation that imposes life without parole sentences on juvenile nonhomicide offenders". The majority also noted that Article 37(a) of the UN Convention on the Rights of the Child (CRC) prohibits life imprisonment without the possibility of release for crimes committed by anyone under 18 years old.

On 14 October, the UN Committee on the Rights of the Child called on the USA to ratify the CRC, the USA and Somalia being the only two countries not to have done so.

Migrants' rights

Human rights organizations, including Amnesty International, expressed concern about a sweeping immigration law passed in Arizona in April. It was feared that the law, which required Arizona police to hand over to the immigration authorities individuals who could not provide immediate proof of their status, would increase "racial profiling". Key provisions of the law were later put on hold, pending a federal lawsuit.

Scores of Mexican and Central American irregular migrants crossing into the USA through the desert border regions died of exposure and exhaustion.

Death penalty

Forty-six prisoners – 45 men and one woman – were put to death in the USA during the year. Forty-four were executed by lethal injection, one by electrocution and one by firing squad. This brought to 1,234 the total number of executions carried out since the US Supreme Court lifted a moratorium on the death penalty in 1976.

■ David Powell was executed in Texas on 15 June, more than three decades after his crime, despite compelling evidence of his rehabilitation. He had been on death row for more than half of his life.

■ Holly Wood was executed in Alabama on 9 September. At his trial, his inexperienced lawyer had presented no evidence to the jury of Holly Wood's significant mental impairments.

■ Brandon Rhode was executed in Georgia on 27 September, six days after he slashed his arms and neck with a razor. He was brought back from the brink of death and killed by lethal injection for a crime committed when he was 18 years old.

■ Jeffrey Landrigan was executed in Arizona on 26 October. Over the years, 13 federal judges argued for a hearing into the failings of his trial lawyer. The execution went ahead after the US Supreme Court voted 5-4 to lift a stay imposed by a lower court concerned by the state's refusal to provide adequate information about one of the lethal injection drugs – of which there was a nationwide shortage – it had obtained from a source overseas.

Four men and one woman facing imminent execution were granted executive clemency during the year.

In October, Anthony Graves was released in Texas, 16 years after he was sentenced to death. A new trial had been ordered by a federal court in 2006, but charges were dismissed in October after the

U

prosecution found no credible evidence linking him to the 1992 crime. He became the 138th person to be released from death row in the USA since 1973 on grounds of innocence.

Amnesty International visits/reports

🚌 Amnesty International delegates observed military commission trials and the trial of Omar Khadr, and visited the USA in October and November.

📄 USA: Still failing human rights in the name of global "war" (AMR 51/006/2010)

📄 Deadly delivery: The maternal health care crisis in the USA (AMR 51/007/2010)

📄 USA: Submission to the UN Universal Periodic Review, November 2010 (AMR 51/027/2010)

📄 USA: Model criminal justice? Death by prosecutorial misconduct and a "stacked" jury (AMR 51/030/2010)

📄 USA: Double standards or international standards? Crucial decision on 9/11 trial forum "weeks" away (AMR 51/034/2010)

📄 USA: Normalizing delay, perpetuating injustice, undermining the "rules of the road" (AMR 51/053/2010)

📄 USA: Secrecy blocks accountability, again – federal court dismisses "rendition" lawsuit; points to avenues for non-judicial remedy (AMR 51/081/2010)

📄 USA: Death penalty, still a part of the "American experiment", still wrong (AMR 51/089/2010)

📄 USA: The case of the Cuban Five (AMR 51/093/2010)

📄 Another door closes on accountability. US Justice Department says no prosecutions for CIA destruction of interrogation tapes (AMR 51/104/2010)

URUGUAY

EASTERN REPUBLIC OF URUGUAY

Head of state and government:	José Mujica
	(replaced Tabaré Vázquez Rosas in March)
Death penalty:	abolitionist for all crimes
Population:	3.4 million
Life expectancy:	76.7 years
Under-5 mortality (m/f):	18/15 per 1,000
Adult literacy:	98.2 per cent

Some positive steps were taken to break the cycle of impunity for human rights violations committed during the nearly 12-year period of civilian and military rule (1973-1985).

Background

In March President José Mujica took office.

Impunity

In October, the Supreme Court of Justice ruled unanimously that the 1986 Law on the Expiration of the Punitive Claims of the State (Expiry Law) was unconstitutional in the case of former President Juan María Bordaberry (1971-1976), thus allowing the trial to continue. He was charged with 10 cases of homicide. This was the Court's second landmark ruling on the Expiry Law, which prevents the prosecution of police and military officials for crimes committed under military rule. However, the ruling applies only to the case at hand and therefore does not provide for the reopening of previously archived cases. In October members of Congress presented a bill that would declare three articles of the Expiry Law null and void. The Chamber of Deputies approved the bill, but it remained pending before the Senate at the end of the year.

■ In November, Uruguay admitted before the Inter-American Court of Human Rights that it had committed human rights violations in the case of María Claudia García Iruretagoyena de Gelman, who was subjected to enforced disappearance in 1976, and her daughter, María Macarena Gelman García, who was born in detention and raised by another family. The case is still pending before the Inter-American Court.

■ General Miguel Angel Dalmao and retired Colonel José Chialanza were provisionally detained in November in connection with the torture and killing in custody of Nibia Sabalsagaray in 1974.

U

Prison conditions

In March, the UN Special Rapporteur on torture presented his report on his visit to Uruguay in 2009. He called on the government, among other things, to undertake fundamental reforms of the criminal justice and penal systems, including the closure of prisons with cruel and inhuman conditions of detention, in particular "Las Latas" in Libertad Penitentiary where prisoners were held in metal boxes, and Modules 2-4 in COMCAR prison.

Concerns about prison overcrowding intensified following a fire in the Rocha prison in July in which 12 inmates died. Days later, an Emergency Prison Law was approved, which provides for increased funding for building and improving prison facilities. The Law also allows, as a temporary and exceptional measure, the housing of prisoners in military facilities.

Violence against women

According to women's rights organizations, 26 women were killed in the first 10 months of the year. The state's response to cases of violence against women remained inadequate and the UN Special Rapporteur on torture drew attention to the failure to implement the national Action Plan on Fighting Domestic Violence.

Sexual and reproductive rights

In September, the President approved a decree on implementation of a 2008 law on sexual and reproductive rights. The decree sets out the obligation of health service providers to give advice on sexual and reproductive health to women and teenagers and confirms that contraception must be provided free of cost.

UZBEKISTAN

REPUBLIC OF UZBEKISTAN

Head of state:	Islam Karimov
Head of government:	Shavkat Mirzioiev
Death penalty:	abolitionist for all crimes
Population:	27.8 million
Life expectancy:	68.2 years
Under-5 mortality (m/f):	63/53 per 1,000
Adult literacy:	99.3 per cent

Reports of torture or other ill-treatment continued unabated. Dozens of members of minority religious and Islamic groups were given long prison terms after unfair trials. Human rights defenders continued to be imprisoned after unfair trials. The authorities forcefully rejected all international calls for an independent, international investigation into the mass killings of protesters.

Torture and other ill-treatment

Despite assertions by the authorities that the practice of torture had significantly decreased, reports of torture or other ill-treatment of detainees and prisoners continued unabated. In most cases, the authorities failed to conduct prompt, thorough and impartial investigations into these allegations.

Several thousand people convicted of involvement with Islamist parties or Islamic movements banned in Uzbekistan, as well as government critics and political opponents, continued to serve long prison terms under conditions that amounted to cruel, inhuman and degrading treatment.

Uzbekistan again refused to allow the UN Special Rapporteur on torture to visit the country despite renewed requests.

■ In June, the authorities released opposition politician Sanzhar Umarov on humanitarian grounds and allowed him to rejoin his family in the USA. Sanzhar Umarov had been sentenced to eight years in prison in 2006 on charges of fraud and embezzlement after an unfair trial. His supporters claimed the charges were politically motivated. In September, he described in the *New York Times* how he had spent months in solitary confinement in small concrete punishment cells with little natural light and no heating. He reported being beaten by prison guards and other prisoners and being denied medical treatment.

U

■ The European Court of Human Rights ruled on 10 June in the case *Garayev v. Azerbaijan* that the extradition of Shaig Garayev from Azerbaijan to Uzbekistan would violate the prohibition of torture under the European Convention on Human Rights. The court stated that "any criminal suspect held in custody [in Uzbekistan] faces a serious risk of being subjected to torture or inhuman or degrading treatment".

Counter-terror and security

Closed trials started in January of nearly 70 defendants charged in relation to attacks in the Ferghana Valley and the capital, Tashkent, in May and August 2009 and the killings of a pro-government imam and a high-ranking police officer in Tashkent in July 2009. The authorities blamed the Islamic Movement of Uzbekistan (IMU), the Islamic Jihad Union (IJU) and the Islamist Hizb-ut-Tahrir party, all banned in Uzbekistan, for the attacks and killings. Among the scores detained as suspected members or sympathizers of the IMU, the IJU and Hizb-ut-Tahrir in 2009 were people who attended unregistered mosques, studied under independent imams, had travelled abroad, or were suspected of affiliation to banned Islamic groups. Many were believed to have been detained without charge or trial for lengthy periods. There were reports of torture and unfair trials.

■ In April, a court in Dzhizzakh sentenced 25 men to terms ranging between two and 10 years in prison in connection with the attacks in 2009. All were convicted of attempting to overthrow the constitutional order and of religious extremism. At least 12 of the men alleged in court that their confessions had been obtained under torture. The trial judge ordered an investigation into these allegations, and then declared they were unfounded. Independent observers reported that the men had admitted to having participated in prayer meetings and practised sports together, but had denied that they were part of a group intent on overthrowing the constitutional order.

■ In April, Kashkadaria Regional Criminal Court sentenced Zulkhumor Khamdamova, her sister Mekhriniso Khamdamova and their relative, Shakhlo Pakhmatova, to between six and a half and seven years in prison for attempting to overthrow the constitutional order and posing a threat to public order. They were part of a group of more than 30 women detained by security forces in counter-terrorism operations in the city of Karshi in November 2009. They were believed to have attended religious classes taught by Zulkhumor Khamdamova in one of the local mosques. The authorities accused Zulkhumor Khamdamova of organizing an illegal religious group, a charge denied by her supporters. Human rights defenders reported that the women were ill-treated in custody; police officers allegedly stripped the women naked and threatened them with rape.

■ Dilorom Abdukadirova, an Uzbek refugee who had fled the country following the violence in Andizhan in 2005, was detained for four days upon her return in January, after receiving assurances from the authorities that she would not face charges. In March, she was detained again and held in police custody for two weeks without access to a lawyer or her family. On 30 April, she was convicted of anti-constitutional activities relating to her participation in the Andizhan demonstrations as well as illegally exiting and entering the country. She was sentenced to 10 years and two months in prison after an unfair trial. Family members reported that she appeared emaciated at the trial and had bruises on her face.

Freedom of expression – human rights defenders and journalists

Human rights defenders and independent journalists were subjected to harassment, beatings, detention and unfair trials. Human rights activists and journalists were summoned for police questioning, placed under house arrest and routinely monitored by uniformed or plain-clothes officers. Others reported being beaten by police officers or by people suspected of working for the security forces.

■ In January 2010, Umida Ahmedova, a prominent Uzbekistani documentary photographer was sentenced to three years in prison for insulting the dignity of Uzbekistani citizens and damaging the country's image on account of photographic and video projects documenting poverty and gender inequality in Uzbekistan. However, the presiding judge gave her an amnesty and she was released from the courtroom. Her continuing appeal against her sentence was rejected in May.

■ In October, courts in Tashkent convicted two independent journalists working for foreign media outlets of criminal defamation and sentenced them to large fines. Vladimir Berezovski, the correspondent of Russian newspaper *Parlamentskaia Gazeta*, was accused of publishing 16 articles on the independent website Vesti.uz which contained defamatory

U

information intended to mislead the Uzbekistani people and could have created panic. The articles focused on the IMU and labour migration and were not authored by Vladimir Berezovski but re-posted from Russian news agencies. Abdumalik Boboev, the correspondent for the US Congress-funded Voice of America Radio Station was sentenced to a large fine. The court found that his print and radio materials insulted the judiciary and the security forces. His articles and reports covered restrictions on freedom of expression, arbitrary detentions and unfair trials of journalists and human rights defenders. Both journalists had their appeals against their sentences rejected.

■ In December, the authorities conditionally released human rights defender Fakhad Mukhtarov, after he had served 11 months of a five-year sentence for bribery and fraud. At least 11 other human rights defenders continued to be imprisoned. Some had new charges brought against them for allegedly violating prison rules and had their sentences extended by several years following unfair secret trials. At least three further human rights defenders were sentenced to long prison terms in 2010 on allegedly fictitious charges brought to punish them for their work.

■ In January, human rights defender Gaibullo Dzhalilov was sentenced to nine years in prison for attempting to overthrow the constitutional order and membership of a banned religious organization. A member of the unregistered, independent Human Rights Society of Uzbekistan, Gaibullo Dzhalilov had been monitoring the detentions and trials of members or suspected members of Islamic movements banned in Uzbekistan and had raised allegations of torture or other ill-treatment. Gaibullo Dzhalilov claimed that he had been forced under duress to confess to being a member of Hizb-ut-Tahrir. His sentence was upheld on appeal in March. In August, new charges were brought against him based, according to the prosecution, on new eyewitness testimony placing him at religious gatherings during which DVDs with extremist religious content were shown. He was sentenced to an additional four years in prison during a closed hearing at Kashkadaria Regional Criminal Court, even though no prosecution witnesses were called.

Freedom of religion

The government continued its strict control over religious communities, compromising the enjoyment of their right to freedom of religion. Those most affected were members of unregistered groups such as Christian Evangelical congregations and Muslims worshipping in mosques outside state control.

■ Suspected followers of the Turkish Muslim theologian, Said Nursi, were convicted in a series of trials that had begun in 2009 and continued into 2010. The charges against them included membership or creation of an illegal religious extremist organization and publishing or distributing materials threatening the social order. By December 2010, at least 114 men had been sentenced to prison terms of between six and 12 years following unfair trials. Reportedly, some of the verdicts were based on confessions gained under torture in pre-trial detention; defence and expert witnesses were not called; access to the trials was in some cases obstructed while other trials were closed.

Refugees and asylum-seekers

The authorities briefly granted temporary shelter to tens of thousands of ethnic Uzbek refugees who fled violence in neighbouring southern Kyrgyzstan in June. The authorities allowed emergency teams from UNHCR, the UN refugee agency, access to Uzbekistan and the refugee camps, the first time since ordering the agency to leave the country in 2006. Security forces tightly controlled the movement of the refugees, including those injured and in hospitals, and their contact with the outside world. At the end of June all but a couple of thousand refugees returned to Kyrgyzstan amid concern that the returns were not genuinely voluntary and that Kyrgyzstani and Uzbekistani local authorities had put pressure on them.

International scrutiny

Five years after the killing of hundreds of mainly peaceful demonstrators by the security forces in Andizhan on 13 May 2005, the authorities continued to reject all calls for an independent, international investigation. The lifting of sanctions by the EU was cited as evidence that the matter was now closed.

At the UN Human Rights Committee's examination of Uzbekistan's implementation of the International Covenant on Civil and Political Rights in March, the Uzbekistani delegation denied that human rights defenders were detained and persecuted. The delegation insisted that Uzbekistan's "enemies" were waging an "information war" against the country and that international NGOs were paid to spread defamation and disinformation.

U

Amnesty International visits/reports

▢ Uzbekistan: Submission to the Human Rights Committee – Update, May 2009-January 2010 (EUR 62/001/2010)

▢ Uzbekistan: A briefing on current human rights concerns, May 2010 (EUR 62/003/2010)

VENEZUELA

BOLIVARIAN REPUBLIC OF VENEZUELA

Head of state and government:	Hugo Chávez Frías
Death penalty:	abolitionist for all crimes
Population:	29 million
Life expectancy:	74.2 years
Under-5 mortality (m/f):	24/19 per 1,000
Adult literacy:	95.2 per cent

Politically motivated charges were brought against those who opposed government policies. Human rights defenders were attacked and intimidated. Human rights violations by the security forces were reported. Progress in combating violence against women was slow.

Background

In the September legislative elections the ruling party lost its two-thirds majority.

Demonstrations were held throughout the year, in most cases sparked by discontent over labour rights and public services.

In January, the government took six television channels off air amid concerns that the measure was aimed at curtailing the right to freedom of expression. Five were able to resume transmission. An appeal by the sixth, RCTV International, remained pending at the end of the year.

Human rights defenders

Human rights defenders continued to be attacked and threatened. Those responsible were not brought to justice.

■ In May, after publicly criticizing military officials, Rocío San Miguel, President of the civil society organization Citizen Control, was followed by two unidentified men in an unmarked car and was later told that there had been an attempt to issue her with an arrest warrant.

■ In July, Víctor Martínez was beaten in the street by an unidentified man while distributing flyers in which he alleged that the police had been involved in the death of his son, Mijail Martínez, in 2009. No one had been brought to justice for the killing of Mijail Martínez or the attack against Víctor Martínez by the end of the year.

Repression of dissent

Those critical of the government were prosecuted on politically motivated charges in what appeared to be an attempt to silence them.

■ In March, Oswaldo Álvarez Paz, a member of an opposition party and ex-governor of the Zulia State; Guillermo Zuloaga, owner of TV station Globovisión; and Wilmer Azuaje, an opposition candidate for the governorship of Barinas State, were detained for several days on spurious charges. The charges remained pending at the end of the year.

■ Richard Blanco, Prefect of Caracas, was released in April, after four months in prison, but continued to face unsubstantiated charges of inciting violence and injuring a police officer during a demonstration against an education law in 2009.

■ In November, the trial began of trade unionist Rubén González, general secretary of Sintraferrominera, the union representing workers at the state-run iron mine CVG Ferrominera Orinoco in Bolivar State. He was charged with inciting a crime, curtailing people's freedom to work, and violating a security zone following his participation in a strike in 2009. He had been in pre-trial detention for over a year and the charges against him appeared to be disproportionate.

Violence against women and girls

Gender-based crime remained a concern. In October, the attorney general announced the establishment of more prosecutors' offices to deal with these crimes. Between January and August, the Public Prosecutor's Office received more than 65,000 complaints of gender-based violence.

■ Six years after Alexandra Hidalgo was kidnapped, raped and tortured by five men, only two of the suspects had been prosecuted. Despite the authorities' commitment to ensure that those responsible were brought to justice, no progress was made in the case during the year.

■ In April, Jennifer Carolina Viera was stabbed to death by her husband in Valencia. He had been arrested in March in Merida, after Jennifer Viera had been

V

hospitalized, but released on bail and issued with an injunction forbidding him from approaching his wife.

Police and security forces

Public security remained a major concern and, according to latest figures released by the Institute of National Statistics, more than 21,000 people were killed nationwide in 2009. There were allegations of police involvement in killings and enforced disappearances.

■ In September, Wilmer José Flores Barrios became the sixth member of the Barrios family to be killed in circumstances suggesting the involvement of members of the Aragua State Police. At the end of the year, Venezuela had not adopted measures to protect the family, nor had it ordered an effective investigation into these crimes.

■ In March, eyewitnesses saw three labourers – Gabriel Antonio Ramírez, José Leonardo Ramírez and Nedfrank Xavier Cona – being bundled into an unmarked car by a group of between 17 and 20 police officers in the city of Barcelona, Anzoátegui State. At the end of the year, the whereabouts of the men remained unknown. Six police officers were under arrest at the end of 2010 in connection with the incident; a higher-ranking officer remained at liberty.

Independence of the judiciary

Judge María Lourdes Afiuni Mora remained in prison awaiting trial. She had been detained in December 2009 on unsubstantiated charges. Three UN Special Rapporteurs described her arrest as a blow to the independence of judges and lawyers in Venezuela, and demanded her immediate and unconditional release. Judge Afiuni was threatened by inmates, some of whom had been convicted following trials over which she presided. She also reported that she was denied adequate medical treatment.

Prison conditions

In November the Inter-American Commission on Human Rights expressed concern at the number of deaths and injuries in Venezuelan prisons. Between January and November, 352 deaths and 736 injuries were recorded, according to national human rights organizations.

The Commission also reiterated concerns over prison conditions following a riot in March in Yare I prison in Caracas which resulted in scores of deaths and injuries, and reports received in November about violence between inmates in Uribana prison, Lara State.

VIET NAM

SOCIALIST REPUBLIC OF VIET NAM

Head of state:	Nguyen Minh Triet
Head of government:	Nguyen Tan Dung
Death penalty:	retentionist
Population:	89 million
Life expectancy:	74.9 years
Under-5 mortality (m/f):	27/20 per 1,000
Adult literacy:	92.5 per cent

Freedom of expression, association and assembly remained severely restricted. New regulations on internet monitoring were introduced. Harsh repression of peaceful dissidents and human rights activists continued. The authorities increasingly used the charge of attempting to "overthrow" the state against peaceful dissidents. Prisoners of conscience were sentenced to long prison terms after unfair trials. Dissidents were arrested and held in lengthy pre-trial detention, and others under house arrest. Members of some religious groups were harassed and ill-treated. At least 34 people were sentenced to death, but secrecy was maintained over the application of the death penalty.

Background

Viet Nam took over as Chair of ASEAN and hosted a series of regional and international meetings during the year.

More than 17,000 prisoners were released under a large-scale prisoner amnesty to mark National Day. No prisoners of conscience were among those released.

The UN independent experts on minority issues and on the question of human rights and extreme poverty visited the country in July and August respectively at the invitation of the authorities.

Freedom of expression

Severe restrictions on the rights to freedom of expression, association and assembly of those critical of or opposed to government policies continued. Provisions of the national security section of the 1999 Penal Code, including Article 79 ("Carrying out activities aimed at overthrowing the people's administration") were used to criminalize peaceful political and social dissent. In April, new internet monitoring regulations affecting retail locations in the

V

capital, Ha Noi, were introduced, placing further restrictions on freedom of expression and access to information. Vietnamese language dissident blogs and websites suffered widespread hacking which internet companies Google and McAfee alleged may have been politically motivated.

At least 30 prisoners of conscience remained behind bars, including members and supporters of banned political groups, independent trade unionists, bloggers, business people, journalists and writers. A further eight activists were arrested and held in pre-trial detention. Other dissidents were held under house arrest following their release from prison, including prisoner of conscience Le Thi Cong Nhan.

■ Five members of Viet Tan, a Vietnamese group calling for democracy and political reform which is based overseas but has a network in Viet Nam, were arrested. Three were reportedly campaigning on land rights for farmers. Maths lecturer Pham Minh Hoang had protested against bauxite mining in the Central Highlands; and Hong Vo, an Australian national, took part in a peaceful protest against China. Hong Vo was charged with "terrorism" and deported 10 days after arrest.

■ In October, independent labour activists Do Thi Minh Hanh, Nguyen Hoang Quoc Hung, and Doan Huy Chuong were charged and tried under Penal Code Article 89 (Disrupting security), for distributing anti-government leaflets and advocating strike action at a factory. They received seven- to nine-year prison sentences.

Unfair trials

By the end of the year courts had convicted at least 22 pro-democracy and human rights activists in a series of dissident trials that began in October 2009. They were all prisoners of conscience. Trials fell far short of international standards of fairness, disregarding basic rights such as the presumption of innocence and the right to defence. As in previous years, court proceedings were short, and permission for family members, journalists and diplomats to observe was either not given or arbitrarily restricted.

■ In January, Ho Chi Minh City People's Court sentenced four dissidents – lawyer Le Cong Dinh, businessman Le Thang Long, computer engineer and blogger Nguyen Tien Trung and businessman Tran Huynh Duy Thuc – to between five and 16 years' imprisonment after a trial lasting one day. They were convicted of "activities aimed at overthrowing the people's administration". The judges deliberated for 15 minutes before returning with a judgement which took 45 minutes to read out, suggesting it had been prepared in advance. Some family members and journalists observed the trial through a video link in an adjacent room; others were refused entry. Sentences of three of the accused were upheld on appeal in May; Le Thanh Long's prison sentence was reduced from five to three and a half years.

■ Novelist and journalist Tran Khai Thanh Thuy was tried by Dong Da District People's Court in February. She was arrested after being beaten by thugs several hours after police had stopped her from travelling to another town to attend a dissidents' trial in October 2009. In an apparently deliberate distortion of the incident, she was charged with assault and sentenced to three and a half years in prison after a trial that lasted less than a day.

Discrimination – religious minorities

Members of the Unified Buddhist Church of Viet Nam (UBCV) continued to face harassment and restrictions on their freedom of movement in some provinces. Supreme Patriarch Thich Quang Do remained under de facto house arrest. Local authorities and police harassed and used unnecessary force against UBCV members at Giac Minh Pagoda in Quang Nam-Da Nang province in May and August as they attempted to hold special prayers.

Disputes over land ownership between local authorities and the Catholic church continued. In May hundreds of police used batons and electric prods against Catholics of Con Dau parish who were attempting to bury a woman in a cemetery on land designated by the authorities for development. Dozens of people were injured, and around 60 briefly detained. Two were sentenced in October to nine and 12 months' imprisonment, and five received non-custodial sentences after being charged with public order offences. Some 40 parishioners fled Viet Nam to seek asylum in Thailand.

Death penalty

The National Assembly voted in May to change the method of execution from firing squad to lethal injection, claiming that it causes less pain, costs less and reduces psychological pressure on executioners. The change was due to come into effect in July 2011. According to media reports, at least 34 people were sentenced to death. No executions were reported in the media. Official statistics on the death penalty were not made public.

YEMEN

REPUBLIC OF YEMEN

Head of state:	'Ali Abdullah Saleh
Head of government:	Ali Mohammed Mujawar
Death penalty:	retentionist
Population:	24.3 million
Life expectancy:	63.9 years
Under-5 mortality (m/f):	84/73 per 1,000
Adult literacy:	60.9 per cent

Human rights were subordinated to security challenges posed by al-Qa'ida as well as by armed conflict in the northern Sa'dah province and protests in the south. Thousands of people were detained. Most were released quickly, but many were held for prolonged periods. Some were held incommunicado for months and were victims of enforced disappearance. Some received unfair trials before the Specialized Criminal Court (SCC) and were sentenced to death or prison terms. Many detainees said they were tortured. The sixth round of fighting in the Sa'dah conflict, which ended in February, involved heavy military bombardments, including by Saudi Arabian forces, and led to hundreds of deaths, widespread destruction and mass flight of civilians. Government repression increased in the face of continuing protests in the south against perceived discrimination by the northern-based government; security forces used excessive force against some demonstrations and several people were killed in targeted attacks. The media faced repressive laws and practices; several journalists were prisoners of conscience. Women continued to face discrimination and violence. Yemen continued to afford protection to many refugees and asylum-seekers from the Horn of Africa, but moved to end the automatic recognition of Somalis. At least 27 people were sentenced to death and 53 executed.

Background

Several provinces were effectively outside the control of the government. In some areas, the risk of kidnapping remained high. Two German girls taken hostage with seven other foreign nationals in Sa'dah province in June 2009 were freed by Saudi Arabian forces in May. Three of the nine had been found dead in 2009; the fate of three Germans and a Briton remained unclear.

Mass protests were held across the country against the worsening economic situation and substantial rises in fuel, electricity, water and food prices.

A presidential amnesty announced on 21 May appeared to apply to all political prisoners, including journalists, but the government did not give details about those it covered or the timeframe for releases. Later that month, 117 people detained on suspicion of taking part in the Sa'dah conflict and the protests in the south were released under the amnesty, as were four journalists. However, hundreds of other political prisoners remained held at the end of 2010.

New and draft laws undermined human rights protection. The Law on Combating Money Laundering and Financing of Terrorism, passed in January, provides a broad definition of the criminalization of financing terrorism and requires lawyers to disclose to the authorities information about their clients if they suspect them of offences under this law. The draft Counter Terrorism Law lacks provisions to protect the rights of suspects during arrest and detention, and proposes to expand the number of crimes punishable by death. Proposed amendments to the Penal Code could allow the death penalty to be used against juvenile offenders, in breach of international law. Two draft laws relating to the media threaten to further restrict freedom of expression.

Counter-terror and security

Government operations against suspected al-Qa'ida threats increased from the beginning of the year in the wake of an apparent attempt to blow up a US airliner on 25 December 2009 by a Nigerian man allegedly trained by al-Qa'ida in Yemen. There was enhanced US-Yemeni co-operation in such operations, including during air strikes and raids.

Attacks by armed groups continued, including by al-Qa'ida in the Arabian Peninsula. Some of the attacks targeted security forces, others targeted foreign nationals or led to the killings of bystanders.

■ In April the British ambassador narrowly escaped a bomb attack in Sana'a claimed by al-Qa'ida.

■ In June, three women, a child and seven security officers were killed during an attack on a security forces building in Aden that the government alleged was carried out by al-Qa'ida.

Tens of people suspected of links to al-Qa'ida or armed Islamist groups were killed by the security forces, some in circumstances suggesting that no attempt was made to arrest them. No judicial

Y

investigations were known to have been held to establish whether the use of lethal force by the security forces was justified and lawful. Scores of other al-Qa'ida suspects were arrested and subjected to a wide range of abuses, including enforced disappearance, prolonged detention without charge, and torture. Several were under sentence of death or serving long prison terms after unfair trials before the SCC.

■ On 25 May, an air attack by security forces killed four people in a car in Ma'rib. Among the victims was Jaber al-Shabwani, deputy governor of Ma'rib, who was reported to have been travelling to meet al-Qa'ida members to help mediate their surrender. The outcome of an investigation had not been disclosed by the end of the year.

In March, following an investigation by a parliamentary committee, the government acknowledged that an air raid on 17 December 2009 that killed 41 men, women and children in Abyan region had been a mistake and that there was no evidence of a military camp at the site, as first alleged. Photographs apparently taken following the attack suggest that the operation used a US-manufactured cruise missile that carried cluster bombs. Such missiles are only known to be held by US forces, and Yemeni armed forces are unlikely to have the military capability to use such a missile. A diplomatic cable leaked by the organization Wikileaks in November corroborated the images that had been released by Amnesty International earlier in the year.

Sa'dah conflict

The government's military offensive, code-named "Scorched Earth", which began in August 2009, ended with a ceasefire on 11 February 2010. It involved the deployment of military force against the Huthis (followers of Hussain Badr al-Din al-Huthi, a Zaidi Shi'a cleric killed in 2004) on a scale not witnessed before, particularly after Saudi Arabian forces became involved in November. Weeks of heavy bombardment of Sa'dah, by Saudi Arabian and Yemeni forces in December and January, killed hundreds of people not engaged in the fighting and caused widespread damage to homes, other civilian buildings such as mosques and schools, as well as local industries and infrastructure. Some of the attacks appeared to violate international humanitarian law in that they appeared either to deliberately target civilians or civilian objects, or to be indiscriminate or disproportionate attacks that took little or no account of the danger they posed to civilians. Neither the Saudi Arabian nor Yemeni government provided any explanation for the vast majority of such attacks nor explained what, if any, precautions were taken by their forces to spare civilians taking no part in hostilities.

By the end of the year, over 350,000 people from Sa'dah were displaced, according to the UN refugee agency UNHCR, some of them for the second or third time. Only a fraction found refuge in specially constructed camps. The scale of the destruction and unexploded ordnance and landmines hampered the early return of the displaced families. In July, the authorities announced that compensation would be paid to families affected by the destruction. In August, the government and Huthis signed a peace deal in Qatar that began the process of political dialogue.

Hundreds of suspected Huthi fighters or supporters were held in the main prisons in Sa'dah and Sana'a, and in other detention centres. Some disappeared for weeks or months after capture or arrest. Many were said to have been tortured or otherwise ill-treated. Most remained held at the end of the year, although dozens of Huthi fighters were released in May under the presidential pardon. Few details of the detainees still held were available.

Unrest in the south

Mass and generally peaceful protests organized by the Southern Movement continued, and there were growing calls for secession of the south. The authorities used excessive and sometimes lethal force against protesters. They accused elements in the Southern Movement of links with al-Qa'ida and in some cases targeted individuals or communities for attack. The government temporarily blockaded some areas by establishing checkpoints and shutting down mobile phone networks, leading to food shortages, and imposed travel bans on some members of the Southern Movement.

Hundreds of people were detained in waves of arrests. Most were released soon after, but some were held incommunicado or for long periods, and some were sentenced to imprisonment after unfair trials before the SCC.

■ On 1 March, security forces shot dead a prominent member of the Southern Movement, Ali al-Haddi, in his home several hours after they had raided the house, held his family captive and shot him in the leg. His body was later mutilated, apparently by the security forces.

Another relative in the house, Ahmad Muhsen Muhammad, was also shot dead by security forces.

■ Qassem Askar Jubran, a former Yemeni diplomat and supporter of the Southern Movement, was released in July 2010. He had been held since April 2009; he appeared to be a prisoner of conscience.

Freedom of expression – attacks on the press

Restrictive press laws and repressive actions by the security forces continued to undermine freedom of the press. People linked to the media were harassed, prosecuted and imprisoned. Some faced unfair trials before the Specialized Press and Publications Court in Sana'a.

■ Abdul Ilah Haydar Shayi', a freelance journalist who specializes in counter-terrorism affairs and had interviewed alleged al-Qa'ida members, was arrested on 16 August. Kamal Sharaf, a cartoonist who campaigns against corruption, was arrested the next day. They were both held incommunicado until 11 September. Abdul Ilah Haydar Shayi' had injuries on his chest, bruising on his body and a broken tooth, which he said he sustained when he was beaten after arrest. On 22 September, the SCC ordered the release of Kamal Sharaf, but this was ignored until his release on 5 October. The same day it extended the detention of Abdul Ilah Haydar Shayi' who, along with another man, Abdul Kareem al-Shami, was tried on charges that included membership of al-Qa'ida and communicating with "wanted men".

■ On 4 January, staff of *al-Ayyam* and supporters began a sit-down protest outside the newspaper's offices in Aden to mark eight months since the authorities effectively silenced the newspaper. On 5 and 6 January, Hisham Bashraheel, the 66-year-old editor-in-chief, along with his two sons Hani and Muhammad, both of whom work for *al-Ayyam*, were arrested. Hisham Bashraheel was initially held incommunicado and his health deteriorated. He was released on bail on 25 March. His sons were released on 9 May. All three continued to face charges.

Discrimination and violence against women and girls

Women and girls continued to face severe discrimination in law and practice, and particularly in rural areas were still subject to forced and early marriage. A draft law to raise the minimum age for marriage for girls to 17, approved by the parliament in 2009, had not been enacted by the end of 2010. Large rallies were held in support of and against the proposed reform. The government pledged to implement plans aimed at increasing the participation of women in political, social and economic life.

■ Twelve-year-old Ilham al-'Ashi died on 9 April, days after her wedding, as a result of internal bleeding reportedly caused by a violent sexual attack by her husband.

Maternal mortality

Maternal mortality rates remained significantly higher in Yemen than in other countries in the region. The authorities continued to work with international aid agencies to increase provision of free health care to pregnant women. The problem of accessing adequate health care for women in remote rural areas remained acute; for many, there was no antenatal or emergency obstetrics care as the nearest clinic was too far away.

Refugees and asylum-seekers

In February, the authorities established a General Department for Refugee Affairs.

At least 178,000 refugees from Africa, 168,000 of whom were Somalis, were resident in Yemen as of June, according to UNHCR. Yemeni authorities took steps towards ending the automatic recognition of Somalis.

Torture and other ill-treatment

Torture and other ill-treatment by police and prison guards continued to be reported, particularly by National Security officials, in the first weeks of detention. Methods cited included beatings with sticks and rifle butts, kicking, and prolonged suspension by the wrists.

Cruel, inhuman and degrading punishments

Flogging continued to be used as punishment for alcohol and sexual offences.

Death penalty

At least 27 people were sentenced to death and at least 53 prisoners were executed. Hundreds of people were believed to remain under sentence of death.

■ Akram al-Samawy, convicted of raping and murdering a girl, was executed in Ta'izz Central Prison on 5 July.

Y

■ In July, the Supreme Court upheld the death sentence imposed on Abdul Aziz al-Obadi after he was convicted of murder. An appeal court in June 2009 had overturned the lower court's sentence of *diya* (financial compensation), imposed after medical reports found that he was "mentally abnormal", and sentenced him to death.

Amnesty International visits/reports

🚌 Amnesty International delegates visited Yemen in March to conduct human rights research and had meetings with the Minister and Deputy Minister of Human Rights.

📄 Yemen: Security and human rights – media briefing (MDE 31/004/2010)

📄 Yemen: Cracking down under pressure (MDE 31/010/2010)

📄 Yemen: Security at what price? (MDE 31/011/2010)

ZIMBABWE

REPUBLIC OF ZIMBABWE

Head of state and government:	**Robert Mugabe**
Death penalty:	**retentionist**
Population:	**12.6 million**
Life expectancy:	**47 years**
Under-5 mortality (m/f):	**100/88 per 1,000**
Adult literacy:	**91.4 per cent**

Police continued to arbitrarily arrest and detain human rights defenders and journalists undertaking legitimate human rights work. There was some loosening of restrictions on the media and Parliament debated a bill to reform the repressive Public Order and Security Act (POSA). Lesbian, gay, bisexual and transgender (LGBT) people faced persecution. The victims of the 2005 forced evictions continued to live in deplorable conditions with some being targeted for eviction or facing the threat of eviction.

Background

Tension within the government of national unity (GNU) continued to undermine the implementation of some aspects of the Global Political Agreement (GPA) brokered by the leaders of the Southern Africa Development Community (SADC) in September 2008. In August 2010, a meeting was held during the SADC summit in Namibia to break the deadlock within the GNU. Despite several trips to Zimbabwe by the SADC-appointed South African mediation team, there was little movement.

President Mugabe made several unilateral decisions that breached the provisions of the GPA and the Constitution requiring consultation with the Prime Minister. In March, he assigned ministerial functions, leaving some ministers affiliated to the two Movement for Democratic Change (MDC) parties without specific responsibilities. In October, President Mugabe reappointed 10 provincial governors, all from his party ZANU-PF, in breach of a prior agreement to share governorships. Other such decisions included the reassignment of ambassadors and the appointment of judges. The President also continued to refuse to swear in Roy Bennett of the MDC party led by Prime Minister Morgan Tsvangirai as Deputy Minister of Agriculture.

ZANU-PF decided not to make further concessions in the GNU unless sanctions imposed by the EU and the USA were lifted. At its summit in August, the SADC decided to engage with the international community on the issue of sanctions.

Members of the Human Rights Commission, Zimbabwe Media Commission and Zimbabwe Electoral Commission were appointed in March although the Human Rights Commission had not started working by the end of the year.

The drafting of a new Constitution started with public consultations, although some meetings were abandoned because of violence and disruption mainly by supporters of ZANU-PF. At least one person died in Harare after being attacked by alleged ZANU-PF supporters in violence that followed the disruption of a constitutional consultation meeting in September. There was no progress in reforming the security sector.

The economy continued to show signs of improvement, although formal unemployment remained above 80 per cent and an estimated 1.5 million people were in need of food aid.

Statements about a possible election in 2011 by President Mugabe, Prime Minister Tsvangirai and the SADC facilitator, South African President Jacob Zuma, heightened tension in the country. In rural areas there were increased reports of harassment and intimidation of perceived opponents of ZANU-PF. State security agents, implicated in the 2008 political violence, were reported to be assisting ZANU-PF to rebuild its structures.

Z

Human rights defenders

Police continued to arbitrarily arrest and detain human rights defenders and journalists for their legitimate human rights work. Human rights defenders involved in the Constitution-drafting process or engaged in debate on accountability for past human rights violations were specifically targeted. At least 186 members of Women of Zimbabwe Arise (WOZA) and Men of Zimbabwe Arise (MOZA) were arrested during 2010.

■ On 25 January, 22 activists from MOZA and WOZA were arrested in Bulawayo after a peace march to hand in a report on education in Bulawayo. They were forcibly marched to the Drill Hall, beaten with batons by police and then released without charge.

■ On 24 February, Gertrude Hambira, Secretary General of the General Agricultural and Plantation Workers Union of Zimbabwe (GAPWUZ), was forced to go into hiding and later to flee the country after six officers from the Criminal Investigation Department of the Zimbabwe Republic Police raided the GAPWUZ offices in Harare looking for her. Before the raid, on 19 February, Gertrude Hambira was summoned to a meeting at Police Headquarters in Harare with a panel of 17 high-ranking security officials from the police, army, air force and intelligence service. She was interrogated with two other union workers about a GAPWUZ report and video highlighting the plight of farm workers and ongoing violence on farms. She was threatened with imprisonment. By the end of the year she had not returned to Zimbabwe.

■ Okay Machisa, National Director of the Zimbabwe Human Rights Association (ZimRights), temporarily fled the country after being detained by police on 23 March for his role in a photo exhibition about the 2008 political violence. Police confiscated at least 65 photographs from the exhibition, and only returned them to ZimRights following a High Court ruling. Despite the ruling, police in the towns of Masvingo, Gweru and Chinhoyi stopped similar exhibitions being shown. In Masvingo, ZimRights' regional chairperson Joel Hita was arrested, detained overnight and released on bail.

■ On 26 March, Owen Maseko, an artist based in Bulawayo, was arrested after mounting an exhibition which depicted atrocities in the Matabeleland region in western Zimbabwe during the 1980s. He was charged with "undermining the authority of the President", "inciting public violence" and "causing offence to people of a particular tribe, race, religion", under POSA. He was released on bail on 29 March.

■ On 15 April, Jenni Williams, Magodonga Mahlangu, Clara Manjengwa and Celina Madukani, members of WOZA, were arrested by police while attending a peaceful demonstration in Harare against rising electricity prices. They were arrested along with 61 others, and were released after the Attorney General's Office refused to prosecute them.

■ On 3 June, Farai Maguwu, director of the Centre for Research and Development (CRD) based in the town of Mutare, was arrested for exposing human rights violations by the security forces in the diamond fields of Marange. He was charged with "publishing or communicating false information prejudicial to the state" and remanded in custody until 12 July. On 21 October the government dropped the charges. Farai Maguwu was arrested after a meeting with Abbey Chikane, the Kimberly Process Certification Scheme monitor on Zimbabwe, reportedly in the presence of state intelligence officers.

■ On 24 June, two members of the Independent Constitution Monitoring Project (ZZZICOMP), Godfrey Nyarota and Tapiwa Mavherevhedze, plus their driver Cornelius Chengu, were arrested in Mutare. They were charged with practising journalism without accreditation and released on bail. Another activist in Mutare, Enddy Ziyera, was detained for several hours without charge on 25 June after taking food to the three detainees.

■ On 27 June, ZZZICOMP monitors Paul Nechishanu, Artwel Katandika and Shingairayi Garira were taken by ZANU-PF supporters to a farm in Makonde district (Mashonaland West province) where they were beaten with logs. Shingairayi Garira sustained injuries to his eardrum while Paul Nechishanu and Artwel Katandika suffered head injuries.

■ On 20 September, 83 activists from WOZA and MOZA were arrested after police in Harare broke up a peaceful demonstration. The activists were part of an estimated 600 WOZA and MOZA members who had marched on Parliament protesting against police abuses and lack of safety in their communities. As police began arresting some demonstrators, others gave themselves up in solidarity. They were detained at Harare Central police station for two nights in filthy conditions before being charged with "criminal nuisance" and released on bail. On the same day, Jenni Williams, WOZA National Coordinator, was arrested and detained for several hours at Harare Magistrates court as she tried to identify released

Z

activists who needed medical assistance. She was accused of "addressing a gathering in court" and was only released after signing a caution statement under protest.

■ In October, police attempted to revive a case against 14 WOZA activists who were arrested in May 2008 after attempting to hand over a petition at the Zambian embassy in Harare. However, only one of the 14 activists, Clara Manjengwa, received the summons. When she turned up at court on 21 October, there was no record of the case and it was not on the court register. There was no docket, no witnesses and even the police did not turn up. The Magistrate dismissed the case.

Freedom of expression, association and peaceful assembly

On 26 November, the Supreme Court ruled that the 2008 arrest and subsequent detention of Women of Zimbabwe Arise (WOZA) leaders Jenni Williams and Magodonga Mahlangu after a peaceful demonstration was wrongful and that their rights and fundamental freedoms had been violated. The court also ruled that the state had failed to protect the two human rights defenders from abuse.

There was partial reform of the media, with the ending of the state monopoly on daily newspapers. In May, four independent daily newspapers were licensed by the Zimbabwe Media Commission, including the Daily News which was banned in 2002. However, there was no progress in licensing private broadcasters.

In February and October, a private member's bill to amend POSA was debated in Parliament. The bill, introduced by MDC-T Member of Parliament, Innocent Gonese, in November 2009, sought to amend sections of the POSA that have been used to curtail freedom of association and peaceful assembly. If it became law, the bill would limit police powers to arbitrarily ban demonstrations, and would enhance police accountability by requiring them to report to the Minister of Home Affairs and assembly organizers when force was used.

Rights of lesbian, gay, bisexual and transgender people

On 21 May, police raided the offices of the Gays and Lesbians of Zimbabwe (GALZ) organization in Harare and arrested two employees, Ellen Chademana and Ignatius Mhambi. They were held until 27 May when they were granted bail. The two GALZ employees were charged with possessing prohibited materials. They were both acquitted – Ignatius Mhambi in July and Ellen Chademana in December.

Forced evictions

May marked the fifth anniversary of the 2005 mass forced evictions known as Operation Murambatsvina. Five years on, the government failed to provide effective remedies for survivors living in appalling conditions on plots of land allocated by the government under Operation Garikai/Hlalani Kuhle – the government's programme to re-house some of the victims of Operation Murambatsvina.

In most of the settlements, survivors were still living in worn-out shacks which had been provided as temporary shelter by humanitarian organizations. They often had no access to clean water, sanitation, health care, education or means of livelihood. The majority of the survivors of Operation Murambatsvina also lost their livelihoods during the mass forced evictions that directly affected 700,000 people.

■ In Hopley settlement, one of the Operation Garikai settlements in Harare, the health risks for pregnant women and newborn babies were increased by dire living conditions and lack of access to basic services including adequate health care. Survivors reported a high incidence of neonatal mortality, and said that contributing factors included lack of maternal and newborn health care services, prohibitive user fees and lack of transport for women in labour.

Survivors of Operation Murambatsvina were also at risk of further forced eviction by the authorities.

■ In June, about 3,000 leaseholders and their families, an estimated 15,000 to 20,000 people, at Hatcliffe Extension were threatened with eviction by the Ministry of Local Government, Urban and Rural Development if they failed to renew their leases by 30 September. Most of the families could not afford the renewal fees. The threat of eviction was withdrawn by the government after mass appeals by Amnesty International and national human rights organizations who assisted some of the affected people to take legal action.

■ On 25 August, about 250 people living at an informal settlement in Harare's affluent Gunhill suburb were forcibly evicted by police without prior notice. Armed police with dogs arrived at the settlement at about midnight and ordered the community out of their dwellings. Victims reported that police only gave them about 10 minutes to remove their belongings before setting them on fire. Some possessions were burnt after their owners failed to remove them in time. Police arrested 55 people, including five children, and detained them at Harare Central police station. They were held for several hours before being released without charge following intervention by lawyers. No reason was given for the police action. The community was forcibly evicted despite written assurances that this would not happen by the mayor of Harare in December 2009. The mayor denied involvement in the August evictions.

Amnesty International visits/reports

Amnesty International visited Zimbabwe in March, May-June and November-December. In May, Amnesty International representatives met Prime Minister Tsvangirai, the Minister of National Housing and Social Amenities, Fidelis Mhashu, and the Minister of Education, Sport and Culture, Senator David Coltart. In November-December, Amnesty International delegates met Deputy Prime Minister Thokozani Khupe, the Minister of Health and Child Welfare Henry Madzorera and the Mayor of Harare, Muchadeyi Masunda.

📑 Submission for consideration by the Constitutional Parliamentary Committee on the death penalty provisions in the Constitution (AFR 46/016/2010)

📑 No chance to live – newborn deaths at Hopley settlement, Zimbabwe (AFR 46/018/2010)

📑 Submission for consideration by the Constitutional Parliamentary Committee recommending the inclusion of economic, social and cultural rights in the Constitution (AFR 46/022/2010)

📑 Zimbabwe: stop harassing opponents of former government, 10 May 2010

📑 Zimbabwe must release 83 activists detained at peaceful demonstration, 19 September 2010

Z

Newly arrived refugees from Somalia wait for registration at Ifo camp, Kenya, May 2010. During November, 8,000 civilians were ordered to return to Somalia by the Kenyan authorities.

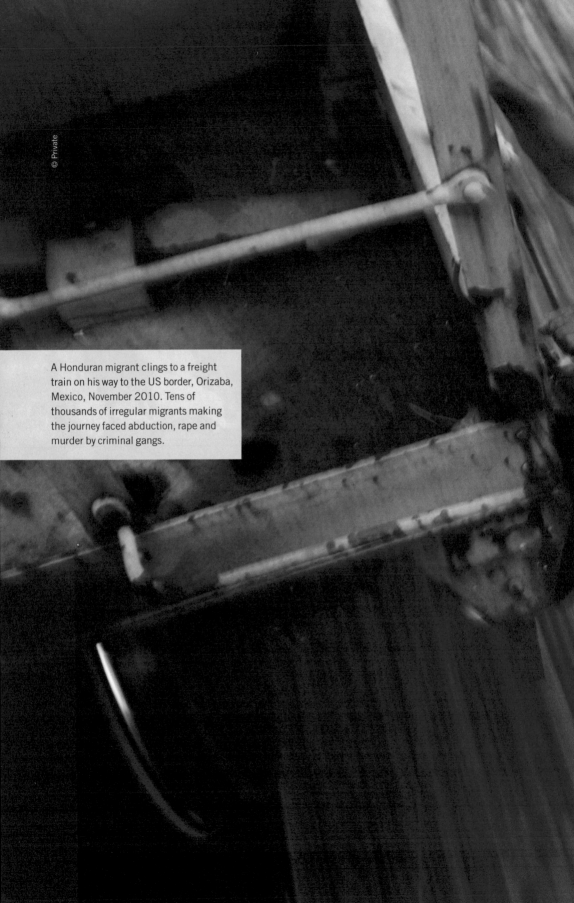

A Honduran migrant clings to a freight train on his way to the US border, Orizaba, Mexico, November 2010. Tens of thousands of irregular migrants making the journey faced abduction, rape and murder by criminal gangs.

AMNESTY INTERNATIONAL REPORT 2011
PART THREE: SELECTED HUMAN RIGHTS TREATIES

11

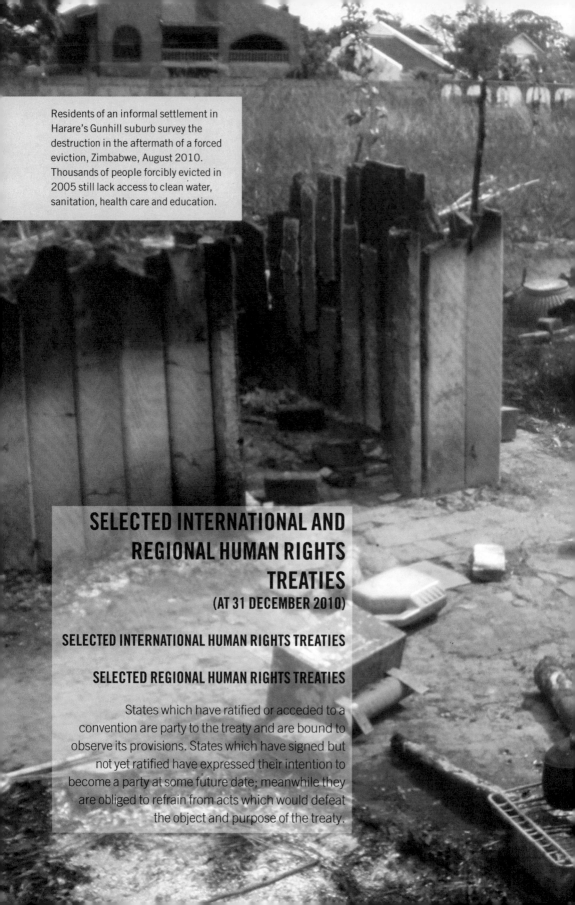

Residents of an informal settlement in Harare's Gunhill suburb survey the destruction in the aftermath of a forced eviction, Zimbabwe, August 2010. Thousands of people forcibly evicted in 2005 still lack access to clean water, sanitation, health care and education.

SELECTED INTERNATIONAL AND REGIONAL HUMAN RIGHTS TREATIES
(AT 31 DECEMBER 2010)

SELECTED INTERNATIONAL HUMAN RIGHTS TREATIES

SELECTED REGIONAL HUMAN RIGHTS TREATIES

States which have ratified or acceded to a convention are party to the treaty and are bound to observe its provisions. States which have signed but not yet ratified have expressed their intention to become a party at some future date; meanwhile they are obliged to refrain from acts which would defeat the object and purpose of the treaty.

	International Covenant on Civil and Political Rights (ICCPR)	(first) Optional Protocol to the ICCPR	Second Optional Protocol to the ICCPR, aiming at the abolition of the death penalty	International Covenant on Economic, Social and Cultural Rights (ICESCR)	Optional Protocol to the ICESCR	Convention on the Elimination of All Forms of Discrimination against Women (CEDAW)	Optional Protocol to CEDAW	Convention on the Rights of the Child (CRC)	Optional Protocol to the CRC on the involvement of children in armed conflict	International Convention on the Elimination of All Forms of Racial Discrimination	Convention against Torture and Other Cruel, Inhuman or Degrading Treatment or Punishment
Afghanistan	●			●		●		●	●	●	●[28]
Albania	●	●	●	●		●	●	●	●	●	●
Algeria	●	●		●		●		●	●	●	●[22]
Andorra	●	●	●			●		●	●	●	●[22]
Angola	●	●		●		●		●	●	●	
Antigua and Barbuda						●		●		●	●
Argentina	●	●	●	●	○	●	●	●	●	●	●[22]
Armenia	●	●		●	○	●	●	●	●	●	●
Australia	●	●	●	●		●	●	●	●	●	●[22]
Austria	●	●	●	●		●	●	●	●	●	●[22]
Azerbaijan	●	●	●	●	○	●	●	●	●	●	●[22]
Bahamas	●			●		●		●		●	○
Bahrain	●			●		●		●		●	●
Bangladesh	●			●		●	●[10]	●	●	●	●
Barbados	●	●		●		●		●		●	
Belarus	●	●		●		●	●	●	●	●	●
Belgium	●	●	●	●	○	●	●	●	●	●	●[22]
Belize	●			○		●	●[10]	●		●	●
Benin	●	●		●		●	○	●	●	●	●
Bhutan						●		●	●	○	
Bolivia	●	●		●	○	●	●	●	●	●	●[22]
Bosnia and Herzegovina	●	●	●	●	○	●	●	●	●	●	●[22]
Botswana	●					●		●	●	●	●
Brazil	●	●	●	●		●	●	●	●	●	●[22]
Brunei Darussalam						●		●			
Bulgaria	●	●	●	●		●	●	●	●	●	●[22]
Burkina Faso	●	●		●		●	●	●	●	●	●
Burundi	●			●		●	○	●	●	●	●[22]

	Optional Protocol to the Convention against Torture	International Convention for the Protection of All Persons from Enforced Disappearance	Convention relating to the Status of Refugees (1951)	Protocol relating to the Status of Refugees (1967)	Convention relating to the Status of Stateless Persons (1954)	Convention on the Reduction of Statelessness (1961)	International Convention on the Protection of the Rights of All Migrant Workers and Members of Their Families	Rome Statute of the International Criminal Court
Afghanistan			●	●				●
Albania	●	●	●	●	●	●	●	●
Algeria		○	●	●	●		●	○
Andorra								●
Angola			●	●				○
Antigua and Barbuda			●	●	●			●
Argentina	●	●	●	●	●		●	●
Armenia	●	○	●	●	●	●		○
Australia	○		●	●	●	●		●
Austria	○	○	●	●	●	●		●
Azerbaijan	●	○	●	●	●	●	●	
Bahamas			●	●				○
Bahrain								○
Bangladesh							○	●
Barbados					●			●
Belarus			●	●				
Belgium	○	○	●	●	●			●
Belize			●	●	●		●	●
Benin	●	○	●	●			○	●
Bhutan								
Bolivia	●	●	●	●	●	●	●	●
Bosnia and Herzegovina	●	○	●	●	●	●	●	●
Botswana			●	●	●			●
Brazil	●	●	●	●	●	●		●
Brunei Darussalam								
Bulgaria	○	○	●	●				●
Burkina Faso	●	●	●	●			●	●
Burundi		○	●	●				●

● state is a party
● state became party in 2010
○ signed but not yet ratified
○ signed in 2010, but not yet ratified

10 Declaration under Article 10 not recognizing the competence of the CEDAW Committee to undertake confidential inquiries into allegations of grave or systematic violations.

22 Declaration under Article 22 recognizing the competence of the Committee against Torture (CAT) to consider individual complaints.

28 Reservation under Article 28 not recognizing the competence of the CAT to undertake confidential inquiries into allegations of systematic torture if warranted.

12 Declaration under Article 12(3) accepting the jurisdiction of the International Criminal Court (ICC) for crimes in its territory.

124 Declaration under Article 124 not accepting the jurisdiction of the ICC over war crimes for seven years after ratification.

* Signed the Rome Statute but have since formally declared their intention not to ratify.

** Ratified or acceded but subsequently denounced the treaty.

	International Covenant on Civil and Political Rights (ICCPR)	(first) Optional Protocol to the ICCPR	Second Optional Protocol to the ICCPR, aiming at the abolition of the death penalty	International Covenant on Economic, Social and Cultural Rights (ICESCR)	Optional Protocol to the ICESCR	Convention on the Elimination of All Forms of Discrimination against Women (CEDAW)	Optional Protocol to CEDAW	Convention on the Rights of the Child (CRC)	Optional Protocol to the CRC on the involvement of children in armed conflict	International Convention on the Elimination of All Forms of Racial Discrimination	Convention against Torture and Other Cruel, Inhuman or Degrading Treatment or Punishment
Cambodia	●	○		●		●	●	●	●	●	●
Cameroon	●	●		●		●	●	●	○	●	●22
Canada	●	●	●	●		●	●	●	●	●	●22
Cape Verde	●	●	●	●		●		●	●	●	●
Central African Republic	●	●		●		●		●	○	●	
Chad	●	●		●		●		●	●	●	●
Chile	●	●	●	●	○	●	○	●	●	●	●22
China	○			●		●		●	●	●	●28
Colombia	●	●	●	●		●	●10	●	●	●	●
Comoros	○			○		●		●		●	○
Congo (Republic of)	●	●		●	○	●	○	●	●	●	●
Cook Islands						●	●	●			
Costa Rica	●	●	●	●		●	●	●	●	●	●22
Côte d'Ivoire	●	●		●		●		●		●	●
Croatia	●	●	●	●		●	●	●	●	●	●22
Cuba	○			○		●	○	●	●	●	●28
Cyprus	●	●	●	●		●	●	●	●	●	●22
Czech Republic	●	●	●	●		●	●	●	●	●	●22
Democratic Republic of the Congo	●	●		●	○	●		●	●	●	●
Denmark	●	●	●	●		●	●	●	●	●	●22
Djibouti	●	●	●	●		●		●	○	○	●
Dominica	●			●		●		●	●		
Dominican Republic	●	●		●		●	●	●	○	●	○
Ecuador	●	●	●	●	●	●	●	●	●	●	●22
Egypt	●			●		●		●	●	●	●
El Salvador	●	●		●	○	●	○	●	●	●	●
Equatorial Guinea	●	●		●		●		●		●	●28
Eritrea	●			●		●		●	●	●	

Optional Protocol to the Convention against Torture	International Convention for the Protection of All Persons from Enforced Disappearance	Convention relating to the Status of Refugees (1951)	Protocol relating to the Status of Refugees (1967)	Convention relating to the Status of Stateless Persons (1954)	Convention on the Reduction of Statelessness (1961)	International Convention on the Protection of the Rights of All Migrant Workers and Members of Their Families	Rome Statute of the International Criminal Court	
●		●	●			○	●	Cambodia
○		●	●			○	○	Cameroon
		●	●		●		●	Canada
	○		●			●	○	Cape Verde
		●	●				●	Central African Republic
	○	●	●	●	●		●	Chad
●	●	●	●			●	●	Chile
		●	●					China
	○	●	●	○		●	●124	Colombia
	○					○	●	Comoros
○	○	●	●			○	●	Congo (Republic of)
							●	Cook Islands
●	○	●	●	●	●		●	Costa Rica
		●	●				○12	Côte d'Ivoire
●	○	●	●	●			●	Croatia
	●							Cuba
●	○	●	●				●	Cyprus
●		●	●	●	●		●	Czech Republic
●		●	●				●	Democratic Republic of the Congo
●	○	●	●	●	●		●	Denmark
		●	●				●	Djibouti
		●	●				●	Dominica
		●	●		○		●	Dominican Republic
●	●	●	●	●		●	●	Ecuador
		●	●			●	○	Egypt
		●	●	○		●		El Salvador
		●	●					Equatorial Guinea
							○	Eritrea

Legend:

● state is a party
● state became party in 2010
○ signed but not yet ratified
○ signed in 2010, but not yet ratified

10 Declaration under Article 10 not recognizing the competence of the CEDAW Committee to undertake confidential inquiries into allegations of grave or systematic violations.

22 Declaration under Article 22 recognizing the competence of the Committee against Torture (CAT) to consider individual complaints.

28 Reservation under Article 28 not recognizing the competence of the CAT to undertake confidential inquiries into allegations of systematic torture if warranted.

12 Declaration under Article 12(3) accepting the jurisdiction of the International Criminal Court (ICC) for crimes in its territory.

124 Declaration under Article 124 not accepting the jurisdiction of the ICC over war crimes for seven years after ratification.

* Signed the Rome Statute but have since formally declared their intention not to ratify.

** Ratified or acceded but subsequently denounced the treaty.

	International Covenant on Civil and Political Rights (ICCPR)	(first) Optional Protocol to the ICCPR	Second Optional Protocol to the ICCPR, aiming at the abolition of the death penalty	International Covenant on Economic, Social and Cultural Rights (ICESCR)	Optional Protocol to the ICESCR	Convention on the Elimination of All Forms of Discrimination against Women (CEDAW)	Optional Protocol to CEDAW	Convention on the Rights of the Child (CRC)	Optional Protocol to the CRC on the involvement of children in armed conflict	International Convention on the Elimination of All Forms of Racial Discrimination	Convention against Torture and Other Cruel, Inhuman or Degrading Treatment or Punishment
Estonia	●	●	●	●		●		●	○	●	●
Ethiopia	●			●		●		●	○	●	●
Fiji						●		●	○	●	
Finland	●	●	●	●	○	●	●	●	●	●	●[22]
France	●	●	●	●		●	●	●	●	●	●[22]
Gabon	●			●	○	●		●	●	●	●
Gambia	●	●		●		●		●	○	●	○
Georgia	●	●	●	●		●	●	●	●	●	●[22]
Germany	●	●	●	●		●	●	●	●	●	●[22]
Ghana	●	●		●	○	●	○	●	○	●	●[22]
Greece	●	●	●	●		●	●	●	●	●	●[22]
Grenada	●			●		●		●		○	
Guatemala	●	●		●	○	●	●	●	●	●	●[22]
Guinea	●	●		●		●		●		●	
Guinea-Bissau	●	○	○	●	○	●	●	●	○	●	○
Guyana	●	●		●		●		●	●	●	●
Haiti	●					●		●	○	●	
Holy See								●	●	●	●
Honduras	●	●	●	●		●		●	●	●	●
Hungary	●	●	●	●		●	●	●	●	●	●[22]
Iceland	●	●	●	●		●	●	●	●	●	●[22]
India	●			●		●		●	●	●	○
Indonesia	●			●		●	○	●	○	●	●
Iran	●			●				●	○	●	
Iraq	●			●		●		●		●	
Ireland	●	●	●	●		●	●	●	●	●	●[22]
Israel	●			●		●		●	●	●	●[28]
Italy	●	●	●	●	○	●	●	●	●	●	●[22]

Optional Protocol to the Convention against Torture	International Convention for the Protection of All Persons from Enforced Disappearance	Convention relating to the Status of Refugees (1951)	Protocol relating to the Status of Refugees (1967)	Convention relating to the Status of Stateless Persons (1954)	Convention on the Reduction of Statelessness (1961)	International Convention on the Protection of the Rights of All Migrant Workers and Members of Their Families	Rome Statute of the International Criminal Court	
●		●	●				●	Estonia
		●	●					Ethiopia
		●	●	●			●	Fiji
○	○	●	●	●	●		●	Finland
●	●	●	●	●	○		●124	France
●	○	●	●			○	●	Gabon
		●	●				●	Gambia
●		●	●				●	Georgia
●	●	●	●	●	●		●	Germany
○	○	●	●			●	●	Ghana
	○	●	●	●			●	Greece
	○							Grenada
●	○	●	●	●	●	●		Guatemala
○		●	●	●		●	●	Guinea
		●	●			○	○	Guinea-Bissau
						●	●	Guyana
	○	●	●				○	Haiti
		●	●	○				Holy See
●	●	●	●	○		●	●	Honduras
		●	●	●	●		●	Hungary
○	○	●	●				●	Iceland
	○							India
	○					○		Indonesia
		●	●				○	Iran
	●							Iraq
○	○	●	●	●	●		●	Ireland
		●	●	●	○		○*	Israel
○	○	●	●	●			●	Italy

- ● state is a party
- ● state became party in 2010
- ○ signed but not yet ratified
- ○ signed in 2010, but not yet ratified

10 Declaration under Article 10 not recognizing the competence of the CEDAW Committee to undertake confidential inquiries into allegations of grave or systematic violations.

22 Declaration under Article 22 recognizing the competence of the Committee against Torture (CAT) to consider individual complaints.

28 Reservation under Article 28 not recognizing the competence of the CAT to undertake confidential inquiries into allegations of systematic torture if warranted.

12 Declaration under Article 12(3) accepting the jurisdiction of the International Criminal Court (ICC) for crimes in its territory.

124 Declaration under Article 124 not accepting the jurisdiction of the ICC over war crimes for seven years after ratification.

* Signed the Rome Statute but have since formally declared their intention not to ratify.

** Ratified or acceded but subsequently denounced the treaty.

	International Covenant on Civil and Political Rights (ICCPR)	(first) Optional Protocol to the ICCPR	Second Optional Protocol to the ICCPR, aiming at the abolition of the death penalty	International Covenant on Economic, Social and Cultural Rights (ICESCR)	Optional Protocol to the ICESCR	Convention on the Elimination of All Forms of Discrimination against Women (CEDAW)	Optional Protocol to CEDAW	Convention on the Rights of the Child (CRC)	Optional Protocol to the CRC on the involvement of children in armed conflict	International Convention on the Elimination of All Forms of Racial Discrimination	Convention against Torture and Other Cruel, Inhuman or Degrading Treatment or Punishment
Jamaica	●	**		●		●		●	●	●	
Japan	●			●		●		●	●	●	●
Jordan	●			●		●		●	●	●	●
Kazakhstan	●	●		●	○	●	●	●	●	●	●22
Kenya	●			●		●		●	●	●	●22
Kiribati						●		●			
Korea (Democratic People's Republic of)	●			●		●		●			
Korea (Republic of)	●	●		●		●	●	●	●	●	●22
Kuwait	●			●		●		●	●	●	●28
Kyrgyzstan	●	●	●	●		●	●	●	●	●	●
Laos	●			●		●		●	●	●	○
Latvia	●	●		●		●		●	●	●	●
Lebanon	●			●		●		●	○	●	●
Lesotho	●	●		●		●		●	●	●	●
Liberia	●	○	●	●		●	○	●	○	●	●
Libya	●	●		●		●	●	●	●	●	●
Liechtenstein	●			●		●	●	●	●	●	●22
Lithuania	●	●		●		●	●	●	●	●	●
Luxembourg	●	●	●	●	○	●	●	●	●	●	●22
Macedonia	●	●	●	●		●	●	●	●	●	●
Madagascar	●	●		●	○	●	○	●	●	●	●
Malawi	●	●		●		●	○	●	●	●	●
Malaysia						●		●			
Maldives	●	●		●		●	●	●	●	●	●
Mali	●	●		●	○	●	●	●	●	●	●
Malta	●	●	●	●		●		●	●	●	●22
Marshall Islands						●		●			
Mauritania	●			●		●		●		●	●28

Optional Protocol to the Convention against Torture	International Convention for the Protection of All Persons from Enforced Disappearance	Convention relating to the Status of Refugees (1951)	Protocol relating to the Status of Refugees (1967)	Convention relating to the Status of Stateless Persons (1954)	Convention on the Reduction of Statelessness (1961)	International Convention on the Protection of the Rights of All Migrant Workers and Members of Their Families	Rome Statute of the International Criminal Court	
		●	●			●	○	Jamaica
	●	●	●				●	Japan
							●	Jordan
●	●	●	●					Kazakhstan
	○	●	●				●	Kenya
				●	●			Kiribati
								Korea (Democratic People's Republic of)
		●	●	●			●	Korea (Republic of)
							○	Kuwait
		●	●			●	○	Kyrgyzstan
	○							Laos
		●	●	●	●		●	Latvia
●	○							Lebanon
	○	●	●	●	●	●	●	Lesotho
●		●	●	●	●	○	●	Liberia
				●	●	●		Libya
●	○	●	●	●	●		●	Liechtenstein
	○	●	●	●			●	Lithuania
●	○	●	●	●			●	Luxembourg
●	○	●	●	●			●	Macedonia
○	○	●		**			●	Madagascar
		●	●	●			●	Malawi
								Malaysia
●	○							Maldives
●	●	●	●			●	●	Mali
●	○	●	●				●	Malta
							●	Marshall Islands
		●	●			●		Mauritania

● state is a party
● state became party in 2010
○ signed but not yet ratified
○ signed in 2010, but not yet ratified

10 Declaration under Article 10 not recognizing the competence of the CEDAW Committee to undertake confidential inquiries into allegations of grave or systematic violations.

22 Declaration under Article 22 recognizing the competence of the Committee against Torture (CAT) to consider individual complaints.

28 Reservation under Article 28 not recognizing the competence of the CAT to undertake confidential inquiries into allegations of systematic torture if warranted.

12 Declaration under Article 12(3) accepting the jurisdiction of the International Criminal Court (ICC) for crimes in its territory.

124 Declaration under Article 124 not accepting the jurisdiction of the ICC over war crimes for seven years after ratification.

* Signed the Rome Statute but have since formally declared their intention not to ratify.

** Ratified or acceded but subsequently denounced the treaty.

	International Covenant on Civil and Political Rights (ICCPR)	(first) Optional Protocol to the ICCPR	Second Optional Protocol to the ICCPR, aiming at the abolition of the death penalty	International Covenant on Economic, Social and Cultural Rights (ICESCR)	Optional Protocol to the ICESCR	Convention on the Elimination of All Forms of Discrimination against Women (CEDAW)	Optional Protocol to CEDAW	Convention on the Rights of the Child (CRC)	Optional Protocol to the CRC on the involvement of children in armed conflict	International Convention on the Elimination of All Forms of Racial Discrimination	Convention against Torture and Other Cruel, Inhuman or Degrading Treatment or Punishment
Mauritius	●	●		●		●	●	●	●	●	●
Mexico	●	●	●	●		●	●	●	●	●	●[22]
Micronesia						●		●	○		
Moldova	●	●	●	●		●	●	●	●	●	●
Monaco	●		●	●		●		●	●	●	●[22]
Mongolia	●	●			●	●	●	●	●	●	●
Montenegro	●	●	●	●	○	●	●	●	●	●	●[22]
Morocco	●			●		●		●	●	●	●[22]
Mozambique	●		●			●	●	●	●	●	●
Myanmar						●		●			
Namibia	●	●	●	●		●	●	●	●	●	●
Nauru	○	○						●	○	○	○
Nepal	●	●	●	●		●	●	●	●	●	●
Netherlands	●	●	●	●	○	●	●	●	●	●	●[22]
New Zealand	●	●	●	●		●	●	●	●	●	●[22]
Nicaragua	●	●	●	●		●		●	●	●	●
Niger	●	●		●		●	●	●		●	●
Nigeria	●			●		●	●	●	○	●	●
Niue								●			
Norway	●	●	●	●		●	●	●	●	●	●[22]
Oman						●		●	●	●	
Pakistan	●			●		●		●	○	●	●[28]
Palau								●			
Panama	●	●	●	●		●	●	●	●	●	●
Papua New Guinea	●			●		●		●		●	
Paraguay	●	●	●	●	○	●	●	●	●	●	●[22]
Peru	●	●		●		●	●	●	●	●	●[22]
Philippines	●	●	●	●		●	●	●	●	●	●

Optional Protocol to the Convention against Torture	International Convention for the Protection of All Persons from Enforced Disappearance	Convention relating to the Status of Refugees (1951)	Protocol relating to the Status of Refugees (1967)	Convention relating to the Status of Stateless Persons (1954)	Convention on the Reduction of Statelessness (1961)	International Convention on the Protection of the Rights of All Migrant Workers and Members of Their Families	Rome Statute of the International Criminal Court	
●							●	Mauritius
●	●	●	●	●		●	●	Mexico
								Micronesia
●	○	●	●				●	Moldova
	○	●	●				○	Monaco
	○						●	Mongolia
●	○	●	●	●		○	●	Montenegro
	○	●	●			●	○	Morocco
	○	●	●				○	Mozambique
								Myanmar
		●	●				●	Namibia
							●	Nauru
								Nepal
●	○	●	●	●	●		●	Netherlands
●		●	●		●		●	New Zealand
●		●	●			●		Nicaragua
	○	●	●		●	●	●	Niger
●	●	●	●			●	●	Nigeria
								Niue
○	○	●	●	●	●		●	Norway
							○	Oman
								Pakistan
								Palau
○	○	●	●				●	Panama
		●	●					Papua New Guinea
●	●	●	●			●	●	Paraguay
●		●	●			●	●	Peru
		●	●	○		●	○	Philippines

● state is a party

● state became party in 2010

○ signed but not yet ratified

○ signed in 2010, but not yet ratified

10 Declaration under Article 10 not recognizing the competence of the CEDAW Committee to undertake confidential inquiries into allegations of grave or systematic violations.

22 Declaration under Article 22 recognizing the competence of the Committee against Torture (CAT) to consider individual complaints.

28 Reservation under Article 28 not recognizing the competence of the CAT to undertake confidential inquiries into allegations of systematic torture if warranted.

12 Declaration under Article 12(3) accepting the jurisdiction of the International Criminal Court (ICC) for crimes in its territory.

124 Declaration under Article 124 not accepting the jurisdiction of the ICC over war crimes for seven years after ratification.

* Signed the Rome Statute but have since formally declared their intention not to ratify.

** Ratified or acceded but subsequently denounced the treaty.

	International Covenant on Civil and Political Rights (ICCPR)	(first) Optional Protocol to the ICCPR	Second Optional Protocol to the ICCPR, aiming at the abolition of the death penalty	International Covenant on Economic, Social and Cultural Rights (ICESCR)	Optional Protocol to the ICESCR	Convention on the Elimination of All Forms of Discrimination against Women (CEDAW)	Optional Protocol to CEDAW	Convention on the Rights of the Child (CRC)	Optional Protocol to the CRC on the involvement of children in armed conflict	International Convention on the Elimination of All Forms of Racial Discrimination	Convention against Torture and Other Cruel, Inhuman or Degrading Treatment or Punishment
Poland	●	●	○	●		●	●	●	●	●	28 ● 22
Portugal	●	●	●	●	○	●	●	●	●	●	●22
Qatar						●		●	●	●	●
Romania	●	●	●	●		●	●	●	●	●	●
Russian Federation	●	●		●		●	●	●	●	●	●22
Rwanda	●		●	●		●	●	●	●	●	●
Saint Kitts and Nevis						●	●	●		●	
Saint Lucia						●		●		●	
Saint Vincent and the Grenadines	●	●		●		●		●		●	●
Samoa	●					●		●			
San Marino	●	●	●	●		●	●	●	○	●	●
Sao Tome and Principe	○	○	○	○		●	○	●		○	○
Saudi Arabia						●		●		●	●28
Senegal	●	●		●	○	●	●	●	●	●	●22
Serbia	●	●	●	●		●	●	●	●	●	●22
Seychelles	●	●	●	●		●	○	●	●	●	●22
Sierra Leone	●	●		●		●	○	●	●	●	●
Singapore						●		●	●		
Slovakia	●	●	●	●	○	●	●	●	●	●	●22
Slovenia	●	●	●	●	○	●	●	●	●	●	●22
Solomon Islands				●	○	●	●	●	○	●	
Somalia	●	●		●				○	○	●	●
South Africa	●	●	●	○		●	●	●	●	●	●22
Spain	●	●	●	●	●	●	●	●	●	●	●22
Sri Lanka	●	●		●		●	●	●	●	●	●
Sudan	●			●				●	●	●	○
Suriname	●	●		●		●		●	○	●	
Swaziland	●			●		●		●		●	●

Optional Protocol to the Convention against Torture	International Convention for the Protection of All Persons from Enforced Disappearance	Convention relating to the Status of Refugees (1951)	Protocol relating to the Status of Refugees (1967)	Convention relating to the Status of Stateless Persons (1954)	Convention on the Reduction of Statelessness (1961)	International Convention on the Protection of the Rights of All Migrant Workers and Members of Their Families	Rome Statute of the International Criminal Court	
●		●	●				●	Poland
○	○	●	●				●	Portugal
								Qatar
●	○	●	●	●	●		●	Romania
		●	●				○	Russian Federation
		●	●	●	●	●		Rwanda
		●					●	Saint Kitts and Nevis
							●	Saint Lucia
	○	●	●	●		●	●	Saint Vincent and the Grenadines
	○	●	●				●	Samoa
							●	San Marino
		●	●			○	○	Sao Tome and Principe
								Saudi Arabia
●	●	●	●	●	●	●	●	Senegal
●	○	●	●	●		○	●	Serbia
		●	●			●	●	Seychelles
○	○	●	●			○	●	Sierra Leone
								Singapore
	○	●	●	●	●		●	Slovakia
●	○	●	●	●			●	Slovenia
		●	●				○	Solomon Islands
		●	●					Somalia
○		●	●				●	South Africa
●	●	●	●	●			●	Spain
						●		Sri Lanka
		●	●				○*	Sudan
		●	●				●	Suriname
	○	●	●	●	●			Swaziland

● state is a party

● state became party in 2010

○ signed but not yet ratified

○ signed in 2010, but not yet ratified

10   Declaration under Article 10 not recognizing the competence of the CEDAW Committee to undertake confidential inquiries into allegations of grave or systematic violations.

22   Declaration under Article 22 recognizing the competence of the Committee against Torture (CAT) to consider individual complaints.

28   Reservation under Article 28 not recognizing the competence of the CAT to undertake confidential inquiries into allegations of systematic torture if warranted.

12   Declaration under Article 12(3) accepting the jurisdiction of the International Criminal Court (ICC) for crimes in its territory.

124   Declaration under Article 124 not accepting the jurisdiction of the ICC over war crimes for seven years after ratification.

*   Signed the Rome Statute but have since formally declared their intention not to ratify.

**   Ratified or acceded but subsequently denounced the treaty.

	International Covenant on Civil and Political Rights (ICCPR)	(first) Optional Protocol to the ICCPR	Second Optional Protocol to the ICCPR, aiming at the abolition of the death penalty	International Covenant on Economic, Social and Cultural Rights (ICESCR)	Optional Protocol to the ICESCR	Convention on the Elimination of All Forms of Discrimination against Women (CEDAW)	Optional Protocol to CEDAW	Convention on the Rights of the Child (CRC)	Optional Protocol to the CRC on the involvement of children in armed conflict	International Convention on the Elimination of All Forms of Racial Discrimination	Convention against Torture and Other Cruel, Inhuman or Degrading Treatment or Punishment
Sweden	●	●	●	●		●	●	●	●	●	●22
Switzerland	●		●	●		●	●	●	●	●	●22
Syria	●			●		●		●	●	●	●28
Tajikistan	●	●		●		●	○	●	●	●	●
Tanzania	●			●		●	●	●	●	●	
Thailand	●			●		●		●	●	●	●
Timor-Leste	●		●	●	○	●	●	●	●	●	●
Togo	●	●		●	○	●		●	●	●	●22
Tonga								●		●	
Trinidad and Tobago	●	**		●		●		●		●	
Tunisia	●			●		●	●	●	●	●	●22
Turkey	●	●	●	●		●	●	●	●	●	●22
Turkmenistan	●	●	●	●		●	●	●	●	●	●
Tuvalu						●		●			
Uganda	●	●		●		●		●	●	●	●
Ukraine	●	●	●	●	○	●	●	●	●	●	●
United Arab Emirates						●		●		●	
United Kingdom	●		●	●		●	●	●	●	●	●
United States of America	●			○		○			○	●	●
Uruguay	●	●	●	●	○	●	●	●	●	●	●22
Uzbekistan	●	●	●	●		●		●	●	●	●
Vanuatu	●					●	●	●	●		
Venezuela	●	●	●	●		●	●	●	●	●	●22
Viet Nam	●			●		●		●	●	●	
Yemen	●			●		●		●	●	●	●
Zambia	●	●		●		●	○	●	○	●	●
Zimbabwe	●			●		●		●		●	

SELECTED TREATIES

INTERNATIONAL

Legend:
- ● state is a party
- ◐ state became party in 2010
- ○ signed but not yet ratified
- ◎ signed in 2010, but not yet ratified

Optional Protocol to the Convention against Torture	International Convention for the Protection of All Persons from Enforced Disappearance	Convention relating to the Status of Refugees (1951)	Protocol relating to the Status of Refugees (1967)	Convention relating to the Status of Stateless Persons (1954)	Convention on the Reduction of Statelessness (1961)	International Convention on the Protection of the Rights of All Migrant Workers and Members of Their Families	Rome Statute of the International Criminal Court	Country
●	○	●	●	●	●		●	Sweden
●		●	●	●			●	Switzerland
						●	○	Syria
		●	●			◐	●	Tajikistan
	○	●	●				●	Tanzania
							○	Thailand
○		●	●			●	●	Timor-Leste
◐	○	●	●				○	Togo
								Tonga
		●	●	●			●	Trinidad and Tobago
	○	●	●	●	●			Tunisia
○		●	●			●		Turkey
		●	●					Turkmenistan
		●	●					Tuvalu
	○	●	●	●		●	●	Uganda
●		●	●				○	Ukraine
							○	United Arab Emirates
●		●	●	●	●		◐	United Kingdom
		●					○*	United States of America
●	●	●	●	●	●	●	●	Uruguay
							○	Uzbekistan
	○							Vanuatu
	○		●				●	Venezuela
								Viet Nam
		●	●				○	Yemen
○	○	●	●	●			◐	Zambia
		●	●	●			○	Zimbabwe

10 Declaration under Article 10 not recognizing the competence of the CEDAW Committee to undertake confidential inquiries into allegations of grave or systematic violations.

22 Declaration under Article 22 recognizing the competence of the Committee against Torture (CAT) to consider individual complaints.

28 Reservation under Article 28 not recognizing the competence of the CAT to undertake confidential inquiries into allegations of systematic torture if warranted.

12 Declaration under Article 12(3) accepting the jurisdiction of the International Criminal Court (ICC) for crimes in its territory.

124 Declaration under Article 124 not accepting the jurisdiction of the ICC over war crimes for seven years after ratification.

* Signed the Rome Statute but have since formally declared their intention not to ratify.

** Ratified or acceded but subsequently denounced the treaty.

	African Charter on Human and Peoples' Rights (1981)	Protocol to the African Charter on the Establishment of an African Court on Human and Peoples' Rights (1998)	African Charter on the Rights and Welfare of the Child (1990)	Convention Governing the Specific Aspects of Refugee Problems in Africa (1969)	Protocol to the African Charter on Human and Peoples' Rights on the Rights of Women in Africa (2003)
Algeria	●	●	●	●	○
Angola	●	○	●	●	●
Benin	●	○	●	●	●
Botswana	●	○	●	●	
Burkina Faso	●	●	●	●	●
Burundi	●	●	●	●	○
Cameroon	●	○	●	●	○
Cape Verde	●		●	●	●
Central African Republic	●	○	○	●	○
Chad	●	○	●	●	○
Comoros	●	●	●	●	●
Congo (Republic of)	●	○	●	●	○
Côte d'Ivoire	●	●	●	●	○
Democratic Republic of the Congo	●	○	○	●	●
Djibouti	●	○	○	○	●
Egypt	●	○	●	●	
Equatorial Guinea	●	○	●	●	○
Eritrea	●		●		
Ethiopia	●	○	●	●	○
Gabon	●	●	●	●	○
Gambia	●	●	●	●	●
Ghana	●	●	●	●	●
Guinea	●	○	●	●	○
Guinea-Bissau	●	○	●	●	●
Kenya	●	●	●	●	○
Lesotho	●	●	●	●	●
Liberia	●	○	●	●	●
Libya	●	●	●	●	●
Madagascar	●	○	●	○	○

	African Charter on Human and Peoples' Rights (1981)	Protocol to the African Charter on the Establishment of an African Court on Human and Peoples' Rights (1998)	African Charter on the Rights and Welfare of the Child (1990)	Convention Governing the Specific Aspects of Refugee Problems in Africa (1969)	Protocol to the African Charter on Human and Peoples' Rights on the Rights of Women in Africa (2003)
Malawi	●	●	●	●	●
Mali	●	●	●	●	●
Mauritania	●	●	●	●	●
Mauritius	●	●	●	○	○
Mozambique	●	●	●	●	●
Namibia	●	○	●	○	●
Niger	●	●	●	●	○
Nigeria	●	●	●	●	●
Rwanda	●	●	●	●	●
Sahrawi Arab Democratic Republic	●	○	○		○
Sao Tome and Principe	●	○	○		○
Senegal	●	●	●	●	●
Seychelles	●	○	●	●	●
Sierra Leone	●	○	●	●	○
Somalia	●	○	○	○	○
South Africa	●	●	●	●	●
Sudan	●	○	●	●	○
Swaziland	●	○	○	◐	○
Tanzania	●	●	●	●	●
Togo	●	●	●	●	●
Tunisia	●	●	○	●	
Uganda	●	●	●	●	◐
Zambia	●	○	●	●	●
Zimbabwe	●	○	●	●	●

● state is a party
◐ state became party in 2010
○ signed but not yet ratified
○ signed in 2010, but not yet ratified

This chart lists countries that were members of the African Union at the end of 2010.

	American Convention on Human Rights (1969)	Protocol to the American Convention on Human Rights to Abolish the Death Penalty (1990)	Additional Protocol to the American Convention on Human Rights in the Area of Economic, Social and Cultural Rights	Inter-American Convention to Prevent and Punish Torture (1985)	Inter-American Convention on Forced Disappearance of Persons (1994)	Inter-American Convention on the Prevention, Punishment and Eradication of Violence Against Women (1994)	Inter-American Convention on the Elimination of All Forms of Discrimination against Persons with Disabilities (1999)
Antigua and Barbuda						●	
Argentina	●[62]	●	●	●	●	●	●
Bahamas						●	
Barbados	●[62]					●	
Belize						●	
Bolivia	●[62]		●	●	●	●	●
Brazil	●[62]	●	●	●	○	●	●
Canada							
Chile	●[62]	●	○	●	●	●	
Colombia	●[62]		●	●	●	●	●
Costa Rica	●[62]	●	●	●	●	●	
Cuba*							
Dominica	●					●	○
Dominican Republic	●[62]		○	●		●	●
Ecuador	●[62]	●	●	●	●	●	●
El Salvador	●[62]		●	●		●	●
Grenada	●					●	
Guatemala	●[62]		●	●	●	●	●
Guyana						●	
Haiti	●[62]		○	○		●	●
Honduras	●[62]			○	●	●	
Jamaica	●					●	○
Mexico	●[62]	●	●	●	●	●	●
Nicaragua	●[62]	●	●	●	○	●	●
Panama	●[62]	●	●	●	●	●	●

	American Convention on Human Rights (1969)	Protocol to the American Convention on Human Rights to Abolish the Death Penalty (1990)	Additional Protocol to the American Convention on Human Rights in the Area of Economic, Social and Cultural Rights	Inter-American Convention to Prevent and Punish Torture (1985)	Inter-American Convention on Forced Disappearance of Persons (1994)	Inter-American Convention on the Prevention, Punishment and Eradication of Violence Against Women (1994)	Inter-American Convention on the Elimination of All Forms of Discrimination against Persons with Disabilities (1999)
Paraguay	●62	●	●	●	●	●	●
Peru	●62		●	●	●	●	●
Saint Kitts and Nevis						●	
Saint Lucia						●	
Saint Vincent and the Grenadines						●	
Suriname	●62		●	●		●	
Trinidad and Tobago						●	
United States of America	○						
Uruguay	●62	●	●	●	●	●	●
Venezuela	●62	●	○	●	●	●	●

SELECTED TREATIES
REGIONAL – ORGANIZATION OF AMERICAN STATES

● state is a party
● state became party in 2010
○ signed but not yet ratified
○ signed in 2010, but not yet ratified

This chart lists countries that were members of the Organization of American States at the end of 2010.

62 Countries making a Declaration under Article 62 recognize as binding the jurisdiction of the Inter-American Court of Human Rights (on all matters relating to the interpretation or application of the American Convention).

* In 2009 the General Assembly of the Organization of American States (OAS) adopted resolution AG/RES.2438 (XXXIX-O/09), which resolves that the 1962 resolution that excluded the Cuban government from its participation in the OAS, ceases its effects. The 2009 resolution states that the participation of Cuba in the OAS will be the result of a process of dialogue initiated at the request of the government of Cuba.

	European Convention for the Protection of Human Rights and Fundamental Freedoms (ECHR) (1950)	Protocol No. 6 to the ECHR concerning the abolition of the death penalty in times of peace (1983)	Protocol No. 12 to the ECHR concerning the general prohibition of discrimination (2000)	Protocol No. 13 to the ECHR concerning the abolition of the death penalty in all circumstances (2002)	Framework Convention on the Protection of National Minorities (1995)	Council of Europe Convention on Action against Trafficking in Human Beings	European Social Charter (revised) (1996)	Additional Protocol to the European Social Charter Providing for a System of Collective Complaints (1995)
Albania	●	●	●	●	●	●	●	
Andorra	●	●	●	●		○	●	
Armenia	●	●	●	○	●	●	●	
Austria	●	●	○	●	●		○*	○
Azerbaijan	●	●	○		●	◉	●	
Belgium	●	●	○	●	○	●	●	●
Bosnia and Herzegovina	●	●	●	●	●	●	●	
Bulgaria	●	●		●	●	●	●	**
Croatia	●	●	●	●	●	●	○*	●
Cyprus	●	●	●	●	●	●	●	●
Czech Republic	●	●	○	●	●		○*	○
Denmark	●	●		●	●	●	○*	○
Estonia	●	●	○	●	●	○	●	
Finland	●	●	●	●	●	○	●	●
France	●	●		●		●	●	●
Georgia	●	●	●	●	●	●	●	
Germany	●	●	○	●	●	○	○*	
Greece	●	●	○	●	○	○	○*	●
Hungary	●	●	○	●	●	○	●	○
Iceland	●	●	○	●	○	○	○*	
Ireland	●	●	○	●	●	◉	●	●
Italy	●	●	○	●	●	◉	●	●
Latvia	●	●	○	○	●	◉	○*	
Liechtenstein	●	●	○	●	●			
Lithuania	●	●		●	●	○	●	

	European Convention for the Protection of Human Rights and Fundamental Freedoms (ECHR) (1950)	Protocol No. 6 to the ECHR concerning the abolition of the death penalty in times of peace (1983)	Protocol No. 12 to the ECHR concerning the general prohibition of discrimination (2000)	Protocol No. 13 to the ECHR concerning the abolition of the death penalty in all circumstances (2002)	Framework Convention on the Protection of National Minorities (1995)	Council of Europe Convention on Action against Trafficking in Human Beings	European Social Charter (revised) (1996)	Additional Protocol to the European Social Charter Providing for a System of Collective Complaints (1995)
Luxembourg	●	●	●	●	○	●	○*	
Macedonia	●	●	●	●	●	●	○*	
Malta	●	●		●	●	●	●	
Moldova	●	●	○	●	●	●	●	
Monaco	●	●		●			○	
Montenegro	●	●	●	●	●	●	●	
Netherlands	●	●	●	●	●	●	●	●
Norway	●	●	○	●	●	●	●	●
Poland	●	●		○	●	●	○*	
Portugal	●	●	○	●	●	●	●	●
Romania	●	●	●	●	●	●	●	
Russian Federation	●	○	○		●		●	
San Marino	●	●	●	●	●	●	○	
Serbia	●	●	●	●	●	●	●	
Slovakia	●	●	○	●	●	●	●	○
Slovenia	●	●	●	●	●	●	●	○**
Spain	●	●	●	●	●	●	○*	
Sweden	●	●		●	●	●	●	●
Switzerland	●	●		●	●	○		
Turkey	●	●	○	●		○	●	
Ukraine	●	●	●	●	●	●	●	
United Kingdom	●	●		●	●	●	○*	

● state is a party

● state became party in 2010

○ signed but not yet ratified

○ signed in 2010, but not yet ratified

This chart lists countries that were members of the Council of Europe at the end of 2010.

* State is a party to the European Social Charter of 1961, which is gradually being replaced by the European Social Charter (revised). The revised Charter embodies in one instrument all rights guaranteed by the Charter of 1961, its Additional Protocol of 1988 and adds new rights and amendments.

** Declaration under Article D of the European Social Charter (revised) recognizing the competence of the European Committee of Social Rights to consider collective complaints.

A Bedouin woman from al-'Araqib village, southern Israel, watches her house being demolished by the Israeli authorities, September 2010. Dozens of Bedouin villages, home to tens of thousands of people, are not formally recognized by the Israeli authorities.

AMNESTY INTERNATIONAL REPORT 2011

PART FOUR

Kashmiri protestors throw stones at armed police during a protest in Srinagar, India, June 2010. More than 100 people were shot dead by security forces in the Kashmir Valley during protests between June and September.

AMNESTY INTERNATIONAL
SECTIONS

Algeria ❖ Amnesty International,
10, rue Mouloud ZADI
(face au 113 rue Didouche Mourad),
Alger Centre,
16004 Alger
email: amnestyalgeria@hotmail.com
www.amnestyalgeria.org

Argentina ❖ Amnistía Internacional,
Av. Pueyrredón 689, Piso 2,
(C1032ABG) Buenos Aires
email: contacto@amnesty.org.ar
www.amnesty.org.ar

Australia ❖ Amnesty International,
Locked Bag 23,
Broadway NSW 2007
email: supporter@amnesty.org.au
www.amnesty.org.au

Austria ❖ Amnesty International,
Moeringgasse 10,
A-1150 Vienna
email: info@amnesty.at
www.amnesty.at

Belgium ❖
Amnesty International (**Flemish-speaking**),
Kerkstraat 156,
2060 Antwerpen
email: amnesty@aivl.be
www.aivl.be
Amnesty International (**francophone**),
Rue Berckmans 9,
1060 Bruxelles
email: aibf@aibf.be
www.aibf.be

Bermuda ❖ Amnesty International,
PO Box HM 2136, Hamilton HM JX
email: aibda@ibl.bm
www.amnestybermuda.org

Canada ❖
Amnesty International (**English-speaking**),
312 Laurier Avenue East,
Ottawa,
Ontario, K1N 1H9
email: info@amnesty.ca
www.amnesty.ca
Amnistie internationale (**francophone**),
6250 boulevard Monk,
Montréal,
Québec, H4E 3H7
www.amnistie.ca

Chile ❖ Amnistía Internacional,
Oficina Nacional, Huelén 164 - Planta Baja,
750-0617 Providencia, Santiago
email: info@amnistia.cl
www.amnistia.cl

Colombia ❖ Amnistía Internacional,
On-line Action Platform
email: AIColombia.Online@amnesty.org

Côte d'Ivoire ❖ Amnesty International,
04 BP 895, Abidjan 04
email: amnesty.ci@aviso.ci

Czech Republic ❖ Amnesty International,
Provaznická 3, 110 00, Prague 1
email: amnesty@amnesty.cz
www.amnesty.cz

Denmark ❖ Amnesty International,
Gammeltorv 8, 5 - 1457 Copenhagen K.
email: amnesty@amnesty.dk
www.amnesty.dk

Faroe Islands ❖ Amnesty International,
Stephanssons Hús, Kongabrúgvin,
Fo-100 Tórshavn
email: amnesty@amnesty.fo
www.amnesty.fo

Finland ❖ Amnesty International,
Ruoholahdenkatu 24, D 00180 Helsinki
email: amnesty@amnesty.fi
www.amnesty.fi

France ❖ Amnesty International,
76 boulevard de la Villette,
75940 Paris, Cédex 19
email: info@amnesty.fr
www.amnesty.fr

Germany ❖ Amnesty International,
Heerstrasse 178, 53111 Bonn
email: info@amnesty.de
www.amnesty.de

Greece ❖ Amnesty International,
Sina 30, 106 72 Athens
email: athens@amnesty.org.gr
www.amnesty.org.gr

Hong Kong ❖ Amnesty International,
Unit D, 3/F, Best-O-Best Commercial Centre,
32-36 Ferry Street, Kowloon
email: admin-hk@amnesty.org.hk
www.amnesty.org.hk

Iceland ❖ Amnesty International,
Þingholtsstræti 27, 101 Reykjavík
email: amnesty@amnesty.is
www.amnesty.is

Ireland ❖ Amnesty International,
Sean MacBride House,
48 Fleet Street, Dublin 2
email: info@amnesty.ie
www.amnesty.ie

Israel ❖ Amnesty International,
PO Box 14179, Tel Aviv 61141
email: info@amnesty.org.il
www.amnesty.org.il

Italy ❖ Amnesty International,
Via Giovanni Battista De Rossi 10,
00161 Roma
email: info@amnesty.it
www.amnesty.it

Japan ❖ Amnesty International,
4F Kyodo Bldg, 2-2 Kandanishiki-cho,
Chiyoda-ku, Tokyo 101-0054
email: info@amnesty.or.jp
www.amnesty.or.jp

Korea (Republic of) ❖ Amnesty International,
Hapjeong-dong, Mapo-gu, 3rd Fl. Geumag Bldg., 454-3,
121-888 Seoul
email: info@amnesty.or.kr
www.amnesty.or.kr

Luxembourg ❖ Amnesty International,
Boîte Postale 1914, 1019 Luxembourg
email: info@amnesty.lu
www.amnesty.lu

Mauritius ❖ Amnesty International,
BP 69, Rose-Hill
email: amnestymtius@erm.mu
www.amnestymauritius.org

Mexico ❖ Amnistía Internacional,
Tajín No. 389, Col. Narvarte, Del. Benito Juárez,
CP 03020 Mexico DF
email: contacto@amnistia.org.mx
www.amnistia.org.mx

Morocco ❖ Amnesty International,
281 avenue Mohamed V,
Apt. 23, Escalier A, Rabat
email: amorocco@sections.amnesty.org
www.amnestymaroc.org

Nepal ❖ Amnesty International,
PO Box 135, Amnesty Marga, Basantanagar,
Balaju, Kathmandu
email: info@amnestynepal.org
www.amnestynepal.org

Netherlands ❖ Amnesty International,
Keizersgracht 177, 1016 DR Amsterdam
email: amnesty@amnesty.nl
www.amnesty.nl

New Zealand ❖ Amnesty International,
PO Box 5300, Wellesley Street, Auckland
email: info@amnesty.org.nz
www.amnesty.org.nz

Norway ❖ Amnesty International,
Tordenskioldsgate 6B, 0106 Oslo
email: info@amnesty.no
www.amnesty.no

Paraguay ❖ Amnistía Internacional,
Manuel Castillo 4987 esquina San Roque González,
Barrio Villa Morra, Asunción
email: ai-info@py.amnesty.org
www.amnesty.org.py

Peru ❖ Amnistía Internacional,
Enrique Palacios 735-A, Miraflores, Lima 18
email: amnistia@amnistia.org.pe
www.amnistia.org.pe

Philippines ❖ Amnesty International,
18 A Marunong Street, Barangay Central,
Quezon City 1100
email: section@amnesty.org.ph
www.amnesty.org.ph

Poland ❖ Amnesty International,
ul. Piękna 66a, lokal 2, I piętro, 00-672, Warszawa
email: amnesty@amnesty.org.pl
www.amnesty.org.pl

Portugal ❖ Amnistia Internacional,
Av. Infante Santo, 42, 2°, 1350 - 179 Lisboa
email: aiportugal@amnistia-internacional.pt
www.amnistia-internacional.pt

Puerto Rico ❖ Amnistía Internacional,
Calle Robles 54, Suite 6, Río Piedras, 00925
email: amnistiapr@amnestypr.org
www.amnistiapr.org

Senegal ❖ Amnesty International,
303/GRD Sacré-coeur II, Résidence Arame SIGA,
BP 35269, Dakar Colobane
email: asenegal@sections.amnesty.org
www.amnesty.sn

Sierra Leone ❖ Amnesty International,
13B Howe Street, Freetown
email: amnestysl@gmail.com

Slovenia ❖ Amnesty International,
Beethovnova 7, 1000 Ljubljana
email: amnesty@amnesty.si
www.amnesty.si

Spain ❖ Amnistía Internacional,
Fernando VI, 8, 1° izda, 28004 Madrid
email: info@es.amnesty.org
www.es.amnesty.org

Sweden ❖ Amnesty International,
PO Box 4719,
11692 Stockholm
email: info@amnesty.se
www.amnesty.se

Switzerland ❖ Amnesty International,
PO Box, CH-3001 Berne
email: info@amnesty.ch
www.amnesty.ch

Taiwan ❖ Amnesty International,
3F., No. 14, Lane 165, Sec. 1,
Sinsheng S. Rd, Da-an District,
Taipei City 106
email: amnesty.taiwan@gmail.com
www.amnesty.tw

Togo ❖ Amnesty International,
2322 avenue du RPT,
Quartier Casablanca,
BP 20013, Lomé
email: aitogo@cafe.tg
www.amnesty.tg

Tunisia ❖ Amnesty International,
67 rue Oum Kalthoum,
3ème étage, escalier B,
1000 Tunis
email: admin-tn@amnesty.org

United Kingdom ❖ Amnesty International,
The Human Rights Action Centre,
17-25 New Inn Yard,
London EC2A 3EA
email: sct@amnesty.org.uk
www.amnesty.org.uk

United States of America ❖ Amnesty International,
5 Penn Plaza, 16th floor,
New York, NY 10001
email: admin-us@aiusa.org
www.amnestyusa.org

Uruguay ❖ Amnistía Internacional,
Wilson Ferreira Aldunate 1220,
CP 11.100,
Montevideo
email: oficina@amnistia.org.uy
www.amnistia.org.uy

Venezuela ❖ Amnistía Internacional,
Torre Phelps piso 17, oficina 17 A,
Av. La Salle,
Plaza Venezuela, Los Caobos,
Caracas 1050
email: info@aiven.org
www.aiven.org

AMNESTY INTERNATIONAL
STRUCTURES

Burkina Faso ❖ Amnesty International,
Quartier Boulmiougou,
Rue 17.548 Villa 27,
08 BP 11344,
Ouagadougou 08
email: aiburkina@fasonet.bf
www.amnesty-bf.org

Hungary ❖ Amnesty International,
Rózsa u. 44, II/4,
1064 Budapest
email: info@amnesty.hu
www.amnesty.hu

Malaysia ❖ Amnesty International,
A-3-3A, 8 Avenue,
Jalan Sungai Jernih,
8/1, Section 8, 46050,
Petaling Jaya,
Selangor
email: aimalaysia@aimalaysia.org
www.aimalaysia.org

Mali ❖ Amnesty International,
Immeuble Soya Bathily,
Route de l'aéroport,
24 rue Kalabancoura,
BP E 3885,
Bamako
email: amnesty.mali@ikatelnet.net

Moldova ❖ Amnesty International,
PO Box 209,
MD-2012 Chişinău
email: info@amnesty.md
www.amnesty.md

Mongolia ❖ Amnesty International,
PO Box 180,
Ulaanbaatar 210648
email: aimncc@magicnet.mn
www.amnesty.mn

Slovakia ❖ Amnesty International,
Karpatska 11,
811 05 Bratislava
email: amnesty@amnesty.sk
www.amnesty.sk

Turkey ❖ Amnesty International,
Abdülhakhamid Cd. No. 30/5,
Talimhane,
Beyoğlu, Istanbul
email: posta@amnesty.org.tr
www.amnesty.org.tr

AMNESTY INTERNATIONAL
PRE-STRUCTURES

Croatia ❖ Amnesty International,
Praška 2/III, 10000 Zagreb
email: admin@amnesty.hr
www.amnesty.hr

Thailand ❖ Amnesty International,
90/24 Lat Phrao Soi 1, Lat Yao,
Chatuchak, Bangkok 10900
email: info@amnesty.or.th
www.amnesty.or.th

AMNESTY INTERNATIONAL
ENTITIES REPORTING DIRECTLY TO THE SECRETARY GENERAL

Benin, Ghana, Kenya, South Africa, Ukraine, Zimbabwe.
For more information on these entities, please contact:
$MSU@amnesty.org

AMNESTY INTERNATIONAL
STRATEGIC PARTNERSHIPS

There are Strategic Partnership projects in the following countries:
Cambodia, Latvia, Indonesia, Timor-Leste, Liberia, Romania.
For more information on Strategic Partnerships, please contact:
Strategic_Partnerships_Team@amnesty.org

AMNESTY INTERNATIONAL
INTERNATIONAL MEMBERSHIP

There are also International Members in several countries and
territories around the world. More information can be found
online at:
www.amnesty.org/en/join
email: online.communities@amnesty.org

AMNESTY INTERNATIONAL
OFFICES

International Secretariat (IS)
Amnesty International,
Peter Benenson House,
1 Easton Street,
London WC1X 0DW,
United Kingdom
email: amnestyis@amnesty.org
www.amnesty.org

Amnesty International Language Resource Centre (AILRC)
Calle Valderribas, 13, 28007 Madrid, Spain
email: AILRC@amnesty.org
French: www.amnesty.org/fr
Spanish: www.amnesty.org/es
Arabic: www.amnesty.org/ar

Amnesty International European Institutions Office
Rue de Trèves 35,
B-1040 Brussels, Belgium
email: amnestyIntl@amnesty.eu
www.amnesty.eu

IS Beirut – Middle East and North Africa Regional Office
Amnesty International,
PO Box 13-5696,
Chouran Beirut 1102 - 2060, Lebanon
email: mena@amnesty.org

IS Dakar – Africa Human Rights Education Office
Amnesty International,
SICAP Sacré Coeur Pyrotechnie Extension, Villa No. 22,
BP 47582, Dakar, Senegal
email: KGaglo@amnesty.org

IS Geneva – UN Representative Office
Amnesty International,
22 rue du Cendrier, 4ème étage,
CH-1201 Geneva, Switzerland
email: uaigv@amnesty.org

IS Hong Kong – Asia Pacific Regional Office
Amnesty International,
16/F Siu On Centre, 188 Lockhart Rd,
Wanchai, Hong Kong
email: admin-ap@amnesty.org

IS Kampala – Africa Regional Office
Amnesty International,
Plot 20A Kawalya Kaggwa Close, PO Box 23966,
Kampala, Uganda
email: ai-aro@amnesty.org

IS Moscow – Russia Resource Centre
Amnesty International,
PO Box 212,
Moscow 119019, Russian Federation
email: msk@amnesty.org
www.amnesty.org.ru

IS New York – UN Representative Office
Amnesty International,
777 UN Plaza, 6th Floor,
New York, NY 10017, USA
email: aiunny@amnesty.org

IS Paris – Research Office
Amnesty International,
76 boulevard de la Villette,
75940 Paris, Cédex 19, France
email: pro@amnesty.org

I WANT
TO HELP

WHETHER IN A HIGH-PROFILE CONFLICT OR A FORGOTTEN CORNER OF THE GLOBE, **AMNESTY INTERNATIONAL** CAMPAIGNS FOR JUSTICE, FREEDOM AND DIGNITY FOR ALL AND SEEKS TO GALVANIZE PUBLIC SUPPORT TO BUILD A BETTER WORLD

WHAT CAN YOU DO?

Activists around the world have shown that it is possible to resist the dangerous forces that are undermining human rights. Be part of this movement. Combat those who peddle fear and hate.

- Join Amnesty International and become part of a worldwide movement campaigning for an end to human rights violations. Help us make a difference.

- Make a donation to support Amnesty International's work.

Together we can make our voices heard.

I am interested in receiving further information on becoming a member of Amnesty International

name

address

country

email

I wish to make a donation to Amnesty International (donations will be taken in UK£, US$ or euros)

amount

please debit my: Visa ☐   Mastercard ☐

number ☐☐☐☐☐ ☐☐☐☐☐ ☐☐☐☐☐ ☐☐☐☐☐

expiry date

signature

Please return this form to the Amnesty International office in your country.
(See pages 394-397 for further details of Amnesty International offices worldwide.)
If there is not an Amnesty International office in your country, please return this form to the International Secretariat in London:
Peter Benenson House, 1 Easton Street, London WC1X 0DW, United Kingdom

amnesty.org

INDEX OF SELECTED TOPICS*

A

abuses by armed groups

Afghanistan 56; Brazil 85; Central African Republic 98-9; Chad 100-1; Colombia 108-11; Côte d'Ivoire 114; Democratic Republic of the Congo 124; Ethiopia 142; Georgia 148-9; India 167; Iraq 177; Mali 220-1; Nepal 241; Nigeria 247; Pakistan 251; Palestinian Authority 256; Senegal 280; Somalia 294-5; Spain 300; Sri Lanka 302; Turkey 329

arbitrary arrests and detentions

Bangladesh 74; Chad 102; Cuba 119; Equatorial Guinea 136-7; Gambia 147; Guinea 157; Guinea-Bissau 159; India 169; Iran 173; Madagascar 216; Malaysia 218; Maldives 220; Mauritania 222; Mozambique 235; Pakistan 252; Palestinian Authority 255; Sri Lanka 302-3; Sudan 306

armed conflict

Africa overview 1-3; Americas overview 13; Middle East and North Africa overview 41-2; Colombia 108; Sudan 305-6; Thailand 320; Uganda 333; Yemen 354

C

child soldiers

Chad 101; Democratic Republic of the Congo 124-5; Somalia 294

children's rights

Albania 59; Bulgaria 88; Chad 102; Czech Republic 122; Holy See 162; Ireland 180; Jamaica 188; Liberia 209; Nigeria 248; Sierra Leone 285-6; Spain 300; Turkey 330; United States of America 345

corporate accountability

Asia-Pacific overview 26; Côte d'Ivoire 115; India 167

counter-terror and security

Americas overview 14; Europe and Central Asia overview 36-7; Albania 59; Algeria 60-1; Bosnia and Herzegovina 83-4; Canada 97; Denmark 127; Egypt 132; Ethiopia 142; Germany 151; Italy 186; Kuwait 200-1; Libya 211; Lithuania 213; Macedonia 214; Mauritania 222-3; Morocco/Western Sahara 233-4; New Zealand 242-3; Oman 250; Poland 264-5; Romania 269; Saudi Arabia 277-8; Slovakia 289-90; Spain 299-300; Swaziland 308-9; Syria 314; Tunisia 326-7; United Kingdom 338-9; Uzbekistan 348; Yemen 353-4

cruel, inhuman and degrading punishments

Iran 175; Qatar 268; Saudi Arabia 278; Sudan 307; Yemen 355

D

death penalty

Americas overview 17; Europe and Central Asia overview 37; Afghanistan 57-8; Algeria 62; Bahamas 71; Bahrain 73; Bangladesh 74; Belarus 75-6; Benin 79; Burkina Faso 89; Cameroon 96; Central African Republic 99; Chad 102; China 106; Cuba 119-20; Democratic Republic of the Congo 125; Egypt 134; Equatorial Guinea 137; Ethiopia 142; Gambia 147; Ghana 152; Guyana 160; India 169; Indonesia 171; Iran 175; Iraq 178-9;

Jamaica 188-9; Japan 189-90; Jordan 192; Kenya 196; Korea (Democratic People's Republic of) 198; Korea (Republic of) 200; Kuwait 201; Lebanon 207; Liberia 209; Libya 212; Malaysia 219; Mali 221; Mauritania 224; Mongolia 229; Morocco/Western Sahara 234; Niger 245; Nigeria 247; Pakistan 254; Palestinian Authority 256; Qatar 287; Saudi Arabia 280; Sierra Leone 288; Singapore 288; Solomon Islands 291; Somalia 295; Sudan 307-8; Swaziland 310; Syria 315; Taiwan 316; Tanzania 319; Thailand 321; Trinidad and Tobago 324; Tunisia 327; Uganda 335; United Arab Emirates 338; United States of America 345-6; Viet Nam 352; Yemen 355-6

deaths in custody

Armenia 66-7; Burkina Faso 89; Egypt 132-3; Eritrea 140; France 144-5; Iraq 177-8; Italy 186-7; Mauritania 223; Swaziland 309; Syria 314; Ukraine 335-6

detention without trial

China 106; Egypt 132; Iraq 177; Israel and the Occupied Palestinian Territories 184; Jordan 191; Korea (Democratic People's Republic of) 197-8; Niger 245; Qatar 267; Singapore 288

discrimination

Africa overview 8-9; Middle East and North Africa overview 47-8; Belgium 78; Bosnia and Herzegovina 83; Chile 104; China 108; Croatia 118; Denmark 128; Egypt 133; France 146-7; Greece 153-4; Indonesia 171; Iran 174; Italy 185; Jordan 191; Kuwait 201; Macedonia 215; Montenegro 231; Nepal 241; Netherlands 241-2; Poland 265; Qatar 267; Serbia 282, 284; Slovenia 290-1; Tanzania 319; Viet Nam 352

discrimination – ethnic minorities

Croatia 118; Iran 174-5; Kyrgyzstan 203-4; Lebanon 206; Liberia 210; Libya 212; Myanmar 236-7; Oman 250; Pakistan 253; Serbia 283-4; Syria 315;

discrimination – Roma

Europe and Central Asia overview 34-5; Bosnia and Herzegovina 83; Bulgaria 87-8; Croatia 118; Czech Republic 121-2; Greece 153-4; Hungary 165; Italy 185; Macedonia 215; Portugal 266; Romania 268-9; Slovakia 288-89; Slovenia 291

discrimination – women

Qatar 267; Spain 300; Syria 315

E

enforced disappearances

Albania 59; Algeria 61; Bosnia and Herzegovina 83; Congo (Republic of) 113; Lebanon 207; Macedonia 214; Nepal 240; Nigeria 246-7; Pakistan 251; Rwanda 275; Serbia 283; Spain 301; Sri Lanka 302; Turkmenistan 332

excessive use of force

Bahrain 72; Bangladesh 74; Belgium 78; Bulgaria 88; Guinea 157-8; India 167-8; Indonesia 170; Israel and the Occupied Palestinian Territories 183; Madagascar 216; Mozambique 235; Nepal 241; Peru 261; Poland 265; Puerto Rico 266; Swaziland 309; Togo 323; United States of America 344

extrajudicial executions

Bangladesh 74; Burkina Faso 89; Burundi 90; Colombia 109; Haiti 162; India 169; Pakistan 251-2; South Africa 296-7; Sri Lanka 303

F

forced evictions

Africa overview 7; Cambodia 93; Chad 102; Egypt 133-4; Equatorial Guinea 138; Haiti 162; Israel and the Occupied Palestinian Territories 182-3; Italy 185-6; Kenya 195-6; Myanmar 237-8; Nigeria 248; Serbia 282; Zimbabwe 358

freedom of assembly

Algeria 60; Angola 64; Azerbaijan 70; Belarus 76; Benin 78-9; Burundi 90; Cameroon 95; Croatia 117-8; Egypt 133; Iran 172-3; Jordan 191; Korea (Republic of) 199; Panama 257; Russian Federation 271; Singapore 287; Togo 323; Tunisia 325; Ukraine 336; Zimbabwe 358

freedom of association

Algeria 60; Azerbaijan 70; Bahrain 73; Burkina Faso 89; Burundi 90; Cambodia 93-4; Cameroon 95; Egypt 133; Fiji 143; Honduras 164; Iran 172-3; Israel and the Occupied Palestinian Territories 184; Jordan 191; Korea (Democratic People's Republic of) 198; Korea (Republic of) 199; Kuwait 200; Palestinian Authority 256; Rwanda 275; Zimbabwe 358

freedom of expression

Americas overview 17; Asia-Pacific overview 22-6; Europe and Central Asia overview 31-3; Algeria 60; Armenia 67; Azerbaijan 69-70; Bahrain 72-3; Belarus 76; Benin 78-9; Bosnia and Herzegovina 83; Burundi 91; Cambodia 93; Cameroon 95; China 105, 106-7; Cuba 119; Egypt 133; Fiji 143; Ghana 151; Honduras 164; Hungary 166; Indonesia 169-70; Iran 172-3; Iraq 179; Israel and the Occupied Palestinian Territories 184; Jordan 191; Korea (Democratic People's Republic of) 198; Korea (Republic of) 199; Kuwait 200; Macedonia 214; Malaysia 218; Montenegro 231; Morocco/Western Sahara 232-3; Namibia 239; Nigeria 248; Oman 250; Pakistan 253; Palestinian Authority 256; Qatar 267; Russian Federation 271; Rwanda 274; Singapore 287; Somalia 294; Sudan 306-7; Swaziland 309; Taiwan 316; Tanzania 318; Togo 323; Tunisia 325; Turkey 328; Uganda 334; Uzbekistan 348-9; Viet Nam 351-2; Zimbabwe 358

freedom of expression – journalists

Middle East and North Africa overview 44-5; Afghanistan 56-7; Azerbaijan 69-70; Burundi 91; Chad 102; Cuba 119; Côte d'Ivoire 115; Democratic Republic of the Congo 126; Dominican Republic 129; Equatorial Guinea 138; Eritrea 139; Ethiopia 141; Gambia 147-8; Madagascar 216; Malawi 217; Mexico 226; Namibia 239; Rwanda 275; Sierra Leone 286; Somalia 295; Sri Lanka 305; Tajikistan 319; Uzbekistan 350; Yemen 356

freedom of movement

Cuba 120; Korea (Democratic People's Republic of) 198; Qatar 267; Turkmenistan 332

freedom of religion

Afghanistan 57; Algeria 62; China 105-6; Eritrea 138-9; Iran 175; Laos 205; Morocco/Western Sahara 234; Pakistan 253; Saudi Arabia 278; Turkmenistan 331-2; Uzbekistan 349; Viet Nam 352

H

housing rights

Middle East and North Africa overview 46-7; Albania 59; Brazil 86; Czech Republic 122; Egypt 133-4; Ghana 152; Hungary 165-6; Israel and the Occupied Palestinian Territories 182-3; Kenya 195; Mongolia 230; Portugal 266; Puerto Rico 266; Romania 269; Slovakia 289; Solomon Islands 291

human rights defenders

Americas overview 12; Brazil 87; Burundi 91; Cambodia 93; Chad 100; China 106; Colombia 111; Democratic Republic of the Congo 125-6; Dominican Republic 129; Ecuador 130; Ethiopia 141-2; Fiji 143-4; Gambia 148; Guatemala 156; Honduras 163; India 168; Iran 174; Kyrgyzstan 204; Mauritania 224; Mexico 226; Niger 245; Paraguay 260; Russian Federation 272; Rwanda 275; Serbia 282-3; South Africa 298; Sri Lanka 304; Tunisia 326; Ukraine 336; Uzbekistan 348-9; Venezuela 350; Zimbabwe 357-8

I

impunity

Americas overview 14-16; Europe and Central Asia overview 37-9; Algeria 61; Argentina 66; Armenia 67; Bangladesh 75; Bolivia 80; Brazil 87; Cameroon 96; Chile 103-04; Colombia 109; Côte d'Ivoire 115; Ecuador 130; El Salvador 135; Guatemala 155-6; Guinea-Bissau 159; India 168; Indonesia 171; Iran 174; Israel and the Occupied Palestinian Territories 183; Kazakhstan 193; Kenya 194; Kyrgyzstan 203; Liberia 208; Libya 211-2; Moldova 228; Mongolia 229; Nepal 240; Peru 261-2; Rwanda 275; Senegal 280; Sri Lanka 303; Syria 315; Tanzania 318; Timor-Leste 322; Togo 323; Turkey 329; United States of America 343-4; Uruguay 346

Indigenous Peoples' rights

Americas overview 12-13; Argentina 66; Australia 68; Bangladesh 75; Brazil 86; Canada 96-7; Chile 103; Ecuador 130; El Salvador 135; Guatemala 155; Guyana 160; Mexico 227; New Zealand 242; Panama 257; Paraguay 259; Peru 261; Philippines 264

internally displaced people

Afghanistan 57; Iraq 178; Democratic Republic of the Congo 125; Georgia 149; Haiti 161-2; Iraq 176; Kenya 196; Somalia 293; Sri Lanka 302

international justice

Americas overview 16-17; Asia-Pacific overview 27-8; Argentina 66; Belgium 78; Bosnia and Herzegovina 81-2; Cambodia 93; Central African Republic 98; Croatia 117; Democratic Republic of the Congo 126; Finland 144; Guinea 156-7; Honduras 163; Kenya 195; Moldova 228; Montenegro 230-1; Norway 249; Rwanda 275-6; Senegal 280-1; Serbia 281-2; Sierra Leone 286-7; Spain 301; Sudan 305; Uganda 333; United Kingdom 340

international scrutiny

Colombia 112; Guinea 157; Holy See 162; Italy 185; Korea (Democratic People's Republic of) 198; Mexico 227; Myanmar 238-9; Singapore 288; United States of America 342; Uzbekistan 349

J

justice system
Americas overview 14-16; Europe and Central Asia overview 39; Afghanistan 57; Albania 59; Bahrain 72; Bosnia and Herzegovina 81; Burundi 92; Canada 97; Colombia 109; Croatia 116-7; Democratic Republic of the Congo 125-6; Finland 144; Ghana 152; Hungary 165; Israel and the Occupied Palestinian Territories 184; Jamaica 188; Japan 189; Kenya 195; Liberia 208-9; Macedonia 214; Maldives 220; Nigeria 247; Palestinian Authority 256; Paraguay 259-60; Russian Federation 271; Rwanda 275; Serbia 282; Sierra Leone 285; Taiwan 316; Timor-Leste 322; United Kingdom 339-40

L

land disputes
Argentina 66; Brazil 86; Colombia 109; Liberia 209-10

legal, constitutional or institutional developments
Australia 68; Bolivia 79; France 146; Mongolia 230; New Zealand 243; Norway 250; Slovenia 290-1; Switzerland 311; United Kingdom 340

M

maternal mortality
Africa overview 7-8; Asia-Pacific overview 26-7; Afghanistan 55; Bolivia 80; Burkina Faso 89; Ecuador 131; Ireland 180; Peru 261; Sierra Leone 286; United States of America 345; Yemen 355

migrants' rights
Africa overview 6-7; Europe and Central Asia overview 33-4; Algeria 62; Angola 64-5; Austria 69; Bahrain 73; Bulgaria 89; Dominican Republic 128-9; Egypt 134; Italy 186; Jordan 191; Korea (Republic of) 199-200; Kuwait 201; Libya 212; Mauritania 223; Mexico 225-6; Morocco/Western Sahara 234; Netherlands 242; Norway 249; Qatar 267; Saudi Arabia 279; Sweden 310; Switzerland 312; Taiwan 316; Ukraine 336; United Arab Emirates 337; United Kingdom 341; United States of America 345

P

police and security forces
Afghanistan 57; Argentina 65-6; Austria 69; Bahamas 71; Bolivia 80; Canada 97; Central African Republic 99; Colombia 109-10; Cyprus 121; Côte d'Ivoire 114; Dominican Republic 128; Ecuador 130; Georgia 149; Ghana 151-2; Jamaica 188; Kenya 194-5; Mexico 225; Mozambique 235; New Zealand 243; Pakistan 251; Paraguay 259; Rwanda 275; Sierra Leone 285; Switzerland 312; Timor-Leste 321-22; Trinidad and Tobago 324; United Kingdom 340; Venezuela 351

political prisoners
Burundi 91; Eritrea 139; Ethiopia 142; Laos 205; Myanmar 237; Togo 323

prison conditions
Albania 59; Benin 79; Brazil 85-6; Burundi 92; Cameroon 95-6; Democratic Republic of the Congo 125; Greece 154; Ireland 180; Israel and the Occupied Palestinian Territories 184; Malawi 217; Mauritania 223; Peru 262; Tanzania 319; Turkey 329; United States of America 344; Uruguay 347; Venezuela 351

prisoners of conscience
Angola 64; Armenia 67; Belarus 77; Central African Republic 99; Cuba 119; Equatorial Guinea 137; Eritrea 139; Ethiopia 142; Finland 144; Israel and the Occupied Palestinian Territories 184; Laos 205; Myanmar 237; Rwanda 275; Singapore 288; Togo 323; Turkey 330

R

racism
Austria 68; Bulgaria 88; Czech Republic 122; France 146-7; Germany 150; Hungary 165; Russian Federation 272; Spain 301

refugees and asylum-seekers
Afghanistan 57; Australia 68; Austria 69; Belgium 77-8; Bulgaria 89; China 108; Congo (Republic of) 113; Cyprus 120; Denmark 127; Egypt 134; Eritrea 139; Finland 144; France 146; Germany 150; Ireland 180; Italy 186; Japan 190; Kenya 196; Laos 204-5; Lebanon 207; Libya 212; Macedonia 215; Malta 221-2; Montenegro 231; Netherlands 242; New Zealand 243; Norway 249; Poland 266; Rwanda 276; Saudi Arabia 279; Slovakia 290; Sweden 310; Switzerland 312; Syria 315; Turkey 330; Uganda 334; United Kingdom 341; Uzbekistan 349; Yemen 355

refugees and migrants
Bahamas 71; Canada 97; Czech Republic 123; Democratic Republic of the Congo 125; Greece 153; Iraq 178; Kazakhstan 193-4; Malaysia 219; Serbia 282; South Africa 298; Spain 300; Tanzania 319; Thailand 320-1

right to health
Asia-Pacific overview 26-7; Argentina 66; Burkina Faso 89; Democratic People's Republic of Korea 197; Ecuador 130; Guyana 160; Ireland 180; Slovakia 290; South Africa 297; Swaziland 309-10; United States of America 345

rights of lesbian, gay, bisexual and transgender people
Cameroon 95; Croatia 118; Cyprus 121; Guyana 160; Honduras 164; Hungary 166; Ireland 180; Italy 186; Jamaica 188; Lithuania 213; Malawi 217; Moldova 228; Poland 266; Serbia 282; Slovakia 290; South Africa 297; Turkey 330; Uganda 334; Zimbabwe 358

S

sexual and reproductive rights
Americas overview 18-19; Argentina 69; Chile 104; Democratic Republic of the Congo 124; Ecuador 131; Indonesia 171; Liberia 209; Malta 222; Mexico 226-7; Nicaragua 244; Paraguay 260; Peru 261; Philippines 264; Poland 265; Slovakia 290; Uruguay 347

T
torture and other ill-treatment

trafficking in human beings

transitional justice

U
unfair trials

unlawful killings

V
violence against women and girls

W
women's rights

workers' rights

* This is an index of topics based around the subheadings that appear in the A-Z country entries. It should be used by the reader only as a navigational tool, not as a statement of Amnesty International's human rights concerns in a particular country or territory.

Police obstruct a cameraman at a Strategy 31 protest against freedom of assembly restrictions, Russian Federation, May 2010. Freedom of assembly and expression continued to come under attack in Russia, through the banning of demonstrations and violent dispersal of individuals.